State and Local Finance for the 1990s:
A Case Study of Arizona

edited by
Therese J. McGuire and Dana Wolfe Naimark

School of Public Affairs • Arizona State University

State and Local Finance for the 1990s:
A Case Study of Arizona

School of Public Affairs
Arizona State University
Tempe, Arizona 85287-0603

Copyright © 1991 by The Arizona Board of Regents

Publisher: School of Public Affairs
Production supervisor: N. Joseph Cayer
Cover and layout design: Cherylene A. Schick
Editors: Sherry S. Dickerson and Kathy Boyd
Printing and binding: Braun-Brumfield, Inc.

ISBN 1-879286-01-7

Foreword

While the full legislative agenda of President Reagan's "New Federalism" failed to achieve the approval of Congress when it was first proposed in 1982, the spirit of that policy initiative -- fiscal decentralization -- seems to have taken firm root in the daily deliberations and operations of today's fiscal policy-making. No longer do we look to Washington for the solution to all our fiscal wants and needs. More and more, and rightly so, I believe, have we turned to state governments as an appropriate center for making and financing public policies. I see the trend continuing. Are state governments and their fiscal institutions up to the task? That is the overriding question addressed by the editors and authors of this thoughtful volume on Arizona's public finances. They have produced a quality product and it should be exported, not only to the other "sunshine states" but to all states concerned with designing a sound fiscal system for an economy undergoing change.

While the study's focus in Arizona, the methodologies employed and the lessons learned reach beyond Phoenix to all state capitals and, just as importantly, to the classrooms presently training our future state leaders. Arizona is now a state in transition, moving from the luxury of high economic growth and low fiscal needs to slower growth and rising demands. How can Arizona cope? This report by a group of the profession's leading analysts of state and local government fiscal policy provides solutions. Here is an outline for a state fiscal system that is both responsible and responsive. It is not driven by gimmicks to attract today's hot industry. Sound and tested economic principles guide the authors' recommendations for reform.

When legislators look beyond their individual interests to the wider good of all state residents, it is important that sound analysis guide the policy discussions. In this volume, policy makers in Arizona and in state governments across the country have an excellent basis on which to build strong financial systems.

Robert P. Inman
Professor of Finance, Economics, and Public Management
Wharton School

Contributors

Michael E. Bell · *Institute for Policy Studies* · *Johns Hopkins University*
R. Bruce Billings · *Department of Economics* · *University of Arizona*
John H. Bowman · *Department of Economics* · *Virginia Commonwealth University*
Robert Carroll · *Office of Tax Analysis* · *U.S. Department of the Treasury*
Alberta H. Charney · *Division of Economic and Business Research* · *University of Arizona*
Jon B. Christianson · *School of Public Health* · *University of Minnesota*
Steven G. Craig · *Department of Economics* · *University of Houston and Hunter College, CUNY*
W. Mark Day · *Demand Management Associates* · *Tucson, Arizona*
Thomas A. Downes · *Department of Economics* · *Northwestern University*
Roger Faith · *Department of Economics* · *Arizona State University*
Daniel Feenberg · *National Bureau of Economic Research* · *Cambridge, Massachusetts*
Ronald C. Fisher · *Department of Economics* · *Michigan State University*
William F. Fox · *Center for Business and Economic Research* · *University of Tennessee*
Mary N. Gade · *Department of Economics* · *Oklahoma State University*
J. Fred Giertz · *Institute of Government and Public Affairs and* · *Department of Economics* · *University of Illinois at Urbana-Champaign*
Craig M. Horn · *College of Business Administration* · *University of Arizona*
Timothy D. Hogan · *Center for Business Research* · *Arizona State University*
Helen F. Ladd · *Institute of Policy Sciences and Public Affairs* · *Duke University*
Therese J. McGuire · *Institute of Government and Public Affairs and* · *School of Urban Planning and Policy* · *University of Illinois at Chicago*
Dana Wolfe Naimark · *Formerly Project Manager* · *Arizona Joint Select Committee on State Revenues and Expenditures*
Wallace E. Oates · *Department of Economics* · *University of Maryland at College Park*
Michael Ormiston · *Department of Economics* · *Arizona State University*
Thomas F. Pogue · *Department of Economics* · *University of Iowa*
Tom R. Rex · *Center for Business Research* · *Arizona State University*
Harvey S. Rosen · *Department of Economics* · *Princeton University*
Don E. Schlagenhauf · *Department of Economics* · *Arizona State University*
Michael Wasylenko · *Department of Economics* · *The Maxwell School* · *Syracuse University*
Mark W. Watson · *Department of Economics* · *Northwestern University*
Dana Weist · *Policy Economics Group* · *KPMG Peat Marwick* · *Washington, D.C.*
David Wyant · *School of Public Health* · *University of Minnesota*

Acknowledgments

The chapters in this volume are based on reports commissioned by the Arizona Joint Select Committee on State Revenues and Expenditures, a temporary, blue-ribbon committee appointed by the Governor and the Legislature to evaluate Arizona's fiscal system and to recommend changes that would result in a simpler, fairer, and more efficient fiscal system for the state. While the work for the Committee was directed toward specific issues and problems in Arizona, much of the research and many of the findings and policy options generated are relevant for states across the country.

Many individuals in Arizona state and local government and in the private sector provided important assistance and information to the authors of the chapters in this volume. To thank each of the many conscientious individuals would make for an exceedingly long list of acknowledgments. We would like to acknowledge here the special assistance and support of two Committee members, Elliott Hibbs and Sharon Megdal.

To ensure that the chapters in this volume would be academically useful as well as policy-relevant, and to ensure that the lessons learned in Arizona would translate, at least partially, to state and local settings across the country, we asked academic public finance economists outside Arizona to read and comment on the chapters. In this regard, we are very grateful to Tim Bartik, Upjohn Institute; Becky Blank, Northwestern University; Howard Chernick, Hunter College; Bob Ebel, U.S. Advisory Commission on Intergovernmental Relations; Jim Hines, Princeton University; Bob Inman, University of Pennsylvania; Bradford Kirkman-Liff, Arizona State University; Jim Poterba, Massachusetts Institute of Technology; Anne Preston, State University of New York at Stony Brook; Bob Schwab, University of Maryland; Ken Small, University of California at Irvine; Jon Sonstelie, University of California at Santa Barbara; Art Sullivan, University of California at Davis; Shelly White, University of Michigan; and Johnny Yinger, Syracuse University.

Finally, we are grateful to the authors who, under great time pressure, provided us with innovative and informative studies of many important issues in state and local public finance, issues policy makers are likely to face in the decade to come.

Therese J. McGuire
Dana Wolfe Naimark

Contents

Part I: Introduction and Context

1   Introduction and Overview   1
Therese J. McGuire and Dana Wolfe Naimark
    Setting The Context   2
    The Revenue System   3
    Expenditures   5
    Financing Local Government   7
    Summary   8

2   Economic Growth And Government Fiscal Behavior 1973-1987   9
Robert Carroll and Michael Wasylenko
    Employment and Output Growth Rates: Arizona Compared   9
    Business Location and Employment Decisions   19
    Appendix A: Data Sources For Variables   30
    Appendix B: Results of the Econometric Analysis   34

3   Demographic Trends and Fiscal Implications   37
Timothy D. Hogan and Tom R. Rex
    Migration Flows - The Key To Arizona's Growth   37
    Population Growth And Economic Activity   38
    Economic Cycle Impacts   38
    Projections   40
    Public Sector Impacts   40
    Summary   43

4   The State Budget: Process and Performance   45
Dana Wolfe Naimark and Mark W. Watson
    An Overview of the Budget Process   45
    Revenue Forecasting   46
    Predicting Expenditures   49
    Budget Flexibility   54
    Making Spending Decisions   56

Part II: State Revenues

5   The Personal Income Tax   59
Daniel Feenberg, Therese J. McGuire, and Harvey S. Rosen
    Issues In The Design Of State PITS   59
    The Structure Of Arizona's Personal Income Tax   62
    Analytical Description Of The Arizona Personal Income Tax   67
    Options For Changing Arizona's Personal Income Tax   71
    Summary   76

6   The Corporation Income Tax   79
     Therese J. McGuire
          Role And Rationale Of Corporation Income Taxes   79
          The Arizona Corporation Income Tax   80
          Arizona Compared   84
          Economic Evaluation Of State Corporation Income Taxes   85
          Summary   88

7   Taxation of Financial Industries In an Era of Change   91
     William F. Fox
          Financial Industry   91
          Current Arizona Tax Structure   98
          Evaluation of the Taxation of Financial Institutions   103
          Summary   113

8   General Sales Taxes   117
     Helen F. Ladd and Dana Weist
          Tax Base And Structure   118
          Reliance On Sales Taxes   122
          Who Pays The Tax?   126
          Revenue Growth And Stability   130
          Policy Issues Related To The Tax Base   133
          Local Sales Taxes   138
          Summary   144
          Appendix   149

9   Selective Sales Taxes   157
     Don E. Schlagenhauf
          Cigarette And Tobacco Taxes   157
          Alcoholic Beverage Taxation   165
          Transient Occupancy Taxes   172
          Real Property Transfer Taxes   177
          Summary   189

10   User Charges and Fees   191
     Roger Faith and Dana Wolfe Naimark
          The Economics Of User Charges And Fees   191
          User Charges in Comparison to General Taxes   192
          User Charges And License Fees
          In Arizona And Other States   196
          Summary   207
          Appendix   210

Part III: State Expenditures

11   Higher Education 211
     J. Fred Giertz
       The Role Of Higher Education:
       A Conceptual Framework 211
       Higher Education In Arizona And The Rest Of The Nation 214
       The Fiscal Structure 221
       Policy Issues 233

12   Government Health Care Expenditures 237
     Jon B. Christianson and David Wyant
       Health Care Expenditures:
         The Changing Role Of Federal, State, And Local Governments 237
       Health Care Expenditures By Arizona State Government 239
       Health Care Expenditures By Counties In Arizona 253
       Summary 256

13   Welfare Policy: Spending and Program Structure 259
     Steven G. Craig
       The Conceptual Role of Government in Providing Welfare 260
       The Current Welfare Policy Environment 268
       Interstate Welfare Expenditure Comparisons 273
       Policy Options Facing Arizona 289
       Summary 293

14   State Recreation And Environmental Quality Programs 295
     R. Bruce Billings and W. Mark Day
       The Economics Of Natural Resources Regulation 296
       Federal, Interstate, And State/Local Comparisons 299
       Analysis Of Current Programs 304
       Policy Issues And Conclusions 315
       Policy Option 316
       Summary 317

15   Public Safety and Criminal Justice 319
     Michael Ormiston
       The Rationale For Government Involvement 319
       The Crisis In Corrections 320
       Interstate Comparisons Of Public Safety Expenditures 321
       Public Safety Expenditures In Arizona 325
       Other Policy Issues 334

16   Financing State and Local Highways 337
     Alberta H. Charney and Craig M. Horn
       The Conceptual Role of Government In Providing Highway Services 337
       The Benefit Principle of Taxation and User Fees 338

Efficient Pricing of Highways 339
Highway Funding Sources 340
Earmarked Highway User Funds 347
Highway Expenditures 351
Policy Implications 355

Part IV: Local Government Finances

17   Financing Local School Districts 361
Thomas A. Downes and Thomas F. Pogue
Trends 361
Rationales For State Aid 366
Arizona's Present System: How Does It Work? 369
Arizona's Present System: Is It Fair? 371
Equality Of Outcome: Another Perspective On Student Equity 377
Conclusion And Potential Policy Changes 383

18   Unrestricted State Aid to Cities and Counties 389
Michael E. Bell
Interstate Comparisons Of State Assistance To Local Government 389
State Assistance To Cities And Counties In Arizona 394
Impact of Intergovernmental Assistance 401
Summary 404

19   The Theory and Rationale of Local Property Taxation 407
Wallace E. Oates
What is Taxed Under the Property Tax? 408
A National Property Tax 408
The Property Tax as a Local Tax 410
"Capitalization" and Its Implications 410
Capitalization and Fairness 411
Property Taxation and Local Fiscal Choice 413
A Note on Property Taxation in Central Cities 414
Land Taxation 415
Local Property Taxation: A Summing Up 417
A Note on State Property Taxation and Fiscal Limitations 421

20   Real Property Classification 425
John H. Bowman
How Is Classification Accomplished? 425
Why Classify Property? 428
How Does Arizona Classification Compare? 429
Evaluation Of Classification: Arizona As A Case Study 437
Summary And Conclusion 444

21 Local Property Tax And Expenditure Limits 449
Ronald C. Fisher and Mary N. Gade
   Description Of Limits 449
   Expenditures 450
   Revenues 453
   Modeling Local Fiscal Behavior In Arizona 457
   School District Property Taxes And The Homeowner's Rebate 460
   Summary 462

Part V: General Fund Projections: Quantifying the Structural Deficit

22 General Fund Projections: Quantifying the Structural Deficit 465
Mark W. Watson
   Revenue and Expenditure Forecasts -- Results 466
   Revenue and Expenditure Forecasts -- Methodology and Assumptions 468
   Revenues and Expenditures -- 10 Year History 475
   Summary 479
   Appendix 479

Tables

2-1 Employment Shares for Arizona, Six Comparison States and
the U.S., By Industry, 1987 11

2-2 Annual Rate of Employment Growth for Arizona, Six Comparison
States And the United States, By Industry, 1973-81 and 1981-87 12

2-3 Annual Rate of Gross State Product Growth for Arizona,
Six Comparison States, And the United States, By Industry,
1973-81 and 1981-86 And the United States, By Industry,
1973-81 and 1981-87 15

2-4 Annual Competitive Employment Effects for Arizona By
Industry, 1973-81, 1981-87, and 1986-87 18

2-5 Names and Definitions of Independent Factors:
Full List of Variables 22

2-6 Arizona Value, Means, and Range for Selected Factors, 1981 24

2-7 Arizona Valuc, Mcans, and Range for Selected Factors, 1987 25

3-1 Arizona Age Distribution 41

4-1 Root Mean Squared Error of GNP Forecasts 47

4-2 Total General Fund Revenues 48

4-3 Department of Education 51

4-4 Department of Economic Security 52

4-5 Department of Corrections 53

4-6 AHCCCS 53

5-1 Personal Income Tax Collections As a Share of Total State Tax Collections . 60

5-2 Arizona Income Taxes in 1988 69

5-3 Federal Taxable Income as the Base for the Arizona Income Tax 72

5-4 A Flat Tax for Arizona With FAGI as the Base 74

5-5 Eliminating the Federal Tax Deduction 75

5-6 Piggybacking on the Federal Tax 77

6-1 Arizona Corporation Income Tax 83

6-2 State Corporation Income Tax Revenue as a
Share of Total State General Revenue 84

6-3 State Corporation Income Tax Revenue as a
Share of State Personal Income 85

6-4 Corporation Income Tax Characteristics of the States 86

7-1 State Interstate Banking Laws 93

7-2 State Diversification Legislation for Interstate Banking 95

7-3 State Taxation of Banks 99

8-1 State Sales and Use Tax Collections and Rates
by Taxable Activity, 1988 120

8-2   State Sales Tax Revenue per Capita,
        1988 Decomposition to Identify Contributing Factors   123
8-3   State Sales Tax Bases and Rates, 1988   125
8-4   Distribution of Arizona Sales Tax by Purchaser   127
8-5   Consumer Expenditure Patterns by Household Income Class
        Share of Income Spent on Taxable Items -- Current Tax Base   129
8-6   Growth in the State Sales Tax Over Time   130
8-7   Stability and Responsiveness of the Arizona Sales Tax   132
8-8   Evaluation of Alternative Sales Tax Bases   134
8-9   Distribution of Arizona City Population By City Sales Tax Rate - 1987   139
8-10 City Sales Taxes on Food, by County   141

9-1   Revenue from Cigarette and Tobacco Taxes in Arizona   158
9-2   Tax Rates Per Pack of Twenty Cigarettes   160
9-3   State Tobacco Tax Revenue and Tax Effort Fiscal Years 1975 and 1987 . . .   161
9-4   Family Income and Consumption of Tobacco Products   162
9-5   Revenue Comparisons Between Per-Unit and *Ad Valorem* Tobacco Tax   164
9-6   Revenue from Alcohol Taxes in Arizona   166
9-7   A Comparison of State Alcohol Tax Rates   167
9-8   State Alcoholic Beverage (Liquor) Tax Revenue and
        Tax Effort Fiscal Years 1975 and 1987   168
9-9   Family Income and Consumption of Alcoholic Products   170
9-10 Revenue From an *Ad Valorem* Tax on Alcoholic Products   172
9-11 Revenue from the Transient Occupancy Tax   173
9-12 A Comparison of Transient Occupancy
        Tax Rates in Selected Cities in 1988   174
9-13 Consumer Spending on Hotel/Motel Rooms   176
9-14 Real Property Transfer Tax by State: Type and Rates, 1988   179
9-15 Real Property Transfer Taxes Assessed by Local Governments   182
9-16 A Comparison of Real Estate Transfer Tax Rates on
        $150,000 House by State: 1988   183
9-17 Estimated Tax Burden of a Real Estate Transfer Tax   186
9-18 Real Estate Transfer Tax Collections for Selected States   187
9-19 Revenue Potential of Alternative Real Estate Transfer Taxes   189

10-1   Sample Sources of Charges and Fees   192
10-2   Comparison of State Revenue Sources   193
10-3   State and Local User Charge Revenue as a
         Percentage of Own-Source Revenue   196
10-4A State Government User Charge and License Fee Revenues -- 1980   198
10-4B State Government User Charge and License Fee Revenues -- 1987   198
10-4C Actual and Representative State User Charge Revenue, FY 1987   199
10-4D Actual and Representative State License Revenue, FY 1987   199
10-5   Percentage Distribution of State User Charge Revenues by Category -- 1987   200
10-6   Percentage Distribution of State License Revenues by Category -- 1987 . . .   200
10-7   License Fee Revenue Capacity and Effort Indices, Selected Categories   201
10-8   State User Charge Revenues as a Percentage of
         State Expenditures By Category -- 1987   202

10-9   Arizona State License Fee and User Charge Revenues By Category -- 1988 . 202
10-10   Arizona State License Fee and User Charge Revenues
            As a Share of Expenditures By Category -- 1988 203
10-11   Percentage of Arizona State License Fee and User Charge
            Revenues Deposited into Special Funds By Category -- 1988 204
10-12   Local Government User Charge Revenues as a
            Percentage of Own-Source Revenues 205
10-13   County User Charges 1982 and 1987 206
10-14   City User Charge Coverage Ratios 1982 and 1987 208

11-1   FTE Enrollment in Public Institutions of Higher Education 215
11-2   Average Undergraduate Tuition (In-State)
            1986-87 Public Four Year Institutions 216
11-3   State Expenditures for Higher Education -- 1987 216
11-4   Combined State and Local Support for
            Public Institutions of Higher Education -- 1985-86 217
11-5   State Appropriations for
            Public Institutions of Higher Education -- 1985-86 218
11-6   Changes in Combined State and Local Support for
            Public Institutions of Higher Education -- 1979-1986 218
11-7   Actual State Expenditures for Higher Education as
            Percentage of Representative State Expenditures -- 1987 220
11-8   State and Local Support for Public Institutions of
            Higher Education as Percentage of Representative
            State and Local Support -- 1986 220
11-9   State Appropriations for Public Institutions of
            Higher Education as Percentage of Representative State - 1986 221
11-10   Enrollment Levels in Arizona Public Universities 223
11-11A General Fund Appropriations for Arizona Universities 225
11-11B General Fund Appropriations for Arizona Universities 226
11-11C General Fund Appropriations for Arizona Universities 227
11-11D General Fund Appropriations for Arizona Universities 227
11-12A Total Educational and General Expenditures 229
11-12B Total Educational and General Expenditures 230
11-13A Tuition and Fees in Arizona Universities 231
11-13B Tuition and Fees in Arizona Universities 232

12-1   Per Capita State Government Expenditures - Vendor Payments 241
12-2   Per Capita State Spending on Health and Hospitals 242
12-3   Per Capita State Government Spending on Hospitals 244
12-4   State Health Care Expenditures 245
12-5   Comparison of Projected Versus Actual
            Arizona State Government Per Capita Expenditures 246
12-6   AHCCCS Acute Care Expenditures by
            Revenue Source FY 1982/83 - FY 1988/89 248
12-7   AHCCCS Enrollment 249
12-8   Department of Health Services -- Federal and State Funds 251
12-9   County Expenditures for Health Care -- FY 87-88 255

13-1 Department of Economic Security Expenditures From 1979-1988 271
13-2 The Largest Children and Families Programs 1988 Expenditures 272
13-3 Comparison of Total State And Local Expenditures For
Public Welfare Arizona, U.S., and Neighboring States -- 1986-87 274
13-4 Variables in the Interstate Model 276
13-5 Interstate Welfare Expenditures Comparison Using 1966-1985 Sample 278
13-6 Interstate Welfare Expenditures Comparison For 1985 Data 280
13-7 AFDC Recipients per 1000 Population Comparisons for 1988-1985 Sample . 282
13-8 AFDC Recipients pre 1000 Population Comparison for 1985 Data 283

13-9 AFDC Expenditures Per Capita Comparison for 1966-1985 Sample 284
13-10 AFDC Expenditures Per Capita Comparison For 1985 Data 285
13-11 Comparison of Western States Total Welfare
Expenditures State Specific Effects 286
13-12 Variables in the Arizona Welfare Model 287
13-13 Arizona Regression Model Results 288

14-1 State Air Quality Programs, 1985 307
14-2 Parks Systems Revenues,
Arizona and Comparison States, FY 1986 Operations 312
14-3 Arizona's Parks Compared to Other State Parks Systems, FY 1986 313

15-1 State and Local Government Public Safety Expenditures 322
15-2 State Government Public Safety Expenditures 323
15-3 State Government Public Safety Expenditures as a
Share of Total State and Local Public Safety Expenditures 324
15-4 1987 Crimes Rates 325
15-5 State Government Public Safety Expenditures in Arizona 326
15-6 Arizona Department of Public Safety Operating Expenditures 327
15-7 Arizona Department of Corrections Operating Expenditures 328
15-8 Arizona Department of Corrections Operating Expenditures Per Inmate 329
15-9 State, County, Municipal, and Federal Funds as a
Percentage of Total Expenditures of the Arizona Judicial System 331
15-10 State Expenditures of the Arizona Judicial System 332
15-11 Probation-Related State Judicial Expenditures 333

16-1 Arizona Registration Fees For Commercial Vehicles 342
16-2 State Tax Rates on Motor Fuel 344
16-3 Revenues Deposited in Arizona Highway User Revenue Fund (HURF)
By Source, Fiscal Years 1976-1989 349
16-4 Per Capita Total State and Local Highway Expenditures Relative to the U.S. 352
16-5 Per Capita Total State and Local Highway Expenditures -
Arizona Relative to Other Western States 353
16-6 10-Year Sum of Highway Expenditures Relative to
10-Year Population Change Real Dollars per Added Person 354

17-1 Arizona School District Expenditures, School Years 1980-88 362
17-2 Arizona School District Revenues School Years 1980-88 363

17-3   Trends in Salaries, Number of Teachers, and Student-Teacher Ratio,
       School Years 1980-88 364

17-4   Long Term Trends in School Finance: Arizona, U.S., and Comparison
       States Distribution of Revenue Sources to School Districts 365

17-5   Elementary and Secondary Education Expenditures
       Interstate Comparisons 1986-1987 366

17-6   Variation in Per-Student Equalization Base SY 1987-88 373

17-7   Ratio of Actual Maintenance, Operation, and Capital Outlay
       Spending to Equalization Base, 1987-88 374

17-8   Ratio of Actual Maintenance, Operation, and Capital Outlay
       Spending to Equalization Base Larger Districts with
       Positive Primary Tax Rate, 1987-88 375

17-9   Number of Students in High and Low Expenditure Districts, 1987-1988 . . . 376

17-10 Variation in Property Tax Rates and Property Tax Bases, SY 1987-88 378

17-11 Distributions of Student Performance Measures in 1987-88 380

17-12 Correlations between Expenditure Measures and
       Performance Measures, 1987-88 380

17-13 Estimates of the Education Production Function Dependent Variable:
       Log of District Mean of Basic Scores of Eleventh Graders 381

18-1   State Assistance To Local Governments:
       Per Capita Aid And As A Share Of General Revenues 390

18-2   Federal Assistance To Local Governments
       Per Capita Aid And As A Share Of Local General Revenues 392

18-3   Local Own-source Revenues:
       Per Capita And As A Share Of Local General Revenues 393

18-4   State Assistance to Local Governments in Arizona 396

18-5   Annual Percent Change in Urban Revenue Sharing Distributions,
       State Personal Income and Population, 1977 to 1988 398

18-6   State Sales Tax Collections by Class, 1988 399

18-7   State Shared Sales Tax Collection And Distribution -- 1988 401

20-1   Selected Features of State Real Property Classification 427

20-2   Summary of Property Classes in Arizona, 1988 431

20-3   History of Assessment Ratios for Arizona Property Classes,
       As Defined by 1988 Law, 1968-1988 432

20-4   Percentage Distributions (by Class) of Arizona Property Tax Base,
       Tax Amounts, and Effective Tax Rates (ETR) Statewide, 1988 435

20-5   Comparisons of Actual Property Tax to a Hypothetical
       Statewide Uniform Property Tax Based on Average Rates for 1988 436

21-1   City Expenditures And Expenditure Limits: 1987 453

21-2   Actual County Levy Limits Compared To Hypothetical Limits
       In The Absence Of New Construction 456

21-3   Percentage Growth Of Per Capita Primary Property Taxes 1982 To 1987 . . 461

22-1   General Fund Revenue and Expenditure Forecast 1988-2000: Summary 466

22-2   General Fund Revenue and Expenditure Forecast 1988-2000 467

22-3   Summary of Annual Forecast Assumptions   470
22-4   Year 2000 Fiscal Impact of Alternative Assumptions   473
22-5   Balanced Budget Alternatives   474
22-6   General Fund New Revenue   476
22-7   General Fund Expenditures   477

Figures

2-1 Tax Burden for Arizona and the
Average of the Contiguous States, 1981-1987   26

2-2 Tax Burden for Arizona and for the Average of the Region, 1981-1987 . . .   27

2-3 Annual Percentage Employment Growth in Arizona and the
Average in 48 Contiguous States, 1981-1987   28

2-4 Annual Percentage Employment Growth in
Arizona and in the Region, 1981-1987   29

3-1 Population change, Net Migration, and
Employment Change in Arizona, 1970-1989   29

5-1 Determination of Arizona Personal Income Tax Liability, 1988   65

5-2 Arizona 1988 Tax Schedules   66

14-1 Natural Resource Programs as a Percent of Federal Budget and GNP   300

14-2 State and Local Commitment to Natural Resources   310

14-3 State and Local Spending *Per Capita* on Natural Resources, 1986-87   302

14-4 State and Local Spending Per $1000 Personal Income
on Natural Resources, 1986-87   303

14-5 State Percentage of State and Local Natural Resources Spending   305

14-6 South Coast Air Quality District *Per Capita* Expenditures By Source   308

22-1 General Fund Revenue and Expenditure Projections: "Best Guess"   469

Part I:
Introduction and Context

Chapter 1

Introduction and Overview

Therese J. McGuire and Dana Wolfe Naimark[*]

The chapters of this book are based on reports prepared for the Arizona Joint Select Committee on State Revenues and Expenditures (otherwise known as Arizona Fiscal 2000), a temporary committee composed of citizens and legislators, charged with making recommendations to the Legislature and the Governor for reform of the fiscal system of Arizona. While the research in this book relates specifically to Arizona, the issues are framed in a general context and are relevant for states across the country. The decade of the 1990s will be critical for state and local governments throughout the nation as they adapt to changes in fiscal federalism implemented in the 1980s, to increasing demands in the areas of health and welfare and public safety, and to changes in local government financing (in particular, but not limited to, financing local school districts). The case study of Arizona presented in this volume illuminates the problems that many states will face throughout the 1990s, and illustrates the application of economic and public finance principles to those problems.

While each of the chapters was researched and written independently, the authors were aware of the interrelationships among various aspects of the fiscal system. In this introductory chapter we attempt to pull the parts together to tell a coherent story of a fiscal system in need of major structural reform. Each of the chapters that follow provides a piece in the fiscal puzzle.

Some of the findings and conclusions described in this volume are unique to Arizona. Arizona's mix of revenues and expenditures, for example, is different from the average state. Arizona has a heavier reliance on sales taxes and a lighter reliance on personal income taxes. Higher than average spending on higher education, public safety, and highways contrasts with much lower than average spending on health and welfare. As discussed below, this mix carries certain implications for the workings of the fiscal system and thus for fiscal reform.

Many of the findings and conclusions, however, apply to most states in the country. Most pervasive, perhaps, and a common conclusion in tax studies (see Ebel and McGuire (1986) for a recent example), is the finding of unnecessary complexity. Years of balancing competing political interests have led many states to fiscal systems full of inconsistencies, irrational rules, confusing loopholes, and procedures that are often incomprehensible to the individuals affected. This complexity greatly increases administration and compliance costs

---

[*]McGuire was director and Naimark was project manager for the Arizona Joint Select Committee on State Revenues and Expenditures. The views and observations expressed in this volume represent those of the authors.

and eventually leads to non-compliance and a distrust of government. It also leads to ineffective fiscal policies. When the system is too complex, it is almost impossible to assess accurately the impact of current policies and proposed policy changes. In Arizona, complexity was particularly notable in the personal income tax system, the school finance rules, the sales tax, and the intergovernmental fiscal relationships, areas of potential complexity in most states.

Probably the most dramatic conclusion of the Arizona Fiscal 2000 study is the existence of a structural deficit. The discovery that revenues are growing much slower than currently planned expenditures with the implication that, if left unattended, the gap between expenditures and revenues will widen over time. Because Arizona has a balanced budget requirement (as do 45 other states), this structural deficit has a major impact on routine state operations.

The structural deficit is a problem that most states will face in the next decade. While Arizona's particular problem is exacerbated by its choice of revenue mix (relying primarily on slow-growth sales taxes rather than fast-growth income taxes), the fast-growth expenditures in Arizona are fast-growth expenditures across the country. Indeed, health care and prisons are issues at all levels of government and in all regions of the nation. The cost of medical care is expected to rise dramatically throughout the next decade, and recent public safety initiatives on mandatory sentencing and stricter drug policy are already having an impact on prisons and the courts. Much uncertainty surrounds predictions for welfare expenditures. With many states proposing innovative programs, the federal government mandating sweeping welfare reform measures (that increase eligibility and extend program coverage), and rapid population growth of many poorer groups in society, the best estimate predicts relatively rapid growth in this category as well. The structural deficit is acute in Arizona because expenditure levels are relatively low in health and welfare, and public safety expenditures are very popular politically leaving little room for expenditure cuts.

In addition to pressures from fast-growing expenditures, many states are likely to face structural deficits in the next decade for two other reasons. First, during the decade of the 1980s, the federal government devolved responsibility to the states for spending in many areas. Some of these spending categories (welfare, for example) involve spending of a cyclical nature. Second, the tax structures of many states are geared toward manufacturing, farming or mining economies rather than service and trade economies, and thus state tax structures are becoming increasingly obsolete as the service and trade sectors grow relative to the manufacturing sectors.

Setting The Context

What is the economic, demographic and institutional context in which Arizona's fiscal system operates? In Chapter 2, Carroll and Wasylenko find that Arizona had one of the fastest growing economies during the 1970s and 1980s. The key question addressed by Carroll and Wasylenko is whether fiscal factors help to explain Arizona's extraordinary growth in the decade of the 1980s. Using data on the 48 contiguous states, they estimate equations similar to those estimated by Wasylenko and McGuire (1985) for the 1970s, and find no consistent, statistical relationship between economic growth and various attributes of the fiscal system (including tax and expenditure levels, changes in tax levels, and expenditure and tax composition). These results differ from the results of Wasylenko and McGuire and of Helms (1985), who find some evidence of fiscal factors being determinants of economic growth. Taken together, these recent empirical results indicate that the effect of fiscal factors on economic growth is likely to be small. Arizona in the 1980s was characterized by economic growth much higher than the national average. At the same time, Arizona had an average level of taxes and spending indicating that fiscal characteristics were not an important force behind economic growth in this period.

In Chapter 3, Hogan and Rex argue that Arizona's rapid population growth in recent decades is both a result and cause of the state's recent booming economy. Demographic projections of large percentage population gains in the next 20 years indicate that the prospects are good for continued strong, secular economic growth. However, demographic changes, such as shifts in the age composition, are likely to require increased state spending to maintain current service levels.

One charge frequently heard in Arizona is that poor revenue forecasting is the cause of Arizona's fiscal problems. However, in Chapter 4, Naimark and Watson find that Arizona's forecasting techniques are sound and that forecasting results over the last decade have been as accurate as can be expected given the inherent uncertainty in the economic phenomena involved. Poor forecasting has not been the cause of Arizona's budget problems. Instead, Arizona's continuing fiscal problems are exacerbated by a lack of procedures to manage unexpected surpluses or deficits. Because unexpected surpluses or deficits will arise no matter how fine the forecasting techniques, states need to develop procedures to accommodate differences in predicted expenditures and revenues. Not surprisingly, Naimark and Watson find much room for improvement in state budget procedures.

The Revenue System

When the revenue sources available to state governments are analyzed, it is obvious that there is no perfect revenue source to finance state expenditures. Different sources of revenue serve different policy goals. These goals are often in conflict so that designing a fiscal system involves policy tradeoffs. While a single revenue source may have undesirable characteristics, it can be one useful component in a well-functioning overall revenue system in conjunction with other revenue sources displaying opposing characteristics.

While economic theory does not justify a specific design for a state personal income tax, Feenberg, McGuire and Rosen (Chapter 5) find that economic principles do argue for taxing all sources of income at the same rate, making the tax base as broad as possible so that marginal effective rates can be as low as possible and making the tax system as simple as possible. The authors find that Arizona's personal income tax system, like most states' personal income tax systems, can use improvement in all three areas. While deductions for specific expenditures are meant to assist certain groups of people or encourage certain activities at the state level where marginal tax rates are low relative to federal tax rates, their impact is probably not worth the extra compliance and administration costs associated with their complexity. Accordingly, the authors present several alternatives to the current Arizona system all of which broaden the base and greatly simplify the tax. The desired degree of progressivity can then be obtained by choosing an appropriate tax rate structure.

In Chapter 6, McGuire finds that simplifying the state corporation income tax is not quite so easy. The tax is inherently complex because of the issues associated with the proper tax treatment of multistate corporations. It is difficult to determine the implications of the tax for equity because it is difficult to determine who bears the burden of the tax. The tax scores poorly on the efficiency criterion distorting investment decisions of corporations. Despite the fact that it fails on many of the generally accepted criteria for good tax design, the state corporation income tax remains popular being employed in 45 states (although at relatively low rates of taxation). Given the political appeal of state corporation income taxes despite so many design defects, a policy prescription of simplicity through general conformity with the federal tax seems warranted.

Because financial industries in the U.S. are in a state of considerable adjustment (regulatory, technological, and economic), it is important to reconsider the tax structures applied to them. In Chapter 7, Fox evaluates Arizona's tax treatment of financial industries in light of these changes. Currently, Arizona taxes financial firms under the corporation income tax statutes. Fox argues that the unique characteristics of financial firms may warrant a tax separate from the corporation income tax, or at least an adaptation of the corporation income tax, that recognizes differences between financial and non-financial firms in the factors of production (tangible versus intangible assets) and the sources of income (taxable earnings versus nontaxable earnings from holdings of federal securities).

The two major policy questions regarding state general sales taxes are how to define the taxable base and how much to rely on sales tax revenue compared to other sources. In Chapter 8, Ladd and Weist find that the sales tax base in Arizona is defined both very broadly, including more business purchases than most states, and not broadly enough, excluding some types of consumer purchases that would logically fit under the tax. In particular, most consumer purchases of services are not taxed precluding Arizona from tapping into this rapidly growing component of the economy. The extent of service taxation under the sales tax is an issue of increasing importance across the country because as the service sector grows allowing a tax distinction between goods and services that provide the same consumption benefit makes increasingly less sense, being costly to state treasuries and causing distortions of many economic decisions. Ladd and Weist find that Arizona lacks an overall conceptual framework for the sales tax leading to piecemeal changes in response to political pressures. Arizona sales tax collections per capita, both at the state and city level, are much higher than average due to a heavy reliance on sales taxes relative to other types of revenue. One possible rationale for this heavy reliance is that much of Arizona's sales tax is exported through the state's large tourism industry. The authors estimate that approximately 11 percent of the sales tax burden is exported meaning that it is borne by people from out of state.

Arizona cities have the authority to impose local general sales taxes. Cities are given the authority to determine not only their own sales tax rates, which is common practice across the country, but also their own sales tax bases, which is not common practice and which creates compliance problems for businesses operating in more than one jurisdiction. Ladd and Weist argue that the economic arguments for allowing each jurisdiction to choose its own sales tax base appear to be outweighed by the simplicity argument for conformity of state and local bases.

In Chapter 9, Schlagenhauf finds that selective sales taxes on liquor, tobacco, hotel rooms, and real estate transfers all score well on simplicity grounds and fairly well on efficiency. In addition, much of the burden of the tax on hotel rooms is exported, borne largely by tourists and business persons from out of state. Cigarette taxes and alcohol taxes are very regressive imposing relatively heavy burdens on low income individuals. However, they provide for stable sources of revenue and enhance efficiency by capturing societal costs associated with alcohol and tobacco consumption. Thus, these taxes have an important role to play in the system as a whole. The author finds the hotel/motel and real estate transfer taxes to be sensitive to both long-term economic growth and short-term economic cycles.

User charges and fees are appropriate public financing mechanisms for a limited set of goods and services. In Chapter 10, Faith and Naimark discuss how user charges enhance economic efficiency by creating a direct link between the costs and benefits of public services. User charges also may enhance government accountability by enabling citizens to communicate their desires about public services through their consumption behavior. To take the greatest advantage of the efficiency that charges can provide, in those cases where the link between provision of the service and revenues generated from the use of the service can be identified, the use of carmarking to special funds is justified.

Expenditures

Our fiscal study of Arizona was unusual in its degree of attention to expenditures in addition to revenues. The research approach on the expenditure side paralleled the revenue approach as much as possible. However, because the chapters did not undertake cost/benefit analyses, the application of objective economic criteria was somewhat limited. In making interstate comparisons of expenditure levels we did not find that Arizona was spending excessively in any important areas, and in fact, we found that Arizona was spending far less than average in some areas. This fact made it difficult to look to adjustments in the level of expenditures as a primary solution to Arizona's fiscal woes.

In Chapter 11, Giertz finds that Arizona has made a clear commitment to high quality, research-oriented higher education. This is a particularly expensive commitment in Arizona because Arizona has a relatively high percentage of students as a share of its population, and Arizona's per capita income is somewhat below the national average. Giertz points out several options available to reduce the expense of this commitment including limiting the state's focus to one major research university, greater utilization of community college districts, limiting enrollment of out-of-state students, and increasing tuition and fees.

As Christianson and Wyant describe health care in Chapter 12, government health care programs in Arizona are in the midst of a major shift in responsibility from the counties to the state. This shift began in 1983 when Arizona became the last state in the union to implement a Medicaid program. Implementation of a state health care program for the indigent was justified because it would bring federal dollars into the state to help pay the costs of public health services, and because the counties were viewed as becoming increasingly incapable of financing a uniform level of health care services across the state.

Arizona's version of Medicaid is a unique experimental program that involves competitive bidding among private providers and payments on a per-patient basis in an attempt to limit indigent health care costs. In the past decade, state health care expenditures in Arizona have increased dramatically, significantly faster than other types of state spending. This increase is due in part to the shift to state responsibility but much of it has been due to factors outside of state control, such as medical care price inflation, technological and demographic changes, and changes in federal laws and programs. Christianson and Wyant expect that these factors, combined with future population growth, will lead to health care cost increases well above general inflation for at least the next decade, a fate to be shared by many other states.

In Chapter 13, Craig finds that Arizona spends less on welfare than the average state, not because it provides a narrower set of welfare services nor because its economic and demographic characteristics require less welfare spending, but because the state's chosen benefit levels are low. Craig presents the argument that the manner in which welfare dollars are spent, rather than simply the level of spending, can make the welfare system an effective tool for promoting the general welfare of the state. State policy changes required by the federal Family Support Act of 1988 ameliorate some of the systematic disincentive effects facing recipients, and Arizona's compliance with the federal mandates will likely narrow the spending gap between Arizona and other states in welfare spending.

Increasing public attention is being paid to the environment and natural resources at local, regional, national and international levels. Public expenditures in this area are likely to increase over the final decade of the 20th century. Arizona is similar to other states in that many environmental issues are a recent concern, but its topography differentiates the state in that water is in scarce supply and the desert landscape is particularly vulnerable to human encroachment. In Chapter 14, Billings and Day describe the many state agencies concerned with environmental and natural resource issues. With the establishment of the Department of Environmental Quality in 1986, Arizona would appear to have a complete apparatus to manage its water, air, land and parks, but Billings and Day find the state to be somewhat deficient in the programs for parks, natural habitat, and wildlife. The authors point out that user charges and fees are often an appropriate source of revenue in this area particularly for internalizing the costs of pollution and for charging for hunting and fishing licenses, groundwater withdrawal rights and park entrance fees. However, user charges are not appropriate for funding pure public goods such as the preservation of wildlife and open space.

Arizona's higher than average expenditures on public safety result from both demographic characteristics and policy choice. In Chapter 15, Ormiston finds that the state has a high crime and high incarceration rate. Like many states, Arizona passed a toughened criminal code and sentencing laws at the beginning of the 1980s. Though the relationship between these laws and escalating prison populations is a matter of controversy, it is clear that the public desire for increased protection and the war against drugs must confront the reality of the incredible costs of court programs and incarceration. Like the federal government and many other states, Arizona faces increasingly overcrowded prisons and a public reluctance to pay for building more.

In recent years, Arizona's total state and local highway expenditures per capita were far above the U.S. average. This level reflects a recent shift for the state into a "catch-up" mode as Arizona's spending in previous decades was far below average. In Chapter 16 Charney and Horn find that Arizona's current structure of highway financing includes many of the basic components of a good highway financing system. One component of the system is a weight-distance tax, a tax which results in higher taxes being paid by those users who cause greater damage to highways, thereby imposing higher highway maintenance and repair costs. However, the current fees and taxes are not designed to keep up with highway construction and maintenance cost inflation leading to potentially major funding problems in the future.

Financing Local Government

Arizona's fiscal system has particularly strong links between the state and local governments, but the components of the intergovernmental system are similar to those in many states including state financing of K-12 education, state revenue distributions to cities and counties, limits on local government property tax levies and expenditures, property tax relief programs, and a statewide system of property classification. This intergovernmental system is characterized by excessive complexity and by mechanisms that are not well designed to serve policy goals. Many of the features were created to limit local property taxes, a goal that has little economic justification. Because of the numerous fiscal interrelationships, potential changes to the state's fiscal system cannot be thoroughly evaluated without examining their impact on local government financing.

Like many other states, Arizona has enacted changes in its school finance system in an attempt to reduce variation in tax rates and spending across school districts. However, in Chapter 17 Downes and Pogue find that there remains considerable unevenness in the treatment of both students and taxpayers. Districts differ substantially in per student spending and in property tax rates levied. The authors discuss several policy options available to enhance uniformity in spending and tax rates without exacerbating the complexity of the school finance system.

The State of Arizona distributes a greater than average share of its revenues as assistance to local governments. This reflects the decentralized system in Arizona and above average spending responsibility at the local level. In Chapter 18, Bell evaluates state aid to counties and cities and finds that the distribution formulas are not well designed to accomplish the goal of equalizing fiscal disparities among jurisdictions. However, because there is a small equalizing effect, reducing state aid would accentuate fiscal disparities between local jurisdictions. In addition, reductions in state aid would require constitutional or statutory changes so that local governments could make up for lost state aid dollars with own-source revenues. A reduction in state aid would represent a shift in tax burden from the state to the local level which could improve accountability in the fiscal system.

Although the property tax is the target of widespread criticism, Oates argues in Chapter 19 that the tax, when properly structured, actually performs very well as a source of local revenue. Local governments need their own major tax source if they are to function as responsible fiscal entities making sensible decisions on local fiscal programs. The property tax is probably the best available tax to serve that role. The objectionable features of the property tax can be dealt with through modifications in its design and through a well structured system of equalizing intergovernmental grants.

While the classification of property often is defended as necessary to achieve equity, Bowman argues in Chapter 20 that the case for uniformity in classification, based on market value, is considerably stronger than that for a classified system that generates effective tax rate differentials across types of property. Differentials in effective property tax rates alter economic decisions and impose non-neutralities on taxpayers. Classification creates complexity and imposes significant administrative and compliance costs. While little economic justification can be found for classification systems, Bowman finds that the Arizona system defines more classes and establishes larger differences in effective tax rates than most other state classification systems. Accordingly, he concludes that to improve simplicity, efficiency and equity, the state should move toward uniformity in classification.

In Chapter 21, Fisher and Gade examine state-imposed limits on local government spending and on property tax levies. These limits in Arizona and throughout the nation resulted from taxpayer revolts of the late 1970s and reflect fear of unrestrained local property taxes. The limits are state-imposed embodying a presumption that voters need protection from their local elected officials. The limits create complexity and can institutionalize inequities among jurisdictions. They also can lead to unintended consequences as localities seek ways to avoid the constraints of the limits. If fiscal limits on local governments are desired, it is important to ensure that local voters have a mechanism for overriding the limits. Such a provision provides for increased autonomy for local governments and recognizes that the political system must not be so rigid as to make it cumbersome for local governments to respond to changing local conditions. Fisher and Gade conclude that Arizona's limits have not constrained the level of local property taxes and expenditures primarily because mechanisms exist for local governments to circumvent the limits when desired and justified by local vote.

Summary

In Chapter 22, Watson provides a sobering conclusion to our study of Arizona's fiscal system. Watson projects expenditures and revenues to the year 2000 and finds that a structural deficit is built into Arizona's fiscal system. Current program expenditures are projected to grow at 5.6 percent a year while the current revenue structure is projected to generate growth of 4.0 percent a year indicating that without structural changes the gap between revenues and expenditures will widen over time. Because the magnitude of the structural deficit is large, minor adjustments to revenues or expenditures will not eliminate it. Finding solutions to the structural deficit will be the key issue in Arizona in the 1990s.

Because fast-growth expenditures and relatively slow-growth state revenues characterize other states as well, restructuring state fiscal systems to accommodate or arrest the growth of expenditure programs is likely to be the greatest challenge facing state and local policy makers and academic researchers across the country in the 1990s. In short, states will need to reexamine their priorities to decide which government programs they both desire *and* are willing to pay for.

References

Ebel, Robert D. and Therese J. McGuire, editors, *Final Report of the Minnesota Tax Study Commission*, Vol. 2, Butterworth, Boston, Massachusetts, 1986.

Helms, L. Jay, "The effect of state and local taxes on economic growth: a time series-cross section approach," *The Review of Economics and Statistics*, November 1985.

Wasylenko, Michael and Therese McGuire, "Jobs and taxes: the effect of business climate on states' employment growth rates," *National Tax Journal*, December 1985.

Chapter 2

Economic Growth And Government Fiscal Behavior 1973-1987

Robert Carroll and Michael Wasylenko

Economic growth benefits a state in many ways. The provision of jobs for the labor force, income and, therefore, goods and services for residents, and tax revenue for financing desired government services, is easier to accomplish in a state with economic growth. Policy decision-makers attempt to encourage economic growth through many means, including fiscal policy. These decisions often are made with an insufficient amount of information to guide effective policy. This attempts to provide factual information regarding the effect of the fiscal system on economic growth.

The methodology employed compares differences in states' long-run economic growth rates to differences across the states in factors influencing business location decisions. The methodology is not appropriate for explaining cyclical changes in growth rates. Rather, the approach used here seeks to explain what causes one state to have *consistently* lower or higher economic growth than the average state. In particular, once we have controlled for many business location factors, does the level or nature of Arizona's fiscal system in the 1980s help to explain its relatively high level of economic growth in the 1980s? The question of whether Arizona's taxes and expenditures put it at a competitive advantage or disadvantage vis-a-vis other states is central to this chapter.

Employment and Output Growth Rates: Arizona Compared

Employment Structure and Growth

The level and growth of economic activity often guide policy-makers' decisions on fiscal matters. In this section, we examine states' employment growth rates for two time periods: 1973 to 1981 and 1981 to 1987. All three years (1973, 1981, and 1987) represent peaks or near-peaks in the business cycle, and 1987 is the last year for which Bureau of Economic Analysis data are available on computer tape. Since 1973, 1981, and 1987 are comparable points in the business cycle, the analysis focuses on secular or long-term growth from 1973 to 1981 and 1981 to 1987.[1] The selection of these two time periods avoids confounding secular or long-run trends in employment growth with short-run employment changes due to business cycle fluctuations. The data for this section are earnings employment, which include employment in wage and salary jobs as well as proprietors' categories. The employment data are from the United States Department of Commerce, Bureau of Economic Analysis. We focus on Arizona, and five neighboring states (California, Colorado, Nevada, New Mexico, and Utah) plus the State of Texas. Table 2-1 reports the distribution of total employment by industry in 1987. Table 2-2 reports the compound annual employment growth rates during the two time periods.

Arizona has relatively high concentrations of employment in Construction and Finance, Insurance, and Real Estate (see Table 2-1). In 1987, about 5.4 percent of the United States workforce was employed in Construction compared to 7.3 percent in Arizona, and about 7.8 percent of the United States workforce was employed in Finance, Insurance, and Real Estate compared to 10.2 percent in Arizona. It is also notable that Arizona had a greater concentration of its workforce in Construction than any other state in the region in 1987. On the other hand, about 6.2 percent of the United States workforce and only 2.5 percent of the Arizona workforce were employed in nondurable manufacturing. For other industries, Arizona's employment concentration does not deviate much from the average in the United States as a whole. Arizona and its comparison states have service-based economies, as all seven states in the region have a lower portion of their workforce employed in manufacturing industries than the United States as a whole. Of the neighboring states, California's employment structure most resembles that of the United States, while Nevada's employment structure, with 43.5 percent of its workforce employed in Services, departs the most from the United States employment structure.

Employment growth rates for these states and for the United States as a whole are displayed in Table 2-2. During the 1973 to 1981 period, employment growth rates in all seven states exceeded the 2.0 percent annual employment growth rate in the United States as a whole. Moreover, in all seven states in the region, non-farm employment in every sector except Mining grew faster than United States employment in that sector during the 1973 to 1981 period. Mining employment in Arizona declined at a 0.2 percent annual rate during the period, compared to an 8.2 percent national rate of growth for Mining.

Turning to the 1981 to 1987 period, employment in the United States grew at an annual rate of 2.2 percent. Five of the seven states in this region experienced higher employment growth than the national average during this period. Arizona had employment growth of 5.2 percent *per annum*, while employment grew 3.5 percent in Nevada, 3.0 percent in California, 2.7 percent in Utah and 2.3 percent in New Mexico. At the same time, employment grew only 2.1 percent per annum in Colorado and a sluggish 1.5 percent in Texas. In the five rapidly growing states, employment in individual industry sectors generally grew faster during the 1981 to 1987 period than the national averages in the corresponding industry sectors during the same period. However, the dominance of the region that is revealed in the 1973 to 1981 employment data is not as evident in the 1981 to 1987 period.

Arizona experienced the most rapid employment growth rate of the seven states from 1981 to 1987. In addition, Arizona's employment growth was more than double the national average in both the 1981 to 1987 period and the 1973 to 1981 period. Employment growth well in excess of that in the nation as a whole relies on a constantly expanding market share, on labor force growth in excess of the national average, and on the infrastructure expanding at a rate sufficient to accommodate rapid growth. Such a high level of growth probably

Table 2-1
Employment Shares for Arizona, Six Comparison States,
And the United States, By Industry, 1987

Industry	United States	Arizona	California	Colorado	Nevada	New Mexico	Texas	Utah
Total Earnings Employment	100.00	100.00	100.00	100.00	100.00	100.00	100.00	100.00
Farm	2.55	1.24	1.62	2.32	0.84	2.75	2.80	2.41
Nonfarm	97.45	98.76	98.38	97.68	99.16	97.25	97.20	97.59
Agricultural, Forestry, & Fishery	0.96	1.45	1.76	0.97	0.70	0.87	0.87	0.62
Mining	0.75	0.76	0.36	1.56	1.43	2.42	3.07	1.09
Construction	5.36	7.33	5.08	5.57	6.12	6.16	6.10	5.05
Manufacturing	15.12	11.01	14.42	9.99	4.03	5.82	11.34	11.89
Nondurable Goods	6.21	2.50	4.71	3.66	1.57	1.97	4.96	3.87
Durable Goods	8.91	8.51	9.71	6.33	2.47	3.85	6.49	8.01
Transportation, Communications, and Public Utilities	4.73	4.08	4.25	5.09	4.94	4.72	5.14	5.03
Wholesale Trade	4.85	4.12	4.87	4.29	3.22	3.52	5.01	4.48
Retail Trade	16.40	17.44	15.63	16.42	15.33	17.54	16.72	16.65
Finance, Insurance, & Real Estate	7.75	10.23	8.92	10.14	7.04	6.82	8.35	7.52
Services	26.06	26.84	28.11	26.70	43.45	25.91	24.64	25.63
Government	15.47	15.50	14.98	16.95	12.89	23.46	15.95	19.62

[a] California, Colorado, Nevada, New Mexico, and Utah were chosen as comparison states because they border Arizona and are generally perceived as economic competitors. Texas is included as a comparison state in this section only since it is in the Southwest region, broadly defined, and it, too, is viewed as an economic competitor.

Source: U.S. Department of Commerce, Bureau of Economic Analysis.

Table 2-2
Annual Rate of Employment Growth for Arizona, Six Comparison States And the United States, By Industry, 1973-81 and 1981-87[a]

Employment Growth, 1973-1981								
Industry	United States	Arizona	California	Colorado	Nevada	New Mexico	Texas	Utah
Total Earnings Employment	1.98	4.55	3.54	4.19	6.84	3.54	4.34	3.70
Farm	-0.68	0.06	-0.77	-0.41	3.67	0.06	-0.63	0.59
Nonfarm	2.08	4.65	3.65	4.35	6.52	3.68	4.56	3.81
Agricultural, Forestry, and Fishery	5.14	6.50	6.77	7.88	9.21	4.57	5.06	7.51
Mining	8.23	-0.19	6.80	14.83	9.36	8.18	13.51	6.55
Construction	1.09	2.10	4.02	2.28	4.60	4.16	5.66	3.10
Manufacturing	0.14	4.98	2.73	3.58	7.03	2.69	4.28	4.32
Nondurable Goods	-0.16	3.98	2.37	1.77	4.62	2.19	2.67	1.96
Durable Goods	0.34	5.29	2.90	4.62	8.44	3.02	5.47	5.54
Transportation, Communications, and Public Utilities	1.46	4.44	2.32	4.15	6.02	3.22	4.05	3.73
Wholesale Trade	3.20	5.78	3.75	5.62	7.39	5.69	5.01	4.93
Retail Trade	2.35	5.10	3.87	4.00	7.16	3.34	4.48	3.45
Finance, Insurance, and Real Estate	3.88	6.50	5.59	6.27	8.67	5.34	5.45	6.17
Services	3.70	6.12	5.20	5.79	7.33	4.84	4.82	5.46
Government	1.17	2.96	1.52	2.10	3.55	1.77	2.08	1.25

Table 2.2 (Continued)

Employment Growth, 1981-1987

Industry	United States	Arizona	California	Colorado	Nevada	New Mexico	Texas	Utah
Total Earnings Employment	2.24	5.15	3.04	2.09	3.50	2.33	1.50	2.72
Farm	-1.82	-0.71	-1.39	-0.12	-2.81	-0.89	-1.83	-0.17
Nonfarm	2.36	5.24	3.13	2.15	3.56	2.43	1.61	2.80
Agricultural, Forestry, and Fishery	5.37	6.73	4.60	5.84	8.55	5.48	3.64	6.50
Mining	-5.35	-10.51	-1.06	-8.28	0.79	-10.57	-5.17	-13.35
Construction	3.82	6.86	5.71	-0.10	3.50	0.79	-0.90	1.07
Manufacturing	-0.89	2.83	0.83	-0.15	2.55	1.89	-2.78	0.78
Nondurable	-0.40	3.06	1.09	1.22	5.31	-0.38	-1.47	1.73
Durable Goods	-1.22	2.76	0.70	-0.89	1.04	3.20	-3.68	0.35
Transportation, Communications, and Public Utilities	1.22	4.13	1.26	1.64	2.24	0.50	0.61	1.95
Wholesale Trade	1.25	4.57	2.62	-0.43	4.80	0.33	-1.21	-0.35
Retail Trade	2.76	4.61	2.63	1.82	2.71	3.25	2.00	3.04
Finance, Insurance, and Real Estate	4.36	9.07	4.75	5.01	4.73	4.85	5.53	4.65
Services	4.96	8.00	5.33	4.98	4.59	5.18	5.01	6.26
Government	1.19	2.53	1.30	1.25	1.50	1.88	2.31	2.33

[a] California, Colorado, Nevada, New Mexico, and Utah were chosen as comparison states because they border Arizona and are generally perceived as economic competitors. Texas is included as a comparison state in this section only since it is in the Southwest region, broadly defined, and it, too, is viewed as an economic competitor.

Source: U.S. Department of Commerce, Bureau of Economic Analysis.

cannot be sustained over the longer run. This observation does not necessarily suggest that the Arizona economy will decline, but its growth rate is likely to slow down and approach the average for the nation as a whole.

The most recent reports on Arizona's job growth relative to the United States should not be viewed as evidence that long-run growth in Arizona has fallen below the United States. For example, from November 1987 to November 1988 total nonagricultural employment increased only 1.6 percent in Arizona compared to 3.1 percent for the United States. This trend represents short-term business cycle responses, driven in this case by a downturn in the construction industry, that occur periodically regardless of the underlying factors that determine long-run growth. Indeed, from November 1988 to November 1989 Arizona's and the United States' employment growth were virtually the same at 2.39 percent and 2.41 percent, respectively. Recent figures for one of the underlying growth factors, population growth, indicate that Arizona is still likely to have an advantage over the average state in long-run growth (although the relative size of the advantage may be declining). From the fourth quarter of 1987 to the fourth quarter of 1988, population in Arizona increased 2.4 percent compared to an increase of 1.0 percent in the United States. Similarly, from the fourth quarter of 1988 to the fourth quarter of 1989, population in Arizona increased 1.9 percent while United States population increased only 1.0 percent.

Gross State Product Growth

Gross State Product measures the sum of payroll plus capital earnings (or value added) in the industry.[2] Conceivably, the rankings and growth rates of states could differ from those obtained using employment growth rates. Data on Gross State Product are not available for 1987. According to data in Table 2-3, Gross State Product for the United States and for five of the seven comparison states, New Mexico and Utah being the exceptions, grew slightly more slowly during the 1973 to 1981 period than employment during the same period (see Table 2-2). The relative ranking of the states changes very little, however. Of the seven states, Nevada, Utah, and Arizona were the fastest growing states when either Gross State Product or employment is used to measure growth. But, from 1973 to 1981 Arizona had the second largest growth rate of employment among the comparison states, while it had the third largest growth rate of Gross State Product.

The reason for the discrepancy between the growth rates of output and employment is difficult to determine without data on the underlying components of Gross State Product. One explanation is that states with a larger manufacturing base will have higher growth in Gross State Product than in employment since manufacturing industries are generally more capital intensive. As a result, Gross State Product in manufacturing industries will grow when capital is added to the production process even though labor is growing more slowly than capital. Service industries have less opportunity to add capital, and Gross State Product growth in services may be more closely tied to increases in employment.

Gross State Product grew more quickly than employment from 1981 to 1986 but the employment growth figures in Table 2-2 are for the 1981 to 1987 period, and they are not strictly comparable to the Gross State Product figures in Table 2-3. During this latter period Arizona and California, but not Nevada, grew faster than the other comparison states when growth is measured using Gross State Product. The main conclusion here is that the results of the regional growth analysis and of Arizona's performance relative to these other states are altered only slightly when output instead of employment is used as the basis of the analysis.

Table 2-3

Annual Rate of Gross State Product Growth for Arizona, Six Comparison States, And the United States, By Industry, 1973-81 and 1981-86[a]

Gross State Product Growth, 1973-1981

Industry	United States	Arizona	California	Colorado	Nevada	New Mexico	Texas	Utah
Total Gross State Product	1.95	4.26	3.22	4.10	6.36	4.19	4.19	4.37
Farm	2.72	7.36	5.90	1.69	0.00	1.43	2.16	2.40
Nonfarm	1.93	4.19	3.16	4.16	6.42	4.26	4.23	4.41
Agricultural, Forestry, and Fishery	3.62	5.84	5.12	7.21	8.09	3.49	4.94	6.82
Mining	0.59	0.92	0.49	2.49	11.36	2.55	-0.06	3.67
Construction	-1.80	0.01	0.27	-0.20	5.34	4.51	4.61	0.08
Manufacturing	1.06	6.37	3.78	5.08	7.04	4.99	5.96	4.71
Durable Goods	0.90	6.66	4.40	6.67	7.41	4.99	8.12	4.60
Nondurable Goods	1.32	5.12	2.63	2.51	6.48	5.03	3.68	4.96
Transportation, Communictions, and Public Utilities	2.51	6.04	2.79	6.55	6.52	5.45	5.90	6.93
Wholesale Trade	2.34	3.97	3.37	4.72	7.71	5.22	6.79	4.21
Retail Trade	1.54	3.85	3.38	3.82	6.36	2.41	4.85	3.29
Finance, Insurance, and Real	3.23	3.82	3.17	4.21	6.81	8.91	5.07	6.05
Estate	3.91	5.67	5.07	6.48	6.89	4.95	6.95	6.36
Services	1.61	4.09	1.48	2.42	4.00	3.18	2.93	2.47
Government								

Table 2.3 (Continued)

Gross State Product Growth, 1981-1986

Industry	United States	Arizona	California	Colorado	Nevada	New Mexico	Texas	Utah
Total Gross State Product	3.06	5.50	4.19	2.99	2.30	0.86	1.64	3.21
Farm	2.27	0.36	1.28	5.54	2.28	4.97	3.71	4.74
Nonfarm	3.08	5.62	4.25	2.92	2.30	0.77	1.60	3.19
Agricultural, Forestry, and Fishery	5.00	5.63	4.11	4.63	6.05	3.71	1.93	4.24
Mining	-3.13	-6.40	-2.52	-1.30	3.61	-5.37	-2.32	-11.21
Construction	2.69	7.42	3.23	0.43	-1.23	1.45	-1.28	1.10
Manufacturing	3.73	7.09	6.11	5.54	6.80	10.46	1.25	7.73
Durable Goods	5.04	7.62	7.87	7.01	7.57	10.80	1.74	8.76
Nondurable Goods	1.66	4.50	2.13	2.44	5.36	10.02	0.61	5.05
Transportation, Communications, and Public Utilities	2.08	2.31	2.97	2.54	2.55	1.46	2.51	2.73
Wholesale Trade	5.28	7.63	7.22	3.46	7.07	3.39	3.64	4.24
Retail Trade	4.63	7.05	5.06	4.04	2.99	4.69	3.92	4.97
Finance, Insurance, and Real Estate	3.06	5.71	3.49	2.41	2.65	-0.43	2.62	2.43
Services	4.08	7.24	4.72	3.67	1.95	4.08	3.55	4.35
Government	0.94	2.97	1.25	1.60	0.57	1.15	2.37	2.26

[a] California, Colorado, Nevada, New Mexico, and Utah were chosen as comparison states because they border Arizona and are generally perceived as economic competitors. Texas is included as a comparison state in this section only since it is in the Southwest region, broadly defined, and it, too, is viewed as an economic competitor.

Source: U.S. Department of Commerce, Bureau of Economic Analysis.

Thus, the conclusion that Arizona was a rapidly growing state during the 1973 to 1987 period remains intact.

Shift-Share Analysis for Arizona

Another method for examining employment growth and economic strength of an economy is shift-share analysis. This method disaggregates employment growth into three components: a national effect, an industry mix effect and a competitive effect. The *national effect* estimates expected employment growth if employment in each industry in the state grows at the same rate as total employment in the national economy. For example, if total national employment growth is 17.0 percent (or 1.98 percent annually) between 1973 and 1981, the national effect would increase expected Arizona employment 17.0 percent in each industry.

Continuing with the above example, the industry *mix effect* measures the expected employment increases for a particular industry from 1973 to 1981, due to the growth of the industry at the national level relative to the growth of total employment in the United States of 17.0 percent. If employment in the nation in services grew 33.7 percent between 1973 and 1981, the industry mix effect is measured as the difference between 33.7 and 17.0 percent, or 16.7 percent additional growth due to the industry mix effect. Intuitively, this measures the effect on a state's economy of having a relatively high concentration of fast or slow growth industries, as measured by the national growth rates for individual industries.

The *competitive effect* is, for this study, the most interesting of the three effects. A positive competitive effect means that the state's employment in the industry is growing faster than national employment in the industry, and a negative competitive effect means that the state's employment is not keeping pace with the national employment growth in the industry. The competitive effect is measured as the difference between the national growth rate of an industry and its local growth rate.

The competitive effects for industries in Arizona for three time periods (1973 to 1981, 1981 to 1987, and 1986 to 1987) are presented in Table 2-4. The competitive effects are expressed as annual averages so that the calculations for the three periods are comparable. The results of this analysis help to illustrate the extent of both the strength of the Arizona economy and the slowdown in certain industries during the 1986 to 1987 period.

In aggregate, the economy of Arizona created 29,286 more jobs on an annual basis between 1973 and 1981 than one would expect if employment in each industry in Arizona grew at the same rate as United States employment growth in each industry. The competitive effect figure for Arizona swelled to 43,328 jobs annually between 1981 and 1987, but slowed down to 11,194 jobs during the 1986 to 1987 period. While there was a slowdown, the Arizona economy still produced more jobs than expected based on national trends in its industries.

The competitive employment effects for the underlying industries were generally positive with the exception of Mining during the two longer time periods, and Agriculture, Forestry and Fishery, and Construction for the 1986 to 1987 period. While the competitive employment effect slowed down in most industries during the 1986 to 1987 period compared to the other time periods, the annual competitive employment effect in Farm; Mining; Transportation, Communications, and Public Utilities; and Wholesale Trade *increased* from 1986 to 1987 compared to the 1973 to 1981 and the 1981 to 1987 time periods. Thus, while overall employment growth in Arizona slowed down in the 1986 to 1987 period relative to the two earlier periods, these four industry sectors increased their contribution to job growth in Arizona.

<table>
<tr><td colspan="4" align="center">Table 2-4
Annual Competitive Employment Effects for Arizona
By Industry, 1973-81, 1981-87, and 1986-87[a]</td></tr>
<tr><td align="center">Industry</td><td align="center">1973-81</td><td align="center">1981-87</td><td align="center">1986-87</td></tr>
<tr><td>Total Earnings Employment</td><td align="right">29,286</td><td align="right">45,328</td><td align="right">11,194</td></tr>
<tr><td>Farm</td><td align="right">162</td><td align="right">238</td><td align="right">1,382</td></tr>
<tr><td>Nonfarm</td><td align="right">28,716</td><td align="right">44,256</td><td align="right">8,885</td></tr>
<tr><td> Agriculture, Forestry and Fishery</td><td align="right">210</td><td align="right">314</td><td align="right">-756</td></tr>
<tr><td> Mining</td><td align="right">-2,970</td><td align="right">-894</td><td align="right">1,003</td></tr>
<tr><td> Construction</td><td align="right">823</td><td align="right">3,409</td><td align="right">-13,351</td></tr>
<tr><td> Manufacturing</td><td align="right">6,429</td><td align="right">6,383</td><td align="right">1,508</td></tr>
<tr><td>   Durable</td><td align="right">5,068</td><td align="right">5,252</td><td align="right">1,248</td></tr>
<tr><td>   Nondurable</td><td align="right">1,268</td><td align="right">1,356</td><td align="right">823</td></tr>
<tr><td> Transportation, Communications
    & Public Utilities</td><td align="right">1,452</td><td align="right">1,871</td><td align="right">2,279</td></tr>
<tr><td> Wholesale Trade</td><td align="right">1,239</td><td align="right">2,118</td><td align="right">4,038</td></tr>
<tr><td> Retail Trade</td><td align="right">5,583</td><td align="right">5,163</td><td align="right">2,798</td></tr>
<tr><td> Finance, Insurance, and Real Estate</td><td align="right">2,405</td><td align="right">6,957</td><td align="right">785</td></tr>
<tr><td> Services</td><td align="right">6,242</td><td align="right">12,357</td><td align="right">2,800</td></tr>
<tr><td> Government</td><td align="right">3,839</td><td align="right">3,460</td><td align="right">3,514</td></tr>
</table>

[a] The competitive effects for individual industries will not sum to the figure listed next to "Total Earnings Employment." The analysis uses different benchmarks for each industry and the competitive effect for total employment is a weighted average of the competitive effects in each industry.

Source: The underlying data are from the U.S. Department of Commerce, Bureau of Economic Analysis.

In summary, Arizona's employment grew at rates far above the United States average over two time periods, 1973 to 1981 and 1981 to 1987. In the latter period Arizona was the fastest growing state among the seven comparison states in the region. Industries that exhibited relatively rapid growth in this more recent period included Construction; Finance, Insurance, and Real Estate; Services; and Retail Trade, all industries in which Arizona has a larger share of its labor employed than does the United States on average. While it is the case that Arizona's employment growth rate from November 1987 to November 1988 was below the United States average, it is reasonably clear that this decline was caused by a cyclical downturn in Construction and related industries, a downturn caused by the overly rapid growth in Construction in the mid 1980s. Arizona's most recent (1989) employment growth rate indicates that this downturn was temporary. Given Arizona's still relatively strong population growth, and growth of other industries, which contribute large proportions of employment and which are less cyclical than construction, it is likely that trend growth rates for Arizona in the next several years will be at or slightly higher than the United States average.

Business Location and Employment Decisions

Theory and Previous Evidence

This section addresses issues which influence businesses in their decisions about where to locate raising such questions as, Do taxes deter and do certain expenditures enhance the economic growth of a state?

The theory of profit maximization underlies most economic models of business location and employment decisions. A firm will choose to locate in a particular site, expand or contract at a particular site, or open or close a branch plant, if the action is profitable. Both the revenue and cost components of a profit equation are relevant because sites will differ along dimensions that affect demand (revenue) and the costs of production. In selecting one site over another, this theory predicts that firms will consider factors such as wages, labor supply, taxes, strength of market demand, public services, and energy costs. Most of these factors will affect profits directly. But some of the public services impact profits indirectly. For example, it may be less costly to attract high quality labor when a high quality public school system is available.

The decisive factors in a location decision depend on the type of location or employment decision under consideration. For example, if a firm has selected a particular state for its new branch plant, but must yet decide in which community within the state to locate, revenue or cost factors common to all areas in the state, such as state income taxes, wages, or quality of higher education, would not be decisive for this location decision. On the other hand, factors that vary from community to community such as property taxes, distance to the central business district, and local market demand, may prove important in the final decision.

The analysis in this report is of interregional decisions rather than intraregional decisions as in the example above. The purpose is to explain business location and employment decisions as they affect state employment growth rates. We thus concentrate on revenue and cost factors that may be relevant for a firm deciding to open or close a branch plant, or to expand or contract employment at one plant or another, where its choice set is between various states.

Two recent empirical studies of interregional location and employment decisions (Wasylenko & McGuire, 1985; Helms, 1985) employ general and encompassing measures of economic activity -- employment in one, and personal income in the other, respectively. These studies are representative of the empirical work in this area. The studies by Wasylenko and McGuire and Helms attempt to explain differences observed across the states in measures of overall economic activity. Wasylenko and McGuire use a set of revenue and cost factors to explain a cross section of observed differences in states' employment growth rates between 1973 and 1980. They find wages, electricity costs, education expenditures, tax trends and per capita income to be statistically significant in explaining total employment growth rates. When total employment is broken down into six broad categories, different sets of factors matter. For example, the statistically significant variables for wholesale trade include the effective individual income tax rate and sales tax revenues as a share of total revenues. For retail trade they find wages, electricity costs, expenditures on education and per capita income to be highly statistically significant and economically important.

Helms uses a data set with annual observations on the states from 1965 through 1979. His model attempts to explain differences observed in total state personal income. He finds taxes to be significant negative factors and government expenditures, except welfare, to be significant positive factors. Specifically, he finds that a $1 increase in state and local taxes that is used to finance K-12 or higher education is a net stimulation to personal income. The unionization rate and population density are also significant variables. Both the Helms and Wasylenko and McGuire studies support the hypothesis that public service expenditures and taxes may be important factors when businesses make location and employment decisions.

Factors In The 1980s

Do the factors that appear to explain differences in states' economic growth rates in the 1970s still explain regional differences in the 1980s? For this chapter, a model was specified and estimated for the 48 contiguous states in an attempt to explain observed differences in the employment growth rates of the states from 1981 to 1987. The model was patterned after the model employed in Wasylenko and McGuire (1985). The set of explanatory factors was large and diverse. The factors employed are listed and defined in Table 2-5, and mean, minimum, and maximum values and values for Arizona for selected factors are displayed in Table 2-6.

The methodology employed allows for the determination of which, if any, of the factors (taking into account the effect of all other factors) explain the observed differences in employment growth rates in the states over the period. The results of the analysis were disappointing in that few of the factors were significant in explaining total employment growth rates or the growth rates of broadly defined industries. Many versions of the model were tested and factors that were significant in one version were insignificant in another. This lack of consistency and robustness of the results leads to the conclusion that these factors explain very little of the regional differences observed in employment growth rates between 1981 and 1987.[3] One version of the estimated model using employment data is reported in Appendix B.

A possible explanation of these results is that, by the 1980s, the states looked very much like one another on the factors that mattered in the 1970s. For example, differences in wage rates can help to explain the differences in employment growth rates only if there is sufficient variability in wages across the states. By one measure of variability, the coefficient of variation, wage rates varied less across the states in the early 1980s than in the mid 1970s. Thus, it is not surprising that wages did not help explain the variation in employment growth rates across the states.

Of major interest to this study are the results for the fiscal factors. The fiscal factors tested here, including total expenditures, expenditures on higher education and K-12, total taxes as a percentage of income, the average income tax rate, and measures of economic development tax incentive programs, did not appear to be important factors explaining differences in total employment growth rates or in the growth rates of major industries during this period.[4]

<table>
<tr><td colspan="2" align="center">Table 2-5
Names and Definitions of Independent Factors:
Full List of Variables[a]</td></tr>
<tr><td align="center">Variable Name</td><td align="center">Definitions</td></tr>
<tr><td>Labor Climate</td><td></td></tr>
<tr><td>Earnings Per Worker</td><td>Average 1981 earnings of the state's employees in each of eleven industries: construction; manufacturing; durable manufacturing; nondurable manufacturing; transportation; communication and public utilities; wholesale trade; retail trade; finance, insurance, and real estate; services; and the total of these industries.</td></tr>
<tr><td>Unionization</td><td>Percentage of the state's workforce unionized in 1980.</td></tr>
<tr><td>Right-to-Work Law</td><td>Dummy variable equal to unity if the state has a right-to-work law and equal to zero otherwise.</td></tr>
<tr><td>Graduation from High School</td><td>Percentage of the state's population over 25 years of age that completed high school in 1980.</td></tr>
<tr><td>Energy Prices</td><td></td></tr>
<tr><td>Average Electric Bill</td><td>Average electric bill for the 300 KWH to 60,000 KWH industrial service electric bill in the state for 1981. (The average commercial electric bill is used for nonmanufacturing industries.)</td></tr>
<tr><td>Average Natural Gas Price</td><td>Average price per 1000 cubic feet of natural gas in the state in 1981.</td></tr>
<tr><td>Fiscal Variables</td><td></td></tr>
<tr><td>Direct General Expenditures/PI</td><td>State and local direct general expenditure in the state as a percentage of income in the state for 1981.</td></tr>
<tr><td>Non-Education Expenditures/PI</td><td>State and local expenditure in the state other than that on primary, secondary, and higher education as a percentage of income in the state for 1981.</td></tr>
<tr><td>Local EducationExpenditures/PI</td><td>State and local expenditure in the state on primary and secondary education as a percentage of income in the state for 1981.</td></tr>
<tr><td>Per Pupil Education Expenditure</td><td>Per pupil state and local expenditure on primary and secondary education in the state for 1981.</td></tr>
<tr><td>Per Capita Education Expenditure</td><td>Per capita state and local expenditure on primary and secondary education in the state for 1981.</td></tr>
</table>

<table>
<tr><td colspan="2" align="center">Table 2-5 (Continued)</td></tr>
<tr><td align="center">Variable Name</td><td align="center">Definitions</td></tr>
<tr><td>Higher Education Expenditures/PI</td><td>The sum of total expenditure by public and private higher education institutions in the state as a percentage of income in the state for 1981.</td></tr>
<tr><td>Total Tax Revenues/PI</td><td>State and local government total taxes as a percentage of state income in 1981.</td></tr>
<tr><td>Effective Property Tax Rates</td><td>Average effective local property tax rate (in percent) in the state in 1981.</td></tr>
<tr><td>Personal Income Tax Rates</td><td>Personal income tax rate (in percent) at $25,000 of taxable income in 1981.</td></tr>
<tr><td>Maximum Corporate Tax Rates</td><td>Maximum state corporate income tax rate (in percent) after accounting for whether the state allows the deductibility of the federal corporate income tax.</td></tr>
<tr><td>Per Capita Sales Tax Revenues</td><td>Per capita state and local sales tax revenues in 1981.</td></tr>
<tr><td>Financial Incentive Programs</td><td>Numbers of different financial incentive programs that the state can use to foster economic development.</td></tr>
<tr><td>Tax Incentive Programs</td><td>Number of different tax incentive programs that the state can use to foster economic development.</td></tr>
<tr><td>Special Incentive Programs</td><td>Number of different special incentive programs that the state can use to foster economic development.</td></tr>
<tr><td align="center">Market</td><td></td></tr>
<tr><td>Population Density</td><td>Population density in the state in 1980.</td></tr>
<tr><td>Per Capita Income</td><td>Per capita income in the state in 1981.</td></tr>
<tr><td>Population Growth</td><td>Population growth (in percent) in the state between 1977 and 1981.</td></tr>
<tr><td align="center">Agglomeration</td><td></td></tr>
<tr><td>Agglomeration Economies</td><td>Industry employment in the state as a proportion of total employment in that industry in all states in 1981.</td></tr>
<tr><td colspan="2">[a] Different subsets of these variables were employed in different versions of the model. The entire set cannot confidently be tested at once because of a lack of degrees of freedom.

Source: See appendix.</td></tr>
</table>

<table>
<tr><td colspan="5" align="center">Table 2-6
Arizona Value, Means, and Range for Selected Factors, 1981</td></tr>
<tr><th>Variable Name</th><th>Arizona</th><th>Mean Value</th><th>Minimum Value</th><th>Maximum Value</th></tr>
<tr><td>Earnings Per Worker:</td><td></td><td></td><td></td><td></td></tr>
<tr><td>Total ($)</td><td>15,291</td><td>15,489</td><td>12,526</td><td>19,430</td></tr>
<tr><td> Construction</td><td>21,538</td><td>19,610</td><td>14,325</td><td>27,463</td></tr>
<tr><td> Manufacturing</td><td>21,928</td><td>20,711</td><td>15,268</td><td>29,562</td></tr>
<tr><td>   Durable</td><td>16,641</td><td>19,140</td><td>13,669</td><td>28,868</td></tr>
<tr><td>   Nondurable</td><td>23,452</td><td>21,545</td><td>15,378</td><td>31,074</td></tr>
<tr><td> Transportation, etc.</td><td>25,290</td><td>23,451</td><td>19,655</td><td>26,832</td></tr>
<tr><td> Wholesale Trade</td><td>19,493</td><td>19,837</td><td>15,763</td><td>23,085</td></tr>
<tr><td> Retail Trade</td><td>9,971</td><td>9,496</td><td>8,350</td><td>11,309</td></tr>
<tr><td> Finance, etc.</td><td>10,812</td><td>12,078</td><td>9,200</td><td>20,508</td></tr>
<tr><td> Services</td><td>12,940</td><td>12,862</td><td>10,165</td><td>15,903</td></tr>
<tr><td>Right-to-Work Law (Dummy)</td><td>1</td><td>0.38</td><td>0</td><td>1</td></tr>
<tr><td>Graduation from High School (%)</td><td>72.4</td><td>67.0</td><td>53.1</td><td>80.0</td></tr>
<tr><td>Average Electric Bill ($)</td><td></td><td></td><td></td><td></td></tr>
<tr><td> Commercial</td><td>424.88</td><td>381.95</td><td>136.12</td><td>711.50</td></tr>
<tr><td> Industrial</td><td>3659.00</td><td>3357.58</td><td>1400.00</td><td>6614.00</td></tr>
<tr><td>Average Natural Gas Price</td><td></td><td></td><td></td><td></td></tr>
<tr><td> Commercial</td><td>3.53</td><td>4.21</td><td>2.41</td><td>6.85</td></tr>
<tr><td> Industrial</td><td>3.17</td><td>3.68</td><td>1.88</td><td>5.61</td></tr>
<tr><td>Direct General Expenditures/PI (%)</td><td>13.47</td><td>14.08</td><td>10.39</td><td>18.33</td></tr>
<tr><td>Local Education Expenditures/PI (%)</td><td>3.64</td><td>3.80</td><td>2.80</td><td>4.89</td></tr>
<tr><td>Per Pupil Education Expenditures ($)</td><td>2034.31</td><td>2219.10</td><td>1531.08</td><td>3264.59</td></tr>
<tr><td>Per Capita Education Expenditures ($)</td><td>366.67</td><td>394.79</td><td>276.74</td><td>570.04</td></tr>
<tr><td>Higher Education Expenditure/PI (%)</td><td>2.53</td><td>2.58</td><td>1.67</td><td>4.34</td></tr>
<tr><td>Total Tax Revenues/PI (%)</td><td>9.71</td><td>9.50</td><td>7.16</td><td>13.75</td></tr>
<tr><td>Financial Incentive Programs</td><td>1</td><td>7</td><td>1</td><td>18</td></tr>
<tr><td>Tax Incentive Programs</td><td>6</td><td>7.10</td><td>3</td><td>12</td></tr>
<tr><td>Special Incentive Programs</td><td>16</td><td>14.10</td><td>8</td><td>18</td></tr>
<tr><td>Per Capita Income ($)</td><td>10,071</td><td>10,426</td><td>7652</td><td>13,486</td></tr>
<tr><td>Population Growth, 1977-81 (%)</td><td>16.04</td><td>5.44</td><td>-1.38</td><td>24.77</td></tr>
<tr><td colspan="5">Source: See appendix.</td></tr>
</table>

A closer look at the underlying data is instructive. Figure 2-1 plots the tax burden (state plus local) for Arizona and for the average of the 48 states. After a modest decline in tax burden in Arizona from 1981 to 1983, Arizona's tax burden increased from a level of 9.7 percent to 11.1 percent from 1983 to 1987. (The data for 1981 reported in Table 2-6 are updated to 1987 and reported in Table 2-7.) The average state and local tax burden in the United States during the 1981 to 1987 period increased steadily from 9.5 percent to 10.6 percent. The trends in the Arizona and United States average tax burdens were very similar during the 1980s and the relative burdens in any year never deviated from one another by more than half a percentage point.

Figure 2-2 plots tax burdens for Arizona and the average of its neighboring states. The trend in the tax burden for the regional average is much like the trends for Arizona and the United States average. The regional average increased slightly from 1981 to 1982, decreased slightly from 1982 to 1983, and increased steadily from 1983 to 1987. The average rate for the region rose from 9.2 percent in 1981 to 10.7 percent in 1987, with the greatest difference between Arizona and the region occurring in 1981 when Arizona's tax burden was 9.7 percent and the average for the region was 9.2 percent.

Given the similarity in levels and trends of tax burdens between Arizona, the United States, and the region, it is not surprising that this factor does not help to explain the differences in economic growth between Arizona, the United States average, and the average for the region during this period.

A look at the year-to-year changes in employment in Arizona, the United States and the region indicates that the three series move roughly together and do not appear to be correlated with the year-to-year changes in respective tax burdens. Figures 2-3 and 2-4 plot Arizona's annual employment growth rates against the United States averages and the regional averages, respectively. Throughout the period, Arizona's growth rate exceeds the United States and regional averages. Employment growth rates first increase rather dramatically from 1981 to 1984 and then decrease for all three from 1984 to 1987, a trend inversely related to the trends in tax burdens. As the regression results show, however, this inverse relationship between tax burdens and employment growth is spurious. Differences in tax burdens between Arizona and other states cannot explain differences in average employment growth rates because state and local tax burden differences among Arizona, the other states in the region, and the United States as a whole are essentially nonexistent during the 1981 to 1987 period.

Do these results imply that fiscal factors no longer matter? Not necessarily. If a state gets far out-of-line on either taxes or expenditures, or the mix of taxes and expenditures, then fiscal factors are likely to matter.[5] Businesses do make employment decisions based on the bottom line. Our results indicate that during the period of the early and mid-1980s, most states did not differ enough in their fiscal makeups for fiscal factors to make a difference in the bottom line. Other factors, which are difficult to quantify, such as world market influences on subsectors of regional economies, overwhelmed any fiscal effects in determining regional differences in employment growth rates during this period. But, if a state should suddenly look *very* different from other competing states in its fiscal makeup, fiscal factors may matter for employment growth in the state.

<table>
<tr><td colspan="5">Table 2-7
Arizona Value, Means, and Range for Selected Factors, 1987</td></tr>
<tr><th>Variable Name</th><th>Arizona</th><th>Mean Value</th><th>Minimum Value</th><th>Maximum Value</th></tr>
<tr><td>Earnings Per Worker:[a]</td><td></td><td></td><td></td><td></td></tr>
<tr><td>Total ($)</td><td>18,665</td><td>18,992</td><td>15,013</td><td>24,547</td></tr>
<tr><td>Construction</td><td>23,545</td><td>23,191</td><td>17,027</td><td>31,417</td></tr>
<tr><td>Manufacturing</td><td>27,640</td><td>26,158</td><td>19,286</td><td>37,893</td></tr>
<tr><td>Durable</td><td>20,839</td><td>24,180</td><td>17,758</td><td>36,249</td></tr>
<tr><td>Nondurable</td><td>29,584</td><td>27,234</td><td>19,043</td><td>40,173</td></tr>
<tr><td>Transportation, etc.</td><td>28,549</td><td>28,538</td><td>23,752</td><td>33,177</td></tr>
<tr><td>Wholesale Trade</td><td>24,259</td><td>24,686</td><td>19,970</td><td>30,830</td></tr>
<tr><td>Retail Trade</td><td>12,419</td><td>11,587</td><td>9,727</td><td>14,461</td></tr>
<tr><td>Finance, etc.</td><td>14,083</td><td>16,000</td><td>10,901</td><td>34,144</td></tr>
<tr><td>Services</td><td>16,554</td><td>16,461</td><td>13,088</td><td>21,464</td></tr>
<tr><td>Right-to-Work Law (Dummy)</td><td>1.00</td><td>0.47</td><td>0.0</td><td>1.00</td></tr>
<tr><td>Graduation from High School (%)</td><td>N/A</td><td>N/A</td><td>N/A</td><td>N/A</td></tr>
<tr><td>Average Electric Bill ($)</td><td></td><td></td><td></td><td></td></tr>
<tr><td>   Commercial</td><td>511.97</td><td>473.96</td><td>262.86</td><td>868.78</td></tr>
<tr><td>   Industrial</td><td>3961.00</td><td>4544.85</td><td>2476.00</td><td>8647.00</td></tr>
<tr><td>Average Natural Gas Price</td><td></td><td></td><td></td><td></td></tr>
<tr><td>   Commercial</td><td>4.54</td><td>4.81</td><td>3.02</td><td>6.98</td></tr>
<tr><td>   Industrial</td><td>3.91</td><td>3.61</td><td>1.80</td><td>6.70</td></tr>
<tr><td>Direct General Expenditures/PI (%)</td><td>15.26</td><td>15.18</td><td>6.30</td><td>19.52</td></tr>
<tr><td>Local Education Expenditures/PI (%)</td><td>3.91</td><td>4.10</td><td>3.07</td><td>8.13</td></tr>
<tr><td>Per Pupil Education Expenditures ($)</td><td>3337.48</td><td>3491.04</td><td>2191.27</td><td>5624.27</td></tr>
<tr><td>Per Capita Education Expenditures ($)</td><td>559.03</td><td>587.13</td><td>395.90</td><td>1033.88</td></tr>
<tr><td>Higher Education Expenditure/PI (%)[b]</td><td>2.47</td><td>2.84</td><td>1.17</td><td>4.81</td></tr>
<tr><td>Total Tax Revenues/PI (%)</td><td>11.10</td><td>10.70</td><td>7.92</td><td>18.04</td></tr>
<tr><td>Financial Incentive Programs</td><td>5</td><td>10.58</td><td>1</td><td>18</td></tr>
<tr><td>Tax Incentive Programs</td><td>9</td><td>9.46</td><td>4</td><td>14</td></tr>
<tr><td>Special Incentive Programs</td><td>13</td><td>12.52</td><td>7</td><td>15</td></tr>
<tr><td>Per Capita Income ($)</td><td>14,314</td><td>14,546</td><td>10,291</td><td>21,268</td></tr>
<tr><td>Population Growth, 1977-81 (%)</td><td>13.74</td><td>3.29</td><td>-5.04</td><td>13.74</td></tr>
</table>

[a] Computations based on 1986 data.
[b] Computations based on 1985 data.

Source: See appendix.

Figure 2-1
Tax Burden for Arizona and the Average of the 48 Continguous States, 1981-1987

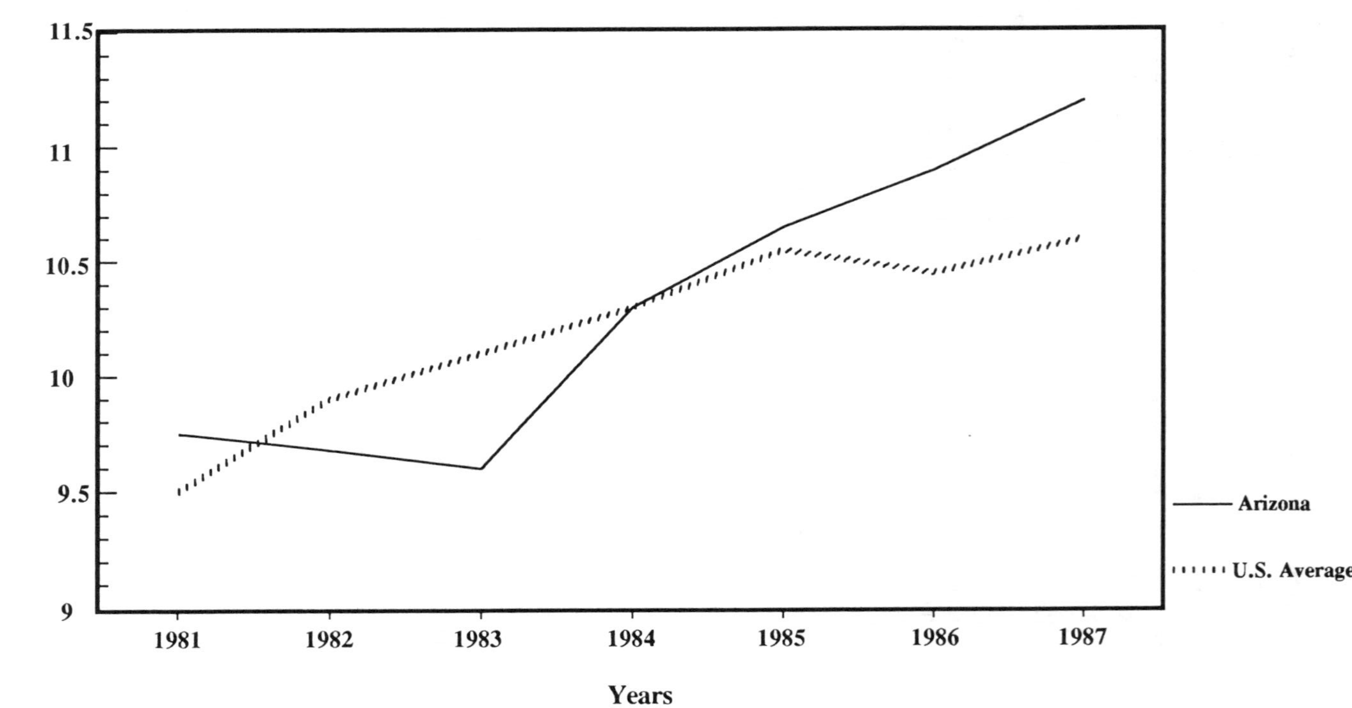

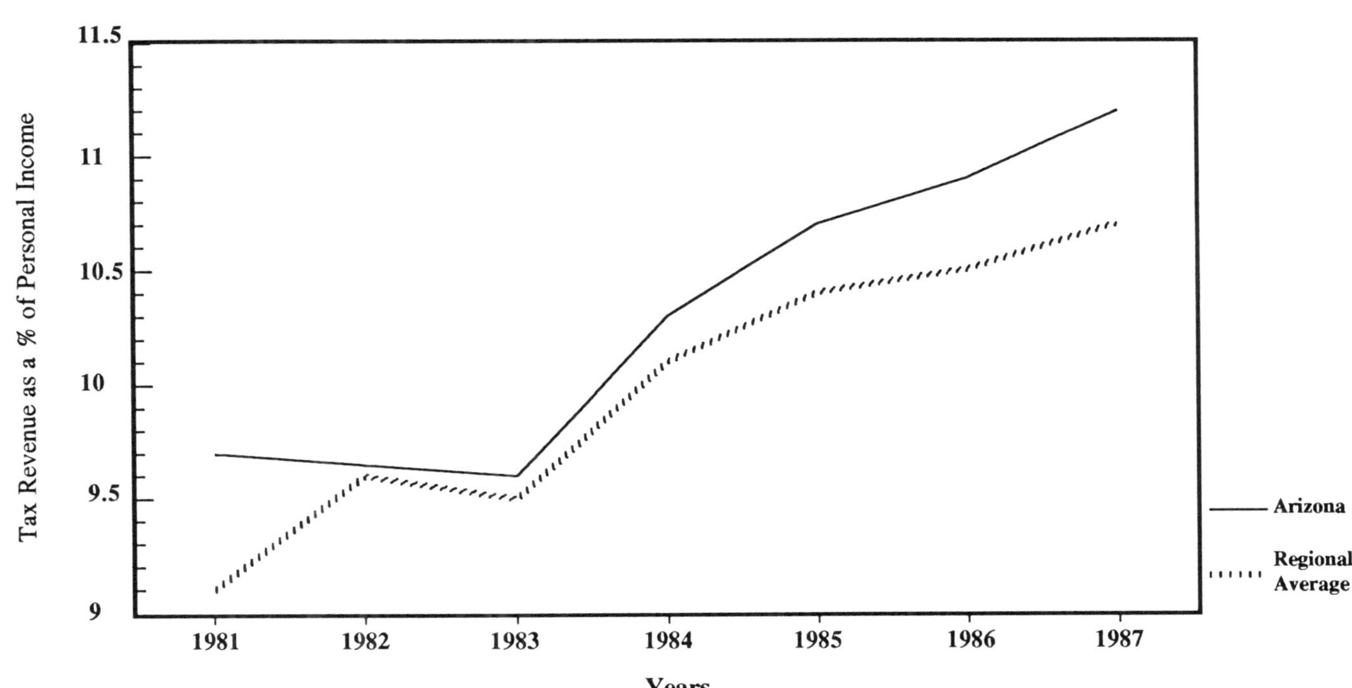

[a] Region includes California, Colorado, New Mexico, Nevada, and Utah.

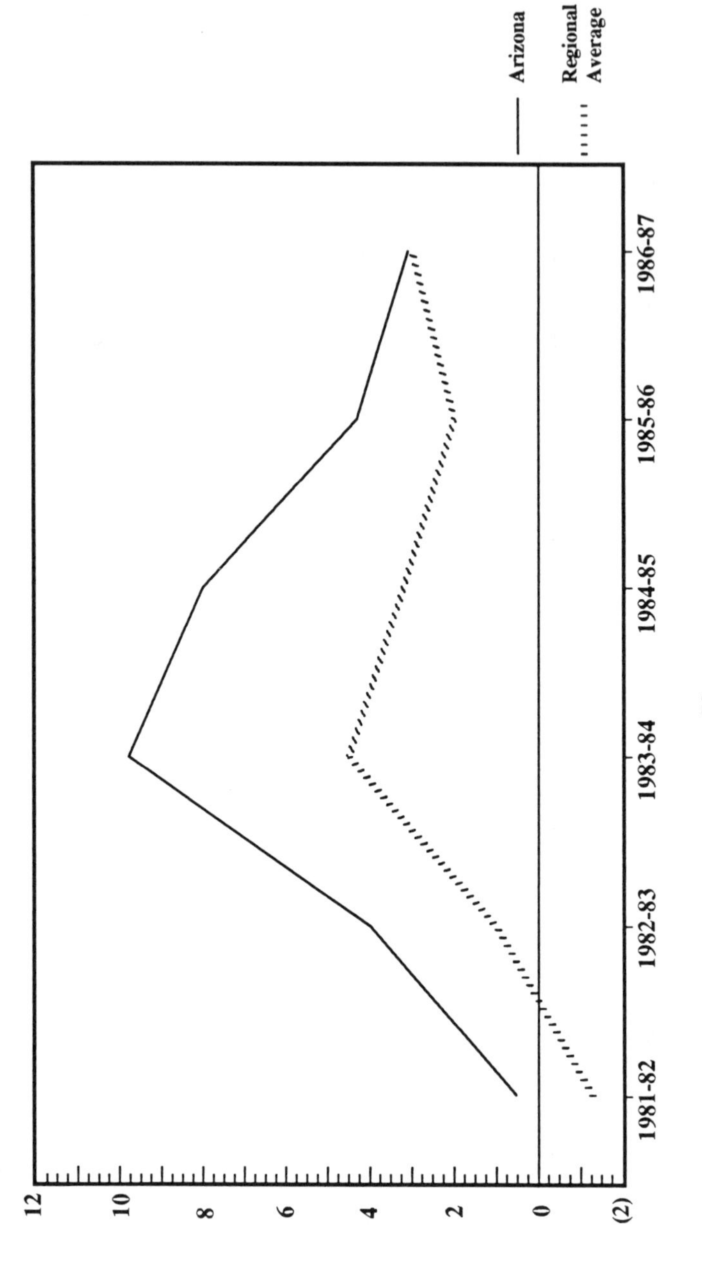

Figure 2-3
Annual Percentage Employment Growth in Arizona
and the Average in the 48 Continguous States, 1981-1987
Arizona
Regional Average
Annual Percent Employment Growth
12
10
8
6
4
2
0
(2)
1981-82
1982-83
1983-84
1984-85
1985-86
1986-87
Years

Figure 2-4

Annual Percentage Employment Growth in Arizona and in the Region[a], 1981-1987

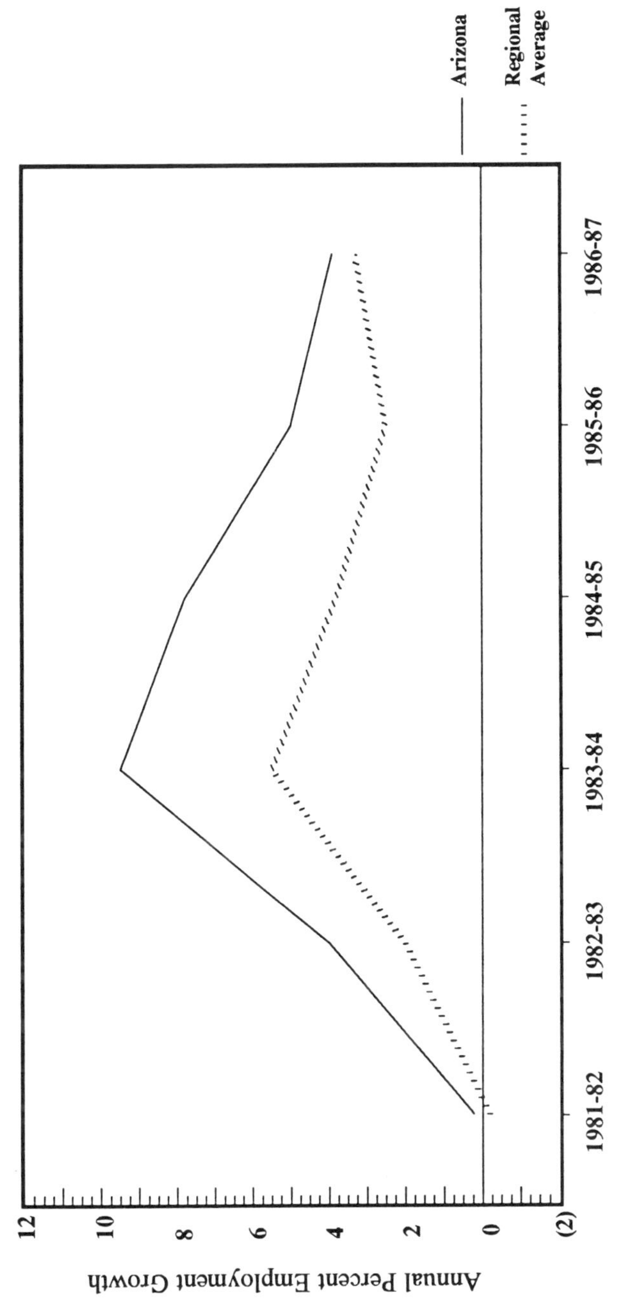

[a]Region includes California, Colorado, New Mexico, Nevada, and Utah.

References

Carroll, Robert and Michael Wasylenko. (forthcoming, 1990). "The Shifting Fate of Fiscal Variables and their Effect on Economic Development." *Proceedings of the Eighty-Second Annual Conference*, National Tax Association-Tax Institute of America.

Genetski, Robert J. and Young D. Chin. "The Impact of State and Local Taxes on Economic Growth." Harris Economic Research Office Service, November 3, 1978.

Helms, L. Jay. (1985). "The Effect of State and Local Taxes on Economic Growth: A Time Series-Cross Section Approach." *The Review of Economics and Statistics* 67 (November): 574-584.

Wasylenko, Michael and Therese McGuire. (1985). "Jobs and Taxes: The Effect of Business Climate on States' Employment Growth Rates." *National Tax Journal* 38 (December): 497-511.

Endnotes

1. The U.S. Department of Commerce indicates that a peak in the business cycle occurred in July 1981, and troughs occurred in July 1980 and November 1982. Some economists have argued that the entire 1980 to 1982 period ought to be regarded as a recession period.

2. This chapter relies on both employment and Gross State Product to measure overall economic activity within a state. Employment measures the use of labor as an input in the production process. Gross State Product includes both payroll and capital earnings and therefore is a more inclusive measure of economic activity. The exclusion of capital usage in the employment measure ignores the direct role of capital in determining the overall level of output within a state. From a government policymaker's perspective, the impact of policy on employment growth may be of greater interest, although from an economist's perspective a measure that accounts for both capital and labor income may be more relevant.

3. We have examined the consistency of the results of a variety of employment growth determinant studies. These studies lead to different conclusions about the role of state and local tax and expenditure policies on economic growth. See R. Carroll and M. Wasylenko (1990), forthcoming.

4. We tested our models using different lag structures for the independent variables and also used measures of employment growth from both the U.S. Bureau of Economic Analysis and U.S. Bureau of Labor Statistics as dependent variables in our models. In all cases, the regression analysis revealed few, if any, consistent results.

5. In his study Genetski and Chin (1978) finds that states where state and local expenditures and policies are out-of-line with the national average also have lower employment growth.

Appendix A Data Sources For Variables	
Labor Climate	
Earnings Per Worker	U.S. Department of Commerce, Bureau of Economic Analysis, Local Area Personal Income: Personal Income for States and Regions, Table SA25, 1969-1987, Table CA35, 1969-1986.
Unionization	Troy, Leo and Neil Sheflin. *Union Sourcebook: Membership Structure, Finance, Directory, First Ed.* NJ: Industrial Relations Data and Information Service, 1985.
Right-to-Work Law	U.S. Bureau of the Census, *Statistical Abstract of the United States*, selected years.
Graduation from High School	U.S. Bureau of the Census, *Statistical Abstract of the United States*, selected years.
Energy Prices	
Average Electric Bill	U.S. Department of Energy, Energy Information Administration, Federal Power Commission, *Typical Electric Bills*, 1981; Unpublished data for 1987 received directly from the Energy Information Administration.
Average Natural Gas Price	U.S. Department of Energy, Energy Information Administration, *Natural Gas Annual*, 1981, 1987.
Fiscal Variables	
Direct General Expenditures/PI	U.S. Department of Commerce, Bureau of the Census, *Governmental Finances* in 1980-81 and 1986-87; U.S. Department of Commerce, Bureau of Economic Analysis, Local Area Personal Income, Table CA25, 1969--1986, computer tape; personal income data for 1987 obtained from, U.S. Department of Commerce, Bureau of Economic Analysis, *Survey of Current Business* Vol. 68, no. 8 (August 1988).
Non-Education Expenditures/PI	U.S. Department of Commerce, Bureau of the Census, *Governmental Finances* in 1980-81 and 1986-87; U.S. Department of Commerce, Bureau of Economic Analysis, Local Area Personal Income, Table CA35, 1969--1986, computer tape; personal income data for 1987 obtained from, U.S. Department of Commerce, Bureau of Economic Analysis, *Survey of Current Business* Vol. 68, no. 8 (August 1988).

Appendix A (Continued)	
Local Education Expenditures/PI	U.S. Department of Commerce, Bureau of the Census, *Governmental Finances* in 1980-81 and 1986-87; U.S. Department of Commerce, Bureau of Economic Analysis, Local Area Personal Income, Table CA25, 1969--1986, computer tape; personal income data for 1987 obtained from, U.S. Department of Commerce, Bureau of Economic Analysis, *Survey of Current Business* Vol. 68, no. 8 (August 1988).
Per Pupil Education Expenditures	U.S. Department of Commerce, Bureau of the Census, *Governmental Finances* in 1980-81 and 1986-87; U.S. Department of Education, National Center of Education Statistics, *Digest of Education Statistics, 1988*, Washington, DC: U.S. Government Printing Office.
Per Capita Education Expenditures	U.S. Department of Commerce, Bureau of the Census, *Governmental Finances* in 1980-81 and 1986-87; U.S. Department of Commerce, Bureau of Census, *Current Population Reports: Population Estimates and Projections*, selected years.
Higher Education Expenditures/PI	U.S. Department of Education, National Center of Education Statistics. *Digest of Education Statistics, 1984-85*, Washington, DC: U.S. Government Printing Office; data for 1985 obtained from U.S. Department of Education, Office of Educational Research and Improvement, Center for Education Statistics, Bulletin CS-87-315B, March 1987; Bureau of Economic Analysis, Local Area Personal Income, Table: data for 1985 obtained from CA 35, 1969-1986, computer tape; personal income data for 1987 obtained from, U.S. Department of Commerce, Bureau of Economic Analysis, *Survey of Current Business* Vol. 68, no. 8 (August 1988).
Total Tax Revenues/PI	U.S. Department of Commerce, Bureau of the Census, *Governmental Finances* in 1980-81 and 1986-87; U.S. Department of Commerce, Bureau of Economic Analysis, Local Area Personal Income, Table CA25, 1969--1986, computer tape; personal income data for 1987 obtained from, U.S. Department of Commerce, Bureau of Economic Analysis, *Survey of Current Business* Vol. 68, no. 8 (August 1988).
Effective Property Tax Rates	Advisory Commission on Intergovernmental Relations, *Significant Features of Fiscal Federalism, 1987* Vol. II, Table 16.

Appendix A (Continued)	
Maximum Corporate Tax Rates	*State Tax Handbook, 1981*, Chicago, IL: Commerce Clearing House, Inc., pp. 670-681
Per Capita Sales Tax Revenues	U.S. Department of Commerce, Bureau of the Census, *Governmental Finances* in 1980-81 and 1986-87; U.S. Department of Commerce, Bureau of Census, *Current Population Reports: Population Estimates and Projections*, selected years.
Financial Incentive Programs	*Site Selection Handbook*, Atlanta, GA: Conway Publications, Inc., selected years.
Tax Incentive Programs	*Site Selection Handbook*, Atlanta, GA: Conway Publications, Inc., selected years.
Special Incentive Programs	*Site Selection Handbook*, Atlanta, GA: Conway Publications, Inc., selected years.
Market	
Population Density	U.S. Department of Commerce, Bureau of Census, Current Population Reports: Population Estimates and Projections, selected years; U.S. Bureau of the Census, Statistical Abstract of the United States, selected years.
Per Capita Income	U.S. Department of Commerce, Bureau of Census, *Current Population Reports: Population Estimates and Projections*, selected years; U.S. Department of Commerce, Bureau of Economic Analysis, Local Area Personal Income, Table CA35, 1969-1986, computer tape; Personal Income data for 1987 obtained from, U.S. Department of Commerce, Bureau of Economic Analysis, *Survey of Current Business* Vol. 68, no. 8 (August 1988).
Population Growth	U.S. Department of Commerce, Bureau of Census, *Current Population Reports: Population Estimates and Projections*, selected years.
Agglomeration	
Agglomeration Economies	U.S. Department of Commerce, Bureau of Economic Analysis, Local Area Personal Income, Table SA25, 1969-1987, floppy disk.

Appendix B
Results of the Econometric Analysis

We specify several models depicting the relationship between employment in a state and the cost, market, and business climate factors in a state. We use the 48 contiguous states as observations and estimate the relationship for the 1981 to 1987 time period. In particular, we relate the natural logarithm of the ratio of the employment level in 1987 to employment in 1981 to the levels of the independent variables in 1981. This specification reduces the potential for simultaneous equations bias, accounts for potential heteroskedasticity introduced from size differences across states, and lends itself to the calculation of interpretable employment elasticities. Regressions are estimated for total employment and employment by major industry. The regressions by major industry account for the differential impact of location factors across industries.

The results for the employment regressions are reported in Table 2-B-1. The Gross State Product regressions yielded very similar results to the employment regressions and are not reported. The results for the Gross State Product regressions may be obtained directly from the authors.

No evidence of heteroskedasticity was found applying the Glesjer method. This finding is not surprising because the dependent variable is the logarithm of an employment ratio, which tends to eliminate heteroskedasticity.

The corrected R^2s or the F-tests for the regressions indicate that the variables in the regression equations explain, in a statistically significant sense, some portion of the employment growth differential among states. But the individual coefficients sometimes do not have the expected sign and often are not statistically significant.

For the labor climate variables, the coefficient for wages is negative as expected but not statistically significant. Similarly, the coefficient for RTW has the expected positive sign in the regressions but is generally not statistically significant. The coefficient for SKILL is positive and statistically significant in the total manufacturing and nondurable goods manufacturing industries. Thus, SKILL, as measured by the percentage of the state's population completing high school, has a significant effect on manufacturing job growth. However, the coefficient on the SKILL variable in the FIRE industry is negative and statistically significant, indicating FIRE employment grows faster in states that have a lower percentage of high school graduates, other things being equal.

The coefficients on ELECTRIC and GAS prices are unexpectedly positive and statistically significant in just under one-half of the equations. These results suggest that during the 1981 to 1987 period higher energy prices do not deter employment growth. Rather, the results indicate that employment grows faster in states with higher energy prices.

The variables used to proxy government fiscal behavior are generally insignificant, have the unexpected sign or both. At first glance, the results suggest that during the 1981 to 1987 period government fiscal variables were not effective as tools of economic development. However, the results may indicate that the differentials or variation in government fiscal variables were not great enough to explain regional differences in employment growth. Following the competitiveness criteria established in this chapter, it is only when state fiscal policies are out-of-line relative to other states that government fiscal policies will play a role in determining the overall level of economic activity within a state. The absence of such differentials should not necessarily lead to the conclusion that fiscal policy is ineffective. Rather, government fiscal policies are simply not far enough out-of-line with one another to reveal a systematic relationship between economic growth and government fiscal behavior. A recent survey (Carroll and Wasylenko, 1990) of the empirical results found in the literature reveals that during the 1980s government fiscal behavior may have played a less significant role for attracting economic activity than in prior periods. The increasing role of an open market between the United States and the world, and increased factor mobility between the states may have been forces leading to less variation in government fiscal packages and, therefore, a less significant role for economic development policies during the 1980s.

Table 2-B-1
Results for the Employment Regressions -- Dependent Variables = 1n (Employment 1987/Employment 1981)
(number of observations = 48)

	Total	Construction	Manufacturing	Durable Manufacturing	Nondurable Manufacturing	Transportation Communication Public Utility	Wholesale Trade	Retail Trade	FIRE	Services
Intercept	0.6536	-0.1291	-0.3162	-0.1788	-0.2321	0.0613	-0.0273	0.2965	-0.7675	0.3138
	(0.30)[a]	(0.31)	(1.49)	(0.71)	(0.85)	(0.23)	(0.08)	(0.97)	(1.03)	(1.68)
W(i)	-0.000011	-0.000022	-0.000006	-0.000010	-0.000009	0.0000057	-0.000016	0.000005	-0.000010	-0.000005
	(1.07)	(1.44)	(0.92)	(1.26)	(1.34)	(0.49)	(0.93)	(0.17)	(0.20)	(0.37)
RTW	0.0011	0.0060	0.0448	0.0172	0.0610	0.0576	0.0269	0.0049	-0.1255	0.0159
	(0.03)	(0.08)	(1.25)	(0.43)	(1.34)	(1.66)	(0.54)	(0.18)	(1.05)	(0.61)
SKILL	-0.0012	-0.0004	0.0078	0.0055	0.0095	-0.0016	-0.0009	-0.0029	-0.0221	0.0004
	(0.47)	(0.6)	(2.74)*	(1.60)	(2.69)*	(0.54)	(0.21)	(1.25)	(2.04)*	(0.21)
ELECTRIC	0.0003	0.0008	0.00002	-0.00001	0.000035	0.00024	0.0004	0.0003	0.0005	0.0002
	(2.39)*	(2.83)*	(1.34)	(0.56)	(1.77)*	(1.70)*	(1.83)*	(2.68)*	(0.96)	(1.57)
GAS	0.0380	0.1180	0.0317	-0.0235	0.0802	0.0605	0.0668	0.0518	0.0637	0.0286
	(2.34)*	(3.25)*	(1.55)	(0.95)	(3.27)*	(3.11)*	(2.30)*	(3.70)*	(1.01)	(2.20)*
EXP	-0.0012	-0.0079	0.0267	0.0239	0.0190	-0.0186	0.0007	-0.0154	0.0472	-0.0195
	(0.09)	(0.23)	(1.78)*	(1.35)	(1.01)	(1.20)	(0.03)	(1.26)	(0.88)	(1.74)*
HIEDEXP	0.0039	-0.0263	-0.0059	0.0147	-0.0354	0.0096	0.0151	0.0041	0.0683	-0.0007
	(0.16)	(0.46)	(0.22)	(0.46)	(1.06)	(0.35)	(0.37)	(0.18)	(0.68)	(0.03)
TAX	-0.0170	-0.0316	-0.0537	-0.0526	-0.0400	-0.0150	-0.0439	-0.0045	-0.0252	0.0054
	(0.87)	(0.68)	(2.50)*	(2.06)*	(1.49)	(0.73)	(1.37)	(0.26)	(0.32)	(0.33)
FINCENT	-0.0021	-0.0047	-0.0045	0.0003	-0.0086	-0.0015	-0.0044	0.0030	-0.0078	-0.0012
	(0.53)	(0.52)	(1.03)	(0.07)	(1.56)	(0.33)	(0.67)	(0.82)	(0.49)	(0.37)
TINCENT	0.0035	0.0025	0.0103	0.0080	0.0142	0.0064	0.0064	0.0088	-0.0110	0.0032
	(0.46)	(0.15)	(1.20)	(0.78)	(1.31)	(0.74)	(0.52)	(1.29)	(0.37)	(0.51)
SPINCENT	0.0037	0.0072	-0.0003	-0.0050	0.0045	0.0036	0.0068	0.0028	-0.0008	0.0053
	(0.73)	(0.64)	(0.05)	(0.75)	(0.640)	(0.66)	(0.83)	(0.63)	(0.04)	(1.27)
PCY	0.000013	0.000037	-0.00003	0.00002	-0.00006	-0.000005	0.000025	-0.000016	0.0001	-0.000006
	(0.74)	(0.93)	(1.40)	(0.81)	(2.68)*	(0.29)	(0.76)	(1.06)	(1.88)*	(0.40)
GROWTH	0.0060	-0.0045	0.0039	0.0018	0.0049	0.00098	0.00058	0.0037	0.0294	0.0042
	(2.08)*	(0.67)	(1.30)	(0.49)	(1.30)	(0.31)	(0.13)	(1.15)	(2.75)*	(1.64)
AG(i)		0.0137	0.8409	0.4526	1.3089	-0.7322	0.7522	0.1026	1.09	0.1787
		(0.009)	(1.06)	(0.52)	(1.52)	(0.87)	(0.71)	(0.16)	(0.48)	(0.32)
R²	0.32	0.49	0.41	0.15	0.49	0.39	0.34	0.49	0.20	0.27

[a] Figures in parentheses are absolute values of the t-statistics, and "*" indicates statistical significance at the 0.05 level or better for a one-tail test.

Source: Computed by authors.

Chapter 3

Demographic Trends and Fiscal Implications

Timothy D. Hogan and Tom R. Rex

Since the formation of the United States, its population has shifted to the South and the West. Factors influencing this migration have included climate, lifestyle, open spaces, availability of land at low cost, low taxes and other living costs, right-to-work laws and the perception of a better quality of life. Arizona possesses each of these positive features, but the state did not begin to attract migrants in large numbers until the late 1940s. Two factors, familiarity with the state gained during military service during World War II and availability of efficient, relatively inexpensive home cooling devices, initiated Arizona's rapid population growth. Arizona has remained among the most rapidly growing states since that time.

Despite periods of slower growth in the early and late 1980s, the state's population exceeded 3.6 million in 1990 - an increase of 937,000 during the decade, making Arizona the third fastest growing state in the nation during the 1980s. Arizona is expected to be the second-fastest growing state during the 1990s, with the population projected to top 4.7 million by 2000 (Rex, 1990; U.S. Bureau of Census, 1988).

Migration Flows - The Key To Arizona's Growth

While population growth of 2 percent per year is considered slow by Arizona standards, it is twice the national average. During boom periods, growth in Arizona approaches 4 percent per year. Net natural increase, the excess of births over deaths -- expands the population approximately 1 percent per year, but net in-migration accounts for at least as much, and generally much more, of the growth.

Net in-migration averaged more than 60,000 people per year between 1970 and 1990, when the population of Arizona doubled from 1.8 million to 3.6 million (Rex, 1990). Even the 60,000+ migration figure does not provide much of a clue to the actual degree of mobility of the state's population. Population flows are more of a revolving door: the average net migration figure results from in-migration of 180,000 and out-migration of 120,000 per year. That is, for every three people who come to Arizona, two leave. Thus, impacts of a mobile population on the public and private sectors are large. For example, bank employees spend more time opening and closing accounts, post office employees forward more mail, and Department of Transportation workers issue more drivers licenses.

Of more importance is the severe volatility of the migration flows, which have ranged from approximately 35,000 to 95,000 per year between 1970 and 1990. As seen in Figure 3-1, fluctuations in the flows correspond to swings in the economic cycle. The volatility of population growth intensifies the economic cycles, magnifying various problems in the public and private sectors. In the private sector, firms may be overextended when growth slows and unprepared when growth accelerates. In the public sector, large differences between budgeted and actual revenues and expenditures may occur at turning points in the cycle.

Population Growth And Economic Activity

Though retirees make up an important segment of Arizona's in-migration, the bulk of Arizona's new residents are working people and their dependents. In particular, many are young adults, for whom jobs and economic conditions are high on a list of priorities. Thus, population growth and economic growth are closely intertwined. Just as Arizona's population growth, which generally is much higher than the national average, is highly cyclical, economic growth rates greatly exceed national norms on average and are subject to severe swings.

In terms of cause and effect, jobs clearly come first in the short run, with migration flows reacting to changes in employment opportunities (Hogan & Rex, 1988). In the longer term, however, job creation and economic opportunity attract people to the state at the same time that people moving to Arizona create jobs both by attracting employers to the state and by consuming goods and services.

Migration is somewhat self-perpetuating, as is Arizona's rapid economic growth. In part, this is due to migrants generally being "pulled" to a new location by its attractiveness rather than being "pushed" from their old homes by poor conditions. This "pulling" effect, however, is temporarily reduced when economic slowdowns reduce employment opportunities.

Economic Cycle Impacts

As an economic recovery proceeds, jobs become readily available in Arizona and large numbers of people move to the state, stimulating the economy further. These boom conditions are not without certain costs; for example, governments may have difficulty providing adequate, timely services to a rapidly expanding population.

Because rapid growth has been the norm, Arizona's private and public sectors have come to expect further rapid growth, in some cases becoming dependent upon it. When economic conditions worsen, with a resultant sharp decline in net migration, many public and private sector entities find themselves overextended.

In the last economic slowdown, which began late in 1986, net migration to Arizona declined 27 percent in the first year and an additional 39 percent the next year. The budgets of most governmental units are heavily dependent on revenues from new residents, from sources such as taxes on building contractors, property taxes, taxes on motor vehicle registrations and sales taxes. This dependence, coupled with an economic slowdown and

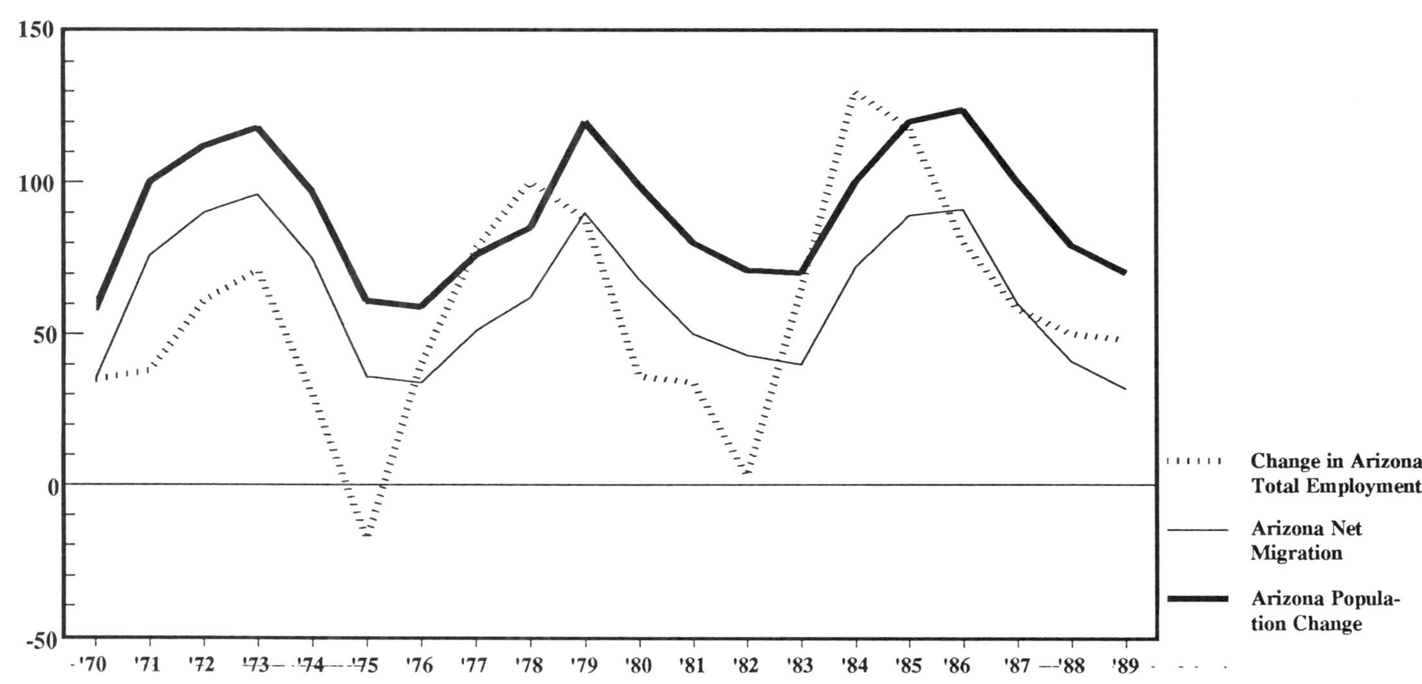

Source: Center for Business Research, College of Business, Arizona State University

greatly reduced population inflows, led to lower revenues than projected, with budget deficits occurring among a variety of governmental units in 1987 and 1988.

Projections

Arizona is expected to remain among the most rapidly growing states in the nation. The number of people added to the Arizona population in the 1990s is likely to be similar to that of the 1980s, though a chance exists that net migration may decline somewhat in response to the aging of the baby-boom generation. (People in their thirties and forties are less likely to migrate than those in their twenties.) Growth rates on a percentage basis will continue to slip as the total population base gets larger (Rex, 1990).

Though aggregate growth of the population likely will be comparable to that of the recent past, the number of people added to different cohorts of the population will be considerably different in the 1990s than in the 1970s and 1980s (U.S Bureau of Census, 1983; U.S. Bureau of Census, 1988; U.S. Bureau of Census, 1988). For example, growth will be greater in the 45-64 age bracket, especially among those aged 45-54.   The school age population will increase more in the 1990s, and the number of elderly at least 75 years old will continue to rise rapidly. In contrast, the number of adults 25-34 probably will decline and the number of 65-74 year olds will increase much less in the 1990s (see Table 3-1).

The overall racial/ethnic composition of the population also is unlikely to change much in the 1990s, continuing the pattern of the 1970s and 1980s. Interstate migration is overwhelmingly white, offsetting immigration from Latin America. Nonetheless, higher birth rates among some minority groups should cause the percentage of children who belong to minority groups to increase.(Hogan & Rex, 1988)

Economically, Arizona is likely to grow somewhat more slowly in the 1990s than in the previous two decades because of less growth in the working age population, particularly among young adults. However, because a greater proportion of the working age population will be older, productivity gains should be better and unemployment rates lower in the 1990s. Per capita income growth thus should be somewhat faster in the 1990s (Espenshade & Serow, 1978; Hogan & Rex, 1986; Russell, 1979; Wascher *et al.*, 1986; The WEFA Group, 1988).

The close link between population and economic growth likely will continue in the next decade. Cycles in each also are likely to persist, though they may be muted somewhat by the demographic shift to an older, more stable workforce and economic shifts to higher productivity and more employment in less cyclical service industries. The public sector thus will continue to be buffeted by swings in growth rates and would be wise to adopt a more conservative view of growth, with the expectation that boom conditions will not persist for long. Beyond these generalized effects on the public sector, the demographic changes will have specific additional consequences on public finances.

Public Sector Impacts

Almost all of the recent growth in total state revenues and expenditures can be explained by inflation and population increases. Between 1970 and 1989 general fund revenues rose 606 percent and expenditures increased 637 percent (Arizona Joint Legislative Budget Committee, 1990). Population growth during this period totaled 99 percent while inflation was 219 percent. Thus, real per capita spending levels grew little (14 percent) during this period. If this pattern continues through the 1990s, the projected slowing in population growth (on a percentage basis) implies that neither state revenues nor spending will grow as fast in the next decade as they have in the past. However, demographic changes will require increased spending to maintain current service levels for several of Arizona's major public programs.

<table>
<tr><td colspan="6" align="center">Table 3-1
Arizona Age Distribution</td></tr>
<tr><td align="center">Age</td><td align="center">1980
Census</td><td align="center">1990
Projection</td><td align="center">2000
Projection</td><td align="center">1980-1990</td><td align="center">1990-2000</td></tr>
<tr><td></td><td colspan="3" align="center">Number in Thousands</td><td colspan="2" align="center">Percent Change</td></tr>
<tr><td>Less than 5</td><td align="right">214</td><td align="right">299</td><td align="right">320</td><td align="right">40</td><td align="right">7</td></tr>
<tr><td>5-17</td><td align="right">578</td><td align="right">690</td><td align="right">894</td><td align="right">19</td><td align="right">30</td></tr>
<tr><td>18-24</td><td align="right">369</td><td align="right">376</td><td align="right">442</td><td align="right">2</td><td align="right">18</td></tr>
<tr><td>25-34</td><td align="right">444</td><td align="right">628</td><td align="right">616</td><td align="right">41</td><td align="right">-2</td></tr>
<tr><td>35-44</td><td align="right">298</td><td align="right">530</td><td align="right">725</td><td align="right">78</td><td align="right">37</td></tr>
<tr><td>45-54</td><td align="right">252</td><td align="right">343</td><td align="right">617</td><td align="right">36</td><td align="right">80</td></tr>
<tr><td>55-64</td><td align="right">257</td><td align="right">307</td><td align="right">428</td><td align="right">19</td><td align="right">39</td></tr>
<tr><td>65-74</td><td align="right">201</td><td align="right">296</td><td align="right">362</td><td align="right">47</td><td align="right">22</td></tr>
<tr><td>75 and older</td><td align="right">105</td><td align="right">186</td><td align="right">306</td><td align="right">77</td><td align="right">65</td></tr>
<tr><td>Total</td><td align="right">2,718</td><td align="right">3,655</td><td align="right">4,710</td><td align="right">34</td><td align="right">29</td></tr>
<tr><td></td><td colspan="3" align="center">Percentage Distribution</td><td colspan="2" align="center">Change in Percentages</td></tr>
<tr><td>Less than 5</td><td align="right">7.9</td><td align="right">8.2</td><td align="right">6.8</td><td align="right">0.3</td><td align="right">-1.4</td></tr>
<tr><td>5-17</td><td align="right">21.3</td><td align="right">18.9</td><td align="right">19.0</td><td align="right">-2.4</td><td align="right">0.1</td></tr>
<tr><td>18-24</td><td align="right">14.6</td><td align="right">10.3</td><td align="right">9.4</td><td align="right">-3.3</td><td align="right">-0.9</td></tr>
<tr><td>25-34</td><td align="right">16.3</td><td align="right">17.2</td><td align="right">14.1</td><td align="right">0.9</td><td align="right">-4.1</td></tr>
<tr><td>35-44</td><td align="right">10.9</td><td align="right">14.5</td><td align="right">15.4</td><td align="right">3.6</td><td align="right">0.9</td></tr>
<tr><td>45-54</td><td align="right">9.3</td><td align="right">9.4</td><td align="right">13.1</td><td align="right">0.1</td><td align="right">3.7</td></tr>
<tr><td>55-64</td><td align="right">9.5</td><td align="right">8.4</td><td align="right">9.1</td><td align="right">-1.1</td><td align="right">0.7</td></tr>
<tr><td>65-74</td><td align="right">7.4</td><td align="right">8.1</td><td align="right">7.7</td><td align="right">0.7</td><td align="right">-0.4</td></tr>
<tr><td>75 and older</td><td align="right">3.9</td><td align="right">5.1</td><td align="right">6.5</td><td align="right">1.2</td><td align="right">1.4</td></tr>
<tr><td>Total</td><td align="right">100.0</td><td align="right">100.0</td><td align="right">100.0</td><td align="right">0.0</td><td align="right">0.0</td></tr>
<tr><td colspan="6">Note: Percentages do not add to 100.0 because of rounding.</td></tr>
<tr><td colspan="6">Source: U.S. Bureau of the Census (1980). Center for Business Research College of Business, Arizona State University (1990-2000).</td></tr>
</table>

Education

For example, the quality of education in Arizona is an issue of growing public concern, and the state's education systems will be affected by shifting demographic trends in the 1990s. During the 1970-85 period, K-12 enrollments rose by only 24 percent and higher education enrollments increased 88 percent (U.S. Bureau of Census). These increases are consistent with growth of the 5-17 year age group (25 percent) and the 18-24 year age group (76 percent). Projections of growth in the school-age population for the 1990s imply that K-12 enrollments will grow faster than was the case in the 1980s. The number of 5-17 year olds is projected to grow 30 percent between 1990 and 2000 -- an average annual growth rate of 2.7 percent per year compared with the 0.8 percent annual growth during the 1970-85 period.

The effect of this change will be even greater because the majority of the projected increase is expected to occur during the 1990-95 period. The annual average growth rate of the 5-17 year population for the first five years of the decade is projected to be 3.4 percent per year, slowing to 1.9 percent during the 1995-2000 period. Further, a disproportionate number of these children will likely come from minority populations who have higher birth rates than the general population.

Growth in post-secondary enrollments also can be expected to rise sharply in the 1990s. The size of the 18-24 age group increased by only 2 percent during the 1980s (an average annual growth rate of 0.2 percent per year), but will grow by nearly 20 percent between 1990 and 2000 (an average of 1.7 percent per year).

Corrections

Due to criminal code changes, stricter sentencing, and other factors, the number of inmates in Arizona state prisons rose sharply from 1.7 in 1980 to 3.7 per 1000 population in 1985 -- a much larger increase than experienced in the U.S. as a whole during the same period (U.S. Bureau of Census). Between 1980 and 1985, the number of persons in Arizona State prisons increased more than 150 percent, while the total population grew by 16 percent.

Nationwide data show that nearly two-thirds of those persons sentenced for serious crimes in 1985 were under the age of twenty-five (U.S. Bureau of Census). The dramatic increase in Arizona's prison population between 1980 and 1985 occurred at a time when the size of the total population 15-24 did not change, but the population in this age group is projected to increase by 133,000 during the 1990s. The expected surge in the number of young adults within Arizona makes it likely the corrections system will remain under severe pressure to house a growing prison population.

Welfare/AHCCCS

The population receiving payments from the state's Aid to Families with Dependent Children (AFDC) program increased from 60,000 in 1980 to 83,000 in 1986 (U.S. Bureau of Census). This 38 percent increase was much larger than either the 22 percent growth in total population or the 26 percent increase in persons less than 18 years of age in Arizona during the same six-year period. Cyclical economic conditions have significant impacts upon the size of the AFDC population, but two factors tend to indicate that the program will not grow as rapidly in the next decade: the 0-17 age group is projected to grow slightly more slowly during the 1990s; and nationwide household/income projections indicate that the number of households in the lowest income category will increase much more slowly than the total number of households (*American Demographics*, 1986). But the number of female single-parent households is projected to grow by 38 percent during the 1990-2000 period (U.S. Bureau of Census, 1986).

Given the complex eligibility requirements for the Arizona Health Care Cost Containment System (AHCCCS), the state's indigent medical care program, it is very difficult to project future growth of the program population. Obviously, the projected 29 percent growth in total population provides substantial pressure for big increases in the AHCCCS population during the 1990s. The dramatic increase in the size of the 75+ population by 2000 is also likely to produce rapidly growing numbers of medically indigent elderly needing long-term care.

Major Revenue Sources

The slower percentage rate of population growth projected for future years implies a relative slowdown in the rate of growth of most major sources of state revenue. The growth of some sources will slow more than population growth, while deceleration in the growth rate will be less for other revenue sources.

The projected shifts in age composition should not have significant impacts upon the growth rate of retail sales (U.S. Department of Labor, 1988). The probable slowdown in the pace of construction activity associated with less rapid population growth will mean slower growth in tax collections from contracting. Over time, slower economic/population growth also may imply a decline in the rate of growth of property tax revenues, since the stock of homes, apartments, office buildings, and such will not grow at the rate experienced during the 1980s (Hogan & Rex, 1986). However, the increase in the average value of new construction may offset slower growth in the volume.

The relative growth of the 45-64 age groups, with their higher income levels, in combination with continued increases in labor force participation should have positive effects upon the growth rate of total personal income during the 1990s, as well as in the state's income tax collections (Russell, 1979; Wascher *et al.*, 1986).

Summary

Demographics play an important role in public finance in Arizona. The fiscal implications of the population's rapid growth and high mobility are magnified by the extreme cyclicality of the migration flows. Beyond these underlying effects, demographic changes in coming years, particularly in the age structure of the population, will have major impacts on a variety of public programs, such as education and corrections, and on sources of revenue.

References

Arizona Joint Legislative Budget Committee, unpublished data, 1990.

"Demographic Forecasts," *American Demographics*, May-October 1986.

Espenshade, Thomas J. and William J. Serow, *The Economic Consequences of Slowing Population Growth*, New York: Academic Press 1978.

Hogan, Timothy D. and Tom R. Rex, "Aging of U.S. Population to Impact Arizona Economy," *Arizona Business*, March 1986, 33, 1-3.

Hogan, Timothy D. and Tom R. Rex, *Arizona Population: Demographic and Migration Trends*, Tempe, AZ: Center for Business Research, Arizona State University, 1988.

Rex, Tom R., *Population Estimates and Projections*, Tempe, AZ: Center for Business Research, Arizona State University, 1990.

Russell, Louise B., "The Macroeconomic Effects of Changes in the Age Structure of the Population," in M.B. Ballabon, ed., *Economic Perspectives: An Annual Survey of Economics*, Vol. 1, 1979.

U.S. Bureau of Census, *1980 Census of Population*, Vol. 1: *Characteristics of the Population, Part 4: Arizona*, Washington: USGPO, 1983.

U.S. Bureau of Census, *Current Population Reports*, Series P-25, No. 986, "Projections of the Number of Households and Families: 1986-2000," Washington: USGPO, 1986.

U.S. Bureau of Census, *Current Population Reports*, Series P-25, No. 1017, "Projections of the Population of State, by Age, Sex, and Race, 1988 to 2010," Washington: USGPO, 1988.

U.S. Bureau of Census, *Current Population Reports*, Series P-25, No. 1024, "State Population and Household Estimates, With Age, Sex, and Components of Change, 1981-87," Washington: USGPO, 1988.

U.S. Bureau of Census, *Statistical Abstract of the United States*, Washington: USGPO, various issues.

U.S. Department of Labor, Bureau of Labor Statistics, "Consumer Expenditure Survey Results From 1986," *BLS News*, No. 88-175, April 14, 1988.

Wascher, William L., *et al.*, "Economic Implications of Changing Population Trends," *Federal Reserve Bulletin*, December 1986, 72, 815-826.

The WEFA Group, *U.S. Long-Term Forecast, 1988-1998, Trend and Cycle*, September 1988.

Chapter 4

The State Budget:
Process and Performance

Dana Wolfe Naimark and Mark W. Watson

Governments raise revenues to finance expenditures and address citizens' needs. Much of the work of governments is accomplished through the collection and outlay of public monies and occurs regularly through a political budgeting process. The quality of the process influences the quality of the services that governments provide their citizens.

The balanced budget requirement in Arizona (and 46 other states) forces the legislative and executive branches to agree each year on a balanced revenue and expenditure program. In any given year, general fund expenditures by the state cannot exceed general fund revenues. During the mid-1980s this requirement led to a series of midyear "fiscal crises," as realized expenditures exceeded or actual revenues fell short of initial projections. Several aspects of the budget process were blamed for these fiscal crises. This chapter examines and evaluates the state budget process in Arizona, viewing the process in relation to budgetary outcomes. We focus on four major aspects of budgeting: predicting future revenues, predicting future expenditures for established programs, ensuring flexibility in the execution of the budget, and setting the framework for determining the allocation of funds to various programs.

An Overview of the Budget Process

Two separate entities in Arizona provide estimates of state revenues and technical support for determining expenditures: the Executive Budget Office (EBO) serves the Governor, and the Joint Legislative Budget Committee (JLBC) staff serves the Legislature. The EBO does most of its forecasting work in the fall preceding the next fiscal year. So, for example, much of the EBO's forecasting work for fiscal 1990 (July 1, 1989 - June 30, 1990) was carried out in the fall of 1988. These forecasts are used by the Governor in the preparation of the budget presented to the Legislature in January. Beginning in September, the JLBC staff analyzes the agency budget requests and, when available, the Governor's budget. The staff then constructs forecasts of revenues and estimates of expenditures assuming no change in current services levels. The JLBC staff's forecasts and estimates serve as input to the legislative budget process. One interpretation of the final budget passed by the

Legislature and signed by the Governor is that it represents a consensus forecast of both the Legislature and the Governor's office.

Revenue Forecasting

Poor revenue forecasting frequently has been blamed for causing Arizona's fiscal woes. To investigate this possibility we studied the methodology underlying the revenue forecasts and their historical performance. Before discussing these results, it is useful to provide a short but general discussion of economic forecasting.

Forecasting Accuracy

A forecaster attempts to predict the future by extrapolating events from the past. The quality of the forecasts (or projections or extrapolations) depends on three things: (1) the inherent uncertainty surrounding the phenomenon being forecasted, (2) the quality of the extrapolation technique used by the forecaster, and (3) the quality and quantity of data used to form the forecast. Only the second and third items can be controlled by the forecaster, so that constructive forecast evaluations emphasize these. However, the overwhelming source of forecast error is often inherent in the phenomenon under study. Even the best forecasting methods using the highest quality data will still be subject to this source of error. The decision maker who uses the forecasts must be aware of the amount of inherent uncertainty surrounding the forecast.

To make these ideas a bit more concrete, consider the problem on January 21 of predicting the outcome of the 1989 Super Bowl played on January 22. More person-years went into forming forecasts of the outcome of this game than of any economic forecast ever constructed. The consensus forecast of the outcome was the 49er's by seven points. (At least this was the consensus forecast of gamblers in Las Vegas.) The forecast was wrong. But, nobody expected it to be exactly right. Everyone realizes that the outcomes of football games can not be perfectly predicted.

Economic forecasting has much in common with football forecasting. Regardless of how hard we try, economic forecasts cannot be perfect; some forecast errors are inevitable. However, not *all* forecasting errors are inevitable. Forecasts can be improved by strengthening their statistical foundation and the data that they employ. Any evaluation of forecasting results must consider that some forecast errors are inevitable.

Accordingly, before evaluating the historical performance of Arizona's revenue forecasts, it is useful to gain some perspective by reviewing the performance of a group of state-of-the-art econometric models used to forecast U.S. gross national product. The forecasting performance of the models from the second quarter of 1980 through the first quarter of 1985 four and five quarters ahead is presented in Table 4-1. The table shows the "root mean squared error" of the forecast. Loosely speaking, this is the average magnitude (either positive or negative) of the forecast errors over the period in question. The conclusion to be drawn from this table is that, when predicting gross national product one year ahead, errors of four percent are typical.

The revenue forecasts used by the state represent a consensus of competing forecasts constructed using a variety of methodologies. There are two primary inputs to the EBO's revenue forecasts. Revenue forecasts are constructed by the Department of Revenue and by a group of independent economists from Arizona State University. These forecasts are reconciled (and potentially modified) by the director of the EBO. Revenue forecasts constructed by the JLBC rely on in-house calculations with input from Wharton's national model and a state econometric model maintained at the University of Arizona. These forecasts are then reviewed and potentially modified by the staff director of the JLBC, with advice from an outside committee of experts (the JLBC's Financial Advisory Committee). Thus, the final official state revenue forecasts are constructed from two econometric models (the models at Arizona State University and the University of Arizona), statistical and intuitive techniques from the Department of Revenue and the JLBC, the judgement of a group of outside forecasting experts, and the judgement of the directors and staffs of the EBO and JLBC.

Overall, there appear to be no major flaws in the way that the forecasts are constructed. Tempering statistical forecasts with judgement is a well established practice that generally improves the quality of forecasts. In general, combining a number of independent forecasts also improves the quality of the forecast.

<table>
<tr><td colspan="3" align="center">Table 4-1
Root Mean Squared Error of GNP Forecasts</td></tr>
<tr><td rowspan="2" align="center">Forecaster</td><td colspan="2" align="center">Forecast Horizon (quarters)</td></tr>
<tr><td align="center">4</td><td align="center">5</td></tr>
<tr><td>Bureau of Economic Analysis</td><td align="center">4.1</td><td align="center">4.0</td></tr>
<tr><td>Chase Econometrics</td><td align="center">4.3</td><td align="center">4.2</td></tr>
<tr><td>Data Resources Inc.</td><td align="center">3.8</td><td align="center">3.9</td></tr>
<tr><td>Georgia State University</td><td align="center">3.9</td><td align="center">3.8</td></tr>
<tr><td>University of Michigan</td><td align="center">3.8</td><td align="center">3.8</td></tr>
<tr><td>Wharton</td><td align="center">4.3</td><td align="center">4.3</td></tr>
<tr><td colspan="3">Note: Forecast period 1980:2-1985:1. Percentage points, cumulative growth at annual rates.

Source: "Forecasting Accuracy of Alternative Techniques: A Comparison of U.S. Macroeconomic Forecasts," by Stephen K. McNees, Journal of Business and Economic Statistics, 4, pp. 5-15.</td></tr>
</table>

Historical Performance

The historical performance of the state's revenue forecasts is illustrated in Table 4-2. At the bottom of the table are summary statistics that can be used to assess the quality of the forecasts.

First, is there a systematic bias in the revenue forecasts? Put another way, is there a systematic tendency for revenue forecasts to be too high or too low? In the past ten years the revenue forecasts have been too low four times and too high six times. The average error is 0.2 percent. These results provide no significant statistical evidence suggesting systematic bias in the forecasts.

Second, how accurate have the forecasts been? The root mean squared error (r.m.s.e.) over the ten year period is 4.2 percent. Loosely speaking, this implies that the average magnitude of the forecast errors (either positive or negative) over the period in question is 4.2 percent. Thus, over the entire ten year period, the forecasts are approximately as accurate as the major econometric models' forecasts of U.S. GNP. (Recall their r.m.s.e. was around 4 percent.) Arizona's forecasts appear to be improving. Over the past eight years the r.m.s.e. has fallen to 2.7 percent.

Table 4-2				
Total General Fund Revenues				
	Revenues		**Forecast Error**	
FY	**Actual**	**Forecast**	**Dollars**	**Percent**
1979	1,136,466,900	1,042,798,200	(93,668,700.0)	(8.2)
1980	1,278,331,800	1,190,286,600	(88,045,200.0)	(6.9)
1981	1,358,394,300	1,381,002,000	22,607,700.0	1.7
1982	1,481,707,600	1,530,021,400	48,313,800.0	3.3
1983	1,581,530,200	1,646,420,200	64,890,000.0	4.1
1984	1,832,646,500	1,802,836,100	(29,800,400.0)	(1.6)
1985	2,124,192,400	2,086,588,500	(37,603,900.0)	(1.8)
1986	2,274,179,400	2,332,464,500	58,285,200.0	2.6
1987	2,422,315,700	2,508,134,100	85,818,400.0	3.5
1988	2,559,301,000	2,607,226,000	47,925,000.0	1.9
		79-88	**81-88**	
Average Percent Error		(0.2)	1.7	
Root Mean Squared Error		4.2	2.7	
Source: *Annual Appropriations Report of the Joint Legislative Budget Committee*, State of Arizona, Selected Years.				

Three major conclusions follow from the analysis in this section. First, the methods used to produce the revenue forecasts are generally sound. Second, the historical forecasting record suggests that there is no systematic bias in the revenue forecasts. Third, the forecasts appear to be at least as accurate as forecasts of GNP constructed by state-of-the-art econometric models.

Can the forecasts be improved? Based on discussions with individuals at the EBO, the Department of Revenue, Arizona State University, and the JLBC, there appears to be only one area where major improvements are possible: forecasts of the corporation income tax. This has been a very volatile and difficult source of revenue to predict. While it accounts for only roughly 6 percent of general fund revenues, the forecasting errors in the category have been very large; they amount to as much as 2 percent of total general fund revenues.

Currently, simple extrapolative models are used to forecast corporation income tax revenues, because the data have not been compiled to construct more elaborate models. Most of the state's revenue forecasters agree that a more accurate forecasting model could be constructed if corporate profits could be determined by sector of the economy (e.g., how much of the tax is being generated from mining, from tourism, etc.). This knowledge of the industry mix underlying corporate profits would allow the forecaster to use data on the relative strengths of the sectors in Arizona's economy to improve the total forecast. A major effort in this area could potentially reduce the corporation income tax forecasting error by 50 percent.

Thus, despite this one notable weakness, Arizona's forecasting results have been accurate by national standards. In other words, the forecasts have been as accurate as can be expected, given the underlying uncertainty involved with the economic activity that determines tax revenues. We found no evidence to support the hypothesis that poor forecasting has caused Arizona's fiscal problems.

Predicting Expenditures

In addition to mid-year budget cuts due to lack of revenues, Arizona frequently has made mid-year supplemental budget appropriations to provide state agencies with the resources necessary to finance mandated programs. Again, there is a common belief that the need for these adjustments arises from poor performance in predicting future expenditures.

Budget estimation is not directly comparable to revenue forecasting since it involves several processes, only one of which is forecasting the underlying economic and demographic variables. The final budget expenditures reflect both technical and political concerns. Budgeted expenditures differ from forecasted revenues in another respect: they are meant to be ceilings for the agencies, not best estimates of actual expenditures. Absent supplemental spending authority, agencies are obligated to stay within their enacted budgets each fiscal year. For most agencies and most of the time, this works well. Yet, programs and departments such as the Arizona Health Care Cost Containment System (Arizona's unique form of Medicaid, known as AHCCCS) and the Department of Economic Security are mandated by law to provide certain pre-determined benefits to people who meet certain eligibility requirements. Thus, the expenditures of these agencies depend to a large extent on the number of applicants who qualify for benefits. Although by law, these agencies also must abide by their budgeted spending ceilings, their spending is, to a large degree, out of their control. Recognizing this, the Legislature and Governor have been somewhat willing to provide supplemental funding to these agencies during a fiscal year if demographic forces have increased benefit payments beyond their anticipated amounts. Thus, the budgets of these agencies rely to a much greater extent than other agencies on the quality of predictions, forecasts of demographic trends influencing expenditure patterns.

Arizona's Methodology

The process of predicting and planning expenditures begins more than a full year before the beginning of the fiscal year. In June, thirteen months before the start of the fiscal year, each department begins work on its annual budget request to the Governor. General guidelines for preparing these budget requests are supplied by the EBO. These requests contain the following information:

1. The department's expenditures during the previous fiscal year.
2. The department's expenditure budget for the current fiscal year.
3. The department's projection of the expenditures during the next fiscal year that would be necessary to supply the same level of service that it is offering this year. (Differences between this expenditure level and the level in item 2 arise from changes in inflation and fixed costs such as rent and insurance. The EBO provides detailed guidelines about these costs.)
4. Proposed changes in the program of services to be offered by the department in the next fiscal year and the cost of these program changes. (This includes, for example, new programs, expansions in staff and changes that arise from increases in population.)

Each department's request is reviewed and modified by the EBO. The EBO's recommendations serve as input for the Governor's budget, which is submitted to the Legislature one week after the Legislature convenes in session. The JLBC staff follows shortly after that with its analysis of the Governor's budget and alternative recommendations.

The framework underlying the budget process is standard, and is the same framework used throughout business and government. There are two steps in the budgeting process where projections play an important role. First, in step 3, projections concerning the rate of inflation and the "cost of doing business" are factored into the budget request. Next, the cost of new programs and projections of increased demand for existing services form the basis of step 4. The major source of uncertainty undoubtedly comes from this step. The uncertainty in next year's fixed costs or the rate of inflation is small relative to the uncertainty in the number of new AHCCCS claimants or the number of welfare applicants.

To pinpoint specific potential problem areas in expenditure budgeting, data were compiled on the major expenditure categories in the general fund budget. Included are data on the historical performance of the Department of Education (which accounted for 39 percent of the 1988 fiscal year general fund appropriations), the Department of Economic Security (DES, 8 percent), the Department of Corrections (DOC, 8 percent), and AHCCCS (7 percent). These four departments account for 62 percent of the fiscal year 1988 budget. These departments were chosen for analysis because of their size or because of media attention concerning particular problems associated with their recent budget projections.

In the tables to follow, budgeted amounts as of June 30 immediately preceding the relevant fiscal year are compared to actual amounts expended. Though it is not uncommon for budget amounts to be reduced during the fiscal year or for agencies to receive supplemental budget appropriations midstream, the June 30 figures were chosen because they represent the best estimates of the agency expenditures *before* the start of the fiscal year.

Table 4-3 presents data on actual expenditures made by the Department of Education during the past 10 years and the expenditures initially budgeted for the same year. On average, budgeted expenditures have been close to actual expenditures; the average budget error is 0.6 percent. The r.m.s.e. of the estimates is 2.1 percent. The estimate errors range from an overestimate of 3.3 percent (1980) to an underestimate of 2.0 percent (1985). At FY 1988 expenditure levels, these correspond to overestimates as large as $34 million and underestimates as large as $22 million. Because the bulk of the Department of Education spending is state aid to local school districts, and because this aid is provided on a per-student basis, Department of Education budgets are dependent on forecasts of student enrollment.

Table 4-3 Department of Education				
	Expenditures		**Budgeted Minus Actual**	
FY	**Actual**	**Budgeted**	**Dollars**	**Percent**
1979	441,483,250	437,140,900	(4,342,340.0)	(0.9)
1980	461,184,015	476,493,100	15,309,085.0	3.3
1981	630,140,300	643,021,800	12,881,500.0	2.0
1982	675,980,600	663,021,800	(12,958,800.0)	(1.9)
1983	723,813,700	712,537,750	(11,275,950.0)	(1.5)
1984	752,807,450	754,025,150	1,217,700.0	0.1
1985	935,991,600	916,363,300	(19,628,300.0)	(2.0)
1986	986,802,700	997,934,900	11,132,200.0	1.1
1987	991,862,500	1,018,004,100	26,141,600.0	2.6
1988	1,029,973,200	1,059,827,200	29,854,000.0	2.8
Mean Percent Error		0.6		
Root Mean Squared Error (percent)		2.1		

Note: In FY 1987 the Department experienced a midyear budget cut of over $21 million. In FY 1988 over $56 million was deferred to FY 1989.

Source: *Annual Appropriations Report of the Joint Legislative Budget Committee*, State of Arizona, Selected Years.

Corresponding data for the Department of Economic Security are shown in Table 4-4. The table shows a persistent overestimate of expenditures. On average, actual expenditures fall short of budgeted expenditures by 3.8 percent. The corresponding r.m.s.e. of the estimates is 5.9 percent. Over the last ten years, the estimate errors have ranged from an overestimate of 11.5 percent (1982) to an underestimate of 4.1 percent (1981). At 1988 expenditure levels, these percentage errors correspond to $26 million and $9 million, respectively.

The data for the Department of Corrections are shown in Table 4-5. On average, budgeted expenditures exceed actual expenditures by 1.9 percent. The forecast r.m.s.e. is 4.3 percent. Over the ten years, the errors have ranged from an overestimate of 12.1 percent (1987) to an underestimate of 2.8 percent (1982). At 1988 expenditure levels, these errors correspond to dollar amounts of $25 million and $6 million, respectively. DOC is another agency whose budget relies heavily on demographic forecasts: expenditures are driven by the number of inmates.

The AHCCCS data are shown in Table 4-6. Because AHCCCS is a new department in Arizona, fewer data are available than for the other departments. It is clear from the table that budgeting performance during 1986 and 1987 was quite good. In 1988 it was quite poor. Indeed, the 1988 error of $47 million is the largest error among any of the departments analyzed over the ten years. Because AHCCCS is so new, state officials have little experience to help predict the future. In addition, AHCCCS programs have been changing rapidly since the inception of the department. This constant programmatic change has exacerbated the uncertainty involved in projected numbers of benefit applicants.

Two important conclusions follow from this analysis. First, the size of the supplementals appropriated for FY 1989 ($36.1 million for AHCCCS, $3.9 million for DOC, and $18.7 million for DES) were large by historical standards. In no year during the past ten have DES and DOC required supplemental appropriations this large. This suggests that FY 1989's expenditure problems may have been unique, explained perhaps by the diversion of lawmakers' attention to impeachment proceedings, changes in legislation affecting eligibility for benefits in DES, or the sudden economic downturn in Arizona. Second, AHCCCS is plagued by serious underestimates. A major problem is obtaining accurate predictions of the size of the population using AHCCCS services.

Table 4-4 Department of Economic Security				
	Expenditures		**Budgeted Minus Actual**	
FY	**Actual**	**Budgeted**	**Dollars**	**Percent**
1979	104,655,800	112,353,700	7,697,900.0	7.3
1980	113,881,500	120,608,400	6,726,900.0	5.9
1981	144,419,000	138,410,200	(6,008,8900.0)	(4.1)
1982	151,771,100	169,317,600	17,546,500.0	11.5
1983	148,049,800	156,009,200	8,877,400.0	5.9
1984	155,194,300	156,009,200	814,900.0	0.5
1985	168,954,000	170,207,200	1,253,200.0	0.7
1986	201,667,000	203,144,800	1,477,800.0	0.7
1987	212,708,300	231,234,200	18,525,900.0	8.7
1988	231,038,500	232,842,500	1,804,000.0	0.7
Mean Percent Error		3.8		
Root Mean Squared Error (percent)		5.9		

Note: In FY 1983, 1987, and 1988 the Department experienced small midyear budget cuts.

Source: *Annual Appropriations Report of the Joint Legislative Budget Committee*, State of Arizona, Selected Years.

Table 4-5 Department of Corrections				
	Expenditures		Budgeted Minus Actual	
FY	Actual	Budgeted	Dollars	Percent
1979	41,184,781	40,621,500	(563,281.0)	(1.3)
1980	50,425,283	50,051,100	(374,183.0)	(0.7)
1981	66,292,228	69,311,600	3,019,372.0	4.5
1982	88,733,500	86,171,200	(2,562,300.0)	(2.8)
1983	95,483,902	101,084,000	5,600,098.0	5.8
1984	109,204,100	110,899,700	1,695,600.0	1.5
1985	133,707,123	135,179,300	1,472,177.0	1.1
1986	163,368,000	159,228,200	(4,139,800.0)	(2.5)
1987	183,493,600	205,719,000	22,225,400.0	12.1
1988	209,496,100	212,953,000	3,456,900.0	1.6
Mean Percent Error		1.9		
Root Mean Squared Error (percent)		4.3		

Note: In FY 1987 and 1988 the Department experienced midyear budget cuts of $19.8
million and $6.2 million respectively.

Source: *Annual Appropriations Report of the Joint Legislative Budget Committee*, State
of Arizona, Selected Years.

Table 4-6 AHCCCS				
	Expenditures		Budgeted Minus Actual	
FY	Actual	Budgeted	Dollars	Percent
1984	81,270,100			
1985	124,620,647			
1986	141,553,500	141,533,496	(4.0)	(0.0)
1987	127,822,300	129,479,300	129,479,300.0	1.3
1988	187,193,300	140,010,300	140,010,300.0	(25.2)

Note: In FY 1988 AHCCCS received a supplemental appropriation of $47.2 million.

Source: *Annual Appropriations Report of the Joint Legislative Budget Committee*, State
of Arizona, Selected Years.

Budget Flexibility

The inherent uncertainty of future economic events means that revenue and expenditure forecasts will never be perfect. With the possible exception of corporation income taxes and AHCCCS expenditures, Arizona's revenue and expenditure forecasts will not significantly improve in the near future. One year ahead forecast errors leading to deficits amounting to 3 percent of the budget (approximately $75 million in 1988) are, and will continue to be, typical. Since forecasting errors of the magnitude experienced in recent years are not unusual, the fiscal system must be flexible enough to accommodate these errors. If the fiscal system falls into a crisis whenever a revenue or expenditure forecast turns out to be wrong, then the fiscal system will continually move from one crisis to another.

This crisis mode accurately characterizes the Arizona state budget for the past several years. The Arizona system is not designed to respond to expenditure costs that exceed the amount budgeted or to revenues that fall short of the amount forecast. The state usually appropriates nearly 100 percent of the amount of revenue that is forecast, leaving little or no leeway to handle the unexpected. Despite sound forecasting techniques, the state has had to make mid-year budget adjustments in 4 of the last 6 fiscal years. Because there is no stabilizing mechanism in place, these adjustments have had a negative impact on fiscal policy.

The mid-year changes are made under severe time pressure with an eye toward expediency; they are not made to serve the long-term goals of state programs. Budget reductions are often made very broadly affecting many or most agencies in the state. This inhibits effective program planning and service delivery in a wide range of services throughout the state.

These crises reflect structural faults in the fiscal system. The incorporation of flexibility into the system is an issue that must be addressed by Arizona policymakers and budget experts. One option is to appropriate funds only up to an amount that is less than the best revenue estimate. In other words, the legislature could conservatively assume each year that revenues will be collected at the low end of the expected range. This option is politically difficult to accomplish. Lawmakers get credit for funding worthwhile programs that provide desirable benefits. Therefore, there is little incentive for lawmakers to hold back making appropriations when their budget experts predict that a certain amount of revenue will be forthcoming.

State Contingency Funds

In the past decade, many states have developed contingency funds to rely on during tough fiscal times. These funds are known as budget reserves and "rainy day" funds. These funds cushion the impact of fiscal imbalances caused by forecasting errors in revenues or expenditures. None of these funds is designed to pull a state through a major recession. The intent is to provide a cushion so that minor fiscal fluctuations do not lead to fiscal crises.

These contingency funds prevent the temporary changes to program funding that would be required by revenue shortfalls. This allows more consistent financing and improves program planning and service delivery. The contingency funds also reduce the need for special legislative sessions and quick-fix tax increases or budget cuts when fiscal imbalances are imminent.

While contingency funds are useful for adjusting to unforeseen changes in revenues and expenditures, there are two notable arguments against the use of these funds. Some argue that the funds represent government mandated savings by taxpayers that are set aside in assets chosen by the government. The argument suggests that temporary revenue shortfalls can be financed by temporary taxes which each taxpayer can finance out of his or her "rainy day" fund rather than a government mandated and administered fund. Second, some contingency funds are structured so that they lock legislatures into predetermined fiscal policies and eliminate some annual fiscal decisions that legislators are elected to make.

Currently, 34 states have a contingency fund (National Conference of State Legislatures [NCSL], 1988). In establishing such funds, three major design issues need to be considered. First, how should revenue be deposited into the funds? Second, how should revenue be withdrawn from the funds, and finally, how large should the funds be? We discuss each of these issues in turn.

Most states deposit money into a contingency fund in one of three ways. The first is through annual discretionary appropriations by the legislature. The second is through the transfer of some specified portion of general fund surplus balances into the contingency fund. The third employs a formula to trigger deposits into the fund. (The most commonly used trigger is real personal income growth relative to a target growth rate.) The discretionary appropriations method is the most flexible, but is the least likely to result in significant deposits into the contingency fund, because legislatures face so many other demands for annual appropriations. Transferring surplus fund balances under the surplus transfer method is relatively painless to accomplish and, thus, more likely to occur. The existence of surplus balances after a fiscal year is dependent on the accuracy of the revenue forecast. This method saves funds collected when revenues are under-forecasted or expenditures come in under budget, for use in years when revenues are over-forecasted or expenditures come in over budget. The formula method is the most systematic, but least flexible, deposit method.

Similarly, withdrawals from budget contingency funds can be achieved in a variety of ways including appropriations from the fund at legislative discretion, automatic appropriations to cover budget deficits caused by forecasting errors in revenues or expenditures, and transfers based on sluggish growth in real personal income.

Most fiscal experts in both the public and private sectors agree that 5 percent of expenditures (or revenues) is a reasonable size for an effective contingency fund. Funds should be large enough to cover typical forecast errors, usually 3 to 5 percent of general fund revenues based on the historical data shown above. The ideal size of any state contingency fund depends on political choices about desired levels of fiscal insurance and stability. It is desirable to place a maximum limit on the size of a contingency fund so that pressures to tap the fund for unintended spending programs or tax reductions do not become too great.

Currently, the State of Arizona has no formal budget contingency fund. Several proposals have been introduced in the Legislature to create reserve funds. Because the state constitution allows the legislature to collect taxes "to defray the necessary ordinary expenses of the state for each fiscal year," there is a legal question about whether the state can collect more than is "needed" in one fiscal year to save for a future fiscal year. Thus, the creation of a contingency fund in Arizona may require a constitutional amendment.

Fiscal crises in Arizona have resulted from design flaws in the fiscal system. If the system is not changed to provide the necessary insurance against unexpected deficits, frequent crises are inevitable.

Making Spending Decisions

Forecasting future costs and demand for state services and establishing flexibility to respond to changing circumstances are only part of the total budget process. Sound forecasting does not necessarily produce sound budgets. Flexible budgets can be bad budgets. The crux of good budgeting is good decision-making. While people may disagree about any policy choice, there is general agreement on what constitutes a good decision-making process. A good decision-making process uses timely and accurate information, includes input from a variety of parties who will be affected by the outcome, includes consideration and comparison of available alternatives and the various consequences arising from each, and is based on a clear set of agreed upon goals or criteria.

Budget procedures can be designed to improve the decision-making process, enhancing these elements. The last two elements listed above are perhaps the most difficult to achieve in a state budget process. In Arizona, there are 91 budget decision-makers (the legislators and the governor) representing a wide spectrum of political values and beliefs about government. Thus, having "agreed upon" goals may be impossible. And because of the large volume of information and number of issues, the goals often become lost during the process anyway. Similarly, the volume of data and the varying incentives of different parties involved may obscure realistic alternatives and their likely consequences.

Below we discuss several budget reform options that may help to clarify the goals of budgeting. These procedural changes may help lawmakers make better budgetary decisions.

Program Budgeting

This reform involves altering the budget process to increase the focus on agency programs rather than administrative divisions and general line items. Two of the major focuses of the current budget process are line item amounts and incremental dollar changes from year to year. This puts the focus on the value of dollars spent, abstracting from what those dollars are supposed to do. Program budgeting and variations of zero-based budgeting shift the focus to government programs and services, treated as whole packages. This reform could involve a wide range of new procedures from simply requiring agencies to submit a list of the services they perform to a total reworking of the budget and accounting formats.

The advantage of program budgeting is that it makes the connection between dollar amounts and service output more explicit; it becomes clearer what outcomes are purchased with tax dollars. It also becomes easier to identify how the same tax dollars can be spent in different ways to purchase alternative outcomes. The disadvantage is that it makes accounting and oversight more difficult. As funds become grouped into service packages, it becomes more difficult to identify the specific input items that are being purchased. This loss of input tracking can lead to the potential for mismanagement and improper or unnecessary expenditures. Another disadvantage is that, depending on how it is structured, zero-based or program budgeting can require significant additional resources for budget preparation and analysis.

Budget by Objectives

This type of budget system incorporates program objectives directly into the budget process. Performance measures are developed to evaluate the fulfillment of the objectives, and the objectives and measures are included on budget forms.

The advantage of linking funding to explicit program objectives is that it establishes clear governmental goals and allows the legislature and executive to hold agencies accountable for meeting these goals. It also stresses long-term strategic planning rather than short-term reaction. There are two disadvantages. First, legislative priorities often change very quickly so that it may not be feasible to hold agencies accountable in March for goals that were established the prior July. Second, it often is difficult to develop reliable measures to evaluate the accomplishment of goals. As less relevant measures are substituted, agency efforts may be directed toward improving those measures rather than achieving the true programmatic goals.

Link Between Audit Process and Budget Process

Performance audits evaluate the effectiveness and efficiency of state agencies and programs. These audits identify incidents of fraud, waste, and abuse, and recommend actions that save money, enhance revenue, or improve agency management. In Arizona, agency audits and agency budgets are conducted on two different time cycles with different (though overlapping) players. Linking the two could help lawmakers identify policy alternatives and judge how well agencies are meeting programmatic goals. The link might involve something as simple as making the budget staff more aware of audit findings and the audit process. Florida, for example, places audit findings into a computerized data base so that they are instantly available to legislative budget staff. The link might involve something more formal, such as appointing fiscal committee members to audit oversight committees or requiring budget staff to include audit findings in their budget analysis. Other possible links include having audit staff brief appropriations committees on relevant findings and conducting a more in-depth budget review of an agency immediately following a performance audit.

Many public goals require investments to obtain long-term gains. Several features of the state budget process reduce the likelihood that these investments will be made. The need to balance the budget each year, together with the frequency of legislative elections, naturally introduces a short-run view of the budget cycle. Direct program needs take precedence over investment since long-term improvements are difficult to measure and evaluate. This makes it hard to prove their value to elected officials and voters. These tendencies can be countered by a variety of procedures, including the development of long-term strategic plans, the creation of relevant efficiency measures, and the establishment of a revolving fund to finance investment projects.

Conclusion

Our evaluation suggests that Arizona does very well at forecasting revenues and reasonably well at forecasting expenditures. Arizona displays unusual weaknesses, however, in dealing with budget surprises. Like many states, Arizona could improve its budget procedures to facilitate better budget decisions.

References

Annual Appropriations of the Joint Legislative Budget Committee, State of Arizona, Selected Years.

"Contingency Measures and Fiscal Limitations: The Real World Significance of Some Recent State Budget Innovations," Steven D. Gold, Fiscal Studies Program of National Conference of State Legislatures, Denver, CO, Legislative Finance Paper #43, May 22, 1984.

Legislative Budget Procedures in the 50 States: A guide to Appropriations and Budget Processes;Fiscal Affairs Program; National Conference of State Legislatures, September, 1988; Table III-2 "State Budget Stability Funds."

"Legislative Program Evaluation in the States," comments to the Idaho Legislature, January 25, 1988; Rich Jones, Director of Legislative Programs, National Conference of State Legislatures, Denver, CO.

"Proceedings of the Conference on Legislative Oversight." October 13-15, 1985, published by the Joint Legislative Audit and Revenue Commission; Virginia General Assembly.

Part II: State Revenues

Chapter 5

The Personal Income Tax

Daniel Feenberg, Therese J. McGuire, and Harvey S. Rosen

Personal income taxes (PITs) are an important component of states' revenue systems. In 1987, the states collectively raised $76 billion from personal income taxation, about 30.8 percent of their total state tax collections. The prominence of PITs is a relatively recent phenomenon. In 1922, only 4.5 percent of total state tax collections were attributable to PITs, and as late as the mid-1950s, the figure was under 10 percent. In the last three decades, there has been a steady and pronounced increase in reliance on personal income taxation (Tax Foundation, Inc., 1988).

The states differ substantially with respect to the extent to which they rely on PITs. As Table 5-1 indicates, seven states have no PIT at all: Alaska, Florida, Nevada, South Dakota, Texas, Washington, and Wyoming. On the other hand, Oregon collected 65 percent of its state taxes from the PIT. In 1987, Arizona collected 22 percent of its state taxes from the PIT. The average reliance among the states that have PITs was 31 percent. Some of Arizona's neighbors rely more on this form of taxation (California at 39 percent, Colorado at 40 percent and Utah at 37 percent), but New Mexico collected only 15 percent of its taxes from a PIT, and Nevada does not have one at all.

Issues In The Design Of State PITS

Before discussing issues in personal income tax design, it is necessary to clarify the definition of progressivity and regressivity. A natural way to define these terms is with the *average tax rate*, the ratio of taxes paid to income. If the average rate increases with income, the system is progressive; if it falls, the tax is regressive.

Confusion arises because people think of progressivity in terms of the *marginal tax rate* -- the *change* in taxes paid with respect to a *change* in income. To illustrate this distinction, consider the following very simple PIT structure. Each individual computes his or her tax liability by subtracting $5,000 from income and paying an amount equal to 10 percent of the remainder. An individual with $10,000 of income has a tax liability of $500 [= .10 x (10,000 - 5,000)]; the average tax rate is 5 percent (= 500/10,000). An individual with $30,000 of income has a tax liability of $2,500 [= .10 x (30,000 - 5,000)]; her average tax rate is 8.33 percent (= 2,500/30,000). Note that the *average* tax rate increases with income. However, the *marginal* tax rate is constant at 0.10 because for each additional dollar earned, people pay an additional 10 cents regardless of income level. Hence, a tax system can be progressive even if marginal tax rates do not increase with income.

The design of tax systems revolves around criteria of fairness, efficiency, and simplicity. These characteristics are the framework for our discussion of tax design.

Table 5-1 Personal Income Tax Collections As a Share of Total State Tax Collections					
Alabama	0.28	Louisiana	0.13	Ohio	0.33
Alaska	0.00	Maine	0.33	Oklahoma	0.25
Arizona	0.22	Maryland	0.42	Oregon	0.65
Arkansas	0.28	Massachusetts	0.47	Pennsylvania	0.24
California	0.39	Michigan	0.33	Rhode Island	0.34
Colorado	0.40	Minnesota	0.42	South Carolina	0.32
Connecticut	0.11	Mississippi	0.16	South Dakota	0.00
Delaware	0.38	Missouri	0.32	Tennessee	0.02
Florida	0.00	Montana	0.33	Texas	0.00
Georgia	0.40	Nebraska	0.30	Utah	0.37
Hawaii	0.32	Nevada	0.00	Vermont	0.30
Idaho	0.32	New Hampshire	0.02	Virginia	0.44
Illinois	0.30	New Jersey	0.27	Washington	0.00
Indiana	0.30	New Mexico	0.15	West Virginia	0.26
Iowa	0.36	New York	0.51	Wisconsin	0.39
Kansas	0.30	North Carolina	0.41	Wyoming	0.00
Kentucky	0.26	North Dakota	0.14		

Source: U.S. Bureau of the Census, *Governmental Finances*, 1987.

Fairness

One criterion for fairness is *vertical equity* -- the tax system should distribute burdens fairly among people with different abilities to pay. Unfortunately, this simple statement raises a host of issues, some of which are difficult or impossible to resolve. Suppose, for example, that we believe that a household's income is the best index of its ability to pay. Income can be hard to measure. For example, some people receive part or all of their incomes "in-kind" in the form of goods and services rather than cash. Farmers often provide field hands with food, corporations give employees subsidized lunches, access to a company car, etc. Such forms of income may be very difficult to measure. Moreover, even if people have identical incomes, their "abilities-to-pay" may not be equal. Just think of the comparison between two households, one of which is headed by a person who is healthy and the other by a disabled person with large medical bills.

Considerations like these make it clear that it is impossible to define a base that perfectly reflects ability-to-pay. Public finance economists have generally agreed, however, that it is sensible to define income as broadly as possible in designing a PIT, and to allow deductions from this base for factors that obviously reduce ability-to-pay.

As suggested above, even after ability-to-pay has been defined, a good tax system should allocate tax burdens "fairly" on the basis of ability-to-pay. Whether a "fair" distribution is regressive, proportional, or progressive, whether average tax burdens should fall, remain the same or rise as income increases, is primarily a political and ethical question.

Efficiency

In a free market system, prices serve as signals that induce both consumers and producers to act efficiently. For example, if wheat prices rise because of a drought, this is simultaneously a signal for consumers to purchase fewer products that contain wheat (e.g., bread) and a signal for farmers to plant more wheat. In economics, a tax system is said to be efficient when it distorts competitive market signals as little as possible. In the phrase that was popular during the last round of federal tax reform, the tax system should leave a "level playing field." Taxes should neither encourage nor discourage various types of economic behavior.

Two caveats are necessary. First, no real world tax is perfectly efficient. A tax on wages, for example, will tend to make the "commodity" labor more expensive than its market price. Similarly, a tax on capital income will distort incentives to save. Given that no feasible tax is perfectly efficient, the appropriate goal is to make the tax system as efficient as possible. Under a broad variety of circumstances, such a system requires that marginal rates be as low as possible (while raising the desired level of revenue and achieving the desired degree of progressivity), and that all forms of income be taxed at about the same marginal rate. The second caveat is that, in certain cases, we know that market signals will *not* lead to efficiency. For example, when a certain activity pollutes the atmosphere, the full costs of that activity are not included in its price. In this case, the price of the associated commodity is "too low," and putting a tax on it may enhance efficiency. Hence, efficiency does not always require that all tax rates be the same.

Simplicity

The collection of income taxes requires government expenditures on administration. At the same time, taxpayers incur costs in complying with the tax system. These include outlays for accountants and tax lawyers as well as the taxpayers' time spent on filling out tax returns and keeping records. In order to minimize these costs, as well as to maintain taxpayer morale and encourage compliance, the tax system should be as simple as possible.

The phrase "as simple as possible" requires a bit of elaboration. Consider a tax system under which every household's tax liability is $1,000 per year regardless of its income or any other of its circumstances. Such a system would certainly be simple. But most people would reject it out of hand because it is unfair. This example makes the important point that our three criteria for tax design can and do conflict. In particular, attempts to achieve more "fairness" in the tax structure, either by increasing marginal tax rates or by exempting certain activities from taxation, are likely to decrease the efficiency and increase the complexity of the system. Policymakers should be aware of these tradeoffs when designing a tax system.

The Rest of the Revenue System

So far we have been considering the design of a state PIT in isolation. In fact, a state PIT exists in the context of an already existing state and federal tax system and should be evaluated in that context. For example, taxpayers who itemize on their federal tax returns can deduct payments of state personal income taxes. Hence, states may be able to "afford" more progressivity than otherwise would be the case because the impact of high taxes on wealthy taxpayers is lessened by deductibility. On the other hand, if state policy makers believe that the federal system has an adequate amount of progressivity built into it, they may decide that there is no need to redistribute income further via a state PIT.

The existence of the federal income tax also has implications for the simplicity of state PITs. *Given* that households have to document and compute their federal taxable income, it may make sense for the state tax base to conform to the federal base. The more conformity there is the fewer additional computations are required.

Design of the state PIT should also take into account other elements of the state tax system. In particular, the advantages and disadvantages of the main competitor to state PITs, general sales taxes, must be evaluated. Relative to PITs, general sales taxes are considered to be stable, regressive, unresponsive and less likely to drive away high income taxpayers. Some of these characteristics are desirable, others not, and all are debatable. In particular, there is little persuasive statistical evidence to support the contention that high income taxes induce interstate mobility. In any case, it should be noted that if one migrates to a state with a lower PIT, one should expect to find either higher levels of other taxes or lower levels of public service provision.

By including both a PIT and a general sales tax in a well-diversified tax system (as 37 states did in 1989), the advantages of one tax can counterbalance the disadvantages of another. For example, a progressive PIT may be a relatively unstable revenue source in the sense that revenue collections are highly responsive to changes in income. This might make a PIT seem undesirable. However, as part of a "portfolio" of taxes that includes relatively stable sources like a general sales tax, such instability problems are of less concern. In the same way, concern with the regressivity of a sales tax can be addressed by including the sales tax as part of a system that includes a progressive PIT. The lesson is clear, although analysis of the PIT by itself is a crucial starting point, ultimately policymakers should evaluate the tax in the entire fiscal context.

The Structure Of Arizona's Personal Income Tax

Although state PITs differ significantly from state to state, they share the basic general structure of the federal tax. That is, deductions and exemptions are subtracted from adjusted gross income to obtain taxable income. A schedule converts taxable income to income tax before credits from which a variety of credits (sometimes refundable) are subtracted. Even with this common skeleton, the state taxes are not generally clones of the federal system or of each other. Thirty-five states, including Arizona, tie their definitions of income fairly closely to that of the federal system. An extreme case is Colorado, where most taxpayers' state income tax liability is simply 5 percent of their federal taxable income. On the other hand, eight states require their taxpayers to go through a rather different set of calculations to determine taxable income. For example, Massachusetts has no itemized deductions and the tax rate depends upon the type of income. Eleven states, including Arizona, allow their citizens to deduct their payments of federal income taxes on their state tax returns; 32 do not. Child-care credits, rent credits, and minimum and maximum taxes are among other features that have found expression in at least one state (Advisory Commission on Intergovernmental Relations [ACIR], 1990).

The states also differ substantially in their rate structures. In North Dakota, there are 8 brackets; in the top bracket (over $50,000 of taxable income) the marginal tax rate is 12 percent. In Indiana, there is only one rate of 3.4 percent. In Arizona, the marginal rates on joint returns start at 2 percent on the first $2,458 of taxable income. For incomes over $14,748, joint filers pay a marginal tax rate of 8 percent (ACIR, 1990).

The Tax Base In Arizona: 1988 Tax Year

As suggested above, the starting point for the calculation of taxable income in Arizona is the taxpayer's *federal adjusted gross income*, a fairly broad measure that includes income from all taxable sources: wages, interest, rents, dividends, profits, realized capital gains, and some other items. To federal adjusted gross income the taxpayer adds refunds from the federal and Arizona income taxes, non-Arizona state and local bond interest, and a few other items. The resulting sum is called *Arizona Income*.

The next step is to subtract certain sums from Arizona Income. First is a series of exemptions: $2,125 for each person in the household aged 65 and over, $1,063 for each blind person, and $1,275 for each dependent. Next are subtractions of federal income taxes paid. Also, subtractions are allowed for some distributions from Individual Retirement Accounts, net operating losses, and a few miscellaneous items. Finally, there is an additional special subtraction for 63 percent of 1988 federal income tax liability or $600, whichever is greater, up to a maximum of $20,000. (The maximum deduction allowed for 1989 was reduced to $5,000.) This special subtraction was designed to respond to the effects of the Federal Tax Reform Act of 1986, which resulted in automatic revenue windfalls or revenue losses for states tied to the federal system. The amount remaining after all these subtractions are made is *Arizona Adjusted Gross Income*.

In order to obtain taxable income, there are two sets of subtractions from Arizona Adjusted Gross Income, deductions and personal exemptions.

Deductions and Personal Exemptions

Just as with the federal tax return, a household has its choice between itemizing its deductions or taking a standard deduction. The household can take whichever deduction is greater. The standard deduction is the minimum of 21.25 percent of Arizona Adjusted Gross Income and $2,125 (for joint returns) or $1,063 (for other returns). The itemized deduction is the sum of the following items: medical expenses; Arizona real estate taxes, general sales taxes and license fees; interest expenses; charitable contributions; casualty or theft losses; moving expenses (if incurred for a job change); some dividends paid by Arizona corporations; contributions to elections held in Arizona; unreimbursed business expenses; and miscellaneous expenses such as tax preparation fees and some adoption expenses.

It should be noted that Arizona's provisions for itemizable deductions are considerably more generous than those embodied in federal tax law under the Tax Reform Act of 1986. For example, under federal law, only medical expenses in excess of 7.5 percent of federal Adjusted Gross Income can be deducted while Arizona allows full deduction. Moreover, on federal returns, sales taxes are not deductible, and the deduction for interest paid on consumer debt such as credit card charges and car loans is being phased out. Finally, Arizona allows the deduction of all unreimbursed employee business expenses, while Federal law only allows those expenses that exceed two percent of Adjusted Gross Income. Presumably, one motivation for these deductions is to influence individuals' behavior, e.g., to encourage charitable donations. However, given that state marginal tax rates are low relative to federal rates, it is doubtful that these deductions affect behavior very much.

The household also subtracts from Arizona Adjusted Gross Income an exemption of $4,250 if the return is joint or a head of household, or $2,125 if the return is for a single individual or a married person filing separately.

Taxable Income and Tax Liability

After subtracting the relevant deductions and personal exemptions from Arizona Adjusted Gross Income, one obtains Taxable Income. A tax table shows how to find the *amount of tax before credits* associated with each taxable income.

The last step is to subtract a series of credits. These are credits for taxes paid to other states or countries and credits for carryovers on earlier purchases of solar energy and groundwater measuring devices. Finally, there are special credits associated with the costs of obtaining shelter: a credit on a portion of property taxes paid by low income elderly households and a renter's tax credit, which is the minimum of 5 percent of rental payments and $85. After the credits are subtracted, the household's *tax liability* is obtained. For easy reference, these steps are summarized in Figure 5-1.

The Tax Rate Schedule in Arizona: 1988 Tax Year

As noted above, the tax rate schedule shows how to calculate the tax liability associated with each level of taxable income. In Arizona, married couples filing joint returns and unmarried heads of households have one schedule (Table Y); single taxpayers and married individuals filing separate returns have another schedule (Table X). Both schedules have seven brackets with marginal tax rates running from 2 percent to 8 percent. The difference between the two schedules is that the brackets in Table Y are twice the size of the brackets in Table X. The two tax schedules are exhibited in Figure 5-2.

To illustrate, suppose that a husband and wife file a joint return and their taxable income is $12,000. Because the return is joint, the relevant schedule is Table Y. Note that $12,000 falls within the fifth bracket. Hence, the tax liability is 6 percent of $12,000 minus $246 or $474. If this family's taxable income increased by one dollar, its tax liability would increase by six cents. Hence, its marginal tax rate is six percent.

Figure 5-1
Determination of Arizona Personal Income Tax Liability, 1988

Federal Adjusted Gross Income
    plus Additions to Income:

        Federal Income Tax Refunds
        Arizona Income Tax Refunds
        Non-Arizona State and Local Bond Interest
        Certain Retirement Income

Arizona Income
    minus Exemptions:

        Age 65 and Over x $2,125
        Blind x $1,063
        Dependents x $1,275
    minus Federal Income Taxes
    minus Net Operating Losses Carried Forward
    minus Special Subtraction for 1988 Federal Taxes*
    minus Employers Air Quality Act Deduction

Arizona Adjusted Gross Income (AAGI)
    minus Standard Deduction:

        Minimum of 0.2125 x AAGI and $2,125 (joint return)
          or $1,063 (other returns)
OR
    minus Itemized Deductions:

        Medical Expenses
        Other Arizona Taxes
        Interest Expenses
        Contributions
        Casualty or Theft Losses
        Some Moving Expenses
        Some Dividends from Arizona Corporations
        Arizona Election Contributions
        Unreimbursed Employee Business Expenses
        Misc. (Tax Prep. Fees, Some Adoption Expenses)
    minus Personal Exemptions:

        $4,250 if Joint Return or Head of Household
        $2,125 if Single Return or Married Filing Separately

Taxable Income
    apply Tax Schedule (See Figure 5-2)

Amount of Tax Before Credits
    minus Credits:

        Taxes Paid to Other States or Countries
        Carryover from Solar and Groundwater Measuring
Devices
        Property Tax Credit for Low Income Elderly
        Renter's Tax Credit (Minimum of 0.05 x rent or $85)

Tax Liability

---

* 63 percent of 1988 federal income tax liability or $600, whichever is greater, up to a maximum of $20,000.

Source: State of Arizona (1988), *Booklet X -- Individual and Corporate Income Tax Forms and Instructions.*

<table>
<tr><td colspan="4" align="center">Figure 5-2
Arizona 1988 Tax Schedules</td></tr>
<tr><td colspan="4" align="center">Table Y
(Married Taxpayers Filing Joint Return and Unmarried Heads of Household)</td></tr>
<tr><td colspan="2" align="center">Taxable Income Between:</td><td colspan="2" align="center">Amount of Tax Before Credits[*]</td></tr>
<tr><td>$ 0</td><td>$ 2,458</td><td colspan="2">2% TI</td></tr>
<tr><td>2,458</td><td>4,916</td><td colspan="2">3% TI minus $25</td></tr>
<tr><td>4,916</td><td>7,374</td><td colspan="2">4% TI minus $74</td></tr>
<tr><td>7,374</td><td>9,832</td><td colspan="2">5% TI minus $147</td></tr>
<tr><td>9,832</td><td>12,290</td><td colspan="2">6% TI minus $246</td></tr>
<tr><td>12,290</td><td>14,748</td><td colspan="2">7% TI minus $369</td></tr>
<tr><td>14,748</td><td>and over</td><td colspan="2">8% TI minus $516</td></tr>
<tr><td colspan="4" align="center">Table X
(Single Taxpayers and Married Taxpayers Filing Separate Returns)</td></tr>
<tr><td colspan="2" align="center">Taxable Income Between:</td><td colspan="2" align="center">Amount of Tax Before Credits[*]</td></tr>
<tr><td>$ 0</td><td>$ 1,229</td><td colspan="2">2% TI</td></tr>
<tr><td>1,229</td><td>2,458</td><td colspan="2">3% TI minus $12</td></tr>
<tr><td>2,458</td><td>3,687</td><td colspan="2">4% TI minus $37</td></tr>
<tr><td>3,687</td><td>4,916</td><td colspan="2">5% TI minus $74</td></tr>
<tr><td>4,916</td><td>6,145</td><td colspan="2">6% TI minus $123</td></tr>
<tr><td>6,145</td><td>7,374</td><td colspan="2">7% TI minus $184</td></tr>
<tr><td>7,374</td><td>and over</td><td colspan="2">8% TI minus $258</td></tr>
</table>

[*] TI stands for "Taxable Income." Hence, "3% TI -$25" means "Take 3 percent of Taxable Income and then subtract $25."

Source: State of Arizona (1988), *Booklet X -- Individual and Corporate Income Tax Forms and Instructions*.

Other Aspects of Arizona's Tax Design

Indexing. In the presence of a progressive tax schedule, inflation leads to unlegislated increases in the *real* burden of the income tax. This process is popularly known as "bracket creep" -- taxpayers are pushed into higher tax brackets as their incomes rise with inflation even though their real purchasing power has not changed. To address this problem, several states, including Arizona, have adopted *tax indexing*, a formula that automatically removes the influence of inflation on real tax liability. Arizona's law is indexed quite thoroughly. The tax brackets, standard deduction and personal exemptions are all adjusted enough to counterbalance the effects of inflation. (The price index used is the Phoenix Consumer Price Index [CPI] for the fiscal year ending in the tax year.) The implied changes in bracket widths, etc., are rounded down to the nearest $10.

One peculiarity of the Arizona law is that the standard deduction is *over*-indexed. In 1978, the standard deduction was 10 percent of Adjusted Gross Income, with a maximum of $1,000. The Arizona statute indexes not only the maximum amount, but also the percentage rate used in the calculation. By 1988, the percentage rate was 21.25 percent with a maximum of $2,125. Given that the maximum standard deduction is indexed, it simply makes no sense to index the percentage rate as well.

Many economists think that indexing is a very desirable feature of an income tax system. One reason is that it is sensible to have a stable and predictable tax law. Moreover, indexing proponents stress that allowing the real tax schedule to be changed systematically by a nonlegislative process like inflation, which occurs with unindexed systems, is bad tax policy. With an indexed income tax system, the share of the income "pie" kept by taxpayers in after-tax income stays constant as income rises. On the other hand, some economists are opposed to indexing, especially during periods of low inflation, because of difficulties with measuring the Consumer Price Index (CPI).

Tax Treatment of Marriage

Suppose that two unmarried people are filing single income tax returns (see Table X in Figure 5-2). Now suppose that the two people marry and file a joint return. If their joint tax liability stays the same, the tax system is said to be "marriage neutral" -- it neither penalizes nor rewards marriage. If joint tax liabilities increase, the tax system is said to embody a "marriage tax;" if liabilities decrease, there is a "marriage subsidy."

Under Arizona law, bracket intervals, the taxpayer exemption and the standard deduction are all twice as large for a joint return as for a single taxpayer. In effect, the law provides for full income splitting on joint returns. Such a tax structure provides a marriage subsidy when taxpayers in different tax brackets marry. The maximum subsidy occurs when a taxpayer with taxable income of $14,748 or greater marries someone with $1,224 or less of taxable income. In this case, the couple's Arizona tax liability (not accounting for subsequent changes in deductions for taxes paid) decreases by $258. However, if both incomes are equal or both exceed $7,374, there is no marriage tax or subsidy.

Analytical Description Of The Arizona Personal Income Tax

This evaluation of the Arizona PIT is based on the National Bureau of Economic Research's TAXSIM model. A sample of the 1985 federal tax returns of Arizona residents was adjusted to approximate 1988 values and to reflect Arizona's specific PIT characteristics. The model applies the tax law to the new data base. A computer program of the tax law is used to do this. The tax law program does, in effect, what H & R Block does for any taxpayer for a fee. It takes the raw data, places it in the appropriate "line" on the tax return and calculates the taxes owed.

Like any data base, our model is reflective of taxpayer behavior in the year the data were collected. A number of factors may have intervened to change taxpayer behavior between the year the tax model file was created and the year of the extrapolation. In particular, the federal tax system has been changed significantly. Both economic theory and empirical tests indicate that this may change taxpayer behavior. These changes range from labor supply decisions and capital gains realizations to the level of charitable giving (Pechman, 1987a). While these changes probably have only slight effects on effective tax rates within an income category, they may have a noticeable effect on the measured distribution of incomes and total revenues.

In short, the simulations of alternative tax reforms discussed below are as accurate as possible, given currently available data. However, to project the revenue impact of changes to the PIT, more recent data on Arizona filers should be employed.

Tax Payments By Income Class

This section describes how tax payments vary by income class under the *status quo*. This information is important in its own right, given the complexity of Arizona's tax system, it is not at all obvious how tax rates relative to *gross* income differ across income groups. In addition, the *status quo* is the "base case" against which various alternatives to the current system are compared.

The results for the *status quo* are displayed in Table 5-2. The table groups taxpayers by their *Federal* Adjusted Gross Income Class (FAGI). The first column in the table shows the range of FAGI being considered. The second column shows the number of returns in that FAGI class. The third column shows the average FAGI level for Arizonans in that class. Thus, for example, the average Arizona FAGI for returns in the lowest income class was $1,670. The column labelled "Taxinc" shows the average Arizona taxable income, using the rules for computing taxable income that are embodied in Figure 1. "Tax Liab" shows the average Arizona tax liability in each FAGI class. The table indicates that people in the very lowest FAGI class paid an average of $3 in 1988, while those with incomes of $200,000 or more paid an average of $20,122. It would be more appropriate to compare tax liabilities to a more comprehensive measure of income than FAGI, but data limitations prevented such an analysis.

Of course, assessing the progressivity of the system requires understanding how taxes as a *proportion* of income vary with income. The column headed "Avg Rate" shows the average value of the ratio of tax liability to Federal Adjusted Gross Income. Importantly, even though more deductions are available to upper income people, this does not undo the basically progressive nature of the Arizona rate schedule. The *average* tax rate generally trends up with income starting at only 0.20 percent and attaining a maximum of 4.17 percent in the highest income class. It is important to note here that while the top *marginal statutory* tax rate in Arizona is 8 percent, taxpayers with over $200,000 in Federal AGI paid an average of 4.17 percent of FAGI.

Although the *average* tax rate is of primary importance in assessing the distributional implications of the tax, the *marginal* tax rate is needed to predict how an *addition* to a taxpayer's income will affect his or her tax liability. To compute the marginal tax rate, we increased each taxpayer's wage income by $100 and recalculated the tax liability. The increase in tax liability associated with the extra income is shown in the column headed "Full MTR." It indicates that a $100 increase in income for people in the very lowest income class would lead, on average, to a 62 cents increase in their Arizona income tax liability. On the other hand, in the highest income category, every $100 increase in income leads to a $7.36 increase in tax liability.

Table 5-2
Arizona Income Taxes in 1988

FAGI Class	Returns	FAGI	Taxinc	Tax Liab	Avg Rate	Full MTR	Fed Rdtn	Net MTR
$ <5,000	136,718	$ 1,670	$ 194	$ 3	0.20	0.62	$ 0	0.62
5-10,000	166,112	7,657	2,426	43	0.56	2.46	0	2.46
10-15,000	165,269	12,562	5,206	202	1.61	4.79	1	4.74
15-20,000	119,523	17,434	6,734	279	1.60	4.85	6	4.70
20-25,000	114,619	22,408	10,178	449	2.01	5.71	12	5.48
25-30,000	91,138	27,402	11,155	475	1.73	6.08	34	5.42
30-35,000	74,727	32,322	13,283	644	1.99	6.53	63	5.78
35-40,000	67,644	37,385	15,902	821	2.20	6.91	142	5.69
40-45,000	74,582	42,617	17,807	925	2.17	6.96	108	6.00
45-50,000	33,795	47,637	18,332	930	1.95	7.04	175	5.63
50-75,000	109,330	59,627	23,975	1,360	2.28	7.42	310	5.57
75-200,000	47,008	103,927	38,052	2,524	2.43	7.18	710	5.13
over	7,219	482,576	257,863	20,122	4.17	7.36	4,687	5.44
Means:		$29,268	$12,061	$ 651	2.22	4.96	$ 111	4.39
Totals:	1,207,685	$35.35 bil.	$14.57 bil.	$785.9 mil.			$134.4 mil.	

FAGI	Federal adjusted gross income.
Taxinc	Arizona taxable income. Figures are the average in each bracket.
Tax Liab	Arizona tax liability under 1988 law. Figures are the average in each bracket.
Fed Rdtn	Reduction in federal liability due to Arizona income tax deduction. Figures are the average in each bracket.
Avg Rate	Average tax rate with respect to adjusted gross income.
Full MTR	Marginal effect on Arizona revenue of an increase in wages of $100.
Net MTR	Net incidence after federal deduction on Arizona taxpayer of a $100 increase in wages.

Source: National Bureau of Economic Research, TAXSIM model.

As emphasized above, it is important to evaluate a state income tax in the context of the existing federal system. In particular, the fact that itemizers can subtract state income taxes on their federal tax returns reduces the effective burden of the state income tax. The column headed "Fed Rdtn" shows the reduction in federal income tax liability associated with the deduction of Arizona income taxes. The results indicate that low income people get virtually nothing for this deduction. This is for two reasons -- first, their Arizona income tax liabilities are low to begin with; and second, low income people have a low propensity to itemize on their federal returns. Conversely, for upper income people, the federal deduction is quite valuable. For people in the highest income group, on average, their federal tax liability gets reduced by $4,687 by virtue of the deduction. The availability of the federal deduction also reduces the *effective* Arizona marginal tax rate. When the taxpayer receives extra income, there is an extra federal deduction associated with the extra Arizona tax liability. The column headed "Net MTR" shows the marginal tax rate for an additional dollar of income after taking into account this deduction. Comparing the results to those under "Full MTR" shows that, due to federal deductibility, the incremental burden on the taxpayer is less than the incremental flow into the Arizona treasury.

The row near the bottom of the table labelled "Means" shows the average value for each of the corresponding columns. Thus, for example, the average tax liability in Arizona was $651, the mean "Avg Rate" was 2.23 percent, etc. The last row, "Totals," gives aggregate values of the variables for which this is a relevant figure. Thus, the simulation model is calibrated to produce personal income tax revenues in 1988 of $785.9 million.

Other Attributes of the Status Quo

It is impossible to summarize completely the vast amount of information behind Table 5-2 in a single number. Nevertheless, for purposes of making comparisons across tax systems, it is sometimes useful to have a single summary statistic. One popular measure is the *elasticity* of tax revenues with respect to income. The elasticity shows the percentage increase in tax liability induced by a one percent increase in income. If the elasticity is greater than one, then an increase in income leads to an increase in taxes that is proportionately greater. The elasticity is one measure of how progressive the tax system is. The elasticity also serves as a measure of the stability and responsiveness of the tax system. Elasticities greater than one mean that revenues vary more than income, and vice versa.

To compute the elasticity of the Arizona tax system, we increased each taxpayer's income by one percent and then calculated the associated increase in tax liability. The implied value of the elasticity is 1.53. Thus, whenever real incomes in Arizona increase by 10 percent, Arizona personal income taxes increase by 15.3 percent. This shows that Arizona's PIT system is progressive and quite responsive to changes in income.

As a second, simple measure of the progressiveness of Arizona's PIT, we compare the average tax rates in two income classes. The ratio of the average tax rate in the $75,000 - $200,000 bracket to the average tax rate in the $5,000 - $10,000 bracket is 4.3, indicating that individuals in the higher bracket bear average tax burdens more than four times larger than individuals in the lower bracket.

Options For Changing Arizona's Personal Income Tax

This section discusses several alternative approaches to Arizona's Personal Income Tax. As stressed above, economic theory alone cannot dictate what the tax structure should look like. This depends to a large extent on political and ethical considerations. The options presented here score differently on the three criteria, equity, efficiency and simplicity, and the trade-offs among the three must be weighed in evaluating each option.

It is important to stress that all of the simulations of alternative tax structures are based on the assumption of *revenue neutrality*; the alternatives raise about as much revenue for Arizona as the *status quo*. Without imposing revenue neutrality, comparing two systems is like comparing apples and oranges. In order to obtain revenue neutrality, we adjust bracket rates upwards or downwards proportionately until the particular system under consideration yields the same amount of revenue as the *status quo*.

The following alternatives are considered:
1. A federal tax base.
   a. Federal Taxable Income.
   b. Federal Adjusted Gross Income.
2. Elimination of the deduction for federal income taxes.
3. Piggybacking on federal tax liability.

Each option is now discussed in turn.

A Federal Tax Base

Federal Taxable Income. The discussion above showed that federal taxable income and Arizona taxable income are determined quite differently. Thus, after computing his or her federal taxable income, an Arizona citizen must face a whole new set of calculations. One way to simplify things is for Arizona to adopt the federal definition of taxable income. (Equally simple would be for Arizona to adopt FAGI as its tax base. Either method of conformity would greatly reduce compliance costs for Arizona taxpayers.) In this simulation, we apply the Arizona rate schedule to the federal definition of taxable income. In addition, we eliminate Arizona tax credits. Because the federal government allows fewer deductions, this would tend to increase revenues. To obtain revenue neutrality, we scale down the bracket rates by a factor of 0.598, that is, the top marginal rate is 4.78 (the current top rate of 8 times 0.598).

The results are presented in Table 5-3. The pattern of average tax rates is similar to the *status quo*. Average rates are negligible at the bottom end of the income scale, and enter the 2 and 3 percent range at the top. Compared to the *status quo*, however, we see that the expanded federal tax base allows most citizens to have lower marginal tax rates which may help to diminish any inefficiency of the personal income tax. Overall, the use of the federal tax base leads to a slightly more progressive system than the *status quo*. The elasticity of tax revenues with respect to income is 1.58, rather than 1.53 under the *status quo*, and with the federal tax base, the average rate increases consistently as income brackets increase. The ratio of the average tax rate in the $75,000 - $200,000 bracket to the average tax rate in the $5,000 - $10,000 bracket is 7.8 compared to 4.3 for the *status quo*. Thus, using the federal tax base greatly enhances simplicity and leads to a more progressive tax.

Federal Adjusted Gross Income (Flat Tax). During the debate that preceded the Tax Reform Act of 1986, one option that received considerable attention was a flat tax, an income

Table 5-3
Federal Taxable Income as the Base for the Arizona Income Tax

FAGI Class	Returns	FAGI	Taxinc	Tax Liab	Avg Rate	Full MTR	Fed Rdtn	Net MTR
$ <5,000	136,718	$ 1,670	$ 105	$ 0	0.00	1.20	$ 0	1.20
5-10,000	166,112	7,657	1,733	28	0.37	1.83	0	1.83
10-15,000	165,269	12,562	5,127	131	1.04	3.20	1	3.15
15-20,000	119,523	17,434	7,271	205	1.18	3.31	6	3.18
20-25,000	114,619	22,408	12,210	379	1.69	3.93	12	3.75
25-30,000	91,138	27,402	14,931	483	1.76	4.23	37	3.78
30-35,000	74,727	32,322	17,733	605	1.87	4.45	58	3.93
35-40,000	67,644	37,385	22,697	842	2.25	4.63	148	3.81
40-45,000	74,582	42,617	26,049	963	2.26	4.71	110	4.04
45-50,000	33,795	47,637	30,623	1,168	2.45	4.78	207	3.85
50-75,000	109,330	59,627	37,898	1,513	2.54	4.74	354	3.57
75-200,000	47,008	103,927	68,459	2,991	2.88	4.69	827	3.36
over	7,219	482,576	379,349	17,871	3.70	4.76	4,241	3.53
Means:		$29,268	$17,164	$652	2.23	3.44	$119	3.06
Totals:	1,207,685	$35.35 bil.	$20.73 bil.	$786.9 mil.			$143.4 mil.	

FAGI	Federal adjusted gross income.
Taxinc	Arizona taxable income. Figures are the average in each bracket.
Tax Liab	Arizona tax liability under 1988 law. Figures are the average in each bracket.
Fed Rdtn	Reduction in federal liability due to Arizona income tax deduction. Figures are the average in each bracket.
Avg Rate	Average tax rate with respect to adjusted gross income.
Full MTR	Marginal effect on Arizona revenue of an increase in wages of $100.
Net MTR	Net incidence after federal deduction on Arizona taxpayer of a $100 increase in wages.

Source: National Bureau of Economic Research, TAXSIM model.

tax with a very broad base, and which taxes everyone at the same marginal tax rate. An important appeal of a flat tax is its simplicity, because itemized deductions are eliminated, so are record-keeping chores. Moreover, because of the broad tax base, any given amount of revenue can be raised with relatively low marginal tax rates. This reduces incentives for tax avoidance and tax evasion. On the other hand, opponents of a flat tax are concerned about its effects on progressivity. It is important to note that the simplicity advantages of a broad base can be achieved while imposing a graduated rate structure thus alleviating progressivity concerns.

A flat tax was simulated using for a base Federal Adjusted Gross Income minus Arizona exemptions and the standard deduction. Itemized deductions and credits were eliminated. Our calculations indicate that with this tax base, Arizona could raise about the same amount of revenue with a flat rate of 2.78 percent.

The detailed results are exhibited in Table 5-4. Note that despite the fact that the marginal rate stays at 2.78 percent over most of the income range, the average rate tends to increase with income. This illustrates that a flat tax with a portion of income exempted is progressive. However, the elasticity is only 1.28, and the ratio of the average tax rates in the comparison income brackets is only 2.2, indicating that the flat tax exhibits considerably less elasticity and progressivity than the *status quo*.

Eliminate Deduction for Federal Taxes Paid

An important aspect of the *status quo* is that it allows a deduction for federal taxes paid. While Arizona is by no means unique in having this provision, it is part of a distinct minority. (Only 11 states allow full or partial deductibility of federal taxes, ACIR, 1989).

Eliminating deductibility of federal taxes (both the ordinary and special provisions) and keeping the same bracket structure intact allows a reduction of the bracket rates by a factor of 0.630. The detailed results are presented in Table 5-5. The elasticity of this system is 1.54 compared to 1.53 for the base case. The ratio of the average tax rate in the $75,000 - $200,000 bracket to the average tax rate in the $5,000 - $10,000 bracket is 4.9 compared to 4.3 for the *status quo*. Thus, this system is about as elastic and progressive as the *status quo*.

It is interesting to note that because federal taxes paid increase by a greater percentage than increases in income, eliminating their deduction disproportionately benefits middle and lower income individuals. Individuals in the FAGI range of $10,000 to $45,000 have lower average tax rates without deductibility, while those with incomes between $45,000 and $200,000 have higher average tax rates. In other words, the deduction for federal taxes paid and the special subtraction reduce the progressivity of the Arizona Personal Income Tax.

Piggybacking on Federal Tax Liability

As the options described above indicate, one way to simplify the computation of Arizona personal income tax liability is adoption of a federal definition of taxable income. Another change in the same spirit is to make each household's Arizona tax liability a fixed proportion of its federal tax liability. This would make the computation of state taxes trivial -- just multiply the federal tax liability by one number and out pops the state tax liability.

Table 5-4
A Flat Tax for Arizona With FAGI as the Base

FAGI Class	Returns	FAGI	Taxinc	Tax Liab	Avg Rate	Full MTR	Fed Rdtn	Net MTR
$ <5,000	136,718	$ 1,670	$ 436	$ 11	0.66	1.12	$ 0	1.12
5-10,000	166,112	7,657	3,274	89	1.16	2.40	0	2.39
10-15,000	165,269	12,562	7,478	205	1.63	2.78	3	2.73
15-20,000	119,523	17,434	11,177	308	1.77	2.78	11	2.68
20-25,000	114,619	22,408	15,711	434	1.94	2.78	17	2.65
25-30,000	91,138	27,402	20,412	565	2.06	2.78	44	2.49
30-35,000	74,727	32,322	25,815	715	2.21	2.78	78	2.45
35-40,000	67,644	37,385	31,037	860	2.30	2.78	142	2.29
40-45,000	74,582	42,617	34,831	966	2.27	2.78	122	2.39
45-50,000	33,795	47,637	39,301	1,090	2.29	2.78	191	2.23
50-75,000	109,330	59,627	51,889	1,440	2.41	2.78	325	2.10
75-200,000	47,008	103,927	96,294	2,674	2.57	2.78	698	2.01
over	7,219	482,576	476,414	13,242	2.74	2.78	2,984	2.06
Means:		$29,268	$23,541	$652	2.23	2.54	$107	2.30
Totals:	1,207,685	$35.35 bil.	$28.43 bil.	$787.3 mil.			$128.6 mil.	

FAGI	Federal adjusted gross income.
Taxinc	Arizona taxable income. Figures are the average in each bracket.
Tax Liab	Arizona tax liability under 1988 law. Figures are the average in each bracket.
Fed Rdtn	Reduction in federal liability due to Arizona income tax deduction. Figures are the average in each bracket.
Avg Rate	Average tax rate with respect to adjusted gross income.
Full MTR	Marginal effect on Arizona revenue of an increase in wages of $100.
Net MTR	Net incidence after federal deduction on Arizona taxpayer of a $100 increase in wages.

Source: National Bureau of Economic Research, TAXSIM model.

Table 5-5
Eliminating the Federal Tax Deduction

FAGI Class	Returns	FAGI	Taxinc	Tax Liab	Avg Rate	Full MTR	Fed Rdtn	Net MTR
$ <5,000	136,718	$ 1,670	$ 1,697	$ 5	0.29	0.54	$ 0	0.54
5-10,000	166,112	7,657	2,790	45	0.58	1.91	0	1.91
10-15,000	165,269	12,562	5,924	180	1.43	3.35	1	3.31
15-20,000	119,523	17,434	7,982	244	1.40	3.27	5	3.16
20-25,000	114,619	22,408	13,212	416	1.86	4.01	11	3.85
25-30,000	91,138	27,402	14,533	469	1.71	4.09	33	3.66
30-35,000	74,727	32,322	17,617	610	1.89	4.34	59	3.84
35-40,000	67,644	37,385	21,839	811	2.17	4.41	141	3.63
40-45,000	74,582	42,617	24,230	899	2.11	4.48	101	3.86
45-50,000	33,795	47,637	26,125	971	2.04	4.64	177	3.73
50-75,000	109,330	59,627	35,053	1,414	2.37	4.60	324	3.46
75-200,000	47,008	103,927	64,185	2,932	2.82	4.55	804	3.26
over	7,219	482,576	380,738	18,901	3.92	4.63	4,371	3.43
Means:		$29,268	$16,631	$651	2.23	3.34	$114	2.98
Totals:	1,207,685	$35.35 bil.	$20.09 bil.	$786.6 mil.			$137.4 mil.	

FAGI	Federal adjusted gross income.
Taxinc	Arizona taxable income. Figures are the average in each bracket.
Tax Liab	Arizona tax liability under 1988 law. Figures are the average in each bracket.
Fed Rdtn	Reduction in federal liability due to Arizona income tax deduction. Figures are the average in each bracket.
Avg Rate	Average tax rate with respect to adjusted gross income.
Full MTR	Marginal effect on Arizona revenue of an increase in wages of $100.
Net MTR	Net incidence after federal deduction on Arizona taxpayer of a $100 increase in wages.

Source: National Bureau of Economic Research, TAXSIM model.

The tax simulation model indicates that Arizona could obtain the same amount of revenue as it currently does by assessing a tax equal to 18.5 percent of the federal tax liability. The outcome of such a system is presented in Table 5-6. Because the federal tax system is progressive, so is any tax structure that is based on a simple proportion of federal taxes. As Table 5-6 indicates, average Arizona tax rates would range from 0.44 percent at the bottom to 4.41 percent at the top of the income distribution. This system is about as progressive as the current system. The elasticity of tax liability with respect to income is 1.51 as opposed to 1.53 under the *status quo*. The ratio of the average tax rates in the comparison income brackets is 4.3, the same as under the *status quo*. Note that marginal tax rates are less under this system than under the *status quo*.

One possible objection to piggybacking on the federal tax liability is that it would make Arizona revenues too sensitive to changes in the federal tax law. However, it would probably not be too difficult to adjust the factor that is applied to federal tax liability so as to achieve any desired level of revenue. Moreover, all of the systems considered here, including the *status quo*, are sensitive to changes in federal tax law.

Comparing the Options

As noted earlier, there is generally no single number that can be employed to characterize an entire tax system. The elasticities reported above are informative and useful, but a necessary by-product of their simplicity is that they do not convey a lot of information. A more comprehensive view can be gained by examining the average tax rates for the *status quo* and each of the four options displayed in Tables 5-2 through 5-6. For each system, average tax rates rise relatively rapidly at low levels of income. They continue to rise through the middle and upper income brackets but at a more moderate rate. Despite this qualitative similarity, there are key differences among the various systems. The flat tax on FAGI imposes higher average tax rates at low income levels than any other of the options. Using federal taxable income as the tax base imposes the highest relative burden on people whose FAGI's fall in the $30,000 to $80,000 FAGI range. And either using federal taxable income as the tax base or piggybacking on the federal tax liability results in the highest average tax rates for upper income individuals. Interestingly, the current tax structure exhibits increases and decreases in average tax rates between the $25,000 and $75,000 FAGI classes.

Summary

The personal income tax is currently an important component of Arizona's fiscal system as it is in many other states. Economic theory does not provide a definite blueprint for constructing a state income tax. One important reason for this is that the degree of tax progressivity is not something that can be determined "scientifically;" it depends on the state's ethical and political norms. However, economics does indicate that it generally makes sense to tax all sources of income at the same rate, to make the marginal effective rates as low as possible, and to make the tax system as simple as possible.

Arizona's system is, in many respects, similar to those of other states. First, the computation of taxable income follows the same general procedure employed in other states.

Table 5-6
Piggybacking on the Federal Tax

FAGI Class	Returns	FAGI	Taxinc	Tax Liab	Avg Rate	Full MTR	Fed Rdtn	Net MTR
$ <5,000	136,718	$ 1,670	$ 1,697	$ 7	0.44	0.00	$ 0	0.00
5-10,000	166,112	7,657	2,790	56	0.74	1.85	0	1.83
10-15,000	165,269	12,562	5,924	137	1.09	2.19	2	2.14
15-20,000	119,523	17,434	7,982	226	1.30	2.64	7	2.53
20-25,000	114,619	22,408	13,212	366	1.63	3.03	12	2.89
25-30,000	91,138	27,402	14,533	462	1.69	3.25	33	2.83
30-35,000	74,727	32,322	17,617	538	1.66	3.35	53	2.91
35-40,000	67,644	37,385	21,839	735	1.97	3.73	127	2.99
40-45,000	74,582	42,617	24,230	827	1.94	4.02	98	3.46
45-50,000	33,795	47,637	26,125	962	2.02	4.38	164	3.48
50-75,000	109,330	59,627	35,053	1,376	2.31	4.72	316	3.49
75-200,000	47,008	103,927	64,185	3,289	3.16	5.32	874	3.76
over	7,219	482,576	380,738	21,265	4.41	5.04	4,791	3.71
Means:		$29,268	$16,631	$652	2.23	2.80	$117	2.43
Totals:	1,207,685	$35.35 bil.	$20.09 bil.	$786.8 mil.			$141.2 mil.	

FAGI	Federal adjusted gross income.
Taxinc	Arizona taxable income. Figures are the average in each bracket.
Tax Liab	Arizona tax liability under 1988 law. Figures are the average in each bracket.
Fed Rdtn	Reduction in federal liability due to Arizona income tax deduction. Figures are the average in each bracket.
Avg Rate	Average tax rate with respect to adjusted gross income.
Full MTR	Marginal effect on Arizona revenue of an increase in wages of $100.
Net MTR	Net incidence after federal deduction on Arizona taxpayer of a $100 increase in wages.

Source: National Bureau of Economic Research, TAXSIM model.

Second, like most other states, the distribution of tax liabilities is fairly progressive and the response to income changes quite elastic; on average, a 10 percent increase in income leads to about a 15 percent increase in Arizona tax liabilities. One way that Arizona's system differs from most other states is that it is thoroughly indexed. This is a desirable feature although over-indexing of the standard deduction is unnecessary.

Another feature that Arizona's tax system has in common with many other states is that compliance is time-consuming. Even after the household's federal tax liability is determined, a whole new set of computations are necessary. We used a microsimulation model to assess the consequences of several changes that would simplify Arizona tax computations to a greater or lesser extent: using the federal definition of taxable income or federal adjusted gross income as the Arizona tax base, removing the deduction for federal taxes paid, and piggybacking on federal tax liability. It is important to emphasize that the choice over tax base is independent of the choice over degree of progressivity. By applying appropriate tax rates, any of the PIT tax structures described in this chapter (except piggybacking) could result in tax burdens distributed in a more or less progressive manner. Thus, Arizona's personal income tax could be greatly simplified while maintaining any desired degree of progressivity.

Piggybacking is the simplest option, resulting in the lowest compliance costs, but it requires the state to adopt the federal degree of progressivity. Adoption of a federal definition of the tax base (either FAGI or Federal Taxable Income) would greatly reduce taxpayer compliance costs, while the choice of tax rates and thus progressivity remains with the state.

References

Advisory Commission on Intergovernmental Relations, *Significant Features of Fiscal Federalism. Volume I.* Washington DC: U.S. Government Printing Office, 1990.

Bradford, David F., *Blueprints for Basic Tax Reform*, Second Edition, Revised, Tax Analysts, Arlington, Virginia, 1984.

Bradford, David F., *Untangling the Income Tax*, Harvard University Press, Cambridge, Massachusetts, 1986.

Courant, Paul N., and Daniel R. Rubinfeld, "Tax Reform: Implications for the State-Local Public Sector," *Journal of Economic Perspectives*, Vol. 1, No. 1, 1987.

Pechman, Joseph A., *Federal Tax Policy*, Fifth Edition, The Brookings Institution, Washington, DC, 1987a.

Pechman, Joseph A., "Tax Reform: Theory and Practice," *Journal of Economic Perspectives*, Vol. 1, No. 1, 1987b.

Rosen, Harvey S., *Public Finance*, Second Edition, Irwin, Homewood, Illinois, 1988.

Sunley, Emil M., and Mary M. Walz, "Simplification of Minnesota's Personal Income Tax," in *Final Report of the Minnesota Tax Study Commission, Volume 2*, edited by Robert D. Ebel and Therese J. McGuire, Butterworth Legal Publishers, St. Paul, Minnesota, 1986.

Tax Foundation, Inc., *Facts and Figures on Government Finance -- 1988-1989 Edition*, The Johns Hopkins University Press: Baltimore, 1988.

Chapter 6

The Corporation Income Tax

Therese J. McGuire

Arizona first imposed a tax on corporate net income in 1933. In 1978 the State adopted the federal definition of taxable income and has used it as the starting point for determining tax liability ever since. The purpose of this chapter is to evaluate the corporation income tax as a source of revenue for the State. The rationale for state corporation income taxes and their role in state finances are briefly described. The chapter provides a detailed description of the tax as it is applied in Arizona, a comparison of Arizona's tax to corporation income taxes in other states, and an economic evaluation of state corporation income taxes.

Role And Rationale Of Corporation Income Taxes

In 1988 Arizona raised over $131 million in revenues net to the state from its corporation income tax. This represented 5.1 percent of state general fund revenues. In 1987, Arizona's gross corporation income taxes represented 3.8 percent of total state general revenues, and 0.41 percent of total state personal income. In comparison, the national average share of total state general revenues attributable to the corporation income tax in 1987 was 4.9 percent, and this represented 0.55 percent of total personal income. Thus, the corporation income tax has a relatively small role to play in financing state and local government in Arizona and in most other states (Advisory Commission on Intergovernmental Relations [ACIR], 1989).

There are two major economic rationales for taxing the net income of corporations. First, the corporation income tax acts as a device for protecting the base of the individual income tax. Without it, certain types of corporate source income, in particular, retained earnings or unrealized capital gains, escape taxation. The result is that individuals can hide income within the corporation and avoid taxation. This treatment results in horizontal inequities, because two individuals of equal income pay different taxes if the source of one individual's income is taxable wages while the income of the other individual is derived from unrealized capital gains.

However, a corporation income tax is an imperfect means of taxing this source of individual income. Retained earnings are taxed at the rate applied to corporate income rather than the rate applicable to the individual shareholder which may result in inequities and inefficiencies. If the corporation income tax is not paid by shareholders in the form of reduced retained earnings but, rather, is borne by workers or consumers in the form of lower wages or higher prices, then the corporation income tax does not even imperfectly plug this tax loophole.

The second economic rationale for the taxation of corporate income is based on the "benefits-received principle." Because corporations receive benefits from government services such as roads, sewers, and education for their workers, they should help pay the costs of providing these services. Under the benefit principle, taxes paid should be related to the value of the benefits received. The problem with viewing a corporation income tax as a benefit tax is that net income, or profits, is a poor measure of the value of the services provided. A corporation with a negative net income may receive just as many government services as a profitable corporation, but is not taxed for them. Similarly, unincorporated forms of businesses also benefit from government-provided services and they are not subject to the corporation income tax.

Neither of these rationales is particularly convincing, and they are further diluted by recognition of an additional problem with the taxation of corporate income at the level of the corporation. It is nearly impossible to determine with certainty who actually pays the corporation income tax. The tax may be borne by the shareholders in the form of lower earnings, by workers in the form of lower wages, or by consumers in the form of higher prices. Because it is difficult to determine the actual distribution of the tax burden, it is difficult to evaluate the equity of the tax.

Despite these difficulties in rationalizing the tax, forty-five states and the federal government employ corporation income taxes (ACIR, 1989). The pervasiveness of the tax can be attributed to historical precedence, revenue convenience, and a sense of fairness, whether valid or not, implying that corporations should help pay for government. An additional, important reason for states to rely on corporation income taxes is that much of the burden of a state corporation income tax is likely to fall on those outside the state.

The Arizona Corporation Income Tax

Unitary Formula Apportionment

Arizona employs a domestic unitary formula apportionment corporation income tax. Beginning with formula apportionment, each of these terms is explained in detail.

Formula apportionment is a method of determining the fraction of a multistate corporation's income that is taxable in Arizona. The method is an attempt to proxy the business activity or presence of the corporation in Arizona relative to its business activity in other states. The method assumes that the amount of income taxable by Arizona is determined by business activity in Arizona as measured by the formula.

Arizona has a typical apportionment formula in that it relies on three factors, sales, property, and wages, and it employs the arithmetic average of the three factors to determine the business presence of the corporation in Arizona. For example, suppose that one half of a multistate corporation's sales are made in Arizona, one quarter of its property is in Arizona, and one quarter of its wages are paid in Arizona. The fraction of the corporation's income that will be taxed by Arizona is one third $[(1/2 + 1/4 + 1/4)/3 = 1/3]$.

The alternative to formula apportionment for determining Arizona's share of a multistate corporation's income is separate accounting. Under separate accounting, the corporation determines, *for each state*, the value of gross sales, the cost of goods sold, wages, and the cost of other factors of production to arrive at the corporation's total net income in each state (presumably, the sum of the state allocations of net income equals the multistate corporation's total net income).

The problem with separate accounting is that, for many items transferred between divisions in a corporation, it is difficult to determine arm's length values for transfer prices. The amount of income allocated to any one state depends on the transfer prices set between divisions of the corporation. In order to avoid paying taxes, transfer prices can be set to allocate most of the corporation's income to low tax rate states and less or none to high tax rate states, even though the operations in the high tax rate state may contribute in a significant way to the generation of the income.

The problem with formula apportionment, on the other hand, is that because states employ different formulae and some do not have a corporation income tax, the apportioning of income to the many states in which a corporation operates can result in double taxation of income (income taxed by more than one state) or "nowhere income" (income that is not subject to tax). Double taxation can occur when more than 100 percent of income is allocated to the various states. "Nowhere income" occurs when a fraction of the corporation's income is allocated to states without corporation income taxes or when nexus laws prohibit a state from taxing a corporation whose only activity in the state is solicitation of sales. In this case, less than 100 percent of the corporation's income is subject to state taxation.

Currently, all states use formula apportionment to determine the amount of a multistate corporation's income that is taxed by the state with several states also allowing the use of separate accounting. Fairness and simplicity favor formula apportionment, but the method does create the possibility of distortions to economic behavior, which are discussed below.

In Arizona, a multistate corporation is required to file as part of a unitary group if the members of the group form a "functionally integrated business." Two thresholds, which are necessary but not sufficient for membership in a unitary group, are fifty percent control of the voting stock of a subsidiary and common management. Arizona is a domestic unitary state because only corporations created or organized in the United States can be included in the unitary group. The incomes of the members of a unitary group are combined, and formula apportionment is used to apportion Arizona's share of the total unitary group income to each of the various corporation members, the tax-paying units.

The unitary definition of a business entity is appealing for two reasons. First, as with formula apportionment, unitary combination precludes the ability of functionally related corporations to set transfer prices for goods and services passed between the corporations so as to avoid paying taxes in high tax rate states. Within a corporation the potential for abuse is between divisions; within a unitary group the potential for abuse is between affiliated corporations. Unitary formula apportionment precludes both forms of potential tax avoidance.

A second appealing aspect of unitary combination is that it treats two business entities the same whether they are organized as divisions or as affiliated corporations. That is, if the definition of a unitary group approximates the definition of a functionally integrated business entity, then the corporate structure of the firm will not, in and of itself, affect the tax liability of the firm or the tax rules it is subject to.

This leads to the major problem with unitary combination: any definition of "functionally integrated business" is bound to be somewhat arbitrary. Joint ownership and flow of intermediate products between two corporations would seem to justify determination of a unitary group. But, what percentage of ownership is sufficient and how strong a flow of products is needed to be functionally integrated? Under unitary combination, an affiliated corporation can be pulled into a group (and thus subject to taxation) when the operations of the affiliate in the state have contributed little or nothing to the generation of the net income of the affiliate. A second problem with unitary combination is tax compliance. Because states employ different and changing definitions of a unitary group, taxpayer compliance can be difficult and costly.

In Arizona the definition of a unitary group is based on the Uniform Division of Income for Tax Purposes Act (UDITPA) of the Multistate Tax Compact, and the definition is contained in rules and regulations as allowed by statute. The regulation (R15-2-1131) states that "the activities of the taxpayer will be considered a single unitary business if there is evidence to indicate that the basic operations of the components under consideration are integrated and interdependent." The rule lists fourteen factors that indicate "basic operational integration" such as transfer of products and technology, vertical or horizontal development of a product, and centralized purchasing of inventory and equipment. A unitary business may consist of one or many corporations. "The entities comprising the unitary business must be united by a bond of direct or indirect ownership or control of more than fifty percent of the voting stock of a subsidiary corporation." (R15-2-1131).

As of 1988, 18 states employed unitary combination. Six states, including California, employed worldwide combination, which allows domestic and foreign corporations to be combined into a unitary group for tax purposes. Unitary combination is an attempt to define the business entity properly. It is an imperfect system, but it does result in a tax system that is invariant with respect to corporate form.

Tax Base and Tax Rates

Table 6-1 provides a description of how Arizona tax liability is determined for corporations doing business in Arizona. To calculate taxable income, Arizona begins with the federal definition of taxable income. Several additions and subtractions are made. The additions include interest paid on obligations to other states and foreign countries, federal income tax refunds received, and expenses paid to a Domestic International Sales Corporation (DISC). The subtractions from federal taxable income include dividends received from corporations doing 50 percent or more of their business in Arizona, dividends received from foreign corporations or from a DISC, dividends received from 50-percent-or-more controlled corporations, and interest on U.S. obligations. The result of these adjustments is Arizona adjusted income for wholly Arizona corporations. Multistate corporations must first apportion the Arizona share of the total to arrive at Arizona adjusted income. To arrive at Arizona net taxable income, a deduction for federal taxes paid (or the portion associated with Arizona apportioned income for multistate corporations) is allowed. A schedule of rates is applied to Arizona net taxable income that ranges from 2.5 percent to 10.5 percent with the top bracket being reached at a net taxable income of only $6,000. A few credits are allowed against the gross tax to arrive at the net tax liability. Arizona also imposes a minimum tax of $50 per taxpayer.

A few of the adjustments to the federal taxable income base, including the treatment of dividends from foreign corporations and 50-percent-or-more controlled corporations, represent minor differences from standard tax practice in other states. The deduction for federal taxes paid is a significant characteristic of the tax system that is employed in only six other states. Because of this deduction, the top statutory tax rate is approximately two percentage points higher than it would need to be without the deduction, while still raising the same amount of revenue. The graduation of tax rates (a feature common to personal income tax systems that is used for injecting progressivity into the systems) makes little sense when the tax unit is a corporation.

Table 6-1
Arizona Corporation Income Tax

Step 1.   <u>Federal Taxable Income</u>
       plus   - interest on obligations
              - federal income tax refunds received
              - other additions
       minus - dividends received from foreign corporations
              - foreign tax credit
              - other subtractions
       yields Arizona adjusted income

Step 2.   <u>Arizona Adjusted Income</u>
       (For multi-state corporations, the three factor formula is used to apportion Arizona's share of the corporation's total adjusted income.)
       minus - Arizona basis net operating loss carryforward
              - federal income tax on Arizona taxable income
              - accrued Arizona income tax
       yields Arizona net taxable income

Step 3.   <u>Arizona Net Taxable Income</u>
       apply tax schedule:

Taxable Income		Tax Rate
At Least	But Less Than	
0	$1,000	2.5%
$1,000	2,000	4.0% less $ 15.00
2,000	3,000	5.0% less 35.00
3,000	4,000	6.5% less 80.00
4,000	5,000	8.0% less 140.00
5,000	6,000	9.0% less 190.00
6,000 and over		10.5% less 280.00

       yields gross tax

Step 4.   <u>Gross Tax</u>
       subtract commercial tax credits
       yields <u>Tax Liability</u>

Source: State of Arizona, Booklet X, *Individual and Corporate Tax Forms and Instructions*, 1988.

Arizona Compared

In 1987, the corporation income tax in Arizona contributed 3.8 percent of total state general revenues. This share was below the U.S. average of 4.9 percent (see Table 6-2). Of the four neighboring states with corporation income taxes, California had the heaviest reliance on this source of revenue at 8.5 percent, while Colorado (2.5 percent), New Mexico (3.0 percent), and Utah (2.2 percent) relied less on this source than Arizona and the U.S. average.

	Table 6-2 State Corporation Income Tax Revenue as a Share of Total State General Revenue		
	FY 1987	**FY 1982**	**FY 1978**
Arizona	3.8%	4.0%	3.2%
U.S.	4.9%	5.1%	5.7%
California	8.5%	7.7%	8.7%
Colorado	2.5%	2.9%	3.8%
New Mexico	3.0%	2.2%	2.5%
Utah	2.2%	2.2%	2.5%

Source: State Finances volumes of *Governmental Finances*, U.S. Department of Commerce, Bureau of the Census, selected years.

Between 1978 and 1987 Arizona's reliance on this tax increased from 3.2 percent to 3.8 percent, while the U.S. average reliance declined from 5.7 percent to 4.9 percent. California's and Utah's reliance on this form of revenue declined slightly over the period, while Colorado's reliance declined rather dramatically and New Mexico's reliance increased.

Table 6-3 displays corporation income tax revenue as a share of total state personal income. The relative standings and trends over time are similar to those discussed for Table 6-2. In 1987, Arizona corporation income tax revenue as a share of total state personal income was 0.41 percent. The comparable figure for the U.S. average was 0.55 percent. The range over the neighboring states over the ten year period was between a quarter of one percent and one percent.

Table 6-4 lists several important features of the corporation income tax structures employed by the states. Twenty-nine of the states use one flat tax rate, the remaining sixteen employ a graduated tax structure. The highest statutory rate is imposed in Iowa, but Iowa allows a deduction for federal taxes paid and employs an apportionment formula that relies on the sales factor only, thus Iowa's effective average tax rate will be much lower than their top statutory rate of 12 percent. As mentioned above, only seven states, including Arizona, allow a deduction for federal income taxes paid.

<table>
<tr><td colspan="4">Table 6-3
State Corporation Income Tax Revenue as a
Share of State Personal Income</td></tr>
<tr><td></td><td>FY 1987</td><td>FY 1982</td><td>FY 1978</td></tr>
<tr><td>Arizona</td><td>0.41%</td><td>0.38%</td><td>0.34%</td></tr>
<tr><td>U.S.</td><td>0.55%</td><td>0.52%</td><td>0.59%</td></tr>
<tr><td>California</td><td>0.96%</td><td>0.80%</td><td>0.96%</td></tr>
<tr><td>Colorado</td><td>0.24%</td><td>0.24%</td><td>0.37%</td></tr>
<tr><td>New Mexico</td><td>0.56%</td><td>0.46%</td><td>0.45%</td></tr>
<tr><td>Utah</td><td>0.32%</td><td>0.29%</td><td>0.32%</td></tr>
<tr><td colspan="4">Source: State Finances volumes of Governmental Finances, U.S. Department of Commerce, Bureau of the Census for tax revenue, and Significant Features of Fiscal Federalism, 1989 Edition, Volume 1, Advisory Commission on Intergovernmental Relations for state personal income.</td></tr>
</table>

Most of the states use the three factor arithmetic average formula for apportioning income. Fourteen states use a formula that gives a heavier weight to the sales factor than to either property or wages. These formulae result in preferential tax treatment of corporations that sell little of their product in the state relative to the amount of labor and property employed in the state. Of the four neighboring states with corporation income taxes, only Colorado uses a formula that differs from the arithmetic average of the three factors, and none of the neighboring states allows a deduction for federal taxes paid.

Economic Evaluation Of State Corporation Income Taxes

An efficient tax should have two characteristics. First, if the tax is meant to be a benefits tax, the tax payment should relate to the benefits received. Second, the tax should not significantly distort economic decisions from those that would be made in the absence of the tax. As already mentioned, a state corporation income tax is likely to be a poor benefits tax. The correlation between corporation net income and benefits received from government provision of services is likely to be small. Also, corporations with no net income or negative net income and unincorporated businesses also benefit from government services, but pay no corporation income tax.

Several potential distortions to economic decisions are possible under a state corporation income tax. First, like the federal corporation income tax, state corporation income taxes affect the cost of investment differently for different firms and for different types of investment. Second, state corporation income tax systems based on formula apportionment give multistate corporations an incentive to open or expand operations in low tax rate states in order to lower their tax liability in high tax rate states. By opening

Table 6-4
Corporation Income Tax Characteristics of the States

State	Range Of Rates	Minimum Taxible Income for Top Bracket	Federal Income Tax Deductible	Apportionment Formula	1987 CIT Revenue Share of Total State General Revenue
Alabama	5%	All	Y	3 factor average	2.7%
Alaska	1 - 9.4%	$90,000	N	3 factor average	3.3%
Arizona	2.5 - 10.5%	$6,000	Y	separate accounting or 3 factor average	3.8%
Arkansas	1 - 6%	$25,000	N	3 factor average	3.6%
California	9.3%	All	N	3 factor average	8.5%
Colorado	5.25 - 6%	$200,00	N	average of sales & property or 3 factor average	2.5%
Connecticut	11.5%	All	N	3 factor formula with double weighted sales	9.9%
Delaware	8.7%	All	N	3 factor average	6.2%
Florida	5.5%	All	N	3 factor formula with double weighted sales	4.1%
Georgia	6%	All	N	3 factor average	5.2%
Hawaii	4.4 - 6.4%	$100,000	N	3 factor average	2.9%
	11.7%	Financial Co.'s			
Idaho	8%	All	N	3 factor average	3.3%
Illinois	4%	All	N	3 factor formula with double weighted sales	5.0%
Indiana	3.4 - 4.5%	Variable	N	3 factor average	2.9%
Iowa	6 - 12%	$250,000	Y	sales factor only	3.2%
Kansas	4.5%	All	N	3 factor average	4.0%
Kentucky	3 - 7.25%	$250,000	N	3 factor formula w/double weighted sales	4.6%
Louisiana	4 - 8%	$200,000	Y	separate accounting or 3 factor average	2.5%
Maine	3.5 - 8.93%	$250,000	N	3 factor average	3.0%
Maryland	7%	All	N	separate accounting or 3 factor average	3.2%
Massachusetts	9.5%	All	N	3 factor formula w/double weighted sales	9.2%
Michigan	2.35%	All	N	3 factor average	9.4%
Minnesota	9.5%	All	N	3 factor formula with 70% weighted sales	4.8%
Mississippi	3.0 - 5.0%	$10,000	N	Unavailable	2.8%
Missouri	5%	All	Y	3 factor average or sales factor only	3.6%

Table 6-4 (Continued)

State	Range Of Rates	Minimum Taxible Income for Top Bracket	Federal Income Tax Deductible	Apportionment Formula	1987 CIT Revenue Share of Total State General Revenue
Montana	6.75%	All	N	3 factor average	2.4%
Nebraska	4.75 - 6.65%	$50,000	N	3 factor average or sales factor only	3.0%
Nevada	NO	CORPORATION INCOME TAX			-.--
New Hampshire	8%	All	N	3 factor average	11.0%
New Jersey	9%	All	N	3 factor average	6.8%
New Mexico	4.8 - 7.6%	$1,000,000	N	separate accounting or 3 factor average	3.0%
New York	9%	All	N	3 factor average	4.8%
North Carolina	7%	All	N	3 factor formula w/double weighted sales	5.8%
North Dakota	3 - 10.5%	$50,000	Y	3 factor average	2.5%
Ohio	5.1 - 8.9% or .582% stock value	$25,000	N	3 factor formula w/double weighted sales	2.8%
Oklahoma	5%	All	N	3 factor average	1.7%
Oregon	6.6%	All	N	3 factor average	2.9%
Pennsylvania	8.5%	All	N	3 factor average	5.4%
Rhode Island	8% or 0.4 per $100 net worth	All	N	3 factor average	4.1%
South Carolina	6%	All	N	3 factor average	3.6%
South Dakota	NO	CORPORATION INCOME TAX			2.3%
Tennessee	6%	All	N	3 factor average	4.7%
Texas	NO	CORPORATION INCOME TAX			-.--
Utah	5%	All	N	3 factor average	2.5%
Vermont	5.5 - 8.25%	$250,000	N	separate accounting or 3 factor average	3.3%
Washington	NO	CORPORATION INCOME TAX			-.--
West Virginia	9.75%	All	N	3 factor formula w/double weighted sales	2.8%
Wisconsin	7.9%	All	Y	3 factor formula w/double weighted sales	5.1%
Wyoming	NO	CORPORATION INCOME TAX			

Source: *Significant Features of Fiscal Federalism*, Advisory Commission on Intergovernmental Relations, 1989 Edition, Vol 1 and *State Tax Guide*, Commerce Clearing House Publishers, updated 1/89.

operations in low tax rate states, the factor ratios in the high tax rate states drop, those in the low tax rate states rise and the overall tax liability of the corporation falls. This tax incentive for firms to open operations in low tax rate states is not likely to be strong, however, as state corporation income taxes are generally low relative to other taxes and other costs of doing business, and they do not vary greatly from state to state.

It is difficult to evaluate corporation income taxes in terms of their effect on vertical equity because it is difficult to determine who bears the burden of the tax. Corporations do not pay taxes, people do, and the question is which individuals bear the burden: shareholders, workers, owners of land, or consumers. If the tax is paid by shareholders in the form of a lower after-tax rate of return (less after-tax income to be reinvested or distributed), the tax will create horizontal and vertical inequities. Horizontal inequities result because corporate source income is taxed differently from other sources of income. Vertical inequities result because the corporate source income is taxed at the corporate rate rather than individual tax rates.

Corporation income taxes may not be paid by the shareholders. Instead, the burden of the tax may be shifted to consumers in the form of higher prices or to workers and property owners in the form of lower wages and rents. In these cases horizontal and vertical equity are both likely to be violated because individuals in similar positions will bear different burdens and burdens are not likely to vary in a systematic way with income.

To summarize, state corporation income taxes are likely to be inefficient because they do not approximate benefit taxes, and they may distort decisions concerning where to open or expand new operations. They are likely to be inequitable because, regardless of who actually pays the tax, the resulting burdens may differ across similar individuals and may not vary with income in a fair manner.

Summary

The Arizona corporation income tax is similar in structure and revenue yield to the corporation income tax systems used in other states. The tax is inherently complex because of the issues associated with the proper tax treatment of multistate corporations. It is difficult to determine the implications of the tax for equity and efficiency. Despite the fact that it fails on many of the criteria set out for good tax design, the tax is popular, being employed in forty-five states and at the federal level.

References

Auerbach, Alan J., "The Tax Reform Act of 1986 and the Cost of Capital," *Journal of Economic Perspectives*, Vol. 1, No. 1, 1987.

Advisory Commission on Intergovernmental Relations, *Significant Features of Fiscal Federalism, Volume II.* (1989) Washington D.C.: U.S. Government Printing Office.

Auerbach, Alan J., and James M. Poterba, "Why Have Corporate Tax Revenues Declined?" in *Tax Policy and the Economy, Volume 1*, edited by Lawrence H. Summers, MIT Press, Cambridge, Massachusetts, 1987.

Bradford, David F., *Blueprints for Basic Tax Reform*, Second Edition, Revised, Tax Analysts, Arlington, Virginia, 1984.

Bradford, David F., *Untangling the Income Tax*, Harvard University Press, Cambridge, Massachusetts, 1986.

Gordon, Roger H., "A Critical Look at Formula Apportionment," in *Final Report of the Minnesota Tax Study Commission, Volume 2*, edited by Robert D. Ebel and Therese J. McGuire, Butterworth Legal Publishers, St. Paul, Minnesota, 1986.

Chapter 7

Taxation of Financial Industries In an Era of Change

William F. Fox

The tax structure imposed on the financial industry was developed in an environment where most financial services were offered within the state of residence and where federal legislation placed significant limitations on the state's flexibility in taxing the service. This environment has changed radically during the past two decades necessitating new consideration of the tax structure. The purpose of this chapter is to describe and evaluate taxation of the financial industry in Arizona given the new environment. The focus is on banks and savings and loans. Other financial institutions, such as insurance companies and brokers, are not considered.

This chapter is separated into three sections. The first is a description of the financial industry in Arizona and of trends towards diversification and interstate provision of services. Second, the legal basis and current taxation of the industry is discussed. Finally, an analysis of economic issues related to the tax structure is provided with emphasis on definition of income and tax neutrality.

Financial Industry

Arizona's Banks and Savings and Loans

Banks and savings and loans operating in Arizona reported combined assets of $56.14 billion as of September 30, 1988 (Office of the Superintendent of Banks, 1988a and 1988b). Assets of Arizona banks were 24th highest among the states (including D.C.) in 1986 and savings and loan assets were 12th in the nation (U.S. Bureau of the Census, 1987, pp. 472, 478). In both cases Arizona is the largest among the eight mountain states. Nonetheless, value added in the finance sector (excluding insurance and real estate) only represented 2.2 percent of total Arizona gross state product (GSP) in 1986, compared with the sector's 2.7 percent contribution to U.S. gross national product (U.S. Department of Commerce 1988). GSP in the financial sector has grown at a robust compound annual 6.5 percent since 1963 (net of inflation), compared with an overall increase in GSP of 5.5 percent. This indicates that the financial sector is slowly increasing as a share of the state's economy. Arizona has

39 banks with $27.49 billion in assets. Twenty-seven of the banks are state chartered, but they account for only $9.49 billion of the assets. The state banks are generally small, as only seven have assets over $100 million. Exceptions include Security Pacific Bank Arizona ($4.3 billion in assets) which purchased Arizona Bank in 1987, Citibank (Arizona) with assets of $2.9 billion, and Bank of America Arizona (acquired Merabank and Western Savings and Loan in 1990) with $2.8 billion in assets. The twelve federally chartered banks have combined assets of $17.99 billion. Valley National Bank of Arizona ($9.38 billion in assets) and First Interstate Bank of Arizona ($6.66 billion in assets) dominate the national banks as only one other bank has more than $100 million in assets.

The state's seven remaining savings and loans have assets of $8.24 billion. Four of the savings and loans have assets of $2.89 billion and are state chartered. The remaining three are federally chartered and have assets of $5.35 billion. The largest savings and loans are Pima with $2.13 billion in assets, Primerit with close to $3 billion in assets, and Southwest with $1.53 billion in assets (*Arizona Business Gazette*, Sept. 7, 1990).

Trends in Interstate Banking

One of the most important trends among financial institutions has been the movement toward the delivery of interstate financial services. According to the McCarran Act, the ability of nondomiciled banks to branch into a state is determined by the state's banking laws. Savings and loans, credit unions, and other financial institutions are not limited by the McCarran Act and must abide by guidelines of their regulatory agencies. Generally they can engage in interstate branching. Also, banks can undertake many interstate activities without branching, and the McCarran Act only limits their branching activities. For example, banks can solicit customers across state lines or offer services through automatic teller machines (ATM) owned by other institutions without violating the McCarran Act.

Forty-five states including the District of Columbia allow some form of interstate banking.[1] Sixteen states have legislation to permit *de novo* interstate banking, though it becomes effective at different dates (Table 7-1). Arizona currently permits interstate banking through holding companies, but will permit *de novo* banking effective June 30, 1992. (*De novo* banking means that interstate banking can occur through the creation of new banks; current law permits interstate banking only by acquisitions of existing banks.) According to Arizona's statutes, banks established after May 1984 must be in operation at least five years before they can be acquired. Though no statistics are available to allow a precise measure of the current share of Arizona financial assets owned by out-of-state holding companies, 46.6 percent of assets were held by banks which were owned by holding companies in 1986 (U.S. Bureau of the Census). Robert Hawkins (undated) estimated that 65 percent of state chartered banks across the nation are owned by bank holding companies.

Arizona also allows state chartered banks which are not members of the Federal Reserve System relatively broad powers to diversify. For example, Arizona is one of 15 states permitting securities underwriting by banks, one of 19 allowing securities brokerage, and one of 24 permitting banks to engage in real estate development (Table 7-2).

Table 7-1		
State Interstate Banking Laws		
State	**Permits Nationwide Banking**	**Permits Multistate Regional Banking**
Alabama		X
Alaska	X	
Arizona	6/92	
Arkansas		1/89
California		X
Colorado		7/93
Connecticut		X
Delaware		X
District of Columbia		X
Florida		X
Georgia		X
Hawaii		
Idaho	X	
Illinois		X
Indiana		X
Iowa		
Kansas		
Kentucky	X	
Louisiana		X
Maine	X	
Maryland		X
Massachusetts		X
Michigan		X
Minnesota		X
Mississippi		X
Missouri		X
Montana		
Nebraska		1/90
Nevada		7/90
New Hampshire		X
New Jersey	X	

Table 7-1 (Continued)		
State	**Permits Nationwide Banking**	**Permits Multistate Regional Banking**
New Mexico	7/92	
New York	X	
North Carolina		X
North Dakota		
Ohio		X
Oklahoma	X	
Oregon		X
Pennsylvania		X
Rhode Island	X	
South Carolina		X
South Dakota	X	
Tennessee		X
Texas	9/2001	
Utah	X	
Vermont		X
Virginia		X
Washington	X	
West Virginia	X	
Wisconsin		X
Wyoming	X	

Note: Dates evidence a change in interstate banking authority as taken from Kincaid and McCray (1988).

Source: Conference of State Bank Supervisors (1988).

Table 7-2
State Diversification Legislation for Interstate Banking

State	Insurance Underwriting	Insurance Brokerage	Real Estate Equity Participation	Real Estate Development	Real Estate Brokerage	Securities Underwriting	Securities Brokerage/No Underwriting
Alabama		X					
Alaska							
Arizona			X	X	X	X	
Arkansas			X	X			
California			X	X	X		
Colorado			X	X			
Connecticut			X	X	X		
Delaware	X				X	X	
District of Columbia							
Florida			X	X		X	X
Georgia							X
Hawaii							
Idaho							
Illinois							
Indiana		X				X	X
Iowa		X			X	X	X
Kansas						X	X
Kentucky			X	X			
Louisiana							

Table 7-2 (Continued)

State	Insurance Underwriting	Insurance Brokerage	Real Estate Equity Participation	Real Estate Development	Real Estate Brokerage	Securities Underwriting	Securities Brokerage/No Underwriting
Maine			X	X	X	X	
Maryland						X	
Massachusetts			X	X	X	X	
Michigan							
Minnesota						X	
Mississippi							
Missouri			X	X		X	
Montana						X	
Nebraska		X				X	
Nevada			X	X			
New Hampshire			X	X			
New Jersey		X	X	X	X	X	X
New Mexico							
New York			X	X		X	
North Carolina	X	X	X	X	X	X	X
North Dakota							
Ohio		X	X		X		
Oklahoma							
Oregon		X			X		
Pennsylvania							

Table 7-2 (Continued)

State	Insurance Underwriting	Insurance Brokerage	Real Estate Equity Participation	Real Estate Development	Real Estate Brokerage	Securities Underwriting	Securities Brokerage/No Underwriting
Rhode Island			X	X			
South Carolina	X	X					
South Dakota	X	X	X	X			
Tennessee			X				
Texas						X	
Utah	X		X	X			
Vermont						X	
Virginia			X	X			
Washington			X	X		X	
West Virginia			X	X		X	X
Wisconsin		X	X	X	X		
Wyoming		X					

Source: Conference of State Bank Supervisors (1988).

Current Arizona Tax Structure

Historical Limitations on Taxing Banks

Constitutional restrictions and congressional action have formed state taxation of financial institutions. Commerce Clearing House (1988, p. 1811) has said it well, "The methods prescribed for the taxation of national banks set the pattern for taxation of all important members of the group." Constitutional restrictions on taxing national banks go back to the case of *McCulloch vs. Maryland* (1819) which limited the ability of one level of government to tax another. The court finding in the McCulloch case has been interpreted to mean that states can only tax national banks to the extent permitted by Congress.

Congress made its first step towards reducing immunity of national banks from state taxation in 1864. Numerous other court cases and legislative acts took place in the intervening years until 1969 when Congress acted to unify its position on immunity provisions. Moratoriums on the 1969 legislation prevented its application until 1976. Since 1976, the only limitation on state taxation of banking is that "such taxation must not discriminate against national banks" (McCray 1986, p. 294). Similar legislation has existed for savings and loans since the 1930s. This does not require that national banks necessarily be taxed using the same structure as state banks only that there be no discrimination. Administratively though, states have been prone to tax state and national banks using the same structure in order to avoid discrimination. This legislation offers states the opportunity to restructure their banking taxes using added flexibility, though only Indiana, Minnesota, and New York have made significant revisions to date.

Taxation of Arizona's Financial Industry

State bank taxes usually are structured using some combination of corporate income, franchise, or share taxes. Base definitions for the corporate income tax often are a variant of the federal definition, but the specific characteristics differ by state. The base for share taxes is the value of banking shares, deposits or another indicator of intangible personal property. Franchise taxes either have a corporate income tax, in which case the tax may appear as a franchise tax, or a share tax base. Thus, state taxes either have an income or an intangible property base, and the franchise tax is a legal distinction rather than a conceptually different tax base.

Seventeen states use a corporate income tax, 34 employ a franchise tax, and seven have share taxes (see Table 7-3). Banks are taxed in Michigan using the single business tax. These totals include 12 states which use some combination of income, franchise, and share taxes, and three states which have no tax on banking firms. Several states have franchise taxes which use both an income and intangibles base.

Tax rates on income (using either an income or income based franchise tax) range from a high of 12.54 percent in Massachusetts (which uses a franchise tax) to no tax in 13 states. Rates on assets are harder to compare because the bases often differ, but they range from as high as the 1.5 percent business and occupations tax in Washington to 0 percent in 31 states.

Table 7-3
State Taxation of Banks

| | | | | | | Apportion Franchise Interest From Government | | | |
| | | | | | | | | Securities Taxable | |
State	Corporate Income Tax Rate	Franchise Tax Rate	Effective Tax Rate on Corporate Income (1980)	Share Tax Rate	Bank Tax Liability	Tax Based on Income	Federal	State & Local
AL	0.0	6.0	4.12	0.0	Y	Y	Y	Y
AK (l)	9.4	0.0	3.99	0.0	Y	N/A	N	Y
AZ (k,l)	10.5	0.0	5.31	0.0	Y	N/A	N	Y
AR (l)	6.0	0.27	0.42	0.0	Y	N	N	N
CA	0.0	10.644	9.52	0.0	Y	Y	Y	Y
CO (l)	6.0	0.0	1.09	0.0	N	N/A	N	N
CT (h)	0.0	11.5	8.88	0.0	Y	Y	Y	Y
DE (l)	0.0	8.7	4.69	0.0	N	Y	Y	Y
DC (k)	0.0	10.5	14.49	0.0	Y	Y	N	Y
FL (c)	0.0	5.5	U	0.2	Y	Y	Y	Y
GA (d,i,k)	6.0	0.0	U	0.0	Y	N	N	Y
HI	0.0	11.7	3.99	0.0	N	Y	Y	Y
ID (k)	7.7	0.0	4.99	0.0	Y	N/A	N	Y
IL	6.5	0.0	U	0.0	Y	N/A	N	Y
IN (d)	3.4	0.0	U	0.25	Y	N/A	N	N
IA	0.0	5.0	4.63	0.0	N	Y	Y	Y
KS	0.0	6.375	4.77	0.0	Y	Y	Y	Y
KY	0.0	0.0	U	0.95	N	N/A	N	Y
LA	0.0	0.0	U	0.0	N	N/A	N	N
ME (a)	0.0	1.0	U	0.015	Y	Y	Y	Y
MD	0.0	7.0	U	0.0	Y	Y	Y	Y

Table 7-3 (Continued)

State	Corporate Income Tax Rate	Franchise Tax Rate	Effective Tax Rate on Corporate Income (1980)	Share Tax Rate	Apportion Franchise Interest From Government		Securities Taxable	
					Bank Tax Liability	Tax Based on Income	Federal	State & Local
MA	0.0	12.54	10.66	0.0	N	Y	Y	Y
MI (j)	0.0	0.0	2.10	0.0	Y	N/A	N	Y
MN	0.0	9.5	9.49	0.0	Y	Y	Y	Y
MS (f,l)	5.0	0.25	U	0.0	N	N	N	N
MO	0.0	7.0	U	0.0	N	Y	Y	Y
MT	0.0	6.75	U	0.0	Y	Y	Y	Y
NE	0.0	0.0	U	0.0004	N	N/A	N	N
NV	0.0	0.0	U	0.0	N	N/A	N	N
NH	8.0	1.0	U	0.0	N	N	N	N
NJ (a)	0.0	9.0	4.53	0.2	Y	Y	Y	Y
NM (b,d,l)	7.6	0.0	4.08	0.0	Y	N/A	N	N
NY	0.0	9.0	8.92	0.0	Y	Y	Y	Y
NC	7.0	0.15	U	0.0	Y	N	Y	Y
ND	0.0	10.0	5.16	0.0	Y	Y	Y	Y
OH	0.0	1.5	U	0.0	Y	N	Y	Y
OK	5.0	0.125	2.23	0.0	Y	N	Y	Y
OR	7.75	0.0	8.16	0.0	Y	N/A	N	N
PA	0.0	0.0	U	1.075	N	N/A	N	Y
RI	8.0	0.00025	9.42	0.000695	N	N	N	N
SC	0.0	4.5	1.29	0.0	N	Y	Y	Y
SD	0.0	6.0	4.35	0.0	Y	Y	Y	Y
TN	6.0	0.25	U	0.0	Y	N	Y	Y

Table 7-3 (Continued)

| State | Corporate Income Tax Rate | Franchise Tax Rate | Effective Tax Rate on Corporate Income (1980) | Share Tax Rate | Apportion Franchise Interest From Government | | Securities Taxable | |
					Bank Tax Liability	Tax Based on Income	Federal	State & Local
TX	0.0	0.525	U	0.0	N	N	N	N
UT (g)	0.0	5.0	2.98	0.0	Y	Y	Y	Y
VT	0.0	0.00024	U	0.0	N	N	N	N
VA	0.0	1.0	U	0.0	N	N	Y	Y
WA (e,k)	0.0	0.0	U	1.5	Y	N/A	N	Y
WV	9.45	0.75	U	0.0	Y	N	N	N
WI	0.0	7.9	7.13	0.0	Y	Y	Y	Y
WY	0.0	0.0	U	0.0	N	N/A	N	N

N/A = Not applicable
U = Unavailable
a = The share tax is a franchise tax levied on assets.
b = Levies a $50 franchise tax.
c = Levies an intangible property tax.
d = Levies a gross receipts tax.
e = The share tax is the business and occupation tax.

f = Levies a share tax, but it is a credit against the personal property tax.
g = Has a supplemental income tax.
h = Minimum tax is levied in the event no income is earned.
i = The gross receipts tax is a credit against the income tax.
j = Levies the Single Business Tax.
k = Not all state and local government interest is taxable.
l = This is the highest marginal tax rate levied on income.

The Arizona financial industry is taxed under general corporate income tax statutes as opposed to industry-specific statutes. The corporate income tax is levied on state chartered banks, national banks, and savings and loans. Credit unions generally have no tax liability because they are exempt from federal income taxes and those insurance companies which are subject to a premium tax (representing all but title insurance companies) are exempt. Twenty-three states, including Arizona, tax banking in the same manner as other corporations and 27 do not. Arizona is one of 19 states that use a direct net income tax for the banking industry (Kincaid and McCray, 1988, p. 19).

Taxation of Multistate Income

State taxation of financial institutions across the U.S. was generally developed to tax the principal office of banks located in the state since each state was prohibiting interstate banking. As a result, income from the interstate operations of banks historically has been given little consideration in tax legislation by most states. Arizona's approach to defining taxable income appears to have developed in the same manner though the logical basis for the state's tax structure is better than in most other states. Currently, the taxable income of interstate financial institutions operating in Arizona is based on the income earned in the state regardless of the state in which the financial institutions are domiciled. The method for measuring income is the same for financial institutions and other corporations.

Arizona's approach to taxing bank income is referred to as "source based" because the goal is to tax income which has its source in Arizona. The alternative is a residence based structure which would tax Arizona domiciled financial institutions on their income earned regardless of the state in which it is earned. Nondomiciled firms would not be taxable in Arizona if the state had a residence structure. Approximately one-third of the states use a residence based approach (McCray, 1987, p. 932).

One potential disadvantage of a source based tax is that little of the tax revenues may be exported to residents of other states though it is unlikely that the state can export much of the tax with either a residence or source based tax. The tax will be paid substantially by Arizona residents or businesses if it is shifted into higher interest rates on borrowers or lower rates for lenders since the tax generally will be imposed on income earned in the state from these transactions. Shifting of the tax to one of these two seems to be the likely result, at least in the short run, for marginal increases in the tax meaning most of it is paid by residents. The alternative is for the tax to be paid by owners of financial institutions through lower rates of return.[2] Owners may be more likely to reside out-of-state than consumers particularly if the financial institution (or its parent) is domiciled outside the state. The recent trend towards Arizona financial institutions being purchased by nondomiciled holding companies means the owner's share is likely being exported more. In any event, there may be no legislative intent to export the tax since it is aimed at income generated in the state.

Apportioning Multistate Income

Arizona's share of multistate corporate income is measured by apportioning income into Arizona using the arithmetic average of the proportion of a corporation's tangible and real property, receipts, and payroll which are located in Arizona. Beginning in 1984, a unitary approach under the Uniform Division of Income for Tax Purposes Act (UDITPA) was adopted for defining the total income subject to apportionment. The unitary rules employ a test of the operational linkage between tied businesses to determine if they are to be combined for measurement of income (see Chapter 6). A water's edge definition is also used in Arizona which essentially means only domestic corporate income is included.

Despite existence of the apportionment formula, it is unlikely that Arizona generates significant revenue from taxation of nondomiciled banks or loses significant revenue by allowing domiciled banks to apportion income out of state. One reason why little revenue is gained from taxing nondomiciled banks is that only domiciled banks can branch in the state though these banks may be owned by a nondomiciled holding company. Thus, nondomiciled banks are only operating in the state through branchless means, such as via the mail or telecommunications.

The Arizona Department of Revenue has concluded that nexus exists for tax purposes if a nondomiciled bank (or any bank) earns income and has property in the state. Bank credit cards, which are owned by a bank, represent property and interest earnings and represent the source for income, so the Department could regard provision of credit cards to Arizona residents as taxable activity for nondomiciled firms. However, there are probably few nondomiciled firms filing returns and the Department is probably collecting little revenue from these sources.

The revenue lost from apportioning income out of state from domiciled banks probably also is limited. Domiciled banks are branching very little outside the state (though their holding companies may be) so any non-Arizona income earned is likely generated through branchless means. This income may be apportioned outside the state using Arizona's rules and may be escaping taxation completely. The interest on loans which are repackaged into securities and resold outside the state also may be escaping taxation.

Evaluation of the Taxation of Financial Institutions

Ultimately, the goals for taxation are accomplished by choosing an appropriate tax base and applying the necessary tax rates. The first topic addressed here is an examination of various aspects of defining taxable income, or in other words, defining the tax base. The second topic is tax neutrality which depends on both the base chosen and the tax rates applied. This section is an evaluation of the current Arizona tax structure as applied to financial institutions, relative to the goals of revenue generation, tax neutrality, and limited costs for administration and compliance. Normative conclusions are reached using these goals as guidelines, but the advantages and disadvantages of each option are listed.

Definition of Taxable Income

Definition of the tax base is the most complex concern in the design of any tax structure, yet it is vitally important because it determines the tax rates which must be imposed to raise a given amount of revenue. It is also the most important determinant of the compliance and administrative efforts which are required to collect the revenues. Generally, it is argued that the base should be as broad as possible to permit lower rates. One advantage is that lower rates reduce incentives to evade taxation, defined as not paying taxes that are legally due. A second advantage is that a broad base precludes avoiding taxes through legal means. For example, if all interest income is taxed at a constant rate, there is no incentive for people to place their assets in one instrument versus another because of differences in the tax rate. A second basic tenet followed is that the tax base should be income which has its source in Arizona.

The Arizona tax base for financial institutions is defined by the corporate income tax regulations in the same manner as for other corporations. Four aspects of this definition as applied to financial institutions must be considered in evaluating the current tax structure: interest on federal obligations, apportionment, interest on securitized loans and branchless banking. The conclusion for each of these is that the state is failing to tax some of the income of financial institutions even though collecting that income could increase revenue in a neutral way with minimal administrative cost, which is consistent with maximizing revenues, maintaining a neutral tax system and minimizing collection and administrative efforts. Arizona may want to consider steps to revise its tax system accordingly. In some ways Arizona's tax structure is better designed than many, but some restructuring may be appropriate.

Interest on Federal Obligations

A significant omission from the Arizona tax base is the interest which financial institutions earn from holding federal obligations. Arizona banks held $1.9 billion in such securities in 1986, representing about 6.9 percent of bank assets (Board of Governors, 1987). This is likely a much greater percentage than nonfinancial corporations thereby reducing the taxation of banks relative to other corporations. Further, banks increased their holding of federal securities by 95 percent between 1978 and 1986. There is significant potential to broaden the base by taxing this interest thus creating a tax structure which taxes corporations more even-handedly. Additional revenue would also accrue to the state if tax rates were not reduced. Unfortunately, conditions under which interest on federal obligations can be taxed are set by Congress and the interest cannot be included in the base of a corporate income tax.

Congress has not totally limited the states' ability to tax interest from federal obligations. It can be taxed by states that use a nondiscriminatory franchise tax or other non-property tax as the revenue instrument for banks. States are free to measure the franchise tax base using income and can use federal taxable income as the starting point for defining the tax base. Many states already use this approach to taxation of banks. Thirty-four states and the District of Columbia currently employ a franchise tax, of which 22 measure the franchise tax base with net income. Twenty-six of the total 34 include the income from federal obligations in the tax base. However, states in the western region of the U.S. are much less likely to use a franchise tax than are states in other parts of the U.S.

Arizona could consider the strategy of exempting financial institutions from the corporate income tax and creating a franchise tax structure specific to them. Though a different tax structure from other firms, it would result in more even taxation. The tax could be legally imposed on financial institutions in interstate commerce as long as it meets the requirements laid out by the courts in *Complete Auto Transit vs. Brady* 420 U.S. 274 (1983). These conditions are that the tax is on an activity with substantial nexus in Arizona, the tax is fairly apportioned, the tax does not discriminate against interstate commerce, and the tax is fairly related to services provided by Arizona (see McCray 1986, p. 326). None of these conditions pose a serious obstacle.

In the 1983 *Memphis Bank & Trust* 103 S.Ct. 692 (1983) case, the U.S. Supreme Court ruled that a state including federal interest in its base also must include interest earned on its own and on its political subdivisions' obligations. Thus, changing to the franchise tax structure also would require the inclusion of interest from Arizona state and local government obligations in the base. This is likely to raise fears of higher interest rates for these governments, but any effect should be very small.

Additional administrative expenses would arise from adopting a different tax structure for financial and other corporations. New guidelines and new forms would be necessary. A particular definitional problem occurs when a unitary firm includes subsidiaries that produce in both types of industries. For example would General Motors, which has both financial and manufacturing subsidiaries, be taxed as a financial or as a general corporation? Application of the unitary concept would require detailed rules to determine in which industry firms are to be taxed.

Apportionment of Multistate Income

The corporate income tax is intended to tax income which has its source in Arizona. Thus, the income of Arizona domiciled financial institutions arising from operations outside Arizona must be excluded in calculation of their Arizona tax base, and the income of nondomiciled firms arising from operations in the state must be measured as their Arizona tax base. Each of these can be achieved through separate accounting of firms' activities or formulary apportionment. As described above, the state has chosen the formulary approach. This section reviews Arizona's current approach and discusses several reasons why the formula that is applied to nonfinancial corporations may be poor when it is applied to financial institutions. The basic conclusion is that the apportionment formula and situs regulations could be revised to better reflect the way financial institutions earn income and to shift more of a firm's taxable income to Arizona.

The share of income which is attributed to Arizona depends on the factors in the formula and the situs rules used to measure where the factors are located. The factors included in the formula are intended as proxies for how income is generated and the situs rules are to determine the state in which income is earned. Wide variation exists in how states approach these two issues and compliance by firms would be greatly enhanced if uniformity with regard to apportionment and situs was achieved. These two aspects of the formula are addressed separately.

Apportionment. Forty-five states (Hellerstein 1983, pp 496-498) use a three- factor formula to apportion general corporate income. The factors are the percentage of corporate property, percentage of corporate receipts, and percentage of corporate payrolls which are located in the state. An average of the percentage of each factor in the state is multiplied times corporate income to determine the income earned in the state. This approach was codified in UDITPA in the late 1950s. In practice the three-factor formula is applied in different ways across those states using it. For example, 12 states choose not to give equal weight to the factors when determining their average.

Thirty-two states use an apportionment method of some type for interstate bank income, though only 11 use the three-factor approach (Kincaid and McCray 1988, p. 22). One reason for treating financial institutions differently is that the UDITPA agreement specifically excludes bank income. Arizona is one of the states which apply the three-factor formula to financial corporations.

Three concerns regarding the use of the three factors must be examined in this regard. These are that the property factor is a poor surrogate for how financial income is earned, the focus on tangible property shifts income to a bank's state of domicile and away from its market states, and the weighing scheme for factors in the formula must be chosen to achieve the desired set of goals.

First, the formula may not be well designed for apportioning financial income because the property factor is a poor representation of how financial income is earned. Only tangible property is included in the property factor but financial income is more closely linked to intangible property. Hellerstein (1983, p. 673) noted that deposits may play the role for banks that factories serve for other producers since they are the basis for making loans. Though this parallel is becoming less true as banks are able to use securitization (repackaging loans for resale to a secondary market) as a mechanism for generating loanable funds, there is still a strong case that intangible assets or deposits are a better indicator of where bank income is earned than is tangible property. Intangible assets are the loans and securities that financial institutions hold in their portfolio.

Second, it would appear that Arizona's use of the property factor without including intangible assets and without proper situs rules tends to shift some taxes on interstate income that could legitimately be taxed in Arizona to the states in which the firms are domiciled. This may become even more of an issue with *de novo* banking. As described below, careful development of the situs rules and the apportionment formula can shift a greater share of revenues into Arizona.

The problem is not necessarily that bank income remains untaxed, but that it might not be apportioned to the state where the income is earned. Conceptually, all income of financial institutions could be taxed in one state or another regardless of whether intangible property is used in defining the property factor. The effect of omitting intangibles is to increase the relative amount of property in the state where financial institutions have tangible property. The physical property of most banks is likely to be in the state of domicile. Thus, Arizona's share of the tax revenues is probably reduced by exclusion of intangibles from the property factor since it is a market state with relatively few domiciled banks.

There is no perfect apportionment formula and one should not be expected since it is merely intended as a proxy not an identical representation of how financial institutions earn their income. Still, it is apparent that if a property factor is included, intangible assets must be used in order to have a good proxy for the method of generating financial income. Other states have begun making adjustments in their formula to account for this distinction between general and financial corporations. New York recently revised its bank income apportionment formula to use all three factors but replaced the property factor with deposits. Minnesota revised its formula by using both tangible and intangible property in the property element of the three-factor formula.

A difficulty with including intangible assets in the property factor is they are mobile, and banks can move them in a manner which lowers their total tax cost.[3] A tax on immobile factors, such as real property, would be preferred on this basis, but a tax on real property is inferior on other grounds. Thus, the task is to write careful situs rules to ensure that intangible property can be used in apportionment. Arizona will probably want its situs rules to favor the state where the market is located because this will increase the state's tax base.[4] Note that both New York and Minnesota use measures of bank revenues as the sales factor and this requires similar rules on situs.

Third, once the factors have been chosen, a decision must be made on how to weight each of them. Again, there is no *a priori* correct set of weights,[5] and the choice is substantially open to a decision based on goals for the tax system. For example, states often double-weight the sales component in their general corporate income tax formula because this tends to lower the taxes for firms which have a relatively large share of their production capabilities (payroll and property) in the state. This approach raises taxes for firms which have a relatively large share of their sales in the state.

New York double-weights its receipts and deposits factors and reduces the weight on the payroll factor in its bank formula. Minnesota's bank formula adds 70 percent of the share of receipts in the state to 15 percent of the shares of property and payroll to determine the percentage of income earned in the state. Clearly, both states have chosen to reduce the tax for banks which locate a large share of their workers in state as an incentive to choose the state as a location for employment. Both increase the tax on banks which have a significant share of receipts in-state.

Arizona could make a similar decision to weight its factors in favor of domestic production though it has not done so with regard to its general corporate income tax. One advantage is that firms with a greater share of receipts than of property and payroll in the state would pay more taxes. This should raise Arizona's collections since it is a market state. A second advantage of such a weighting system is it would reduce taxes for banks with significant physical presence in the state and this would encourage the location of jobs in Arizona. However, the influence of the apportionment formula's weighting scheme on the location of jobs is probably very small. Another potential advantage of unequal weights is that they could modestly increase exporting of the tax since the tax burden would be heavier on nondomiciled firms. A disadvantage is that this scheme probably increases the chance that a bank would pay taxes on more than 100 percent of its income.

Situs. The situs rules for the factors can be of equal importance as the factors themselves to the amount of income taxable in each state. Establishing rules for situs is most difficult for receipts and intangible property. The rules are likely to be written such that there is either a bias towards the state of bank domicile or towards the state where the market is located. To maximize revenues, it is generally in a state's best interest to lean to the bias which it possesses. Thus, it would be most desirable to create a bias towards the market state in Arizona's situs regulations. This would have the effect of increasing Arizona's revenues and of creating an incentive for banks to domicile in Arizona. Further, the market state approach appears to be consistent with the rules used for determining sales tax liability, since 40 of 45 sales-taxing states use a destination principle for the tax liability.

The market state bias can be created through a variety of mechanisms. For receipts, this can be accomplished by identifying the situs where a credit card is billed, where the property is located which serves as security for a loan, or where the proceeds of loans are to be applied, rather than the situs of the institution making the loan or housing the asset. Deposits can be handled in a similar fashion by identifying their situs at the account's address. Minnesota has adopted these types of situs provisions. At least some aspects of Arizona's situs rules operate in this fashion. *Walter E. Heller Western, Inc. vs. Arizona Department of Revenue* affirms Arizona's ability to tax interest earned in the state using market-oriented rules.

Administrative and compliance burdens imposed by the situs provisions should be given consideration in any final decision. Complicated rules or rules requiring difficult data collection would be undesirable for tax collectors and payers. Compliance would be enhanced if all states used consistent rules. Since few states have acted as yet to revise their bank taxes, the set of rules which minimizes compliance and administration is not yet certain. A state can play a role in formulating the best pattern if it gives early attention to reconsidering its situs rules.

Securitization of Loans

There is a strong trend towards financial institutions making loans and then repackaging these loans into securities that are subsequently resold to investors through secondary markets. Resale of packaged home mortgages has been done for some years, and auto and other consumer loans are frequently resold as well. This practice is referred to as securitization of loans and means that financial institutions often make loans but do not hold the loan until the borrowers have repaid them. The tax concern with such practices is the difficulty in identifying which state has jurisdiction for tax purposes over interest earned on the securities. With securitization, Arizona retains the ability to tax income from making and reselling loans but it may lose the ability to tax interest paid on loans since the interest paid on the loan may go to an out-of-state investor. The financial institution selling the loan would no longer receive the interest if the loan were resold so the institution would pay no tax on the interest. The interest would escape Arizona taxation completely if the security is sold to a firm without nexus in the state. Further, the interest could escape all state taxation unless all tax structures are very carefully designed. This would happen if the situs rules for interest in the state where the security purchaser is domiciled considers the interest on a market basis which presumes Arizona would tax it.

At present the issue of securitization may be of limited importance in Arizona. Nationwide, large banks are engaging in reselling loans, but smaller banks generally are not. Further, banks may be holding relatively little securitized debt as they seek to make loans and resell them. But the issue may be of growing importance.

One approach to taxing the securitized interest is to establish a dual tax structure for financial institutions (see McCray 1988). A residence-based system could be levied on in-state domiciled banks and a source-based system on out-of-state domiciled banks. The source-based part of a dual system would tax out-of-state banks on their Arizona income just as is done today. The residence-based system would tax domiciled banks on their entire income (wherever earned) and allow them a credit for any taxes paid to other states. This could increase tax revenues by raising taxable income for domiciled corporations, and would not place the domiciled firms at a competitive disadvantage in the sale of in-state financial services. Also, it would ensure that Arizona banks operating in states using a residence-based system are taxed by Arizona since these banks would not be taxed by the other residence-based state. This system would prevent domiciled firms from escaping taxation on interest from securitized loans.

Finally, the residence-based system appears to reduce administrative burdens for domiciled firms because situs rules are unnecessary, and since there are no situs rules, domiciled banks would be unable to shift their tax burden by relocating intangible assets. Still, situs rules will remain necessary for nondomiciled firms and the potential for them to relocate intangibles remains in place. Further, domiciled institutions must abide by situs rules in other states so there is little compliance savings.

Several potentially undesirable effects of the residence-based system should be noted. First, it would effectively tax Arizona-domiciled firms operating outside the state at the higher of the Arizona or other state tax structure.[6] This could place the Arizona firms at a competitive disadvantage when operating in other states. It also places Arizona's collections at the mercy of other states since the value of credits depends on taxation by other states. Thus, revenues become unpredictable as they depend on the tax policies of 49 other states.

A related concern is the effect on Arizona's ability to export taxes. A greater share of taxes could be exported if higher tax costs can be shifted to consumers in another state. However, it would appear unlikely that higher taxes paid only by Arizona-domiciled banks could be shifted to residents of other states in which these banks operate given competitors do not pay the same taxes. Thus, the increased taxes from use of a residence approach probably would be paid by owners of Arizona financial institutions and potentially by Arizona residents and businesses.

Next, the residence system would raise the tax costs to banks which have their domicile in Arizona and thereby give banks the incentive to be domiciled outside the state or at least to offer their interstate services from banks located in other states. This is unlikely to have a significant effect on the availability of banking services in the state. However, it may reduce the Arizona presence of central office banking positions and may be regarded as a negative for economic development.

A more limited approach to taxing the securitized interest would be to introduce a direct allocation to Arizona for the income on securities held by domiciled institutions which is totally untaxed in other states. This would be sufficient to prevent Arizona financial institutions from avoiding taxes through purchasing securitized loans.

However the state seeks to tax interest related to securitization, the decision must be made simultaneously with the state's nexus and situs rules. If the nexus rules follow the market approach, it may be difficult for Arizona firms to resell their securities. This issue arose in Minnesota because of the fear that purchase of securitized loans from a Minnesota financial institution would give the purchaser nexus in the state. Of course, this is only of concern for purchasers which have not as yet established nexus in the state. Minnesota adopted the approach of providing safe harbor for a purchaser which had no nexus connection other than ownership of securitized loans (Geis 1988). Thus, the interest is taxed in the state only if nexus exists for other reasons.

<u>Branchless Banking</u>

Another problem with the definition of taxable income arises because of branchless banking which refers to the receipt of financial services by Arizona residents from an institution without a physical presence in the state. Examples of branchless banking are financial services offered by an out-of-state bank to Arizona residents through an automatic teller machine, the mail, and telephone. Credit cards are probably the major service provided in this manner today. Expansion of these types of services has been very rapid and new telecommunications technology will increase the potential for branchless banking. Currently, Arizona is unlikely to tax the income derived from these services because there is no physical presence in the state although the Arizona Department of Revenue has concluded that nexus exists for credit card interest since the issuer owns the cards.

There are several reasons for Arizona to tax the income of branchless activities in the state: the source of branchless income is Arizona, their taxation overcomes any problems with tax neutrality in the state, and their taxation can generate additional revenues for Arizona. Each of these deserve a brief explanation. First, the case for Arizona being the source of income rests on following the market rather than domicile approach to defining the generation of income. Simply, the income is regarded as earned where proceeds of the loans are used rather than where the home office of the lending institution is located.

The neutrality concern is that branchless services could go completely untaxed if they are delivered by a financial institution domiciled in a state which uses a source approach to tax banking income and if Arizona fails to tax the income. If neither the state of domicile nor Arizona tax the income, financial institutions either domiciled in or having a physical presence in Arizona are placed at a competitive disadvantage because they must compete in Arizona with financial institutions that are not taxed on the income earned on their Arizona activities. The result would be lower costs for the untaxed firms and this should permit them to offer better rates to attract deposits, offer lower rates on loans, or provide greater return to owners.

The only way to ensure that neutral taxation can be imposed on all institutions operating in Arizona is for the income generated there to be taxed by Arizona regardless of the financial institution's state of domicile or banking techniques. Even if no competitive disadvantage existed for any financial institution operating in Arizona, the state loses tax revenues if it fails to tax branchless activities. The amount of revenue loss from failing to collect these taxes is likely to grow rapidly over time as branchless activities expand.

To date, only Minnesota has chosen to extend its tax on financial institutions to explicitly include branchless services, although, as noted above, the Arizona Department of Revenue holds that credit card income is taxable in the state. Minnesota's approach is to use a solicitation basis for defining nexus rather than requiring physical presence. This is accomplished by levying the tax on banks with a physical presence in the state or which regularly solicit for business in the state. Activity must be conducted with at least 20 persons during the tax year or deposits must exceed $5,000,000 in order for such regular solicitation to have been deemed to occur.

Establishing nexus on the basis of solicitation does not appear to raise a constitutional problem. Hellerstein (1983, pp. 664-665) concluded that "making regular loans on a continuing basis is sufficient" nexus under the Due Process Clause. McCray (1986, pp. 305-306) extends this by noting that "an out-of-state bank that has purposefully solicited deposits and loans from a host state and earns income therefrom has created sufficient contacts with that state and its residents upon which to base taxing jurisdiction." She extends this to credit card business as well (pp. 310-311).

Taxing branchless activities may create administrative problems because of the need to identify taxpayers. However, much of the burden may be placed on the potential taxpayers by establishing clear legislation requiring that they report their activities in the state. Some court cases have brought into question the penalties included in the reporting statutes used in other states. New Jersey was sued in the *First Family Mortgage* case and the court appeared to accept reporting requirements in certain circumstances but this remains an open issue (Geis 1988). Rules which exclude nondomiciled firms with minimal activities should be developed to limit administrative and compliance problems and to ensure that constitutional limitations regarding nexus are met.

Tax Neutrality

Interindustry Neutrality

Interindustry tax neutrality means that taxes are imposed such that their incidence on businesses is even across financial and nonfinancial industries. This presumably means that taxes will not make investment in one industry more attractive than in another. Economists assert that such decisions are made by comparing marginal rates of return, so neutrality should be examined in terms of marginal rather than average rates of return.

On the surface, a way to measure whether neutrality exists would be to determine whether taxes are equal to a constant share of before tax income for all industries. An obvious problem with this is it compares average rather than marginal tax rates. Also, consideration of whether taxes are neutral requires understanding how much of the tax is shifted away from the firm. A tax which can be fully shifted to consumers by one industry may have less effect on the marginal after-tax rate of return than a much lower tax which is borne totally by the firms. Unfortunately, no studies are available on whether Arizona taxes are neutral across industries.

Attaining neutrality does not require that all industries be taxed using exactly the same structure, only that the effect on marginal rates of return is the same. The economic literature on optimal taxation (though focusing mostly on consumption taxes) concludes that different tax rates should be levied on industries depending on the demand and supply conditions in each industry. However, the information is generally unavailable for setting rates separately for each industry and the administrative problems of doing so are considerable. Thus, the most practical public policy approach to neutrality is to impose a tax which generally has the same initial incidence on all industries unless some very specialized information is available on incidence within an industry.

The above discussion on defining bank income illustrates that the historical approach to taxing financial company income in Arizona, using the same definitions as for nonfinancial corporations, is likely to leave taxes nonneutral because the proportion of income subject to the tax is not equal. Many of the reasons why corporate taxes will not be neutral arise because of unique characteristics of the financial industry. As a result, different tax structures are probably necessary for financial and other corporations in order to obtain neutrality. Thus, making reforms in the tax structure as described above may be necessary to achieve a neutral tax structure across industries.

The importance of neutral taxation across industries is growing because the lines between industries have been blurring with recent diversification of nonfinancial firms into financial markets and vice versa. For example, Sears owns Allstate Insurance, Coldwell Banker real estate, Dean Witter Securities, the Discover Card, and Dean Witter and Sears Savings Banks (Waren 1988, p. 23). General Electric owns the investment banking firm of Kidder Peabody. Diversification increases the risk that investment in industries is at least partially determined by tax differentials as the lines between the industries become less obvious.

<u>Financial Industry Neutrality</u>

Neutrality within the financial industry also requires that marginal tax burdens for individual segments of the industry be even. Practically, this has been applied to mean that all institutions in the industry should be subject to the same tax structure. Arizona's current tax structure is effective for taxing most financial institutions which have physical presence within the state, but there are three cases where neutrality may be violated.

First, credit unions generally operate untaxed and yet they compete with other financial institutions for many of the services that they offer. This exemption would appear to have no merit. Second, a lack of neutrality may exist between the depository institutions, which are generally the topic of this chapter, and the nondepositories such as insurance companies and brokers. In Arizona, most of these nondepositories are currently subject to the general corporate income tax structure with the exception of those insurance companies which are taxed with the premium tax. The premium tax is probably a greater share of insurance profits or value added than is the corporate income tax for other financial institutions. This may indicate that insurance companies bear a heavier tax burden.[7] Third, intraindustry neutrality is likely to be violated for financial institutions that operate in Arizona without a physical presence. As described above, Arizona can increase the chance for neutrality by broadening its laws to tax these branchless banking activities.

Interstate Neutrality

Differences in taxation of financial institutions across states is another issue which frequently arises. Interstate neutrality of taxes exists whenever taxes do not influence the behavior of financial institutions in terms of where they locate, where they conduct economic activity, and how they engage in financial practices. Generally, the interstate neutrality of taxes is examined by identifying tax differentials across states.

Two reasons may be posited for why unusually high or low tax rates relative to other states may be a concern for Arizona. First, high (low) taxes may make it difficult (or easier) for Arizona domiciled banks to operate in interstate markets. However, this concern is probably of little relevance in Arizona. The ability of Arizona banks to compete outside the state largely depends on the banks' goodwill, economies of scale, and specialized banking expertise while taxes are of much less significance (Tannenwald 1988). Further, Arizona taxes will not influence costs of doing business or the profitability of activities outside the state as long as Arizona uses source-based taxation which precludes taxing income generated outside the state.

Second, high taxes are posited as a concern because they may make it difficult for the state to attract the location of specialized activities of nondomiciled banks. Many market related financial service activities must be located near their consumers. However, telecommunications (and other) technologies permit financial institutions some flexibility in locating certain specialized operations in states with low tax rates, and future technologies are likely to increase this flexibility. For example, banks may have the potential to offer services, such as their credit card operations, through subsidiaries located far from their place of domicile.

Considerable study has been undertaken on the effects of taxes and other factors on the location of industry (see a review in Wasylenko and McGuire, 1985). Unfortunately, little of this analysis has focused specifically on the factors which enter siting decisions for financial institutions. Fox and Black (1990) found that Delaware and South Dakota were very effective at attracting employment and assets of financial institutions by creating a tax structure and regulatory package which is conducive to the location of firms. However, they concluded there was little evidence that changes in marginal tax rates influenced the situs of banking activity. Wasylenko and McGuire (1985) examined the effect of taxes on employment change in the combined finance, insurance, and real estate industries of states. They found no evidence that corporate tax rates were a factor in the location of employment although they concluded that high personal income tax rates could discourage employment growth in these industries.[8]

Though the limited amount of analysis causes current research evidence to be inconclusive on the relationship between taxes and financial industries, the preponderance of studies focused on other industries indicates that tax differentials at most have a very modest influence on the location of even the specialized functions of financial firms. Other factors, such as quality and availability of labor and access to quality infrastructure, are likely to be much more important. Thus, the influence of interstate tax differences on economic development should be a minor consideration in today's design of the tax structure. However, tax influences can be expected to grow with banks' ability to shift assets and liabilities between members of a holding company.

The extent to which Arizona taxes may be even a modest concern can be determined through a comparison of relative tax burdens with other states. Arizona's 10.5 percent rate on corporate income (above $6000) is only exceeded by Massachusetts, Hawaii, and Connecticut among the 36 states and the District of Columbia which tax bank income in some manner (see Table 7-3). The median rate across all states in the table is 7.5 percent. Also note that Arizona's rate is higher than any neighboring state.

The tax rates described above are statutory rates and fail to reflect the relative burdens placed on banks in Arizona vis-a-vis those operating in other states. One reason is that states have differing definitions of taxable income. For example, the Arizona statute which permits banks to subtract federal income tax payments in determination of taxable income significantly narrows the tax base and thereby reduces the effectiveness of the high rates. It is necessary to consider both the size of rates and breadth of the base in measuring tax burdens. Also, it would be useful to examine the full range of taxes levied by states on the financial industry.

Average effective tax rates, which are measured by dividing actual tax payments by a broad measure of corporate income, are a better indicator of relative tax burdens.[9] A study conducted several years ago by the Massachusetts Executive Office for Administration and Finance sought to measure effective tax rates on bank income for 27 states (see Table 7-3).[10] A finding of the study was that the effective tax rate on Arizona bank income was 5.31 percent which was 10th highest of the states and approximately at the national average rate of 5.32 percent. Thus, Arizona's tax burden is comparable to that imposed by other states. However, only California had a higher effective rate among the nearby states.

Several conclusions arise from this section. First, firms would not choose Arizona if they were seeking a very low tax rate environment for their operations because the corporate taxes are near the national norm. Second, financial entities are not unusually disadvantaged by high taxes in Arizona. Finally, the average effective tax rate paid by financial institutions appears to be approximately one-half of the stated nominal tax rate.

Summary

In summary, the definition of taxable income for financial institutions must be reevaluated if the goals for the tax system are to be met. The combination of federal legislation and changing industry structure means that traditional approaches to taxing firms in the financial industries are inadequate. The result is that Arizona collects less revenue than it could, financial institutions have ready means to avoid taxes legally, and firms are treated unevenly for tax purposes. Restructuring the taxes can overcome these problems but likely at the expense of greater administrative and compliance burdens.

References

Amel, Dean F. and Daniel G. Keane. 1987. "State Laws Affecting Commercial Bank Branching, Multibank Holding Company Expansion, and Interstate Banking." *Mimeo*, April, 42 pp.

Board of Governors of Federal Reserve System. 1987. "Call and Income Report." Report PB85-219673, April.

Commerce Clearing House. 1988. *State Tax Guide.* Chicago, Illinois.

Conference of State Bank Supervisors. 1988. *State of the State Banking System*, May.

Fox, William F. and Harold A. Black. 1990. "Economic Impact of State Taxation and Regulation on Banking." *Mimeo*, 29 pp.

Geis, Jerome A. 1988. "Financial Institutions: Nexus, the Exception for Secondary Market Transactions and the Business Activities Report." St. Paul, Minnesota: Briggs and Morgan, *Mimeo*.

Hawkins, Robert B., Jr. undated. "Relating to Regulations Y; Docket No. R-0652." Statement of the Advisory Commission on Intergovernmental Relations before the Federal Reserve Board.

Hellerstein, Jerome R. 1983. *State Taxation.* Warren, Gorham and Lamont: Boston and New York.

Kincaid, John and Sandra B. McCray. 1988. "State Taxation and the Rise of Interstate Banking: A Survey of States." Intergovernmental Perspective, Volume 14, Fall, pp. 18-22.

McCray, Sandra B. 1986. "State Taxation of Interstate Banking," *Georgia Law Review*, Vol. 21, Fall, pp. 283-327.

_______________. 1987. "Constitutional Issues in State Income Taxes: Financial Institutions," *Albany Law Review*, Volume 51, pp. 895-933.

_______________. 1988. "State Taxation of Banks: Issues and Options." Study Prepared for the Advisory Commission on Intergovernmental Relations, mimeo October.

Office of the Superintendent of Banks. 1988a. "Condensed Statement of Reports: State and Federal Savings and Loan Associations." Phoenix: AZ, September, mimeo.

Office of the Superintendent of Banks. 1988b. "Condensed Statement of Reports: State and National Banks of Arizona." Phoenix: AZ, September, mimeo.

Special Commission Relative to the Taxation of Banks. 1987. "The Thirteenth Interim Report." Boston, MA: Commonwealth of Massachusetts, April 9, 1987.

Tannewald, Robert. 1988. "Should Massachusetts Reform its Bank Taxes," *New England Economic Review*, Federal Reserve Bank of Boston, September/October, pp. 23-35.

U.S. Bureau of the Census. 1987. *Statistical Abstract of the United States*: 1988. Washington, D.C., 108th edition.

U.S. Department of Commerce. 1988. Gross State Products Diskettes. Bureau of Economic Analysis, April.

Waren, William T. 1988. "Bank Wars," *State Legislatures*, September, pp. 22-26.

Michael Wasylenko and Therese McGuire. 1985. "Jobs and Taxes: The Effect of Business Climate on State's Employment Growth Rates" *National Tax Journal*, December, pp. 497-511.

Endnotes

1. Amel and Keane (1987) provide a detailed description of interstate banking practices.
2. The national "average" rate of tax may be borne by owners and only the differential from the average may be borne by consumers. If this occurs, Arizona consumers may bear little of the tax because the burden may be near the average.
3. Fox and Black (1990) find limited evidence that banks shift the location of their intangible property in response to taxes.
4. Situs rules are addressed below.
5. There is no particular reason to believe that equal weights are necessary.
6. This can be likened to the effects of the retaliation component of state insurance taxes. One difference is that revenues corresponding to retaliatory taxes would go to the state of domicile rather than the state of operations.
7. Life companies are more likely to be in competition with other financial institutions than are property/casualty companies and are less likely to be able to shift the tax to consumers.
8. Financial institutions may be more concerned about whether a state uses residence-based or source-based taxation than with the level of rates. The tax burden for an institution in interstate commerce may be much greater if the state of domicile has a lower rate with a residence-based system than a higher rate with a source-based system. This issue has not been studied to date.
9. Marginal tax rates rather than average should be used to examine neutrality but the data are unavailable.
10. The study is described in Special Commission Relative to the Taxation of Banks (1987).

Chapter 8

General Sales Taxes

Helen F. Ladd and Dana Weist

Arizona relies heavily on general sales taxes. Technically called business privilege taxes, these Arizona taxes can be viewed as general sales taxes because they apply to the gross receipts, or equivalently to the total sales, of firms. Together, Arizona's state and local sales taxes accounted for 25 percent of state and local revenue from own sources in 1988 with the proportion for the state alone being much higher at 37 percent.

Compared to other states, Arizona defines the state tax base broadly and gives its cities considerable autonomy with respect to the definition of base and choice of tax rate. The specific characteristics of the Arizona sales tax raise certain policy issues that are peculiar to Arizona, but more generally highlight a variety of conceptual and policy issues that arise with sales taxes throughout the country. Policymakers in Arizona and elsewhere need to consider whether to include food in the tax base, how to treat business purchases, and whether to expand the tax base to include services. In addition, they need to address a number of issues with respect to local government use of the sales tax.

Sales taxes are fundamentally taxes on consumer spending. As such, well-designed sales taxes can be an appropriate vehicle for generating substantial revenue. The recent proliferation in Europe and elsewhere of value-added taxes, which are virtually equivalent to retail sales taxes, attests to this fact. Within the United States, sales taxes are particularly appropriate for use by state and local governments because they are not used by the federal government. This situation contrasts to that for income taxes whose use at the state level is inhibited by federal use of the tax. General sales taxes are also appropriate for use by states because they permit a state to obtain revenue from visitors. Because these visitors (tourists, winter residents, and business people) benefit from the state's public services, it makes sense for them to pay some taxes to the state.[1]

Public finance experts evaluate revenue sources by a variety of standard criteria. How well a sales tax meets these standard criteria for good tax policy depends on how the tax base is defined.

Simplicity. Much of the literature on sales taxes treats them as if they are exclusively taxes on consumer purchases, but in fact many states, like Arizona, include substantial amounts of business purchases in the tax base. This inclusion of business purchases interferes with the criterion that taxes be simple and easy to understand. According to the simplicity criterion, an ideal sales tax would apply a uniform tax rate to a broad base of final sales with few exclusions. A tax that applies only to sales to final consumers and to all such sales at a uniform rate meets that criterion. A tax that applies to a variety of intermediate business purchases violates this criterion; some business purchases, such as manufacturing equipment in Arizona, are commonly excluded from the tax base. Further, the nature of business purchases as inputs to production makes it difficult to determine who ultimately bears the burden of the tax. How well Arizona does with respect to this criterion is discussed in the section on the structure of the tax.

Vertical Equity. As a tax on consumer spending, sales taxes suffer from the charge of regressivity, that is, that they impose disproportionately large burdens on low-income households. This criticism is valid. Because the portion of income spent on consumption of most items declines as income rises, a broad-based tax on consumption will be regressive. Exactly how regressive a state's sales tax is, however, depends on the definition of the base. For example, a tax base that includes food and drugs will be more regressive than one that exempts them. Regressivity is generally undesirable, but need not by itself rule out use of the tax. The tax should be analyzed relative to the overall tax structure, and the disadvantages of regressivity need to be weighed against the advantages of the tax. Moreover, mechanisms such as refundable tax credits against the state's income tax can be used to reduce the burden on low-income households.

Neutrality. The degree to which a sales tax treats like activities differently depends on what is included in the tax base. In general, the tax will be more neutral the broader is its coverage of consumer purchases and the more that it avoids the taxation of business purchases.

A closely related issue is the potential for a tax to distort geographical patterns of economic activity. In states where sellers near the border compete with sellers across the border, a state's sales tax can induce consumers to alter their shopping patterns to avoid the tax. This "border" effect is not very important in Arizona and is not analyzed in this paper. Mail order sales and sales on Indian reservations, however, present similar potential distortions.

Stability and Responsiveness. As a tax on consumer purchases, sales taxation could potentially provide a relatively stable but not overly responsive source of revenues. When state income or population rises, consumer spending will rise and when it falls, consumer spending will fall -- but in both cases the change is likely to fall short of the change in income. Once again, however, one must be careful with generalizations; how stable or responsive the tax is depends on what is included in the tax base.

Given the dependence of a sales tax evaluation on how the tax is designed, we begin by summarizing the structure of Arizona's sales tax. We then explore the reasons for Arizona's relatively high per capita sales taxes, analyze who bears the burden of the tax, and evaluate its stability and responsiveness to economic growth. We next turn to the major policy issues related to the structure of the state tax base and to the use of sales taxes by local governments.

Tax Base And Structure

This section focuses on the structure of the state tax. Since the introduction of the tax in 1933, some of the state's sales tax revenue has always been shared with local governments. However, the proportion distributed to local governments has changed over time, especially since 1959 when the transaction privilege tax was augmented by special excises for education and other purposes. In 1986, the original transaction privilege tax was combined with the special excise taxes into a single consolidated sales tax. This combined tax has two components: a distribution base, the revenue from which is shared with local governments, and a non-shared base, the revenue from which is allocated exclusively to the State General Fund. Except where explicitly noted, we refer to revenue from the consolidated sales tax without distinguishing between the distribution and the non-shared base.

Taxable Activities and Rates

In many states, the sales tax is legally imposed on the retail sale and retailers simply serve as the collection agents. In contrast, the liability for Arizona's sales tax is legally placed on the gross receipts of registered vendors for the privilege of engaging in business in the state. This fact accounts for the Arizona Department of Revenue's practice of reporting sales revenue by activity class as shown in Table 8-1. This table lists total collections and tax rates by activity, ranked by size of collections.

The table shows that the tax is more than simply a tax on retail sales. Nonetheless, retail sales are the single largest category and account for 50 percent of the total collections. Other major categories of the sales tax include contracting services such as homebuilding and the construction of buildings and roads (13.5 percent); utility services such as electricity, gas, oil, and water (10.0 percent); food and drink at restaurants and bars (8.4 percent); rentals of personal property such as tuxedos and office equipment (4.1 percent); and rentals of real (primarily) commercial property (3.7 percent). Together, these next five categories represent about 40 percent of the total collections. In addition, the state receives almost $62 million, or 4 percent of the total, from its use tax which applies to goods purchased outside the state but used in Arizona.

As shown in the table, the gross receipts of most taxable activities are subject to the basic 5 percent rate. The exceptions are rentals of real property which were taxed at 3.75 percent until July, 1988, hotels and motels which were taxed at 4 percent and are now taxed at 5.5 percent, and feed for livestock which is taxed at wholesale at a rate of about 0.5 percent in lieu of taxation at retail.

From the perspective of registered vendors, the Arizona sales tax applies to gross receipts. These gross receipts represent sales to final consumers, business firms, nonprofit organizations, and governments. Because the policy issues related to sales taxation differ by category of purchaser, the following discussion shifts away from the focus on activity classes to categories defined by type of purchaser. (See Appendix Tables 8-A-1 through 8-A-3 for detailed descriptions of the State's base relative to those of other states.)

Consumer Purchases

Most tax experts advocate broad coverage under the sales tax of the goods and services sold to consumers. Broad coverage makes sense for several reasons. First, the broader the coverage, the lower the tax rate that is needed to raise a given amount of revenue. Because people have more incentive to avoid a high tax rate than a low rate, keeping the tax rate down minimizes undesirable changes in behavior and thereby makes the tax more neutral. Second, broad coverage minimizes the incentive for consumers to avoid the tax by favoring untaxed over taxed goods. With coverage extended to movies, for example, people cannot avoid the tax on home videos by going to movies. Third, broad coverage often makes the tax cheaper to collect; neither tax administrators nor vendors need worry about making fine distinctions about what is taxed and what is exempt. This logic does not rule out the possibility that other considerations, such as minimizing the burden on poor people, the administrative and compliance costs associated with small vendors, or concerns about social policy, might push in favor of exempting certain items. Nonetheless, the starting presumption for the taxation on consumer purchases is that the tax should be comprehensively applied.[2]

Table 8-1
State Sales and Use Tax Collections and
Rates by Taxable Activity, 1988
(Ranked by size of collections)

Taxable Activity	Gross State Collections	Activity as Share of Total (%)	Tax Rate (%)
Sales			
Retail	$ 787,687,342	50.0	5
Contracting	212,684,042	13.5	5
Utilities	157,463,224	10.0	5
Restaurants and Bars	132,103,378	8.4	5
Rentals of Personal Property	64,015,576	4.1	5
Rentals of Real Property	58,770,776	3.7	3.75[1]
Communications	36,139,388	2.3	5
Hotel/Motel	28,471,088	1.8	4[2]
Printing	15,550,571	1.0	5
Amusements	14,071,827	0.9	5
Railroads and Aircraft	1,163,556	0.1	5
Transporting & Towing	1,023,134	0.1	5
Wholesale Feed	992,678	0.1	0.4687
Publishing	920,557	0.1	5
Agricultural Equipment	517,384	0.0	1[3]
License Fees	379,479	0.0	--
Private Car & Pipeline	123,635	0.0	5
Rental Occupancy	88,163	0.0	3
Local Advertising	18,177	0.0	--
Use Tax	61,797,123	3.9	5
Total	1,573,981,098	100.0	

[1] Raised to 5 percent effective July 31, 1988.
[2] Raised to 5.5 percent effective July 31, 1988.
[3] Tax on new equipment phased out by 1989, used equipment placed in retail category.

Source: Arizona Department of Revenue, *1988 Annual Report.*

The coverage of goods sold at the retail level in Arizona is comparable to that of many other states. The two main consumer exemptions are 1) food consumed at home which was eliminated from Arizona's tax in 1980 and is currently exempt in 27 other states, and 2) prescribed drugs and medical supplies which are exempt in all states except New Mexico. The total consumer base is broader in Arizona than in many other states in that it includes the services provided by building contractors (with deductions for land costs and typical labor costs) and utility services such as the gas and electricity used by households.

In addition, Arizona includes cigarettes and alcohol in the general sales tax base (as well as subjecting them to special excise taxes), but follows most other states in exempting motor vehicle fuel. Arizona also taxes food and drink at restaurants and bars and taxes admissions for movies and other entertainment. Like most other states, however, Arizona does not tax a wide array of personal and professional services such as dry cleaning and consulting or accounting services.

Business Purchases

Many sales tax experts argue that state sales taxes should be structured to tax consumer expenditures alone and that business purchases should not be taxed. This approach can be justified on the grounds that a tax limited to final sales to consumers applies to a clearly defined base which, along with income and net wealth, is generally deemed to be an appropriate base for taxation. Any sales taxation of business purchases leads to tax pyramiding in that taxes are paid at the production stage as well as at final sale with the result that the total tax burden in an industry varies with the volume of taxed inputs used in production. Tax-related price increases that differ across industries distort consumer decisions and make it unclear who bears the burden of the tax.

However, Arizona and many other states do tax a wide variety of business purchases. A major reason for this practice in Arizona is that sales taxes were initially justified in terms of payment for the privilege of doing business in the state. Hence, the tax applied to the gross receipts of all firms regardless of their stage in the production process and regardless of who purchased the goods. Recognizing the disadvantages of a multi-stage tax, Arizona has reduced over time the worst pyramiding effects of its gross receipts tax by exempting all sales for resale. Nonetheless, many sales by one firm to another are still included in the tax base, the major ones being equipment sales to nonmanufacturing firms, contracting and utility services sold to firms, and inputs such as industrial fuel or chemicals consumed in the production process. In response to concerns about the state's ability to compete with other states, or possibly simply in response to political pressure, the state has exempted from the sales tax most equipment used in manufacturing, utility production and transmission, and mining. In addition, the state exempts the purchase of agricultural equipment and, like most other states, does not tax professional services. Despite these exemptions, Arizona continues to have broader coverage of business purchases than most other states.

Governments and Charitable Organizations

Because Arizona taxes the privilege of engaging in sales, rather than the sale itself, the tax logically extends to governments and charitable organizations. Hence, the starting presumption is that such sales will be taxed in Arizona unless they are specifically exempted. In general, Arizona fully taxes the purchases of nonprofits and state and local governments, taxes retail sales to the federal government at half the standard rate, and exempts purchases by public or nonprofit hospitals and sales to the federal government made directly by a manufacturer.[3] Overall, Arizona's coverage of purchases by governments and charitable organizations is broader than that in most other states.

Reliance On Sales Taxes

Whether measured by state sales taxes alone or by state and local sales taxes combined, Arizona relies heavily on sales taxes for revenue. In 1988, it ranked fourth behind Washington, Hawaii, and Connecticut in terms of total state and local sales taxes per capita and sixth in terms of state sales taxes per capita. In this section, we focus on state taxes alone.[4]

Fiscal Structure and Composition of State Tax Revenues

Per capita state sales tax collections in a particular state can deviate from the national average for at least three reasons. First, state and local governments in the state may spend more or less on public services per capita than the average state. If one ignores differences across states in the share of revenue received from the federal government, state and local spending can be measured by the revenue collected by state and local governments.[5] Second, the state's revenue-raising structure may be more or less centralized than that of other states. The more centralized is the revenue-raising responsibility in a state, the greater is the burden on state revenue sources relative to local sources. And third, the state may rely more or less heavily on sales taxes relative to other state revenues.

To determine which of these reasons best explains the heavy reliance of Arizona's state government on sales taxes, Arizona's per capita sales tax revenue can be decomposed into three multiplicative components which might be labeled measures of spending, centralization, and revenue-mix, as follows:

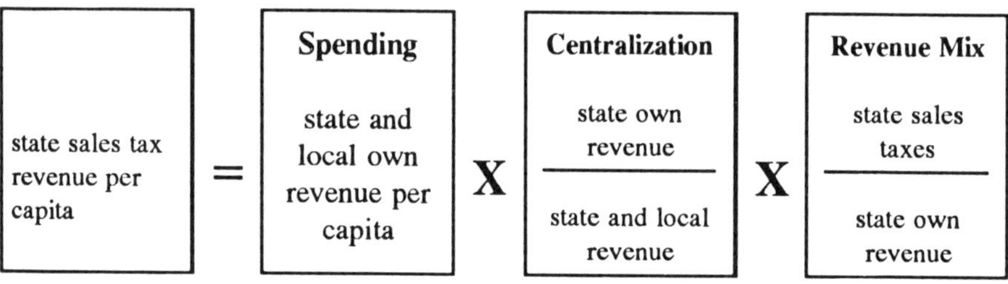

By comparing each of these components to the U.S. average, one can determine the approximate contribution of each component to Arizona's above-average state sales tax burden. (The estimated contribution only approximates the true contribution of each component because it ignores the interaction of the three components.)

The top panel of Table 8-2 shows first that Arizona's 1988 sales tax collections of $482 per capita exceeded the U.S. average by 36.5 percent. The fact that state and local own-source revenue per capita in Arizona is slightly below the U.S. average rules out high spending as a cause of the high state sales tax burden. In addition, Arizona's relatively decentralized fiscal system also rules out high state government revenues relative to local revenues as a cause of its high state sales taxes.

Table 8-2
State Sales Tax Revenue per Capita, 1988
Decomposition to Identify Contributing Factors
(Arizona and other high sales tax states)

	Collections	Spending	Centralization	Revenue Mix
	State sales tax revenue per capita	*State and local own revenue per capita*	*State own revenue/state and local own revenue*	*State sales tax revenue/state own revenue*
Arizona	$482	$2,378	0.550	0.368
United States Total(50 states)	$353	$2,476	0.553	0.258
% Above/Below U.S.	36.5	-4.0	-0.5	42.9
Other High Sales Tax States				
Connecticut	614	2,871	0.612	0.349
% Above/Below U.S.	73.7	16.0	10.6	35.4
Hawaii	838	2,937	0.815	0.350
% Above/Below U.S.	137.1	18.6	47.4	35.6
Nevada	518	2,448	0.555	0.382
% Above/Below U.S.	46.7	-1.1	0.3	47.9
New Mexico	491	2,592	0.747	0.254
% Above/Below U.S.	39.0	4.7	35.0	-1.7
Washington	765	2,473	0.616	0.502
% Above/Below U.S.	116.4	-0.1	11.3	94.6

Note: Sales tax revenue includes general sales and gross receipts as defined by the U.S. Census Bureau. Refer to the text for peculiarities of the Washington data. Arizona sales tax figures have been adjusted to exclude revenue from severance taxes.

Source: U.S. Bureau of the Census, *Governmental Finances in 1987-88.*

Most importantly, the table shows that Arizona's above-average state tax burden is attributable to its above-average reliance on sales taxes relative to all own-source revenues. Holding the other components constant, Arizona's sales tax burden is 42.9 percent higher than the national average because of this factor alone. Stated differently, if Arizona decided to reduce its reliance on sales taxes as a share of state tax revenues to the national average, the state would reduce its per capita sales tax burden well below the U.S. average.[6]

The bottom panel of the table presents comparable numbers for other high sales tax states. Four of these states (Connecticut, Hawaii, Nevada, and Washington) impose heavier state sales tax burdens than Arizona and partly with the same explanation as in Arizona, namely, the policy decision to rely heavily on sales taxes relative to other state revenue sources. Arizona's neighbor, New Mexico, is interesting because its above-average sales tax burden reflects not its choice of revenue mix, but rather its above-average state and local revenues per capita and its highly centralized revenue-raising structure.

Tax Rates and Tax Bases

Arizona's 5 percent state sales tax rate is currently the same as that of the median state nationally and also is in line with rates in its neighboring states. Because tax revenues equal the product of the state's tax base and its tax rate, the conclusion that Arizona's state sales tax rate is not out of line with those of other states implies that Arizona's above-average sales tax burden must be attributable to the size of its tax base. We can look at this relationship more formally with the following multiplicative decomposition:

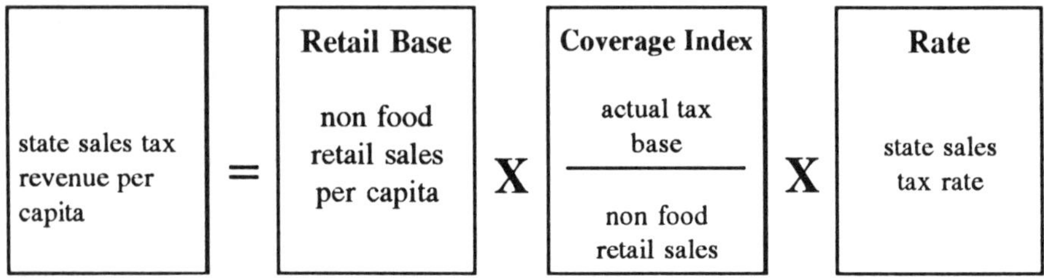

Together, the first two components following the equal sign characterize a state's per capita tax base. Per capita nonfood retail sales (estimated as total retail sales minus 80 percent of the sales of food stores) represent the essential or basic component of a state's sales tax base since most states include the bulk of retail sales in their tax bases.[7] The second term measures the coverage of the sales tax. For example, this ratio will exceed one if a state's sales tax base includes food, if the tax applies to nonretail purchases such as utilities or services, or if the base includes some purchases by business. In principle, this ratio could fall below one. This outcome would occur if a state excluded some major retail sales categories such as clothing from the tax base without sufficient broadening in other dimensions to offset the shortfall.

The top panel of Table 8-3 compares Arizona with the other 44 states that have sales taxes according to this decomposition. The results are clear and striking. Little of Arizona's high revenue is attributable to an above-average tax rate; Arizona's state tax rate is only 0.1 percentage points or 1.3 percent above the average of states with sales taxes. The main point is that Arizona has an average retail sales base only slightly above average, but as already noted defines its base much more comprehensively than average. Specifically, Arizona's nonfood retail sales are 4.2 percent above the average of states with sales taxes, but its base is 29.5 percent broader than average.

Comparing Arizona to the other high-tax states at the bottom of the table shows that above-average tax rates and retail sales account for the high collections in some of the other states, but that broad coverage of the base is also important in Hawaii, New Mexico, and Washington.

<table>
<tr><td colspan="5">Table 8-3
State Sales Tax Bases and Rates, 1988
(Arizona and other high sales tax states)</td></tr>
<tr><td></td><td>Collections</td><td>Capacity</td><td>Coverage</td><td>Rate</td></tr>
<tr><td></td><td>State sales tax revenue per capita</td><td>Estimated retail sales per capita</td><td>Actual tax base/retail sales</td><td>State sales tax rate</td></tr>
<tr><td>Arizona</td><td>$482</td><td>$5,653</td><td>1.710</td><td>0.050</td></tr>
<tr><td>United States Total (45 states)</td><td>$362</td><td>$5,425</td><td>1.320</td><td>0.049</td></tr>
<tr><td>% Above/Below U.S.</td><td>33.1</td><td>4.2</td><td>29.5</td><td>1.3</td></tr>
<tr><td>Other High Sales Tax States</td><td></td><td></td><td></td><td></td></tr>
<tr><td> Connecticut</td><td>614</td><td>7,239</td><td>1.13</td><td>0.075</td></tr>
<tr><td>   % Above/Below U.S.</td><td>69.6</td><td>33.4</td><td>-14.4</td><td>52.0</td></tr>
<tr><td> Hawaii</td><td>838</td><td>6,038</td><td>3.47</td><td>0.040</td></tr>
<tr><td>   % Above/Below U.S.</td><td>131.5</td><td>11.3</td><td>162.8</td><td>-18.9</td></tr>
<tr><td> Nevada</td><td>518</td><td>6,285</td><td>1.43</td><td>0.0575</td></tr>
<tr><td>   % Above/Below U.S.</td><td>43.1</td><td>15.9</td><td>8.6</td><td>16.5</td></tr>
<tr><td> New Mexico</td><td>491</td><td>4,635</td><td>2.23</td><td>0.0475</td></tr>
<tr><td>   % Above/Below U.S.</td><td>35.6</td><td>-14.6</td><td>68.9</td><td>-3.7</td></tr>
<tr><td> Washington</td><td>765</td><td>5,323</td><td>2.21</td><td>0.065</td></tr>
<tr><td>   % Above/Below U.S.</td><td>111.3</td><td>-1.9</td><td>67.4</td><td>31.7</td></tr>
</table>

Note: Sales tax revenue includes general sales and gross receipts as defined by the U.S. Census Bureau. Refer to the text for peculiarities of the Washington data. Arizona sales tax figures have been adjusted to exclude revenue from severance taxes.

Source: U.S. Bureau of the Census, *Governmental Finances in 1987-88*. Retail sales data are from Sales and Marketing Management, *Survey of Buying Power* (August 7, 1989), p.B7, with adjustments for food made by the authors.

Summary

Two conclusions emerge from this analysis of Arizona's reliance on sales taxes relative to other states. First, its above-average per capita revenue reflects, not high spending, but rather the state's choice about its revenue mix. Second, the state is able to raise above-average amounts of revenue, not through tax rates that are out of line with others, but rather by defining the tax base much more broadly than other states. Part of the broad coverage reflects the inclusion in the base of many business purchases. This analysis shows that including such purchases in the base is desirable in that they generate substantial tax revenue for the state at reasonable tax rates. This revenue advantage, however, needs to be weighed against some of the disadvantages discussed elsewhere in this chapter.

Who Pays The Tax?

Arizona statutes state clearly who is legally liable for Arizona's general sales tax; the legal burden falls on vendors (not the consumers) firms, and governments that purchase goods and services. However, this legal clarity does not answer the more important policy question of who ultimately bears the burden of the tax. The point is that firms and governments do not bear tax burdens. People do. After markets have fully adjusted to sales taxes, people bear the burden of taxes either in their capacity as consumers who pay higher gross-of-tax prices, or in their capacity as suppliers of inputs such as land, labor, or investment capital who receive lower net-of-tax income.

A standard economic assumption is that, in the long run, sellers can fully shift the burden of a state sales tax forward to consumers in the form of higher prices. Because sellers have many alternatives, such as investing more heavily in a lower-tax state or in untaxed activities, they can change their behavior enough to avoid bearing the burden of the tax; by reducing the supply of the taxed good, they induce consumers to pay a higher price than they would pay in the absence of the tax. Although it cannot easily be verified, this assumption is generally reasonable and serves as the basis for much of the analysis in this section.

The outcome is complicated, however, because a large portion of taxable sales in Arizona, and in most other states, represent sales not to final consumers but instead to business firms and governments. Following the same logic leads to the reasonable conclusion that business firms and governments will face higher (gross-of-tax) prices for the taxable goods they purchase. Thus, the taxation of intermediate goods sold to firms raises the costs of production for the affected firms, who in turn may be able shift the burden to consumers in the form of higher prices, lower wages, or lower returns on investments. Similarly, the taxation of sales to governments raises the cost of providing public services, which in turn may increase the taxes required to provide public services. Hence, the taxation of sales to firms and governments complicates enormously the task of determining who ultimately bears the burden of the sales tax.

Distribution by Type of Purchaser

The first step, therefore, in analyzing the distribution of the tax burden is to separate taxable sales, and consequently taxes paid, by type of purchaser. Consumer spending on taxable items by Arizona residents, tourists, and winter residents was estimated from detailed information on consumption patterns from various sources and then converted into tax payments by multiplying by the tax rate. (See appendix for the methodology and sources.) The taxes paid by business firms, governments, and nonprofit organizations were estimated as a residual.

Table 8-4 reports our estimated distribution of the tax burden by purchaser for 1986. The table shows that approximately 47 percent of the tax applies to sales to Arizona residents in their capacity as consumers of taxable goods and selected services, and that about 11 percent applies to sales to nonresidents including both tourists and winter residents.[8] The remaining 42 percent, which was calculated as a residual, represents taxes on sales to all other purchasers including business firms, charitable organizations, local governments, and the federal government.

<table>
<tr><td colspan="3" align="center">Table 8-4
Distribution of Arizona Sales Tax by Purchaser
(1986)</td></tr>
<tr><td></td><td align="center">Amount
(in thousands)</td><td align="center">Percent
of Total</td></tr>
<tr><td>Total Sales Taxes</td><td align="center">$1,443,282</td><td align="center">100.0</td></tr>
<tr><td>Taxes on Sales to:
  Arizona Residents</td><td></td><td></td></tr>
<tr><td>   Goods and taxable services</td><td align="center">549,056</td><td align="center">38.0</td></tr>
<tr><td>   Contracting</td><td align="center">133,969</td><td align="center">9.3</td></tr>
<tr><td> Tourists and short-term visitors</td><td align="center">151,379</td><td align="center">10.5</td></tr>
<tr><td> Winter residents</td><td align="center">9,182</td><td align="center">0.6</td></tr>
<tr><td> Other (residual)</td><td align="center">599,696</td><td align="center">41.6</td></tr>
<tr><td colspan="3">Note: Total sales taxes exclude severance taxes.

Source: Authors' estimates. See text and appendix for explanation.</td></tr>
</table>

The results in Table 8-4 are important for two reasons. First, they document that a substantial portion of the sales tax, namely about 11 percent, is ultimately borne by people who are not permanent residents of Arizona. Because these visitors, whether they be tourists, winter residents, or business people, benefit from the state's public services, it is appropriate, according to the benefits-received notion of equity, that they pay some taxes to the state. Unlike permanent residents who also pay income and property taxes, these visitors pay few direct taxes to the state. Nonetheless, during their stay they benefit from the quality of the state's public services. The sales tax then becomes an appropriate way to have them contribute to the cost of those public services.

The second reason the results are important is that they highlight once again the fact that Arizona's general sales tax applies to much more than the purchases of individual consumers. In particular, the estimates suggest that Arizona would lose substantial revenue if it chose to redefine the tax base to apply only to sales to final consumers while maintaining the current 5 percent tax rate.

Distribution of Tax Burden on Arizona Households by Income Class

The second step is to estimate the distribution by income class of the tax burden on Arizona households. Following standard methodology, we estimated household consumption patterns by income class from the Bureau of Labor Statistics Survey of Consumer Expenditures for the Western Region. We then used these consumption patterns to determine the distribution by income class of the 38 percent of the tax collections that are attributable to the purchases of taxable items by Arizona residents (excluding contracting). In addition, rough estimates are available of the distributional impact of the 9.3 percent attributable to residential contracting services.

Before we report these patterns by income class, however, we emphasize once again that Arizona households may also bear a significant portion of the "other" component, through higher taxes to support the higher (tax-inclusive) price of providing state and local services, or in the form of lower wages or lower profits. In fact, the difficulty of determining the final incidence of taxes levied on business purchases provides a strong rationale for exempting them from the tax base. This rationale rests on the reasonable proposition that a good tax is one for which the distribution of the burden is relatively clear.

Table 8-5 presents patterns of consumer spending on all taxable items and selected components by income class for the Western Region for 1985-86, the latest year for which data are available. The entries in the table are not tax burdens. Instead, they are the percentages of total income (before taxes) spent on the indicated category. For example, the first row shows that Arizona residents with 1986 income between $5,000 and $10,000 spent about 57 percent of their income on taxable items. Because sales tax burdens are a fixed proportion of spending on taxable items, the fact that this percentage declines monotonically to 26 percent in the highest income category indicates that the current tax is quite regressive.

The final column summarizes the degree of regressivity by the ratio of the burden for households with incomes between $5,000 and $10,000 to that for households with income above $40,000. If this summary measure exceeds one, the tax burden is regressive across the indicated range of income, while an index value below one indicates a progressive burden. The estimated index of 2.17 indicates that the tax is regressive and that the tax burden relative to income of low-income households is more than twice as high as that of high-income households.

This finding that the burden is regressive is hardly surprising. As noted in the introduction, consumption spending declines as a share of income as income rises. Hence, taxes on consumption spending are likely to be regressive. As shown in the next section of the table, the regressivity of the overall tax burden reflects the regressivity of each of the selected components. The three most regressive components (by our simple summary measure) are tobacco and smoking supplies, personal care products, and utility purchases. The least regressive components are fees and admissions, purchases of cars and trucks, and spending on entertainment.

The results reported in this section ignore the fact that in 1986, households that itemized their federal income tax returns could deduct general sales taxes from their federal taxable income. Because high-income households are more likely than low-income households to itemize and because they face higher marginal federal tax rates, the benefit of deductibility per dollar of sales taxes paid was greater for high than for low-income households. Hence, incorporating the effects of deductibility would have produced an even more regressive distribution of the tax burden across income classes. Because the federal Tax Reform Act of 1986 eliminated the deductibility of sales taxes, deductibility is no longer an issue. Hence, the results reported in the section represent the best estimates of the current distribution of the consumer portion of Arizona's sales tax.

Table 8-5
Consumer Expenditure Patterns by Household Income Class
Share of Income Spent on Taxable Items -- Current Tax Base
(in percentages)

	All Consumer Units	$5,000 to 9,999	$10,000 to 14,999	$15,000 to 19,999	$20,000 to 29,999	$30,000 to 30,000	$40,000 and over	Index of Regressivity
Current Total Tax Base	32.9	56.5	49.0	41.1	34.8	30.1	26.0	2.17
Selected Components								
Cars and trucks	8.7	12.4	13.1	12.2	9.2	9.6	6.9	1.80
Utilities	5.1	12.7	9.4	7.1	5.7	4.6	3.3	3.92
Apparel	4.2	6.6	5.3	4.8	4.3	3.8	3.5	1.90
Food and drink at restaurants/bars	4.0	6.6	6.0	4.9	4.2	3.5	3.1	2.14
Household furnishings	3.6	5.5	4.5	3.4	3.5	3.2	3.3	1.68
Entertainment	3.1	4.4	4.5	3.3	3.5	2.9	2.7	1.62
Fees and admissions	0.7	0.8	0.8	0.8	0.8	0.6	0.7	1.21
Tobacco and smoking supplies	0.6	1.9	1.3	1.1	0.7	0.5	0.4	5.22
Personal care products	0.5	1.0	0.7	0.7	0.5	0.5	0.4	2.67
Spending on new homes		0.0	3.6	5.9	8.8	16.3	17.8	020*

Notes: All entries except the last column are consumer expenditures as a share of income before taxes. The income class below $5,000 was deleted from this analysis because of the unreliability of data.

The Index of Regressivity is calculated as the ratio of the expenditure burden in the $5,000-9,999 class to that in the $40,000 and over class. Thus, higher numbers represent greater regressivity.

*For spending on new homes, the Index of Regressivity is the ratio of the burden in the $10,000-14,999 class to the 40,000 and over class.

Source: U.S. Bureau of Labor Statistics, Consumer Expenditure Survey (CES), Western Interview Data, 1985-86 augmented by more detailed breakdowns on consumption from U.S. interview data. Percent of households estimated by authors based on the U.S. Bureau of the Census, *1980 Census of Population*. Tax burden on new homes estimated from data supplied in Dennis Hoffman, "Arizona Sales Tax and Regressivity," *Arizona Business*, Vol. 35 (August 1988).

Revenue Growth And Stability

During the ten-year period between 1978 and 1988, revenues from Arizona's sales tax increased at an average annual rate of 10.7 percent in nominal dollars and 4.1 percent in dollars adjusted for inflation. Table 8-6 documents this growth, both for sales tax collections in current dollars in column 1 and inflation adjusted collections (in 1988 dollars) in columns 2 and 5. Total collections (in 1988 constant dollars) increased slightly relative to population over the period, to $443 per capita in 1988, but exhibited no secular growth as a percentage of personal income.

<table>
<tr><td colspan="6" align="center">Table 8-6
Growth in the State Sales Tax Over Time
(in millions of dollars)</td></tr>
<tr><td></td><td colspan="2" align="center">Gross Sales Tax Collections</td><td></td><td></td><td></td></tr>
<tr><td>Fiscal Year</td><td>Nominal Dollars (1)</td><td>Real Dollars (2)</td><td>Annual Percent Change (Real) (3)</td><td>Gross Sales Taxes As Percent of Income (4)</td><td>Real Gross Sales Taxes per Capita (5)</td></tr>
<tr><td>1987-88</td><td>1,598</td><td>1,598</td><td>-0.3</td><td>3.36</td><td>$443</td></tr>
<tr><td>1986-87</td><td>1,530</td><td>1,602</td><td>1.3</td><td>3.32</td><td>460</td></tr>
<tr><td>1985-86</td><td>1,459</td><td>1,581</td><td>2.8</td><td>3.30</td><td>470</td></tr>
<tr><td>1984-85</td><td>1,364</td><td>1,538</td><td>13.7</td><td>3.51</td><td>487</td></tr>
<tr><td>1983-84</td><td>1,143</td><td>1,353</td><td>28.8</td><td>3.29</td><td>445</td></tr>
<tr><td>1982-83</td><td>848</td><td>1,051</td><td>-0.5</td><td>2.71</td><td>360</td></tr>
<tr><td>1981-82</td><td>805</td><td>1,056</td><td>-0.4</td><td>2.77</td><td>369</td></tr>
<tr><td>1980-81</td><td>751</td><td>1,060</td><td>-16.3</td><td>2.81</td><td>379</td></tr>
<tr><td>1979-80</td><td>817</td><td>1,267</td><td>4.9</td><td>3.48</td><td>522</td></tr>
<tr><td>1978-79</td><td>706</td><td>1,208</td><td>12.5</td><td>3.49</td><td>458</td></tr>
<tr><td>1977-78</td><td>579</td><td>1,074</td><td>7.4</td><td>3.39</td><td>426</td></tr>
<tr><td colspan="6">Average Annual Growth Rates (Percent)</td></tr>
<tr><td>1978-88</td><td>10.7</td><td>4.1</td><td>--</td><td>--</td><td>0.4</td></tr>
<tr><td>1985-88</td><td>5.4</td><td>1.2</td><td>--</td><td>--</td><td>-3.1</td></tr>
</table>

Note: Gross sales tax collections include sales, use, and severance taxes. To calculate real dollar figures, nominal values were deflated by the GNP implicit price deflator for state and local government purchases.

Source: Arizona Department of Revenue, *1988 Annual Report* (and various other issues); BEA personal income data on computer diskettes.

As shown in the third column of the table, year-to-year growth in total collections fluctuated considerably over the period. These variations are attributable either to discretionary policy changes or to cyclical movements in the Arizona economy. The largest swings in total collections occurred between fiscal years 1980 and 1981, 1983 and 1984, and 1984 and 1985, and correspond to some of the major discretionary changes in the sales tax code. For example, the removal of food from the retail sales tax base in July 1980 accounts for much of the 16.3 percent decline in collections between 1980 and 1981. Conversely, the 25 percent increase in sales tax rates from 4 to 5 percent accounts for the sharp increases in collections between 1983 and 1985.[9] The average annual growth since 1985, after these discretionary changes, is only 1 percent per year.

Secular Growth and Cyclical Changes

Changes in sales tax revenues take two forms: long-run, or secular growth and short-run variation around the long-run growth path. Secular growth helps assure that the state's revenues will be sufficient to meet expenditure needs that typically grow over time and with the economy. The degree of sensitivity of sales tax revenues to short-run fluctuations in the Arizona economy indicates the stability of the sales tax. More stable revenue sources are better suited to maintaining balanced budgets during economic downturns.

Using data provided by the Arizona Department of Revenue on quarterly sales tax collections from 1981:III through 1988:I (the only period for which data were available), we separated the secular growth in sales tax collections from cyclical fluctuations by fitting a smooth time trend to the quarterly data.[10] This estimated trend showed that, on an annual basis, total sales tax collections grew 8.7 percent per year during this time period.

Remember, however, that total collections include the effect of discretionary changes, like the 1983-84 rate increase, as well as underlying changes in the size of the base. To better capture the characteristics of the tax base alone, we examined changes in revenues from what Arizona calls the distribution base.[11] Since tax rates on the distribution base of the sales tax were uniform during the period, changes in revenues from the distribution base exclude the influence of rate changes and better reflect changes in the size of the tax base itself. Revenues from the distribution base grew at an average annual rate of 4.5 percent. In other words, roughly half of the growth in sales tax collections from 1981:III - 1988:I reflected discretionary changes in tax rates, while the remaining half reflected underlying growth in the state sales tax base.

The difference between actual quarterly collections and the smooth secular trend line indicates the cyclical movement in collections. The magnitude of this deviation from trend indicates the stability of the revenue source. The greater is the average absolute deviation from long-term trend in sales tax collections, the more unstable is the tax. The absolute deviation from trend is expressed in percentage form in the first column of Table 8-7 for those activities characterized by a significant long-term trend. The table shows that total collections varied from the trend on average by 8.0 percent. Of course, part of this deviation reflects the discretionary rate changes made in 1983-84; the average deviation of the distribution base, which factors out the rate changes, was 4.3 percent.

Of the large classes of taxable activity, retail and restaurants and bars are the most stable. Individuals purchase retail items throughout all phases of the business cycle, and spending at restaurants and bars may not be overly responsive to changes in the economy. In contrast, contracting activity is highly responsive to swings in the economy and revenue from this source is less stable.[12] Overall, the state's sales tax revenues move in conjunction with the Arizona economy falling during economic downturns and growing during economic expansions. A 4.3 percent fluctuation in sales tax collections would result in a revenue change in the \$65 to \$70 million range.

	Table 8-7 Stability and Responsiveness of the Arizona Sales Tax (Percent)		
	Stability and Cyclical Movement	**Economic Responsiveness**	
	Mean Absolute Deviation From Trend	**To Personal Income**	**To Gross State Product**
Total Collections	8.0	1.5*	1.4*
Revenues Retained by State	10.4	1.5*	1.4*
Distribution Base Revenues	4.3	0.8*	0.7*
Retail	4.7	0.8*	--
Contracting	8.8	1.6*	1.5*
Utilities	--	0.1	0.2
Restaurants & Bars	3.8	1.0*	--
Rentals of Personal Property	12.4	1.2*	--
Rentals of Real Property	--	0.1	0.0
Communications	--	0.1	0.0
Printing	--	--	-0.1
Amusements	--	1.9	--
Railroads & Aircraft	38.0	--	-1.5*
Transportation & Towing	--	--	1.9
Wholesale Feed	12.6	--	-0.9*
Publishing	159.6**	--	-8.5*

* Designates that the coefficient was statistically different from zero with 90% certainty. The secular growth trend was based on a regression of collections (in natural logarithms) against a time trend variable and three dummy variables for seasonal adjustments; the income responsiveness was based on a regression of collections (in natural logarithms) against personal income (in natural logarithms); the production responsiveness was based on a regression of collections (in natural logarithms) against gross state product (in natural logarithms).

** Extremely high value due to changes in the definition of the base.

Source: Computed by authors based on quarterly data for 1981:III through 1988:I supplied by the Arizona Department of Revenue.

<u>Responsiveness to Economic Growth</u>

We measure the level of economic activity in Arizona by personal income and the total value of production (gross state product). Using regression analysis to estimate the effect of these economic measures on sales tax collections, we find that on average, every 10 percent increase in personal income was associated with a 15 percent increase in total collections while a 10 percent increase in gross state product was associated with a 14 percent increase in total collections. Table 8-7 displays these results: the revenue-income elasticity equals 1.5 and the revenue-production elasticity equals 1.4. However, these two elasticities include the effects of discretionary changes in tax rates. Without the effects of tax rate changes, every 10 percent increase in personal income is associated with only an 8 percent increase in total collections while every 10 percent increase in gross state product is associated with a 7 percent increase in total collections. (See Distribution Base Revenues in Table 8-7.) Thus, without policy changes, sales tax collections would grow more slowly than the economy.

Among the largest classes of taxable activity, contracting stands out as a highly responsive source of revenue with a revenue-income elasticity of 1.6 and a revenue-production elasticity of 1.5. This high responsiveness, however, is a double-edged sword. Revenues from contracting activities will rise *and* fall more than proportionately than changes in income and production. In other words, the flip side of this high degree of responsiveness is the high instability of contracting activities that has already been mentioned. Retail activities lie at the opposite end of the spectrum -- relatively unresponsive to changes in economic activity and relatively invariant to cyclical fluctuations. Note that because retail sales constitute nearly half of the total base, the distribution base is also relatively stable and relatively unresponsive. The main point is that a tradeoff arises between responsiveness and stability; the more responsive a tax base is, the less stable it is.

Policy Issues Related To The Tax Base

One set of policy issues in Arizona relates to what should be included in the state sales tax base. This section concentrates on two policy issues: removal of business purchases, and expansion of the base to include food and personal services. Table 8-8 provides a summary statement of the discussion that follows. The section ends with a brief discussion of other miscellaneous policy issues related to the base and tax collections.

<u>Eliminating the Taxation of Business Purchases</u>

The broad coverage of Arizona's sales tax largely reflects quite extensive taxation of business purchases. The state has made a number of changes over the years that appropriately eliminate the worst features of a multistage tax. Nonetheless, the continued taxation of inputs used up in production such as industrial fuel and chemicals, of many equipment purchases, and of real property rentals complicates the tax, leads to differential burdens across industries, may distort business production decisions, and produces an unclear and capricious distribution of the tax burden among individuals. One additional effect of this taxation is that the industries most burdened by this taxation have strong and legitimate reasons to complain about the sales tax.

Table 8-8
Evaluation of Alternative Sales Tax Bases

	Estimate of 1988 Revenue Change at Current Tax Rate (in millions)	Revenue Neutral Tax Rate (percent)	Simplicity	Neutrality (*Efficiency*)	Vertical Equity	Stability	Responsiveness
Current Base	$0.0	5.0	low	medium	2.17	high	low
Removal of Business Purchases	-$399.4	6.7	medium	high	?	?	?
Base Expansions:							
Food for Home Consumption	$163.1	4.5	high	high	2.57	high	low
Personal Services and Repair	$68.3	4.8	medium	high	2.22	medium	medium

Note:	With the current tax rate and tax base, Arizona raised $1,598 million with the general sales tax in FY 1987-88. A higher value for the vertical equity measure indicates a more regressive sales tax system. The vertical equity index for the current base does not include the tax on contracting; the vertical equity index for food overstates the regressivity, because it includes purchases with food stamps. The revenue estimates are based on a combination of tax expenditure estimates reported by the Department of Revenue and data from the *Consumer Expenditure Survey*. Revenue estimates represent gross sales tax collections which are currently divided between cities, counties, and the state general fund.

How adversely such taxes affect economic development and the competitive situation of the state is hard to determine. For example, the exemption of equipment used in manufacturing and of new equipment purchases in agriculture mitigates the disincentive effects on those industries, but then distorts the taxation of those industries relative to others. Hence, the elimination of all business purchases from the sales tax base would simplify the tax, reduce production distortions, and clarify the incidence of the tax.

Complete removal of all business purchases from the sales tax base, however, would be difficult to administer. Attempting to remove all purchases, including those such as office supplies that could also be used for personal use, could lead to abuses in that individuals would have an incentive to purchase such supplies through their firms rather than as individual consumers. Nonetheless, exempting most large business purchases, such as heavy equipment, should be administratively feasible. Business purchases of industrial fuel and electricity present few administrative problems. Similarly, rentals of real property and non-residential contracting could easily be eliminated.

To exempt business purchases most effectively, many states require formal certificates of exemption. Vendors are held liable for taxes not collected from purchasers who do not hold a certificate of exemption. West Virginia is currently the only state to exclude from the sales tax virtually all producers' goods in manufacturing, retailing and agriculture. Apparently, West Virginia has managed to administer its tax without major problems (see Due and Mikesell, 1983, p.52).

The disadvantage of removing business purchases from Arizona's tax base is clear; it would involve a large revenue loss for the state. The exact amount of revenue loss is hard to determine, but it could be as high as 20-30 percent of total collections. (As reported in Table 8-4, about 42 percent of total sales tax revenue is estimated to come from sales to private business, governments, and nonprofits.) If these purchases were eliminated, the state would have to make up substantial revenue shortfalls through other means. Alternatives include increasing the sales tax rate, taxing business more directly through business profits taxes, or increasing reliance on other state revenue sources.

Taxation of Food

Like 27 other states, Arizona exempts food for home consumption from its state sales tax.[13] The arguments for and against food taxation were well rehearsed in Arizona in 1980 when the state switched from taxing food to exempting it. The main argument for taxing food is that it would generate substantial revenue (between $140 and $150 million in 1986) or alternatively would permit a substantial reduction in the tax rate (to 4.5 percent). In addition, taxing food would eliminate the current incentives for consumers to substitute in favor of the untaxed good, food-consumed-at-home away from food purchased at restaurants, and thereby would make the sales tax more neutral. Taxing food would also reduce administration and compliance costs since vendors and administrators would no longer have to make fine distinctions between taxable items and nontaxable food. Finally, estimates of the responsiveness of food spending to changes in state income indicate that adding food to the tax base would increase the stability of the sales tax over the economic cycle. In particular, our analysis shows that every 10 percent increase in income is met by only a 7 percent increase in food purchases.[14]

However, political pressures have led many states, including Arizona, to exempt food from the sales tax base in order to reduce the burden on poor households. The regressivity of taxing food is indisputable; our analysis shows that the burden of food spending for low income households is almost 3.9 times that for high income households (based on an estimated regressivity index for food of 3.88), and that if food were added to the current sales tax base, the overall regressivity index of the sales tax would increase from 2.17 to 2.57.[15]

Note, however, that exempting food from the sales tax base provides benefits to all consumers of food, including residents and nonresidents, and poor and nonpoor. As an alternative policy, three states that tax food (Vermont, New Mexico, and Hawaii) provide a refundable income tax credit against the state income tax for low-income households. Compared to the general exemption, a tax credit targets tax relief more efficiently on the poor. In addition, a tax credit could be expanded to offset the burden of the tax not only on food purchases but also on other purchases, such as utilities, that disproportionately burden the poor. Because it would be targeted to low-income households, the cost to the state of the credit would be only a small fraction of the potential revenue gain from taxing food. Concerns that many low income people might not take advantage of the credit and therefore would be disproportionately hurt by the policy change are substantially mitigated by the fact that food bought with foodstamps cannot be taxed.

Expansion of the Base to Include Services

Currently, Arizona is in step with much of the rest of the country in not taxing a wide array of services. But the recent growth of the service sector has made sales taxation of services an increasingly popular option, not only for Arizona but for other states as well. During the early 1980s, output from service industries in Arizona accounted for over 15 percent of total gross state product. Between 1981 and 1986, total gross state product grew at an annual rate (adjusted for inflation) of 5.5 percent, output from retail trade grew by 7.05 percent, and output from services grew by 7.24 percent.[16] Thus, expanding the sales tax base to include services could potentially produce significant new revenue, or permit a substantial reduction in the sales tax rate. Moreover, if services continue to grow faster than retail trade, the taxation of services would allow the state to capture a greater portion of the growth in the state economy.

However, the desirability of including services in the sales tax base depends on the type of service considered. Some services are for personal use such as dry cleaning and haircutting. Others represent the professional services of lawyers, accountants, and doctors that are used by both individuals and firms. And finally, business services such as advertising are used only by businesses. In Arizona, spending on professional services is twice as large as spending on business services and four times as large as spending on personal services.

The case for taxing consumer services, especially personal services and repair, is strong. First and most important, consumer spending on services is similar to consumer spending on retail goods; they simply represent two different ways of satisfying consumer wants. For example, a consumer may choose to satisfy her desire for a good sound system by buying a new stereo or by having an old one repaired. Taxing one approach to satisfying wants but not another distorts the consumer's consumption decision. Hence, using the criterion of neutrality, taxation of consumer services makes sense. Second, expanding the tax to include personal services facilitates the administration of some parts of the tax. Service providers who now charge taxes only on the parts or materials they sell would no longer have to distinguish between parts and services. Third, the taxation of personal services barely increases the regressivity of the sales tax. (Our estimate of the regressivity index for personal services and repair is 2.22.) The tradeoff here is that broad expansion of the base to personal services would require the registration of many additional small vendors.

The case for taxing consumers' purchases of professional services is less compelling since many of these professional services (such as medical and legal services) relate to the misfortune of individuals. Despite their large potential base, many professional services probably should be excluded from the tax based on social policy concerns. Further, the inclusion of health and education services in the sales tax base increases its regressivity. Taxing the legal and accounting services used by individuals would be the least regressive option and deserves further investigation.

The drawbacks of taxing business services were well illustrated by the recent fiasco in Florida. Florida tried to expand dramatically its sales tax on services but quickly repealed the tax in response to pressures from out-of-state advertisers. Florida's problem was not that it tried to tax services, but rather that it tried to tax the services purchased by businesses.[17]

For two reasons, the taxation of business services is even more inappropriate than the taxation of business purchases. First, if business services such as accounting, bookkeeping or legal services were taxed, firms, especially large ones, would have a strong incentive to use their own employees for in-house services rather than to use employees from specialized firms. Because a firm would find it easier to produce services internally than to produce commodities (such as office supplies) internally, the potential for distortions, tax avoidance, and inequities across firms is more serious for the taxation of business services than for the taxation of commodity purchases.

Second, for out-of-state transactions, taxes on services would be even more difficult to collect than taxes on physical commodities. This fact would provide a strong incentive for Arizona service firms to move outside the state. Florida tried to offset these incentives for in-state firms by including out-of-state services in the service tax base. Florida's experience clearly indicates the difficulties with that approach; out-of-state advertising firms launched a strong and politically successful attack on the state's tax.

In sum, we advocate the taxation of personal services, but not services used by business firms. Taxing personal services (including repair) would have increased 1988 tax revenues by about 4 percent, or would have permitted a reduction in the sales tax rate to 4.8 percent. In addition, taxing personal services would increase the responsiveness of the sales tax base to economic growth, but by less than if business services were also included.[18]

Other Policy Issues Related to the Tax Base

Several other policy issues related to the tax base and revenue collection arise in the Arizona context. These issues are briefly identified and discussed in this section.

Motor Fuel. Although motor fuel is subject to a separate excise tax, logically it could also be included in the general sales tax. It would make sense for consumers of motor fuel, like consumers of other products, to pay the state's 5 percent general sales tax to help pay for the state's general public services, and then, if deemed desirable, to pay an additional tax on that consumption as a charge for the use of highways. Expanding the base to include motor fuel would have generated about $68 million in 1988 or about 4 percent of total collections.

Casual Vehicle Sales. Current Arizona law exempts all casual activities or sales from the sales tax base where casual sales are defined as those that are not part of the ordinary, regular function or business of the seller. Expanding the base to include such sales makes sense in terms of the neutrality of the tax, since similar transactions would be treated similarly and distortions in consumer spending would be reduced. The major problem with such a tax is enforcement of collections. Casual sales of vehicles, however, carry a built-in enforcement mechanism, because the state already regulates ownership through the issuance of titles, licenses, and registrations. Hence, imposing the sales tax on casual sales of vehicles makes sense for Arizona and would bring it in line with practice in 28 other states including California, Florida, Texas, and Utah.

Interstate Sales of Electricity and Telephone Calls. The U.S Supreme Court recently upheld the constitutionality of an Illinois tax on long-distance telephone calls originating or terminating in Illinois that are billed to service addresses in Illinois. The Court unanimously rejected the argument that the tax creates a barrier to interstate commerce. This ruling increases the attractiveness of such a tax for Arizona and the other 32 states that do not currently tax interstate phone calls.

Sales on Indian Reservations. New York State recently enacted a pact with the Seneca Indians whereby the state could tax sales on reservations but had to return the revenues to the reservation. If this practice were followed in Arizona, taxing sales on Indian Reservations would produce no additional revenue for the state. Nonetheless, such taxation would be desirable. As long as sales on reservations are not taxed, consumers have an incentive to avoid the state sales tax by purchasing goods on the reservation.

Mail-Order Sales. Although technically subject to use taxes, mail order purchases from out-of-state firms frequently escape taxation. According to a 1987 study by the Advisory Commission on Intergovernmental Relations, full enforcement by Arizona of the use tax on mail order purchases would have generated about $36 million in 1988, or about 2 percent of total collections. Unfortunately, however, the Supreme Court's 1967 Bellas Hess ruling severely limits the ability of states to collect these taxes at this time. The Court ruled that states cannot require out-of-state mail order firms to collect sales or use taxes unless the firm has some minimum connection or link -- called nexus -- with the state. The Court ruled that a physical presence in the state was necessary for nexus to exist. Accordingly, a firm such as Sears, with retail outlets in every state, can legally be forced to collect the taxes, but a firm such as Spiegel, which conducts transactions through mail order without retail outlets, cannot.

Because the technology and practical reality of out-of-state sales have changed substantially since 1967, a future court decision could reverse Bellas Hess. Or federal legislation could be enacted that reaffirms the right of states to enforce the collection of use taxes. Because mail order sales are likely to continue their rapid growth, especially with the emergence of cable T.V. shopping channels, catalogs on home computer software, and the advertisement of 800 area code telephone numbers, states like Arizona would do well to push for new federal legislation in this area.

Local Sales Taxes

A second set of policy issues arises in connection with local use of the sales tax in Arizona. Local governments in Arizona collect almost twice as much sales tax revenue as local governments nationally. Since counties in Arizona were not empowered to use the sales tax until 1990, this outcome reflects heavy reliance by cities.[19] In 1988, Arizona cities collected $99 per capita from sales taxes while cities nationally collected an average of $41 per capita. This high average level of city sales tax collections in Arizona is achieved primarily through widespread city usage of the tax and broadly defined tax bases.

Arizona cities have the power to set their own local tax rates. As shown in Table 8-9, local city tax rates varied from 1 percent to 3 percent in 1987. About half the cities had a rate of 1 percent. The other 38 cities with sales taxes had rates ranging from 1.2 percent in Phoenix to 3.0 percent in a few small cities. The 21 percent of the state's population in cities with rates greater than or equal to 2.0 percent faced a combined city and state tax rate of 7.0 percent or above.

<table>
<tr><td colspan="3">Table 8-9
Distribution of Arizona City Population
By City Sales Tax Rate - 1987</td></tr>
<tr><td>City Sales Tax Rate (Percent)</td><td>Number of Cities</td><td>Percent of City Population (Percent)</td></tr>
<tr><td>3.02</td><td>3</td><td>0.2</td></tr>
<tr><td>.0</td><td>31</td><td>20.9</td></tr>
<tr><td>1.5</td><td>3</td><td>0.4</td></tr>
<tr><td>1.2</td><td>1</td><td>35.8</td></tr>
<tr><td>1.0</td><td>39</td><td>42.4</td></tr>
<tr><td>0.0</td><td>3</td><td>0.2</td></tr>
<tr><td>Total</td><td>80</td><td>100.0</td></tr>
</table>

Note: The table is based on the population living in 80 of Arizona's 83 cities. This excludes the newly-incorporated cities of Cave Creek, Fountain Hills, Litchfield Park, Queen Creek, and Sedona.

Source: League of Arizona Cities and Towns, *Sales Tax Survey*, May 1988.

Local sales taxation in Arizona raises three policy issues: whether local tax bases should be brought into conformance with the state base, how food should be treated, and whether the emphasis of local sales taxes should be shifted away from cities toward counties.

Local Non-Conformance

Arizona's municipal sales taxes are unusual in that cities have authority to define their own tax bases. This authority arises from Arizona's strong tradition of local home rule and the fact that sales taxes were initially collected at the local level. In the other 30 states that authorized local sales taxes as of 1987, state revenue departments collect the tax on behalf of the local governments in 24 and typically require that the local tax base conform to the state tax base. Atypically, Arizona cities can opt for state collection even when their tax base differs from the state base.

Local control over the definition of the tax base is advantageous to cities because it allows them to tailor the sales tax base to their particular circumstances and preferences. For example, a city hard-pressed for funds may choose to include food even though the state exempts it. In addition, this arrangement insulates the cities somewhat from changes in the state sales tax base enacted by the state legislature. Even if a state tax change can be justified as good tax policy, changes that reduce the local tax base can be devastating to local governments that often have less flexibility than the state government to offset the associated loss of sales tax revenue.

The disadvantages of this approach are that it complicates tax compliance and can lead to problems of tax collection and enforcement. A business firm incurs additional compliance costs when its taxable sales under the state tax differ from those under the city tax. For a firm operating in more than one Arizona city, the problem is magnified further as the firm must determine the taxable sales in each of the cities in which it has offices and must prepare for audits from multiple agents. Differences in the tax base also make the tax more difficult and more expensive to administer fairly. For example, economies of scale and expertise typically make state collection of local sales taxes more cost effective than local collection, especially for small cities. But differences between state and local tax codes may lead to uneven enforcement of local tax codes when the state collects the local tax.

In terms of revenue impact, the largest differences between city tax bases and the state base come from the frequent taxation at the local level of food for home consumption, residential rentals, and local advertising, all of which are exempt from the state sales tax. If it were deemed desirable to make city tax bases conform to the state tax base by requiring cities to exempt these categories from local taxation, cities would face large revenue losses unless they chose to offset the loss of the base with an increase in the city sales tax rate. These potential revenue losses are important since Arizona cities have little flexibility to raise revenue through other mechanisms.

Thus, a tradeoff arises between the goal of simplifying the state-local tax structure to reduce compliance and administrative costs and the goal of assuring that local governments have adequate revenue sources to meet the expenditure needs of their local residents. A closer look at the local decision to tax food illustrates this tradeoff.

Local Taxation of Food

The Model City Tax Code, a document developed by the League of Arizona Cities and Towns, attorneys, and business groups to provide uniform language on definitions, tax imposition, and exemptions, supports the exemption of food from local taxation. Such exemption can be justified both because taxing food puts a heavier burden on low-income than high-income households, and because food is exempt from the state tax. Nonetheless, 63 out of the 81 Arizona cities with a sales tax include food in the tax base.

The local decision to tax food represents a balance between considerations of fairness, the need for revenue, competitive pressures from nearby cities, and the availability of alternative tax revenues. The primary consideration is likely to be the city's need for revenue. Food typically accounts for about 20 percent of retail sales, and from 10-20 percent of a broadly defined sales tax base of the type used in Arizona. Hence, exempting food from the base either lowers sales tax revenue by 10 to 20 percent (and possibly by much more in small non-metropolitan cities) or requires an offsetting increase in the sales tax rate or other revenues. Because a city's per capita income is a main contributor to its revenue-raising capacity, we would expect a city with low per capita income to have low revenue-raising capacity, and, hence, all else held constant, to experience greater pressure to include food in its sales tax base.

Second, a city might choose to exempt food if its local retailers were concerned about the adverse impact of a food tax on their sales. For example, a tax on food in a city that borders a state that exempts food from sales taxes (such as Colorado or Nevada), might encourage some local residents to buy food over the border. Even more important in some cases, the tax on food might reduce the inflow of people from Mexico or other states into the border city, thereby reducing the profits of local retailers.

Finally, a city may be influenced by the actions of other nearby cities. If all cities in the area tax food, a city can be less concerned about adverse responses to its food tax than if none of the surrounding cities taxes food. Table 8-10 sheds light on the proximity issue where proximity is crudely defined by county boundaries. In 12 of Arizona's 15 counties, nearly all cities tax food. In two counties, Mohave and Pima, almost all the cities do not tax food. Only in the tiny county of Santa Cruz is there an even split between those taxing and those not taxing food. Hence, city decisions about the taxation of food appear to be influenced by the actions of nearby cities. Phoenix stands out as an exception. Despite the taxation of food in nearby cities, Phoenix has chosen to follow the state tax practice of exempting food.

| | Table 8-10 | |
	City Sales Taxes on Food, by County	
County	**Number of Cities That Tax Food/All Cities In County With Sales Taxes**	**Cities With Sales Taxes That Do Not Tax Food**
Apache	3/3	None
Cochise	5/7	Huacha City, Tombstone
Coconino	3/5	Flagstaff, Sedona
Gila	4/4	None
Graham	3/3	None
Greenlee	2/2	None
La Paz	0/1	Parker
Maricopa	20/22	Phoenix, Youngtown
Mohave	0/4	Bullhead City, Colorado City, Kingman, Lake Havasu City
Navajo	6/6	None
Pima	1/4	Marana, Oro Valley, Tucson
Pinal	5/7	Florence, Superior
Santa Cruz	1/2	Patagonia
Yavapai	6/7	Camp Verde
Yuma	4/4	None

Source: League of Arizona Cities and Towns, *Model City Tax Code.*

A more formal statistical analysis shows that both personal income and proximity to the state border influence a city's decision to tax food. In general, we find that the probability of taxing food is inversely related to the per capita income of city residents, and that proximity to the state border decreases the probability of taxing food. More specifically, we obtain the following regression model:

Probability Of

Taxing Food $= 3.54 - 0.299^* \text{PCY} - 0.201^* \text{Border}$

where

    Probability Of Taxing Food takes on the value of 1 if the city taxes food and 0 otherwise;

    LPCY is the natural logarithm of city per capita income; and

    Border takes on the value of 1 for 17 cities near state boundaries and 0 for all other cities.

    and * indicates the estimated coefficient is statistically significant with 95 percent certainty.

The equation implies that a city with a per capita income 10 percent below that of another city is approximately 3 percentage points more likely to tax food. Similarly, being near the border decreases by about 20 percentage points the probability that a city will tax food relative to an interior city. Stated differently, a low-income city in the middle of the state is more likely to tax food than a high-income city on the border.

The finding that low-income cities are more likely than high-income cities to tax food is relevant for policy discussions. Because a tax on food places a heavier burden on low-income households relative to their income than on high-income households, the case for exempting food would be stronger in low-income areas where more of the benefits of the tax exemption would go to needy households. However, the regression model suggests that exempting food is a luxury that low-income cities cannot afford. Thus, the very cities that would benefit the most from not taxing food are less likely to choose to exempt it.

To counter this situation, the state should consider providing tax credits for low-income households subject to local food taxes. The availability of such credits might encourage other cities to tax food, but this outcome need not be undesirable, especially if the state itself were to begin taxing food again. As already noted, tax credits have the advantage of targeting the assistance to people who are most needy and, in this intergovernmental context, have the additional advantage of placing the burden of helping poor people not on local governments, but rather on the state government where most fiscal experts believe it belongs.

City vs. County Sales Taxes

Arizona empowers cities rather than counties to levy local sales taxes. Should the emphasis be shifted to counties?

To the extent that rates or the coverage of the tax base vary across communities, local sales taxes can significantly distort consumer behavior. For example, a person living in a community with a high sales tax rate can avoid that tax simply by shopping in a nearby community with a lower rate. Avoiding taxes in this manner is much easier for sales taxes than for local income or property taxes. To avoid paying a local income tax, one must take the much larger step of changing one's place of work or residence (depending on whether the tax is imposed by place of work or by residence). The only way to avoid the burden of local property taxes is to move, but even this may not work if the community's high property tax rate is capitalized into the value of the land. With capitalization, even if she moves, the individual bears the burden of the higher tax in the form of a lower sale price for her house.

The efficiency consideration of minimizing changes in behavior has led some states to empower counties, rather than cities, to levy local sales taxes, and has led other states, in which counties have few powers, to eschew local sales taxes completely. Counties can be the preferred level of government to tax sales because their larger geographic size helps to minimize the adverse locational effects of local differentials in tax rates.

Sales taxation works better for Arizona cities than it might for cities in other states because, with the exception of cities in the two metropolitan counties of Maricopa (Phoenix) and Pima (Tucson), cities are relatively spread out. The large distances between many cities reduces the distortionary effects of variation in city tax rates. In the two metropolitan counties, which are home to 75 percent of the population, distortions are minimized by the fact that most cities in each county impose the same tax rate. In Pima County, for example, all 4 cities impose a 2 percent rate. In Maricopa County, many cities impose a 1.0 percent rate. Phoenix is able to have a slightly higher rate because of its unique character as the center of the metropolitan area, but any attempt to raise the rate beyond 1.2 percent might adversely affect the city's sales. Thus, in Maricopa and Pima counties, tax competition among cities constrains the tax rate choices that a city can make.

A second argument in favor of county rather than city taxes is that city tax bases are likely to exhibit much more variation than county bases from one jurisdiction to another. This variation is undesirable because it implies that to raise the same amount of revenue, cities have to impose different tax rates which produces the locational distortions just discussed. Or, if they impose similar tax rates, they have to make do with different amounts of sales tax revenue per capita, which creates a problem for jurisdictions with low revenue-raising capacity relative to their expenditure needs.

An analysis of sales tax bases in Arizona cities (adjusted so that food is excluded from the base in all cities) indicates substantial variation in per capita bases. The complete range is from $17,117 per capita to $926 with more than a 6 to 1 variation in the more meaningful 90th to 10th percentile range. The wide range implies that Tempe (the 90th percentile city) can raise 6 times as much revenue per capita with a given sales tax rate as Taylor (the 10th percentile city). Moreover, the sales tax base varies much more widely across cities than does per capita income.

Not surprisingly, estimates for Arizona counties yield a smaller variation in potential sales tax bases: the estimated range is from $9,941 in Maricopa to $2,118 in Apache. However, the variation is still substantial and it exceeds the variation of per capita personal income. Hence, even if sales taxes were imposed at the county rather than the city level, a given tax rate would generate very different revenue amounts in different counties and these differences are even greater than those that would be generated by a proportional tax rate on income.

Because county governments in Arizona are currently severely restricted in their revenue sources and consequently are turning more and more toward user charges regardless of their desirability, the state has empowered counties to use sales taxes on a limited basis.

However, coordination of the new sales taxes with existing city taxes to avoid complicated problems of overlapping tax administration is a concern. Ideally, the city and county sales taxes would be coordinated to prevent the combined rate from being higher in cities than in unincorporated areas where only county and state rates apply. This coordination would maintain competitive tax rates, and would recognize that city residents receive a narrower range of county services than residents of unincorporated areas.

Summary

The two major policy issues in Arizona regarding sales taxation at the state level are how to define the taxable base and how much to rely on sales taxes relative to other types of revenue. Arizona's heavy reliance on state sales taxes reflects not excessive state spending or high state responsibilities relative to local governments, but rather a decision about the appropriate mix of revenues at the state level. This heavy reliance on sales taxation enables the state to collect taxes from non-resident visitors and makes the revenue system quite stable. At the same time, it magnifies the regressivity of the fiscal system and diminishes the responsiveness of state revenues to long-term growth in the economy.

The current Arizona sales tax continues to reflect its origin as a gross receipts tax and applies to a broader base than in many other states. Starting from the conceptual framework of the sales tax as a tax on final consumption, we believe that a strong case can be made for eliminating many of the business purchases still included in the base and for expanding the base to include personal services and food, with the latter accompanied by a refundable credit against the state income tax for low income households.

The variation across Arizona cities in the definition of city tax bases is clearly undesirable from the perspective of simplicity and minimizing compliance and administrative costs. However, such variation allows Arizona cities to tailor their tax bases to their own revenue needs and circumstances and is firmly rooted in Arizona's strong tradition of local autonomy. In our view, more conformity is desirable, but can only be achieved if state officials are sensitive to the revenue needs of local governments.

References

Arizona State University, College of Business, Center for Business Research. "Slow Growth Next Few Years, Then More Rapid." *Arizona Business.* 36 (February 1989).

______________________. "Arizona Sales Tax and Regressivity." *Arizona Business.* 35 (August 1988).

______________________. "Winter Residents Add 10 Percent to Valley's Population." *Arizona Business.* 35 (June 1988).

______________________. "'86-87 Winter Residents Spend $400 Million in Valley." *Arizona Business.* 34 (May 1987).

______________________. "Valley's Winter Residents Spend $381 Million." *Arizona Business.* 33 (June 1986).

______________________. "East Valley Winter Migration Up 6 Percent in '85." *Arizona Business.* 32 (May 1985).

Arizona Tax Research Association. "Estimated Individual Tax Burdens: Major Federal, State and Local Taxes and Selected Alternatives." Mimeo, April 27, 1988.

Auerbach, Alan. "The Theory of Excess Burden and Optimal Taxation," in Alan Auerbach and Martin Feldstein, eds., *Handbook of Public Economics*, vol. 1. Amsterdam: North Holland, 1985.

Blume, Lawrence E. "The Sales and Use Taxes," in Harvey E. Brazer, ed. *Michigan's Fiscal and Economic Structure*. Ann Arbor, MI: University of Michigan Press, 1982.

Due, John F. and Loretta Fairchild. "The Nebraska State and Local Sales and Use Taxes." in *The Final Report of the Nebraska Comprehensive Study*, Michael Wasylenko and John Yinger, co-directors. Syracuse, NY: Maxwell School of Citizenship and Public Affairs, 1987.

Due, John F. and John L. Mikesell. *Sales Taxation: State and Local Structure and Administration*. Baltimore, MD: Johns Hopkins University Press, 1983.

Fairchild, Loretta and John F. Due. "The Operation of the Nebraska State and Local Sales and Use Taxes," in *The Final Report of the Nebraska Comprehensive Study*, Michael Wasylenko and John Yinger, co-directors. Syracuse, NY: Maxwell School of Citizenship and Public Affairs, 1987.

Fox, William and Matthew Murray. "Economic Aspects of Taxing Services." *National Tax Journal*. March 1988: 19-36.

Francis, James. "The Florida Sales Tax on Services: What Really Went Wrong." in Steven D. Gold, ed., *The Unfininished Agenda for State Tax Reform*. Denver, CO: National Conference of State Legislatures, 1988.

Heller, Vic. "The Arizona Travel and Tourism Industry: 1984." Phoenix, AZ: Travel and Tourism Studies, Arizona State University, February 1985.

Hellerstein, Walter. "Florida's Sales Tax on Services." *National Tax Journal*. March 1988:1-18.

Hibbs, J. Elliot. "Report on the Taxation of Services." Undated mimeo.

Hogan, Timothy D. and McPheters, Lee R. *Tourism and Travel in Arizona, 1981*. Phoenix, AZ: Arizona State University, Bureau of Business and Economic Research, 1981.

League of Arizona Cities and Towns. *Sales Tax Survey*. 1988.

__________________. *Model City Tax Code* 1988.

Mikesell, John L. "The Cyclical Sensitivity of State and Local Taxes." *Public Budgeting and Finance*. Spring 1984: 32-39.

__________________. "Retail Sales and Use Taxation in Minnesota," in Robert D. Ebel and Therese J. McGuire, eds., *Final Report of the Minnesota Tax Study Commission*. Vol. 2. St. Paul, MN: Butterworth, 1986.

Peat, Marwick and Mitchell & Company. *Report to the American Retail Federation on costs to Retailers of Sales and Use Tax Compliance*. New York: NY, Peat Marwick and Mitchell & Company, November 1982.

Phoenix and Valley of the Sun Convention and Visitors Bureau. *Valley Visitor Profile: 1987/88 Survey Results* (1988).

Quick, Perry and McKee, Michael. "Sales Tax on Services: Revenue or Reform." *National Tax Journal*. September 1988:395-410.

Reschovsky, Andrew *et al. State Tax Policy: Evaluating the Issues*. Cambridge, MA: Lincoln Institute of Land Policy, 1983.

Sales and Marketing Management. *Survey of Buying Power*. August 7, 1989.

State of Arizona, Joint Legislative Budget Committee. *Tax Handbook* 1985, and 1988 Update.

State of Arizona, Department of Revenue. "The Revenue Impact of Arizona's Tax Expenditures." November 15, 1987.

_______________________. *Annual Report*, (various years).

"The Seneca's Pact with New York on Sales Taxes Could Set a National Standard." *Wall Street Journal*, 11 January 1989, p.1.

United States Advisory Commission on Intergovernmental Relations. *Significant Features of Fiscal Federalism*, 1989 edition, volumes I and II. Washington, DC: ACIR, 1989.

_______________________. *Significant Features of Fiscal Federalism*, 1988 edition. Washington, DC: ACIR, 1988.

_______________________. "Estimates of Revenue Potential from State Taxation of Out-of-State Mail Order Sales." Report SR-5. Washington, DC: ACIR, September 1987.

_______________________. *State and Local Taxation of Out-of-State Mail Order Sales*. Washington, DC: ACIR, April 1986.

United States Department of Commerce, Bureau of Economic Analysis. Personal income data on computer diskettes.

_______________________. *Survey of Current Business*. 68 (August 1988).

United States Department of Commerce, Bureau of the Census. *1980 Census of Population*. Washington, DC: USGPO, 1982.

_______________________. *1987 Census of Service Industries*. Washington, DC: USGPO, 1989.

_______________________. *1982 Census of Service Industries*. Washington, DC: USGPO, 1984.

_______________________. *1977 Census of Service Industries*. Washington, DC: USGPO, 1979.

_______________________. *1988 County and City Data Book*. Washington, DC: USGPO, 1989.

_______________________. *Governmental Finances in 1987-88*. Washington, DC: USGPO, 1990.

United States Department of Commerce, Bureau of Labor Statistics. *Consumer Expenditure Survey*, Western Interview Data and U.S. Interview Data. Washington, DC: USGPO.

U. S. Travel Data Center. *Impact of Travel on State Economies*. June 1988.

The Urban Institute and Price Waterhouse. *Fiscal Affairs of State and Local Governments in Nevada*. November, 1988.

Waren, William T. "Closing the Bellas Hess Loophole." *State Legislatures*. February 1989: 10-14.

White, Fred. "Tradeoff in Growth and Stability in State Taxes." *National Tax Journal*. March 1983: 103-14.

Endnotes

1. State sales taxes have become slightly less desirable as a revenue source now that sales taxes, but not income and property taxes, have been eliminated as a deductible item for the purposes of federal income taxation. However, the magnitude of the change should not be overstated. First, the change hurts only itemizers. Second, higher-income people are much more likely than low-income people to itemize deductions and therefore to benefit from the deductibility of sales taxes. But high income people bear relatively low

sales tax burdens and consequently did not benefit as much from deductibility of sales taxes as they do from the deductibility of property and income taxes. Hence, the perceived increase in their net tax burden is likely to be relatively small.

2. Recent developments in the theory of "optimal taxation" imply that one might want to design a tax on consumer goods with differential tax rates by type of good. According to this approach, in order to minimize the behavioral distortions associated with raising a given amount of revenue, one should apply higher tax rates to those goods for which consumers are relatively unresponsive to price changes and lower tax rates to other goods. But this approach is generally not acceptable in practice. Not only does it call for a complex system of differentiated rates, but it also calls for higher tax rates on goods such as food that burden low income people more heavily than high income people. See, for example, Alan Auerbach, "The Theory of Excess Burden and Optimal Taxation," in Alan Auerbach and Martin Feldstein, eds., *Handbook of Public Economics*, vol. 1. (Amsterdam: North Holland, 1985), pp. 61-127.

3. Thus, the sales tax would not apply to a federal contract to purchase IBM computers directly from IBM, but it would apply to such purchases from a retail or wholesale outlet. The reduced rate for federal purchases presumably minimizes the incentive for the federal government to make purchases from firms in other states.

4. Because our interstate comparisons are based on 1988 Census data, we use the Census definition of general sales taxes. This definition leads to inappropriate treatment of sales taxes in some states, most notably Washington and West Virginia. In both states, reported sales tax revenues include business occupation taxes which are more similar to business taxes than to general sales taxes. Estimates by Due and Mikesell (1983) for 1981 and by Mikesell (1986) for 1983 indicate that the inappropriate inclusion of such taxes overstates general sales taxes by about 35 percent in Washington and by 194 percent in West Virginia. (Due and Mikesell, p.6 and Mikesell, p. 161.) Without state-specific information to adjust the data correctly, we use the sales tax data provided by the Census for all states other than Arizona. However, for Arizona, we have made one minor adjustment to make its sales tax collections more comparable to those in other states. Namely, we have subtracted from the reported total the revenue that Arizona collects from its severance taxes on minerals and timber. Arizona's practice of listing severance taxes as sales taxes (which is reflected in the Census numbers for Arizona) is unusual. Hence, for comparability across states in sales tax collections, severance tax revenues are appropriately deleted.

5. One must be careful, however, not to assume that spending translates directly into service levels. Because of differences across states in the cost of providing a standard package of public services, a state that spends a lot could in fact be providing below-average services.

6. Note that the percentage differences relative to the U.S. average do not sum exactly to the overall difference of 36.5 percent because of the interactions mentioned above. Nonetheless, the basic point of the comparison remains valid.

7. Food has been deleted to reflect current sales tax practice in many states.

8. The percentage attributed to tourists and other visitors is relatively high, and places Arizona among the top eight states in terms of its ability to collect general sales tax revenue from visitors per dollar collected from residents. This judgement is based on the ratio of total expenditures by domestic visitors expressed as a percentage of state personal income. In 1986, Arizona had $4,815.3 million in domestic travel expenditures, which represented 10.7 percent of personal income. Other states with higher

percentages in 1986 included Florida, Hawaii, Maine, Nevada, Vermont, and Wyoming. Expenditure data were obtained from the U.S. Travel Data Center, *Impact of Travel on State Economies* (June 1988), Table 2; and personal income data were obtained from the U.S. Department of Commerce, Bureau of Economic Analysis, *Survey of Current Business* 68 (August 1988), p. 30.

9. The retail sales tax rate was increased to 5 percent effective June 1983, while the rates on the remaining classes of taxable activity were increased to 5 percent effective June, 1984.

10. The data were reported on a collection basis, which lags a month behind sales activity. For example, January collections are based on December sales activity. Our quarterly data are adjusted to reflect this lag.

11. As noted above, revenues from the distribution portion of the base are shared with the local governments.

12. Note, however, that there have been some discretionary changes in the definition of the contracting base that may have biased upward the measure of cyclicality.

13. The states that tax food are Kansas, Missouri, South Dakota, Alabama, Arkansas, Georgia, Hawaii, Idaho, Mississippi, New Mexico, North Carolina, Oklahoma, South Carolina, Tennessee, Virginia, Utah, and Wyoming.

14. This estimate is based on the same time period and methodology reported in Table 8-7. The data were provided by researchers at the University of Arizona.

15. This figure overstates the burden on the poor of including food in the base because federal laws prohibit taxing food purchased with food stamps.

16. Refer to Chapter 2 on the Arizona Economy for further detail.

17. A detailed review of the Florida experience is found in James Francis, "The Florida Sales Tax on Services: What Really Went Wrong," in Steven D. Gold, ed., *The Unfinished Agenda for State Tax Reform* (Denver CO: National Conference of State Legislatures, November 1988), pp.129-152.

18. Data for the whole U.S. indicate that business services (as measured by the receipts of firms) grew nearly twice as fast as personal services between 1977 and 1982 but only slightly faster between 1982 and 1987. Source: U.S. Bureau of the Census, *Census of Service Industries*, United States 1977, 1982, 1987.

19. Although countywide sales taxes are levied in Maricopa and Pinal counties for transportation, this revenue is earmarked for highway construction and is not available for county use.

Appendix: Methodology For Estimating Taxable Spending By Type Of Purchaser

Spending on taxable items by Arizona residents was derived from the consumption patterns reported by income class in the Bureau of Labor Statistics, 1985-86 Survey of Consumer Expenditures for the Western Region, supplemented with more detailed data from the comparable U.S. survey.[1] This survey reports average consumption expenditures by consumer spending unit on a wide variety of goods and services by income class for the 13 states in the Western region. After first categorizing each expenditure item as taxable or nontaxable in Arizona, taxable spending by Arizona residents was estimated by multiplying the average spending on each taxable item in each income class reported in the survey by the number of Arizona households in each class.[2] Although a consumer survey for Arizona alone would have been preferable, had one been available, we are quite comfortable using the survey for the Western Region; any differences between the distribution of households by income class in Arizona and the rest of the region are irrelevant given that we use the Arizona distribution of households to estimate taxable sales in each expenditure category.

This approach yields an estimate of spending on taxable items by Arizona residents. Because the spending levels in the survey include the sales taxes paid by consumers, they overstate the base to which the tax rate applies. To adjust for this overestimate, we divided the estimates of total spending by $1/(1+.067)$ to convert them to spending amounts that are subject to state sales taxes. This adjustment assumes that state consumers are paying an average combined state and local rate of 6.7 percent, the current rate in Phoenix. We then multiplied our estimate of taxable spending by the state's 5 percent sales tax rate. This procedure yields the tax payments of $549 million reported in the table.

Information about resident spending on new housing, which is subject to the tax on the gross receipts of contractors, is not available in the Survey of Consumer Expenditures. Hence, to determine how much of the tax on contractors should be allocated to Arizona residents, we relied on data on the distribution of construction activity. Based on the breakdown of the total valuation of construction authorized by building permits in Arizona in 1986 (*County and City Data Book*, 1988, Table A), we estimate that about 63 percent of contracting activity and hence 63 percent of the taxes collected from contractors are attributable to the building and renovation of residential structures.

The estimates on tourism come from a 1984 study of the Arizona travel and tourism industry by Heller (1985), inflated to 1986 using the Consumer Price Index for Phoenix. To

---

[1] The more detailed data for the U.S. survey permitted a finer allocation of purchases to the taxable and nontaxable categories than would have been possible with the Western data alone. For a spending category such as fees and admissions, for which the breakdown between taxable fees and admissions and nontaxable dues to clubs was not available for the Western Region, we used the national survey to estimate the national average percentage of entertainment expenditures used for each purpose and multiplied those percentages by the reported expenditures on entertainment by income group in the Western region. For service categories such as personal care, we typically assumed that 20 percent of the expenditures were for taxable materials and the rest for nontaxable labor. The one exception is transportation repair, for which we allocated 40 percent to taxable parts.

[2] More precisely, we used an estimate of the number of consumer spending units in each class because those, rather than households, are the unit of observation for the survey. We obtained the total number of spending units in Arizona by multiplying Arizona's share of total households in the Western Region by the number of spending units in the region. We then estimated the Arizona distribution of households (and hence consumer units) by income class by updating the distribution reported in the 1980 Census of Housing for increases in the price level.

estimate tax burdens for winter residents, we assumed that approximately 90,000 such households lived in Arizona for about four months in 1986 and that the typical household in this category was between 65 and 74 years old. We then used the same method discussed above for resident spending to estimate the taxable expenditures of these winter visitors, with the important modification that we used the consumption patterns for Western households in the age category 65-74, rather than all ages. The average annual income before taxes for people in this age range is about $27,000, a number that seems relatively consistent with the widely reported estimate that such winter residents spend about $1,000 per month per household while they are in Arizona.

Finally, taxes on sales to the category of "other" purchaser is calculated as a residual. This category includes sales to governments, charitable organizations, and private firms. Without a more direct way to estimate taxable sales to these other types of purchasers, the best estimate is simply the difference between total taxes and the sales to residents, tourists, and winter visitors.

Table 8-A-1
Comparison of Sales Tax Bases for Consumer Purchases

Category	Tax Treatment in Arizona	Tax Treatment in the 44 Other States With Sales Taxes
1. Goods at retail		
Most goods	Taxed at 5% rate	Fully taxed
Food for home consumption	Exempt since 1980	Exempt in 27 states(A)
Prescription drugs and medical supplies	Exempt	Exempt in all states except New Mexico(A)
Clothing	Taxed at 5% rate	Exempt or partially exempt in 6 states(A)
2. Contracting services (*e.g.* new houses and renovations)	Services of prime contractors taxed at 5% rate; 35% deduction for labor; land costs excluded	Contractors in 42 states pay tax on materials; 5 states tax contractors' receipts(B)
3. Utility services		
Gas, oil, and electricity	Taxed at 5% rate	No tax in 29 states,(A) some states impose special taxes(B)
Water	Taxed at 5% rate	No tax in 16 states(B)
Telephone and telegraph	Intrastate calls taxed at 5% rate; interstate calls exempt	Telecommunications exempt in 8 states(A); interstate calls taxed in 13 states(D)
4. Food and drink at restaurants and bars	Taxed at 5% rate	Generally taxed(A)
5. Hotel/motel	Taxed at 5.5% rate	See chapter on selective sales taxes

Table 8-A-1 (Continued)

Category	Tax Treatment in Arizona	Tax Treatment in the 44 Other States With Sales Taxes
6. Amusements		
Admissions to movies, and other entertainment	Taxed at 5% rate	Included in sales tax in 27 states; special taxes apply in 5 states(B)
Dues for country clubs	Exempt	Taxed in 10 states(B)
Activities sponsored by nonprofits	Exempt for religious, educational, and other enumerated charitable organizations	Not Available
7. Rental of personal property	Taxed at 5% rate	Taxed in most states
8. Printing		
Newspapers and magazines	Taxed at 5% rate	Exempt in 38 states(B)
Books	College texts exempt; other books taxed at 5% rate.	All textbooks sold to students exempt in 11 states; textbooks through high school exempt in 4 states; many states exempt all purchases by school boards(B)
9. Auto repair	Parts taxed at 5% rate	Typically, differential treatment of establishments depending on importance of materials in repair work(B)
10. Personal services (*e.g.* dry cleaning, barber shops)	Exempt	Some taxation in 21 states(C)

Table 8-A-1 (Continued)

Category	Tax Treatment in Arizona	Tax Treatment in the 44 Other States With Sales Taxes
11. Computer software	Canned software taxed at 5% rate	Trend toward taxation; 19 states tax all software; 16 states tax canned software(B)
12. Casual vehicle sales	Exempt	Taxed in 28 states(B)
13. Professional services (*e.g.* Legal, Medical, Accounting)	Exempt	Exempt in most states; only South Dakota, Florida, New Mexico, and Hawaii have extensive taxation(C)
14. Goods subject to special excises		
Moter vehicle fuel	Exempt	Exempt from general sales tax in all but 10 states(B)
Cigarettes	Taxed at 5% rate	Exempt only in Vermont(E)
Alcohol	Taxed at 5% rate	In general subject to taxation(B)

Sources: (A) Advisory Commission on Intergovernmental Relations, *Significant Features of Fiscal Federalism*, 1989 Edition, Vol. I, Table 24. Information is for October 1989.

(B) John F. Due and John L. Mikesell, *Sales Taxation: State and Local Structure and Administration* (Baltimore: The Johns Hopkins University Press, 1983). Data are for 1982.

(C) Advisory Commission on Intergovernmental Relations, *Significant Features of Fiscal Federalism*, 1988 Edition, Vol. I, Table 22. Based on ACIR designation of general broad, or substantial taxation of services.

(D) Advisory Commission on Intergovernmental Relations, *Significant Features of Fiscal Federalism*, 1990 Edition, Vol. I, Table 46.

(E) Tobacco Merchants Associations of the U.S., Inc., May 1, 1989.

Table 8-A-2
Comparison of Sales Tax Bases, Business Purchases

Category	Tax Treatment in Arizona	Tax Treatment in the 44 Other States With Sales Taxes
1. Items for resale	Exempt	Exempt in all states except Hawaii and Mississippi; also taxed in Washington and West Virginia under separate taxes(A)
2. Equipment used in:		
Manufacturing	Exempt	Exempt in 21 other states; trend toward exemption(B)
Agriculture	Used equipment taxed at 5% rate; exemption for new equipment	Trend toward exemption; distinction made between heavy and light equipment(A)
Mining	Exempt	Not Available
Other - retail, distribution, and wholesale	Taxed at 5% rate	Taxed in most states; exempt in West Virginia(A)
3. Inputs used up in production		
General (*e.g.* ehemicals)	Taxed at 5% rate	Fully taxed in 17 states, limited or wide exemption in 27 states(A)
Industrial Fuel and Electricity	Taxed at 5% rate	similar to treatment of general category with some exceptions(A)
Feed, seed, fertilizer	Seed, fertilizer taxed at 5% rate; livestock feed taxed at wholesale at 0.46875% rate	In part or fully exempt in most states; common rule exempts sales for farm use(A)

Table 8-A-2 (Continued)

Category	Tax Treatment in Arizona	Tax Treatment in the 44 Other States With Sales Taxes
4. Contracting services (*e.g.* new buildings)	Services of prime contractor taxed at 5% rate; 35% deduction for labor; land cost excluded	Contractors pay tax on materials in 39 states; contractors treated as vendor in 5 states(A)
5. Transportation		
Railroad rolling stock	Exempt	Exempt in all states(A)
Purchases by commercial airlines	Exempt	Exempt(A)
Moter transport vehicles	Buses or other urban transport vehicles exempt; trucks taxed at 5% rate	Exempt(A)
6. Rental of real property	Taxed at 5% rate	Taxed in 4 other states and taxed by cities in 2 additional states(D)
7. Computer software	Canned software taxed at 5% rate	Trend toward taxation(A)
8. Professional services (*e.g.* Local advertising, accounting, legal)	Exempt	Exempt in most states; only South Dakota, Florida, New Mexico, and Hawaii have extensive taxation(C)

Sources: (A) John F. Due and John L. Mikesell, *Sales Taxation: State and Local Structure and Administration* (Baltimore: The Johns Hopkins University Press, 1983). Data are for 1982.

(B) John L. Mikesell, "Retail Sales and Use Taxation in Minnesota," *Final Report of the Minnesota Tax Study Commission*, Vol. 2 (St. Paul: Butterworths). Information is from 1984.

(C) Advisory Commission on Intergovernmental Relations, *Significant Features of Fiscal Federalism*, 1988 Ed., Vol. I, Table 22.

(D) Survey by Ernst & Whinney, Phoenix, Arizona, prepared by Phoenix Chamber of Commerce, December 7, 1988.

Table 8-A-3

Comparison of Sales Tax Bases Coverage for Purchases by Government and Charitable Organizations

Category	Tax Treatment in Arizona	Tax Treatment in the 44 Other States With Sales Taxes
1. Federal government	Sales by manufacturer, modifier, or assembler exempt; retail sales taxed at 2.5% rate	Exempt in some states by constitution and in others by statute; taxed only in South Carolina
2. State and local governments	Purchases taxed at 5% rate; public hospitals exempt	Taxed in 8 states
3. Charitable institutions	Purchases taxed at 5% rate; nonprofit hospitals exempt	Commonly exempt in states with consumer tax

Source: John F. Due and John L. Mikesell, *Sales Taxation: State and Local Structure and Administration* (Baltimore: The Johns Hopkins University Press, 1983). Data are for 1982.

Chapter 9

Selective Sales Taxes

Don E. Schlagenhauf

The State of Arizona selectively taxes certain transactions. These taxes are known as selective sales taxes. Purchases of tobacco products and alcoholic beverages are taxed selectively (these taxes are also called luxury taxes or sin taxes in Arizona). The State also imposes transient occupancy taxes (known as hotel/motel or bed taxes) which are treated differently from general sales taxes. Although the State of Arizona does not presently have a real estate transfer tax, this type of selective tax is frequently mentioned as a potential new revenue source and is quite common throughout the country. This chapter examines the characteristics of these four types of selective sales taxes and discusses their contribution to an overall revenue structure.

Cigarette And Tobacco Taxes

In 1933, the State of Arizona passed its first law concerning the taxation of cigarettes and tobacco products. The amount of tax collected was based on the number of cigarettes and cigars and on the ounces of other tobacco products sold. The tax was paid through the purchase of stamps that were affixed to each product package. Interestingly, this tax was intended as a temporary tax and was scheduled to expire on March 1, 1935. Needless to say, the tax has never expired.

From its beginning, collections from this tax generally have been earmarked for specific purposes rather than for supporting general governmental expenditures. At various points in time, these revenues have been dedicated to public welfare, unemployment, and school aid.

The Current Arizona Law and Interstate Comparisons

Since the passage of the first luxury tax on cigarettes and tobacco products, the rates have been modified periodically. The FY 1989-90 law establishes the following tax rates:
- 15 cents per package of 20 cigarettes;
- 2 cents per ounce on tobacco and snuff products;
- 1/2 cent per ounce on cavendish, plug or twist;

- 4 cents on each 20 of small cigars;
- 2 cents on each 3 cigars retailing at 5 cents each or less; and
- 2 cents on cigars retailing over 5 cents.

Through June 30, 1994, 50 percent of the funds collected from the tobacco products tax and 2 cents of the 15 cent cigarette tax are to be deposited into the Corrections Fund and used for the maintenance and construction of prison facilities; the remaining revenue is deposited in the State General Fund with 3.5 cents of the cigarette tax to be spent on school aid. Beginning July 1, 1994, all of the collections are scheduled to be deposited in the General Fund.

Table 9-1 presents the amount of revenue generated from cigarette and tobacco taxes for each of the past 10 years. In fiscal year 1987/88, revenue from the taxation of tobacco products was $52.4 million. The table also displays the tobacco tax revenue as a share of total General Fund revenue. Although the portion of tobacco tax revenue actually deposited into the General Fund varied from year to year, this percentage provides a useful measure to gauge the growth in tobacco tax revenue relative to the growth in the overall State budget.

Table 9-1 **Revenue from Cigarette and Tobacco Taxes in Arizona**		
Fiscal Year	**Gross Tobacco Products Revenue (in millions)**	**Gross Tobacco Products Revenue as Fraction of State General Fund (percent)**
1978/79	$37.8	3.3
1979/80	39.9	3.1
1980/81	39.7	2.9
1981/82	40.8	2.8
1982/83	40.9	2.6
1983/84	41.5	2.3
1984/85	49.5	2.3
1985/86	50.1	2.2
1986/87	51.2	2.1
1987/88	52.4	2.0
Source: State of Arizona, Department of Revenue.		

While the revenue from tobacco products has increased, the more important fact is that tobacco taxes have grown more slowly than total General Fund revenues. Tobacco taxes were equal to 3.3 percent of General Fund revenue in fiscal year 1978/79 and only 2.0 percent of General Fund revenue in FY 1987/88. The decline in the relative importance of this revenue source is due to the fact that tobacco taxes are levied on a per unit rather than *ad valorem* basis. A general sales tax is an *ad valorem* tax; revenue depends on the *price* of the good being taxed. Tobacco taxes, on the other hand, depend on the *quantity* of cigarettes sold, irrespective of price. *Ad valorem* taxes automatically respond to price changes, as prices increase so do tax collections. Per-unit taxes do not respond to price changes, so during inflationary times, policy makers must increase the tax rate frequently in order to maintain the same real tax burden. If per-unit rates are not increased, revenue will decline in relative magnitude.

Tables 9-2 and 9-3 present interstate data on the taxation of tobacco products. Table 9-2 presents the selective cigarette tax rates employed by the various states, effective May 1, 1989. The highest tax on a pack of twenty cigarettes is 38 cents in Minnesota. The lowest tax rates are in the tobacco-producing states, such as Virginia and North Carolina, where the tax rates are 2.5 and 2.0 cents per pack, respectively. Arizona, which presently imposes a 15 cent tax per pack of twenty cigarettes, is below the national average of 22 cents. Arizona's tax rates also are low relative to most of the neighboring states. On January 1, 1989, the State of California raised its tax rate from 10 cents per pack to 35 cents per pack. The tax rate in New Mexico is 15 cents per pack, Utah's is 23 cents per pack, Colorado's is 20 cents per pack, Nevada's is 20 cents per pack, and Texas' rate is 26 cents per pack.

Like most states, Arizona includes cigarettes in its general tax base in addition to imposing a selective sales tax. Arizona's general sales tax rate is average to high. Thus, the total tax burden on cigarette sales in Arizona is not quite as low as it appears from the selective tax alone.

Table 9-3 presents tobacco tax revenue data for Arizona and comparison states in selected fiscal years. As can be seen, total revenues from tobacco taxes have increased in each state since 1975. However, the fraction of state tax revenue accounted for by tobacco taxes has decreased in almost every state. In 1975, states raised an average of 4.1 percent of their tax revenue from tobacco taxes. By 1987, this average had fallen to 1.9 percent. Of course, the declining importance of tobacco taxes is due to the fact that these taxes are on a per-unit basis. Compared to the 1.9 percent average over all states, the State of Arizona generated 1.5 percent of total state tax revenue from tobacco taxes in fiscal year 1987. (It should be pointed out that the differences in the relative importance of tobacco taxes that appear in Table 9-1 and Table 9-3 are due to differences in the definition of total tax revenue in the two sources.) Thus, Arizona does not rely on this revenue source as heavily as other states.

Another way to judge the importance of tobacco taxes is to calculate measures of tax effort. Two such measures frequently used to calculate tax effort are revenue per capita and revenue as a percentage of state personal income. Both measures are presented in Table 9-3. The national average tobacco tax yield per capita rose from $15.47 in 1975 to $18.97 in 1987. In contrast, yield per capita in Arizona has declined slightly since 1975.

The U.S. average tobacco tax revenue as a share of personal income shows a decrease in total effort between 1975 and 1987. The decline in Arizona's tax effort from tobacco taxes has been even greater than the national average, falling from 0.31 percent in 1975 to 0.11 percent in 1987. In summary, the facts presented in Table 9-3 suggests that Arizona's reliance on tobacco taxes has fallen over time and is below the average of the states.

Simplicity, Efficiency and Equity Considerations

The tax on cigarettes and tobacco products is levied on licensed distributors. Distributors of cigarettes pay the tax through the purchase of tax stamps from the Department of Revenue. No cigarettes can be sold without the stamp affixed to the package. The law establishes a 2 to 4 percent discount on the stamps, depending on volume, so that the actual tax is slightly less than 15 cents per package. The Department of Revenue estimates that this discount resulted in a revenue loss of approximately $1.3 million in FY 1988. (Forty-eight other states provide similar discounts.) Distributors of cigars and other tobacco products pay the tobacco tax by filing a monthly tax return. Thus, the tax is simple and easy to administer.

Table 9-2 Tax Rates Per Pack of Twenty Cigarettes (as of May 1, 1989)			
State	**Rate**	**State**	**Rate**
Alabama	16.5¢	Montana	16¢
Alaska	29¢	Nebraska	27¢
Arizona	15¢	Nevada	20¢
Arkansas	21¢	New Hampshire	21¢
California	35¢	New Jersey	27¢
Colorado	20¢	New Mexico	15¢
Connecticut	40¢	New York	33¢
Delaware	14¢	North Carolina	02¢
Florida	24¢	North Dakota	30¢
Georgia	12¢	Ohio	18¢
Hawaii	40% of wholesale price	Oklahoma	23¢
Idaho	18¢	Oregon	27¢
Illinois	30¢	Pennsylvania	18¢
Indiana	15.5¢	Rhode Island	37¢
Iowa	30¢	South Carolina	07¢
Kansas	24¢	South Dakota	23¢
Kentucky	03¢	Tennessee	13¢
Louisiana	16¢	Texas	26¢
Maine	28¢	Utah	23¢
Maryland	13¢	Vermont	17¢
Massachusetts	26¢	Virginia	2.5¢
Michigan	25¢	Washington	34¢
Minnesota	38¢	West Virginia	17¢
Mississippi	18¢	Wisconsin	30¢
Missouri	13¢	Wyoming	12¢
U. S. Average 22¢			
Source: Tobacco Merchants Association of the U.S., Inc., Princeton, New Jersey.			

In a perfectly competitive world, marginal rates of substitution and marginal rates of transformation among all commodities are equal. As a result, resources will be used optimally. Imposing a tax on selective sales changes relative prices between goods and, thus, may alter purchasing decisions and result in consumer benefits and/or economic profits being lost. To minimize these inefficient changes in behavior, taxes should be imposed on goods with inelastic demands or supplies. Houthakker and Taylor (1970) estimate the long-run price elasticity of demand for cigarettes in the United States to be -0.35. In other words, a 10 percent increase in the price of cigarettes would lead to a 3.5 percent decrease in consumption. Because the percentage change in consumption is considerably less than the percentage change in price, the taxation of cigarettes satisfies this efficiency criterion.

<table>
<tr><td colspan="5" align="center">Table 9-3
State Tobacco Tax Revenue and Tax Effort
Fiscal Years 1975 and 1987</td></tr>
<tr><td colspan="5" align="center">1975</td></tr>
<tr><td></td><td align="center">Tobacco Tax
(in millions)</td><td align="center">Tobacco
Revenue as
Percent of
Total State
Tax Revenue</td><td align="center">Tobacco Tax
Revenue Per
Capita</td><td align="center">Tobacco Tax
Revenue as
Percent of
Personal In-
come</td></tr>
<tr><td>Arizona</td><td align="center">$ 34.2</td><td align="center">3.6</td><td align="center">$15.37</td><td align="center">0.31</td></tr>
<tr><td>California</td><td align="center">253.1</td><td align="center">2.6</td><td align="center">11.75</td><td align="center">0.17</td></tr>
<tr><td>Colorado</td><td align="center">31.4</td><td align="center">3.6</td><td align="center">12.14</td><td align="center">0.19</td></tr>
<tr><td>Nevada</td><td align="center">11.3</td><td align="center">4.2</td><td align="center">18.23</td><td align="center">0.27</td></tr>
<tr><td>New Mexico</td><td align="center">13.4</td><td align="center">2.6</td><td align="center">11.52</td><td align="center">0.23</td></tr>
<tr><td>Utah</td><td align="center">7.0</td><td align="center">1.7</td><td align="center">5.67</td><td align="center">0.11</td></tr>
<tr><td>U.S. Average</td><td></td><td align="center">4.1</td><td align="center">$15.47</td><td align="center">0.29</td></tr>
<tr><td colspan="5" align="center">1987</td></tr>
<tr><td></td><td align="center">Tobacco Tax
(in millions)</td><td align="center">Tobacco
Revenue as
Percent of
Total State
Tax Revenue</td><td align="center">Tobacco Tax
Revenue Per
Capita</td><td align="center">Tobacco Tax
Revenue as
Percent of
Personal In-
come</td></tr>
<tr><td>Arizona</td><td align="center">$ 51.2</td><td align="center">1.5</td><td align="center">$15.13</td><td align="center">0.11</td></tr>
<tr><td>California</td><td align="center">268.3</td><td align="center">0.7</td><td align="center">9.69</td><td align="center">0.05</td></tr>
<tr><td>Colorado</td><td align="center">80.2</td><td align="center">3.1</td><td align="center">24.33</td><td align="center">0.16</td></tr>
<tr><td>Nevada</td><td align="center">21.1</td><td align="center">1.9</td><td align="center">20.95</td><td align="center">0.13</td></tr>
<tr><td>New Mexico</td><td align="center">18.6</td><td align="center">1.2</td><td align="center">12.40</td><td align="center">0.10</td></tr>
<tr><td>Utah</td><td align="center">15.9</td><td align="center">1.1</td><td align="center">10.49</td><td align="center">0.08</td></tr>
<tr><td>U.S. Average</td><td></td><td align="center">1.9</td><td align="center">$18.97</td><td align="center">0.13</td></tr>
<tr><td colspan="5">Source: U.S. Bureau of Census, State Tax Collections 1987 (GF87, No. 1) and earlier volumes.</td></tr>
</table>

If perfect competition does not hold, then an optimal allocation of resources may not occur and taxes can be imposed to improve the allocation of resources. Differences in the competitive structure of industries, external economies in the production and use of some commodities, or external diseconomies in the production or use of commodities all can result in a nonoptimal allocation of resources. The consumption of tobacco products creates external costs that are not included in the price of the products. Individual smokers may not fully realize the harm that smoking does to themselves and others. The link between cigarette smoking and lung cancer has now been well established. There is growing evidence that second-hand smoke is harmful to non-smokers.

This means future medical costs are higher for the smoking individual and for society. Without government intervention in the market, the prices of these products are too low and consumption is too great because users are not paying all the costs associated with the use of the product. By imposing a tax, the government can force consumers to pay the costs they are imposing on society.

Of course efficiency is not the only relevant criterion for evaluating taxes. Cigarette taxes must also be evaluated on equity grounds. The tax on tobacco products is legally imposed on the distributor, but because the demand for these products is insensitive to price, the major portion of the tax is shifted to the consumer. Vertical equity can be evaluated under the assumption that the consumer bears the full burden of the tax.

The central vertical equity issue is how much consumers at different income levels pay in taxes. Unfortunately, detailed family expenditure patterns are not available specifically for Arizona. The Bureau of Labor Statistics assembles such data for the United States and publishes these statistics in the *Consumer Expenditure Survey*. This analysis examines expenditure patterns for the entire United States under the assumption that the expenditure patterns in the United States do not vary greatly from the expenditure patterns in Arizona. Table 9-4 presents the percentage of income spent on tobacco products for households of various income levels. The data show that low-income families spend a higher percentage of their income on tobacco products. Families with incomes between $5,000 and $9,999 spend approximately 2.5 percent of their income on tobacco products, while families with incomes over $40,000 spend 0.4 percent of their income on tobacco products. Because the percent of income spent on tobacco products decreases as income rises, tobacco taxes are regressive.

<table>
<tr><td colspan="4" align="center">Table 9-4
Family Income and Consumption of Tobacco Products</td></tr>
<tr><td align="center">Family
Income Class</td><td align="center">Average Income
Before Taxes</td><td align="center">Tobacco
Product
Expenditures</td><td align="center">Tobacco
Expenditures
as Percentage of
Average Income</td></tr>
<tr><td>$ 5,000 - 9,999</td><td align="right">$ 7,388</td><td align="right">$188</td><td align="right">2.5</td></tr>
<tr><td>10,000 - 14,999</td><td align="right">12,426</td><td align="right">241</td><td align="right">1.9</td></tr>
<tr><td>15,000 - 19,999</td><td align="right">17,341</td><td align="right">228</td><td align="right">1.3</td></tr>
<tr><td>20,000 - 29,999</td><td align="right">24,676</td><td align="right">257</td><td align="right">1.0</td></tr>
<tr><td>30,000 - 39,999</td><td align="right">34,283</td><td align="right">270</td><td align="right">0.7</td></tr>
<tr><td>40,000 and above</td><td align="right">61,693</td><td align="right">270</td><td align="right">0.4</td></tr>
<tr><td colspan="4">Source: Bureau of Labor Statistics, Consumer Expenditure Survey, 1986.</td></tr>
</table>

The extent of regressivity over all income classes can be measured with a regressivity index. One such index is the ratio of the burden for households with incomes between $5,000 and $9,999 to that for households with incomes above $40,000. This calculation results in an index of 6.25 for tobacco products meaning that low income households bear a tax burden that is more than six times as high as the burden on high income households. By this measure, the tax on tobacco products is regressive.

Revenue Responsiveness and Revenue Stability

When evaluating a fiscal system, it is important to know how revenue responds to changes in income. From a long-run point of view, it is preferable to have a revenue source that grows to match the growth in the state's economy and desired growth in expenditures. We have already seen that tobacco product taxes tend to decline in importance over time unless the tax rate is repeatedly increased to keep up with inflation.

The income elasticity of a tax measures its sensitivity to changes in income. An accurate measure of an income elasticity cannot be based on revenue data because changes in revenue could be due to changes in tax rates as well as changes in the quantity of cigarettes purchased. Therefore, the more accurate measure is the sensitivity of the quantity of cigarettes purchased to changes in income. A regression equation can be used to estimate the relationship between annual percentage changes in the quantities of cigarettes purchased in Arizona and annual percentage changes in State personal income. The results indicate that a 1 percent increase in real income leads to only a 0.73 percent increase in the quantity of cigarettes sold. Because consumption rises more slowly than real income, tobacco tax collections will not grow as fast as income even if the rates are continually adjusted for inflation. This means that tobacco taxes are relatively unresponsive to economic growth.

One way to measure the stability of a tax source is to examine how much actual collections vary each quarter from the long-term trend. Large deviations from the trend suggest a volatile or unstable revenue source. For quarterly tobacco tax revenues adjusted for tax rate changes in Arizona over the period 1970:III through 1988:III, the average deviation from the trend is only 0.44 percent which is substantially smaller than the same statistic for the personal income tax. This finding suggests that the tobacco tax is a very stable revenue source. This result is not surprising because taxes with lower income elasticities (less responsiveness) are more stable.

Because Arizona's cigarette tax rate is now more than 25 percent below the average, raising the rate appears to be a reasonable option. Indeed, raising the rate will help make up for the past erosion of tobacco tax revenues due to inflation.

Policy Issues

Selective tobacco taxes are normally a per-unit tax. Tradition and administrative necessity are often given as reasons why a per-unit rather than an *ad valorem* tax is employed. In 1989, Hawaii was the only state that exclusively used an *ad valorem* tax on tobacco. In fact, *ad valorem* sales taxes on tobacco are probably just as easy to administer especially given the current prevalence of computerization. Hawaii reports no significant administrative problems with its *ad valorem* tax at the wholesale level. Arizona and most other states already impose general sales taxes on cigarettes at the retail level; so, an *ad valorem* selective tax at the retail level would not increase administrative costs significantly. (Administrative costs may actually decrease as the need for issuing stamps would be eliminated.) An *ad valorem* tax would prevent inflation-induced erosion of revenue over time. Tobacco products could still be treated selectively by adjusting the tax rate to any level desired.

In order to stress the inflation-induced erosion that occurs with a per-unit tax, the effective tax rate of the per-unit tax in fiscal year 1980/81 is calculated. Given an estimated price of $1.08 per pack (including general sales tax) and a per-unit selective tax of 13 cents, the effective selective *ad valorem* tax rate was approximately 12 percent (0.13/1.08). Using this tax rate for subsequent fiscal years, an estimate of revenue from an *ad valorem* tax can be calculated. As shown in Table 9-5, revenue from this type of tax exceeds revenue from a per-unit tax in each fiscal year. (Note that the revenue displayed from the 12 percent tax does *not* include revenue from the general sales tax.)

Table 9-5 **Revenue Comparisons Between** **Per-Unit and *Ad Valorem* Tobacco Tax**				
Fiscal Year	**Actual Tobacco Revenue (in millions)**	**Millions of Packs Sold**	**Price per Pack**[*]	**Hypothetical Revenue with 12% *ad valorem* tax**
1980/81	$39.7	305.7	$1.08	$39.6
1981/82	40.8	313.6	1.15	43.3
1982/83	40.9	314.6	1.20	45.3
1983/84	41.5	323.9	1.24	48.2
1984/85	49.5	331.7	1.26	50.2
1985/86	50.8	335.7	1.32	53.2
1986/87	51.2	338.8	1.37	55.7
1987/88	52.4	346.6	1.40	58.2

[*] Price includes general sales tax but excludes the selective sales tax. Prices are based on a local survey of 1988 prices and the national consumer price index for cigarettes published by the U.S. Bureau of Labor Statistics.

For instance, in fiscal year 1987/88 the taxation of tobacco products generated revenue of $52.4 million. A 12 percent *ad valorem* tax is estimated to generate an additional $5.8 million in revenue. There was, however, a 2 cent per package tax increase effective in FY 1984/85. If the tax had remained 13 cents per package, it would have generated only $45.1 million in FY 1987/88. Thus by FY 1988, the *ad valorem* tax at a constant rate would have generated $13.1 million more than the per-unit tax at a constant rate. This estimate should be considered an upper bound as no allowance for a decline in consumption due to a price response or movement of purchases to a lower tax area (*e.g.*, an Indian Reservation) is considered.

Alcoholic Beverage Taxation

The same year that a tax on tobacco products was imposed in Arizona a "temporary" tax on alcoholic beverages was passed. The tax rates were different for malt extracts, spirituous liquor, and vinous liquor and were based on the number of gallons sold.

Like the tobacco tax collections, revenues from the tax on alcoholic beverages historically have been earmarked for specific purposes such as public welfare, unemployment benefits, and state aid to schools.

The Current Arizona Law and Interstate Comparisons

As with the tax on tobacco products, the temporary tax on alcoholic beverages was extended and made permanent in 1935. Since that time there have been numerous revisions in the tax structure. The current tax rates on alcoholic beverages are:

- $3.00 on each gallon of spirituous liquor, with a proportionate rate for greater or lesser quantities;
- 25 cents on each container of eight ounces or less of vinous liquor having an alcoholic content greater than 24 percent. Containers exceeding eight ounces are taxed at a rate of 25 cents per eight ounces;
- 84 cents per gallon for vinous liquor having an alcohol content of 24 percent or less with a proportionate rate for greater or lesser quantities; and
- 16 cents on each gallon of malt liquor with a proportionate rate for greater or lesser quantities.

Currently 3.5 cents of the tax on spirituous liquor and 3.5 cents of the tax on vinous liquor with more than 24 percent alcohol content are dedicated to state school aid (approximately 1.2 percent and 14 percent of the taxes respectively). Twenty percent of the spirituous liquor tax and 50 percent of all other liquor taxes are deposited into the Corrections Fund for prison maintenance and construction. The remainder is deposited into the General Fund for general governmental purposes.

Table 9-6 presents the amount of revenue generated by this tax since fiscal year 1979/80. In addition, total collections are shown relative to total General Fund revenue. (Note that the total collections amount was not deposited into the General Fund, but the measure is used here to illustrate the magnitude of liquor tax collections relative to the size of the State budget.) In fiscal year 1987/88, revenue from the taxation of alcoholic beverages totaled $40.9 million. Of the three types of alcoholic products, the smallest source of revenue is wine which accounts for approximately 19 percent of the total alcohol tax collections. The taxation of malt products and spirits account for 38 and 42 percent, respectively, of alcohol tax revenues. Although revenue from this source has increased, alcoholic beverage taxes as a share of General Fund revenues have fallen from 1.7 percent in 1979/80 to 1.5 percent in 1987/88. In fact, if the tax rates had not been increased in FY 1984/85, the revenue from alcoholic beverage taxes would have fallen even more relative to total General Fund revenues. One explanation for the diminished importance of alcohol taxes is the fact that, like tobacco taxes, they are on a per-unit basis.

<table>
<tr>
<td colspan="7">Table 9-6
Revenue from Alcohol Taxes in Arizona
(In thousands of dollars and percentages)</td>
</tr>
<tr>
<td>Fiscal
Year</td>
<td>Revenue
from
Spirit.
Liquor</td>
<td>Fraction
of General
Fund
Revenue
(percent)</td>
<td>Revenue
from
Vinous
Liquor</td>
<td>Fraction
of General
Fund
Revenue
(percent)</td>
<td>Revenue
from Malt
Liquor</td>
<td>Fraction
of General
Fund
Revenue
(percent)</td>
</tr>
<tr><td>1979/80</td><td>$13,227.2</td><td>1.0</td><td>$2,480.9</td><td>0.2</td><td>$ 6,386.7</td><td>0.5</td></tr>
<tr><td>1980/81</td><td>13,593.5</td><td>1.0</td><td>2,632.7</td><td>0.2</td><td>6,574.8</td><td>0.5</td></tr>
<tr><td>1981/82</td><td>13,482.0</td><td>0.9</td><td>2,967.2</td><td>0.2</td><td>6,891.2</td><td>0.5</td></tr>
<tr><td>1982/83</td><td>13,891.0</td><td>0.9</td><td>3,008.5</td><td>0.2</td><td>6,813.1</td><td>0.4</td></tr>
<tr><td>1983/84</td><td>14,600.1</td><td>0.8</td><td>3,663.6</td><td>0.2</td><td>7,235.4</td><td>0.4</td></tr>
<tr><td>1984/85</td><td>17,049.4</td><td>0.8</td><td>6,785.0</td><td>0.3</td><td>14,102.9</td><td>0.7</td></tr>
<tr><td>1985/86</td><td>18,034.7</td><td>0.8</td><td>7,563.3</td><td>0.3</td><td>15,250.8</td><td>0.7</td></tr>
<tr><td>1986/87</td><td>17,059.1</td><td>0.7</td><td>7,832.6</td><td>0.3</td><td>15,927.2</td><td>0.6</td></tr>
<tr><td>1987/88</td><td>17,287.3</td><td>0.6</td><td>7,901.9</td><td>0.3</td><td>15,705.7</td><td>0.6</td></tr>
<tr><td colspan="7">Source: State of Arizona, Department of Revenue.</td></tr>
</table>

The alcoholic beverage taxes in neighboring states and in Arizona are presented in Table 9-7. Comparisons are difficult because of the variety of tax approaches employed. Some states sell alcoholic products directly through state liquor stores. These states are known as control states. Arizona is not a control state. Hence, most comparisons that are made in the following discussion will be with respect to noncontrol states only. The table illustrates that Arizona's tax rate on beer is at the high end of the neighboring states. The national average tax rate on beer, however, is approximately 19 cents per gallon; so, Arizona's rate of 16 cents per gallon is somewhat lower than average. In Alaska, Florida, Georgia, Hawaii, Louisiana, Oklahoma, South Carolina and Utah, the tax is over 30 cents per gallon.

The calculation of an average tax rate for either spirituous or vinous liquor is much more complicated because the tax is dependent on alcoholic content. The U.S. average tax on vinous products with less than 24 percent alcohol is 63 cents per gallon. Arizona imposes a tax of 84 cents per gallon, 33 percent above average. Again, Arizona is at the high end of the rate scale compared to neighboring states. Florida and Georgia have the highest tax on these products. California imposes a tax of only one cent per gallon; the low rate no doubt being related to the fact that the state is a large wine producer. The U.S. average tax for spirituous products, based on alcoholic content less than 15 percent, is $2.83 per gallon. Here again, Arizona's tax rate of $3.00 per gallon is slightly above average and above most of the neighboring states. Three states (Alaska, Hawaii, and Minnesota) impose a tax of over $5.00 per gallon.

Table 9-8 presents revenue data by state for selected fiscal years. As shown, total revenue from alcoholic beverage taxes has increased in each state since 1975. However, the fraction of total state tax revenue accounted for by this tax has decreased in almost every state.   In 1975, states on average raised 2.4 percent of their tax revenue from taxes on alcoholic products. However, by 1987 this average had fallen to 1.3 percent of total taxes, reflecting the per-unit nature of these taxes.

<table>
<tr><td colspan="5">Table 9-7
A Comparison of State Alcohol Tax Rates
(as of July, 1987)</td></tr>
<tr><td>State</td><td>Control State</td><td>Beer (Over 3.2%)</td><td>Wine</td><td>Spirits</td></tr>
<tr><td>Arizona</td><td>No</td><td>$0.16/gal</td><td>$0.84/gal ≤ 24%
$2.00/gal > 24%</td><td>$3.00/gal</td></tr>
<tr><td>California</td><td>No</td><td>$0.04/gal</td><td>$0.01/gal ≤ 14%

$0.02/gal > 14%</td><td>$2.00/gal proof strength or less
$4.00/gal above proof strength</td></tr>
<tr><td>Colorado</td><td>No</td><td>$0.08/gal</td><td>$0.28/gal</td><td>$2.28/gal</td></tr>
<tr><td>Nevada</td><td>No</td><td>$0.09/gal</td><td>$0.40/gal ≤ 14%
$0.75/gal 14-22%
$2.95/gal > 22%</td><td>$2.05/gal</td></tr>
<tr><td>New Mexico</td><td>No</td><td>$0.18/gal</td><td>$0.95/gal</td><td>$3.94/gal</td></tr>
<tr><td>Utah</td><td>No</td><td>$0.355/gal
68.5% state store markup</td><td>$0.17/gal ≤ 14%
$0.67/gal 14-21%
$2.25/gal 21-24%</td><td>$12.50/proof gal
103% markup</td></tr>
<tr><td colspan="5">Source: Commerce Clearing House, State Tax Guide.</td></tr>
</table>

In 1987, Arizona collected $12.06 per capita from liquor taxes, compared to the U.S. average of $12.73 per capita.   Another measure of tax effort is tax revenue as a percentage of state personal income.   Both Arizona and the average for all states show a *decrease* in tax effort between 1975 and 1987, again indicating the erosion of per-unit tax revenues over time.

<u>Simplicity, Efficiency and Equity Considerations</u>

Liquor wholesalers (and domestic farm wineries and domestic microbreweries) pay the alcohol tax through monthly returns filed with the Department of Revenue (DOR). Distillers and manufacturers who sell alcoholic products to wholesalers in Arizona are required to send copies of their sales invoices to the DOR.   This provides the Department a simple means with which to audit the taxes paid by wholesalers.   Thus, the tax is very simple and easy to administer.

Table 9-8
State Alcoholic Beverage (Liquor) Tax Revenue and Tax Effort
Fiscal Years 1975 and 1987

1975

State	Liquor Tax Revenue (in millions)	Liquor Tax as Percent of State Tax Revenue	Liquor Tax Revenue Per Capita	Liquor Tax Revenue as Percent of Personal Income
Arizona	$ 15.9	1.7	$ 7.16	0.14
California	120.7	1.3	5.60	0.08
Colorado	15.7	1.8	6.07	0.09
Nevada	8.9	3.3	14.35	0.21
New Mexico	6.4	1.2	5.50	0.11
Utah	4.3	1.1	3.48	0.07
U.S. Average		2.4	9.22	0.17

1987

State	Liquor Tax Revenue (in millions)	Liquor Tax as Percent of State Tax Revenue	Liquor Tax Revenue Per Capita	Liquor Tax Revenue as Percent of Personal Income
Arizona	$ 40.8	1.2	$12.06	0.09
California	131.3	0.4	4.75	0.03
Colorado	23.2	0.9	7.04	0.05
Nevada	13.3	1.2	13.21	0.08
New Mexico	17.5	1.1	11.67	0.10
Utah	16.7	1.2	9.64	0.09
U.S. Average		1.3	12.73	0.09

Source: U.S. Bureau of Census, *State Tax Collections 1987* (GF87, No. 1) and earlier
volumes.

In the discussion of the efficiency of cigarette taxes, it was pointed out that to enhance efficiency, taxes should be imposed on goods with unresponsive demands or supplies. Browning and Browning (1989) report that the long-run price elasticity of demand for beer is between -0.7 and -0.9. This indicates that alcohol consumption is not very sensitive to changes in price although it is more sensitive than tobacco consumption.

Like cigarette smoking, the consumption of alcoholic products creates internal costs to the consumer and external costs to society that are not fully considered in the market decision process. Internal costs to the consumer include increased medical expenses, lost income, increased health and automobile insurance premiums, and emotional and physical stress. The costs to society range from injury to others to damage to property. Harwood, Napolitano, Kristiansen and Collins (1984) estimate these costs nationally at $116.7 billion in 1983. The study identifies the main costs as alcohol-related treatment and support, deaths, reduced productivity, motor vehicle crashes, and crime. Thus, taxing liquor may enhance efficiency by making the product prices better reflect the costs imposed on society.

There is one efficiency issue that is relevant to the taxation of alcoholic products that was not relevant to the taxation of tobacco products. The State of Arizona imposes different per-unit tax rates on beer, wine and hard liquor. If the per-unit taxes are expressed as effective tax rates, they can be evaluated to see if a bias is introduced that can influence the consumption of these commodities. In order to calculate the effective tax rates, an estimate of the net-of-tax price for each of these products is required. Prices at various convenience stores in Phoenix and Tempe were sampled in an ad hoc manner in February, 1989. These average prices should be considered as illustrative. The net-of-tax price of beer, wine, and hard liquor per gallon was $5.64, $8.00, and $45.17, respectively. Using the price of beer and the current per-unit tax of 16 cents per gallon, the effective tax rate is 2.8 percent. The effective tax rate on wine is 10.5 percent, while the tax rate on spirituous products is 6.6 percent. The range in effective tax rates means the current tax structure on alcoholic products encourages beer consumption relative to wine and hard liquor consumption.

Liquor taxes are often criticized based on equity considerations. The following discussion of equity assumes alcohol taxes are paid by the consumer. Table 9-9 presents the percentage of income spent on alcoholic products by income class. The data for this table are national values from the 1986 *Consumer Expenditure Survey*. It is assumed that expenditure patterns for the United States are representative of Arizona expenditure patterns. Low-income families spend the highest percentage of their income on alcoholic products. Families with incomes between $5,000 and $9,999 spend approximately 1.8 percent of their income on these products, while families with incomes over $40,000 spend 0.7 percent of their income on alcoholic beverages. An examination of other income classes indicates that the fraction of income allocated to alcoholic products declines as income increases. This finding suggests that alcohol taxes are regressive. Calculation of a regressivity index (the ratio of tax burdens in the $5,000-$9,999 income category to the over $40,000 category) yields a regressivity index of 2.57 meaning that low income households pay over twice as large a fraction of their incomes in alcohol taxes as high income households.

Calculation of a second regressivity index further supports the argument that this tax is regressive. The regressivity index is calculated by regressing the natural log of the amount of alcoholic expenditures on the natural log of average family income by class. The index equals 0.566. Hence, a family with income one percent higher than another family would bear a tax burden higher by only 0.566 percent.

Recently there has been criticism of this traditional approach to determining the regressivity of a tax. Poterba (1990) has argued that the burden of a tax should not be based on income at a point in time but rather on income over a lifetime. The reasoning is that families move in and out of income classes over a lifetime. He argues if a measure of lifetime income is employed, federal excise taxes on alcoholic products appear to be roughly proportional. This criticism is important as it lessens the impact of equity considerations with taxation of these products.

<table>
<tr><td colspan="4" align="center">Table 9-9
Family Income and Consumption of Alcoholic Products</td></tr>
<tr><td align="center">Family
Income Class</td><td align="center">Average Income
Before Taxes</td><td align="center">Alcoholic
Product
Expenditures</td><td align="center">Fraction of
Income Allocated to
Alcoholic Products</td></tr>
<tr><td>$ 5,000 - 9,999</td><td align="right">$ 7,388</td><td align="right">$133</td><td align="right">1.8</td></tr>
<tr><td>10,000 - 14,999</td><td align="right">12,426</td><td align="right">181</td><td align="right">1.4</td></tr>
<tr><td>15,000 - 19,999</td><td align="right">17,341</td><td align="right">223</td><td align="right">1.3</td></tr>
<tr><td>20,000 - 29,999</td><td align="right">24,676</td><td align="right">303</td><td align="right">1.2</td></tr>
<tr><td>30,000 - 39,999</td><td align="right">34,283</td><td align="right">327</td><td align="right">0.9</td></tr>
<tr><td>40,000 and above</td><td align="right">61,693</td><td align="right">491</td><td align="right">0.7</td></tr>
<tr><td colspan="4">Source: Bureau of Labor Statistics, Consumer Expenditure Survey, 1986.</td></tr>
</table>

Revenue Responsiveness and Stability

As discussed previously, revenue from the alcohol tax declines over time relative to other revenue sources because it is a per-unit tax and does not automatically increase with inflation. It is also useful to know whether the *tax base*, the quantity of alcohol sold, increases proportionate to personal income. Using statistical regression techniques, the real income elasticity is estimated to be less than one for all three alcohol product groups subject to the tax. For wine, a ten-percent increase in income will result in an 8.7 percent increase in gallons sold. A ten percent increase in income will yield a 7.1 percent increase in gallons of beer sold, and a 7.3 percent increase in gallons of spirits. The fact that consumption does not grow proportionate to income for any of the alcohol products means that even if tax rates were adjusted for inflation, revenues would not grow as fast as state personal income, making alcohol taxes relatively unresponsive.

The cyclical characteristics of a tax can be measured by examining the quarterly deviations of collections from the long-term trend. For each alcoholic beverage, a summary statistic can be generated that reflects the extent of deviations from the trend. A large value of this measure indicates a cyclical or unstable revenue source. The average absolute percentage deviation from trend for malt beverages is 0.82 percent while the values of this measure for vinous and spirituous alcohol are 1.28 and 1.23 percent, respectively. All three values are small indicating that alcohol consumption is a relatively stable tax source.

Policy Issues

In this section, an estimate of the revenue increase that can be generated from a per-unit tax increase is presented. In addition, the revenue potential of an *ad valorem* alcoholic beverage tax is discussed.

In order to analyze the revenue change that would result from an increase in the taxation of alcoholic products, a per-unit tax increase has to be assumed for each product. The tax on beer is assumed to increase to 20 cents per gallon from 16 cents, the tax on vinous products is increased to $1.05 per gallon from $0.84, and the tax on spirituous liquor is increased to $3.75 per gallon from $3.00. The tax increase on each product is equal to 25 percent. If the quantity of each product sold in fiscal year 1987/88 remained unchanged, the taxation of malt liquor would generate an additional $3.9 million in revenue. The tax increase on vinous products would generate an additional $2.0 million in revenue, while the tax increase on spirituous products would generate an additional $4.3 million.

Of course, the actual additional revenue that would be collected from such a tax increase would not be at the stated amount. The reason is that the tax increase will result in higher prices which will cause a decrease in consumption of these products. The amount of the consumption decline depends on the price elasticity. Since a price elasticity measure exists only for beer, the price elasticity for each beverage will be assumed to be the same and equal to -0.8. Hence, a twenty-five percent price increase will reduce quantity demanded by twenty percent. This means the tax increase would generate an additional $3.1 million in revenue from beer, $1.6 million from vinous products and $3.5 million from spirituous products. In total, the assumed per-unit tax increase of 25 percent would generate an additional $8.2 million.

The State of Arizona imposes a per-unit tax on alcoholic beverages. An *ad valorem* tax would avoid some of the inflation-induced erosion of revenue that occurs with a per-unit tax. To illustrate the revenue potential that such a taxing approach would have for Arizona, the revenue that would have been generated if an *ad valorem* tax on alcoholic beverages was enacted in fiscal year 1980/81 is calculated. In order to construct such estimates, a number of assumptions are required. An *ad valorem* tax depends on the price of the various alcoholic products. Historical prices for beer, wine, and hard liquor are not readily available for Arizona. A price index for alcoholic beverages does exist in the *CITIBASE* data tape for the entire United States. If one assumes that the behavior of beer, wine, and spirituous prices are the same as the behavior of prices implied by the price index and that the average price of a gallon of beer, wine, and hard liquor in fiscal year 1987/88 is $5.80, $8.84, and $45.17, respectively, price series can be generated. Average net-of-tax series can be calculated by subtracting the appropriate per-unit tax. The number of gallons of each product sold can be calculated from revenue data given the tax rate. These data are presented in Table 9-10.

To estimate the amount of revenue from an *ad valorem* tax, a tax rate must be assumed. The value of the tax that is instituted is assumed to equal the effective tax rate that actually existed in fiscal year 1985/86, the last year the tax was increased. The effective tax rate on beer is assumed to be 3.0 percent while the effective tax on wine and spirits is 11.11 and 7.01 percent, respectively. As can be seen, revenue from an *ad valorem* tax would exceed revenue from a per-unit tax in each fiscal year. For instance, in fiscal year 1987/88, the per-unit taxation of alcoholic products (less license fees) generated $40.87 million of revenue. An *ad valorem* tax is estimated to generate $43.3 million in revenue. In other words, an additional $2.5 million in revenue would have been generated by this type of tax. This estimate should be considered an upper bound as no allowance for a decline in consumption due to higher prices is considered.

<table>
<tr><td colspan="6" align="center">Table 9-10
Revenue From an Ad Valorem Tax on Alcoholic Products
(in thousands of dollars)</td></tr>
<tr>
<td align="center">Fiscal
Year</td>
<td align="center">Actual
Revenue</td>
<td align="center">Quantity
Sold
(gallons)</td>
<td align="center">Price</td>
<td align="center">Price
Less Tax</td>
<td align="center">Revenue from
Ad Valorem
Tax</td>
</tr>
<tr><td colspan="6" align="center">A. Malt Liquor (Ad Valorem Tax of 3%)</td></tr>
<tr><td>1985/86</td><td>$15,250.8</td><td>95,316.9</td><td>$5.51</td><td>$5.35</td><td>$15,250.8</td></tr>
<tr><td>1986/87</td><td>15,927.2</td><td>99,511.1</td><td>5.67</td><td>5.51</td><td>16,449.2</td></tr>
<tr><td>1987/88</td><td>15,705.7</td><td>98,157.0</td><td>5.80</td><td>5.64</td><td>16,608.2</td></tr>
<tr><td colspan="6" align="center">B. Vinous Liquor (Ad Valorem Tax of 11.11%)</td></tr>
<tr><td>1985/86</td><td>$7,563.3</td><td>9,003.81</td><td>$8.40</td><td>$7.56</td><td>$7,563.3</td></tr>
<tr><td>1986/87</td><td>7,563.3</td><td>9,324.40</td><td>8.64</td><td>7.80</td><td>8,080.3</td></tr>
<tr><td>1987/88</td><td>7,901.9</td><td>9,478.69</td><td>8.84</td><td>8.00</td><td>8,424.6</td></tr>
<tr><td colspan="6" align="center">C. Spiritous Liquor (Ad Valorem Tax of 7.01%)</td></tr>
<tr><td>1985/86</td><td>$18,034.7</td><td>6,012.25</td><td>$45.78</td><td>$42.78</td><td>$18,034.7</td></tr>
<tr><td>1986/87</td><td>17,059.1</td><td>5,686.36</td><td>47.06</td><td>44.06</td><td>17,562.9</td></tr>
<tr><td>1987/88</td><td>17,287.3</td><td>5,762.46</td><td>48.17</td><td>45.17</td><td>18,246.4</td></tr>
<tr><td colspan="6">Source: Commerce Clearing House, State Tax Guide.</td></tr>
</table>

Transient Occupancy Taxes

States with a relatively large tourism industry often look to the tourist as a revenue source. Hotel/motel taxes or bed taxes are largely paid by nonresidents. This makes them quite attractive because they provide a way to finance public services without burdening the state's residents (and voters). A bed tax is based on the price of a room that is rented for some temporary period.

<u>Arizona Law and Interstate Comparisons</u>

Effective June 1, 1984, the State of Arizona imposed a transient occupancy tax. The tax rate was set at 4 percent. In contrast to other states that often earmark revenue from bed taxes to tourism advertising or tourism-enhancing development projects, the revenue from this Arizona tax was originally treated like general sales tax revenue and split between cities, counties and the State General Fund according to the sales tax distribution formula set in state statute. Effective July 31, 1988, the transient occupancy tax rate was increased to 5.5 percent. At that time, an annual appropriation of $2 million from state sales tax collections was dedicated to a newly created Tourism Fund.

In Table 9-11, the revenue collected from this tax is presented. The tax raised $15.5 million in the first fiscal year it took effect. In fiscal year 1987/1988 the transient occupancy tax generated $28.5 million in revenue.

<table>
<tr><td colspan="3">Table 9-11
Revenue from the Transient Occupancy Tax</td></tr>
<tr><td>Fiscal Year</td><td>Revenue Collected
(in thousands)</td><td>Tax Rate
(Percent)</td></tr>
<tr><td>1984/85</td><td>$15,454.5</td><td>4</td></tr>
<tr><td>1985/86</td><td>21,098.3</td><td>4</td></tr>
<tr><td>1986/87</td><td>25,271.2</td><td>4</td></tr>
<tr><td>1987/88</td><td>28,470.9</td><td>4</td></tr>
<tr><td colspan="3">Source: The State of Arizona, Department of Revenue.</td></tr>
</table>

The tourism industry frequently argues that a hotel/motel tax is bad for business. Although this issue will be considered in more detail later, one way to address it is to see how the transient occupancy tax in Arizona compares with the tax imposed in other states. Simply comparing state tax rates is not the correct approach to determine the total tax burden on a tourist, because city governments as well as county authorities may also impose transient occupancy taxes. Hence, to determine whether a state's tax burden is low relative to another state, the total state and local tax rate imposed must be calculated.

In Table 9-12, total transient occupancy tax rates for various cities in Arizona and selected other cities are presented. Cities in other states that are viewed as Arizona's competitors for the tourist dollar are included in the sample. In Arizona, cities have the option to impose a transient occupancy tax and counties may impose the tax as part of the sales tax for freeway construction. Twenty-eight cities in Arizona impose a lodging tax with varying tax rates. As of this time, the only county to impose any tax on transient occupancy is Maricopa County (which includes the Phoenix metropolitan area). Lodging in Maricopa County is subject to a 0.55 percent tax which is earmarked for highway development. Hence, the total transient occupancy tax varies from a high rate of 10.50 percent in the City of Sedona to 7.05 percent in the City of Mesa.

As shown, total state and local tax rates vary substantially. In California and New Mexico, the transient occupancy tax is solely a city tax with tax rates varying from 11.5 percent in the City of Los Angeles to 5.0 percent in the City of Albuquerque. The highest total tax rates are in the State of Texas where the state rate alone is 6.0 percent. In Dallas and San Antonio the current tax rate is 13.0 percent while Houston has a total rate of 14.0 percent. Of the cities included in this sample, the lowest tax rates occur in Albuquerque, Las Vegas, Reno, and Salt Lake City. The relatively low transient occupancy taxes in the Nevada cities are understandable when considered in conjunction with the gaming tax. A comparison of the tax rates presented in Table 9-12 indicates that the bed tax rates imposed in Arizona's cities are near the average and are not far out of line with rates in other cities competing for tourism business.

<table>
<tr><td colspan="6" align="center">Table 9-12
A Comparison of Transient Occupancy
Tax Rates in Selected Cities in 1988
(In Percentages)</td></tr>
<tr><td>State</td><td>City</td><td>State Tax</td><td>City Tax</td><td>County Tax</td><td>Total Tax</td></tr>
<tr><td>Arizona</td><td>Glendale</td><td>5.5</td><td>3.0</td><td>0.55</td><td>9.05</td></tr>
<tr><td></td><td>Mesa</td><td>5.5</td><td>1.0[1]</td><td>0.55</td><td>7.05</td></tr>
<tr><td></td><td>Paradise Valley</td><td>5.5</td><td>2.0</td><td>0.55</td><td>8.05</td></tr>
<tr><td></td><td>Parker</td><td>5.5</td><td>2.0</td><td>0.00</td><td>7.50</td></tr>
<tr><td></td><td>Phoenix</td><td>5.5</td><td>3.2[2]</td><td>0.55</td><td>9.25</td></tr>
<tr><td></td><td>Sedona</td><td>5.5</td><td>5.0</td><td>0.00</td><td>10.50</td></tr>
<tr><td></td><td>Scottsdale</td><td>5.5</td><td>4.0</td><td>0.55</td><td>10.05</td></tr>
<tr><td></td><td>Tempe</td><td>5.5</td><td>3.0</td><td>0.55</td><td>9.05</td></tr>
<tr><td></td><td>Tucson</td><td>5.5</td><td>4.0[3]</td><td>0.00</td><td>9.50</td></tr>
<tr><td>California</td><td>Los Angeles</td><td>0.0</td><td>11.5</td><td>0.00</td><td>11.50</td></tr>
<tr><td></td><td>Palm Springs</td><td>0.0</td><td>9.0</td><td>0.00</td><td>9.00</td></tr>
<tr><td></td><td>Sacramento</td><td>0.0</td><td>10.0</td><td>0.00</td><td>10.00</td></tr>
<tr><td></td><td>San Diego</td><td>0.0</td><td>8.0[4]</td><td>0.00</td><td>8.00</td></tr>
<tr><td></td><td>San Francisco</td><td>0.0</td><td>11.0</td><td>0.00</td><td>11.00</td></tr>
<tr><td>Colorado</td><td>Denver</td><td>0.2</td><td>8.0</td><td>0.00</td><td>8.20</td></tr>
<tr><td>Florida[5]</td><td>Ft. Lauderdale</td><td>6.0</td><td>0.0</td><td>3.00</td><td>9.00</td></tr>
<tr><td></td><td>Miami</td><td>6.0</td><td>0.0</td><td>5.00</td><td>11.00</td></tr>
<tr><td></td><td>Orlando</td><td>6.0</td><td>0.0</td><td>3.00</td><td>9.00</td></tr>
<tr><td></td><td>Tampa</td><td>6.0</td><td>0.0</td><td>3.00</td><td>9.00</td></tr>
<tr><td>Georgia</td><td>Atlanta</td><td>3.0</td><td>6.0</td><td>2.00</td><td>11.00</td></tr>
<tr><td>Hawaii</td><td>Honolulu</td><td>9.0</td><td>0.0</td><td>0.00</td><td>9.00</td></tr>
<tr><td>Louisiana</td><td>New Orleans</td><td>4.0</td><td>5.0</td><td>0.00</td><td>9.00</td></tr>
<tr><td>New Mexico</td><td>Albuquerque</td><td>0.0</td><td>5.0</td><td>0.00</td><td>5.00</td></tr>
<tr><td>Nevada</td><td>Las Vegas</td><td>1.0</td><td>6.0</td><td>0.00</td><td>7.00</td></tr>
<tr><td>Texas</td><td>Reno</td><td>1.0</td><td>6.0</td><td>0.00</td><td>7.00</td></tr>
<tr><td></td><td>Dallas</td><td>6.0</td><td>7.0</td><td>0.00</td><td>13.00</td></tr>
<tr><td></td><td>Houston</td><td>6.0</td><td>6.0</td><td>2.00</td><td>14.00</td></tr>
<tr><td></td><td>San Antonio</td><td>6.0</td><td>7.0</td><td>0.00</td><td>13.00</td></tr>
<tr><td>Utah</td><td>Salt Lake City</td><td>3.0</td><td>1.0</td><td>0.00</td><td>4.00</td></tr>
</table>

[1] In addition, the city of Mesa imposes a flat rate daily room charge on motel/hotels based on number of rooms.

[2] Effective in 1989, the city of Phoenix increased its bed tax rate to 4.2 percent to help finance construction of the basketball arena.

[3] The city of Tucson's transient occupancy tax covers trailer pads. A $1 per night surcharge is also imposed on a room rental.

[4] Effective June 1, 1989, the city of San Diego raised the room rate to 9 percent.

[5] In Florida, the transient occupancy tax is often supplemented by a county business license tax based on the number of rooms in the hotel/motel.

Source: Telephone Survey.

<u>Simplicity, Efficiency and Equity Considerations</u>

The transient occupancy tax is an *ad valorem* tax imposed on the dollar value of a transaction. As a result, this tax is simple to understand. More importantly, the cost of administering this selective tax is minimal as the collection process and technologies used for general sales and use tax collections can also be used to collect this tax.

The transient occupancy tax is especially attractive if the tax can be exported without any cost to the local tourism industry. If the tax causes consumers to change their behavior and leads to fewer Arizona hotel bookings, then the tax leads to distortions and is inefficient.

Tax incidence analysis examines the extent to which profit-maximizing hotel operators can pass the bed tax on to customers by raising the price of the room inclusive of the tax. The extent to which a hotel room tax can be passed on depends on the price elasticity of demand for lodging services relative to the price elasticity of supply. If hotel operators are more willing to accept lower rates of return, then they will bear the tax. If consumers are more willing to pay higher prices, then they will pay the tax. As long as both demand and supply exhibit some elasticity, a room tax can be only partially shifted to customers. In this case, the imposition of a tax on lodging would raise the price of the room, reduce the net price received by hotel operators, and reduce the quantity of lodging services bought and sold.

In order to estimate the actual price elasticity of demand and supply for Arizona, data on the average price of a room, the number of rooms available, the occupancy rate, the average length of stay by tourist type, and average expenditures per day are needed. Many states with a large tourism industry, such as Hawaii, collect and maintain such data. Unfortunately, much of the data that are required do not exist for Arizona for a sufficient length of time to permit use of econometric, statistical techniques. As a result, price elasticities of demand and supply for Arizona cannot be calculated at this time.

A number of studies have estimated price elasticities of demand and supply for other states. These studies are considered under the assumption that these estimates are reasonable proxies for these elasticities in Arizona. Combs and Elledge (1979) argue, without empirical evidence, that the demand for lodging in a resort area is inelastic with respect to price. They conclude that a small *ad valorem* tax imposed on motel rooms and other forms of temporary lodging would have very little impact on the volume of business and would generate substantial revenue. Mak and Nishimura (1979) estimate the effects of a hotel room tax on Hawaii's visitor industry using a cross-sectional approach based on survey data. Their conclusions are very similar to the Combs and Elledge results. Hoffman and Low (1980) find that the amount of daily expenditures by visitors to Arizona has relatively little influence on an individual's desire to return for a vacation. Their results suggest that a tax that raised tourist's expenditures an average of $10 per day could be expected to induce approximately one out of every 200 potential returning visitors not to visit Arizona again.

More recent studies, which use time-series data, yield slightly different results. Arbel and Ravid (1983), Fujii, Khaled, and Mak (1985) and Sakai (1985) have computed demand elasticities for lodging that are significantly greater than zero (in absolute value). Arbel and Ravid estimate the price elasticity of demand to be -0.3 for New York State (meaning a 10 percent increase in prices would lead to a 3.0 percent decrease in the number of hotel rooms sold). Fujii, Khaled, and Mak found an estimate of the demand elasticity for lodging in Hawaii that is not significantly different from -1.0. Sakai produced elasticities of -0.887 for pleasure visitors and -0.622 for business visitors to Hawaii. Estimates of supply elasticities are much larger than demand elasticities indicating that consumers are more willing to pay higher prices and, thus, hotel room taxes are easily passed on to room guests and do not result in large inefficiencies. However, the estimated demand elasticities suggest that a hotel/motel tax might have a larger negative impact on hotel sales than previously thought.

Neutral treatment across types of transient lodging is another important efficiency issue. In the State of Arizona, the temporary rental of trailer pads is *not* subject to a transient occupancy tax except in the City of Tucson. The exemption of trailer pads has efficiency implications in the sense that the tax on hotel/motels encourages the use of trailer pads relative to hotel rooms on the margin. The two industries are treated differently and consumer decisions are distorted. Other states, such as Texas, include trailer pads as part of the transient occupancy tax.

Since the purchase of hotel/motel rooms is a luxury rather than a necessity, logic would indicate that a bed tax would result in a proportional to progressive tax burden. The total tax burden is impossible to determine since much hotel lodging is purchased by businesses rather than individuals. The taxes paid by businesses could be borne ultimately by customers of the businesses in the form of higher prices, shareholders in the form of lower net returns, or workers in the form of lower wages.

Table 9-13 presents some evidence on the distribution of the bed tax among household consumers. The data show that expenditures on lodging while out of town do not rise quite as fast as income. Thus the proportion of income spent on hotels/motels tends to fall as income rises. The proportion does rise, however, between some of the income brackets. The regressivity index, comparing the burden on families in the $5,000-$9,999 income class to those with incomes over $40,000, is 1.12. This means that low income households spend only a slightly higher fraction of their incomes on lodging than high income households and, thus, would expend only a slightly higher fraction of their incomes on a bed tax. Although this tax is somewhat regressive, it is much less regressive than the taxes on tobacco and alcohol and less regressive than the general sales tax on other activities. It appears that the tax becomes more progressive at the high end of the income scale.

<table>
<tr><td colspan="4" align="center">Table 9-13
Consumer Spending on Hotel/Motel Rooms</td></tr>
<tr><td align="center">Family Income
Class</td><td align="center">Average Income
Before Taxes</td><td align="center">Spending on
Lodging While
Out-of-Town</td><td align="center">Fraction of
Income Allocated
to Hotels/Motels</td></tr>
<tr><td>$ 5,000 - 9,999</td><td align="center">$ 7,388</td><td align="center">$ 56</td><td align="center">.76</td></tr>
<tr><td>10,000 - 14,999</td><td align="center">12,426</td><td align="center">81</td><td align="center">.65</td></tr>
<tr><td>15,000 - 19,999</td><td align="center">17,341</td><td align="center">97</td><td align="center">.56</td></tr>
<tr><td>20,000 - 29,999</td><td align="center">24,676</td><td align="center">142</td><td align="center">.58</td></tr>
<tr><td>30,000 - 39,999</td><td align="center">34,283</td><td align="center">172</td><td align="center">.50</td></tr>
<tr><td>40,000 and above</td><td align="center">61,693</td><td align="center">417</td><td align="center">.68</td></tr>
<tr><td colspan="4">Source: Bureau of Labor Statistics, Consumer Expenditure Survey, 1986.</td></tr>
</table>

Revenue Responsiveness and Stability

Transient occupancy taxes are an especially attractive revenue source for policy makers in areas where tourism is an important industry. This type of tax has the ability to raise a large amount of revenue without burdening residents to a large extent. It is important, however, to consider the implications of the secular and cyclical behavior of bed tax revenue flows.

Tourism has long been an important industry in Arizona. More importantly, tourism has been a growing industry. This means that revenue based on the tourism industry, such as the transient occupancy tax, will tend to grow in real terms over time. The revenue data presented in Table 9-11 support this contention.

The tourism industry is sensitive to business cycle conditions. Downturns in the economy will influence convention activity to some extent and private tourism to a greater extent. It is likely, then, that bed tax revenues will be relatively unstable and will exhibit wide cyclical fluctuations and a relatively high sensitivity to changes in income. Fujii, Khaled, and Mak (1985) report a lodging income elasticity of 1.03 for visitors to Hawaii, finding evidence to support the theoretical prediction that lodging consumption is very sensitive to changes in income. Between 1985/86 and 1987/88, state bed tax collections in Arizona grew faster than state personal income. Although there are too few years of data to develop a good estimate, it appears that the income elasticity of lodging in Arizona is over 1.0, meaning that lodging expenditures are relatively sensitive to changes in income. This strengthens the conclusion that bed taxes provide a relatively responsive, but relatively unstable, tax source.

Real Property Transfer Taxes

Because of the need for additional revenue sources across the country, there has been a pronounced trend towards increased real property transfer tax rates. Presently, the State of Arizona does not have a real estate transfer tax. A document transfer fee of $6.00 is imposed, but revenue from this source is considered a processing fee and is paid to the County Clerk.

Description and Interstate Comparisons

A real property transfer tax is a tax assessed on real property at the time the ownership of the property is transferred from one party to another. The tax is usually assessed on all classes of property including residential and commercial. Generally, the tax is imposed on the value of the property, but it is separate from the general property tax. Although the tax can be assessed on the buyer or seller, it is generally assessed on the buyer.

There are four basic types of real property transfer taxes: a real estate transfer tax, a documentation or deed recordation fee, a mortgage tax, and a sales tax on real estate agent commissions. The real estate transfer tax is the most common and is assessed on the selling price of the property. Usually, the tax rate is expressed as a percentage of the purchase price or a dollar amount per $1,000 of value. This tax can be assessed on the buyer, seller or both. Another form of the real property transfer tax is the documentation stamp or deed recordation fee. This is a tax that must be paid in order to have a state or local government properly record the transfer of the property on the deed and receive the appropriate stamp making the transfer legal. The tax can be either a flat fee unrelated to value or a dollar amount per $1,000 of value. Generally, this fee is assessed on the buyer.

The third type of transfer tax is the mortgage tax which is assessed on the amount of the mortgage secured to purchase real property. Hence, as the down payment increases, the tax liability declines. Typically, the tax is expressed as a dollar amount per $1,000 of the mortgage amount. The tax is assessed on the party who obtains the mortgage. The last type of real property transfer tax is the sales tax on real estate agent commissions. This type of tax is equivalent to a general sales tax on the value of a service (the service being assistance in finding a buyer and closing a deal). Since real estate agent commissions are assessed against the seller, this tax would also, theoretically, be assessed against the seller. (This latter type of tax stands in contrast to the first three types of real estate transfer taxes as the tax can be collected independent of the transfer of property.)

In Table 9-14, the type of real property transfer tax as well as the tax rate imposed by the various states are presented for 1988. As the table shows, forty states have some type of real property transfer tax. Arizona, which is counted as a state that imposes such a tax, charges only a $6 deed recordation fee.

The most popular type of real property transfer tax is the real estate transfer tax. Thirty states impose this type of tax. State tax rates vary from highs of 2.0 percent in Delaware, 1.34 percent in Washington, and 1.0 percent in Pennsylvania to lows of 0.01 percent in Colorado and North Carolina. The Documentation Stamp/Deed Recordation Fee is the second most common transfer tax with eighteen states imposing it. Of the eighteen states, twelve states impose a flat fee. Arizona is one of these states. The remaining six states impose a deed tax based on the value of the property. The tax rate varies from 0.55 percent of value in Florida to 0.10 percent in Alabama, with the average tax being 0.31 percent. Ten states impose a mortgage tax. Nine states tax the value of the mortgage while Rhode Island imposes a flat fee. The tax rates range from 0.75 percent of the mortgage amount in New York to 0.10 percent in Oklahoma. Only three states, Hawaii, New Mexico, and South Dakota impose a sales tax on real estate commissions. For example, the State of New Mexico assesses a 4.75 percent sales tax on commissions.

In addition to the state taxes on real property transfers, some states also authorize local governments to assess their own property transfer tax. In 1988, at least 18 states had local property transfer taxes and five other states had statewide uniform taxes that were collected at the local level. Table 9-15 summarizes the states that have local taxes and lists selected local governments that assess the tax and their respective tax rates.

As with the state taxes, local government transfer taxes are most prevalent in the eastern states. Of the 18 states that have local transfer taxes, seven are Eastern states. About half of the 18 states have local taxes that are imposed on a statewide basis. In addition, in five other states, select local governments impose such a tax.

Because of the differences in tax rates, different types of transfer taxes, and the existence of local taxes, it is very difficult to get an accurate picture of the relative size of the total real property transfer tax in various states. Table 9-16 helps to put the various taxes into perspective by presenting the total state and local tax obligation of an individual selling a $150,000 house (assuming the buyer finances the purchase with an 80 percent mortgage) in each state. Of the states that impose some form of a real property transfer tax, the State of Arizona has the smallest total transfer obligation. The sale of a $150,000 home generates a tax obligation of $6.00. The largest tax obligation from the sale of a home of the assumed value occurs in the Eastern states. For instance, the tax obligation in Pennsylvania, Delaware, New York, Maryland and Massachusetts for the assumed value of the home would be $7,610, $4,503, $4,350, $3,569, and $3,342, respectively. In the West, the tax obligation is much smaller. In California, the tax obligation would be $750, while in Nevada and New Mexico the obligation would be $165 and $427.50, respectively. The largest transfer tax obligation in the West would occur in the State of Washington where the tax obligation would be $2,010.

Table 9-14
Real Property Transfer Tax by State: Type and Rates, 1988

State	Real Estate Transfer Tax		Stamp/Deed Fee			Mortgage Tax		Sales Tax on Commissions	
	Imposed	Rate (%)	Imposed	Fee ($)	Rate (%)	Imposed	Rate (%)	Imposed	Rate(%)
Alabama	No		Yes		0.10	Yes	0.15	No	
Alaska	No		No			No		No	
Arizona	No		Yes	6.00		No		No	
Arkansas	Yes	0.22	No			No		No	
California[1]	Yes		No			No		No	
Colorado	Yes	0.01	No			No		No	
Connecticut	Yes	0.56	No			No		No	
Delaware[2]	Yes	2.00	Yes	3.00		No		No	
Florida	No		Yes		0.55	Yes	0.15	No	
Georgia	Yes	0.10	Yes	2.00		Yes	0.30	No	
Hawaii	Yes	0.05	No			No		Yes	0.04
Idaho	No		No			No		No	
Illinois	Yes	0.05	No			No		No	
Indiana	No		No			No		No	
Iowa	Yes	0.11	No			No		No	
Kansas	No		No			Yes	0.25	No	
Kentucky	Yes	0.10	No			No		No	
Louisiana	No		Yes	3.00		No		No	
Maine	Yes	0.44	Yes	5.00		No		No	
Maryland[3]	No		Yes		0.50	No		No	
Massachusetts[4]	Yes	0.228	No			No		No	
Michigan	Yes	0.11	Yes	4.00		No		No	

Table 9-14 (Continued)

State	Real Estate Transfer Tax		Stamp/Deed Fee			Mortgage Tax		Sales Tax on Commissions	
	Imposed	Rate (%)	Imposed	Fee ($)	Rate (%)	Imposed	Rate (%)	Imposed	Rate(%)
Minnesota	No		Yes		0.33	Yes	0.23	No	
Mississippi	No		No			No		No	
Missouri	No		No			No		No	
Montana	No		No			No		No	
Nebraska	No		Yes		0.15	No		No	
Nevada	Yes	0.11	No			No		No	
New Hampshire[5]	Yes	0.70	No			No		No	
New Jersey[4]	Yes	0.35	No			No	0.75	No	
New Mexico	No		No			No		Yes	0.0475
New York	Yes	0.40	No			Yes		No	
North Carolina[5]	Yes	0.010	No			No		No	
North Dakota	No		Yes		0.25	No	0.10	No	
Ohio[5]	Yes		Yes	3.50		No		No	
Oklahoma	Yes	0.15	Yes	5.00		Yes		No	
Oregon	No		No			No	$19.45	No	
Pennsylvania	Yes	1.00	Yes	5.00		No		No	
Rhode Island	Yes	0.22	Yes	6.15		Yes		No	
South Carolina	yes	0.22	No			No	0.115	No	
South Dakota	Yes	0.10	Yes	2.00		No		Yes	0.05
Tennessee	Yes	0.33	No			Yes		No	
Texas	No		No			No		No	
Utah	No		No			No	0.25	No	
Vermont	Yes	0.50	No			No		No	

Table 9-14 (Continued)

State	Real Estate Transfer Tax		Stamp/Deed Fee			Mortgage Tax		Sales Tax on Commissions	
	Imposed	Rate (%)	Imposed	Fee ($)	Rate (%)	Imposed	Rate (%)	Imposed	Rate(%)
Virginia	Yes	0.25	No			Yes		No	
Washington	Yes	1.34	No			No		No	
West Virginia	Yes	0.22	No			No		No	
Wisconsin	Yes	0.30	Yes	2.00		No		No	
Wyoming	No		No			No		No	
Total	30		18			10		3	

[1] State does not levy a realty transfer tax. However, counties and cities may levy such a tax.
[2] Transfers under $500 are exempt.
[3] In Maryland, counties also impose additional deed transfer taxes.
[4] Transfers under $100 are exempt.
[5] Counties may also levy transfer tax.

Source: *State Tax Guide*, Commerce Clearing House.

Table 9-15
Real Property Transfer Taxes Assessed by Local Governments[*]

State	Local Governments Assessing a Transfer Tax	Tax Rate (% of Value)
California	Counties	0.11
	Chartered Cities	up to .50
Delaware	Certain Cities	1.00
Florida	Dade County	0.55
Illinois	Counties	0.05
	Cities	0.10-0.70
Louisiana	City of New Orleans	$300 fee
Maryland	Counties	0.22-1.50
Massachusetts	Martha's Vineyard	2.00
	Nantucket Island	2.00
Michigan	Counties	0.11-0.15
New York	Counties	0.75-1.00
	New York City	1.75-2.50
North Carolina	Certain Counties	1.00
Ohio	Counties	0.10-0.40
Oregon	Washington Co.	0.10
Pennsylvania	Philadelphia	4.07
	Allegheny County	2.50
	Other Municipalities	1.00
Rhode Island	Little Compton	2.00
South Carolina	Counties	0.11
Virginia	Counties	up to 1/3 state rate
Washington	Counties	0.25-0.75
West Virginia	Counties	0.11

[*] Does not include the following states that have a statewide uniform tax that is collected at the local level: Colorado, Kansas, Minnesota, Nevada, and North Dakota.

Source: The National Association Of Realtors and Commerce Clearing House, *State Tax Handbook*.

Table 9-16
A Comparison of Real Estate Transfer Tax Rates on $150,000 House by State: 1988
(Including selected local government taxes)

State	Real Estate Transfer Tax (%)	Document Stamp Fee (%)	Mortgage Tax[*] (%)	Total Transfer Tax	Commission Tax	Notes
Alabama	0.10	0.15		$ 330.00		
Alaska				0.00		
Arizona		$6.00		6.00		
Arkansas	0.22			330.00		
California		0.50		750.00		Assumes San Francisco
Colorado	0.01			15.00		
Connecticut	0.56			840.00		
Delaware	3.00	$3.00		4,503.00		Assumes City of Wilmington
Florida		0.55	0.15	1,005.00		Assumes Dade County
Georgia	0.10		0.30	510.00		
Hawaii	0.05			75.00	$360.00	
Idaho				0.00		
Illinois	0.55			825.00		Assumes Chicago
Indiana				0.00		
Iowa		0.11		165.00		
Kansas			0.25	300.00		
Kentucky	0.10			150.00		
Louisiana		$300.00		300.00		Assumes New Orleans
Maine	0.44	$5.00		665.00		Total Tax on Buyer & Seller
Maryland	2.00	0.50		3,569.71		Assumes Baltimore
Massachusetts	2.228			3,342.00		Assumes Martha's Vineyard
Michigan			$4.00	225.00		Assumes Wayne County
Minnesota		0.33	0.23	762.00		State
Mississippi				0.00		
Missouri				0.00		

Table 9-16 (Continued)

State	Real Estate Transfer Tax (%)	Document Stamp Fee (%)	Mortgage Tax[*] (%)	Total Transfer Tax	Commission Tax	Notes
Montana				0.00		
Nebraska		0.15		225.00		
Nevada	0.11			165.00		
New Hampshire	0.70			1,050.00		
New Jersey	0.35			525.00	427.50	
New Mexico						
New York	1.40		$1.50	4,350.00		Assumes New York City
North Carolina	1.10			1,650.00		Assumes Coastal City
North Dakota		0.25		375.00		
Ohio		0.40	$3.50	603.50		Assumes highest county rate
Oklahoma	0.15		0.10	345.00		
Oregon	0.10			150.00		Washington County Only
Pennsylvania	5.07	$5.00		7,610.00		Assumes Philadelphia
Rhode Island	0.22	$6.15	$19.45	355.60		Assumes Little Compton
South Carolina	0.33			495.00		
South Dakota	0.10			150.00	450.00	
Tennessee	0.33		0.115	633.00		
Texas				0.00		
Utah				0.00		
Vermont	0.50			750.00		
Virginia		0.30	0.20	690.00		Assuming Fairfax County
Washington	1.34			2,010.00		
West Virginia	0.22			330.00		
Wisconsin	0.30			450.00		
Wyoming				0.00		

[*] Assumes the mortgage is 80% of sales price

Source: *State Tax Guide*, Commerce Clearing House, and author's calculations.

Simplicity, Efficiency and Equity Considerations

Real estate transfer taxes are appealing to state and local governments because of their ability to raise a large amount of revenue with relatively low tax rates. Since Arizona presently does not impose a tax on the value of real property transfers (beyond the $6 fee), it is important to evaluate this tax on equity, efficiency, and simplicity considerations.

Proponents of this tax frequently refer to its simplicity and ease of administration. As long as the sale of a property is registered, the tax is simple and easy to administer. Hence, a tax on owner-occupied residential housing would meet this criterion. Administrative problems can occur with the taxation of commercial property. Existing data on the transfer of commercial property are suspect due to the fact that this type of property transfer may not always be recorded. If a corporation is sold, the corresponding transfer of commercial property may not be recorded. If a general real estate transfer tax is to be enacted, statutory changes may be required to insure that all property transactions are recorded.

In terms of the efficiency criterion, real estate transfer taxes may be problematic. Economic theory suggests that the imposition of a tax on products with inelastic demands (insensitivity of consumption to changes in price) results in minimal adjustments to optimal market decisions. Price elasticities are not readily available for all of the various types of properties that would be subject to a real estate transfer tax either nationally or in Arizona. The most readily available price elasticity is for housing. Browning and Browning (1989) report that this elasticity is -1.0. While using this estimate for all types of real property and for all types of owner-occupied residential property is an unrealistic assumption, this is still the best estimate of a price elasticity that is currently available. Since the estimate indicates that the demand for housing is not inelastic, the introduction of a real estate transfer tax may influence consumption decisions. However, a *low* real estate transfer tax would not significantly affect the price and would have only small effects on housing demand. Another aspect of efficiency is whether the price of real property relative to other consumption options is distorted by the tax system. Currently, Arizona imposes a sales tax on contracting which, in effect, places a tax on the purchase of a new home. Since there is no tax on the sale of existing homes, the tax system may be encouraging the purchase of existing homes over new homes.

Opponents of a real estate transfer tax often argue against this tax on equity grounds. The argument focuses on vertical equity considerations. Individuals tend to spend a decreasing share of their income on housing as income increases. Of course, the final distribution of the tax burden depends on who would bear the burden of the tax on sales of commercial property, and on the frequency with which different types of property are transferred. The *Consumer Expenditure Survey* reports the estimated market value of owned homes by family income class which provides a partial view of the incidence of a real estate transfer tax. These values are presented in Table 9-17.

In order to estimate the tax burden of a real estate transfer tax, a one tenth of one percent real estate transfer tax rate is assumed. The table shows that the effective tax burden decreases as income increases. The home value for families with incomes between $5,000-$9,999 is $26,385. This means the transfer tax obligation would be $26.39 and the effective tax burden for this income class is 0.357 percent. On the other hand, the home value in the over $40,000 income class is $102,439. The effective tax burden for this income class would be 0.166 percent. Comparing these two tax burdens results in a regressivity index measure of 2.15 meaning that low-income households would bear more than twice as great a burden as high-income households. This suggests that the real estate transfer tax is regressive. However, a closer examination of Table 9-17 suggests that the extent of the regressivity of this type of tax may be overstated. For incomes over $15,000, the real estate transfer tax is nearly proportional. In fact, since the effective tax burden increases for the $40,000 and above income class as compared to the $30,000 to $39,999 income class, a further disaggregation of the highest income class might reveal a progressive aspect of this tax.

Table 9-17 Estimated Tax Burden of a Real Estate Transfer Tax				
Family Income Class	Average Income Before Taxes	Average Home Value	Tax from 0.1% Transfer Tax	Effective Tax Burden (%)
$ 5,000-9,999	$ 7,388	$ 26,385	$ 26.39	0.357
10,000-14,999	12,426	30,071	30.07	0.242
15,000-19,999	17,341	31,079	31.07	0.179
20,000-29,999	24,676	42,294	42.29	0.171
30,000-39,999	34,283	55,978	55.98	0.163
40,000 & above	61,693	102,439	102.44	0.166

Source: U.S. Department of Labor, Bureau of Labor Statistics, *Consumer Expenditure Survey*, 1986.

This analysis suggests that exempting homes selling for $30,000 or less would greatly reduce the regressivity of the real estate transfer tax. Such an exemption would also address another concern about the tax. It prevents first time home-buyers from being able to enter the housing market. By exempting sales below a certain value from the tax, the state could avoid presenting barriers to first-time purchasers. A problem with exemptions, however, is that they introduce distortions into the market and encourage people to adjust the price of their property to avoid the tax.

Another factor to consider in analyzing the distribution of the transfer tax burden is the frequency with which households buy and move into new homes and therefore incur the tax over time. Individuals at higher income levels tend to move slightly more frequently than people at lower income levels. For example, according to the 1983 *Census of Housing*, the average $100,000 income household had lived in their home for an average of 10.3 years. This is compared with 11.6 years for households earning $20,000. This factor tends to add a progressive element to the real estate transfer tax.

Revenue Responsiveness and Stability

In a growing state, the demand for publicly provided goods tends to increase over time. Hence, to avoid fiscal budget imbalance, policy makers desire revenue structures that generate growth in revenues to match expenditure requirements. This long-term need for revenue growth requires that a tax be evaluated on its secular revenue behavior. Real estate transfer taxes are attractive in terms of this particular criterion. From a long-term perspective, the real estate market will mirror the growth and development trends in an area. An area that is characterized by growth and development will find the size of the real estate market increasing. In addition, the value of real estate will likely be increasing. As a result, secular revenue trends for a real estate transfer tax will be positively correlated with growth trends of a state. This is an attractive feature from a policy maker's point of view.

From a cyclical perspective, the real estate transfer tax is less attractive as a stable source of revenue. Table 9-18 presents the real estate transfer tax revenues from 1978 to 1986 for the states of Delaware, Illinois, New Hampshire, Pennsylvania, and Tennessee. These data have been adjusted for tax rate changes. The fluctuations in revenue from this type of tax are highly correlated with changes in economic activity. In the early 1980s, revenues declined in nominal dollars as the economic recession developed and then rose steadily through 1986 as the economy recovered. If the revenue generated by this tax source is added together for the five states, revenue from property transfer taxes in these states declined 8.2 percent from 1978 to 1982 and then increased 133 percent from 1982 to 1986.

Table 9-18
Real Estate Transfer Tax Collections for Selected States
(Adjusted for rate changes, millions of dollars)

State	1978	1979	1980	1981	1982	1983	1984	1985	1986
Delaware	9.5	11.2	12.9	12.3	10.6	12.6	19.2	21.6	25.8
Illinois	3.9	4.1	6.8	5.2	3.5	4.6	6.8	7.2	9.3
New Hampshire	4.0	5.1	4.9	4.5	7.7	5.3	16.1	28.6	34.2
Pennsylvania	81.9	94.9	85.2	77.8	68.4	83.5	107.7	121.9	147.9
Tennessee	19.5	21.3	20.0	19.6	18.9	21.9	29.9	33.6	37.4
Total	118.9	136.6	129.9	119.5	109.2	127.8	179.8	213.0	254.6

Source: U.S. Department of Commerce, Bureau of the Census, *State Government Finances*.

If these revenues are expressed in real terms, the variability of revenue flows from this tax is even greater. In real dollars, real estate transfer tax revenue in these states fell sharply, by 38 percent from 1978 to 1982, and then increased by 105 percent from 1982 to 1986. At the end of this cycle, the 1986 level was 27 percent above the 1978 level.

The volatility of revenues from the real estate property tax over the business cycle can be put in perspective by comparing it to the volatility of the sales and income taxes for these five states. From 1978 to 1983, real income tax collections fell 6.9 percent, and from 1978 to 1982, the sales tax revenues declined 14.5 percent. These declines were much less severe than the 38 percent drop experienced by real transfer tax revenues. From 1983 to 1986, real income tax collections rose 11.1 percent and real sales tax revenue rose 17.3 percent compared to the 105 percent revenue increase from real estate transfer taxes. The real estate transfer tax is a much more volatile revenue source than the sales or income taxes over a business cycle. The primary cause of this volatility is the high sensitivity that real estate sales, in particular residential real estate sales, have to economic conditions. Real estate sales are positively affected when employment and incomes are increasing. When economic conditions worsen and employment and earnings decline, investors are less able to make the major financial commitment that real estate requires. In addition, high interest rates which often are associated with the onset of a recession are a deterrent to real estate activity.

Policy Issues and Revenue Potential

One reason for enacting a real estate transfer tax is its revenue potential. An important question is how much revenue would such a tax raise in the State of Arizona. In this section, data on real estate transactions by various classes for Arizona are used to estimate the amount of revenue that this type of tax could generate.

The Department of Revenue for the State of Arizona provided data on the number of sales and the total value of these sales by county for fiscal year 1986-87. The data are divided into five classes: commercial, vacant land, owned residential, rental residential and mixed usage. In fiscal year 1986-87, a total of 116,532 real estate transactions took place. The recorded value of these transactions was $12.062 billion. As would be expected, the majority of these transactions occurred in Maricopa County and are residential in type. There is some concern over the accuracy of the data for commercial transactions. These values should be considered a lower bound estimate.

Currently, Arizona imposes a $6.00 transfer or recording fee. The revenue from this fee does not go to the State General Fund but rather to the county in which the transaction takes place. As a benchmark, an estimate of revenue from this transfer fee is calculated. The value of revenue is estimated to be $0.7 million. In contrast, three types of real estate transfer taxes are evaluated. Each one of these alternatives imposes a real estate transfer tax on the selling price of the property with a tax rate of 0.10 percent. This would be one of the lowest taxes that states actually employ. At this tax rate, a home buyer or seller of a $150,000 home would have to pay a tax of $150 dollars (a small amount relative to the total price and other closing costs). The alternatives differ by considering the effect of introducing various exemptions to the tax based on the value of the property sold.

Table 9-19 presents the revenue estimates from the three tax possibilities. If there were no exemptions, a real estate transfer tax would have generated approximately $12.1 million in revenue in fiscal year 1986-87 assuming the same number of properties would have been sold. Of course, in reality, the imposition of this tax would have had an effect on the number of transactions that would have taken place. The average price of a real estate transaction over all classes of property for this period was $103,515. With an assumed elasticity of -1.0, the tax increase would have resulted in 117 (.1 percent of 116,532) fewer properties being sold. This would have led to $12.1 million less of total transactions ($103,515 X 117). Taking this demand response into account, the amount of revenue generated from a real estate transfer tax with a 0.10 percent tax rate would be approximately $12.05 million.

An argument made against the real estate transfer tax is that it has deleterious implications for families entering the residential housing market for the first time. One way to minimize such an effect is to exempt housing transactions with values under some given amount. The data assembled by Arizona's Department of Revenue segmented owner-occupied residential property into three value categories: under $25,000, $25,000 to $50,000, and over $50,000. This allows revenue estimates to be generated for real estate transfer taxes that exempt owner-occupied residential housing selling for less than $25,000 or less than $50,000. If price effects are ignored, the exemption of homes selling for less than $25,000 would generate $11.98 million while the exemption for homes selling for less than $50,000 would generate $11.5 million.

<table>
<tr><td colspan="5">Table 9-19
Revenue Potential of Alternative Real Estate Transfer Taxes
(Based on Fiscal Year 1986-87 Values)</td></tr>
<tr><td>County</td><td>Transfer
Fee of $6.00
per Deed
or Contract</td><td>Transfer tax on
all Real Estate
Classes at rate
of 0.10% of
selling price</td><td>Transfer Tax
at 0.10%
(Residential
homes sold for
under $25,000
exempt)</td><td>Transfer Tax
at 0.10%
(Residential
homes sold for
under $50,000
exempt)</td></tr>
<tr><td>Apache</td><td>$ 7,560</td><td>$ 33,032</td><td>$ 31,655</td><td>$ 28,599</td></tr>
<tr><td>Cochise</td><td>19,680</td><td>163,120</td><td>156,892</td><td>140,291</td></tr>
<tr><td>Coconino</td><td>19,524</td><td>238,370</td><td>35,111</td><td>220,549</td></tr>
<tr><td>Gila</td><td>9,276</td><td>76,479</td><td>72,717</td><td>59,544</td></tr>
<tr><td>Graham</td><td>2,820</td><td>26,479</td><td>25,734</td><td>21,751</td></tr>
<tr><td>Greenlee</td><td>930</td><td>2,891</td><td>2,610</td><td>1,987</td></tr>
<tr><td>LaPaz</td><td>2,820</td><td>47,742</td><td>46,955</td><td>45,163</td></tr>
<tr><td>Maricopa</td><td>383,220</td><td>8,345,217</td><td>8,330,106</td><td>8,117,225</td></tr>
<tr><td>Mohave</td><td>51,966</td><td>311,151</td><td>298,840</td><td>260,922</td></tr>
<tr><td>Navajo</td><td>16,836</td><td>134,004</td><td>127,718</td><td>113,089</td></tr>
<tr><td>Pima</td><td>110,844</td><td>1,890,578</td><td>1,879,959</td><td>1,777,598</td></tr>
<tr><td>Pinal</td><td>6,564</td><td>183,526</td><td>181,722</td><td>176,931</td></tr>
<tr><td>Santa Cruz</td><td>2,880</td><td>53,761</td><td>52,411</td><td>48,158</td></tr>
<tr><td>Yavapai</td><td>44,652</td><td>382,282</td><td>371,869</td><td>338,282</td></tr>
<tr><td>Yuma</td><td>16,518</td><td>174,676</td><td>169,609</td><td>147,553</td></tr>
<tr><td>State-Wide Total</td><td>$696,072</td><td>$12,062,800</td><td>$11,983,907</td><td>$11,497,641</td></tr>
</table>

Note: The above estimates do not reflect any reduction in sales caused by the imposition of the tax. Revenue estimates accounting for estimated reductions in the number of houses sold are $12.05 million, $11.97 million, and $11.49 million, respectively.

Source: Author's calculations based on sales data provided by Arizona Department of Revenue.

Summary

All of the selective sales taxes analyzed in this chapter score well on simplicity grounds and fairly well on efficiency. The liquor and tobacco taxes enhance efficiency by making product prices better reflect the cost their consumption imposes on society. The tax on alcohol, however, may introduce some inefficiencies because there are different effective tax rates on the different types of products. The bed tax may be somewhat inefficient because consumers may be willing to purchase fewer room-nights as prices increase. The state and local bed tax rates in Arizona are in line with the total rates in neighboring states and other states with large tourism industries.

Concerning vertical equity, the bed tax appears least regressive and the cigarette tax most regressive. The real estate transfer tax is at approximately the same level of regressivity as Arizona's current general sales tax. In 1988, Arizona had only a $6.00 deed fee for real estate transactions, while thirty states imposed a real estate transfer tax equal to a percentage of the selling price. Cigarette and alcohol taxes are stable sources of revenue that do not respond much to economic growth over time. The hotel/motel and real estate transfer taxes, on the other hand, are sensitive to both long-term economic growth and short-term economic cycles.

References

Arbel, A. and S. A. Ravid, "The Differential Impact of Gas Shortages and Fuel Price Increases on Demand: The Case of the Hotel Industry in New York State," *The Energy Journal*, 32, 1983, 165-171.

Blakemore, Arthur E., and William J. Boyes, "Tourist Taxes: A Potential Source of Revenue for Arizona," *Arizona Business*, July/August 1982, 3-7.

Browning, Edgar K., and Jacqueline M. Browning, *Microeconomic Theory and Applications*, Glenview, Illinois: Scott, Foresman and Company, 1989.

Combs, J.P., and B. Elledge, "Effects of Room Tax on Resort Hotel/Motels," *National Tax Journal*, 32, 1979, 201-207.

Fujii, E., M. Khaled, and J. Mak, "The Exportability of Hotel Occupancy and Other Tourist Taxes," *National Tax Journal*, 38, 1985, 169-177.

Harwood, Henrick J., Diane M. Napolitano, Patricia L. Kristiansen, and James J. Collins, *Economic Costs to Society of Alcohol and Drug Abuse and Mental Illness: 1980*, Research Triangle Park, N.C.: Research Triangle Institute, 1984.

Hoffman, Dennis L., and Stuart Low, "Arizona Tourism and Conventioneer Attitudes," *Arizona Business*, August/September, 1980.

Houthakker, Hendrik S., and Lester D. Taylor, *Consumer Demand in the United States, 1927-1970*, Cambridge, MA: Harvard University Press, 1970.

Mak, James, "Taxing Hotel Room Rentals in the U.S.," *Journal of Travel Research*, Summer 1988, 11-15.

Pogue, Thomas F., and Larry G. Sgontz, "Taxes to Control Social Costs: The Case of Alcohol," *American Economic Review*, 79, March 1989, 235-243.

Poterba, James M., "Lifetime Incidence and the Distribution Burden of Excise Taxes," *American Economic Review, Papers and Proceedings*, 80, May 1990.

Sakai, M.Y. *A Micro-Analysis of Demand for Travel Goods: An Application to the Business Traveler*, unpublished doctoral dissertation, University of Hawaii, 1985.

Chapter 10

User Charges and Fees

Roger Faith and Dana Wolfe Naimark[*]

The Economics Of User Charges And Fees

User charges and fees are direct payments to a governmental body based on actual use of a publicly provided or regulated resource or service. User charges and fees are levied on a myriad of activities and in a variety of forms. Some services are paid for on a per-unit basis, such as university tuition, water and electricity charges, and bus fares. Other services are paid for on a lump-sum basis, such as annual fees for hunting and fishing, business licenses, and drivers' licenses. Table 10-1 presents a partial list of activities that are commonly financed with charges and fees at the state and local levels.

As Table 10-1 shows, user charges and fees are applied to a wide variety of governmentally-provided goods and services. However, user charge and fee financing are appropriate only for specific types of goods and services. To be appropriate for user charge and fee financing, a good or service should have the following characteristics.

1. Measurability -- The good or service is provided in discrete units so that it is possible to distinguish users from non-users and to measure consumption;
2. Excludability -- It is relatively easy, either physically or administratively, to prevent non-payers from receiving the good or service;
3. Non-Redistributional -- If the goal of the service itself is to redistribute wealth or income from wealthier to less wealthy households, then it makes no sense to charge a fee for receipt of the service.

Examples such as bridge tolls, parking fees, and hospital charges meet these criteria very well. Services such as welfare, police protection, non-game wildlife and wilderness programs, and economic development do not meet the criteria and, therefore, are not good candidates for user charge financing. Other services fall in between. Some would argue, for example, that one purpose of community college education is economic improvement for lower-income people, so that charging tuition may be inappropriate. Parks usage may prove difficult to exclude from non-payers, but fees may still be appropriate as they can be easily collected to some extent.

---

[*] Portions of this chapter are based on work performed by Helen F. Ladd and Dana Weist for the Arizona Joint Select Committee on State Revenues and Expenditures.

Table 10-1 Sample Sources of Charges and Fees	
Municipal Government	**State Government**
Golf Courses	College and University Courses
Museums	State Parks and Campgrounds
Hobby Classes	Boating Permits
Building Inspections	Agricultural Inspections
Business Licenses	Occupational Licenses
Public Utilities	Highway and Bridge Use
Parking Meters and Lots	State Hospitals
Accident Reports	Corporation Licenses
Refuse Collection	Motor Vehicle Registration
Emergency Ambulance Services	State-Operated Day Care Centers
Water Use	Hazardous Waste Disposal

The three characteristics described above suggest that user charges are most appropriate for goods and services that are essentially like those goods and services provided by the private sector. This raises the question of why such goods and services are publicly produced to begin with. The most common reasons for government provision are natural monopoly and public goods. With respect to natural monopoly, large economies of scale create decreasing average costs over the relevant range of production. Decreasing cost implies that competitive pricing (*i.e.*, marginal cost pricing), which is efficient, will not be profitable and, therefore, will not be attractive to private producers. Monopoly pricing (price above marginal cost or fixed fee plus marginal cost pricing), on the other hand, is profitable but inefficient. Such goods, therefore, are either governmentally produced or, if privately produced, subject to rate regulation. Utilities, such as electric power generation, water supply and treatment, and natural gas are examples.

With respect to public goods, free-riding by persons who do not pay for consuming the public good may result in revenue shortfalls rendering private production unprofitable. If it is possible to exclude non-payers, non-discriminatory pricing will result in underconsumption from a social efficiency perspective. Museums, parks and recreation areas, police and safety services, roads, and flood control are examples.

User Charges in Comparison to General Taxes

User charges differ from general tax instruments in two major ways. First, user charge revenues depend on the quantity of the service that the individual chooses to consume, and user charges are paid concurrently with the services rendered. General taxes, on the other hand, are collected independently of service provision and the individual's tax liability is determined independently of the individual's consumption. Two people paying the same amount in income and sales taxes, for example, may receive different amounts of public safety services. Second, user charge rates often are set to recover a specific portion of the per-unit cost of providing the service, while general taxes are set to meet the total desired level of expenditures.

These two differences are not always easily distinguishable in practice. Clearly, university tuition is a user charge for a semester's worth of education. Elementary and secondary education are often purchased at the local level through local property taxes paid on an annual basis. Should school property taxes be considered a user charge? The answer is no, because an individual's tax liability is not determined by the amount of educational services one uses directly. State excise taxes on gasoline frequently are earmarked for capital improvements on state highways which is a service consumed by motorists. Such taxes are not pure user charges because the state government supplies road maintenance, not gasoline, and purchasers of gasoline do not necessarily travel on state-constructed highways. In fact, state highway usage is strongly correlated with gasoline consumption, so gasoline taxes act as good proxies for highway user charges.

License and inspection fees have some of the same features as user charges. Like charges, license fees are payments by an individual for a direct service. Instead of being payment for a specific quantity of a good or service, however, these fees often serve as payment for the *privilege* of carrying out a regulated activity. A fishing license, for example, can be viewed as a user charge for permission to catch wildlife. Unlike pure user charges, however, license fees are not based on a strict per-unit basis (*e.g.*, the fishing license fee is not based on the number of fish caught). Some license fees are more like taxes than user charges. Motor vehicle license taxes in Arizona, for example, are based on the value of the vehicle. Thus, they serve as a tax on wealth rather than as a charge for a privilege. Table 10-2 summarizes the features that distinguish user charges and license fees from general taxes.

Table 10-2 Comparison of State Revenue Sources			
	User Charges	**License and Inspection Fees**	**General Taxes**
Assessed on	specified good or service	the privilege of conducting a regulated activity	general wealth or consumption
Revenue collected	concurrent with service provision	on a regularly scheduled, periodic basis	at various times
Rate set to cover	a portion of the cost of providing the service	a portion of the cost of regulation	cost of general government services
Financed service	is discrete like a private market good or service	is regulatory	varies in nature

Characteristics of User Charges and Fees

User charges levied on a per-unit basis are the public analog to prices of goods and services in the private market. As such, user charges bring to the public sector many of the advantages and disadvantages of the competitive market.

In the competitive private market, equilibrium prices (those that equate demand and supply) efficiently allocate resources to their highest-valued uses. Consumers choose the quantity of a good or service they wish to consume at the going market price; they purchase units of the good up to the point where the benefit they gain from the good or service equals the price they have to pay for it. If the benefit to an individual is less than the price, the individual will not buy the good or service. Over time, competitive sellers will not produce more goods than the market demands. Any production capacity over the equilibrium amount will be directed to other products that are in demand. Thus, production is efficient, and each resource is directed to its most valued use.

In contrast, when a good or service is supplied at less than the market-clearing price, or at a zero price, the good will be consumed up to the point where the last unit purchased has little or no value to the consumer. In this case, either demand will exceed supply, leading to shortages and waiting lists, or supply will meet demand and resources will be diverted from their most valued uses. This inefficiency occurs in the provision of government services because consumers do not perceive their general tax liability as a price for public goods. This is an example of "fiscal illusion" (Buchanan, 1967), in which citizens treat taxes simply as lost income and treat public services as costless rights of citizenship.

Because the marginal tax price for most government goods is zero, taxpayers demand an inefficiently large quantity of public goods. User charges make the price of public goods reflect their cost. Taxpayers will only consume such goods to the point where the charge is equal to the benefit they receive from the good. Thus, when set at appropriate rates, user charges avoid the overconsumption of public services, the congestion of public facilities, and delays and waiting lists to receive services.

Another potential type of user charge is a fee for the consumption of a natural resource such as air or water. A pollution fee can be assessed based upon the degree of pollution caused by a specific activity. Pollution always imposes a cost to society, but usually this cost is not directly linked to the polluting activity. By assessing a pollution fee, government can create this direct link and force the private market to take account of societal costs in production and consumption decisions. Many license fees function similarly in efficiently allocating scarce resources. Hunting and fishing license fees help to ration the consumption of limited wildlife. The cost of business and professional licenses is, in part, passed on to consumers. Thus, the people who benefit from the regulation pay its cost, and efficiency is enhanced.

An additional efficiency advantage is that user charges and fees, like private prices, are flexible and can be changed fairly easily to meet changing demand or cost conditions. This is particularly important with respect to governmental services that face peak demand periods. Parks and recreation sites on weekends, roads at rush hour, and electricity demand in afternoons are examples of peak loads. User charges can be tailored to manage these predictable swings in demand efficiently by raising rates during peak load periods.

User charges can provide a strong link between government revenues and expenditures. Often the same agency that collects the revenue also provides the service. User charges, unlike general taxes, can act as signals regarding the value of placing resources into various activities. With "zero-priced" goods (such as those financed with general taxes), it is difficult to know whether the social value of the good exceeds its costs. The consumption of goods or services when the price is zero does not mean the good is providing net value, only that it is cheap. The consumption of goods financed with user charges or fees, however, provides policymakers a way to measure the value of the good to citizens. If consumption of the good is high, then the social value is equal to or above the user charge rate; if consumption is low, the public is indicating that the existing program is not worth the price. Thus, user charges enable policymakers to set appropriate rate levels and to design programs according to citizen desires.

Like private market prices, user charges and fees make no distinction between consumers with respect to income or other personal circumstances. Service quantities are allocated in proportion to the number of dollars spent by the individual consumers, and charges are not based on citizens' ability to pay. Thus, vertical equity norms may be strained under user charge financing especially if the service is one that lower income households spend a proportionally greater share of their income on than higher income households.

Equity problems can be overcome, however, by granting vouchers or income grants to low income persons to spend on public services however they wish. Subsidized rates and discounts for low income households can also help relieve the inequities of user charges, but these features come at the expense of artificially increasing demand and distorting the efficient allocation of public resources. Thus, user charges and fees provide another example of the tension between equity and efficiency.

In sum, user charges and fees score high, relative to general taxes, on efficiency and accountability grounds. They promote the efficient allocation of resources and promote a more responsive government. By promoting efficiency, user charges and fees lower the cost of government and thus help free up resources for the pursuit of other goals. On equity grounds, user charges and fees do not provide an appropriate vehicle for income redistribution.

Design Issues

Two important issues regarding the design of user charges and fees are: what is the appropriate charge and how are the proceeds distributed.

To maximize efficiency, it is desirable to set user fees at the rate where marginal benefit is equal to marginal cost; that is, where the benefit to the user of the last unit purchased is equal to the cost of providing that last unit. If the price is set at this level, resources are being put to their most valued uses and no one can be made better off without someone else being made worse off. It is important to note that services may have benefits for general society in addition to the benefits to specific users. Higher education, for example, improves citizenship and economic productivity in addition to raising the income potential for the student. To maximize efficiency for these types of goods, fees should be set equal to the benefit to specific users while general taxes should finance the portion that benefits society as a whole. Other goods or services may impose costs on general society. Charges on these types of goods can be set to reflect societal costs in addition to the benefits the individual receives. Consuming gasoline, for example, creates air pollution. Thus, gas taxes can be assessed to reflect the costs of controlling air pollution in addition to the benefits of highway use.

One of the advantages of user charges is that they can enhance the responsiveness of public agencies to taxpayer desires. Accountability to the demands of the market is strengthened if the revenues collected by the providing agency stay with the providing agency and are used to finance the service that is being charged for. Incentives to respond to the information contained in user charges are strengthened when the user charge revenues are earmarked to the collecting agency. When user revenues accrue to the general fund, the collecting agency must compete for the monies with other agencies, and the incentive to administer user charges efficiently is reduced. When user charge revenues are not earmarked, and their efficiency advantage is reduced, the only remaining advantage of user fees over general taxes is the ability to reduce the burden of taxes.

User Charges And License Fees In Arizona And Other States

Table 10-3 displays state and local government reliance on user charges in various states in 1980 and 1987. The data demonstrate that user charges are a small, but significant source of revenue, ranging from 13 to 19 percent of own-source revenue for the comparison states in 1987. In both years, Arizona's reliance on user charges was below the U.S. average and below most of the comparison states. In 1987, all of the comparison states except Arizona and New Mexico had a greater reliance on user charges than the U.S. average.

Table 10-3
State and Local User Charge Revenue as a
Percentage of Own-Source Revenue

	1980 (%)	1987 (%)
United States	14.8	15.1
Arizona	12.9	12.8
California	13.8	15.5
Colorado	16.9	17.0
Florida	19.2	18.5
Nevada	18.2	18.7
New Mexico	12.5	13.2
Texas	15.9	15.6
Utah	16.0	16.8

Source: *Governmental Finances*, selected years, U.S. Bureau of the Census.

There was a national move toward greater reliance on user charges in the late 1970s (Lemov, 1989). As shown here, however, there has been virtually no change in the level of user charge reliance since 1980.

Interstate Revenue Comparisons

Tables 10-4A and 10-4B compare state government user charge and license revenues in 1980 and 1987. In 1980, states collected $73.02 per capita from user charges, accounting for approximately 10 percent of own-source revenue. Arizona was essentially identical to the U.S. average. Colorado, New Mexico, and Utah raised more revenue per capita through user charges while the three most populous sunbelt states, California, Florida, and Texas, raised much less in per capita user charge revenues. With respect to per capita license revenues, Arizona was about 16 percent lower than the national average. Three of the comparison states, California, Colorado and Utah, had lower per capita license revenues than Arizona. For both Arizona and the U.S. average, license fee revenue was about half the level of user charge revenue.

Table 10-4B shows that by 1987, Arizona's user fee revenues had declined relative to the U.S. average and the averages of its comparison states, while license fee revenues had risen compared to average. Only Nevada and Texas collected more license fees per capita than Arizona in 1987, indicating some sort of policy shift away from per unit pricing of public services in Arizona.

An alternative method of comparing Arizona to other states is to determine the amount of user charge and license revenue a statistically representative state having some of the same characteristics as Arizona would generate, and to compare "predicted" revenue with Arizona's actual revenue. To arrive at this comparison, the revenue numbers reported in Table 10-4B were regressed on various demographic and economic variables, on a cross-section of the fifty states, to estimate a representative state's user charge and license revenues.

Table 10-4C reports actual user charge revenue, representative user charge revenue, and the percentage difference between the two for Arizona and the comparison states. (See the appendix for a specification of the regressions used to estimate representative user charge and license fee revenues.) Arizona's actual user charge revenue is 41 percent below what a representative state with Arizona's characteristics would produce. This number represents the fourth largest negative percentage difference among the fifty states (the other states being Wyoming, Nevada and Idaho). Table 10-4D reports the same information regarding license fee revenue. In this case, Arizona is on the high side, 23.1 percent higher than a representative state with the same characteristics.

As these results show, Arizona tends to generate more license revenue and less user charge revenue than a "typical state" with Arizona's characteristics. Despite the fact that Arizona collects more license revenue than predicted, when user charge and license revenues are combined, Arizona still ranks third in terms of negative percentage difference from its representative level. This indicates that Arizona generates considerably less revenue in the form of user charges and fees than would a typical state with Arizona's characteristics.

The distribution of user charges by category is illustrated in Table 10-5. For all states, higher education contributed the bulk of user charge revenues through tuition and other student fees. This contribution was greater than average in Arizona, 86 percent of user charge revenues in Arizona compared to an average of 56 percent. On average, hospitals contributed the second greatest share of user charges, but this category provided negligible amounts in Arizona.

The distribution of license revenues by category is shown in Table 10-6. Motor vehicle registrations contributed the greatest share of license revenues, 74 percent in Arizona and 52 percent for the U.S. average. For the U.S. as a whole, corporation licenses contributed the second greatest share. (Corporation license revenues include any flat fees

Table 10-4A
State Government User Charge and License Fee Revenues -- 1980

	User Charges			License Fees		
	Total (millions of $)	$ Per Capita	Percent of Own Source Revenue	Total (millions of $)	$ Per Capita	Percent of Own Source Revenue
U.S.	$16,544	$73.02	9.7	$8,690	$38.35	5.1
Arizona	199	73.21	9.9	88	32.37	4.3
California	1,480	62.53	6.6	629	26.57	2.8
Colorado	339	117.30	16.8	93	32.31	4.6
Florida	343	35.19	6.2	379	38.88	6.8
Nevada	39	48.37	6.5	64	80.12	10.9
New Mexico	127	98.00	8.2	55	42.59	3.5
Texas	761	53.48	8.4	741	52.07	8.2
Utah	163	111.56	15.5	34	22.09	3.1
Arizona Percent of Total		100.3			84.4	

Table 10-4B
State Government User Charge and License Fee Revenues -- 1987

	User Charges			License Fees		
	Total (millions of $)	$ Per Capita	Percent of Own Source Revenue	Total (millions of $)	$ Per Capita	Percent of Own Source Revenue
U.S.	$31,900	$131.06	10.1	$16,000	$65.73	5.0
Arizona	357	105.58	8.5	243	71.81	5.8
California	3,332	120.44	7.7	1,426	51.56	3.3
Colorado	603	183.08	16.4	142	43.03	3.9
Florida	781	64.92	6.8	663	55.12	5.7
Nevada	84	83.47	6.2	123	122.63	9.1
New Mexico	259	172.66	9.7	67	44.60	2.5
Texas	1,530	91.15	10.1	1,816	108.18	12.0
Utah	366	217.59	18.2	69	40.95	3.4
Arizona Percent of Total		80.6			109.2	

Source: *State Government Finances*, 1980 and 1987, U.S. Bureau of the Census.

| Table 10-4C
Actual and Representative State User Charge Revenue, FY 1987 | | |
	Actual Revenue (millions)	Representative Revenue (millions)	Percent Difference Between Actual and Representative
Arizona	$ 357	$ 605.9	-41.0
California	3,331	3,256.5	2.2
Colorado	603	486.7	23.8
Nevada	84	191.3	-56.1
New Mexico	258	278.8	-7.4
Utah	365	273.6	33.4
Florida	780	1,050.5	-25.7
Texas	1,530	1,572.5	-2.7

Source: Bureau of the Census, *State Government Finances*, 1987 and authors' calculations (see appendix).

| Table 10-4D
Actual and Representative State License Revenue, FY 1987 | | |
	Actual Revenue (millions)	Representative Revenue (millions)	Percent Difference Between Actual and Representative
Arizona	$ 243	$ 197.3	23.1
California	1,426	1,543.9	-7.6
Colorado	141	292.6	-51.8
Nevada	123	52.2	135.6
New Mexico	66	104.2	-36.6
Utah	68	152.1	-55.2
Florida	662	843.6	-21.5
Texas	1,816	1,479.4	22.7

Source: Bureau of the Census, *State Government Finances*, 1987 and authors' calculations (see appendix).

imposed on all corporations; occupational and business license revenues include inspection fees, fees required for specific businesses or occupations, and other business fees not included in another category.) Arizona and all of the comparison states except Texas had considerably lower shares of corporation license revenue than average.

Table 10-5
Percentage Distribution of State
User Charge Revenues by Category -- 1987

	Higher Education	Other Education	Hospitals	Highways	Natural Resources	Parks and Recreation	Other	Total
U.S.	56.1	0.7	21.2	6.5	2.5	1.8	11.2	100.0
AZ	86.2	0.6	0.0	0.5	3.7	0.5	8.6	100.0
CA	52.3	0.1	25.9	3.3	10.1	1.1	7.2	100.0
CO	74.3	0.8	16.1	0.7	0.7	0.2	7.2	100.0
FL	44.2	0.4	9.6	20.5	1.6	1.5	22.3	100.0
NV	67.3	0.9	2.6	6.7	1.7	1.0	19.8	100.0
NM	53.1	2.3	29.4	0.4	4.5	1.2	9.2	100.0
TX	69.0	0.2	19.1	1.7	1.2	0.6	8.2	100.0
UT	58.6	0.7	33.5	0.4	1.3	0.6	5.0	100.0

Source: *State Government Finances*, 1987, U.S. Bureau of the Census.

Table 10-6
Percentage Distribution of State License Revenues by Category -- 1987

	Motor Vehicle Registrations	Corporations	Occupations & Business	Hunting/ Fishing	Motor Vehicle Operators	Alcoholic Beverages	Other	Total
U.S.	51.9	19.8	14.4	4.2	4.6	1.6	3.6	100.0
AZ	73.9	1.6	8.2	5.1	2.8	0.9	7.6	100.0
CA	66.3	0.5	17.5	3.9	5.1	2.2	4.4	100.0
CO	54.7	1.8	15.3	19.7	3.4	1.7	3.5	100.0
FL	54.8	3.3	23.6	1.8	8.9	3.4	4.3	100.0
NV	40.4	3.5	10.2	3.7	2.5	0.0	39.6	100.0
NM	54.8	8.3	17.2	10.6	4.8	1.5	2.8	100.0
TX	38.4	49.1	5.9	1.8	2.7	1.3	0.8	100.0
UT	57.9	0.0	14.8	19.3	6.9	0.5	0.6	100.0

Source: *State Government Finances*, 1987, U.S. Bureau of the Census.

Table 10-7 displays revenue capacity and effort indices for licenses. Capacity measures the number of licenses granted per capita compared to the average while effort measures the amount of revenue collected relative to the number of licenses. Arizona's effort was 45 percent above average for vehicle registrations indicating higher than average license fees; Arizona's effort was far below average for licenses to sell alcoholic beverages and for corporation licenses indicating lower than average rates.

	Table 10-7 License Fee Revenue Capacity and Effort Indices, Selected Categories							
	Motor Vehicle Registration		Hunting/Fishing		Alcoholic Beverages		Corporations	
	Capacity Index	Effort Index	Capacity Index	Effort Index	Capacity Index	Effort Index	Capacity Index	Effort Index
U.S.	100.0	100.0	100.0	100.0	100.0	100.0	100.0	100.0
AZ	104.1	145.1	118.5	108.3	114.3	60.5	105.2	8.3
CA	99.3	71.1	57.8	133.8	84.0	135.0	93.8	2.4
CO	121.1	63.9	150.5	238.2	151.9	48.2	131.6	4.4
FL	117.4	78.6	45.1	73.1	61.2	240.8	160.6	8.1
NV	112.8	123.6	147.8	111.7	203.4	1.4	124.8	23.4
NM	138.8	47.4	109.3	195.8	77.3	74.0	78.4	48.6
TX	108.8	123.3	81.2	87.0	61.2	96.1	93.7	464.4
UT	100.1	55.7	167.6	157.9	23.5	78.9	92.1	0.0

Note: Capacity is measured by actual and estimated numbers of licenses for the first three categories and by number of corporations for the last category. Effort is measured by actual fee collections relative to capacity. Indexed with U.S. = 100.

Source: *1986 State Fiscal Capacity and Effort*, Advisory Commission on Intergovernmental Relations.

Table 10-8 reports the extent to which user charges cover expenditures in various categories. The comparison states show great variation in this respect and Arizona differs substantially from the average. Arizona user charges financed 12 to 15 percent of expenditures in education, natural resources, and parks and recreation. For most states, hospital fees cover a substantial portion of expenditures, but Arizona's hospital fees are negligible. Of the comparison states, only Colorado's parks and recreation fees cover a smaller portion of expenditures than Arizona.

<u>Arizona State Charges and Fees</u>

Just under half of all Arizona state agencies collect some fee revenues. Currently, many fee rates are set in statute or in rules. Thus, changing the rates is a very lengthy process. To maximize efficiency, it is necessary for agencies to have flexibility in changing rates to respond to changes in costs and shifts in demand. Flexibility could be enhanced by establishing fee *ranges* in statute and rule, and allowing agencies to shift fees within those ranges, either through a Board action or agency policy. The efficiency advantages of this structure must be balanced against the loss of public input that would result from giving more authority directly to the agencies.

Table 10-8
State User Charge Revenues as a
Percentage of State Expenditures By Category -- 1987

	Education	Hospitals	Highways	Natural Resources	Parks and Recreation
U.S.	12.1	37.4	5.4	10.2	26.6
Arizona	14.3	0.0	0.2	15.3	11.6
California	7.8	53.8	4.2	26.3	15.9
Colorado	23.0	41.5	0.8	3.8	6.4
Florida	6.1	19.1	10.9	2.4	20.0
Nevada	9.3	7.3	2.8	4.9	14.1
New Mexico	11.0	55.1	0.3	20.3	13.7
Texas	10.8	31.9	1.0	6.1	14.3
Utah	15.7	81.9	0.5	3.8	15.4

Source: *State Government Finances*, 1987, U. S. Bureau of the Census.

Table 10-9 reports the actual amounts of user charge and license revenues collected in 1988, by section of government. Total charge and fee revenues retained by the State amounted to approximately 7.5 percent of total State revenues with education and transportation each contributing 2.7 percent in charges. License revenues were approximately 50 percent more than user charge revenues.

Table 10-9
Arizona State License Fee and User Charge Revenues By Category -- 1988

Category	Licenses	Charges	Total	% of Total State Revenue
General Government	$ 1,176,100	$ 64,800	$ 1,240,900	0.03
Health and Welfare	10,026,400	9,972,400	19,898,700	0.51
Inspection & Regulation	43,693,700	990,300	44,684,000	1.14
Education	274,800	103,926,600	104,201,400	2.67
Protection and Safety	168,700	248,200	416,900	0.01
Transportation	103,649,400	354,400	104,003,800	2.66
Natural Resources	16,920,000	741,400	17,661,400	0.45
Total	$175,909,100	$116,198,000	$292,107,100	7.48

Source: *State of Arizona Executive Budget*, FY 1990.

Table 10-10 shows user charge and license revenues as a percentage of total expenditures for each category of government. In total, such revenue financed only 8.6 percent of state expenditures in 1988, but the percentage varied greatly by category. Inspection and Regulation and Natural Resources financed the greatest share of expenditures with charges and fees, 80 percent and 40 percent respectively. Within Inspection and Regulation, the major contributors of license revenues are the Registrar of Contractors, the Commission on Agriculture and Horticulture, the Department of Insurance, and the Banking Department. Within Natural Resources, the major contributing agencies are the Department of Water Resources, the Land Department, and the Game and Fish Department. With respect to user charges, the largest contributors overall are university tuition, the Department of Economic Security, the Department of Health Services, and AHCCCS.

<table>
<tr><td colspan="2" align="center">Table 10-10
Arizona State License Fee and User
Charge Revenues As a Share of
Expenditures By Category -- 1988</td></tr>
<tr><td>General Government</td><td align="right">0.6</td></tr>
<tr><td>Health and Welfare</td><td align="right">2.8</td></tr>
<tr><td>Inspection and Regulation</td><td align="right">80.0</td></tr>
<tr><td>Education</td><td align="right">6.7</td></tr>
<tr><td>Protection and Safety</td><td align="right">0.1</td></tr>
<tr><td>Transportation</td><td align="right">19.0</td></tr>
<tr><td>Natural Resources</td><td align="right">40.1</td></tr>
<tr><td>Total</td><td align="right">8.6</td></tr>
<tr><td colspan="2">Source: State of Arizona Executive Budget FY 1990 and State of Arizona Annual Financial Report, FY 1988.</td></tr>
</table>

The incentives for an individual agency to manage user charges efficiently and to respond to consumer desires depend, in part, on how much of the user revenues the agency can reserve for its own use. An indicator of the existence of these incentives, then, is the percentage of an agency's user charge and fee revenues that accrues to special funds of the State rather than to the General Fund. The General Fund receives general taxes and other types of revenues and finances general governmental activities; special funds are created in statute with revenue sources and revenue uses specifically defined. Usually, the revenue source is related to the allowed uses of the fund. The motor fuel tax, for example, is deposited into a fund for highway construction and maintenance. The agency providing the good or service administers the special fund, with or without annual legislative appropriation, depending on the statutory provisions. When user fees are deposited into the General Fund, they become part of the large pot of State monies and there is no link between revenues and expenditures. When user fees are deposited into special funds, on the other hand, there is a direct link between revenues and expenditures, and agencies are more likely to respond to the messages inherent in the revenue stream.

Table 10-11 reports the percentage of user charge and license fee revenues deposited into special funds in 1988. Overall, 86 percent of such revenues was directed into special funds indicating that the State is taking advantage of the efficiency potential of user charges. The special fund proportion varied considerably by category, however. General Government deposited the lowest percentage into special funds (12 percent), while education and transportation each deposited 100 percent of fee and charge revenues into special funds. More than 60 percent of the fee revenues collected by General Government, Inspection and Regulation, and Protection and Safety agencies are deposited into the State General Fund. To enhance the efficiency advantages of charges and fees, it may be desirable to earmark more fee revenues into special agency funds. These fees should be considered individually as there may be special circumstances or conflicting policy goals that would make earmarking inappropriate.

Table 10-11
Percentage of Arizona State License Fee and
User Charge Revenues Deposited into Special Funds
By Category -- 1988

Category	Licenses	Charges	Total
General Government	9.1	55.7	11.5
Health and Welfare	97.6	20.9	59.5
Inspection & Regulation	35.8	35.9	35.8
Education	100.0	100.0	100.0
Protection and Safety	0.0	40.9	24.3
Transportation	100.0	100.0	100.0
Natural Resources	80.6	23.7	78.2
Total	81.4	92.1	85.6

Source: *State of Arizona Executive Budget*, FY 1990.

Local Government Charges and Fees

Local governments traditionally have relied more heavily on user charges than state governments. This pattern has continued in the 1980s. In 1987, U.S. local governments financed 21 percent of own-source revenues through user charges (on average), while state governments financed 10 percent through charges. Arizona exhibits this same pattern, 18 percent reliance for local governments compared to 8 percent reliance for state government. Table 10-12 compares the local user charge reliance in various states in 1980 and 1987. Arizona local governments relied somewhat less on user charges than average in both years. Like state government reliance (Tables 4A and 4B), local reliance on user charges has remained virtually constant since 1980. The comparison states show no distinct characteristics relative to the U.S. average: half were below the average reliance in 1987 while half were above.

Table 10-12 Local Government User Charge Revenues as a Percentage of Own-Source Revenues		
	1980(%)	**1987 (%)**
U.S.	21.4	21.4
Arizona	16.6	17.9
California	25.1	26.3
Colorado	16.9	17.5
Florida	33.5	28.7
Nevada	30.3	34.7
New Mexico	28.1	22.3
Texas	24.8	20.0
Utah	16.8	14.9
Source: *Governmental Finances*, selected years, U.S. Bureau of the Census.		

Arizona counties collect the bulk of their license fees from building permits, automobile operators' licenses, rabies control licenses and franchise and inspection fees. County user charges primarily include sewer and sanitation and hospital and ambulance charges. Between 1982 and 1987, the use of "other charges" increased significantly from 12 percent of user charge revenues in 1982 to 27 percent in 1987. As shown in the top panel of Table 10-13, the portion of county expenditures financed through user charges increased substantially between 1982 and 1987. For example, counties increased from 33 to 63 percent the share of their sewer and sanitation expenditures financed by user charges. The remaining portions of Table 10-13 present per capita and share-of-revenue figures. These show that charges per capita have risen in nominal dollars, and that the fraction of own-source revenue due to user charges has increased. Thus, although user charges as a share of total (all sources including intergovernmental grants) revenue had fallen, user charges have become a more important source of revenue that is raised internally. This is in contrast to the experience at the state level where user charges have accounted for a declining percentage of state own-raised revenue during the 1980s (see Tables 10-4a and 10-b).

Without more detailed analysis we cannot determine whether this increased reliance on user charges has led to more efficient provision of public services. It is probable, however, that this increase was motivated not by considerations of economic efficiency, but rather by the budgetary pressures faced by counties during the period. With rising expenditure pressures, and few other revenue sources to turn to, counties may have chosen to rely more heavily on user charges simply out of necessity.

Prior to fiscal year 1989, counties had the authority to impose charges for specific items described in statute. In 1988, the Legislature granted counties more general authority to establish user charges, provided that the charge did not exceed the actual cost of providing the service. Currently, the counties are conducting (indirect) cost allocation and user fee studies to determine actual service costs and reasonable fee levels. It is likely then, that county reliance on user charges will increase significantly in the near future.

<table>
<tr><td colspan="3">Table 10-13
County User Charges 1982 and 1987</td></tr>
<tr><td></td><td>1982</td><td>1987</td></tr>
<tr><td colspan="3">Coverage Ratios*</td></tr>
<tr><td>Sewer and Sanitation</td><td>33.2</td><td>62.8</td></tr>
<tr><td>Airports</td><td>19.8</td><td>94.4</td></tr>
<tr><td>Parks and Recreation</td><td>20.7</td><td>49.3</td></tr>
<tr><td>Hospitals</td><td>22.7</td><td>63.9</td></tr>
<tr><td colspan="3">Charge Revenue Per Capita</td></tr>
<tr><td>Sewer System</td><td>$1.19</td><td>$3.39</td></tr>
<tr><td>Sanitation</td><td>0.28</td><td>1.59</td></tr>
<tr><td>Airport</td><td>0.21</td><td>0.53</td></tr>
<tr><td>Parks and Recreation</td><td>0.24</td><td>1.08</td></tr>
<tr><td>Ambulance</td><td>4.78</td><td>2.10</td></tr>
<tr><td>Hospital</td><td>4.79</td><td>14.32</td></tr>
<tr><td>Housing Development</td><td>0.20</td><td>0.14</td></tr>
<tr><td>Other</td><td>2.54</td><td>7.44</td></tr>
<tr><td colspan="3">Charge Revenue as a Share of Revenue</td></tr>
<tr><td>As a Share of Total Revenue</td><td>8.6</td><td>7.4</td></tr>
<tr><td>As a Share of Own-Source Revenue</td><td>11.2</td><td>14.0</td></tr>
</table>

* Coverage ratio = user charge revenue as a share of expenditure in a particular category.

Source: Census survey data collected by Arizona State University and adjusted by Arizona Joint Select Committee on State Revenues and Expenditures.

While, legally, counties can charge an individual user the full cost of the service provided, from an economic perspective this is desirable only when equity concerns are minimal and when there are no benefits that accrue to people other than the individual user. If individual users are asked to pay for full provision costs when the service generates external benefits, they will consume less than the efficient amount from an overall perspective and net benefits to society will be lost. Thus, state rules limiting county use of property taxes, prohibiting other revenue sources, and allowing greater reliance on charges may be encouraging an over-reliance on charge financing and resulting in losses of efficiency and equity.

Approximately half of Arizona municipal license revenue comes from building permits with large amounts added from business and occupational licenses and inspection fees.

On average, half of city user charges come from utilities with significant contributions from garbage collection, parking and airport fees, and parks and recreation. Transit fees contributed only 0.6 percent of total municipal user charge revenues in 1987.

Table 10-14 reports the portion of city expenditures financed through user charges for 1982 and 1987 for 8 categories of charges. As shown, the number of cities that employ user charges varies from one functional category to another. This variation partially reflects differences in city activities and functions. For example, many cities do not provide electricity or gas through the public sector, do not have public bus or transit systems, or do not have airports. The variation also reflects different decisions about the use of charges. For example, most cities spend money on parks and recreation, but they make different choices about how much reliance to place on user charges.

Looking first at the 1987 coverage ratios, we see that, on average, the few cities that provide electricity and gas receive more in charge revenue than their reported expenditures. (Reported expenditures probably do not include indirect costs of administration, so the "profit" from these charges is probably not as great as shown here.) Other categories with high coverage ratios are water, sewers, and garbage collection. On average about 20 percent of spending on parks and recreation was recovered through user charges in 1987.

A comparison of the 1982 averages in the bottom panel of the table with the 1987 averages shows, somewhat surprisingly, that coverage ratios have declined over time in all expenditure categories except garbage collection and gas. Hence, despite increases in per capita charges, cities have not increased their relative reliance on user charges over time; many of the observed increases in per capita user charges simply reflect increased spending on items that are financed by user charges.

Summary

Increased utilization of user charges during the eighties occurred simultaneously with increased deregulation and privatization of public services. Thus, the question arises whether user charges and privatization are substitutes or complements. If they are substitutes, then states in which privatization is successful will show less reliance on user charges than other states. If privatization and user charges are complements, then future reliance on user charges will depend on the popularity of private market principles in the public sector. As of this writing, Arizona state and local governments rely less on charges and fees than average.

What is the future of user charges and license fees? There appears to be a growing feeling among public officials that user charges have run their course as revenue-generating instruments (See Lemov, 1989). As reported in this chapter, user charges account for only 15% of state and local own-revenue nationwide. An important consideration regarding the future of user charges is a political one. The greatest resistance to user charges will come from those who stand to lose as a result. Another consideration is the voters' perception of fairness. Because user charges allocate goods in a manner similar to the private market, the question of equity is frequently waiting around the corner to challenge the desirability of charging direct prices for public services. Finally, as we have emphasized in this chapter, the advantage of user charges over general taxes lies in allocative efficiency. Their usefulness and desirability may be strained if they are employed as revenue generators simply to avoid the political problems associated with raising taxes.

Table 10-14
City User Charge Coverage Ratios 1982 and 1987

	Charges as a Share of Own-Source Revenue	Coverage Ratios[*]								
		Water	Electricity	Gas	Transit and Bus	Sewer	Garbage	Sewer/ Garbage[**]	Airport	Parks and Recreation
1987										
Average (number of cities)	0.366 (74)	0.970 (52)	1.655 (5)	1.195 (4)	0.125 (4)	0.861 (56)	0.877 (53)	0.737 (62)	0.406 (21)	0.201 (55)
1982										
Average (number of cities)	0.364 (75)	1.175 (52)	1.783 (5)	1.068 (3)	0.341 (2)	0.972 (55)	0.817 (50)	0.753 (61)	0.569 (20)	0.213 (47)

[*] Coverage ratio = User charge revenue as a share of expenditures in a particular category.
[**] Some cities reported this as a combined category.

Source: Census survey data collected by Arizona State University and adjusted by Arizona Joint Select Committee on State Revenues and Expenditures.

References

Buchanan, James M., *Public Finance in Democratic Process*, (Chapel Hill, NC: The University of North Carolina Press, 1967).

Lemov, Penelope, "User Fees, Once the Answer to City Budget Prayers, May Have Reached Their Peak," *Governing*, March 1989, pp.24-30.

U.S. Advisory Commission on Intergovernmental Relations, *1986 State Fiscal Capacity and Effort*, (Washington, D.C.: ACIR).

U.S. Bureau of the Census, *Governmental Finances*, (Washington, D.C.: GPO, various years).

__________________, *State Government Finance*, (Washington, D.C.: GPO, various years).

U.S. Conference of Mayors and Arthur Young and Company, *User Fees: Toward Better Usage*, April 1987.

Appendix

The following ordinary least squares regression equation for state user charge revenue was run on a 1987 cross-section of the fifty states:

$$SCH = 46.3 - 25.6\ POP - 2.63\ POPSQ + .092\ STAX - .04\ IGRS$$
$$(43.5)\ \ (26.1)\qquad (0.66)\qquad\qquad (.024)\qquad\quad (.031)$$

$$+\ .139\ SLC + 3.05\ ENROLL,\ R\text{-}SQUARED = .935,\ F = 104.$$
$$(.171)\qquad\quad (.641)$$

Standard errors are in parentheses.

SCH is total state user charge revenue, POP and POPSQ are state population and its square, STAX is total state general tax collections, IGRS is total state intergovernmental revenue, SLC is total state license revenue, and ENROLL is total state enrollment in public higher education. POP and POPSQ control for state size. Bigger states are likely to collect more revenue. IGRS controls for revenue raised outside the state -- a state "income effect". STAX and SLC proxy a state's proclivity to tax as well as controlling for substitute sources of state-raised revenue. ENROLL is included to control for differences in college tuition revenue, a major source of a state's user charge revenue.

The regression equation for license revenue run over the same sample as the user charge equation, is:

$$SLC = 8.05 + 103.6\ POP - .635\ POPSQ - .071\ STAX$$
$$(38.0)\ \ (14.2)\qquad (.529)\qquad\quad (.022)$$

$$+\ .157\ SCH + .007\ IGRS,\ R\text{-}SQUARED = .869,\ F = 58.5$$
$$(.105)\qquad\quad (.027)$$

Standard errors are in parentheses.

Variables are defined identically to those in the SCH equation above. ENROLL is omitted from this equation since there is no obvious connection between license revenue and college tuition.

It should be noted that these equations are included only for descriptive purposes. No normative implications are intended.

Part III:
State
Expenditures

Chapter 11

Higher Education

J. Fred Giertz

This chapter analyzes fiscal aspects of public higher education in Arizona. The rationale for public provision of higher education services is discussed as well as the reasons for the dominance of state governments in these activities. Arizona is compared to other states in the nation on expenditures and financing of higher education. Arizona's higher education policy decisions are compared with those of a representative state having characteristics similar to those of Arizona. The distribution of resources among the various institutions of higher eduction in Arizona is also analyzed. The chapter concludes with a discussion of policy options available to the state.

The Role Of Higher Education: A Conceptual Framework

Higher education has come to play a major role in American society. It obviously is important to current or prospective students and their parents. It also is a concern of both business and government and citizens in general especially for its role in promoting economic development. Higher education can be considered a major industry in the United States with 3,400 institutions providing instruction to 12.5 million students in 1986. Revenues of higher education institutions amounted to over $100 billion dollars or about 2.5 percent of gross national product in 1986. In Arizona in 1986, there were 227,000 (full and part-time) college students (7 percent of the state's population), and institutions of higher education reported current-fund revenues of $1.1 billion.

Despite its size and pervasiveness, fundamental questions about the roles that higher education plays for both the individual as well as society are often taken for granted or misunderstood. In this section, several important questions concerning higher education and its place in society are reviewed. In particular, the division of responsibility for financing education between the individual student (and the student's family) and the rest of society is addressed. The various types of benefits of higher education that are external to the student are described to provide a rationale for the role of government in the provision of these educational services.

Higher Education: The Student and Society

Higher education provides a variety of benefits directly to the student and indirectly to the remainder of society.   The student expects that education will increase lifetime earnings, while also yielding direct consumption benefits (the college experience) during the college years and enhancing the student's future enjoyment and appreciation of life (for example, art, music, literature, and sports).

If these were the only benefits from higher education, education would be little different from many other goods and services that are dealt with efficiently through the private market with limited government involvement.   Students and their parents would be expected to compare the present value of these private benefits with the costs of education (such as tuition and fees, books and supplies, and probably most importantly, foregone income) to determine the most desirable amount of education to undertake.   Studies suggest that the private pecuniary returns to higher education from higher future incomes would be substantial even if students paid the full cost of their education.[1]   In addition to the pecuniary benefits, other studies suggest that educated individuals live longer, have fewer health problems, and report that they have a more positive outlook on life than those with less education.

Clearly, many, if not most, students would pursue various programs of study beyond high school even if they were unsubsidized.   Education would promote economic well-being by increasing the future incomes and enjoyment of life of students with minimal government involvement.   Intervention by government would only be called for if students found it difficult or impossible to borrow to finance educational activities because of imperfections in the financial markets.   Guaranteed student loans often are suggested to address this problem.

The benefits of higher education, however, are not confined to or captured solely by the student.   There are many external benefits from higher education that accrue to members of society who are not students.   These benefits (such as lower crime rates, lower welfare costs, and greater participation in governmental and community affairs) are important, but they are difficult to quantify.   The extent and quantitative magnitude of such benefits are the subject of considerable controversy.

An important external benefit of higher education is its contribution to the growth and development of the economy.   Educated workers not only increase their own incomes (which is a private benefit), but they also contribute to the increased productivity of other human and non-human factors of production.   While estimates are imprecise, higher education may account for from between 5 and 15 percent of economic growth in our society.   The contribution of higher education to economic development comes in many forms and ranges from basic training that provides vocational skills for students to the support of high level scientific and technical research carried out in university laboratories.   Basic and applied research produced in universities may play a role in technological advancement in the private sector.   A high quality system of higher education may also serve to retain talented in-state students and attract out-of-state students who will remain in the state to pursue their careers and thus contribute to the state's economy.[2]

A second rationale for government involvement in higher education is the view that access to higher education, like access to elementary and secondary education, should be guaranteed to all regardless of personal income or community wealth.   Even if this view of higher education as an entitlement were accepted, public provision of higher education services may not be required since government loans and scholarships to students of low income might address the concern.

The Role of Government

Whether external benefits from higher education are sufficiently large in reality to justify the current level of governmental support for higher education is an open question. Some critics suggest that the private benefits to students are so large in comparison to the external benefits that extensive government involvement is not justified. They suggest reduced direct student aid (especially to higher income students), more reliance on private institutions and, in regard to public higher education, greater reliance on tuition and fees from students.

Regardless of the merits of the arguments, these critics have clearly not prevailed. The role played by government in the provision of higher education directly, through the establishment of public universities and colleges, and indirectly, through the support of students and programs in both public and private institutions, remains large. The faith in higher education as a vehicle for both individual and societal progress continues unabated. Access to subsidized higher education is viewed as a means of overcoming past inequities and considered to be a fundamental right not unlike free elementary and secondary education. It is instructive to note that critics of education in the 1980s have focused predominately on the deficiencies of elementary and secondary education not those of higher education.

Over the years, states have become the single most important provider of higher educational services. Higher education in the United States receives more direct state expenditures than any other function except welfare. (Elementary and secondary education is supported primarily indirectly by states through intergovernmental grants to local districts.) Public colleges and universities enroll about three-fourths of all higher education students. There are only a handful of federal institutions of higher education and even fewer municipal universities. In the public arena, almost all four-year institutions are state controlled while the control of two-year colleges varies from state to state. Some are controlled by the state, while others are locally controlled with substantial state financial support.

State governments have become the dominant provider of public higher education for a variety of reasons. States seem to provide an appropriate level of government for the provision of public higher education. Primary provision at the federal level would be unlikely to deal effectively with the diversity of needs and tastes of different regions of the nation. The federal government does, however, have a role to play in the provision of higher education since issues such as competitiveness and access for the poor are national in scope. The federal government tends to promote higher education through grants for particular programs and projects (both to public and private institutions) rather than through the establishment of federal institutions. Federal aid also is available to many students through grants and loans.

At the other extreme, local governments are not well suited to provide comprehensive higher educational services. First, there are important economies of scale in higher education (for example, libraries, laboratories and specialized courses of study). A large number of small institutions could not provide these types of comprehensive services at a reasonable cost. Note that this problem is considerably less severe for elementary and secondary schools because of less need for specialized resources and programs.

In addition, the external benefits generated by higher education have a fairly broad geographic dispersion. Residents of a local community are unlikely to capture many of these benefits thus reducing their incentive for the efficient provision of these services. States are much better suited to pursue economic development policies including those related to education and research than are local governments. To the extent that higher education is provided as a response to redistributional motives, states are better prepared to carry out this function than are local governments.

State provision allows diversity while also providing a level of operation large enough to capture economies of scale and a geographic area large enough to capture most external benefits. Two year colleges are characterized by fewer scale economies and also have a narrower geographic distribution of benefits thereby making local provision more attractive. In such cases, community colleges usually have wider jurisdictions than elementary and secondary schools while also receiving substantial state support.

Higher Education In Arizona And The Rest Of The Nation

Higher education, as measured by money spent on it, is one of the most important functions of state government in Arizona. Although it has declined in importance relative to other state functions in recent years, state expenditures for education exceed those for any other function in Arizona except aid for local elementary and secondary schools. Comparison of higher education activities in Arizona with those in other states and with the nation as a whole puts the size of the state's higher education sector and the state's financial commitment to these activities in perspective.

A word of caution is in order in regard to interstate comparisons. First, national averages are not necessarily ideals. While comparisons may be interesting and useful, they cannot be used to reach a final conclusion as to the appropriateness of a particular state's activities. Furthermore, there are no universally accepted norms for measuring state effort in this area. For example, should a state's support of education be measured in terms of expenditures per capita, or per $1,000 of income, or per student enrolled? Each of these measures provides useful information, yet no one measure can provide a complete picture.

Finally, comparisons are sometimes difficult because of different institutional arrangements and accounting procedures among the states. For example, in some states (such as Arizona) two-year colleges are financed at the local level along with intergovernmental aid from the state. In other states, two-year colleges are solely the responsibility of the state with no local involvement. Comparisons of state government support between two states with differing structures might yield misleading conclusions about the overall level of support for two-year colleges. Similarly, some states have highly developed private higher education sectors while other states rely more heavily on public institutions. In this situation, comparisons of state support may be misleading as evidence about the total commitment of people in the state to higher education.

Descriptive Comparisons

Arizona has three four-year public universities and nine public two-year community college districts. Arizona, with about 1.4 percent of the nation's population, has two of the nation's largest universities. Measured by total enrollment, Arizona State University is the fifth largest university in the country, and the University of Arizona is in the top thirty in size. The share of all college students who are enrolled in public institutions in Arizona is much larger than in most other states. The private college sector is very small. In Arizona in 1986, full time equivalent (FTE) enrollment in public institutions of higher education accounted for 97 percent of all higher education students in Arizona compared to a national average of 75 percent.

Table 11-1 presents information on FTE enrollment in public institutions (both universities and community colleges) in academic year 1986-87 per 1,000 of population for Arizona, Arizona's five neighboring states and the nation. Arizona enrollment was over twenty percent higher than the national average in per capita FTE enrollment in public institutions of higher education.

Table 11-1 FTE Enrollment in Public Institutions of Higher Education		
	(1) **Enrollment** **per 1,000** **Population**	**(2)** **Percentage** **of United States** **Average**
United States	29.1	100.0
Arizona	35.2	120.9
California	35.0	120.3
Colorado	34.6	119.0
Nevada	21.4	73.4
New Mexico	32.1	110.5
Utah	33.1	113.8
Source: *Statistical Abstract of the United States 1988*, U.S. Bureau of Census, Table 247.		

Arizona institutions of higher education are very attractive to in-state students. Of Arizona residents who choose to attend higher education institutions, 97 percent choose to stay within the state. This percentage is the highest in the country at 14 percent above the national average.[3] Arizona also attracts a large number of out-of-state students, ranking seventh in absolute terms and first when compared to population. In 1986-87, in-state tuition at four-year institutions in the state ranked thirty-fifth in the country at about 80 percent of the national average. (See Table 11-2.) In 1986, tuition plus fee revenues per FTE were about 8 percent above the national average for four-year public institutions and 13 percent below the average for public two-year schools. Tuition and fees were above the national average even though in-state tuition was below the average because of the large number of out-of-state students paying higher charges.

State expenditures on higher education for 1986-87 are presented in Table 11-3. These expenditure figures provide a measure of the level of services provided by the state. State expenditures include direct expenditures for current operations (not including auxiliary enterprises such as student housing) plus intergovernmental aid to community colleges. Expenditures are presented on a per capita basis, per FTE enrollment and, finally, per $1,000 of state personal income. Arizona ranked considerably above the national average

(17 percent) in per capita expenditures because of its relatively large enrollment relative to population. It also ranked above the U.S. average compared to personal income (29 percent) because of the large enrollment and relatively low level of state personal income. However, state expenditures per student were somewhat low (3 percent below the national average) because of the high enrollment levels in the state and the fact that local support from community college districts was not included in this state expenditure measure.

Table 11-2
Average Undergraduate Tuition (In-State)
1986-87 Public Four Year Institutions

United States	$1,414
Arizona	1,136
California	1,031
Colorado	1,482
Nevada	988
New Mexico	915
Utah	1,159

Source: *Digest of Education Statistics 1988*, National Center for Education Statistics, page 253.

Table 11-3
State Expenditures for Higher Education -- 1987
(Current Operations less Auxiliary Enterprises plus Intergovernmental)

State	Expenditures Per Capita		Expenditures Per FTE		Expenditures Per $1,000 Of Personal Income	
	Amount	Index	Amount	Index	Amount	Index
United States	$181	100.0	$6,230	100.0	$12.51	100.0
Arizona	212	117.2	6,040	96.9	16.09	128.6
California	239	132.0	6,833	109.7	14.51	116.0
Colorado	221	121.7	6,370	102.2	14.60	116.8
Nevada	168	92.5	7,848	126.0	11.35	90.7
New Mexico	218	120.4	6,787	109.0	19.37	154.8
Utah	296	163.3	8,941	143.5	27.18	217.4

Source: *State Government Finances in 1987*, U.S. Bureau of the Census, Table 12.

Combined state and local support for public higher education is shown in Table 11-4. Support includes state and local appropriations, grants, and contracts to public institutions. When local support is added to that of the state, Arizona spent substantially more than the national average both per capita (22.5 percent higher) and per $1,000 of personal income (34.4 percent higher) and slightly more per full time student. This suggests a substantial commitment to higher education in the state.

<table>
<tr><th colspan="7">Table 11-4
Combined State and Local Support for
Public Institutions of Higher Education -- 1985-86</th></tr>
<tr><th rowspan="2">State</th><th colspan="2">Support Per Capita</th><th colspan="2">Support per FTE</th><th colspan="2">Support Per $1,000
Of Personal Income</th></tr>
<tr><th>Amount</th><th>Index</th><th>Amount</th><th>Index</th><th>Amount</th><th>Index</th></tr>
<tr><td>United States</td><td>$130</td><td>100.0</td><td>$4,467</td><td>100.0</td><td>$8.97</td><td>100.0</td></tr>
<tr><td>Arizona</td><td>159</td><td>122.5</td><td>4,525</td><td>101.3</td><td>12.05</td><td>134.4</td></tr>
<tr><td>California</td><td>178</td><td>137.1</td><td>5,090</td><td>113.9</td><td>10.81</td><td>120.5</td></tr>
<tr><td>Colorado</td><td>118</td><td>91.1</td><td>3,418</td><td>76.5</td><td>7.84</td><td>87.4</td></tr>
<tr><td>Nevada</td><td>99</td><td>76.3</td><td>4,643</td><td>103.9</td><td>6.71</td><td>74.9</td></tr>
<tr><td>New Mexico</td><td>147</td><td>113.3</td><td>4,581</td><td>102.5</td><td>13.07</td><td>145.7</td></tr>
<tr><td>Utah</td><td>153</td><td>117.7</td><td>4,621</td><td>103.4</td><td>14.05</td><td>156.7</td></tr>
<tr><td colspan="7">Source: Digest of Education Statistics 1988, National Center for Education Statistics, Table 229.</td></tr>
</table>

State appropriations alone for 1985-86 are presented in Table 11-5. Because Arizona relies on substantial local support for community colleges, state appropriations are lower than combined state and local support. State appropriations were still over 6 percent above the average per capita and almost 17 percent above per $1,000 of personal income. Because of the large enrollment in Arizona, state appropriations per FTE were almost 12 percent below the national average.

The change in combined state and local support for higher education for 1979 to 1986 is shown in Table 11-6. In current (nominal) dollar terms, combined support in Arizona increased 91.6 percent during this period, which is well above the national average of 80.5 percent. However, on a per FTE basis, the current dollar support increased only 64.1 percent which is slightly less than the national average of 67.7 percent. This suggests that enrollment increases in Arizona were considerably greater than the national average. When the changes are viewed in real (constant dollar) terms, the increases in support are less dramatic. (Support is deflated using the higher education price index.) Real state and local support increased 14.5 percent in Arizona during this period while real support per FTE actually declined slightly.

In summary, these descriptive statistics suggest that the people of the state of Arizona make a major effort to support higher education given the size and wealth of the state, but the resources are spread over an unusually large number of students. Stated differently, support for higher education per person in the state or per $1,000 dollars of personal income is considerably above the national average, yet the support per student in the system of higher education is near the average level.

Table 11-5 State Appropriations for Public Institutions of Higher Education -- 1985-86					
State	**Appropriations Per Capita**		**Appropriations Per FTE**		**Appropriations Per $1,1000 Of Personal Income**	
	Amount	**Index**	**Amount**	**Index**	**Amount**	**Index**
United States	$116	100.0	$3,975	100.0	$7.98	100.0
Arizona	123	106.6	3,504	88.1	9.33	116.9
California	150	129.8	4,286	107.8	9.10	114.0
Colorado	108	93.0	3,108	78.2	7.12	89.3
Nevada	95	81.9	4,438	111.6	6.42	80.4
New Mexico	127	110.0	3,958	99.6	11.29	141.5
Utah	148	127.8	4,465	112.3	13.57	170.1

Source: *Digest of Education Statistics 1988*, National Center for Education Statistics, Table 229.

Table 11-6 Changes in Combined State and Local Support for Public Institutions of Higher Education -- 1979-1986				
State	**Percentage Change Total (Current $)**	**Percentage Change Per Student (Current $)**	**Percentage Change Total (Real $)**	**Percentage Change Per Student (Real $)**
United States	80.5	67.7	7.9	0.2
Arizona	91.6	64.1	14.5	-1.9
California	80.6	79.3	7.9	7.2
Colorado	74.6	55.1	4.3	-7.3
Nevada	107.6	60.7	24.1	-3.9
New Mexico	99.6	34.6	19.3	-19.5
Utah	81.7	39.3	8.6	-16.7

Source: *Digest of Education Statistics 1988*, National Center for Education Statistics, Table 229; and *Digest for Education Statistics 1988*, National Center for Education Statistics, Table 128.

<u>Arizona Compared to a Representative State</u>

While the descriptive data provide some insight into higher education in Arizona as compared to other states, comparisons are difficult because socio-economic differences among the states, as well as differences in institutional structures, influence state needs and demands for public higher education. This section attempts to address these complexities using an adaptation of the representative state expenditure approach developed by the Advisory Commission on Intergovernmental Relations. The concept can be defined in the following terms: a state's representative expenditure for a program function is the level the state would have to undertake in order to match the national average level of spending in relation to the state's underlying need for the service.

The data presented in the previous section were used in conjunction with various demographic and economic indicators to estimate representative expenditures or support levels for higher education for each state. The factors affecting public higher education in each state included: per capita income, the percentage of college-age persons in the population, the relative size of the private higher educational institutions, and various other state demographic measures. Regression analysis was used to estimate the effects of these variables on state support for higher education. It should be noted that the representative expenditure function includes both demand and supply elements and is thus a reduced form equation.

Using these results, a predicted or representative level of support was determined for each state. For example, the level of support for a representative state with the same characteristics as Arizona is determined by inserting Arizona's characteristics into the estimated equation and calculating the resulting Arizona-specific representative level. For each state, this representative level is compared to the actual level of support to determine whether the state provides more or less support than would be expected based on the economic and demographic characteristics of the state. This approach provides a more sophisticated evaluation of state activity compared to the previous section where many relevant socioeconomic factors were not considered.

Tables 11-7, 11-8, and 11-9 present data using the representative-level methodology for state expenditures, state and local support, and state appropriations. Table 11-7 presents the actual level of state expenditures (using the data from Table 11-3) as a percentage of what a representative state with the same characteristics would spend. The results suggest that spending per capita and spending per $1,000 of personal income in Arizona in 1987 were higher than a representative state with the same characteristics, but not as much above average as suggested by the raw comparisons presented earlier. The limited extent of private higher education and the size of the college-age population in Arizona explain, in part, why expenditures appear so high in the previous section.

In combined state and local support for higher education (Table 11-8), Arizona is about 12 to 13 percent above a representative state with characteristics similar to Arizona in per capita and per $1,000 of income, and almost the same per FTE. Compared to the results in Table 11-4, which indicated very high levels of support, the results in Table 11-8 indicate that support was not nearly as much above average when additional demographic factors are taken into account. Arizona's performance compared very closely with that of California, but its commitment was considerably greater than the neighboring states of Colorado, Nevada, and New Mexico and considerably less than Utah. A similar analysis is presented for state appropriations in Table 11-9 where the results indicate that state appropriations per capita and per $1,000 of personal income for Arizona were almost the same as that of a representative state.

<table>
<tr><td colspan="4" align="center">Table 11-7
Actual State Expenditures for Higher Education as Percentage of Representative State Expenditures -- 1987
(Current Operations less Auxiliary Enterprises plus Intergovernmental)</td></tr>
<tr><td align="center">State</td><td align="center">Per Capita</td><td align="center">Per FTE</td><td align="center">Per $1,000 of
Per. Inc.</td></tr>
<tr><td>Arizona</td><td align="center">106.3</td><td align="center">94.6</td><td align="center">104.5</td></tr>
<tr><td>California</td><td align="center">125.1</td><td align="center">103.4</td><td align="center">127.0</td></tr>
<tr><td>Colorado</td><td align="center">83.2</td><td align="center">81.9</td><td align="center">80.5</td></tr>
<tr><td>Nevada</td><td align="center">90.0</td><td align="center">128.1</td><td align="center">99.0</td></tr>
<tr><td>New Mexico</td><td align="center">97.2</td><td align="center">101.5</td><td align="center">99.0</td></tr>
<tr><td>Utah</td><td align="center">131.3</td><td align="center">134.5</td><td align="center">134.5</td></tr>
<tr><td colspan="4">Source: Statistical Abstract of the United States 1988, U.S. Bureau of Census, Table 247 and author's calculations.</td></tr>
</table>

<table>
<tr><td colspan="4" align="center">Table 11-8
State and Local Support for Public Institutions of Higher Education as Percentage of Representative State and Local Support -- 1986</td></tr>
<tr><td align="center">State</td><td align="center">Per Capita</td><td align="center">Per FTE</td><td align="center">Per $1,000 of
Per. Inc.</td></tr>
<tr><td>Arizona</td><td align="center">113.2</td><td align="center">100.4</td><td align="center">112.2</td></tr>
<tr><td>California</td><td align="center">117.4</td><td align="center">96.9</td><td align="center">116.2</td></tr>
<tr><td>Colorado</td><td align="center">64.5</td><td align="center">63.5</td><td align="center">63.1</td></tr>
<tr><td>Nevada</td><td align="center">61.7</td><td align="center">87.9</td><td align="center">64.5</td></tr>
<tr><td>New Mexico</td><td align="center">90.1</td><td align="center">92.5</td><td align="center">93.6</td></tr>
<tr><td>Utah</td><td align="center">128.8</td><td align="center">141.6</td><td align="center">127.0</td></tr>
<tr><td colspan="4">Source: Digest of Education Statistics 1988, National center for Education Statistics, Table 229 and author's calculations.</td></tr>
</table>

Table 11-9			
State Appropriations for Public Institutions of Higher Education as Percentage of Representative State - 1986			
State	**Per Capita**	**Per FTE**	**Per $1,000 of Per. Inc.**
Arizona	100.2	88.5	99.2
California	116.1	94.9	116.7
Colorado	66.0	64.9	64.9
Nevada	68.1	96.4	71.8
New Mexico	89.9	92.2	92.8
Utah	133.7	145.6	132.1
Source: *Digest of Education Statistics 1988*, National Center for Education Statistics, Table 229.			

The Fiscal Structure Of Higher Education In Arizona

Higher education in Arizona has come under close scrutiny in the last several years. There have been several studies dealing with various aspects of higher education including some with controversial findings and recommendations. For example, The Arizona Board of Regents' Task Force on Excellence, Efficiency and Competitiveness produced a report and a massive set of working papers on many facets of higher education in the state. In this chapter, no attempt is made to duplicate the comprehensive work of these previous studies.

The major focus is on the structure of revenues and expenditures in the system of public higher education in Arizona in the 1980s. This study is not intended to be an efficiency analysis to guide internal management decisions at particular institutions of higher education. Nor is it intended to determine the appropriateness of either the distribution of educational resources among the various institutions in the state or the overall level of support for higher education. It should, however, provide an understanding of the level of resources committed to higher education in the state as well as an understanding of the manner in which these resources are distributed among the public institutions of higher education during the decade of the 1980s.

Several unique features of higher education in Arizona discussed in the previous section include:

1. Arizona has an extremely small private higher education sector. Private enrollment per 1,000 of population is 88 percent below the national average in 1986. Only two states (Nevada and Wyoming) ranked lower. Arizona has one 2-year private college, five 4-year private colleges, and 2 specialized graduate schools. As noted, their combined enrollment is very small.
2. A high portion of Arizona students remain in the state to attend college. The 97 percent of students who remain in-state is the highest in the nation.
3. Arizona educates a large number of students coming from out of state. The net in-migration (students arriving less students leaving) is second largest in the country in absolute terms and the largest relative to population.

Higher education in Arizona is virtually synonymous with public higher education. It seems to be meeting the market test in terms of attracting both in-state and out-of-state students.

The Structure of the Public University System

Public higher education is divided into two major systems: four-year universities and two-year college districts. Public four-year universities are the sole province of the Board of Regents. Arizona has only three such institutions: The University of Arizona, Arizona State University, and Northern Arizona University. Arizona has a relatively small number of institutions compared to other states even after adjusting for population. This pattern of centralization may be related to the concentration of population in the urban centers of Phoenix and Tucson combined with sparsely populated rural areas. As noted in the previous section, Arizona State University and the University of Arizona are among the largest universities in the country. Only a handful of states have two or more institutions this large.

The University of Arizona (U of A), located in Tucson, has historically been the major research-oriented, Land-Grant institution in the state. It offers a comprehensive range of programs including a medical school. Arizona State University (ASU) in Tempe, which began primarily as an undergraduate institution, has become very large over the last several decades, fueled by the growth of Phoenix. It now has branch campuses in the area. It also has become a research-oriented institution although its range of programs is less comprehensive than the U of A. This situation can be compared to the relationship between the University of California campuses at Berkeley and Los Angeles. In California, Berkeley was traditionally the dominant comprehensive public university in the state. In recent years, UCLA has become a first-rate research university as well, in part because of the rapid growth in southern California. The division of responsibility between the U of A and ASU is a vital question to be resolved in the future. Northern Arizona University in Flagstaff is the smallest of the state's three institutions. Its focus is on undergraduate education, master's level training, and specialized Ph.D. programs.

Over 90,000 students were enrolled in public universities in the state in 1988. See Table 11-10. (Note that the years referred to in this section are fiscal or academic years. For example, 1988 values are for the academic year 1987-1988.) Full time equivalent enrollment for the system was just over 70,000. (The method of calculating FTE enrollment was changed for the system in 1988. To maintain comparability with past years, FTE levels using the old method are used in this chapter.)

The headcount of students grew 14.5 percent from 1980 to 1988, while FTE growth was 8.2 percent. The higher headcount growth reflects a larger percentage of part-time students perhaps in response to larger numbers of older, non-traditional students. The increase in enrollment during this period is considerably less than the 28 percent increase in population for the state from 1980 to 1988. This lower growth rate is explained in large part by the reduction in the proportion of the primary college-age population (18 through 24 years of age) from 13.6 percent in 1980 to 11.0 percent in 1987, a 19 percent decline.

Arizona State University had the largest headcount enrollment (44,148) in the state in 1988 and has experienced the largest percentage growth in the 1980s. The University of Arizona had an enrollment of 32,505 in 1988, and Northern Arizona University's enrollment was 13,445. The growth rates in FTE enrollment for the three institutions were in a narrow range of 7.7 percent for NAU to 8.6 percent for ASU. The decline in the proportion of college-age students expected in the first half of the next decade will continue to dampen slightly the impact of population growth on enrollments.

Table 11-10 Enrollment Levels in Arizona Public Universities				
Fiscal Year	**University of Arizona**		**Arizona State University**	
	Headcount	**FTE**	**Headcount**	**FTE**
1980	29,310	25,017	37,755	29,581
1981	30,441	25,959	37,828	29,783
1982	30,785	26,059	38,590	29,984
1983	30,292	25,406	39,319	30,629
1984	29,986	25,184	40,239	41,164
1985	29,777	24,846	40,563	30,702
1986	30,374	25,438	40,558	30,230
1987	31,079	25,799	41,540	31,115
1988	32,505	26,984*	44,148	32,124*
Percentage Change 1980-1988	10.9	7.9	16.9	8.6
Fiscal Year	**Northern Arizona University**		**Total System**	
	Headcount	**FTE**	**Headcount**	**FTE**
1980	11,601	10,240	78,666	64,838
1981	12,074	10,675	80,343	66,417
1982	12,090	10,525	81,465	66,568
1983	11,665	10,220	81,276	66,255
1984	11,501	10,141	81,726	66,489
1985	11,826	10,158	82,166	65,706
1986	12,615	10,393	83,547	66,061
1987	13,208	10,973	85,827	67,887
1988	13,445	11,024*	90,098	70,132*
Percentage Change 1980-1988	15.9	7.7	14.5	8.2

* Adjusted for change in FTE calculations.

Source: *Arizona Board of Regents Fact Book* (1980) with additional updated information.

In the previous section, it was suggested that there was no single measure that captured all of the relevant factors for interstate comparisons of educational finance. A similar situation exists for comparisons among institutions within a state and for the analysis of changes over time. Some measures address various sources of support (such as state support or tuition and fees) while others relate to the overall level of activity. It is also necessary to distinguish between current and capital activities and to separate auxiliary activities from primary educational functions.

Price level changes further complicate comparisons between different points in time. To address this problem, information is presented in real or constant dollar terms as well as in nominal or current dollars. In converting to constant dollars (of 1988 purchasing power), the implicit GNP price deflator is used as a general measure of price level changes. This measure often underestimates changes in the costs of educational inputs although it does provide a good measure of the burden to taxpayers of state support.

This discussion first focuses on state general fund appropriations as a measure of state support for public universities. Operating-budget general fund appropriations (total and for each institution) are presented in several ways. In Table 11-11A, current (nominal) dollar appropriations are given, while appropriations are presented in constant 1988 dollars in Table 11-11B. Tables 11-11C and 11-11D provide current and constant dollar appropriations per FTE enrollment.

For the university system, including the Board of Regents, 1988 general fund appropriations amounted to $429 million or $6,124 per FTE student. Appropriations have more than doubled in nominal terms in the 1980s, increasing 113 percent overall and 97 percent per FTE. Adjusting for inflation, overall appropriations have increased by 46 percent while constant dollar appropriations per FTE have increased by 35 percent. For comparison, the total general fund operating budget of the state, adjusted for inflation, increased 63 percent from 1980 to 1988 or 25 percent per capita.

It should be noted that higher education costs in the United States have increased more rapidly in the 1980s than the general price level (a 65 percent increase in the cost of resources used in higher education versus a 46 percent overall increase in prices). In addition, many states in the nation have devoted additional resources to enhance their systems of higher education. The implication is that increases that considerably exceed inflation are necessary for institutions to even retain their competitive position. The figures in Tables 11B and 11D indicate that despite the increased costs of educational inputs, substantial increases in real resources (both total and per FTE) have been provided by the state in the 1980s.

The University of Arizona receives the largest share of appropriations because of the comprehensive nature of its activities. On an FTE basis, total appropriations including the medical school were considerably higher at the University of Arizona ($7,821) as compared to ASU ($4,950) and NAU ($4,945). Much of this difference relates to the large appropriations for both the U of A College of Medicine, with its relatively small enrollment, and for agricultural research activities. Even excluding the medical school, main campus appropriations for the U of A were about $15 million above those for ASU in 1988.

In terms of growth, Arizona State University's appropriations grew at a considerably faster rate (144 percent) than the U of A (96 percent) or NAU (117 percent). (See Table 11-11A.) Part of this growth reflects ASU's more rapid increase in enrollment. However, after adjustment for enrollment changes and inflation, Table 11-11D illustrates that ASU's rate of increase was more than twice that of the U of A from 1980 until 1988 (53 percent versus 24 percent). Some of this differential is accounted for in the relatively slow rate of growth for the U of A College of Medicine during the 1980s. All three of the universities received

Table 11-11A
General Fund Appropriations for Arizona Universities
(Current dollars)

Fiscal Year	University of Arizona			Arizona State University			Northern Arizona University	Board of Regents	Total Universities
	Main Campus	College of Medicine*	Total	Main Campus (Tempe)	West Campus	Total			
1980	$ 83,194,300	$24,769,200	$107,963,500	$65,712,600		$65,712,600	$25,185,600	$3,090,300	$201,952,000
1981	96,326,500	29,061,700	125,388,200	80,511,000		80,511,000	28,578,200	3,367,900	237,845,300
1982	112,649,100	28,928,600	141,577,700	96,357,000		96,357,000	34,741,100	3,359,650	276,035,450
1983	103,949,100	22,076,000	126,025,100	89,226,500		89,226,500	33,511,100	3,126,800	251,889,500
1984	120,673,700	26,575,300	147,249,000	104,663,900		104,663,900	37,905,800	3,451,000	293,269,700
1985	134,300,400	30,831,000	165,131,400	117,383,400	$1,332,800	118,716,200	41,966,000	3,151,600	328,965,200
1986	152,848,900	33,977,000	186,825,900	132,748,900	4,321,700	137,070,600	48,208,800	3,266,100	375,371,400
1987	158,118,100	35,843,700	194,141,000	138,701,500	5,174,100	143,962,000	49,531,600	3,907,900	391,542,500
1988	173,729,800	40,102,600	211,053,000	153,362,800	7,463,700	158,999,000	54,515,500	4,930,800	429,498,300
Percentage Change 1980-1988	108.8	61.9	95.5	133.4		142.0	116.5	59.6	112.7

*Includes University hospital appropriations.

Note: Operating budget only.

Source: *Arizona Board of Regents Fact Book* (1980) with additional updated information and annual financial reports of the universities.

Table 11-11B
General Fund Appropriations for Arizona Universities
(Real-1988 dollars)

Fiscal Year	University of Arizona			Arizona State University			Northern Arizona University	Board of Regents	Total Universities
	Main Campus	College of Medicine*	Total	Main Campus (Tempe)	West Campus	Total			
1980	$121,221,640	$36,090,971	$157,312,610	$ 95,749,281		$ 95,749,218	$36,697,703	$4,502,847	$294,262,379
1981	128,328,125	38,716,589	167,044,714	107,258,394		107,258,394	38,072,460	4,486,785	316,862,353
1982	139,011,312	35,698,489	174,709,801	118,906,525		118,906,525	42,871,234	4,145,877	340,633,437
1983	122,047,153	25,919,541	147,966,694	104,761,276		104,761,276	39,345,549	3,671,191	295,744,710
1984	136,527,806	30,066,762	166,594,568	118,414,639		118,414,639	42,885,863	3,904,392	331,799,462
1985	147,079,212	33,764,599	180,843,811	128,552,543	$1,459,617	130,012,160	45,959,105	3,451,478	360,266,555
1986	162,775,919	36,183,691	198,959,611	141,370,492	4,602,380	145,972,872	51,339,799	3,478,222	399,750,503
1987	163,443,321	37,050,871	200,679,427	143,372,794	5,348,357	148,810,461	51,199,763	4,039,513	404,729,165
1988	173,739,800	40,102,600	411,053,000	153,362,800	7,463,700	158,999,000	54,515,500	4,930,800	429,498,300
Percentage Change 1980-1988	43.3	11.1	34.2	60.2		66.1	48.6	9.5	46.0

*Includes University hospital appropriations.

Note: Operating budget only.

Source: *Arizona Board of Regents Fact Book* (1980) with additional updated information and annual financial reports of the universities.

Table 11-11C
General Fund Appropriations for Arizona Universities
(Current dollars per FTE)

Fiscal Year	University of Arizona	Arizona State University	Northern Arizona University	Regents, Staff and WICHE	Total Universities
1980	$4,316	$2,221	$2,460	$48	$3,115
1981	4,830	2,703	2,677	51	$3,581
1982	5,433	3,214	3,301	50	$4,147
1983	4,960	2,913	3,279	47	$3,802
1984	5,847	3,358	3,738	52	$4,411
1985	6,646	3,867	4,131	48	$5,007
1986	7,344	4,534	4,639	49	$5,682
1987	7,525	4,627	4,514	58	$5,768
1988	7,821	4,950	4,945	70	$6,124
Percentage Change 1980-1988	81.2	122.8	101.1	47.5	96.6

Source: *Arizona Board of Regents Fact Book* (1980) with additional updated information and annual financial reports of the universities.

Table 11-11D
General Fund Appropriations for Arizona Universities
(Real 1988 dollars per FTE)

Fiscal Year	University of Arizona	Arizona State University	Northern Arizona University	Regents, Staff and Miscellaneous	Total Universities
1980	$6,288	$3,237	$3,584	$69	$4,538
1981	6,435	3,601	3,567	68	4,771
1982	6,704	3,966	4,073	62	5,117
1983	5,824	3,420	3,850	55	4,464
1984	6,615	3,800	4,229	59	4,990
1985	7,279	4,235	4,524	53	5,483
1986	7,821	4,829	4,940	53	6,051
1987	7,779	4,783	4,666	60	5,962
1988	7,821	4,950	4,945	70	6,124
Percentage Change 1980-1988	24.4	52.9	38.0	1.2	34.9

Source: *Arizona Board of Regents Fact Book* (1980) with additional updated information and annual financial reports of the universities.

increases in state resources during this period that outpaced the combined effects of inflation and enrollment growth. It should be noted that appropriations for the Board of Regents' activities grew at a much slower rate (even though additional responsibilities were assumed in recent years).

Total educational and general expenditures for each institution are presented in Tables 11-12A and 11-12B. These tables provide a picture of the overall level of current activities (excluding auxiliary enterprises and capital expenditures) from all funding sources including state, federal, tuition and fees, and other grants and contracts. These expenditures amounted to more than $400 million for the U of A and over $300 million for ASU in 1988. As noted with appropriations, the U of A had a considerably larger level of expenditures despite its smaller enrollment than did ASU. As with appropriations, ASU's expenditures increased faster than the U of A especially after adjustments for inflation. All three universities experienced considerable increases in the *real* level of expenditures (both total and per FTE) during the 1980s.

Tables 11-13A and 11-13B present information concerning support from tuition and fees. By almost any measure, the contribution from students increased substantially during the 1980s. Tuition and fees per FTE more than doubled at all three universities from 1980 until 1988. This growth outpaced inflation by more than 50 percent. During this period, tuition and fees per FTE were roughly comparable among the institutions with NAU somewhat below the other two institutions. These differentials among the three institutions reflect, in part, differing portions of graduate and professional versus undergraduate students, and differing ratios of in-state to out-of-state students.

The System of Community Colleges

Unlike the university system, the provision of community college services is shared by the state and local districts. The system is coordinated by the State Board of Directors for Community Colleges which is separate from the Board of Regents. There are nine community college districts in the state. Most district boundaries are the same as county boundaries except for one multiple county district. Five counties do not have community college districts although services are available from districts in other counties. Community colleges provide a wide range of services including preparing students for transfer to four-year colleges, vocational and technical training, and general education for the enrichment of community life.

Each district has an elected governing board exercising a range of independent powers while operating the district within the guidelines established by the state through the State Board of Directors. Most support comes from local property taxes, state funds, and tuition and fees.

On a headcount basis, more students (137,168) in Arizona are enrolled in community colleges than four-year universities. On an FTE basis, enrollment is slightly lower in community colleges than in universities because of the large number of part-time students. Between 1980 and 1988, overall enrollment increased by 26 percent while FTE enrollment increased 12 percent. Both of these figures are above the growth rates for universities, at 15 and 8 percent, respectively.

The Maricopa County Community College District, with its nine campuses and centers, has by far the largest enrollment (78,008) comprising over half the community college students in the state. As of 1988, the Maricopa County Community College District

Table 11-12A
Total Educational and General Expenditures
(all funds)

Fiscal Year	Current Dollars			Real-1988 dollars		
	University of Arizona	Arizona State University	Northern Arizona University	University of Arizona	Arizona State University	Northern Arizona University
1980	$196,232,602	$121,865,887	$38,219,833	$285,928,697	$177,569,649	$55,689,763
1981	227,502,812	141,800,595	50,025,085	303,083,880	188,909,641	66,644,437
1982	256,323,900	164,294,279	54,478,863	316,308,978	202,742,528	67,228,040
1983	260,228,618	171,809,717	55,425,535	305,535,709	201,722,640	65,075,395
1984	276,107,000	193,203,000	62,826,452	312,381,927	218,586,003	71,080,589
1985	309,464,000	225,628,000	70,851,620	338,909,797	247,096,721	77,593,220
1986	350,381,000	249,324,000	78,613,429	373,137,061	265,516,751	83,719,105
1987	378,438,000	272,033,000	86,782,261	391,183,321	281,194,733	89,704,980
1988	418,046,000	302,832,000	92,447,545	418,046,000	302,832,000	92,447,545
Percentage Change 1980-1988	114.0	148.5	141.9	46.2	70.5	66.0

Source: Annual financial reports of the universities.

Table 11-12B
Total Educational and General Expenditures
(all funds)

Fiscal Year	Current Dollars -- Per FTE			Real-1988 dollars -- Per FTE		
	University of Arizona	Arizona State University	Northern Arizona University	University of Arizona	Arizona State University	Northern Arizona University
1980	$7,844	$4,120	$3,732	$11,429	$6,003	$5,438
1981	8,764	4,761	4,686	11,675	6,343	6,243
1982	9,836	5,479	5,176	12,138	6,762	6,387
1983	10,243	5,609	5,423	12,026	6,586	6,367
1984	10,964	6,200	6,195	12,404	7,014	7,009
1985	12,455	7,349	6,975	13,640	8,048	7,639
1986	13,774	8,248	7,564	14,668	8,783	8,055
1987	14,669	8,743	7,909	15,163	9,037	8,175
1988	15,492	9,427	8,386	15,492	9,427	8,386
Percentage Change 1980-1988	97.5	128.8	124.7	35.5	57.0	54.2

Source: Annual financial reports of the universities.

Table 11-13A
Tuition and Fees in Arizona Universities

Fiscal Year	Current Dollars			Real-1988 dollars		
	University of Arizona	Arizona State University	Northern Arizona University	University of Arizona	Arizona State University	Northern Arizona University
1980	$29,520,588	$32,123,956	$ 8,596,629	$43,014,174	$46,807,517	$12,526,068
1981	34,371,017	36,361,516	10,070,560	45,789,769	48,441,552	13,416,205
1982	35,548,824	40,788,645	10,847,687	43,855,642	50,334,029	13,386,269
1983	37,824,093	44,411,489	11,266,912	44,409,455	52,143,749	13,228,537
1984	42,930,453	49,426,889	13,758,651	48,570,654	55,920,592	15,566,262
1985	49,207,000	57,223,000	15,998,670	53,889,093	62,667,823	17,520,959
1986	52,247,000	60,339,000	17,371,703	55,640,266	64,257,814	18,499,936
1987	61,719,000	71,008,000	21,047,957	63,797,619	73,399,461	21,756,826
1988	69,701,000	77,958,000	23,013,763	69,701,000	77,958,000	23,013,763
Percentage Change 1980-1988	136.1	142.7	167.7	62.0	66.6	83.7

Source: Annual financial reports of the universities.

Table 11-13B
Tuition and Fees in Arizona Universities

Fiscal Year	Current Dollars -- Per FTE			Real-1988 dollars -- Per FTE		
	University of Arizona	Arizona State University	Northern Arizona University	University of Arizona	Arizona State University	Northern Arizona University
1980	$1,180	$1,086	$ 840	$1,719	$1,582	$1,223
1981	1,324	1,221	943	1,764	1,626	1,257
1982	1,364	1,360	1,031	1,683	1,679	1,272
1983	1,489	1,450	1,102	1,748	1,702	1,294
1984	1,705	1,586	1,357	1,929	1,794	1,535
1985	1,980	1,864	1,575	2,169	2,041	1,725
1986	2,054	1,996	1,671	2,187	2,126	1,780
1987	2,392	2,282	1,918	2,473	2,359	1,983
1988	2,583	2,427	2,088	2,583	2,427	2,088
Percentage Change 1980-1988	118.9	123.5	148.7	50.2	53.4	70.7

Source: Annual financial reports of the universities.

was the second largest community collete district in the nation. Pima is the next largest district in Arizona with 24,339 students and four campuses. FTE enrollments are approximately 40 percent of these headcount figures because of the importance of part-time students. The seven districts outside the Phoenix and Tucson areas are considerably smaller with headcount enrollments in the four to six thousand range. In general, the smaller districts have had the largest percentage growth rates during the 1980s.

Resources for community colleges come from several sources. In 1988, local property tax levies were the most important source of revenues followed by state aid and tuition. Obviously, the large districts receive more revenue and spend more than small districts, but this is not necessarily the case when comparisons are made on an FTE basis. Because state aid per FTE differs across districts and is inversely related to the local property tax base, state aid per FTE is redistributive in nature and not based solely on enrollments. Maricopa and Pima, with their large property tax bases, receive considerably less per student from the state than the rural districts.

Pima has the lowest per student general fund expenditures and Maricopa is the fourth lowest. These districts are likely to realize economies of scale from the large and relatively concentrated populations resulting in lower-cost educational services. While not directly comparable, total current educational expenditures per FTE for community colleges are approximately one-third that of the university system.

From 1980 to 1988, general fund expenditures more than doubled in current dollars while increasing in real terms by less than 50 percent. On a per student basis, the real increase was 29 percent. State aid increased less rapidly than either local property tax support or tuition and fees, rising by 12 percent in constant dollars per FTE. There was a major increase in reliance on tuition and fees with over a 400 percent increase in the total current dollar amount. In real terms, tuition and fees increased about 250 percent and on a real, per FTE basis, over 200 percent.

To summarize, overall support for community colleges more than kept pace with the combined effects of enrollment growth and inflation although the community college increase in real per student expenditures of 29 percent was smaller than that of 45 percent for the universities. As mentioned, real state aid per student increased only 12 percent making state aid the slowest growing source of support for community colleges during the 1980s. For community colleges, tuition and fees was the revenue source that increased the most rapidly in percentage terms during the 1980s, but it still represented less than half of state aid and less than 25 percent of local property tax revenue.

Policy Issues

The information and analysis presented in this chapter raise several issues relevant to education policy in Arizona. Definitive conclusions regarding these issues cannot be based on this chapter alone, partly because the resolution of the issues involves political and ethical matters. But, the analysis here does shed some light on the many debates.

Arizona has clearly made a commitment to high quality research-oriented higher education. Two issues must be faced in this regard. First, Arizona is relatively small in terms of population, and its per capita income is somewhat below the national average. Unfortunately, higher education quality depends on the absolute level of resources committed to the institutions not on effort per capita or per $1,000 of personal income. This means that

Arizona faces a more difficult task than larger and richer states. Most, if not all, distinguished public institutions are in large and high income states. The burden of support on a per person (or per $1,000 of income) basis will have to be greater in Arizona than many other states to achieve comparable quality goals.

A second question to be resolved is whether the State wants one or two comprehensive research universities. Very few states have more than one really outstanding research institution. Concentrating resources in one institution might provide for one distinguished research institution rather than diluting support between the two institutions. On the other hand, assuming that the University of Arizona is to retain its comprehensive status, it could be argued that a major metropolitan area such as Phoenix should also have a distinguished research institution to serve as a stimulus for further economic development. There are no major private institutions in Phoenix as there are in Boston, Chicago, and New York City to fill this role.

Educating students may be less expensive at community colleges than at four-year institutions. The two are not perfectly comparable because the nature and intent of the education provided at community colleges differs from that provided at the universities. The State has a choice between continuing its policy of expanding the size of the universities to accommodate all qualified students who wish to attend or limiting enrollment at universities and accommodating more students at community colleges. Many of these students would later transfer to the universities to complete their education. It should be noted that Arizona's community college enrollment per capita is already one of the highest in the country.

Limiting university enrollment might be unpopular, but it would provide the state with more flexibility and resources to pursue other education goals such as enhancement of upper division teaching activities or the graduate program and research activities. The fiscal implications for community colleges should not be ignored. What might be a cost saving strategy at the state level would be partially offset by higher property taxes in community college districts or greater state aid to community colleges. These additional resources would be needed to finance the increased responsibilities of community colleges.

As noted earlier, Arizona educates a very large number of out-of-state students. The net flow of students from out of state to public universities in Arizona is greater than any other state in the nation except California. A guideline of limiting out-of-state enrollment to 25 percent has been used in Arizona. Also, the Board of Regents has recently begun a policy of increasing out-of-state tuition faster than in-state tuition. Out-of-state students are charged higher tuition and fees ($4,866 versus for in-state students $1,278 at the U of A and ASU in 1988-89), yet the extra charge probably does not cover the full cost of educating these students. While determining marginal cost within a university is difficult because of the difficulty of allocating costs, the out-of-state charges are clearly much less than the average cost per student of providing educational services.

If out-of-state enrollment were further limited, perhaps by increasing the out-of-state tuition charge even more, more revenue *per student* would be generated while also reducing the demand for services. However, limiting out-of-state enrollment would reduce the influx of young, educated persons into the state. If many out-of-state students contribute to the state's economic vitality by remaining in the state after graduation (and evidence suggests that 20 to 25 percent do), providing a subsidized education for out-of-state students may be a very good bargain for the state.

The level of tuition at Arizona's universities is relatively modest. In-state tuition ranked thirty-fifth in the country in 1987. This raises the question of whether students should bear a greater proportion of the cost of their education. Higher tuition and fees could be used either to increase the overall quality of the universities or to limit the rate of growth of state support.

On the negative side, higher tuition and fees may limit access for some students from poorer families. To maintain access, any substantial increase in costs to students should also be accompanied by increased availability of various types of student aid. A greater reliance on tuition and fees would be a major departure from the historic pattern in Arizona and would contradict the state goal of "tuition as nearly free as possible" as set forth in the State Constitution. However, if funding in the future becomes more limited, it might be an attractive alternative for financing the maintenance or enhancement of the quality of the state's universities.

In one sense, many of the options presented here represent unpleasant choices, such as concentrating resources in one rather than two major research institutions, limiting access to four year institutions with the unserved students directed to community colleges, limiting out-of-state enrollments, and raising tuition. Nevertheless, these are choices that may be impossible to avoid. If state resources in the future prove insufficient (as well they may) to achieve a variety of desirable higher education goals simultaneously, it is vital to know what the trade-offs are. Knowledge of these trade-offs will allow the state to make more informed choices, which can preserve and enhance the most important attributes of the system of higher education.

Endnotes

1. For a fuller discussion of the economic impact of higher education for students and society, see Larry L. Leslie and Paul T. Brinkman, *The Economic Value of Higher Education*, New York: Macmillan, 1988.
2. While there seems always to have been a strong belief on the part of policymakers about the link between higher education and economic development, the relationship is difficult to establish empirically. A recent study by Jones and Vedlitz concludes that there is a linkage between university quality and several measures of regional economic development. See Bryan D. Jones and Arnold Vedlitz, "Higher Education Policies and Economic Growth in the American States," *Economic Development Quarterly*, 2, no. 1, February 1988.
3. *Digest of Education Statistics, 1988*, National Center for Education Statistics, Table 141.

Chapter 12

Government Health Care Expenditures

Jon B. Christianson and David Wyant

The purpose of this chapter is to describe and interpret governmental health care spending in the State of Arizona over the past two decades. The first section reviews the justification for governmental expenditures on health care and provides data on changes in the share of these expenditures paid by state and local governments. The second section, which is the primary focus of the chapter, describes health care expenditures by the State of Arizona. It discusses how health care expenditures by Arizona state government have changed over time, how Arizona state government expenditures compare with the expenditures of other state governments, and how expenditures are distributed across existing programs. The third part of the chapter addresses health care spending by Arizona's county governments with emphasis on its relationship to state spending on health care.

Health Care Expenditures:
The Changing Role Of Federal, State, And Local Governments

The growth of health care expenditures nationwide has been impressive. In 1966, expenditures on health care equaled 6 percent of GNP while, two decades later, they stood at approximately 11 percent of GNP. According to the federal government's Health Care Financing Administration (HCFA), this figure will reach 15 percent by the year 2000. Recent increases in personal health care expenditures can be attributed to a variety of factors, the foremost of which is price inflation. For example, 32 percent of the 32.8 billion increase in expenditures between 1985 and 1986 reflected general price inflation in the economy nationwide, while another 22 percent represented medical care price inflation in excess of general price inflation. Population growth contributed 11 percent of the overall increase. The remainder (35 percent) of the increase was associated with increased consumption of health care per person due to an aging population, rising income levels and increased "intensity" of services provided (Division of National Cost Estimates, 1987, p.11).

Funding for Health Care:
The Role of Federal, State, and Local Governments

Justification for a government role in the financing and regulation of medical services can be found in both economic and social welfare theory. Where competition is effective, the sum of the private benefits received from the consumption of medical care is roughly equal to the benefits received by society as a whole. However, in the area of public health, this is not necessarily the case. For example, if an individual suffers from an infectious disease, the consumption of medical services may cure the disease, but this private benefit represents only a portion of the total benefits from that consumption. People who otherwise might contract the disease also benefit. Therefore, the private market is likely to "under-invest" in disease prevention activities and government investment may be necessary.

For private markets to be efficient, consumers must be able to evaluate the worth of goods and services accurately. Although all actual market decisions are based to some extent on imperfect knowledge, the "information problem" seems particularly important in the case of medical care. The complicated nature of medical services, their infrequent purchase, and the use of the physician as a consumer agent can lead to private consumption decisions that are "inefficient" from society's viewpoint (Marmor & Christianson, 1982). Government licensure of personnel, regulation of inputs, and certification of medical facilities all have been justified as attempts to deal with poor consumer information.

While other efficiency related arguments for a governmental role in medical care delivery can be made, it is also true that this role can be defended for non-efficiency reasons as well. For instance, many would argue that all members of society have a "right" or "entitlement" to medical care. In this view, a government role is necessary to assure that consumers with lower incomes receive the medical care they need. Indigent health care programs such as Medicaid, funded through government tax revenues, reduce the price of medical care for these individuals and thereby address this concern.

Assuming that government has a role to play in the medical care delivery system, what level of government should carry out this role? In theory and in practice, the answer depends on the nature of the specific issue. For instance, it does little good for a local government to allocate funds to fight the spread of communicable disease if neighboring local governments do not undertake similar efforts. Intervention by a higher level of government would be more effective. On the other hand, federal government regulation of health care facilities may be inefficient if it leads to rules that do not adequately take into account variations in local circumstances.

In general, higher levels of government are better equipped to deal with equity issues and the redistribution of resources, while lower levels of government are better able to respond to specific needs and problems within their boundaries. At either level, however, it is not realistic to expect government to function in ways that necessarily improve social welfare. Political considerations or resource limitations can result in ineffective or biased program implementation and administration. Therefore, it is important to acknowledge that medical care delivery will not necessarily be improved by government action, and that neither government nor the private market is likely to operate as effectively as society might wish (Marmor & Christianson, 1982). Defining an appropriate role for government in the financing and delivery of health care is an issue subject to ongoing debate.

Distribution of Aggregate Expenditures by Payment Source

From 1980 through 2000, it is expected that the proportion of total health care expenditures funded through private sources (private health insurers or direct patient payment) will remain approximately 57.5 percent. A substantial change is expected to occur, however, in the division of public expenditures between the federal government and state and local governments. The share of total health care expenditures financed by the federal government is expected to grow from 28.6 percent in 1980 to 32.6 percent in the year 2000. Expenditures by state and local governments will fall from 13.8 percent to 9.9 percent of the total over the same period (Division of National Cost Estimates, 1987). Of course, this decline does not mean a reduction in dollar expenditures on the part of state and local governments. However, the rate of increase in expenditures from 1985 through 2000 for state and local governments is projected to be lower than for the private payers or for the federal government over the same period.

Distribution of Health Care:
Expenditures by Type of Service and Payment Source

With respect to hospital, physician and nursing home care, the relative role of state and local government spending is expected to decrease (Division of National Cost Estimates, 1987). The decrease is expected to be largest for nursing home care (-7.2 percentage points), where Medicaid's role as a purchaser is expected to decline in conjunction with a projected increase in direct private payments and payments through private insurance for nursing home care.

The role of state and local governments in purchasing hospital care is also predicted to decline from 12.6 percent to 6.9 percent. Medicare and direct patient payments will increase over the same period reflecting an aging population and the expectation that private insurance will provide more limited coverage to fewer individuals.

In contrast, the role of state and local government as a purchaser of other personal health care (*e.g.*, dental, drugs, eyeglasses, home health, public health, administration, construction) will increase from 5.9 to 7.6 percent. Similar increases are expected for private insurance and federal government expenditures with direct private payments decreasing. The assumption underlying these projections is that services such as dental care, home health care, and drugs increasingly will be covered by insurance, either public or private.

Health Care Expenditures By Arizona State Government

Historically, state government spending for health care in Arizona has not followed patterns that are typical of other states for at least two reasons. First, Arizona until recently, had no state sponsored program for indigent health care, and the indigent health care program enacted in 1982, the Arizona Health Care Cost Containment System (AHCCCS), differed in many important ways from traditional Medicaid programs. Second, Arizona state government made explicit choices to spend less than other states for health care for some special population groups.

When the federal Medicaid legislation was implemented in 1967, the state of Arizona did not exercise its option to participate. However, by the late 1970's, inflation in the cost of providing health care for indigents had reached a critical level for Arizona counties. Several rural counties reported a doubling of indigent health care costs between FY 1978-1979 and FY 1979-1980 with an average rate of increase of 26.9 percent across all counties. The relatively large rates of increase in health care spending experienced by counties continued into the succeeding year and, together with several expensive cases of catastrophic illness, placed extreme pressure on county budgets, particularly in rural Arizona.

Prior to 1980, it had been possible for counties to meet growing indigent care expenses by raising property tax rates. However, in 1980 the legislature amended the state constitution to impose limits on the rate at which property tax revenues could be increased. As a result, the legislature was forced to provide supplemental appropriations for counties in FY 1980-1981 and FY 1981-1982 to assist them in meeting budget overruns. In part as a response to county fiscal problems related to indigent health care expenses, a legislative consensus formed in support of an "experimental" program that would bring federal funds to Arizona for health care for indigents, and the Arizona Health Care Cost Containment System (AHCCCS) was born (Christianson & Hillman, 1986). AHCCCS was initiated in October, 1982 as a three-year "demonstration" program authorized by the federal government's Health Care Financing Administration (HCFA). The program's authorization has been renewed twice, and AHCCCS now appears to be a permanent feature of Arizona state government.

Comparative Spending Patterns

The U.S. Department of Commerce, Bureau of the Census, publishes annual data on state government spending for health care. It defines vendor payments as expenditures by state governments to private vendors for medical care, burials, and other commodities and services provided by welfare programs for the needy. Most Medicaid program spending is reported in this category. A second category, hospital and health services payments, refers to expenditures made directly by state governments through their own hospitals and health agencies and payments to other governments for such purposes. The value of these data is that they permit a rough comparison of Arizona state government spending to spending by other states.

Unadjusted Comparisons

As Table 12-1 suggests, per capita Arizona *state* government spending for health care vendor payments was low relative to other states until implementation of AHCCCS in late 1982 (Tables 12-1 through 12-5 exclude local government health care expenditures so that they do not compare total public health care programs, but focus on state level spending only). Beginning with 1983 and, especially, 1984, Arizona vendor payments were similar to, but lower than, the average of four neighboring states (Colorado, Nevada, New Mexico, and Utah). Even with AHCCCS, they still were considerably lower than vendor payments in California and the 49 state average for vendor payments from 1984 to 1987. In Arizona, per capita vendor payments by state government grew by 27 percent from 1984-1987 as compared to a 43.8 percent average increase in the four neighboring states. In both cases, most of this increase occurred from 1986-1987. Over the same period, the 49 state average for per capita vendor payments rose by 31 percent, suggesting that recent increases in vendor payments in Arizona have been fairly typical of the national experience.

Per capita state spending on health and hospitals (Table 12-2 excludes transfers to local governments) historically has been low in Arizona compared to the national average and to the expenditures of neighboring states, with the exception of Nevada and California. Despite inflation, per capita spending by Arizona state government in this area actually fell from 1981 to 1987. In the 1984-1987 period, per capita spending decreased by 5.5 percent

Table 12-1
Per Capita State Government Expenditures - Vendor Payments[5]
(dollars)

	Arizona	California	Colorado	Nevada	New Mexico	Utah	4 State Mean[1]	49 State Mean[2]	49 State Median[3]
1965	.50	0	7.71	2.12	5.11	6.76	6.35	2.75	3.40
1970	1.79	45.96	18.77	14.43	16.89	13.85	16.84	17.17	13.94
1975	1.81	83.21	46.83	30.04	29.90	28.39	37.39	44.32	37.91
1980[4]	2.45	129.77	57.89	51.54	44.70	59.88	54.89	86.33	74.68
1981[4]	3.38	158.28	71.32	66.95	55.68	69.55	67.24	99.57	87.67
1982[4]	1.85	165.00	78.32	70.93	60.74	57.34	69.12	108.34	96.79
1983[4]	33.61	157.13	74.53	70.74	68.41	66.28	70.96	118.90	103.02
1984	73.21	148.46	78.27	69.78	71.06	79.93	76.12	127.67	109.89
1985	83.53	155.38	83.58	74.34	78.39	95.25	84.00	136.23	119.41
1986	78.62	146.96	86.07	67.89	82.17	111.16	88.58	145.28	128.87
1987	93.19	154.30	114.80	77.19	97.57	129.07	109.49	159.40	144.21

[1] 4 State Mean (Weighted mean of Colorado, Nevada, New Mexico and Utah).

[2] 49 State Mean (mean spending for 49 states divided by mean population for 49 states -- Arizona excluded).

[3] 49 State Median (per capita spending for 49 states -- Arizona excluded).

[4] Includes all Public Welfare Vendor payments. Other years include only "Vendor Payments Medical Care."

[5] Vendor payments are payments made directly to private vendors for medical care, burials and other commodities and services provided by welfare programs for the needy. Health and hospital services provided directly by the government through its own hospitals and health agencies, and payments to other governments for such purposes are included under those categories and not included in this table.

Source: *State Government Finances*, U.S. Department of Commerce Bureau of Census, Annual Publication; Population data are from the U.S. Department of Commerce, Bureau of Census, as reported in *Statistical Abstract of the United States*.

Table 12-2
Per Capita State Spending on Health and Hospitals[4]
(Excludes transfers to local governments)
(dollars)

	Arizona	California	Colorado	Nevada	New Mexico	Utah	4 State Mean[1]	49 State Mean[2]	49 State Median[3]
1965	6.50	12.32	20.45	11.04	9.78	11.60	15.09	14.08	12.83
1970	10.37	17.13	25.84	17.38	17.01	18.23	21.40	23.76	21.38
1975	30.14	27.91	35.54	31.13	49.36	33.87	37.55	41.89	39.00
1980	48.79	45.20	66.78	48.00	104.14	73.10	73.43	69.60	65.13
1981	60.94	56.96	71.82	50.36	120.15	76.98	79.93	78.94	74.04
1982	65.25	57.70	80.66	52.28	140.18	70.88	86.67	84.08	77.56
1983	58.95	56.24	89.58	52.51	136.38	82.71	92.62	89.55	84.72
1984	60.98	58.74	93.07	54.85	149.48	88.05	98.28	91.85	88.05
1985	42.62	67.72	102.13	53.02	157.42	106.66	107.86	98.22	93.05
1986	52.79	75.63	105.82	58.26	162.18	132.84	117.01	106.68	101.79
1987	57.59	83.52	104.50	56.99	156.55	137.92	116.04	112.82	100.94

[1] 4 State Mean (Weighted mean of Colorado, Nevada, New Mexico and Utah).

[2] 49 State Mean (mean spending for 49 states divided by mean population for 49 states -- Arizona excluded).

[3] 49 State Median (per capita spending for 49 states -- Arizona excluded).

[4] Hospital expenditures are identified in Table 12-9.

Source: *State Government Finances*, U.S. Department of Commerce Bureau of Census, Annual Publication; Population data are from the U.S. Department of Commerce, Bureau of Census, as reported in *Statistical Abstract of the United States*.

as compared to an 18 percent increase in average spending by four neighboring states and a 15 percent increase in the 49 state average.

A major component of spending for health and hospitals is funding for state mental hospitals. When attention is focused solely on hospitals, and transfers to local government are excluded, Arizona's per capita spending relative to other states remains very low (Table 12-3). From 1985-1987, Arizona state per capita spending on hospitals rose by 6 percent as compared to an average of 8 percent in neighboring states and 8 percent for the other 49 states (Table 12-3). The only state with remotely similar levels of state spending in this area is Nevada, but Arizona's spending was only 63.5 percent of Nevada's spending in 1987.

<u>Adjusted Comparisons</u>

Comparison of Arizona's average per capita spending figures to national averages can be misleading. Arizona may differ from other states in factors relating to economic environment (*e.g.*, per capita income) and population demographics (*e.g.*, percent of population living in urban areas) that could influence spending on health care. Using neighboring states for comparison purposes controls for some, but possibly not all, of these factors. Therefore, in further analysis, variables representing the expenditure classifications in Tables 12-1 and 12-2 were related to various state characteristics using regression methods.

Model Specification. In this analysis, data at five year intervals were utilized for the forty-nine states, excluding Arizona. Each dependent variable in the regression analyses, representing a different category of state and local government spending, was related to the same set of independent variables. The set of independent variables was patterned after previous published studies of government expenditures (*e.g.*, Bergstrom & Goodman, 1973; Borcherding & Deacon, 1972; Holcombe, 1978; Ohls & Wales, 1972; Leuthold, 1988). Variables were deflated by state population with the exception of cost per hospital stay and federal matching rate. Two different specifications of a time variable were utilized. In the first, time was entered as a series of binary variables representing the year in which the observation was taken (1970, 1975, 1980, 1985) with 1970 being the omitted category. The second approach specified time as a linear trend, with the estimated coefficient representing the average effect of the passage of five years, controlling for other variables.

Data for all variables pooled over the four years specified above were utilized in estimating the regression models. Table 12-4 displays the regression results. In general, the estimated models fit the data well as indicated by the relatively high R^2 values. (The R^2 value represents the proportion of variation in per capita expenditures explained by the set of independent variables listed.)

The estimated regression model with binary time variables was used to predict the average expenditure levels for a state with Arizona's characteristics (see Table 12-5). The comparisons between these predictions and Arizona's actual values indicate that Arizona state government spent much less than was predicted for a state with Arizona's characteristics. This disparity diminished between 1975 and 1985 with respect to vendor payments; after the implementation of AHCCCS, actual state vendor payments were much closer to the predicted values (1985). In fact, given that long term care and behavioral health services were not included in AHCCCS at that time, it is somewhat surprising that there was not a larger difference.

Table 12-3
Per Capita State Government Spending on Hospitals[4]
(excludes transfers to local government)
(dollars)

	Arizona	California	Colorado	Nevada	New Mexico	Utah	4 State Mean[1]	49 State Mean[2]	49 State Median[3]
1985	17.87	50.51	70.91	27.16	90.87	65.65	68.06	67.61	64.59
1986	18.27	52.81	65.85	30.09	91.72	80.50	69.67	71.86	67.35
1987	18.92	58.00	70.58	29.79	92.09	88.93	73.52	74.90	69.28

[1] 4 State Mean (Weighted mean of Colorado, Nevada, New Mexico and Utah).

[2] 49 State Mean (mean spending for 49 states divided by mean population for 49 states--Arizona excluded).

[3] 49 State Median (per capita spending for 49 states--Arizona excluded).

[4] Hospital expenditures are identified in Table 12-9.

Source: *State Government Finances*, U.S. Department of Commerce Bureau of Census, Annual Publication; Population data are from the U.S. Department of Commerce, Bureau of Census, as reported in *Statistical Abstract of the United States*.

Table 12-4 **State Health Care Expenditures ($ per capita)** **Coefficient Estimates[1]**				
Independent Variables	**Time Trend Specifications**		**Binary Variable Time Period Specifications**	
	Vendor Payment	**Health & Hospitals[2]**	**Vendor Payment**	**Health & Hospitals[2]**
Time	-4.027	14.909**		
Binary 1			-17.491*	16.467*
Binary 2			-9.681	30.419**
Binary 3			-17.610	35.325
Percent SMSA	.096	-.183	.104	-.194*
Percent Over 65	-2.226	-3.224**	-2.752	-2.793*
Percent Under 18	-.095	.006	-.402	.446
Percent Poverty	.356	.807	-.153	.776
P.C.[3] Income	.003	-.001	.003	-.001
P.C. Nursing Home Beds	5.923**	.698	6.309**	.593
P.C. Hospital Beds	-.186	-2.776	.024	-3.179
P.C. Physicians	25.580**	16.116**	27.966**	14.279**
Cost per Hospital Stay	.028**	.018	.026**	.025**
Matching Rate	1.336*	-.203	1.635**	-.179
Percent Unemployed	2.926**	-.451	4.078**	-.746
Constant	-153.003**	38.128	-160.949**	36.274
F. Statistic	53.29**	37.96**	49.91**	32.54**
R²	.78	.71	.78	.72

[1] **Significant at less than .05; *Significant at less than .1.
[2] Excludes Transfers to Local Government.
[3] P.C. = per capita

State Health Care Programs: Arizona Health Care Cost Containment System

The largest share of Arizona state government spending for health care occurs under the auspices of the Arizona Health Care Cost containment System (AHCCCS). This program, which became a separate department in Arizona state government in 1984, provides financial access to health care for various categories of low income Arizona residents. Since its inception, it has grown rapidly in terms of expenditures and the number of individuals receiving services.

<table>
<tr><td colspan="5">Table 12-5
Comparison of Projected Versus Actual
Arizona State Government Per Capita Expenditures</td></tr>
<tr><td rowspan="2">Category of Expenditure</td><td colspan="4">Year</td></tr>
<tr><td>1970</td><td>1975</td><td>1980</td><td>1985</td></tr>
<tr><td>Vendor Payments</td><td></td><td></td><td></td><td></td></tr>
<tr><td> Projected</td><td>11.58</td><td>45.20</td><td>69.89</td><td>93.57</td></tr>
<tr><td> Actual</td><td>1.79</td><td>1.81</td><td>2.45</td><td>83.53</td></tr>
<tr><td> Difference[1]</td><td>-9.80</td><td>-43.39</td><td>-67.43</td><td>-10.04</td></tr>
<tr><td>Health & Hospitals[2]</td><td></td><td></td><td></td><td></td></tr>
<tr><td> Projected</td><td>23.88</td><td>49.17</td><td>89.98</td><td>116.60</td></tr>
<tr><td> Actual</td><td>10.37</td><td>30.14</td><td>48.79</td><td>42.62</td></tr>
<tr><td> Difference[1]</td><td>-13.52</td><td>-19.03</td><td>-41.19</td><td>-73.98</td></tr>
<tr><td colspan="5">[1] Difference = Actual-Projected
[2] Excluding transfers to local governments</td></tr>
</table>

<u>Coverage</u>

Until 1989, AHCCCS covered the full range of acute medical services found in the Medicaid programs of other states but did not provide coverage for mental health or long term care services. (Long term care coverage was added in 1989, as described below). AHCCCS is further distinguished from Medicaid in other states in that all services are delivered by prepaid health plans under contract to the state. These plans receive a per person, per month ("capitated") payment from AHCCCS for each individual who enrolls with them or is assigned to them by the state. (Prepaid plans enroll Medicaid beneficiaries in some other states, but only in Arizona are all program beneficiaries served by organizations of this type.) The plans are selected for participation in the program, and their payment levels are established through a competitive process. This competition for state contracts, along with the fixed, per person payment approach, was intended to create incentives for cost containment on the part of providers.

AHCCCS provides services to several different groups of people identified in different ways. The "categorically eligible" are specified by federal law, and federal funds pay a portion of their cost. They include individuals eligible for Aid to Families with Dependent Children (AFDC), AFDC Medical Assistance Only (MAO) eligible, and individuals qualified for Supplemental Security Income (SSI). In January, 1988, program eligibility was extended, through federal legislation, to a relatively small group of pregnant women and children under six years of age.

In addition to program eligible determined by federal statutes, Arizona law defines rules under which the "medically needy/medically indigent" (MN/MI) qualify for AHCCCS. Individuals in these groups are eligible for AHCCCS based primarily on annual incomes that fall below predetermined income levels that vary by household size. The federal government does not share in the funding of medical services for the MN/MI.

<u>Costs</u>

Although AHCCCS suffered severe implementation problems (Christianson & Hillman, 1986) and has been an extremely controversial program since its inception, the best available evidence suggests that it has been successful in containing costs relative to traditional Medicaid programs without damaging quality of care or patient satisfaction. A federally sponsored evaluation of the program (SRI International, 1989) reported that, from 1983-1987, AHCCCS program costs averaged 6 percent less than estimates of what the cost of a traditional Medicaid program would have been in Arizona over the same period, and increases in average per capita costs were 23 percent versus a projected 37 percent for traditional Medicaid. The authors of the report acknowledge that it is very difficult to assess accurately what a traditional Medicaid program in Arizona would have cost. In order to compare AHCCCS costs to potential Medicaid costs, one has to make numerous assumptions about how Medicaid would have been implemented in Arizona, and it is impossible to make these assumptions totally free of error. Thus, the margin of error could well be greater than 6 percent, and AHCCCS costs may have been either somewhat above or somewhat below traditional Medicaid costs. In addition, the study examined only federally-shared costs and did not compare AHCCCS MN/MI costs to traditional Medicaid MN/MI program costs. Thus, total cost differences to the state have not been estimated.

The evaluation also found that quality of care for children in AHCCCS was comparable to care received by children in other Medicaid programs. Access to routine care under AHCCCS was superior relative to a comparison state. However, more problems were reported with access to emergency services. In addition, as discussed below, AHCCCS succeeded in stabilizing the contributions of counties for indigent care (at least as measured by contributions to the AHCCCS program) while bringing a substantial amount of federal dollars to the state through program cost-sharing arrangements. Nevertheless, AHCCCS has been controversial in part because its program costs in some years exceeded budgeted figures by a substantial amount, and because these costs have increased rapidly.

<u>Financing</u>

The funding for AHCCCS comes from federal, state, and local governments. County governments contributed 40 percent of their 1980-81 fiscal year indigent health care budget (or actual expenditures, whichever was lower) in the first year of AHCCCS and 50 percent of this base figure in subsequent years. Thus, their direct contributions to the acute care portion of AHCCCS were effectively "capped." The federal government's contributions to AHCCCS pertain only to the "categorical" populations and are now based on past actual AHCCCS costs per person per month. These costs were trended forward, accounting for inflation and programmatic changes, to calculate a "capitation rate." The federal government pays 62 percent of this capitation rate, multiplied by the estimated number of enrollees, with quarterly adjustments for discrepancies between actual and expected numbers of enrollees. (In the early years of AHCCCS, the federal government based its contribution on estimates of future costs.) A significant feature of this funding scheme is that the state is responsible for program expenditures in excess of projections (although the federal government shares payment responsibility for numbers of enrollees over projections). In traditional Medicaid programs, state and federal governments share all expenditures.

Federal, state, and county funding for AHCCCS since its inception is displayed in Table 12-6. County contributions, as expected, have been relatively stable in magnitude and have declined as a percentage of total funds over time. Since July, 1984, state funds as a percentage of total AHCCCS funds, have been relatively stable at between 44.5 and 51.5 percent (consistent with relative stability in the enrollment of the MN/MI population, Table 12-7) although growing in absolute amount over the last two fiscal years. Federal funds have increased in absolute and percentage terms reflecting strong growth in the number of AFDC enrollees after 1985.

Table 12-6
AHCCCS Acute Care Expenditures by Revenue Source
FY 1982/83 - FY 1988/89
(In Millions of Dollars)

Fiscal Year	State		County		Federal		Other		Total
	$	%	$	%	$	%	$	%	$
1982-83	22.0	19.1	50.5	43.9	37.8	32.8	4.8	4.2	115.1
1983-84	81.3	37.2	63.1	28.8	57.0	26.0	17.4	8.0	218.8
1984-85	124.6	48.6	63.1	24.6	66.7	25.9	2.2	0.9	256.6
1985-86	141.3	51.5	60.8	22.2	70.1	25.5	2.1	0.8	274.3
1986-87	127.8	44.5	58.3	20.3	87.2	30.3	13.8	4.8	287.1
1987-88	182.1	49.1	57.5	15.5	120.6	32.5	2.8	0.8	370.7
1988-89*	216.5	50.3	58.4	13.6	153.4	35.6	2.2	0.5	430.5

* Figures represent estimates of expenditures.

Source: AHCCCS Administration

As in any entitlement program, a major factor relating to increases in expenditures under AHCCCS is growth in the number of enrollees. Enrollment figures are displayed in Table 12-7. Under AHCCCS, enrollment has increased steadily with the exception of the period from October 1, 1984 to October 1, 1985. The decrease in enrollment during this period was due to changes instituted in December, 1984, that made eligibility for the MN/MI category more restrictive. At the same time, SSI allowable income standards were increased, increasing the AFDC pool of eligible. The net result was a 17 percent decrease in total AHCCCS enrollment during 1985. After 1985, enrollment increased most rapidly in the AFDC category while MN/MI enrollment remained relatively stable. In October, 1986, AFDC coverage was extended to children in households that met some, but not all, AFDC requirements and in January, 1987, a new state program for children ages 0-5 was instituted.

A rough sense of the impact of enrollment growth on AHCCCS expenditures can be provided by calculating cost per AHCCCS enrollee over time. In FY 1984/1985 (from July, 1984 to June, 1985) AHCCCS expenditures were $256.6 million. Using October, 1984 enrollment as an estimate of average enrollment for the fiscal year, the cost per enrollee was $1,799. AHCCCS expenditures increased by 44 percent between FY 1984/1985 and FY 1987/1988, but the number of enrollees grew by 57 percent during the same period. Consequently, cost per enrollee declined to $1,634 by 1988. While the addition of new categories of enrollees changed the enrollee mix somewhat, and influenced the cost per enrollee, these calculations suggest the importance of enrollment as a factor contributing to AHCCCS expenditure increases.

<table>
<tr><th colspan="7">Table 12-7
AHCCCS Enrollment</th></tr>
<tr><th>Enrollment[1]
as of</th><th>AFDC</th><th>SSI</th><th>MI/MN</th><th>Other[3]</th><th>Total</th><th>Percent
Change[4]</th></tr>
<tr><td>1/1/83[2]</td><td>98,898</td><td></td><td>61,430</td><td>0</td><td>160,327</td><td></td></tr>
<tr><td>10/1/84</td><td>74,140</td><td>31,631</td><td>67,100</td><td>0</td><td>172,871</td><td>+8</td></tr>
<tr><td>10/1/85</td><td>69,116</td><td>32,859</td><td>40,655</td><td>0</td><td>142,630</td><td>-17</td></tr>
<tr><td>10/1/86</td><td>78,781</td><td>35,318</td><td>43,834</td><td>0</td><td>157,933</td><td>+11</td></tr>
<tr><td>10/1/87</td><td>88,120</td><td>37,225</td><td>46,667</td><td>20,492</td><td>192,504</td><td>+22</td></tr>
<tr><td>10/1/88</td><td>106,800</td><td>39,248</td><td>47,786</td><td>32,378</td><td>226,212</td><td>+18</td></tr>
</table>

[1] In addition to enrollees in prepaid plans, enrollment data includes a relatively small number of persons served through the Indian Health service and fee-for-service recipients of long term care.

[2] Disaggregated enrollment data for 1983 were not reported from AFDC/SSI.

[3] The "other" category includes AFDC-MOA and state children's program enrollees.

[4] Percentage change using previous year as base.

Source: SRI International, Final Report, January, 1989.

The AHCCCS budget has presented two challenges to the State. First, as a major new program, AHCCCS expenditures have been difficult to predict. During the program's second fiscal year (FY 1983/84), expenditures exceeded the AHCCCS budget by approximately $40 million primarily due to larger than expected fee-for-service and administrative expenditures. After passing a supplemental appropriation to cover the shortfall, the state responded by reducing the rates at which hospitals were reimbursed for those AHCCCS enrollees not yet in prepaid plans and the length of time allowed for enrollees to select a plan. Another supplemental appropriation of $47 million was required in FY 1987/88, primarily to cover unexpected increases in the number of program eligibles. And, a third supplemental appropriation of over $30 million was enacted for FY 1988/1989. The second budgetary challenge of AHCCCS has been to finance the dramatic expenditure increases from year to year. Between FY 1984 and FY 1988, state general fund expenditures on AHCCCS rose 124 percent. Total general fund operating expenditures, by contrast, rose only 32 percent.

<u>Extensions of AHCCCS</u>

Several programmatic developments are likely to have a substantial long term impact on state expenditures under the AHCCCS program (AHCCCS White Paper, 1988). These developments are described briefly below.

Welfare Reform. Under the provisions of the federal Welfare Reform Act, beginning on April 1, 1990, Arizona was required to extend AHCCCS participation for one year to AFDC recipients who leave the AFDC program because they have secured employment. (A premium related to income may be collected by the state during the second six months of the year.) Also, beginning in October 1, 1990, AHCCCS benefits must be offered to low income, two-parent families where the principal wage earner is unemployed.

Children's Care Program. Beginning in January, 1987, AHCCCS benefits were extended to (1) children up to 13 years old in families certified for the Federal Food Stamp Program and (2) children in families that do not receive food stamps but whose income exceeds state MN/MI income but is less than federal poverty guidelines. Care for these children under AHCCCS is funded entirely with state dollars, and its impact on AHCCCS expenditures is just beginning to be felt.

Mental Health. Mental health care is a component of traditional Medicaid programs that is not currently covered under AHCCCS except for limited, acute care, crisis intervention. The legislature directed AHCCCS and the Arizona Department of Health Services (DHS) to study the possible inclusion of mental health care beginning in October, 1989. This study concluded that, while incorporating mental health coverage would increase the flow of federal dollars to AHCCCS, it would also result in a substantial increase in state funding for these services. Total cost estimates for such a program were $155 million in 1989 growing to $209 million in 1993. The non-federal portion of these costs was expected to increase form $82 million to $111 million over the same period.

Long Term Care. The recent change in the AHCCCS program that is likely to have the most significant impact on state expenditures is the addition of long term care coverage under state legislation passed in May, 1988 that establishes the Arizona Long Term Care System (ALTCS). It is projected that 13,508 individuals will receive services under ALTCS during its first year, with that total increasing to 18,070 by year three (1990-1991) of the program. Total program costs (including administration) are estimated at $330 million in the first program year growing to $478 million by year three. The non-federal share of those costs is expected to increase from $128 million to $185 million over the same period.

State Health Care Programs: Arizona Department of Health Services

The Arizona Department of Health Services (DHS) has undergone several organizational changes over the past ten years that make interpretation of changes in its expenditures somewhat difficult. In two instances, AHCCCS and Environmental Quality, divisions within DHS became separate departments in state government. Substantial restructuring also occurred relating to behavioral health, emergency services, and laboratory services. At present, there are six divisions within DHS: Division of Disease Prevention Services; Division of Laboratory Services; Division of Family Health Services; Division of Emergency Medical Services and Health Care Facilities; Department Support Services; and Division of Behavioral Health Services.

The Department is funded from a variety of sources with the most prominent being state and federal appropriations (Table 12-8). In 1989, DHS received $121 million in state appropriations and $42 million in federal appropriations. State appropriations represented 74 percent of total state and federal appropriations, up from 65 percent in 1980. In percentage terms, the most rapid growth in state funding from 1980 to 1989 occurred for emergency services (306.7 percent) and disease prevention (212.2 percent). However, in absolute terms, by far the greatest increase occurred for behavioral health care ($54.5 million).

<table>
<tr><td colspan="7" align="center">Table 12-8
Department of Health Services -- Federal and State Funds
(in millions of $)</td></tr>
<tr><td></td><td colspan="2" align="center">State Funds</td><td colspan="2" align="center">Federal Funds</td><td colspan="2" align="center">Total</td></tr>
<tr><td></td><td align="center">1980</td><td align="center">1989</td><td align="center">1980</td><td align="center">1989</td><td align="center">1980</td><td align="center">1989</td></tr>
<tr><td>Non-Behavioral</td><td></td><td></td><td></td><td></td><td></td><td></td></tr>
<tr><td>   Management</td><td>4,761.7</td><td>9,108.1</td><td>169.2</td><td>127.8</td><td>4,780.9</td><td>9235.9</td></tr>
<tr><td>   Emergency Services</td><td>1,438.5</td><td>5,849.8</td><td>1,664.6</td><td>2,329.7</td><td>3,103.1</td><td>8,179.5</td></tr>
<tr><td>   Disease Prevention</td><td>1,823.3</td><td>5,691.9</td><td>1,571.2</td><td>3,569.2</td><td>3,394.5</td><td>9,261.1</td></tr>
<tr><td>   Family Health</td><td>12,423.5</td><td>14,823.4</td><td>21,978.2</td><td>24,185.2</td><td>34,401.7</td><td>39,008.6</td></tr>
<tr><td>   Laboratory</td><td>958.1</td><td>2,241.7</td><td>--</td><td>--</td><td>958.1</td><td>2,241.7</td></tr>
<tr><td>Sub-Total:</td><td>21,405.1</td><td>37,714.9</td><td>25,383.2</td><td>30,211.9</td><td>45,680.2</td><td>67,926.8</td></tr>
<tr><td>Behavioral</td><td>29,229.9</td><td>83,757.1</td><td>2,875.6</td><td>11,955.1</td><td>32,105.5</td><td>95,712.2</td></tr>
<tr><td>Total[1]</td><td>50,635.0</td><td>121,472.0</td><td>28,258.8</td><td>42,167.0</td><td>77,785.7</td><td>63,639.0</td></tr>
<tr><td colspan="7">[1] Combined DHS expenditures for behavioral and nonbehavioral health services.

Source: Arizona Department of Health Services, White Paper, November 9, 1988.</td></tr>
</table>

State behavioral health funding grew by 185.6 percent from 1980 to 1989, as compared to a 76.2 percent growth rate in all DHS non-behavioral health expenditures combined. In 1989, behavioral health expenditures accounted for 68.9 percent of all DHS expenditures from state funds and 58.5 percent of expenditures from state and federal funds combined. The percentage of state DHS funds spent for non-behavioral health care declined from 42.3 percent to 31.1 percent during the 1980s. Federal funds expended on behavioral health care grew by 315.7 percent from 1980-1989 as compared to a 19 percent increase in federal funding for DHS non-behavioral health care programs. Nevertheless, federal funds were only 12.5 percent of total federal and state funds projected to be spent by DHS for behavioral health care in 1989 as compared to 44.4 percent of DHS state and federal funds expended for non-behavioral health care.

<u>Behavioral Health Services</u>

The Division of Behavioral Health Services (BHS) of the Arizona Department of Health Services consists of the Arizona State Hospital, the Southern Arizona Mental Health Center, and Community Behavioral Health Services and Chronic Mental Illness with associated support services relating to research, community relations and management information. For the period from 1981-1988, state government funding for the State hospital increased from $16.39 million to $25.90 million. There was a much larger proportionate increase in state government funding for the provision of services to the chronically mentally ill (from $3.2 million to $17.1 million) and smaller increases for mental health ($6.3 million to $8.1 million) and for substance abuse treatment ($6.6 to $9.8 million).

When these state expenditures are adjusted for inflation and divided by the state's population to obtain per capita figures, the trends look somewhat different. Spending (in 1981 dollars) for the chronically mentally ill (CMI) continued to show a substantial increase from 1981-1988 from $1.15 to $3.70 per Arizona resident. However, per capita spending in the remaining three categories declined; from $5.85 to $5.60 for the Arizona State Hospital; from $2.73 to $2.13 for substance abuse; and from $2.37 to $1.75 for mental health services. A third way of portraying state spending for behavioral health services is on a "per client served basis." Using this method (without inflation adjustment) spending rose in all categories. For Arizona State Hospital residents, annual state costs per resident increased from $18,147 in 1981 to $22,249 in 1987. State spending per CMI client rose from $646 in 1981 to $1784 in 1988, a substantially greater increase than for substance abuse ($293 versus $344) or mental health ($217 versus $288), (ADHS, BHS, Budget Justification Package, FY 1988-1989).

Arizona state government funds the entire cost of the Arizona State Hospital and approximately 49 percent of costs in the other three areas combined. In these areas, about 31 percent of funds are provided by local government matching dollars and 12 percent by federal dollars. It is estimated that 16 percent of spending for behavioral health services in Arizona is done directly by county governments (ADHS, BHS, Budget Justification Package, FY 1988-1989).

State funding for behavioral health services is likely to increase in the future. One reason relates to a class action suit, filed in 1981, against the state and Maricopa county, alleging that they failed to provide adequate care for chronically mentally ill persons. In 1985, Maricopa County Superior Court issued a ruling in support of the suit requiring that the state and county must provide a continuum of care to chronically mentally ill persons. This ruling was appealed to the Arizona Supreme Court where it was affirmed in March, 1989. Estimates of the total impact have ranged from $70 million to $600 million, with the expectation that the state will increase expenditures over a number of years, rather than all at once, to comply with the ruling (Winters & Van Der Were, March 14, 1989).

A second reason relates to Arizona's ranking with respect to many indices associated with mental health need. For instance, among the 50 states, Puerto Rico and the District of Columbia, Arizona has the second highest rates of teenage suicide, crime, and child abuse. And, it ranks seventh in divorce rates. In contrast to these indicators of need, Arizona ranks near the bottom in utilization of services and expenditures of funds for mental health care. The Division of Behavioral Health Services estimates that, even if a requested $17.7 million (5.9 percent) increase for FY 1990 were approved, only a small portion of the existing unmet needs of Arizona's residents for behavioral health services would be met. These unmet needs, together with the recent court ruling, will create pressure for larger future increases in state spending for behavioral health services (*Phoenix Gazette*, March 16, 1989).

<u>DHS Programs, Excluding Behavioral Health Care</u>

In 1989, about 31 percent of state appropriations for the Department of Health Services were expected to be spent in areas other than behavioral health including: family health (12.1 percent), disease prevention (4.7 percent), emergency medical services/health resources (4.8 percent), state laboratory (1.8 percent), and overall department management (7.5 percent). Within these general categories, DHS manages a number of programs targeted at specific disease or population groups. In most cases, these programs do not involve direct service delivery nor are they entitlement programs. Where services are funded, they are delivered by private providers under contract with the state. The degree to which legislators have supported individual programs in the past has varied with constituent demands and the state's economic climate.

Of particular interest are programs relating to the health care of children, who comprised 30 percent of the state's population in 1987. Arizona ranks 13th in the nation in percent of babies born to single mothers. Also, Arizona's divorce rate is 32 percent higher than the national average, with over half of state divorces involving children. And, Arizona ranks high in numerous other factors contributing to stressful environmental circumstances for children (Division of Family Health Services, 1987). In 1987, DHS initiated a statewide appraisal of child health needs as part of an effort to develop a children's health plan. As a result of this appraisal, it was recommended that "...the state promote and ensure the development of a universal child health care plan" (p.2). Additional DHS activities were also proposed to minimize the impact of childhood injuries, support potentially dysfunctional families, minimize exposure to hazardous substances, promote child health planning at the state and local levels, and implement a statewide data collection and reporting system.

Health Care Expenditures By Counties In Arizona

In most states, the Medicaid program removed much of the funding responsibility for health services from county governments in the late 1960s. In Arizona, these responsibilities remained with counties until the early 1980s, when they were modified by the implementation of AHCCCS.

AHCCCS and County Governments

The AHCCCS legislation was intended to provide financial relief to the counties by setting each county's contribution legislatively at 40 percent of the amount budgeted or expended (whichever was less) on indigent care in FY 1980-1981 to be increased to 50 percent for subsequent years of the demonstration. Individual counties benefitted from this arrangement to various degrees. Since county contributions were determined as a percentage of total expenditures for all care including long term care (which was not a covered service under AHCCCS), counties that spent a relatively high proportion of their funds on long term care in FY 1980-1981 benefitted less from AHCCCS. Also, the AHCCCS legislation required counties to fund those services in effect January 1, 1981 that were not covered by AHCCCS. And, counties retained statutory responsibility for the provision of health services to those individuals with income and medical expenses that did not qualify them for AHCCCS but did permit them to meet existing county eligibility requirements for medical assistance. For individuals who received medical services on an emergency basis and subsequently qualified for AHCCCS, counties are liable for all costs of care incurred prior to completion of an AHCCCS application. Initially, AHCCCS assumed responsibility for financing this care for 30 days prior to completion of an application. This was subsequently changed to five days and then to one day. The reduction to one day transferred considerable financial exposure from the state to the counties.

County governments have responsibility for determining eligibility for AHCCCS with the state conducting the actual enrollment into the program. The new costs associated with this activity were substantial. During the month prior to the actual delivery of care under AHCCCS, Pima County tripled the number of its eligibility workers (*Tucson Citizen*, September 29, 1983) and Maricopa County also reported a large increase in its staff.

The AHCCCS legislation gave counties the option to participate as a provider, contracting with the state to deliver health care to indigents in return for a fixed payment per month in this way. By 1985, three counties remained as contractors, including Maricopa (Phoenix) and Pima (Tucson) Counties. The county plans have reported varying experiences with their contracts under AHCCCS. For instance, from July 1984 through December 1985, the Pima County plan had $1.6 million in losses versus a $2.6 million surplus in Maricopa County's plan for the same period. However, it should be noted that the county hospitals and county sponsored plans are so interrelated politically and organizationally that it is difficult to separate the actual financial performance of the plans from the hospitals' performance (Kirkman-Liff, Christianson & Kirkman-Liff, 1987).

In April, 1985, the Pima County Board of Supervisors, in a largely symbolic action, voted to quit AHCCCS. It asserted that the county could save the state $8 million and provide better care if it were once again the sole provider of health services for its indigents (*Arizona Republic*, April 24, 1985). The validity of such assertions is virtually impossible to ascertain since one doesn't know what would have happened in the absence of AHCCCS. However, a rough sense of how the counties have fared under AHCCCS can be obtained by comparing spending for health care as a proportion of total county budgets before and after AHCCCS. Health care related expenditures have gone down as a percentage of total county expenditures in both urban counties and, on average, in rural counties as well. Health care related revenues as a percentage of total county revenues have gone up in urban counties but have fallen in rural counties. As a result, net health care expenditures (defined as health care expenditures minus health care revenues) as a percentage of county expenditures have declined for urban counties but risen slightly in rural counties. These calculations, based on budget numbers reported by the counties to the U.S. Bureau of the Census, suggest that although health care spending by Arizona counties has continued to rise in absolute dollars, urban counties now spend a lower portion of their budgets on health care than they did prior to AHCCCS, while the portion spent by rural counties has remained about the same.

County expenditures for health care during FY 1987-88 are presented in Table 12-9. On average, health care expenditures constituted 38 percent of county budgets in FY 1987-88, ranging from a high of 43 percent in Pinal County to a low of 8 percent in Apache County. In general, the more populous counties spend a larger share of their budgets on health care. In counties with county hospitals, expenditures for acute hospital care constituted the largest single health care budget category. Excluding this category, long term care spending exceeded spending in other areas for most counties. Clearly, even with AHCCCS contributions, health care related expenditures continue to be a major budget item for county governments.

County governments anticipated some relief from expenditures on long term care with the implementation of ALTCS on January 1, 1989. However, as with AHCCCS, the counties have residual responsibilities under ALTCS. In particular, counties remain liable for the provision of long term care to individuals they were serving or who applied for services prior to January 1, 1989, but were not eligible for ALTCS (KPMG, 1989). It has been estimated that as many as 35 percent of individuals receiving care from counties in 1988 could fall into this group. In addition, Pima and Maricopa counties are mandated to be program contractors

Table 12-9
County Expenditures for Health Care -- FY 87-88
(millions of dollars)

County	AHCCCS	Acute Care Contribution	LTC Eligibility	Public Hospital	Other	Total	Health Care Expenditures as Percentage of Total County Expenditures
Maricopa	32.93	4.27	113.85	69.55	31.45	252.05	42
Pima	11.05	2.45	56.09	28.09	10.03	107.71	41
Pinal	2.65	3.06	13.95	4.95	1.77	26.38	43
Cochise	2.16	.37	.29	3.15	1.72	7.69	27
Yuma	1.29	.33	2.36	3.23	.91	8.12	25
Coconino	.72	.33	.00	.53	1.63	3.21	12
Yavapai	1.39	.32	.45	2.73	1.14	6.03	19
Mohave	.21	.31	.38	2.28	.50	4.68	16
Navajo	.30	.46	.06	1.16	.31	2.29	12
Apache	.26	.11	.00	.22	.24	.83	8
Gila	1.49	.31	.53	2.61	.37	5.31	29
Santa Cruz	.43	.12	.00	.90	.93	1.95	20
Graham	.52	.05	.00	.56	.40	1.53	22
LaPaz	.21	.13	.10	.37	.10	.91	14
Greenlee	.19	.10	.00	.29	.47	1.05	23
Total	56.34	12.74	188.06	120.63	51.98	429.80	38

Source: County Budget Forms, Arizona Association of Counties.

for long term care, with the other thirteen counties given the option to be sole program contractors for their jurisdictions. Where county governments choose not to contract with ALTCS, private contractors will provide services.

Because of the residual responsibilities of the counties, it is not clear at this point how total county expenditures for long term care ultimately will be affected by the implementation of ALTCS. It is expected that county contracts and obligations to ALTCS will total $95.4 million in FY 1989-1990 (AHCCCS Waiver, 1988). The contribution of each individual county will be determined by its share of total county spending on long term care prior to implementation of the ALTCS. The legislature is expected to review the level of county expenditures for ALTCS and either continue it at $95.4 million or fix county contributions at a percentage of total ALTCS spending.

Summary

Government health care programs in Arizona are in the midst of a major transformation. The transformation began with the implementation of AHCCCS in 1982, continued with the addition of children's programs (1987) and the Arizona Long Term Care System (1989) to AHCCCS, and will likely be extended through the development of new programs for the provision of behavioral health services. The implications of this transformation for health care expenditures by state and local governments in Arizona cannot be assessed completely at this time, but they are likely to be enormous. Major shifts in expenditures have already occurred, and will continue to occur, between state and local government to conform to federal regulations and accommodate new federal funds flowing to the state. Indeed, one of the stated motivations for development of AHCCCS was to constrain the growth of county spending on indigent health care. However, although federal funding for health care in Arizona is increasing as a result of the transformation currently underway, expansion of program eligibility and coverage, along with constraints on county contributions, has created an environment in which continued rapid growth in state spending is almost certain.

Many factors affecting state health care expenditures, including the actions of the federal government, are essentially beyond the influence of state governments. And, because state government in Arizona is, in effect, the "residual payer" under the structure of its new programs, it bears most of the financial risk for budget overruns caused by unanticipated growth in enrollment, service use, or inflation. This situation, along with the strong potential for the institution of new programs in the behavioral health care area, means that state government will continue to face periodic short falls in its health care budgets.

Since it is likely that health care costs will continue to grow more rapidly than other governmental costs for at least the next ten years, health care expenditures will comprise a growing share of the total state budget in Arizona and in other states as well. As this occurs, state governments will be able to call on a limited number of policy options if they hope to constrain increases in their health care costs.

Ration Eligibility

Under this approach, total expenditure increases would be constrained by changing program disability standards to reduce the number of individuals eligible to receive state-financed services. Of course, this would increase the number of uninsured in the state and presumably the number of untreated health care problems in the low income population. Some costs would be shifted to county governments, where county-run facilities would become providers of last resort to growing numbers of individuals.

Limit Coverage

State expenditures could also be constrained by reducing the scope of covered services in public medical care programs. This could have an adverse effect on access to services for the poor and, ultimately, their health status. The state could refuse to cover medical care services that had questionable cost-effectiveness. However, it may not be possible to limit coverage enough using this criterion to have a significant impact on cost increases. If it could be accomplished, the major impact of this strategy would be on the incomes of health care providers.

Reduce Provider Payments

States could attempt to constrain costs by reducing payments to health care providers for services delivered to program beneficiaries. In many states, this approach has been implemented to the point that further reductions might substantially reduce the number of providers willing to deliver services. Rather than reduce the choice of providers available to program participants indirectly by lowering payments, states might instead establish limited provider panels authorized to treat participants. In return for an increased volume of patients, these providers would be required to accept lower reimbursements. Besides reducing provider incomes, this strategy risks creating a two-tier medical care system where the poor do not have access to mainstream medical care.

Mandate Employer Provided Insurance

Studies have shown that many individuals covered by state-financed medical care programs have employment, but their positions are part-time and they are paid low wages. Often, employer provided health insurance is not available for these individuals. By making it mandatory for employers to provide some type of health insurance coverage to all employees, the state could shift some of its public program costs to the private sector. However, since this would increase the effective cost of labor to the employer, it could reduce the number of low-wage employment opportunities. In turn, this might increase the number of individuals eligible for state-financed medical care.

Clearly, as the discussion of these options suggests, rising health care costs will force many states to make politically difficult programmatic choices. While all of their consequences are not obvious, each strategy is likely to limit access to services on the part of program participants, reduce payment to providers and/or possibly shift costs to the private sector. The mix of strategies likely to be adopted in a given state is difficult to predict, since it will depend in part on the relative political power of the affected parties within that state and in part on the state's economic climate.

References

Arizona Association of Counties, *County Expenditures*, FY 1987-1988.

Arizona Department of Health Services, "White Paper," November 9, 1988.

Arizona Department of Health Services, Division of Behavioral Health Services, *Budget Justification Package*, FY 1988-1989.

Arizona Health Care Cost Containment System Waiver Package submitted to the Health Care Financing Administration, May 19, 1988.

Arizona Health Care Cost Containment System, "White Paper," November 21, 1988.

Arizona Republic, "Pima County Votes to Quit AHCCCS; Actual Exit 'Doubtful'!" April 24, 1985.

Bergstrom, T. and R. Goodman. "Private Demands for Public Goods," *American Economic Review*, Vol. 63 (June, 1973), pp. 280-296.

Borcherding, T. and R. Deacon. "The Demand for the Services of Non-Federal Governments," *American Economic Review*, Vol. 62, No. 5 (December, 1972), pp. 891-901.

Christianson, J. and D. Hillman. *Health Care for the Indigent and Competitive Contracts: The Arizona Experience.* Health Administration Press Perspectives: Ann Arbor, MI, 1986.

Division of Family Health Services, Arizona Department of Health Services. *The Health of Arizona's Children: A Challenge for Action*, 1987.

Division of National Cost Estimates, Office of Actuary. "National Health Expenditures, 1986-2000," *Health Care Financing Review*, Vol. 8. No. 4 (Summer, 1987), pp.1-36.

Firebaugh, G. and J. Gibbs. "User's Guide to Ratio Variables," *American Sociological Review*, Vol. 50, (October, 1985), pp. 713-722.

Holcombe, R. "Public Choice and Public Spending," *National Tax Journal*, Vol. 31, No. 4 (December, 1978), pp. 373-384.

Kirkman-Liff, B., J. Christianson, and T. Kirkman-Liff. "The Evolution of Arizona's Indigent Care System," *Health Affairs*, Winter, 1987, pp.46-58.

KPMG Peat Marwick, *Information and Recommendations Concerning the Issue of Maintenance of Effort for Long Term Care Services in Arizona, Phase I*, report to the Arizona State Legislature, Joint Legislative Council Committee on the Arizona Health Care Cost Containment System, January 15, 1989.

Leuthold, J. "A Forecasting Model for State Expenditures," *Public Choice*, Vol. 56, No. 1 (January, 1988), pp. 45-55.

Marmor T. and J. Christianson. *Health Care Policy: A Political Economy Approach*, Sage Publications, Beverly Hills, 1982.

Ohls, J. and T. Wales. "Supply and Demand for State and Local Services," *The Review of Economics and Statistics*, Vol. 54, No. 4 (November, 1972), pp. 424-430.

Peat Marwick Main and Company, *Medicaid Mental Health Study: Summary and Final Report*, report to the State of Arizona, Department of Health Services, Division of Behavioral Health Services, September 28, 1988.

Phoenix Gazette, "Mental Health: More Bad News," March 16, 1989.

SRI International, "Evaluation of the Arizona Health Care Cost Containment System: Final Report," January, 1989.

Tucson Citizen, "ACCESS Was to 'Save' Counties, But They Still Feel Pinch," September 26, 1983.

Tucson Citizen, "ACCESS Helps But Counties Still Pay," September 29, 1983.

Winters, J. and M. Van Der Were. "Full Services Ordered for Mentally Ill," *Arizona Republic*, March 14, 1989.

Chapter 13

Welfare Policy:
Spending and Program Structure

Steven G. Craig[*]

This chapter examines welfare spending in Arizona, with the exception of medical care (discussed in Chapter 12). Welfare is certainly one of the most complex activities undertaken by state governments. Welfare policy and welfare design issues have been at the forefront of federal and state policy discussions in the 1980s and promise to remain so throughout the 1990s. This chapter places the central issues in the design of a welfare system into perspective through both a theoretical discussion of the design complexities of welfare systems and a statistical analysis of how Arizona fits into the national picture.

One reason for complexity in the welfare system is the fundamental paradox inherent in welfare. If people are paid because they are not working, there exist incentives for individuals to avoid work to get paid by the state. Similarly, if unmarried women with children receive aid, there is an incentive for unmarried women to have children. A central issue in welfare design is to assist those who most need help while minimizing the socially undesirable incentives inherent in any welfare system.

There are two primary causes of low incomes. One is nonemployment (or underemployment), the second is social dislocation. Nonemployment can be caused by a host of problems from lack of desire for work to lack of opportunity for work caused by either a deficiency in skills or deficiency in ability. Social dislocations include divorce, having a child, or other family changes or problems such as old age and disability. It has been estimated that about 25% of U.S. society uses the welfare system some time during a decade even though only about eight percent of the population is on welfare in any one year. These

---

[*] I would like to acknowledge the enormous assistance of several people in state government for providing an excellent overview of the successes and problems that characterize welfare spending in Arizona. Therese McGuire, the Executive Director of the Arizona Fiscal 2000 Committee did an excellent job of providing an organized framework in which to conduct the analysis, and provided much needed editorial assistance. Rebecca Blank also provided useful and stimulating comments. Richard Stavneak of the Joint Legislative Budget Committee provided a useful overview of welfare spending. The cooperation of Gordon Mulleneaux of the Department of Economic security is gratefully acknowledged. I benefitted from conversations with Andy Genualdi of the Department of Economic Security, who also made available some of the data for this study. Rick Ferreira of the DES kindly provided some of the excellent internal studies of welfare and AFDC. I gratefully acknowledge the excellent research assistance of Russel Burge and Jiang Yu. Finally, the research support of the NSF is also gratefully acknowledged.

figures illustrate that the poverty population is dynamic reflecting the myriad causes for needing government assistance and illustrating that a large number of people successfully leave the welfare system.

Public attention has focused on the fact that Arizona is a low welfare spending state. To put the welfare expenditure ranking of Arizona into perspective, a detailed statistical model is presented that captures the primary determinants of welfare spending in the 48 mainland states over the twenty year period 1966-1985. This model shows that, while Arizona is indeed a low welfare spending state, it has made considerable progress over the last decade in narrowing the gap between itself and the rest of the nation.

The Conceptual Role of Government in Providing Welfare

The primary function of state welfare assistance, as with any good insurance plan, is to provide an opportunity for needy individuals to get through a bad period and emerge as productive members of society. State efforts serve to focus the aggregate desire of society to provide insurance for both social and economic distress. Successful efforts, even if difficult to measure, result in more smoothly functioning labor markets as well as providing an increased sense of safety and well-being to society. This section discusses the rationale for state government provision of low income assistance and some of the consequences of welfare aid on individual behavior.

Low income assistance in the United States has been a governmental function for a long time, at least since 1898 (Lynn, 1977). The modern welfare system began to evolve in 1935 with federal government establishment of the Aid to Families with Dependent Children (AFDC) Program. There are two types of income transfer programs that currently characterize the U.S. welfare system. Social insurance programs aim to prevent poverty by replacing (at least partially) income lost through unemployment, retirement, disability, or death. Traditional public assistance programs, on the other hand, aim to assist those already in poverty. These welfare programs are "means-tested" meaning that low income is a condition for receipt of aid. Because the federal government has been the primary financier of social insurance programs, with the exception of Unemployment Insurance, the analysis in this chapter is confined to a discussion about state operated means-tested programs.

The Causes of Poverty

While there are many potential causes of low income for an individual or a household, social science has not yet been able to model the causes of poverty reliably. Nonetheless, most agree the primary causes of poverty revolve around demographic changes and the lack of what are called human capital investments (education and training).

Demographic changes in the economy can be central to determining aggregate measured poverty rates. Elderly households tend to have relatively low incomes even though they may have a high level of assets. Young people just entering the labor force tend to have low incomes since first jobs will generally pay less than jobs later in life. The presence of children can also result in lower measured income because of the increased importance of "household production" required to provide care for children. While this is true for families that remain intact as well as for separated or divorced parents, the problems are greater for single parents. Finally, for a variety of reasons, people in minority groups tend to have a higher incidence of poverty. All four of these demographic groups have grown at very rapid rates over the last twenty years, more so for Arizona than for most of the rest of the country.

In 1988, elderly (defined as over 65 years old) individuals in Arizona accounted for 12.7 percent of the population. Compared to the 1970 share of 9.1 percent, this is almost a 30 percent growth rate in the *share* of the population and represents a 270 percent growth in the number of elderly individuals in the state. Families headed by females also have grown very rapidly from 6.1 percent of the households in 1970 to 8.3 percent in 1988, over a doubling of the size of this group. The minority share of the population has also grown more rapidly than the state as a whole from 9.4 percent of the population in 1970 to 17.6 percent in 1980 (these figures do not include the growth in the Hispanic share). Recent statistics indicate that the minority share of the population will remain roughly constant as a higher proportion of Whites are migrating to Arizona offsetting a higher birth rate among other groups.

The most important of the demographic groups in terms of the impact on low income assistance expenditure levels are the elderly and female headed households. Both of these groups are growing rapidly in Arizona and most likely will continue to grow at a rate fast r than the general population. These trends can be expected to add significant pressure n welfare programs.

Elderly households are not all poor especially when the greater asset levels of this segment of the population are accounted for. Further, due to rapid increases in the level of Social Security Old Age Assistance, poverty rates for elderly householders have actually fallen in the last fifteen years. Nonetheless, elderly households are still more likely to have low incomes than is the general population. Single parent households are an even greater problem as less success has been made in helping this group out of poverty. The magnitude of both problems can be seen by looking at household income. Using data from the last complete Census year, over 43 percent of the single parent households in Arizona had 1979 incomes less than $10,000 compared to only 28.9 percent of all households. Similarly, 52 percent of households headed by a person over the age of 65 had 1979 incomes less than $10,000.

A central problem affecting poverty rates among female headed households is family dissolution. For example, Duncan (1984) finds that divorce or separation causes family income to fall by over 9 percent per year in real terms (after inflation) for the seven years following divorce. Families that remain married, on the other hand, on average experienced income gains greater than inflation. A similar impact on children is found. Children in homes of divorced parents had family incomes fall by 8.7 percent per year over the seven year period of the study. This same study finds that most of the income losses can be made up by remarriage.

A second hypothesized cause of poverty is a lack of sufficient education and training. While education and training are clearly central to the prevention or elimination of poverty, a key question is whether education and training are sufficient by themselves to eliminate poverty. Education and training have been central elements of the War on Poverty since 1965 and are of growing importance with the recent changes in federal welfare legislation. Expenditures on training programs are usually called investments in human capital since the goal of training programs is to increase the earning power of individuals. There are two types of programs: those that aim at children and those that attempt to train or retrain adults. Virtually all studies find that both types of training programs have positive benefits although it is much more difficult to show that they have positive net-of-cost benefits (see Sawhill, 1988 for a recent review). More important, however, is that it is difficult to ascertain why they succeed.

One counter-argument to the notion that education leads to higher income is that even though people need some certification in order to obtain a job, on-the-job training is the only training of value. The argument is that a policy of providing human capital by itself will be insufficient. Also, it is difficult to differentiate the contribution to earnings of training, other environmental factors, and pure ability. The point of these arguments is not to say that education and training are not helpful. But, education and training are only a part of an overall strategy for dealing with the poverty problem. Further, care should be taken when extrapolating the results of a demonstration training project to the population as a whole because it is unclear whether newly trained people simply displace other workers, or whether new jobs are created to harness additional people.

Finally, the level of economic activity is central to observed levels of income. Recent research shows that when unemployment rises, working heads of poor families suffer about three times the income loss as middle class families, both through unemployment and through reduced wages and hours (Gramlich and Laren, 1984a). There is voluminous research literature on the causes of wages and hours worked and why they differ between people. For the purposes here, it is sufficient to say that those with restricted opportunities are more likely to need public assistance.

Can the Private Sector Provide Welfare-Type Insurance?

The basic issue addressed in this section is to determine why the government should provide insurance in the form of welfare assistance. There are two private sector alternatives to publicly provided economic and social insurance that are worth discussing. The first is to rely on private charitable contributions. The other is to provide some type of private insurance. Each of these alternatives, however, has basic problems that lead to a serious underprovision of low income assistance care.

The underlying economic problem behind private charitable contributions is termed the "free rider problem" that plagues the provision of what are called "positive externalities." The term positive externalities refers to goods in society that provide benefits to others besides the direct purchasers. For example, suppose two high income people both care about the income levels of the poor. One of them makes a contribution to the poor. The other person is now made better off because the income levels of the poor have now improved even though that second person has not yet done anything to help. Thus the person that made the contribution to the poor has provided "positive externalities" to the second. This second person is likely to contribute less than otherwise (or even zero) because of the actions of the first person. This second person is the "free rider" because he/she benefitted from another's contribution without doing anything. In a complex society like ours, however, we do not directly know about the actions of others. Nonetheless, we are likely to assume that others will care for the problem, and we will neglect to take any direct action ourselves.

This explanation of the effect of positive externalities provides one justification for government intervention. Through the actions of the government, all people are required to contribute to the poor through the tax system. In theory, at least, this avoids the free rider problem. The government decides what level of assistance to provide the poor while accounting for the desire for low income assistance by the population as a whole. Thus, the government simply acts as the social collection agency for the entire population.

Government action in this fashion may result in reduced private contributions. In fact, there is some evidence that there has been considerable substitution of public for private care in the case of cash assistance (Roberts, 1984). On the other hand, to the extent that some people feel government levels of assistance are too paltry, they will engage in some private charitable contributions. Maybe even more important, it is possible that some types of government services allow a greater role for private charitable actions because the public sector provides a better environment for private actions (Schiff, 1985). This may be because the government provides some basic facilities or because the government provides a reliable screening device in its determination of truly needy individuals.

The free rider argument is based on an altruism model where some people care about others. The other argument for welfare is that it acts as an insurance mechanism. One alternative to public provision of social and economic insurance is private insurance. Indeed, many people have insurance for some of the types of problems that welfare programs address, for example medical and disability insurance. There are two separate problems with private insurance, however, that especially afflict people at the lower end of the income scale. One, it is highly probable that such insurance might not be profitable if provided privately. Second, those who most need insurance may not purchase it if they cannot afford it.

Private insurance for economic disasters might not be profitable because the only people that would buy it are those most likely to use it. To the extent that it is difficult for an insurance company to determine how likely it is for a person to need it, the insurance company would find that its only customers are those for whom the insurance is a good deal which is to say those whose benefits from the insurance exceed its cost. To see this, consider two individuals. The first knows he/she is about to lose his/her job. The second knows that he/she will keep his job for the foreseeable future. If the insurance company offers a contract that pays when a person loses his/her job, the first individual will think it is a good deal and will buy it. The second person will not. The insurance company will find that it only sells to people who claim soon after purchase and the insurance company will lose money.

In the context of the state-wide economy, the government forces all of its citizens to contribute to the insurance fund. Thus, both those who will need the insurance shortly as well as those that may not need it for a long time contribute.

The other problem with private insurance is that people who most need it cannot afford it. Even though a person knows that insurance is needed, it is easy to postpone the decision when there is no immediate crisis. Further, for those in the lowest income brackets, day-to-day survival may mean that they are not able to afford concerns about the future. Thus, the other role of the government may be to force individuals to buy what is needed. This occurs when all workers are required to pay state and federal taxes which then are available to fund welfare benefits.

One startling statistic is that a very high proportion of people use a means-tested welfare program at some time in their lives as children, as adults, or when elderly. According to Duncan (1984), almost one-fourth of the population uses the welfare system at least once in a decade. This is because the U.S. population is quite mobile across income classes. For example, about 45 percent of the individuals in the lowest 20 percent income bracket in 1971 had raised their incomes above that range by 1978 including 6 percent into the top 20 percent income bracket.

Another conceptual issue to consider is the desired output of state welfare programs. The appropriate definition of success in welfare programs is neither how many people are on welfare nor how many people are not on welfare. The success of the welfare system can only be measured by the success of individuals after they have "graduated" from welfare. Recent policy changes are cognizant of this point and are directed at both targeting individuals with different needs and at easing the transition out of welfare.

The Federal and State Roles

More than any other state level activity, low income assistance activities represent a partnership between the federal government and state and local governments. The relationship between the levels of government is sometimes an uneasy one as the nature of the responsibility of each level of government has changed over time. The central decisions that characterize this relationship are overall funding levels, benefit levels per recipient, and eligibility rules. This section discusses the motivation for federal intervention in welfare policy and presents a brief history of the evolution of federal welfare policy.

The United States is relatively unique in that welfare benefit levels and eligibility standards vary greatly across the country. Interstate variation arises due to differences in what programs are offered and due to differences in the level of benefits within a program. For example, AFDC benefit levels are set by each state, and each state sets most of the eligibility standards. Additional variation arises because only about one-half of the states have implemented the Unemployed Parent (UP) segment of AFDC (see below). For Food Stamps, on the other hand, benefit levels and eligibility standards are set by the federal government. Supplemental Security Income (SSI) now (since 1974) also has federally dictated benefit levels and eligibility standards although states can choose state supplementation. In addition, there are a host of smaller programs and there is considerable variation among states in which programs are offered. In addition to programmatic variation, each state is responsible for administrating each program. Even under the Food Stamp Program, for example, the federal government only pays for 50% of the administrative costs. State level administration undoubtably causes further differences by state.

While the federal government occasionally has attempted to influence the degree of interstate variation, it has been much more concerned with the overall level of welfare benefits. Federal policy intervention can come in a variety of forms. If state funded benefit levels are considered too low, the federal government can choose among various policy options. More liberal funding under cost sharing arrangements (such as with AFDC), mandating changes in eligibility standards (such as requiring that all AFDC participants be eligible for medical assistance), and new programs (such as requiring participation in AFDC-UP) are all possible. Because of the large number of means-tested welfare programs, state welfare policy can be understood only when all program benefits are aggregated together including both state and federally directed programs.

Federal policy with respect to the degree of interstate variation in benefits, and with respect to the overall level of benefits, has been influenced by interstate competition. Interstate competition can affect both sides of the welfare financing equation. On the one hand, states hope to attract residents by offering a low tax environment. On the other hand, states fear the in-migration of low income individuals if welfare benefit levels are higher than elsewhere. These forces, driven by interstate competition, serve to keep welfare expenditures lower than an individual state might otherwise prefer. The federal government therefore has attempted to raise base welfare levels, through provision of a nationally fixed level of Food Stamp benefits, while still allowing state governments to individually determine supplemental expenditures (through for example the AFDC program). There are two different policy levers the federal government has employed to accomplish this goal. One is to offer cost sharing with state governments. The other is to initiate new federally financed programs that expand the recipient base.

The cost sharing arrangements work through "matching aid." Matching aid means that the federal government agrees to match each state dollar with a predetermined number of federal dollars. The primary matching aid program is AFDC. The purpose of the matching aid subsidy is to encourage state governments to provide more generous assistance than they otherwise would. In this sense, matching aid works like a price subsidy. Each $2 increase in AFDC expenditures costs the state only about $1 (in the case of Arizona, the state only pays about $.72 for each $2 of total expenditure). The goal of this price subsidy is to cause all states to raise their expenditure levels even if relative expenditures between states stay constant.

Matching aid has been a feature of AFDC since its inception in 1935. Starting in 1965, the federal government attempted to narrow welfare expenditure differences among states by matching low expenditure states at a higher level than high expenditure states. While the matching aid rate still varies among states, the rate is no longer based on state expenditure levels but instead is based on *per capita* income with lower income states receiving a greater federal share. This change occurred when the federal government allowed states to choose the Medicaid matching formula which is somewhat more generous on average than the older AFDC formula. With the initiation of the AHCCCS program (Arizona's version of Medicaid) in 1982, Arizona (along with Texas) was among the last states to convert to the Medicaid formula. There are no other extant federal efforts to narrow state expenditure differences through cost sharing arrangements.

In setting welfare benefit levels, one of the primary concerns of state governments has been the migration of recipients. Despite the finding of no migration effects in early studies, recent research by Gramlich and Laren (1984b) and Blank (1988) has shown that differences in welfare benefit levels between states do impact migration decisions on the margin. In general, these impacts are relatively small and occur over several years, but show that potential welfare recipients tend to leave low benefit states for high benefit states. Blank has found the largest effects. Her results show that for a state with welfare benefit levels similar to Arizona (or Texas), an increase in benefits to the mean of all states (about a doubling of benefits) would cause a 6 percent increase in the probability that a family would remain in the state over a four year period (from about 86 percent to about 92 percent). She also finds that, for individuals with a high risk of welfare participation, changes in labor market opportunities are as least as important in impacting migration decisions and even more important for relatively low welfare benefit states such as Arizona. Thus, it appears that differences in welfare benefit levels are important in affecting migration decisions although more so for high benefit states. Nonetheless, the current federal policy judgement appears to be that migration is not so prevalent a problem as to abandon state choice over welfare benefit levels.

The federal government has also attempted to change welfare policy existing in the states through the implementation of new federally financed programs (Craig and Kohlhase, 1985). The first in the series of federally financed programs was Food Stamps which began in 1964 on the county level and did not achieve virtual nationwide coverage until 1974. In 1971, the federal government established uniform eligibility standards for Food Stamps across all states. In 1974, the federal government established SSI as a replacement for previously state-controlled Aid to the Blind, Aid to the Permanently and Totally Disabled, and Old Age Assistance programs. The Omnibus Budget Reconciliation Act (OBRA) of 1981 continued the trend for greater federal government involvement in setting eligibility standards by tightening AFDC requirements. The Family Support Act of 1988 is the most recent example of federal intervention. The Act has mandated a series of changes that narrows programmatic variation between states. This Act will be discussed in much more detail below. As an example, however, the AFDC Unemployed Parent (UP) program was initiated in 1962, but state participation was voluntary. Implementation of AFDC-UP is now required of all states by October 1, 1990.

Despite the growing federal role, state governments continue to have an important and independent role in welfare policy. There are still many programs that can be implemented at the option of the state. Further, states still have considerable control over benefit levels and eligibility standards in one of the major welfare programs, AFDC. Flexibility in individual state welfare programs reflects the varying needs of recipients across states and the varying tastes of state residents for supporting welfare expenditures. It must be recognized, however, that the federal-state relationship is evolving toward federal financing and state administration of many welfare programs.

Current Trends and Emerging Issues

The conceptual role of welfare has developed considerably during the decade of the 80s. The problem for the 1990s and beyond is to operationalize the new understanding about welfare expenditures into effective public policy. The primary focus of public policy change is twofold: first, to design welfare programs to cope effectively with the diverse population in need of assistance, and second, to design welfare programs to minimize the disincentive effects of the system. This section discusses the primary undesirable disincentives built into the welfare system, and where appropriate, discusses the role of recent policy changes in attempting to reverse these problems.

There are several important sources of disincentives inherent in the welfare system. The most difficult challenge, perhaps, is to design a program without the work disincentive effects that exist in any system that, effectively, rewards low income. There are additional disincentive effects, however, that need to be addressed. One is the extent to which publicly provided welfare substitutes for other sources of family support. A second crucial set of issues involves the family; there are currently incentives to split the family unit as well as incentives to have more children. Finally, there is the problem of creating a permanent welfare class; the "underclass." This group is composed of those individuals who are more or less permanently on welfare, and it has been characterized as being symptomatic of the "culture of poverty" (Sawhill, 1988).

Work disincentives have been the most extensively studied of the problems in welfare program design. This is because work disincentives fly in the face of the primary goal of welfare policy. The desired output of a welfare program is a productive citizen who can obtain satisfactory, stable employment. A difficulty for individuals on welfare is that work experience is crucial to finding better, and higher paying, jobs.

Work disincentives are created through the fundamental design of virtually all assistance programs. A basic level of income support is provided to those with no income which is then reduced as an individual's income rises. The reduction in assistance in response to earned income creates what is called the "implicit tax rate." The implicit tax rate is the rate at which the basic income support grant is reduced for each $1 of earned income. For example, if $100 of earnings reduces the AFDC award to an individual by $50, then the implicit tax rate is 50 percent. This means that the $100 of earnings only increased the net income of the recipient by $50. The implicit tax rate in most welfare programs is much higher than most low income individuals would face if they were not on welfare. This is especially true when the impact of several programs is combined, for example AFDC and Day Care assistance.

In addition to the implicit tax rate, people tend to consume more leisure (work less) when they have higher incomes even assuming wage rates are constant (that is, even assuming there is no implicit tax rate). Most research finds that this non-wage income is more important for altering the working behavior of individuals than is the implicit tax rate (Sawhill, 1988). One of the crucial components of non-wage income affecting working behavior is medical care. AFDC eligibility also allows a recipient to obtain Medicaid assistance (AHCCCS in Arizona) if needed. Since many low income jobs do not provide health insurance, medical necessity may be one of the central factors causing people to forego work for the benefits of welfare.

The education and training programs that are part of the Family Support Act of 1988 are, in part, attempts to alter the work disincentives. The idea behind them is that as people obtain a better set of skills, their market opportunities increase. This makes working more attractive relative to welfare participation.

One policy option that has not been attempted on a wide scale that is beginning to receive serious attention is to consider "matching grants" for earned income. Under this type of program, an individual would be rewarded for a transitional period of time with extra payments that rise with the amount of earned income, and not fall as under the traditional implicit tax rate type of program design (Gramlich, 1988). The Earned Income Tax Credit (EITC) in the federal income tax code does this to a certain extent. Nonetheless, the implicit tax rate problem cannot be avoided altogether because at some level of income publicly provided benefits will be phased out. Other programmatic changes in the recently passed Family Support Act also attempt to lower work disincentives. For example, people who leave the welfare rolls for work will be allowed to maintain eligibility for Medicaid (AHCCCS) and Day Care for up to twelve months in an effort to reduce any loss in purchasing power from obtaining employment.

The other important set of incentives that is built into the welfare system involves family issues. There are two primary problems that deserve mention. One is the impact on family structure. This includes divorce and separation, remarriage, and the number of independent households. The other involves fertility, especially by young women out of wedlock.

The primary welfare program, AFDC, is only available in Arizona to single parents with children. Virtually all of the single parents are women, less than 1 percent of AFDC recipients are men with children. There has been considerable concern that a couple, when faced with economic distress, is more likely to separate or divorce because of the availability of AFDC. Recent research indicates that this problem is potentially important. For example, Ellwood and Bane (1985) find that AFDC benefit levels have a significant effect on the incidence of divorce, and that a 38 percent increase in benefit levels over the average causes about a 10 percent increase in separated or divorced female heads of households. Further, they find that the probability of remarriage also falls resulting in a total increase in female headed households of 15 percent. Other studies find different magnitudes but generally support the Ellwood and Bane findings.

There are two possible welfare policy responses to the problem. One is to do nothing. This argument says that divorce is not necessarily bad and that the presence of the welfare system allows the affected women the economic freedom to do what they most desire. The contrary argument is that families are an important part of the economic relations in society, and an increase in divorce increases the economic burden on the existing welfare programs.

The Family Support Act of 1988 has attempted to address the family composition problem by requiring that the AFDC-UP program be provided by all states beginning in 1990. AFDC-UP allows two parent households to receive welfare payments when the head of the household is unemployed. While this program should reduce the number of people who separate or divorce simply to receive welfare, the payments only last six months. Another important policy change included in the federal Family Support Act of 1988 is the heightened emphasis on child support payment enforcement. This provision may alter the father's behavior to the extent that fathers are unable to avoid the financial consequences of family participation.

A further effect of AFDC on household composition arises due to the "independence effect." The presence of AFDC benefits allows more single mothers to live independently from other family members such as their parents. Ellwood and Bane estimate that this effect is about equal in size to the increase in female headed households caused by separation and divorce. It is difficult to ascertain whether independence should be classified as a major social problem.

It must also be recognized that the increase in the divorce rate among the low income population cannot be accounted for solely by the presence of AFDC because the national divorce rate has risen considerably. Garfinkel and MacLanahan (1986) estimate that no more than 10-15 percent of the total increase in female-headed households can be explained by AFDC. Their estimate excludes the independence effect but nonetheless shows the difficulty of separating programmatic effects from overall demographic trends.

Another policy problem that may be affected by welfare program design is increased fertility. Of particular concern is the dramatic increase in children born to young mothers out of wedlock. Most research that has examined the issue of whether potential welfare participation encourages childbirth has not been able to find any significant effect. In part, this may be because welfare payments are too small to cause such dramatic behavioral changes. A recent study by Antel (1988), however, explores the problem in a slightly different way. This study finds that, while welfare payments have little direct effect on fertility, young women whose parents are on welfare are much more likely to have children and children out of wedlock than are young women whose parents are not on welfare. This may be because young women from families on welfare are uninformed about the deleterious effects of childbirth on labor market opportunities or because they are more aware of the opportunities that child bearing brings for welfare participation. Irrespective of the fundamental cause, out of wedlock fertility by young women is a potentially serious problem especially if it is linked to the inter-generational transmission of welfare participation. This aspect of the incentives built into the welfare system structure has not been completely addressed in the current program reforms although more administrative emphasis is being placed on at-risk individuals and on poverty prevention.

The Current Welfare Policy Environment

The welfare system in Arizona consists of over sixty separate programs reflecting the diverse needs of the recipient population. The Department of Economic Security (DES) divides its programs into four major categories: children and families (C&F), adults and elderly (A&E), developmental disabilities (DD), and other disabilities (OD). Many of the current welfare programs are the joint financial responsibility of the state and federal governments. This section briefly describes the structure of the welfare system and discusses some of the policy developments that have created this system.

Poverty in Arizona

In 1980, over 13 percent of the population in Arizona was estimated to earn annual incomes below the federal poverty line. By 1988, over 475,000 people were estimated to be in poverty, almost 13.6 percent of the population (Governor's Task Force, 1989). The primary characteristic of the poverty population is that it is a diverse group. As discussed above, there are many reasons why an individual may receive a low income, and these reasons are reflected in the diversity of the poverty group at any one time. It must further be remembered that there is no "poverty group" per se. People in poverty at any one time are made up of people in poverty on both a temporary and a relatively permanent basis. Because of the diversity, it is worthwhile to discuss some of the characteristics of individuals in poverty.

A large number of welfare recipients use the system as a form of temporary assistance. Over 39 percent of AFDC recipients, for example, are on welfare for less than one year (DES, 1986). On the other hand, about 22 percent of the recipients are on welfare for five years or more. This latter group is often referred to as the underclass because of the wide spectrum of problems that afflict those on welfare for an extended period. One concern with the underclass population is that although they only represent one-fifth of the welfare rolls, they account for a significantly greater share of expenditures. This is because members of the underclass are always on welfare while other recipients are on welfare only temporarily.

Some groups in the population are disproportionately represented among the poor. Although the majority of people in poverty in Arizona are White, minorities are disproportionately represented. Hispanics represent about 16 percent of the state's population but about 26 percent of those in poverty. American Indians comprise about 5 percent of the state population and about 17 percent of the poverty population. Similarly, Blacks are about 3 percent of the state population but about 5 percent of the poverty group.

One of the distressing aspects of the poverty population is the number of children in poverty. Over 52 percent of Food Stamp recipients in Arizona are children (100,000 individuals), and about 70 percent of AFDC recipients are children. These children represent a large number of families as about 75 percent of Arizona's AFDC families have two or fewer children. The heightened emphasis on Day Care assistance was brought about, in part, by recognition of these numbers.

As shown in the next section, the diversity of the recipient base is fully reflected in the diversity in the programs. While program diversity results in somewhat higher administrative costs, the advantages of targeting assistance appear to be substantial since this is one of the primary methods for overcoming some of the disincentive effects of the standard welfare programs.

Arizona Welfare Programs

Table 13-1 presents the breakdown of the four categories of expenditures. This table includes all Department of Economic Security (DES) expenditures with the exception of Unemployment Insurance. Policies to assist children and families (C&F) represented over two-thirds of 1988 total welfare expenditures. Adults and elderly (A&E), which includes services for the elderly as well as job programs, comprised 14.6 percent of total expenditures. Developmental disabilities was about 12.6 percent of the total. Other disabilities was the smallest category, accounting for a little over 4 percent of total expenditures.

The largest program in the C&F category is Food Stamps (see Table 13-2). Arizona is only required to finance a share of the administrative costs; the benefits to individuals under this program are entirely financed by the federal government. The state share of administrative costs alone, however, amounted to $15.45 million in 1988. The Food Stamps program provides coupons that recipients exchange for food. About 50 percent of Food Stamp recipients also participate in Aid to Families with Dependent Children (AFDC). AFDC requires the largest share of state resources because the state participates in cost sharing for direct assistance as well as administrative costs. Other important C&F programs shown in Table 13-2 include Children Services, Day Care, Adoptive Services, General Assistance, Child Support Enforcement (CSEA), and the Comprehensive Medical and Dental Program (CMDP). Social Services Block Grants (SSBG) under Title XX of the Social Security Act can be used for a variety of purposes and are listed separately.

One fact readily evident from Table 13-2 is that the federal government is an important participant in low income assistance policies. Two-thirds of C&F programs are paid for by the federal government. A large part of the financial participation by the federal government arises because it uses state governments as the administrative agents for its programs (such as with Food Stamps). On occasion, however, the federal government uses financial incentives to influence state behavior. This is especially true with respect to Medicaid (not considered in this chapter) and AFDC which provide interesting case studies on how federal incentives can change the financial situation facing state welfare agencies.

Starting in 1965, there were two different cost sharing arrangements, or formulas, offered by the federal government for AFDC. In order to be able to use the more advantageous formula, the federal government required that states implement a Medicaid program. In 1982, Arizona paid $30.78 million directly to AFDC recipients which amounted to over 63 percent of total AFDC payments of $48.52 million. By offering the AHCCCS program, however, Arizona was allowed to switch to the more advantageous cost sharing formula in 1983. Total AFDC payments in that year rose to $57.18 million yet Arizona was required to spend only $22.19 million, or 38.8 percent of the total, from its own funds. This represented a savings of about $14 million if the old formula had been in effect and was actually over $8 million less than was spent the previous year.

As with most incentives, however, the AFDC story has another side. One is that the state is required to support the AHCCCS program. The other is that there may be repercussions on the AFDC program due to AHCCCS availability as recipients are more likely to attempt to qualify for AFDC because it confers automatic eligibility for AHCCCS. The state welfare model for Arizona discussed more fully below finds strong statistical evidence that implementation of AHCCCS raised AFDC costs by about $4.7 million annually, a considerable offset to the $8 million in savings.

Table 13-1 has another tale to tell which is the trend in state as compared to federal responsibility for financing low income assistance. Ten years ago the federal government total of $77 million was about 55 percent of the total C&F costs in Arizona. In 1988, this share had climbed to 66 percent representing a 13 percent growth rate over the ten year period. This growth rate in federal funding is misleading, however, because it masks the important departure from the trend during the Reagan Era.

<table>
<tr><th colspan="6">Table 13-1
Department of Economic Security Expenditures From 1979-1988</th></tr>
<tr><th></th><th>1979
Millions
of Dollars</th><th>1983
Millions
of Dollars</th><th>1988
Millions
of Dollars</th><th>5-Year*
Annual %
Change</th><th>10-Year
Annual %
Change</th></tr>
<tr><td>Children and Families</td><td></td><td></td><td></td><td></td><td></td></tr>
<tr><td>State Program</td><td>$ 46.76</td><td>$ 59.17</td><td>$ 96.84</td><td>10.35</td><td>7.55</td></tr>
<tr><td>State Administration</td><td>16.43</td><td>23.13</td><td>35.91</td><td>9.20</td><td>8.10</td></tr>
<tr><td>Federal Program</td><td>68.68</td><td>199.88</td><td>232.72</td><td>3.08</td><td>13.00</td></tr>
<tr><td>Federal Administration</td><td>8.32</td><td>16.82</td><td>27.83</td><td>10.60</td><td>12.80</td></tr>
<tr><td>Total</td><td>140.19</td><td>299.00</td><td>393.30</td><td>5.63</td><td>10.90</td></tr>
<tr><td>Adults and Elderly</td><td></td><td></td><td></td><td></td><td></td></tr>
<tr><td>State Program</td><td>0.41</td><td>2.52</td><td>6.85</td><td>22.14</td><td>32.50</td></tr>
<tr><td>State Administration</td><td>1.70</td><td>1.21</td><td>2.00</td><td>10.57</td><td>1.60</td></tr>
<tr><td>Federal Program</td><td>17.53</td><td>42.97</td><td>74.74</td><td>11.69</td><td>15.80</td></tr>
<tr><td>Federal Administration</td><td>0.31</td><td>0.37</td><td>2.22</td><td>43.10</td><td>21.80</td></tr>
<tr><td>Total</td><td>19.95</td><td>47.07</td><td>85.81</td><td>12.75</td><td>15.90</td></tr>
<tr><td>Developmental Disabilities</td><td></td><td></td><td></td><td></td><td></td></tr>
<tr><td>State Program</td><td>4.40</td><td>16.40</td><td>37.82</td><td>18.18</td><td>24.00</td></tr>
<tr><td>State Administration</td><td>23.35</td><td>29.26</td><td>33.46</td><td>2.74</td><td>3.70</td></tr>
<tr><td>Federal Program</td><td>0.00</td><td>0.69</td><td>0.85</td><td>4.26</td><td>-0.00</td></tr>
<tr><td>Federal Administration</td><td>0.00</td><td>0.00</td><td>0.00</td><td>0.00</td><td>10.00</td></tr>
<tr><td>Total</td><td>27.75</td><td>46.35</td><td>72.13</td><td>9.25</td><td></td></tr>
<tr><td>Other Disabilities</td><td></td><td></td><td></td><td></td><td>3.80</td></tr>
<tr><td>State Program</td><td>1.31</td><td>1.34</td><td>1.94</td><td>7.23</td><td>6.10</td></tr>
<tr><td>State Administration</td><td>1.00</td><td>1.42</td><td>1.78</td><td>4.86</td><td>-0.00</td></tr>
<tr><td>Federal Program</td><td>0.00</td><td>13.29</td><td>19.59</td><td>8.68</td><td>26.00</td></tr>
<tr><td>Federal Administration</td><td>0.00</td><td>0.00</td><td>0.00</td><td>0.00</td><td></td></tr>
<tr><td>Total</td><td>2.31</td><td>16.05</td><td>23.31</td><td>7.74</td><td>11.69</td></tr>
<tr><td>Total DES Expenditures</td><td>190.20</td><td>408.47</td><td>574.55</td><td>7.06</td><td></td></tr>
<tr><td>% Admin. (Fed+State)</td><td>26.85</td><td>17.68</td><td>17.96</td><td></td><td></td></tr>
<tr><td>% Federal</td><td>49.96</td><td>67.08</td><td>62.30</td><td></td><td></td></tr>
<tr><td colspan="6">* The five year annual change is from 1983 to 1988.</td></tr>
<tr><td colspan="6">Source: Department of Economic Security.</td></tr>
</table>

<table>
<tr><td colspan="4" align="center">Table 13-2
The Largest Children and Families Programs 1988 Expenditures
(millions of dollars)</td></tr>
<tr><td></td><td align="center">Federal</td><td align="center">State</td><td align="center">Total</td></tr>
<tr><td>Food Stamps</td><td align="right">158.77</td><td align="right">15.45</td><td align="right">174.22</td></tr>
<tr><td>AFDC</td><td align="right">68.84</td><td align="right">41.19</td><td align="right">110.03</td></tr>
<tr><td>Children Services</td><td align="right">3.45</td><td align="right">23.25</td><td align="right">26.70</td></tr>
<tr><td>Day Care</td><td align="right">*</td><td align="right">12.75</td><td align="right">12.75</td></tr>
<tr><td>Adoptive Services -- Title IV-E</td><td align="right">3.76</td><td align="right">7.14</td><td align="right">10.90</td></tr>
<tr><td>SSBG -- Title XX</td><td align="right">11.38</td><td align="right">-</td><td align="right">11.38</td></tr>
<tr><td>General Assistance</td><td align="right">0.00</td><td align="right">8.88</td><td align="right">8.88</td></tr>
<tr><td>CSEA</td><td align="right">6.69</td><td align="right">0.11</td><td align="right">6.80</td></tr>
<tr><td>CMDP</td><td align="right">-</td><td align="right">6.40</td><td align="right">6.40</td></tr>
<tr><td>State Administration</td><td align="right">-</td><td align="right">14.93</td><td align="right">14.93</td></tr>
<tr><td>Other</td><td align="right">7.66</td><td align="right">9.05</td><td align="right">16.71</td></tr>
<tr><td>Total</td><td align="right">260.55</td><td align="right">139.15</td><td align="right">399.70</td></tr>
<tr><td>Percent Share</td><td align="right">66.25</td><td align="right">33.75</td><td align="right">100.00</td></tr>
<tr><td colspan="4">* SSBG funds are used here.</td></tr>
<tr><td colspan="4">Source: Department of Economic Securities</td></tr>
</table>

The growth rate in federal programmatic assistance (excluding administrative costs) over the last five years is only about 3.1 percent per year, about equal to the rate of income growth. This attenuation in federal aid growth has put considerable pressure on the state budget, and the 10 percent per year growth in state C&F expenditures over the last five years illustrates this. These trends are relevant for the discussion below of future policy directions and the likelihood of additional pressure on this portion of the state budget. Federal financing, however, remains quite important to Arizona. The federal government spent over $230 million in Arizona in 1988 to care for children and families at a cost to Arizona of only $97 million.

State responsibility for the A&E category primarily consists of adult services which is pre-institutional care for the elderly. This program is matched by federal funds from the Older Americans Act. Other federal government programs constitute the bulk of this category of spending. The largest segment is the Job Training and Placement Administration which receives over $29 million. Over $21 million in Title XX social service block grant funds are used in this category. Other important programs include job services (which are declining in importance due to programmatic change) and the Disability Determination Services Administration.

In contrast to the A&E category, Developmental Disability (DD) is entirely a state supported category with the exception of a very small amount of Title XX funds. Purchase of Care for institutionalized recipients accounts for over $30 million and Foster Care for over

$6 million. Purchase of Care has grown quite rapidly as shown in Table 13-1 by the 18 percent and 24 percent five and ten year growth rates in the state program category for DD. Purchase of Care will exert additional budgetary pressure in the near future because of Title XIX requirements associated with long term care.

The final category of Other Disabilities primarily includes various vocational rehabilitation service programs. The largest is Section 110 funding (over $16.3 million), some Title XX funds ($1.8 million), and the Comprehensive Services for Independent Living program from Title VII with a little over $1 million. Vocational Rehabilitation has grown quite rapidly over the last ten years (at a 26 percent annual rate), one reason being that the federal government pays 80 percent of program costs through Section 110 funding, a program that did not exist in 1979.

All four of these categories of spending are growing faster than the rate of inflation indicating that expenditures in real terms are increasing. Administrative costs are growing at a slower rate than assistance to individuals; total federal and state administrative costs grew 7.3 percent over the last ten years. In part this reflects the fact that it takes no additional personnel to administer budgetary increases due to inflation. It also reflects some economies of scale in administration as the individual programs grow. While federal requirements impose considerable administrative burdens, the federal government paid 29.1 percent of the total administrative costs in 1988 compared to only 16.9 percent ten years earlier.

Interstate Welfare Expenditure Comparisons

There has been a great deal of concern about how Arizona compares to other states in terms of its *per capita* assistance to the low income population. This concern is well placed to the extent that welfare expenditures contribute to a smoothly operating economy and to the well-being of society. Concentrating first on levels of expenditures, Arizona appears to lag most of the nation. In FY 1987, welfare expenditures *per capita* were $121.26 in Arizona while the U.S. average was $167.54 (see Table 13-3). As a share of personal income, Arizona spent 0.85 percent while the U.S. average was 1.10 percent. Of the neighboring states, California and Colorado spent considerably more than Arizona; New Mexico and Utah spent amounts similar to Arizona; and Nevada spent considerably less than Arizona ($85.05 *per capita*). As illustrated in Table 13-3, AFDC expenditures per capita in Arizona were less than half the U.S. average ($5.20 for Arizona compared to a U.S. average of $12.78). While a comparison with other states is certainly not sufficient for determining the "best" level of spending, it is helpful for examining how other states have made the difficult trade-offs involved in setting welfare expenditures.

The Causes of Arizona's Relative Expenditure Level: Modelling

The problem with looking solely at averages, however, is that other factors are not accounted for in determining the comparable level of spending. Factors that might influence interstate comparisons include the level of federal aid, cost of living, population, and other socio-demographic characteristics. In order to facilitate a more complete study of how Arizona compares to other states, a detailed statistical model has been constructed in an attempt to control for many of the determinants of welfare expenditures.

The interstate comparison model is a regression analysis based on published research by Craig and Inman (1982, 1986). What is useful about regression analysis is that the effect of each factor is calculated conditional on holding the level of all the other determinants constant. By this procedure, each potential determinant of welfare spending can be examined separately to ascertain why Arizona might differ from other states.

Table 13-3
Comparison of Total State
And Local Expenditures For Public Welfare
Arizona, U.S., and Neighboring States -- 1986-87

	Total[*] State & Local (in thousands)	Expenditures *Per Capita*	Percentage of State Personal Income	1985 AFDC Recips Per 1000	1985 AFDC Real Expend. *Per Capita*[**]
U.S.	41,616,262	167.54	1.10	37.97	12.78
Arizona	410,583	121.26	0.85	22.56	5.20
California	7,023,804	253.91	1.42	61.85	31.63
Colorado	544,807	165.29	1.06	25.78	7.91
Nevada	85,657	85.06	0.52	16.35	3.41
New Mexico	182,684	121.79	1.03	35.45	9.23
Utah	175,722	104.60	0.92	22.98	8.10

[*] Expenditures for all means-tested public welfare programs except Medicaid (AHCCCS).
[**] Measured in 1965 dollars.

Source: *1987 Government Finances Series, 1987 Governmental Finances, State and Local Finances, State Government Finances.* Population and state personal income statistics derived from *Significant Features of Fiscal Federalism 1989 Edition*, Vol. 1, Advisory Commission on Intergovernmental Relations.

The model underlying the regression procedure is called a "reduced form" model. Reduced form means that the regression equation contains determinants of welfare spending from several different underlying forces. In particular, one cause of welfare expenditures is the state legislature which acts through setting certain program parameters such as maximum benefit levels and eligibility standards. Another set of factors that determines welfare expenditures, however, results because many welfare programs are entitlement programs, meaning that once the program parameters are set the actual level of expenditures depends on the circumstances affecting the welfare-using population. Important causes of welfare expenditures are factors such as the unemployment rate or the number of female headed households that determine the need for welfare by individuals. The reduced form statistical model, therefore, attempts to combine the choice variables that influence state level decision making as well as variables affecting the welfare population. These sets of variables may very well be intertwined, and no attempt is made to separate them. The regressions measure the extent to which a variable influences welfare spending irrespective of whether the influence comes from a change in legislative behavior, a change in the welfare population, or both (thus the impact of each variable is "reduced" to a single number that measures the joint influence).

The regression model that is applied to welfare spending statistically describes how real (adjusted for inflation) expenditures *per capita* vary with respect to certain aspects of each state's economy. The variables that serve to explain welfare spending can be divided into four groups. One group is the basic socio-demographic variables that describe the population such as education, racial composition, and the age structure of the population. Second are the economic variables such as the level of income, its distribution, and the unemployment rate. Third are variables that describe the level and structure of federal welfare assistance. Finally, a set of year specific and state specific effects are estimated. These effects (called "fixed effects") allow a separate constant term to be estimated for each state and year and capture factors specific to each state and year that are omitted from the regression variables. One of the items of interest from estimation of the welfare regression model is the state specific effect for Arizona.

The data used for the regressions are for the twenty year period 1966-1985 for all 48 mainland states. The total number of observations is therefore 960 (48x20). Each of the dollar variables is defined in *per capita* terms. In addition, a state cost-of-living index is constructed based on urban and rural cost-of-living indices from the U.S. Department of Labor. The dollar variables are all deflated by the cost-of-living index.

The Census variables are often available only for the ten year intervals of the Census. The 1960 Census values are used for the years 1966-68, the 1970 Census values are used for 1969-1975, and the 1980 values are used for 1976-1985. It should be noted that because these variables are only available at ten year intervals, the estimated effects are approximate. When possible, however, values available annually are used. Table 13-4 describes each of the variables used in the welfare spending model and indicates whether a variable is available annually or on a ten year basis.

The final aspect of the model to be discussed is federal aid. Federal programs that provide financial assistance to states vary considerably depending on the programmatic "strings" that are attached. AFDC has already been discussed. It is a matching aid program where the rate of cost sharing between a state and the federal government varies depending on a three year average of state income *per capita* and where low income states pay a lower share than do high income states up to a maximum state share of 50 percent. The appropriate method to estimate the effect of AFDC is through the matching rate "price term." Other federal aid programs for welfare are non-matching aid that have been aggregated into one variable, federal categorical aid for welfare. Federal aid for Food Stamps is treated separately. In addition, the impact of the Earned Income Tax Credit (EITC) is included because it is federal aid to the working poor. Even though it is outside of the state budget, state governments may respond to the EITC when setting welfare program benefits. Finally, categorical federal aid to states for other purposes is included since a higher level of aid may indicate a general easing of the state budget and allow more generous welfare assistance.

The model can be summarized by the equation:

$$\text{WELEX} = f \, (\text{OFA, WELAID, FS, EITC, MAT, Demog, Econ, State, Year})$$

where WELEX is state welfare expenditure in real terms *per capita*, OFA is other federal non-welfare categorical aid, FS is Food Stamp expenditures, EITC is the level of real *per capita* earned income tax credit, MAT is the state cost share for AFDC, Demog are the socio-demographic variables, Econ are the state economic characteristics, State is the state specific effects not accounted for by the previous variables, and Year is the year specific effects. All dollar variables are in real terms *per capita*.

The Causes of Arizona's Relative Expenditure Level: Results

Our purpose is to use the regression results to examine the reasons why Arizona is a low welfare spending state. In particular, we will use the regression results to differentiate between two hypotheses. The first is that Arizona is a low spending state because of its particular socio-demographic and economic variables. The second hypothesis is that Arizona is a low welfare spending state by explicit policy design irrespective of its characteristics. The key to determining which hypothesis holds is to compare the regression estimates for the variables described in the model to the estimate for the state specific effect for Arizona.

<table>
<tr><td colspan="2" align="center">Table 13-4
Variables in the Interstate Model</td></tr>
<tr><td align="center">Variables</td><td align="center">Definition</td></tr>
<tr><td>Federal Aid Variables
 OFA</td><td>Non-welfare categorical aid, excludes highway aid (which is matching); annual, real per capita</td></tr>
<tr><td> WELAID</td><td>Categorical welfare aid; annual, real per capita</td></tr>
<tr><td> FS</td><td>Food Stamp aid; annual, real per capita</td></tr>
<tr><td> EITC</td><td>Earned Income Tax Credit; annual, real per capita</td></tr>
<tr><td> MAT</td><td>Matching rate (state cost share) for AFDC; annual</td></tr>
<tr><td>Demographic Variables
 POP</td><td>State population; annual</td></tr>
<tr><td> OLD</td><td>Percent of population over 65 years; annual</td></tr>
<tr><td> METRO</td><td>Percent of population in urban areas; census years</td></tr>
<tr><td> RICH</td><td>Percent of population over $15,000 income; census years</td></tr>
<tr><td> HS</td><td>Percent of population with high school education or over; Census years</td></tr>
<tr><td> POVLN</td><td>Percent of population below the poverty line; census years</td></tr>
<tr><td> PCWH</td><td>Percent of population White; census years</td></tr>
<tr><td> FFAM</td><td>Percent of families headed by a female; census years</td></tr>
<tr><td>Economic Variables
 INC</td><td>State per capita income; annual, real</td></tr>
<tr><td> UNEMP</td><td>Percent of labor force unemployed; annual</td></tr>
<tr><td> CPI</td><td>State cost of living index; 1965=1.00; annual</td></tr>
<tr><td> MANPC</td><td>Percent of population working in manufacturing; annual</td></tr>
<tr><td>Dependent Variables
 STWPC</td><td>State welfare spending; annual, real per capita</td></tr>
<tr><td> AFPART</td><td>AFDC participation per capita; annual</td></tr>
<tr><td> AFEXP</td><td>AFDC expenditures; annual, real per capita</td></tr>
<tr><td colspan="2">Source: U.S. Census; State Government Finances; AFDC Finances.</td></tr>
</table>

We would expect the first hypothesis to hold, for example, if Arizona has a low need for welfare (a small welfare-using population) or has a low level of resources to support welfare expenditures (low income or low levels of federal aid). That is, if Arizona has both a welfare-using population that is average size and has an average level of resources to support welfare expenditures, then we would expect it to have an average level of welfare expenditures. To the extent that Arizona is a low welfare spending state even after accounting for its level of need and resources, then only the state specific estimate for Arizona will capture the lower than average spending effect. The state specific effect means that there has been an explicit policy choice in Arizona, one that is different from that taken by other states, to keep welfare spending low.

Table 13-5 presents the regression results in column one. The estimated coefficient on each of the individual variables in Table 13-5 measures how a marginal change in that variable affects welfare spending. The coefficient for each variable is reported, and statistically significant variables are indicated by an asterisk. If the variable name does not have an asterisk, the statistical results are considered to be imprecise in that there is a greater than 5 percent chance that the coefficient is not different from zero. Several of the coefficient estimates are significantly different from zero, however, and they have an interesting tale to tell about welfare expenditures in Arizona.

The variables with statistically significant coefficients are important for explaining the level of welfare spending in Arizona. The magnitude of the coefficients determines their importance with larger (in absolute value) coefficients having a larger effect on welfare expenditures. To determine whether the variables listed in Table 13-5 explain why Arizona is a low welfare spending state (the first hypothesis explained above), we need to compare Arizona's level to the national average for each variable. If Arizona is different from the national average, then the estimated coefficient from column one will determine how important that difference is for explaining Arizona's relative welfare spending level.

Columns two through four in Table 13-5 show how Arizona compares to the national average value for each of the socio-demographic and economic characteristic variables in the model. The second column presents the average value for all states over the 20 year period for each variable. The third column presents the 20 year average value for Arizona. If the mean for Arizona is the same as the national mean for a particular variable, then that variable will not describe why Arizona spends considerably less than other states on welfare. On the other hand, a large difference between the national mean and that for Arizona indicates a potentially important difference, depending on the coefficient estimate. The fourth column of the table presents the difference between the nationwide average (column 2) and Arizona (column 3).

The fifth column of Table 13-5 combines potential causes of the difference between Arizona and the national average welfare expenditure level. Column one is the coefficient level (the importance of the variable for explaining welfare spending). Column four is the difference between Arizona and the national average for each variable (whether Arizona has different characteristics than the nation). The fifth column, therefore, multiplies the coefficient estimate in column one times the difference in column four. The result in column five is the dollar amount of *per capita* welfare spending by which Arizona is expected to differ from the national average because of its socio-demographic and economic characteristics. The sixth column is simply this expected dollar amount of difference divided by the actual average Arizona welfare expenditure level.

Columns 5 and 6 of Table 13-5 show that the two largest socio-demographic factors explaining interstate welfare differences are population and the percentage of the population

Table 13-5
Interstate Welfare Expenditures Comparison Using 1966-1985 Sample

Variable	(1) Coeff	(2) Average For All States	(3) Average For Arizona	(4) Arizona Minus All States Average	(5) Expected Dollar Difference in Arizona Level	(6) Arizona Difference as a Percent of Arizona Welfare Expenditures
OFA	0.051	41.06	36.99	-4.07	-0.208	-0.945
Welfare Aid*	0.491	13.09	4.178	-8.912	-4.376	-19.928
EITC	-0.764	1.51	1.695	0.185	-0.141	-0.644
Food Stamps	-	10.64	6.348	-4.292	0.001	0.002
State Cost Share	0.0001	0.407	0.408	0.001	-0.01	-0.047
Population*	2	4454.96	2305.34	-2149.62	6.019	27.411
Percent Old	-17.24	0.104	0.094	-0.01	0.004	0.018
Percent Urban	-0.0028	0.575	0.748	0.173	0.098	0.449
Percent Unemployed*	-0.399	0.06	0.061	0.001	0.209	0.952
Price Index	0.571	2.147	2.209	0.062	0.129	0.585
Income *Per Capita*	160.83	3089.68	2919.40	-170.28	0.494	2.249
Percent Manufacturing	2.08	0.082	0.051	-0.031	-1.632	-7.432
Percent Rich	-0.0029	0.025	0.028	0.002	0.344	1.565
Percent H.S. Education*	52.64	0.592	0.646	0.054	6.116	27.853
Percent Poverty Line*	137.5	0.106	0.101	-0.005	-0.655	-2.982
Percent White*	113.47	0.885	0.878	-0.008	-0.639	-2.911
Percent Female Families	130.94	0.099	0.094	-0.005	0.326	1.485
Welfare Expenditures	85.24	49.37	21.958	-27.412	6.078	
State Specific Effect*	-65.22	-5.470	-39.240	-33.770		

* Indicates statistically significant variable at 95% level.

with a high school or above education. Education in particular should be viewed with caution as it is a Census variable that varies only every ten years. With this caveat, these two factors indicate Arizona would be expected to spend more than average, not less. Population is estimated to have a negative impact on welfare expenditures. That is, larger states tend to have smaller levels of *per capita* welfare expenditures than smaller states. Since Arizona has a smaller population than the average state, it is expected to spend over 27 percent more than an average size state. Similarly, states with higher education levels tend to support more welfare expenditures. Since Arizona has a higher education level than average, it is expected to spend more than the average state, again by over 27 percent.

Among other significant factors, Arizona received less categorical federal aid for welfare than average, so this variable indicates one explanation for Arizona's below average spending. Nonetheless, the sum of all the effects shows that Arizona should be spending over 12.3 percent more than average on welfare ($6.08 more than the nationwide average of $49.37). In other words, given Arizona's characteristics, this model predicts that Arizona should be a high spending state. Thus, neither demographic factors, economic factors, nor federal aid explain why Arizona spends less than average for welfare. The hypothesis that Arizona has characteristics that cause it to be a low spending state is therefore rejected. We are thus forced to turn to the second hypothesis, that there is a state specific policy choice in Arizona resulting in relatively low welfare expenditures.

The last row of Table 13-5 shows, indeed, that Arizona has a large, and statistically significant negative state specific effect. The state specific effect estimated for Arizona is $39.24. This state effect is measured against the constant term and is difficult to evaluate on its own. The average of all the state constant terms, however, is only -$5.47. The statistically significant effect for Arizona says that in addition to the variables in the equation, Arizona spent $33.77 ($39.24 - 5.47) in real terms *per capita* less than would be expected given the other factors in the model.

The Arizona state specific effect does not fully explain why Arizona is a low welfare spending state. The state specific effect measures all influences except those that are included in the other variables of the model. Because the variable list is rather extensive, however, there is little reason to expect that there is an unmeasured factor peculiar to Arizona that causes either a low need for welfare or low resources available to support welfare. The negative $33.77 state specific effect for Arizona, thus, most likely captures political tastes for welfare spending in the state.

While Arizona may have been lagging other states, the data and model indicate that this difference is narrowing over time. The nationwide annual growth rate in real *per capita* welfare spending for the first ten years of the data set, from 1966-75, is 7.5 percent. The comparable rate for Arizona is only 0.6 percent per year. On the other hand, for the 1976-85 period average state welfare expenditures are virtually constant showing only a 0.05 percent annual growth rate. During this time, Arizona experienced relatively rapid growth in welfare expenditures at almost 6.6 percent per year. This trend is reinforced by examining the individual factors influencing welfare in Table 13-6. The estimated coefficients are the same as presented in Table 13-5, but 1985 averages are used for the comparisons in Table 13-6. While the same three factors are most important, categorical aid in Arizona in 1985 is considerably less than average causing Arizona to be below the all-states average in expected expenditures. Population and education, however, make up this loss to some extent. The aggregate of all factors indicates that, given its characteristics in 1985, Arizona should be expected to spend almost $4.63 *less* than average or about 8 percent less than the nationwide average of $58.43. This does not fully account for the 36.3 percent difference between

Table 13-6
Interstate Welfare Expenditures Comparison For 1985 Data

Variable	(1) Coeff	(2) Average For All States	(3) Average For Arizona	(4) Arizona Minus All States Average	(5) Expected Dollar Difference in Arizona Level	(6) Arizona Difference as a Percent of Arizona Welfare Expenditures
OFA	0.051	43.370	26.510	-16.860	-0.860	-2.309
Welfare Aid*	0.491	26.250	4.940	-21.310	-10.463	-28.097
EITC	-0.764	2.395	2.250	-0.145	0.111	0.297
Food Stamps	-0.00012	12.020	9.680	-2.340	0.000	0.001
State Cost Share	-17.24	0.402	0.388	-0.014	0.236	0.634
Population*	-0.0028	4927.875	3187.000	-1740.875	4.874	13.089
Percent Old	-0.399	0.119	0.123	0.004	-0.002	0.004
Percent Urban	0.571	0.614	0.750	0.136	0.078	0.209
Percent Unemployed*	160.83	0.071	0.065	-0.006	-0.901	2.418
Price Index	2.08	3.696	3.920	0.224	0.466	1.251
Income *Per Capita*	-0.0029	3527.260	3268.800	-258.460	0.750	2.013
Percent Manufacturing	52.64	0.077	0.057	-0.020	-1.032	-2.771
Percent Rich	137.5	0.039	0.040	0.001	0.179	0.480
Percent H.S. Education*	113.47	0.669	0.723	0.054	6.127	16.454
Percent Poverty Line*	130.94	0.095	0.087	-0.008	-1.048	-2.813
Percent White*	85.24	0.867	0.824	-0.043	-3.665	-9.842
Percent Female Families	-65.22	0.118	0.110	-0.008	0.522	1.401
Welfare Expenditures		58.430	37.240	-21.190	-4.627	

* Indicates statistically significant variable at 95% level.

Arizona's actual spending of $37.24 and the $58.43 average, but the difference has narrowed considerably over time. The 20 year average characteristics in Table 13-5 show a 55.5 percent differential between Arizona and the national average (actual spending of $21.96 vs. the national average of $49.37).

Tables 13-7 through 13-10 present a comparable analysis for the AFDC program, the first two tables for AFDC recipients and the next two for AFDC expenditures. AFDC is the cornerstone program that is substantially under the control of state governments. For both AFDC recipients and for expenditures, Arizona is considerably below the nationwide average as evidenced by the all-states average of 37.56 recipients per 1,000 population over the period compared to 26.76 recipients per 1,000 population in Arizona (Table 13-7) and AFDC expenditures *per capita* of $13.74 for all states and $6.96 for Arizona (Table 13-9). As we found for welfare spending as a whole, the state specific estimate seems to be more important than other variables for explaining the difference between Arizona and the nation.

Considering individual variables, Arizona would be expected to have an *above* average level of participants due to its relatively small population, its relatively urban concentration, and its high level of education. The 1985 analysis (see Table 13-8) shows that the expected difference between Arizona and the national average has narrowed to 7.7 additional recipients per 1,000 population expected in 1985 from 10.6 expected additional recipients for the 20 year period. As with the total welfare expenditure equation, Arizona has significantly fewer recipients than average because of its state specific effect not because of its measured characteristics. The state specific estimate for recipients is -24.31 recipients per 1,000 population compared to an average of state effects of -2.96. The conclusion is that Arizona could make the policy choice to be considerably more lenient in its AFDC eligibility rules and still have participation rates below the nationwide average.

The analysis of AFDC expenditures in Tables 13-9 and 13-10 confirms these results. The tables show that, given its characteristics, Arizona is expected to spend about $2.90 *per capita more* than average. This amount is almost 42 percent of Arizona's actual expenditure of $6.96 *per capita*. The difference has narrowed only a little from 1966 to 1985; the $2.15 difference in 1985 still represents 41 percent of Arizona's spending level. For the twenty year period, the state specific effect is estimated to be -$8.43 compared to an average for all states of $1.27. Thus Arizona is spending $9.70 less than would be expected given its other characteristics. As found previously, the low spending levels appear to be due to explicit policy choices.

Another way to examine Arizona with this statistical model is to compare Arizona expenditures to the five neighboring states of California, Colorado, Nevada, New Mexico, and Utah. Table 13-11 presents the state specific effects from the overall welfare spending model for each of these five states plus Arizona. This table indicates that only California has significantly higher spending than would be expected. Utah has the lowest state specific estimate followed by Nevada and Arizona. Colorado and New Mexico are somewhat above the lowest group but still quite a bit below the nationwide average of -5.47.

The Interaction Between Programs and Expenditures

This section outlines the method and results of attempting to explain welfare expenditures using Arizona specific data. This process will allow an examination of some specific policy questions and provides another perspective by which to judge the interstate comparison model of the previous section. A statistical model is constructed that attempts to

Table 13-7

AFDC Recipients per 1000 Population Comparisons for 1966-1985 Sample

Variable	(1) Coeff	(2) Average For All States	(3) Average For Arizona	(4) Arizona Minus All States Average	(5) Expected Difference in Arizona Level	(6) Arizona Difference as a Percent of Arizona Welfare Recipients
OFA*	0.153	41.060	36.990	-4.070	-0.623	-2.327
Welfare Aid	-0.028	13.090	4.178	-8.912	0.250	0.932
EITC	-0.056	1.510	1.695	0.185	-0.010	-0.039
Food Stamps	0.0031	10.640	6.348	-4.292	-0.013	-0.050
State Cost Share	-11.92	0.407	0.408	0.001	-0.007	-0.027
Population*	-0.0014	4454.960	2305.340	-2149.620	3.009	11.246
Percent Old	-0.049	0.104	0.094	-0.010	0.000	0.002
Percent Urban*	15.34	0.575	0.748	0.173	2.646	9.888
Percent Unemployed*	168.78	0.060	0.061	0.001	0.219	0.820
Price Index	5.106	2.147	2.209	0.062	0.316	1.179
Income *Per Capita**	-0.0052	3089.680	2919.400	-170.280	0.885	3.309
Percent Manufacturing*	71.37	0.082	0.051	-0.031	-2.212	-8.268
Percent Rich	107.39	0.025	0.028	0.002	0.268	1.003
Percent H.S. Education*	133.34	0.592	0.646	0.054	7.187	26.857
Percent Poverty Line*	89.31	0.106	0.101	-0.005	-0.447	-1.669
Percent White	12.95	0.885	0.878	-0.008	-0.097	-0.363
Percent Female Families*	149.04	0.099	0.094	-0.005	-0.745	-2.785
Welfare Recipients		37.560	26.760	-10.800	10.627	
State Specific Effect*		-2.960	-24.310	-21.350		

* Indicates statistically significant variable at 95% level.

Table 13-8
AFDC Recipients per 1000 Population Comparison for 1985 Data

Variable	(1) Coeff	(2) Average For All States	(3) Average For Arizona	(4) Arizona Minus All States Average	(5) Expected Difference in Arizona Level	(6) Arizona Difference as a Percent of Arizona Welfare Recipients
OFA*	0.153	43.370	26.510	-16.860	-2.580	-11.434
Welfare Aid	-0.028	26.250	4.940	-21.310	0.597	2.645
EITC	-0.056	2.395	2.250	-0.145	0.008	0.036
Food Stamps	0.0031	12.020	9.680	-2.340	-0.007	-0.032
State Cost Share	-11.92	0.402	0.388	-0.014	0.163	0.724
Population*	-0.001	4927.875	3187.000	-1740.875	2.437	10.803
Percent Old	-0.049	0.119	0.123	0.004	0.000	-0.001
Percent Urban*	15.34	0.614	0.750	0.136	2.068	9.248
Percent Unemployed*	168.78	0.071	0.065	-0.006	-0.945	-4.190
Price Index	5.106	3.696	3.920	0.224	1.144	5.070
Income *Per Capita*￼*	-0.005	3527.260	3268.800	-258.460	1.344	5.957
Percent Manufacturing*	71.37	0.077	0.057	-0.020	-1.399	6.201
Percent Rich	107.39	0.039	0.040	0.001	0.140	0.619
Percent H.S. Education*	133.34	0.669	0.723	0.054	7.200	31.916
Percent Poverty Line*	89.31	0.095	0.087	-0.008	-0.714	3.167
Percent White*	12.95	0.867	0.824	-0.043	-0.557	2.468
Percent Female Families*	149.04	0.118	0.110	-0.008	-1.192	5.285
Welfare Recipients		37.970	22.560	-15.410	7.725	

* Indicates statistically significant variable at 95% level.

Table 13-9
AFDC Expenditures *Per Capita* Comparison for 1966-1985 Sample

Variable	(1) Coeff	(2) Average For All States	(3) Average For Arizona	(4) Arizona Minus All States Average	(5) Expected Dollar Difference in Arizona Level	(6) Arizona Difference as a Percent of Arizona AFDC Expenditures
OFA*	0.038	41.060	36.990	-4.070	-0.155	-2.222
Welfare Aid	0.043	13.090	4.178	-8.912	-0.383	-5.506
EITC*	-0.61	1.510	1.695	0.185	-0.113	-1.621
Food Stamps	-0.00013	10.640	6.348	-4.292	0.001	0.008
State Cost Share*	-10.19	0.407	0.408	0.001	-0.006	-0.088
Population*	0.00044	4454.960	2305.340	-2149.620	-0.946	-13.590
Percent Old	-1.03	0.104	0.094	-0.010	0.010	0.148
Percent Urban	-0.634	0.575	0.748	0.173	-0.109	-1.571
Percent Unemployed*	62.58	0.060	0.061	0.001	0.081	1.169
Price Index	3.9	2.147	2.209	0.062	0.241	3.463
Income *Per Capita*	-0.002	3089.680	2919.400	-170.280	0.341	4.893
Percent Manufacturing	-1.95	0.082	0.051	-0.031	0.060	0.869
Percent Rich	36.68	0.025	0.028	0.002	0.092	1.318
Percent H.S. Education*	78.75	0.592	0.646	0.054	4.245	60.986
Percent Poverty Line*	24.41	0.106	0.101	-0.005	-0.122	-1.754
Percent White	10.01	0.885	0.878	-0.008	-0.075	-1.079
Percent Female Families	52.57	0.099	0.094	-0.005	-0.263	-3.777
Welfare Expenditures		13.740	6.960	-6.780	2.899	
State Specific Effect*		1.270	-8.430	-9.700		

* Indicates statistically significant variable at 95% level.

Table 13-10
AFDC Expenditures *Per Capita* Comparison For 1985 Data

Variable	(1) Coeff	(2) Average For All States	(3) Average For Arizona	(4) Arizona Minus All States Average	(5) Expected Dollar Difference in Arizona Level	(6) Arizona Difference as a Percent of Arizona AFDC Expenditures
OFA*	0.038	43.370	26.510	-16.860	-0.641	-12.321
Welfare Aid*	0.043	26.250	4.940	-21.310	-0.916	-17.622
EITC*	-0.61	2.395	2.250	-0.145	0.088	1.701
Food Stamps	-0.00013	12.020	9.680	-2.340	0.000	0.006
State Cost Share*	-10.19	0.402	0.388	-0.014	0.140	2.685
Population*	0.00044	4927.875	3187.000	-1740.875	-0.766	-14.730
Percent Old	-1.03	0.119	0.123	0.004	-0.004	-0.079
Percent Urban	-0.634	0.614	0.750	0.136	-0.086	-1.658
Percent Unemployed*	62.58	0.071	0.065	-0.006	-0.350	-6.739
Price Index	2.9	3.696	3.920	0.224	0.874	16.800
Income *Per Capita**	-0.002	3527.260	3268.800	-258.460	0.517	9.941
Percent Manufacturing	-1.95	0.077	0.057	-0.020	0.038	0.735
Percent Rich	36.68	0.039	0.040	0.001	0.048	0.917
Percent H.S. Education*	78.75	0.669	0.723	0.054	4.252	81.779
Percent Poverty Line*	24.41	0.095	0.087	-0.008	-0.195	-3.755
Percent White	10.01	0.867	0.824	-0.043	-0.430	-8.278
Percent Female Families	52.57	0.118	0.110	-0.008	-0.421	-8.088
AFDC Expenditures		12.780	5.200	-7.580	2.147	

* Indicates statistically significant variable at 95% level.

explain the growth path of welfare over time in Arizona. Because of data limitations, this analysis will focus exclusively on the AFDC program. Since AFDC is the primary welfare program mainly under state control this focus is appropriate from a policy standpoint. Further, AFDC participation generally entitles a recipient access to most other state provided services. Statistically, the close relationship between AFDC and total welfare expenditures is also evident. AFDC has maintained a virtually constant share of total welfare expenditures over the last decade averaging 17.38 percent of the total.

Table 13-11 Comparison of Western States Total Welfare Expenditures State Specific Effects	
Arizona	-39.24
California	70.47
Colorado	-28.32
Nevada	-39.95
New Mexico	-29.48
Utah	-45.85
All State Average	-5.47

Two regression models are discussed in this section. The first estimates the causes of changes in the number of AFDC recipients. The second model estimates the causes of AFDC total expenditures. The results of the total expenditures model are similar to the results of the recipient model, but there are more important differences.

The model constructed to estimate changes in welfare spending in Arizona is based on the same methodology as the interstate comparison model. A separate regression equation is developed for AFDC recipients and for total AFDC expenditures. The variables included in these two regression equations are an attempt to capture both changes in the underlying welfare-using population as well as changes in state behavior. An important limitation of this methodology is that the regression model only captures systematic effects over time. Nonetheless, where possible, important policy changes are incorporated into the model.

The data available to model Arizona welfare spending are described in Table 13-12. These data are used to estimate a time series regression model for the years 1971-1987 using monthly observations. Some of the data is available quarterly rather than monthly; these data are assumed to be constant for all three months of the quarter.

The causes of welfare program growth are derived in large measure from the state budget model of the previous section. Population, *per capita* income, economic structure, socio-demographic change, the inflation rate, and major programmatic change are used as the explanatory variables. State population is included because of its importance in the state budgeting model. The percentage of the population in Maricopa county is included to capture urbanization trends. Current dollar *per capita* income is included as a measure of the economic health of the state. Also of potential economic importance is the labor force participation rate. As measures of economic structure the percentages of the labor force working in manufacturing, mining, retail, and service industries are included. The unemployment rate is also added as a measure of the economic environment. The divorce rate is constructed primarily from annual measures although monthly statistics were available for 1972-74, 1980, and 1987. This variable is an attempt to capture socio-demographic change in the number of female headed households. While it has important limitations, this variable is likely to be correlated with the other causal elements of family dissolution. Finally, the inflation rate is included as a measure of fiscal stress on households and on the state government. In addition to these basic explanatory variables, dummy variables that take on a value of one or zero are included for each month and year. This allows specific seasonal (for monthly) or annual effects to be measured that are not captured by the basic regression variables. Finally, a dummy variable is added that takes on a value of one starting with the advent of the AHCCCS program and zero for the time period preceding implementation of AHCCCS. DES (1987) has speculated that an important cause of AFDC recipient growth is the immediate availability of AHCCCS for AFDC recipients. If so, this variable should be estimated to have a positive impact on AFDC expenditures and recipients.

Table 13-12
Variables in the Arizona Welfare Model

Variables	Definition
MARICOPA	Percent of state population in Maricopa County; quarterly
STATEPOP	Arizona population; quarterly
TOTEMP	Percent of state population working; monthly
MNFPCT	Percent of labor force in manufacturing; monthly
MINPCT	Percent of labor force in mining; monthly
RETPCT	Percent of labor force in retail; monthly
SRVPCT	Percent of labor force in service industries; monthly
UERATE	Unemployment rate; monthly
CURCAP	Current *per capita* Gross State Product; quarterly
DIVORCES	Percent of population divorced; annually, monthly for 72-74, 80-87
DEFLATOR	Gross State Product deflator, '82=100; quarterly
AFDCPER	AFDC recipients; monthly
AFDCTOT	AFDC total expenditures; monthly

Source: Center for Business Researach, Arizona State University; Department of Economic Security.

Table 13-13 presents the estimation results for the AFDC recipient model in the first column. On the whole, the results are as expected and paint an interesting picture of welfare recipient growth in Arizona. An increase in the urbanization rate, as indicated by the percentage of the population in Maricopa County, causes an increase in welfare recipients. An increase in the population of the state of 1,000 people is estimated to cause 8 additional monthly AFDC recipients without any other changes in the economy. Increases in nominal *per capita* income (CURCAP) cause a somewhat imprecisely estimated increase in welfare recipients. This result may indicate that the state is able to afford more generous welfare eligibility standards as income rises. (As evidence that a change in eligibility standards is likely to have a large effect on the number of recipients only about 95,000 of the 475,000 people in poverty in Arizona in 1988 are on AFDC). An increase in the divorce rate is not estimated to have a significant impact on AFDC recipients, although the sign on the coefficient is positive. An increase in the inflation rate is estimated to cause a decrease in recipients due perhaps to increased fiscal pressure on the state. Movements in the retail sector of the economy are most important for determining welfare recipients. When the retail sector share declines more people require the services of the welfare system. The unemployment rate has the expected positive sign, but its effect is imprecisely estimated. It appears that the sectoral composition of employment, as shown by the retail sector result, is the most important economic indicator affecting the potential welfare recipient population.

Table 13-13 **Arizona Regression Model Results**		
Variables	**AFDC** **Recips Coeff**	**AFDC** **Expenditure Coeff**
CONSTANT	-20206.2	-1.4E+07*
MARICOPA	333817*	59807450*
STATEPOP	0.0081	1.945*
TOTEMP	-5874	265371
MNFPCT	-73067	-2.0E+07*
MINPCT	73570	674116
RETPCT	-184677*	-1.5E+07*
SRVPCT	-22853	-49461
UERATE	28401	15960
CURCAP	1.606	366.16*
DIVORCES	2400690	9.5E+08*
DEFLATOR	-63706*	-9931837*
AHCCCS	1821.6*	389282*
MONTHLY DUMS	-	-
YEARLY DUMS	-	-
R-SQUARED	0.9632	0.9833
* indicates statistically significant at the 95% level.		

The empirical results indicate that economic variables constitute a relatively important contribution towards explaining welfare participation. These results reinforce the notion that welfare users come from a variety of causes. Temporary economic hardship is clearly one of them. It should be noted, however, that the divorce rate is the only variable able to capture socio-demographic changes in the population. While not reported, the time trend effects show about 1,000 additional recipients per year are added to the welfare rolls for reasons not accounted for in the regression variables. It is highly likely that this time trend is due to changes in the socio-demographic make-up of the population not captured by the available data.

There is one other empirical result of note in the regression. The dummy variable that accounts for implementation of the state AHCCCS program is estimated to be positive with a high degree of statistical reliability. The coefficient of 1,822 indicates that the availability of AHCCCS increased AFDC participation by about 1,822 participants a month, over 2.7 percent of the average participants during the time period under study, or about 1.9 percent of 1988 recipients. While AHCCCS is clearly important for determining welfare recipients, it is not sufficient by itself to explain the 7.8 percent per annum growth in AFDC during the 1980s.

The AFDC total expenditure equation looks very similar to the recipient equation and also is reported in Table 13-13. Urbanization and state population growth both have positive effects on AFDC expenditure. *Per capita* nominal income growth (CURCAP) also is a significantly positive factor. The impact of the divorce rate is more precisely estimated in this equation, perhaps indicating that women who are separated from their husbands are more likely to require the maximum payment levels. A higher inflation rate is found to decrease welfare expenditures.

One slight difference between the expenditure and recipient equations is the impact of different economic sectors. Unlike the recipient equation, the retail sector has an insignificant impact on expenditures even though the sign is the same. On the other hand, the manufacturing sector's share of employment is statistically important where growth in the manufacturing sector reduces welfare spending. The time trend in expenditures as observed through the year dummy variables is slightly more pronounced with a sharp increase in expenditures occurring after 1981 despite the effects of OBRA. Nonetheless, like the recipient equation, the effect of AHCCCS implementation is an important explanatory variable showing that AFDC expenditures increased by about $390,000 per month. This is about 4.5 percent of average monthly AFDC expenditures in 1988. This estimate is somewhat higher than the estimated effect of AHCCCS on recipients of 1.9 percent but describes a range within which implementation of AHCCCS impacted the AFDC program.

Policy Options Facing Arizona

The major policy options facing the State of Arizona in the immediate future have been dictated by recently passed federal Family Support Act legislation or raised by the recently released report from the Governor's Task Force on Welfare Reform (1989). The changes due to federal legislation are mandatory and will be phased in over the next three years. This section provides a discussion of some of the implications of both the mandatory and the discretionary policy changes as they affect individual recipient behavior and as they affect state government financing.

The Family Support Act of 1988

The federal Family Support Act of 1988 mandates a series of actions that address many of the individual incentive concerns raised in this chapter. The primary changes in Arizona welfare provision as a result of the Act are: implementation of the AFDC-UP program by October 1, 1990; implementation of transitional AHCCCS and Day Care payments for twelve months for individuals leaving the welfare system; and implementation of the Job Opportunities and Basic Skills Training Program (JOBS).

The AFDC-UP program is anticipated to have several effects on welfare in Arizona. The potential problems raised by implementation of this policy are:

- Increased migration of recipients to Arizona as the interstate variation in welfare programs narrows.
- The basic cost, of which over 1/3 will be paid by Arizona, estimated to be $11.33 million by 1990 (Governor's Task Force, 1989).
- Potential spillovers, in that availability of AFDC-UP will increase overall welfare participation rates by the poverty population.

On the other hand, there are some important potential benefits of the AFDC-UP program:

- A reduction in the rate of family dissolution, reducing the overall burden on state welfare programs, particularly among children.
- Providing a supplement to Unemployment Insurance for uncovered industries thus increasing the attraction of jobs in uncovered sectors.
- An increase in overall welfare participation rates by the poverty population allowing a greater reach to those in need.
- Allowing a greater number of federally provided dollars to enter the state.

An examination of these issues shows that the major trade-off is between the cost of the program and the direct benefits to the recipients.

One change attributable to mandatory AFDC-UP is that the programmatic variation between states will narrow as all states, rather than only about half as is currently the case, will have this program. Arizona can afford to narrow the welfare payment difference between itself and other states without fear of an in-migration of potential recipients since Arizona is already one of the least generous states. Further, migration due to welfare benefits has been found to be small, and the AFDC-UP program in particular will only provide benefits for six months, not providing much of a long term incentive to migrate.

AFDC-UP allows two parent households to receive welfare payments for up to six months when the head of the household is unemployed. One goal of this program is to reduce the number of people who separate or divorce simply to receive welfare. Reducing incentives for family dissolution is an integral part of current welfare design. It is important not to have excessive expectations in this regard, however, as AFDC-UP by itself will not go very far in addressing the heart of the long-term welfare recipient problem.

Estimates based on the Arizona AFDC model developed for this chapter indicate that implementation of an AFDC-UP program would add about $11.83 million in 1988 dollars to Arizona's AFDC total costs. The same effect estimated in the overall welfare expenditure model is less precisely estimated but indicates an increase in total expenditures of $11 million. These figures are remarkably close to the full year estimate contained in the Task Force report. In 1988 dollars, the Task Force estimates the full-year cost to be about $10.375 million. The difference between the estimated $11.83 million which includes spillover effects on other programs, and the Task Force estimate of $10.375 million indicates that no more than $1.45 million will have to be spent on other welfare programs due to AFDC-UP. Thus, there do not appear to be any major hidden costs or program interactions lurking behind the decision to implement AFDC-UP.

Implementation of the JOBS program also is mandated by the Family Support Act. This is a separate training program that is directed at long term welfare recipients, or those at risk of being long term recipients. The purpose of this proposal is to attempt to break the "cycle of poverty" that characterizes the underclass population. All of the recent research indicates that specifically targeted programs are the type needed. To the extent that this program is successful, welfare costs may be reduced substantially since long term welfare recipients account for a disproportionate amount of total welfare funding. One policy change that is important to the success of the JOBS program is that Day Care assistance will be made available to JOBS participants. This provision significantly reduces the costs of participating in the program and considerably increases the chance that it will reach the intended recipient population. On the other hand, training programs in general have had mixed success in accomplishing their objectives. While clearly targeted at the right area, it is impossible at this time to project the ultimate financial impact of the JOBS program.

The transitional provision of AHCCCS and Day Care to those leaving welfare for work is an important addition to the welfare system as it attempts to reduce work disincentives for welfare recipients. People who leave the welfare rolls to take a job will be allowed to maintain eligibility for AHCCCS and Day Care for up to twelve months in an effort to reduce any loss in purchasing power from obtaining employment. Nonetheless, potential problems with the policy are:

- The cost, which has been estimated in the Task Force report at over $28.4 million, including $11.4 million from the state.
- Potential impact on the basic AFDC program as program participation will now be more attractive.

Some of the goals of the program, however, are seen in the potential benefits:

- Work effort, rather than welfare participation, is subsidized.
- Increased human capital for recipients through improved health and better care for children (the largest single group on welfare).
- The benefits of the program go to those who represent success in the welfare system.

The transitional provision of AHCCCS and Day Care significantly increases the benefits of taking a job compared with staying on a welfare program. This type of incentive is central to development of a welfare system that accomplishes the objective of moving people from dependency on the public sector to self supporting status. This change is consistent with the provisions of the Earned Income Tax Credit in the federal income tax code. One caveat is that these transitional provisions, like the implementation of the AHCCCS program, make overall AFDC participation more attractive to recipients. Thus, it is likely that there will be some feedback onto the AFDC recipient base although the size of this feedback is likely to be smaller than the 1,822 monthly participants estimated to have been caused by the implementation of AHCCCS.

Governor's Task Force on Welfare Reform

In addition to the federally mandated changes in welfare policy, other policy changes under discussion in Arizona include those in the recently released Task Force study. These policy changes include: an increase in AFDC benefit payments of about 20 percent; a poverty prevention program; and strengthened child support enforcement policies.

The poverty prevention proposal is a relatively modest proposal to establish a set of poverty prevention programs aimed at children and school drop out prevention. The purpose of this proposal, like implementation of the JOBS program, is an attempt to break the "cycle of poverty." This specifically targeted program has been shown to be the type needed to attack the long-term welfare recipient program. The program proposed in the Task Force report is quite modest, however. If it shows successful results, it will most likely need to be increased considerably to make an appreciable dent in the at-risk population.

In addition to the AFDC-UP program, the other part of the attack that attempts to reduce the incidence of welfare households headed by females is the renewed emphasis on child support payment enforcement. Policies in this area can be expected to evolve throughout the 1990s as attempts are made to make enforcement more certain, less costly, and more direct between parents. There are two goals embedded in child support enforcement. One is to reduce the financial burden on the public sector. It is possible that this will occur although there are substantial administrative costs to the program (see the Task Force Report). Nonetheless, the other more important goal of the program is to reduce the prevalence of divorce and/or unwed mothers by making the father share financial responsibility for the children. To the extent that this occurs, it is possible that lower AFDC costs will result.

An important additional provision in the Task Force Report, not mandated by the federal government, is an increase in overall AFDC benefit levels. The trade-off between benefits and costs is difficult to quantify for this proposal. Some potential problems, however, are:

- It is costly. The Task Force estimates that 1991 costs will be $56.9 million of which the state will have to finance about $20.5 million.
- Increased payment levels will increase the participation rate of the poverty population so that the costs of the benefit change may have been underestimated.
- The money is misplaced in that more targeted programs, such as JOBS, would make better use of the funds compared to an increase in payments to the basic welfare population.

Conversely, the benefits of the proposed change are:

- Arizona is one of the lowest welfare spending states, and benefits could be increased consistent with the economic growth of the state.
- For a person temporarily on welfare, a higher level of payments makes it easy to recover financially from whatever disaster caused a need for welfare.
- To the extent welfare operates as an insurance policy for bad economic conditions, a higher level of welfare benefits represents improvement in the overall social return that a worker in a low wage occupation faces.
- Specifically targeted programs are difficult to design and implement, and an increase in AFDC benefits is the most direct way to redress deficiencies in welfare assistance.

An increase in the basic AFDC payment level is a direct way to accomplish the goal of reducing the disparity between Arizona and its neighbors in terms of the amount of welfare assistance that is provided. In 1988, Arizona would have had to increase AFDC spending by $76 million to reach the national average of AFDC expenditures *per capita*.

One important issue in determining welfare expenditures is whether the desire is to concentrate resources on temporary or long-term recipients. For a person temporarily on welfare, a higher level of payments makes it easy to recover financially from whatever disaster caused a need for welfare. Given the other changes in incentives to reward starting back to work, an increase in benefits should not significantly change the incentives regarding increased welfare participation. On the other hand, a large share of AFDC expenditures goes to long-term recipients, and the effect of increased benefits to these recipients is more difficult to determine.

Recent welfare reform efforts have attempted to construct a consistent set of incentives to insure that those that need welfare obtain assistance while making it difficult to choose to be on welfare rather than to work or remain in a self-supporting family unit. The set of policy options currently under consideration make significant progress at achieving these goals. Future expenditure levels, however, depend on the complex interactions between programs and depend on further policy changes.

Summary

Welfare is a complex system of programs designed to provide insurance to those experiencing a variety of social and economic problems. This chapter presents an overview of welfare policy and some of the factors that are important for designing effective policy. The key factors in designing welfare policy are the set of incentives that individual welfare recipients face. Policy changes required by 1990 in the Family Support Act of 1988 go a long way toward ameliorating some of the systematic disincentive effects facing recipients. The question facing the State of Arizona, is how will these and other changes affect the expenditure requirements of the state?

The discussion of the current programmatic environment illustrates that federal financial assistance is central to the financing of poverty assistance in Arizona. Nonetheless, the period of growth in federal aid appears to be over, increases at about the rate of inflation are most likely. The only method for Arizona to increase federal financial participation is through increases in the commitment of its own resources in areas where the federal government provides cost sharing arrangements. This fact makes increases in AFDC benefit rates relatively attractive. Nonetheless, increased spending on Day Care and other subsidies to working parents would appear to be the programmatic direction most consistent with the objectives of the state.

The interstate comparison statistical model shows that Arizona has a good deal of distance to go before its expenditure levels match those of the average state in the country. Of the neighboring states, only Utah spends less than Arizona given its characteristics. Some further increase in expenditure levels thus appears to be consistent with the developing economy of the state. This will narrow the difference between Arizona and the all-state average while the rest of the nation is experiencing low rates of expenditure growth due to federal welfare restrictions. Arizona has an advantage over some of the older states in that it is able to learn from past programmatic errors and direct its increased effort into areas that appear to have the highest social rate of return without promoting some of the serious disincentives of the past.

The analysis of the causes of welfare spending in Arizona illustrates the interrelationship inherent among welfare programs. Implementation of AHCCCS increased the AFDC participation rate by between 2 and 4 percent. Another aspect of this interrelationship is the potential power of utilizing the incentive effects of the system to promote worthwhile objectives. Welfare recipients do respond to incentives in the welfare system showing that programs such as subsidizing work effort may achieve some of the desired effects. At the same time it provides a warning in that increases in one program can have feedback effects on others.

It is clear that the manner in which welfare dollars are spent, rather than simply the level of spending, can make the welfare system an effective tool promoting the general welfare of the state.

References

Antel, John J., "Mother's Welfare Dependency Effects on Daughter's Early Fertility and Fertility Out of Wedlock," University of Houston mimeo, 1988.

Arizona Joint Select Committee on State Revenues and Expenditures, *Characteristics of Arizona's Population*, March 8, 1989.

Blank, Rebecca M., "The Effect of Welfare and Wage Levels on the Location Decisions of Female-Headed Households," *Journal of Urban Economics*, 24, September, 1988, pp. 186-211.

Craig, Steven G. and Robert P. Inman, "Federal Aid and Public Education: An Empirical Look at the 'New' Fiscal Federalism," *Review of Economics and Statistics*, 64, November, 1982, pp. 541-552.

Craig, Steven G. and Robert P. Inman, "Education, Welfare, and the 'New' Federalism: State Budgeting in a Federalist Public Economy," in Rosen, Harvey (ed.), *Studies in State and Local Public Finance*, University of Chicago Press, Chicago, 1986.

Craig, Steven G. and Janet E. Kohlhase, "Why There is Not a Unified Welfare System: Fiscal Federalism from an Agency Approach," in John Quigley, John (ed.), *Perspectives on Local Public Finance and Public Policy*, Vol. 2, JAI Press, 1985, pp. 81-99.

Department of Economic Security, *Human Services in Arizona*, 1986.

Department of Economic Security, *Analysis of Aid to Families with Dependent Children: Recipient Growth in Arizona SFY 1971-1987*, 1987.

Department of Economic Security, *White Paper on Welfare Programs*, December, 1988.

Duncan, Greg J., *Years of Poverty, Years of Plenty*, Institute for Social Research, University of Michigan, Ann Arbor, 1984.

Ellwood, David T. and Mary Jo Bane, "The Impact of AFDC on Family Structure and Living Arrangements," in Ehrenberg, Ronald G. (ed.), *Research in Labor Economics*, Vol 7, JAI Press, Greenwich, CT, 1985.

Garfinkel, Irwin and Sara MacLanahan, *Single-Mothers and Their Children: A New American Dilemma*, Urban Institute Press, Washington, 1986.

Governor's Task Force on Welfare Reform, *A Family Investment Strategy for Low Income Families in Arizona*, January, 1989.

Gramlich, Edward M., "Economists' View of the Welfare System," *American Economic Review*, 79, May, 1988, pp. 191-96.

Gramlich, Edward M. and Deborah S. Laren, "How Widespread are Income Losses in a Recession," in Bawden, D. Lee (ed.), *The Social Contract Revisited*, Urban Institute Press, Washington, 1984a.

Gramlich, Edward M. and Deborah S. Laren, "Migration and Income Redistribution Responsibilities," *Journal of Human Resources*, 19, 1984b.

Lynn, Lawrence E. Jr., "A Decade of Policy Developments in the Income Maintenance System," in Haveman, Robert H. (ed.), *A Decade of Federal Antipoverty Programs*, Academic Press, New York, 1977.

Roberts, Russell D., "A Positive Model of Private Charity and Public Transfers," *Journal of Political Economy*, 92, February, 1984, pp. 136-48.

Sawhill, Isabel V., "Poverty in the US: Why is it So Persistent?" *Journal of Economic Literature*, 26, September, 1988, pp. 1073-1119.

Schiff, Jerald, "Does Government Spending Crowd Out Charitable Contributions," *National Tax Journal*, 38, December, 1985, pp. 535-546.

Chapter 14

State Recreation And Environmental Quality Programs

R. Bruce Billings and W. Mark Day

Arizona presents an image to the world of wide open spaces, monumental cliffs, magnificent canyons, majestic mountains, deep forests, and sweeping deserts. Its wildlife and vegetation are unique, varied, plentiful and renowned. Its mineral wealth is still considerable after a century of production. Its cities are vibrant, providing cultural and economic activity in spectacular settings.

But, all is not well. After a century of exploitation, some of the resources that make Arizona a state to be envied are rapidly diminishing. Given that tourism and travel are a large part of Arizona's economy, serious attention must be paid to maintaining this natural heritage. Even the saguaro cactus and the Grand Canyon, symbols of Arizona to all the world, stand in jeopardy of environmental deterioration or destruction from human causes. The Grand Canyon suffers from reduced visibility due to smoke from a nearby power plant and the saguaro is threatened by the loss of a primary pollinator, a tiny bat, and other stresses possibly linked to air pollution.

Chemical waste dumping, groundwater overuse and contamination, air pollution and pollens from imported plants jeopardize the health of residents in Arizona, a former haven for asthma sufferers. Becoming more visible are rural and urban blight, murky urban air, and loss of wilderness, wetlands and natural vistas. Arizonans are discovering that too much freedom for some can mean loss and damage to others.

Arizona's residents are concerned about the natural environment and are willing to increase spending to take care of problems according to a 1988 poll conducted by Arizona State University's Morrison Institute. Respondents also felt that government should encourage growth but not at the expense of the environment. In two 1988 polls conducted by Arizona Newspapers, Inc. and Rocky Mountain Poll, environment/air quality was ranked as the second most serious issue facing Arizona. Perhaps most telling is a recent poll published by Senator Dennis DeConcini, indicating the *only* area in which Arizonans want increased federal spending is the environment.

Concern is rising for such problems as the "brown cloud" over Phoenix, groundwater contamination, water availability and transfer, and toxic and solid waste disposal. The possible effects of these problems on tourism and the attractiveness of the state to relocating industries are emerging as political issues. For instance, while current efforts to resolve the water transfer debate revolve around the loss of tax base and future water sources for development in rural areas, conservation and rural interest groups are also concerned about the potential impact of withdrawals on stream-side (riparian) habitat of diverse wildlife populations.

This chapter presents the economic rationale for government involvement in regulating and managing the environment. It also provides interstate comparisons of expenditures and finances of state and local governments in the area of natural resources and a description of the major Arizona state agencies with responsibilities for natural resources and environmental quality. Emphasis is placed on agencies with responsibility for air and water quality and for parks and recreation.

The Economics Of Natural Resources Regulation

The Environment as a Public Good

In a market economy with private property rights, each person uses his or her time and resources to maximize the benefit derived from their use. Thus, each resource is used to provide the greatest benefit to its owner which tends to maximize the total value of production and material wealth of society. When no one owns and controls a resource and many people have the right to use the resource, the private market mechanism is unable to put that resource to its best and most valued use. When a resource is privately owned, the owner has an incentive to maintain its value, but if private ownership is lacking there is little economic incentive to preserve values. People generally do not dump trash in their own back yards but along road sides or on unfenced land.

The same phenomenon occurs in cattle grazing. If a specific family owns or has long-term control of a range, its members will limit the herd size on that range to maximize long-term production. However, if many people are given grazing rights, each will have an incentive to add to his or her herd as long as some short-term, personal benefit is derived, resulting in overgrazing and destruction of the range.

This phenomenon is often referred to as the "tragedy of the commons," and occurs whenever several people have the rights to use a resource but none have the right to limit the use of others. This lack of property rights prevents any individual from refraining from current use in order to preserve future use. The tragedy of the commons occurs throughout Arizona's natural resource environment and is particularly evident in declining water tables and overgrazed public lands.

An alternative and equally useful way to look at the problem of non-market effects is to examine the impacts that one person's activities have on others. Such commonplace actions as use of a transistor radio to produce music have spillover or "external" effects on those around us. Depending on the preferences of our neighbors, the sounds emanating from a radio will be considered either noise or music. Those preferring silence would consider this noise a "negative externality." On the other hand, for someone enjoying the music, it is a "positive externality."

An externality occurs whenever one person's actions impose a cost or benefit for a second person over which the second person has no control. The automobile is often considered a necessity and makes our very culture possible, but at the same time it is central to many environmental problems. The problem lies in the automobile's numerous negative externalities: its exhaust is poisonous; the production and delivery of its fuel create serious environmental impacts; the number of cars on many of our streets and highways exceeds their capacity, resulting in congestion and slowed travel; and the more fuel we burn to drive us to our ever-more-remote homes or other destinations, the greater the chance of bringing on the much discussed "greenhouse effect."

Environmental Costs

The pollution caused by the automobile and its supporting industries is a cost. Ignoring this cost does not make it go away. The social cost of pollution will be borne in the end, either directly through dollar costs or indirectly through a diminished environment. The significant policy question is, *who will bear this cost*? Will it be those persons, places or things which happen to be in the path of the resulting pollution, or will society force the producers of these costs to bear them?

Currently, the answer is a mixture of these two alternatives. Several steps have been taken, in the case of air pollution, to reduce pollution by imposing some costs on those causing it: automobile manufacturers are required to install pollution reduction equipment on new cars; most automobiles are required to pass emissions tests; and oil refineries are required to meet environmental standards. The remaining costs of pollution, however, are absorbed by the general public, by being forced to breath polluted air, to repaint their corroded houses more often, and to suffer reduced enjoyment of outdoor activities due to smog.

It is often less expensive to regulate production or consumption to mitigate negative externalities than it is to clean up the mess left behind or to pay damages to those injured. Consider what the choices were for the State of Alaska, as regulator, and Exxon, as producer/supplier of petroleum products, prior to the Exxon Valdez oil spill. Perhaps tighter shipping regulations on the part of the state or additional navigational precautions on the part of the firm would have saved 11 million gallons of crude oil, hundreds of millions of dollars of clean-up costs, a damaged ship, the reputation of the firm, a major fishing industry, and uncalculated damage to the wildlife and environment of Prince William Sound. The cost of cleanup disclosed in the media was $500 million or $45 per gallon.

Optimum regulation of pollution might be achieved by applying the "polluter-pays" principle to "internalize" the externalities of polluting industries. This may be achieved by imposing a fee or tax on pollution based on the marginal (or unit) value of the damage caused by the pollution or on the cost of cleaning it up. When this price is properly assigned, the state will have a source of funds for cleaning up or improving the environment, and producers or consumers will have an incentive to reduce their pollution production. Other methods for controlling negative externalities include subsidies to reduce pollution and direct regulation.

A special problem, somewhat unique to Arizona and other western states with wide open spaces, is visual pollution. Whether it is the appearance of a hillside home, a road cut, or a pile of mine tailings, actions of others frequently degrade the quality-of-life of all within a radius of 50 or more miles. Thin desert vegetation hides little. Much of the native vegetation recovers slowly from destruction and reminds us of careless land use practices. Although a landscape with fewer saguaro cactus may not be tangibly polluted, it nonetheless has diminished visual value. We need only consult a realtor to learn the value placed on "views" by the marketplace. Well-considered controls may mitigate or minimize these environmental damages.

In the case of extractive industries which remove value from the public resource base, a severance tax can be assessed on the activity. Several states raise substantial revenues for resource programs through use of a severance tax on mineral extraction. Levying a severance tax may serve environmental policy as well as revenue goals.

For instance, Arizona's groundwater costs the user almost nothing. Aside from minimal taxes, the user simply pays delivery costs. Assessing a scarcity rent could approximate the social cost of using the water now as opposed to preserving it for future generations. Removing groundwater contributes to potential land subsidence, and, for the most part, groundwater is much higher in quality than new surface water sources. So, these benefits are lost to future residents.

Given the stated goal of wise use and conservation of water, a scarcity value placed on water and collected for its use through a severance tax or fee, would aid in achieving these goals. Since numerous studies have shown substantial conservation response to price increases for water use, and imply wasteful use when prices are relatively low, it makes sense to charge what water is worth. Price elasticities (measurements of the response to price changes) for residential water use in Arizona are reported as yielding between three and seven percent reduction in use for every ten percent increase in average price. Therefore, by not undervaluing (underpricing) water, it will be more wisely used. So, there are both financial and performance reasons for assigning a scarcity price or rent for groundwater.

Governmental Role

From the economic and public policy standpoint, there are a number of natural resource and environmental problems or situations that warrant public sector involvement. These situations may call for regulation, taxes on polluting activities, public ownership and operation of production processes (like some types of recreational facilities), or public governance of the production processes (for example, public utilities serving water users). Sometimes there is a problem even when government itself is the owner, the inability (physically or financially) to exclude those who would damage or use a protected resource. Governmental agencies are often no more willing than private companies to spend resources for pollution prevention. Before federal intervention with the Clean Water Act, cities were frequently the primary source of untreated sewage in rivers and lakes.

There is also a role for government in providing goods and services that individuals cannot provide for themselves and that are not effectively provided through the private market. Some natural resource-related services may be provided by government because they are non-rival in consumption or because of the inability (or prohibitive cost) of excluding those who do not agree to pay. Thus, government provides forest fire protection, highways, parks, hiking and bicycle trails, toxic waste disposal, and urban-area planning and zoning. Private provision of these goods would be difficult or impossible because sufficient user fees to make the service profitable could not be collected or because society does not wish to exclude anyone from using them. Once the service is provided, anyone who wants to may use it without payment. In addition, with parks or highways, use is often non-rival since there is generally no additional cost from an extra user, and additional users do not prevent others' enjoyment of the resource. In this case there is no reason, and it is inefficient, to exclude anyone who wants to use the service or facility.

The provision of environmental amenities and regulations can be viewed as public goods, characterized as both non-rival and non-exclusive, from which many people benefit and where those who choose not to pay cannot be excluded. If an urban area has an effective planning and zoning program, all residents benefit from well-ordered urban development.

Those who may not wish to pay *cannot* be excluded from the benefits of this service. Similarly, if environmental regulations result in cleaner air, all residents of the area receive the same benefit; there is no way to exclude anyone.

It is the responsibility of government to protect the rights of all to enjoy, but not destroy, the environmental benefits of Arizona. Preservation of the natural heritage for current and future generations will always be a difficult area of public policy because it will always be a process of dividing the pie, deciding which generation or which interest group will have how much of what is left of the various resources. For example, pumping groundwater from beneath flowing streams, and thereby drying them up, would mean a virtually permanent change in an ecosystem that might be more valuable, intact, to tourists and those who serve them than is the value of the extracted water to immediate users.

The most prominent methods for controlling the production of negative externalities include: taxation of negative externalities; taxation of activities known to produce negative outputs; and regulations to limit negative externalities. Fortunately, policy instruments are flexible and allow for considerable creativity in establishing policy as follows: Information and suasion, public appeals from political leaders, or advertisements, can be very effective for some issues. Emissions taxes charged to polluting parties can provide an incentive for reducing emissions as well as funding for needed remedial activities. Abatement subsidies, payments to potential polluters to give them means to comply with pollution regulations, can speed up the use of cleaner technology in both production and consumption. Auctioned or marketable emission permits which designate rights to produce specified amounts of pollution can be used to set total allowable pollution without the need for government regulators to decide who should be allowed how much pollution. Regulatory allocation of abatement requirements allows government officials to distribute the costs of pollution control to those best able to afford the extra costs.

Federal, Interstate, And State/Local Comparisons

Figure 14-1 provides a picture of the commitment of the federal government to natural resource and environmental programs in recent years. It reveals that these programs' share of the federal budget and Gross National Product has steadily decreased since 1978 and is projected to continue decreasing. These declines have occurred despite small gains in absolute dollars spent. In real terms, these program budgets have been declining. Grants to state and local governments for natural resource programs have not only declined in real terms but also as a proportion of total federal natural resource programs. The proportion of state and local budgets devoted to natural resource functions has also decreased during the 1980's for Arizona and a set of comparison states (Figure 14-2).

While a thorough analysis of program needs is beyond the scope of this chapter, some sense of Arizona's response to environmental needs can be gained from expenditure comparisons with selected states that are thought to have similar problems or characteristics. Figures 14-3 and 14-4 indicate that Arizona's combined state and local expenditures on natural resources exceed the comparison states' average for "Total Natural Resources" and "Solid Waste," but not for "Parks and Recreation," both on a per capita basis and as a share of total state personal income. Arizona's combined governments also out spent the U.S. average for categories other than parks while the comparison states' average exceeded the U.S. average for all categories except solid waste.

Figure 14-1
Natural Resource Programs As Percent of Federal Budget and GNP

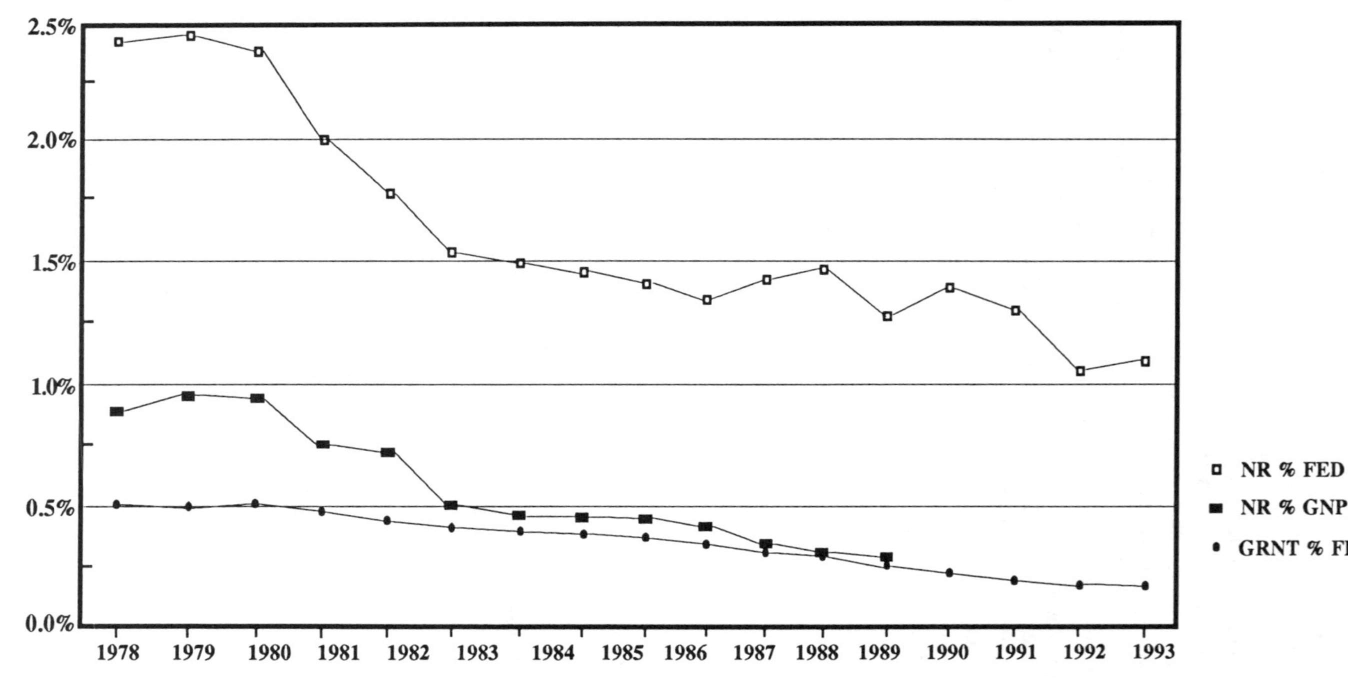

Note: NR=Natural Resource Programs; FED=Federal Budget; GNP=Gross National Product; and GRNT=Grants to state and local governments.

Source: Historic Table 3.3, U.S. Budget FY 1990 and Special Analysis H (same).

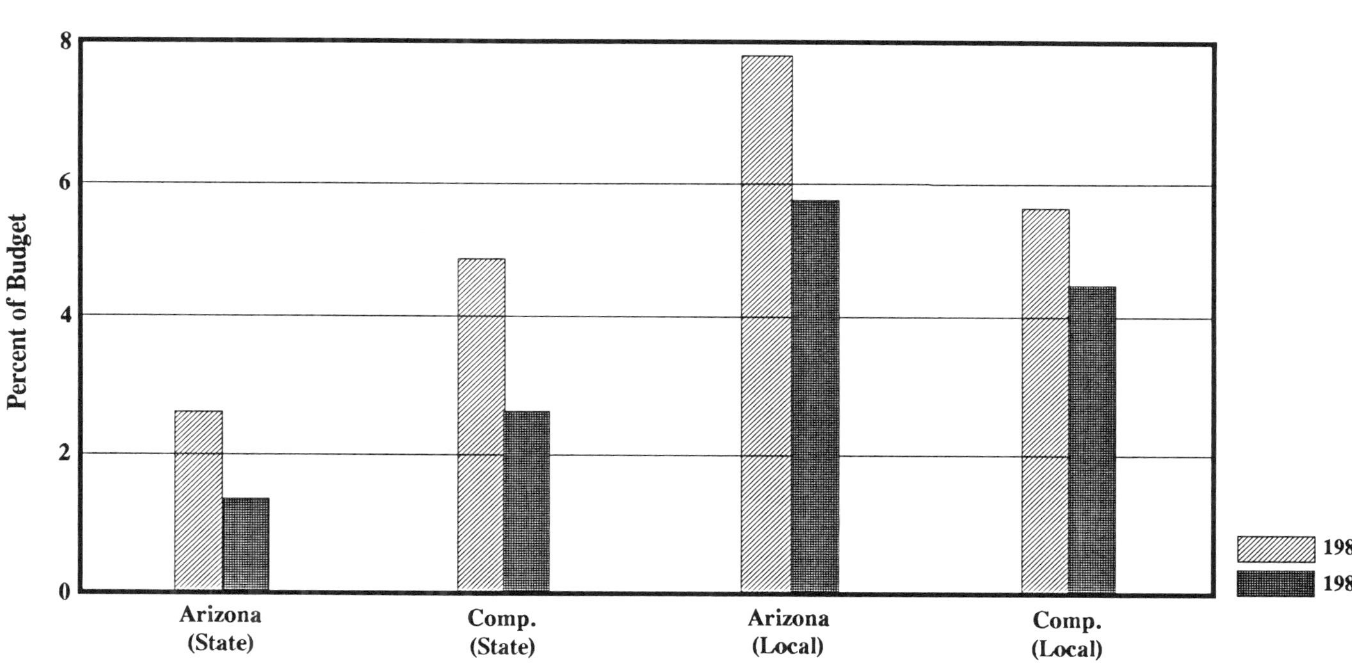

Source: Census GF5 Series. Comp. = Comparison States: Washington, Utah, Texas, Oregon, New Mexico, Nevada, Florida, Colorado, California, and Arizona.

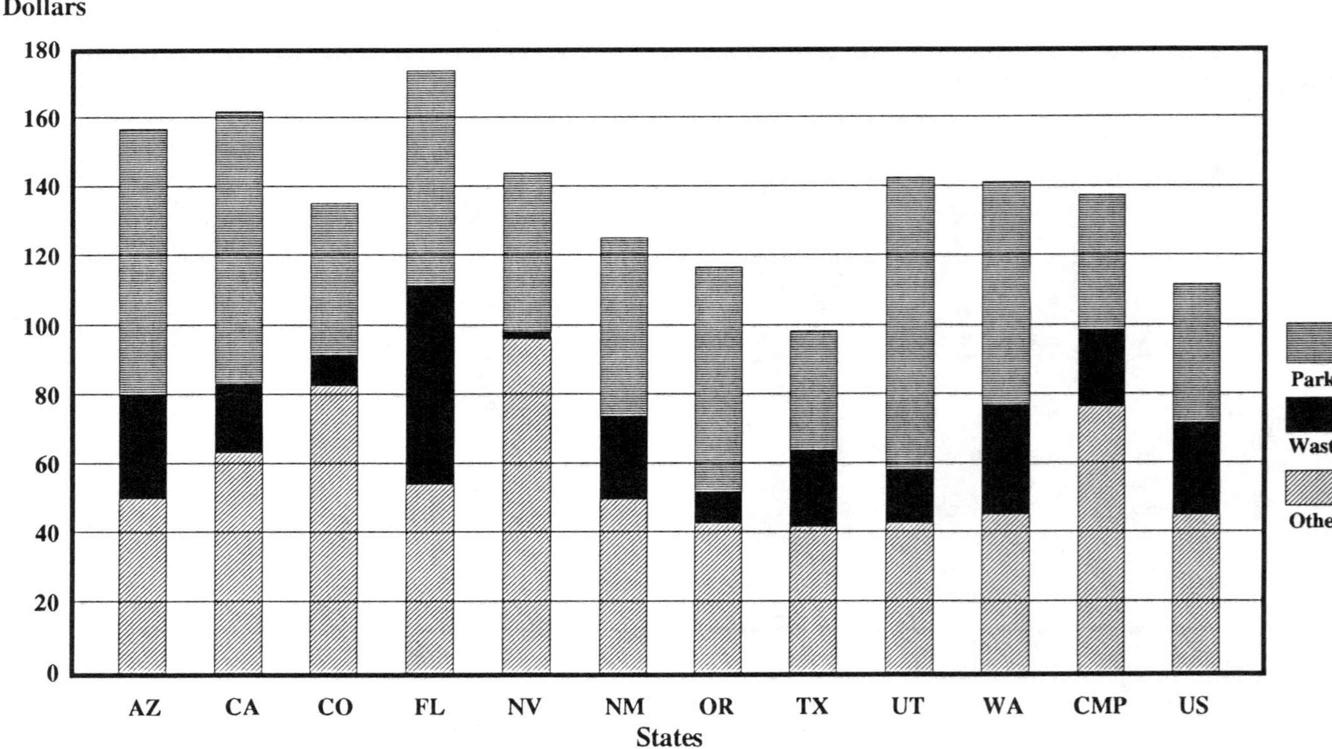

Source: Census GF5 Series. CMP = Average of Comparison States.

Figure 14-4

State and Local Spending Per $1,000 Personal Income On Natural Resources, 1986-87

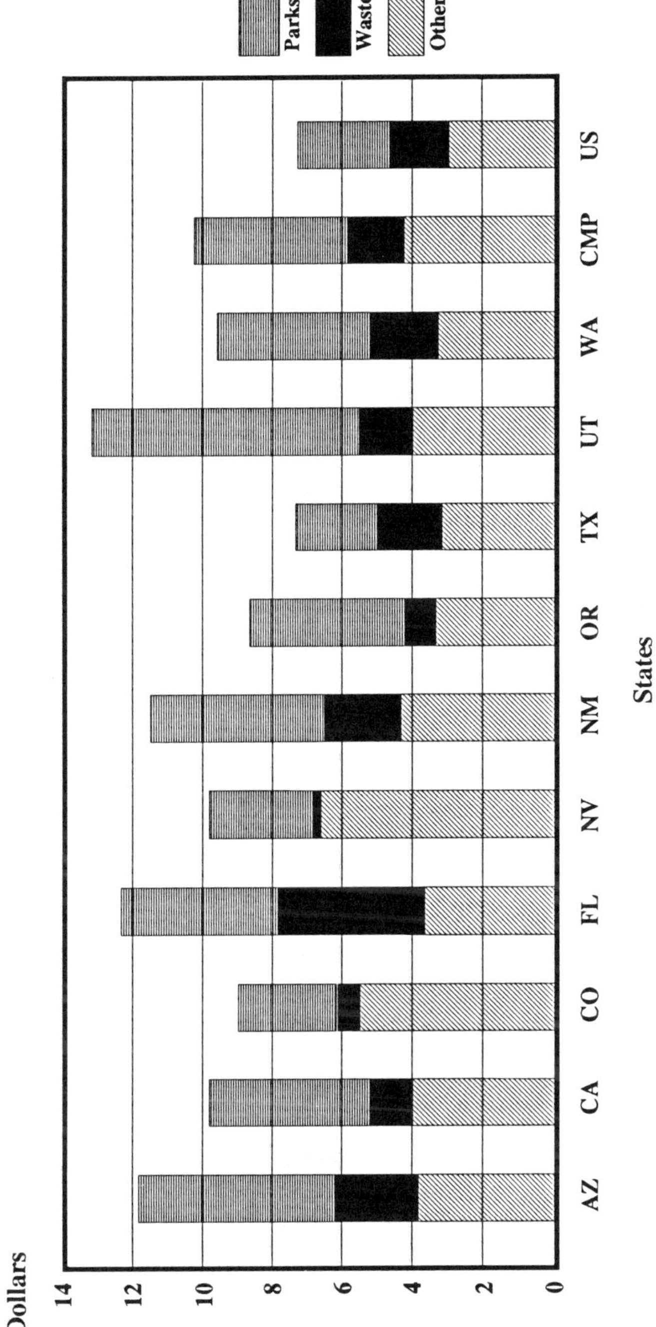

Source: Census GF5 Series. CMP = Average of Comparison States.

Arizona relies far less on state government and far more on local government than the comparison states, many of which, like Arizona, contain federal parks, monuments and reserves to help meet their residents' demand for outdoor recreation and have similar capabilities to meet the demands for the use of natural resources (Figure 14-5).

Analysis Of Current Programs

Department of Environmental Quality

The Department of Environmental Quality is the newest major state agency. It was established by the Environmental Quality Act of 1986. The Department of Environmental Quality's responsibilities include many that were previously under the Department of Health Services' Environmental Health Division which was abolished when the Department of Environmental Quality was created. Responsibilities include regulation of water and air quality, regulation of hazardous and solid wastes, and implementation of remedial programs intended to restore an environment damaged due to past polluting practices.

In FY 1988, total expenditures amounted to $16.7 million of which 71 percent was financed by the state. Estimated expenditures for FY 1989 were $22.6 million, of which 53 percent (including $2.8 million from the Water Quality Assurance Revolving Fund [WQARF]) was state funded. Federal aid (primarily from the Environmental Protection Agency) and user charges and fees (deposited into other state funds such as the Air Quality Fund, [AQF]) are the most important non-appropriated sources of revenue for the Department. Many of the fees and charges collected by the Department of Environmental Quality are deposited into the state General Fund and are available to the agency only by legislative appropriation.

The WQARF, funded by state appropriation, is the state Superfund set up to finance detection and cleanup of hazardous substances that may pollute the waters of the state. The AQF is financed by a $1.50 air quality fee paid by residents of Maricopa and Pima counties when they register their vehicles each year. The AQF is used to finance projects to improve air quality in areas where health standards for carbon monoxide or ozone are violated. The WQARF and the AQF are revolving funds with estimated balances for the 1989 FY of more than $12 million and $4 million, respectively.

Substantial uncertainty surrounds the future expenditures of the Department of Environmental Quality which, along with a number of its program elements, is still quite new. The Department of Environmental Quality is composed of five offices, three with program responsibilities. Many of the problems and issues facing the Department of Environmental Quality are not well developed and solutions are often unclear. Program needs are often driven by federal regulatory requirements as health standards are revised, by the discovery of inappropriate past practices in waste disposal, and by environmental emergencies.

For instance, the regulation of leaking underground storage tanks has recently received much attention from federal regulators. Federal mandates and funding programs have spawned both state and local programs.

Office of Air Quality was expected to spend $3.9 million during FY 1989 on programs to maintain and improve air quality. High quality air is important for aesthetic, health and economic development purposes. A decline in air quality in the Phoenix metropolitan area (which contains more than half the state's population) is a cause for concern for current and potential residents and businesses.

Figure 14-5
State Percentage of State and Local Natural Resource Spending

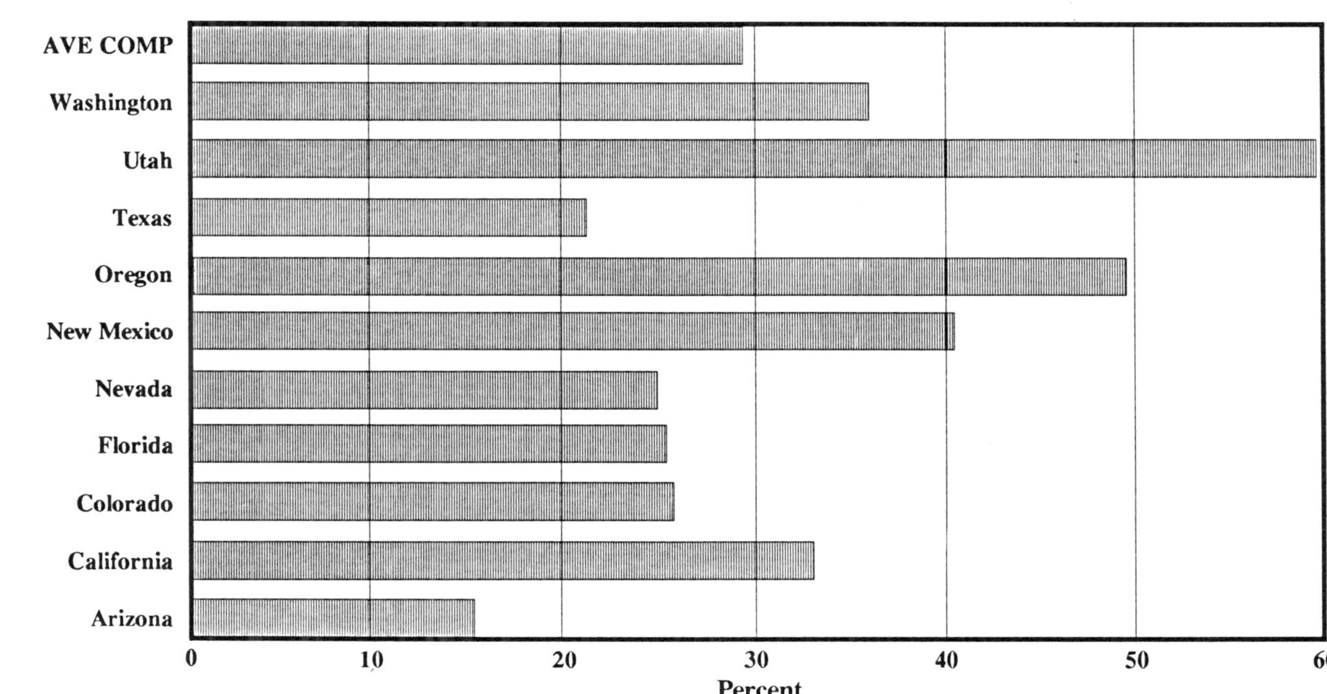

Source: Census GF4 Series data. AVE COMP = Average of Comparative States

The Office of Air Quality is responsible for air quality assessment through statewide data collection and analysis of trends and through special studies such as the Pilot Brown Cloud Study for Phoenix. The Office also regulates industrial and other sources of air pollution via permits and compliance enforcement and administers a contract with a private firm for the Vehicle Emissions Inspection programs in Phoenix/Maricopa County and Tucson/Pima County.

Table 14-1 compares the 1985 state air quality program budgets of Arizona and several other states. With the exception of Washington, Arizona had the lowest per capita state expenditures on air quality programs at $0.55 while Oregon was highest at $2.37 followed by California at $1.80. Arizona relied almost equally on federal aid and state appropriations and relied very little on fees. California and Florida relied heavily on state appropriations while Colorado's largest source of revenue was fees. Combined state and local expenditures per capita on air quality for 1988 were nearly the same in Colorado (state-wide at $1.79) as in Arizona ($1.46 in Maricopa County and $1.71 in Pima County). Those in coastal California were much greater, at $6.46 in the Los Angeles area and $5.09 in the San Francisco Bay area both of which have severe air pollution problems.

State and local government air quality expenditures have been responsive in recent years to ongoing concerns for environmental protection including concerns for indoor air pollution as buildings become tighter and more energy efficient. Population increases bring more cars and more industry which are both likely to increase air pollution. The recent experience of Los Angeles (South Coast Air Quality District) shown in Figure 14-6 may suggest the long-term trend for these programs in metropolitan Arizona.

Office of Waste Programs. This Office was expected to spend $4.8 million in FY 1989 to monitor, control and manage the state's solid waste disposal efforts. The Office is responsible for issuing permits, performing inspections, and monitoring compliance with hazardous waste regulations. This authority extends from generators and transporters of wastes to treatment and disposal facilities including landfills. The Office will regulate the construction and eventual operation of a hazardous waste disposal site by a private contractor.

Both WQARF and Federal Superfund funds are used for emergency and remedial efforts including assessment, investigation and decontamination of hazardous substances, such as those often found in old landfills, that may cause water pollution.

Office of Water Quality. This Office, with 1989 expenditures of $11 million, is the largest division of the Department of Environmental Quality. It implements all state, and most federal, water quality laws and is responsible for monitoring and regulating the quality of surface water and groundwater, inspecting regulated water and wastewater facilities, approving plans for public water and wastewater systems, and reviewing permits and complaints to determine compliance with water quality standards. Protected water uses include drinking, industrial, agricultural, recreational and wildlife habitat needs.

Water quality programs have become more controversial in recent years due to public awareness of discoveries of groundwater contamination. The Department of Environmental Quality reports that, due to the large number of wells (73,000 estimated) and relatively recent public focus on groundwater contamination in Arizona, the extent of groundwater pollution problems on a statewide basis is not yet known. However, hundreds of wells are known to have been contaminated by various chemicals, and efforts are underway to discover additional contamination, to clean up known sites, and to prevent future contamination. A program to clean up leaking underground chemical and gasoline storage tanks is also being implemented. The water quality programs have become more rigorous by requiring each discharger to use the best available demonstrated control technologies.

Table 14-1
State Air Quality Programs, 1985

State	Population	Budget Per Capita	Federal Percentage	State Percentage	Fee Percentage	Local Area Programs?	Emissions Tests (Auto)?
			Source of Funds				
Arizona	3,193,000	$0.55	42.0	51.6	6.4	Yes	Yes
California	26,358,000	1.80	5.5	93.7	0.8	Yes	Yes
Colorado	3,234,000	1.46	28.6	14.7	56.7	No	Yes
Florida	11,364,000	0.59	10.4	89.6	0.0	Yes	No
Nevada	937,000	0.57	48.4	51.6	0.0	No	No
New Mexico	1,451,000	1.21	50.1	49.9	0.0	No	No
Oregon[*]	2,686,000	2.37	28.7	24.1	47.2	Yes	Yes
Texas	16,389,000	0.86	24.4	75.6	0.0	No	Yes
Utah	1,645,000	0.93	69.2	30.8	0.0	No	Yes[*]
Washington	4,408,000	0.37	47.1	52.9	0.0	Yes	Yes

[*] Oregon fees include auto inspection fees. Utah emmissions test program is run by counties.

Source: *Air Permit and Emission Fees*, April, 1987, State and Territorial Air Pollution Program Administrators and the Association of Local Air Pollution Control Officials.

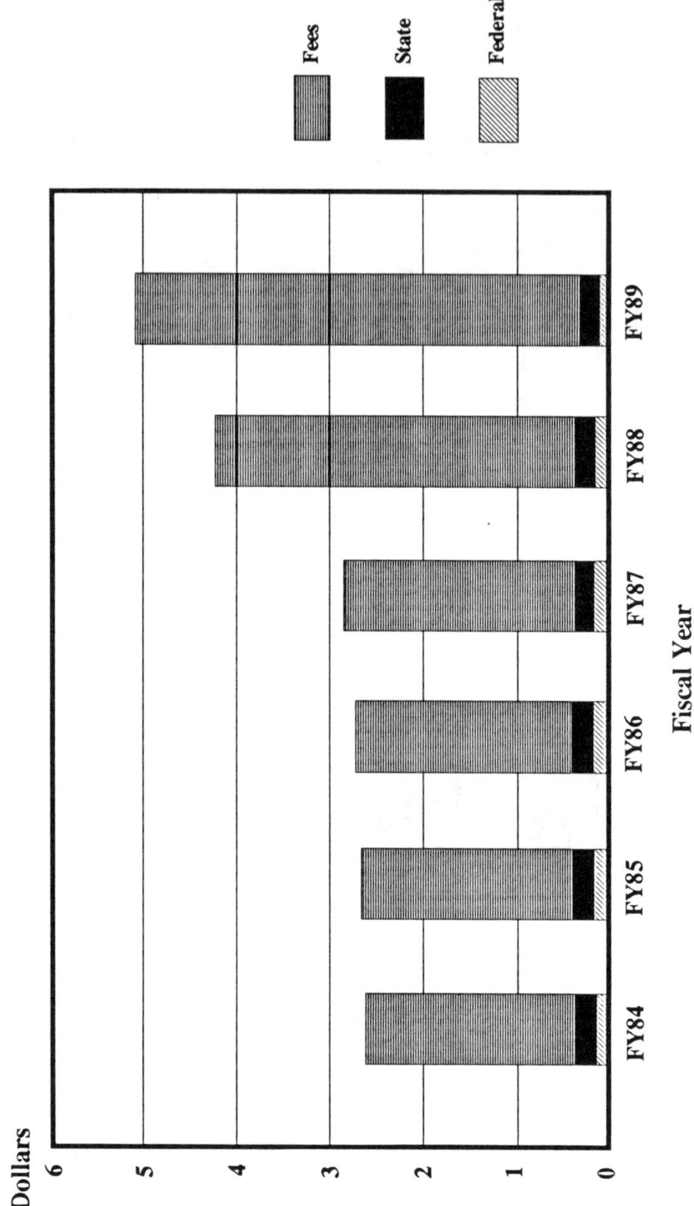

Figure 14-6

South Coast Air Quality District Per Capita Expenditures By Source

Source: Published agency data.

Because of these and related programs, new Federal requirements set or anticipated, and expected termination of current Federal funding (for example, elimination of the huge Wastewater Treatment Facility Construction Grants Program), the revenue requirements for water quality programs are expected to grow rapidly during the next decade.   For instance, new Federal requirements for the Safe Drinking Water Program have been assessed (by a national survey) to require at least a doubling of Arizona's program staff over the next 5 years.

Department of Water Resources

The Department of Water Resources was established to "assure a dependable water supply for Arizona's future, and protect against floods by developing and implementing programs to conserve, control, protect, augment, allocate and understand our water resources" (Groundwater Management Act, June 12, 1980). Under this legislation, four active management areas (AMAs) were established in the state's two major metropolitan centers and two other areas.   Additional AMAs may be established in the future if the director of Department of Water Resources determines that management is necessary to preserve existing groundwater supplies.   An AMA may also be designated through an initiative process by voters residing in a water basin.

Each AMA consists of one or more water basins where groundwater pumpage has resulted in a falling water table and where, without intervention, the groundwater supply would diminish to the point where it would become virtually unusable either because of deteriorating water quality with extreme depths or because pumping costs would have become exorbitant.   To prevent this from happening, the Department, through the AMAs, is required to implement controls on allowable water use for virtually all water users within each AMA. The Department is primarily a regulatory agency.   It is not involved in building physical structures or in operating water supply systems.

The objective of the Department of Water Resources and the AMAs is to make the best use of limited supplies of water from whatever source derived.   Within this general objective, existing water use rights have been formalized, water withdrawals are being quantified and current water use is being limited.   The Department of Water Resources has the responsibility of developing and implementing a series of ten-year management plans to obtain increasingly severe conservation action by water users by 2025.

Currently, most of the funding for the Department of Water Resources is obtained from state general fund appropriations.   Relatively small amounts are derived from various fees and federal funds.

The most important source of revenue generated by the Department of Water Resources, which is reverted to the General Fund, is the groundwater withdrawal fee. It is currently $1.00 per acre foot of groundwater pumped and is imposed only within the AMAs. Department of Water Resources is a good example of an agency that could be totally financed by those receiving its services.   An increase in the groundwater withdrawal fee to about $1.60 per acre foot, which would still make this fee a small percentage of the cost of pumping and transporting groundwater for most users, could fund the entire department.   Similarly, it would be appropriate to finance the water quality activities of the Department of Environmental Quality from an additional modest increase in the groundwater withdrawal fees since the primary purpose of these activities is to protect groundwater from contamination.   An increase in the groundwater withdrawal fee would serve the added purpose of making alternative water supplies more economically attractive.

The principal alternative supplies are Central Arizona Project (CAP) water and processed effluent. The CAP is a federal project that delivers water from the Colorado River to Phoenix, other parts of central Arizona, Indian reservations, and, eventually, to Tucson. The CAP is financed by federal loans and grants, property taxes, capacity charges for those with subcontracts for CAP water (used to repay the federal loans), and volume charges based on operating costs.

The primary rationale for building the CAP is to reduce the overdraft of Arizona's groundwater. However, under the current pricing system, users of CAP water or processed effluent pay the delivery and processing costs which in most cases are much higher than the cost of pumping groundwater even when the current groundwater withdrawal fee is added in. For example, groundwater can usually be pumped for $10-$40 per acre foot compared to canal side delivery of CAP water at over $100 per acre foot and purchase of treated effluent for as much as $400 per acre foot. Thus, groundwater, often the highest quality water and an increasingly scarce source, is the cheapest source.

Efficient resource use requires that prices include not only production cost but a payment for the use of the resource itself. This extra payment is often referred to as a scarcity rent which accrues due to the market value of the resource exceeding production cost. For privately owned resources, these appear as mineral royalties to owners which help ration the resource to its most valuable present and future uses.

Efficient use of groundwater, which is not privately owned, could be achieved by the imposition of an appropriately determined "scarcity rent" in the form of a withdrawal fee. This would provide a solution to the current inefficient pricing scheme with its governmentally-created anomalies in the pricing of water from various sources. Such a fee would cause large redistributions of wealth among whose with pre-existing use rights requiring some adjustment for equity considerations.

Arizona State Parks Board

The Arizona State Parks Board was established in 1957 to "select, acquire, preserve, establish and maintain areas of natural features, scenic beauty, historical and scientific interest, and zoos and botanical gardens, for the education, pleasure, recreation, and health of the people." (ARS 41-511.03) State parks include campgrounds, recreational lakes for swimming, fishing and boating, Colorado River camping sites, and historical sites and edifices. The State Parks Board also administers recreation-related programs.

The State Parks Board received $5.3 million for operations from the General Fund and collected $1.5 million in gate and concessions revenues (which were largely deposited into the General Fund) in FY 1988. That year $857,610 was expended for capital projects with most of the money coming from General Fund appropriations. The State Parks had 1,394,653 paid visitors during FY 1988.

The State Parks Board also administers the State Lake Improvement Fund which provides capital improvement funding for projects statewide at all levels of government and is funded with a share of motor fuel taxes (in proportion to marine fuel sales).

Arizona's parks are far less than average in a number of important dimensions and have been roundly criticized in several recent reports including the 1986 *Performance Audit* by the Arizona Auditor General and the 1989 *State Comprehensive Outdoor Recreation Plan*

(SCORP). A State Parks System Plan was developed as a direct result of these reports, and the legislature responded by establishing the Acquisition and Development Fund. Starting in April 1988, all park entry fees and concessions royalties are deposited in this fund dedicated to park system expansion.

Arizona's spending for state parks was only $1.53 per capita in 1986, nearly 10 cents less than the next lowest comparison state (Table 14-2). The per capita average of nine comparison states was $4.03, a bit higher than the national average of $3.40. Parks also claimed a smaller percentage of Arizona's total operating budget than for any other western state reviewed (at 0.181 percent) and higher only than Florida (at 0.138 percent). The average of the nine states reviewed was 0.337 percent, a bit higher than the national average of 0.313 percent. Arizona funded 88 percent of operations with state appropriations compared to 65 percent for the national average and 62 percent for the average of the comparison states.

Arizona also has less than one-fifth the number of recreational sites or facilities of the average comparison state (24 vs. 125) and fewer sites per capita than any of the comparison states (Table 14-3). Compared to the other "Four Corner" states and Nevada, Arizona has slightly less than one-third as many sites per capita and about one-tenth the average park acreage per capita. A recent Auditor General's report characterizes Arizona's parks as often inappropriate or insignificant facilities for the state parks system. In short, Arizona not only has fewer sites than the average state, and smaller sites than adjacent states, but some of the sites it has are below par for what they offer the public. Park usage in Arizona is correspondingly low, less than a fifth of the national average and less than Nevada's park visitation, a state with less than one-third the population of Arizona. Arizona's parks revenues are correspondingly low even though fee structures are similar. Recently, however, there has been a steady to rapid increase in park visitation and fees received (15 percent per year) with the opening of unique new parks (such as the very popular Slide Rock Park in Oak Creek Canyon).

Surveys indicate that camping is the most popular form of outdoor recreation for Arizonans yet Arizona has less than half as many campsites as the average comparison state. A large excess demand for developed campsites is revealed by spillover from state and national campgrounds. Numerous areas are being damaged by those who camp in fragile areas when campgrounds are unavailable. The Tonto National Forest north of Phoenix is the most heavily visited forest in the nation, and foresters are concerned about damage caused by extensive, uncontrolled use.

Parks systems can contribute substantially to local economies especially in rural areas. New parks, like Kartchner Caverns (a beautiful cave which was obtained with a combination of private donations and state funds), are being recommended as economic development tools. State Parks Board surveys indicate popular facilities can contribute to economic development (with the average family spending $203 within 50 miles of the park per visit). Regional economic development professionals emphasize the strategy of tourism-based rural development. Tourism is a major economic activity state-wide and protection of the natural resource and environmental endowment of the state is a key factor in preserving the industry.

Game and Fish Department

The Game and Fish Department is responsible for assuring the health and safety of Arizona's wildlife and for regulation of hunting, fishing, boating and related outdoor activities. It operates fish hatcheries, provides hunter education programs, issues publications

Table 14-2
Parks Systems Revenues, Arizona and Comparison States, FY 1986 Operations

States	Fees	State Appropriation	Tax and License	Federal Revenues	Miscellaneous	Total	Parks Operating Budget	
							Percent of State Budget	Per Capita
Arizona*	$0	$4,457,777	$363,179	$194,210	$76,973	$4,876,946	0.181	$1.53
California	31,807,000	75,014,000	6,550,000	968,000	197k,500	114,536,500	0.534	4.35
Colorado	3,308,804	1,814,417	210,000	169,807	1,947,500	7,450,528	0.199	2.30
Florida	0	20,423,548	0	0	0	20,423,548	0.138	1.80
Nevada	684,755	1,300,417	740,000	332,030	5,000	3,062,202	0.237	3.27
New Mexico	1,990,400	3,789,000	3,569,000	107,600	76,900	9,532,900	0.259	6.57
Oregon	5,145,000	2,634,000	5,467,000	895,000	309,000	14,450,000	0.222	5.38
Texas	13,130,783	13,283,847	0	145,303	0	26,559,933	0.301	1.62
Utah	1,717,330	5,752,000	1,302,900	740,088	180,430	9,692,748	0.866	5.89
Washington	4,111,789	17,815,467	317,288	170,899	0	22,415,443	0.280	5.09
Comparison States Average							0.337	$4.03
Fifty States Average							0.313	3.40

* Arizona generated $1,264,206 in gate revenues in FY 1986, but these were deposited to the General Fund. Beginning in FY 1988, Parks' gate revenues were deposited in the Acquisition and Development Fund for new capital facilities.

Source: National Association of Park Directors, *Annual Information Exchange 1987.*

and licenses, investigates wildlife incidents, registers watercraft and performs numerous other activities. What is remarkable is that this department functions without state general funds. Its funding derives entirely from sales of licenses, tags, permits, registrations, taxes on watercraft, and federal funds. The Department's FY 1988 Annual Report indicates total revenues of $24,980,969 including federal funding of $6,797,090.

<table>
<tr><td colspan="7">Table 14-3
Arizona's Parks Compared to Other State Parks Systems, FY 1986</td></tr>
<tr><td>States</td><td>Total
Sites</td><td>Total
Acres</td><td>Sites Per
100,000
Population</td><td>Acres
Per
Capita</td><td>Campsites
Per 1,000
Population</td><td>Visitation
Per
Capita</td></tr>
<tr><td>Arizona</td><td>24</td><td>39,480</td><td>0.75</td><td>0.01</td><td>0.45</td><td>0.32</td></tr>
<tr><td>California</td><td>283</td><td>1,247,069</td><td>1.07</td><td>0.05</td><td>0.54</td><td>0.87</td></tr>
<tr><td>Colorado</td><td>61</td><td>328,178</td><td>1.89</td><td>0.10</td><td>0.76</td><td>2.39</td></tr>
<tr><td>Florida</td><td>133</td><td>272,351</td><td>1.17</td><td>0.02</td><td>0.25</td><td>0.97</td></tr>
<tr><td>Nevada</td><td>22</td><td>144,521</td><td>2.35</td><td>0.15</td><td>0.36</td><td>2.30</td></tr>
<tr><td>New Mexico</td><td>39</td><td>118,951</td><td>2.69</td><td>0.08</td><td>1.34</td><td>4.25</td></tr>
<tr><td>Oregon</td><td>2234</td><td>89,267</td><td>8.30</td><td>0.03</td><td>2.10</td><td>0.72</td></tr>
<tr><td>Texas</td><td>124</td><td>206,340</td><td>0.76</td><td>0.01</td><td>0.37</td><td>1.04</td></tr>
<tr><td>Utah</td><td>48</td><td>115,746</td><td>2.92</td><td>0.07</td><td>0.04</td><td>1.28</td></tr>
<tr><td>Washington</td><td>188</td><td>249,476</td><td>4.26</td><td>0.06</td><td>1.77</td><td>0.49</td></tr>
<tr><td>Comp States Avg</td><td>125</td><td>307,989</td><td>2.82</td><td>0.04</td><td>0.61</td><td>1.07</td></tr>
<tr><td>50 State Avg</td><td>119</td><td>274,524</td><td>2.49</td><td>0.06</td><td>0.76</td><td>1.06</td></tr>
<tr><td colspan="7">Source: National Association of Park Directors, Annual Information Exchange 1987.</td></tr>
</table>

Expenditures and revenues of the Game and Fish Department have shown steady growth in the 1980s. Federal funds have increased slightly as a percentage of total funding which is unusual in today's era of reduced federal funding. Game and Fish's organization and funding may be inadequate in the future to support fully nongame (not related to hunting, fishing or other fee supported) program needs. Wildlife or other programs without a substantial revenue source, or a strong mandate and organized support, tend to receive less attention in an agency that is geared to, and dependent on, programs funded primarily by hunting and fishing.

Game-related revenues are not tracking population growth in the state as a decreasing proportion of new arrivals are sportsmen, hunters, and fishers. Thus, revenues are flattening out just when nongame programs are becoming increasingly important. A 1985 survey by the U.S. Fish and Wildlife Service indicates 599,000 Arizonans either hunted or fished while 620,000 backpacked and 812,000 enjoyed camping. Presumably, the number of Arizonans that enjoy nongame species in "nonconsumptive" ways is several times higher than any of these figures. What may be equally important is the number of nonresidents visiting Arizona who are charmed back every year by the chance to see another quail, roadrunner or hawk.

Should nongame programs be funded with revenues from game-related activities? If wildlife is considered a socially owned resource, perhaps it should be treated as other resources, and scarcity rents should be collected from those who hunt and fish. The fees charged by private hunting preserves as well as the sometimes large queue of potential hunters seeking licenses suggest that at least some publicly regulated wildlife has a very high value. If the part of this value exceeding "production cost" of game related programs is viewed as an economic rent, then revenue from game-related sources could appropriately be used for non-game programs. The auctioning of hunting licenses (especially for elk) would be one method of capturing some of these rents.

The public favors increases in nongame programs. More than 80 percent of respondents to a 1988 Game and Fish survey (*Wildlife for Tomorrow*) favored expanded programs to preserve habitat from development. Considering Arizona has one of the most diverse wildlife populations in the United States, unique habitat areas such as riparian lands and mountain tops often constitute inexpensive yet extremely valuable natural resources. Even if current revenue sources are used for these new programs, it may be necessary to find additional funding. The nongame income tax check-off, which asks income tax filers for a voluntary contribution, is one such mechanism already in existence, but it has not been a very effective source of revenue. Few people are aware of the check-off especially those who rely on a tax preparation service. The check-off also gives people an incentive to be free riders. The non-game programs will be available to an individual with or without a contribution, and each person's contribution has a negligible effect on total funding.

The state's administrative structure has also retarded programs to protect habitat. The Arizona Natural Areas Program is operated by the State Parks Board which has no funding to support it, while the Game and Fish Department has funds but no authority. The result is summarized in the SCORP, *Natural Areas Study*, p. 141, as follows: "...while boasting some success in registering sites and working with Federal agencies, [this program] has been ineffective in long-term protection of natural areas ... only a single wholly privately-owned natural area has been registered with the state in the past twelve years."

This is one of several indications favoring reorganizing several (perhaps all) of the natural resources departments into an umbrella agency, a department of natural resources.

State Land Department

The State Land Department manages state trust lands and is required by the federal Enabling Act and the State Constitution to maximize the revenues from these lands for the trust beneficiaries. The beneficiaries include public schools, universities, and state hospitals. The operating budget of the Land Department ($6.84 million in 1988) is provided by annual legislative appropriations out of the general fund. Revenue from the trust fund is *not* used to operate the Department. This method of funding allows for significant annual oversight of agency operations by the legislative and executive branches of government which determine annual budget amounts.

Arizona's trust lands are an extremely valuable asset. There are 9.6 million acres scattered throughout the state with extensive holdings located near many Arizona cities and towns. The Federal Enabling Act and State Constitution provide for the lease and sale of these trust lands and resources to provide revenues for the designated programs.

Revenues from the sale of land or land-based assets such as minerals are deposited into a permanent fund which is invested to produce income. Investment income from the trust, along with revenues from the use of these lands, is made available to the trust beneficiaries on an annual basis. The Department sold an average of $22 million worth of land per year over the past ten years and earned over $50 million of current income in 1988 from its investments.

The Land Department has come under periodic scrutiny. The March 1989, *Report of the Governor's Oversight Committee on the State Land Department*, together with a September 1987 *Performance Audit* by the Auditor General, recommended a number of procedural changes, including the hiring of outside consultants to help evaluate proposed land transactions (sales and trades). It recommended improvement in dealing with trespassing on trust lands which often results in preventable or recoverable damages to the land. The Department apparently had only one trespass officer at the time of the audit, and he estimated that his work brought in $87,500 during fiscal 1986-87, more than twice his salary and related costs.

Policy Issues And Conclusions

<u>The Appropriate Use of User Charges and Fees</u>

Governmental provision of air and water quality programs and parks and recreation often lends itself readily to funding through user charges and fees. While many of the activities of the Department of Environmental Quality, the Department of Water Resources, Parks, and the Game and Fish Department are currently subject to charges and fees, not all possible charges and fees are currently utilized to their full potential. At the same time, natural resources expenditures illustrate the limits of user charge financing.

The ideal user fee taps those who are directly responsible for a problem, such as air pollution, or who directly benefit from a program, such as a park visit. Indirect contributors to a problem or beneficiaries of a service should bear some of the costs in proportion to their indirect contribution to the problem or benefit from the service. All water users, for example, should bear the costs of water programs while special recreation facility users should bear a reasonable portion of facility operation and maintenance costs. For a user fee system to be feasible there must be an identifiable user group of sufficient size to make the program cover a significant portion of day-to-day operating and maintenance costs; a measurable benefit that can be readily denied to those unwilling to pay the fee; ease of enforcement; and political acceptance.

User fees or taxes based on benefits received can improve governmental efficiency by providing a direct measure of demand for individual services. If the demand for a service goes up, the agency providing it receives more funds and can expand. Conversely, if demand falls, so will revenue and the agency will be forced to reduce service levels. When user charges are feasible, they provide a clear signal of people's shifting demands for specific services. In the absence of user charges, agencies may attempt to provide as much service as people want to use for free thus extending service levels when the cost of added services far exceeds the extra benefit.

Many recent Federal programs mandate user fees to improve efficiency. This Federal policy has forced the establishment of user fees by many state and local agencies. All of these user fees are earmarked for the program that mandates them. For instance, all sewer user fees must go for wastewater programs. However, among state agencies reviewed here, some have state mandated user fees that are turned over to the General Fund and are not linked to department appropriations. In several instances it is apparent that greater revenue collections could be obtained from current fees if departments responsible for collecting each revenue source received at least part of the resulting income. This policy would give program managers an incentive to be more attentive to revenue enhancement efforts because their programs would thereby receive increased funding.

There has been some movement toward the use of fees and charges that are dedicated to specific natural resource and environmental programs. The Department of Game and Fish, for instance, is entirely funded with fees, grants and contributions. The Department of Environmental Quality uses an air quality fee for special air quality projects. The State Parks Board administers the State Lake Improvement Fund which provides for marine capital improvement funding out of marine fuel taxes.

While there are additional opportunities for user fees for these and other departments, user fees are not appropriate for many of the services provided. For example, it is not possible to identify all polluters of water and air nor all individuals who benefit from wilderness preservation. A good example of a pure public good, for which it is impossible to exclude those who do not pay from enjoying the good, is the sight of a hawk soaring overhead. The inability to identify the affected group and to exclude those who do not pay renders the use of charges and fees ineffective. Programs not conducive to user charge financing include wildlife habitat preservation, endangered species programs, beautification of highways and publicly owned lands and wilderness, and clean-up of illegal waste disposal. For these environmental and recreational services, general taxes funded by the entire population are appropriate.

Fees which are viewed as excessively high may also generate perverse incentives. Campground fees, for example, may result in overuse and consequent deterioration of non-fee areas. Similarly, high fees for waste disposal may result in increased "wildcat" dumping with its resulting environmental degradation. This problem is sufficiently serious that several Arizona counties have hired full-time staff to locate illegal dumping, fine and prosecute the perpetrators, and supervise clean-up efforts.

The use of fees may also conflict with the goal of equitable availability of some governmental services. Fees for the use of parks, for example, may cause some low income families to stay away. Equity concerns have frequently prevented a more widespread imposition of user charges and resulted in many fees being set far below the cost of providing the service.

Policy Options

The Groundwater Withdrawal Fee

Arizona is in a position to provide both water program funding and improved performance in attainment of a major state goal: water conservation. The current fee for withdrawal of groundwater is minuscule in comparison with the costs of alternative sources of water. A much more significant fee or tax on pumped or transferred groundwater would provide incentives for conservation of this scarce water supply and would provide funding for related programs. With increased prices, water users are well known to increase the efficiency of use and consume less water. The revenue from a groundwater withdrawal fee could be tied to conservation programs and water quality programs (Department of Water Resources and Department of Environmental Quality).

Gasoline Tax for Department of Environmental Quality Programs

In accord with the logic of user fees, tax revenues generated by an activity that causes the need for a program are often earmarked for the program. California has created a Motor Vehicle Account that is funded by motor vehicle related fees and taxes. It is used to fund a variety of programs such as the Highway Patrol, the Department of Motor Vehicles, Highway Construction, and the Air Resources Board. The Air Resources Board must justify its budget request for Motor Vehicle Account funds, but it is eligible to receive such funds. In Arizona, this would be somewhat equivalent to the Highway User Revenue Fund (HURF), but the uses of the fund in Arizona are much more limited. If HURF were funded with additional gas taxes and its disbursement formula readjusted, it could fund a substantial part of Department of Environmental Quality or other program areas. It is a large, stable source of revenues that could reasonably be diverted to motor vehicle/environment-related programs such as air quality programs.

Funding Nongame and Wildlife Habitat Programs

Programs in the Parks and Game and Fish departments that are concerned with preservation of wildlife and wilderness areas cannot be funded with user charges and fees due to the nonexclusive nature of these public goods. Current nongame programs in these departments do not have a steady source of revenue, and it is clear that the fees and permits collected under the game programs are likely to fall relative to the demand for nongame programs. Earmarking a general tax (or portion thereof) for nongame programs may be justified.

Use Parks Admission Fees for Operating Expense Not Capital

Parks admissions fees are currently deposited in a fund for purchase and development of parks. These fees would more logically be used to fund operations since operating cost can be expected to be somewhat related to usage and, therefore, to fee revenue. In contrast, operating expenses are funded by general fund appropriations. This situation often leads to a problem with parks systems, where it is politically expedient to provide more parks to constituents but very difficult to increase "soft" operation and maintenance funds from competitive sources.

Summary

The Natural Resource programs of Arizona state government, like those of many other states, are very likely to require substantial increases in funding in real terms in the decade to come. With increasing public awareness of environmental problems, the pressure on existing programs and resources will continue to increase. For example, the Department of Environmental Quality administers a number of health-related mandates that are being strengthened by the Environmental Protection Agency and may be enforced by the courts as in the past. These programs are likely to expand dramatically over the next ten years following the pattern set by the air quality programs in Southern California.

Population growth will put additional pressures on many environmental programs. Recreationists' demands for substantial new camping and hiking facilities are likely to exceed significantly the growth rate of many rapidly growing states, including Arizona's. Rural interests, focusing on economic development, will continue to push for more park facilities in their own areas.

Arizona is in a position to be a leader in adopting funding mechanisms that could improve the efficiency of natural resource and environmental programs. It is also within the grasp of today's leaders to improve Arizona's environmental and natural resource programs to offset past and present wasteful behavior and to pass a generous endowment of environmental amenities on to future generations. The alternative is to remain behind in a competitive sense and eventually be forced to play catch-up with other states that exercised greater foresight in providing environmental services to their residents.

Chapter 15

Public Safety and Criminal Justice

Michael Ormiston

Governments are organizations created to exercise control over individuals living together in a society and to finance and provide essential goods and services. One of the most basic functions of government is the provision of *public safety*. In most societies, the provision of public safety entails the enforcement of laws and contracts as well as the administration of justice through a system of courts and the punishment and/or restraint of criminals. Government power is used to establish and enforce the rules that regulate the social interaction of individuals. The existence of rules that establish law and order are essential for the production and exchange of goods and services in a free enterprise economy as well as for the security and well being of individuals. In Arizona, public safety is primarily provided by three government agencies: the Department of Public Safety (DPS), the Department of Corrections (DOC), and the Arizona Judiciary. In this chapter we analyze the expenditure patterns of these three departments and we discuss the impact of recent policy changes on these expenditures.

The Rationale For Government Involvement

A society could not function well with several different private entities establishing and enforcing different sets of rules in the same geographic area. Citizens in a given society must agree to be subject to one set of laws. Thus, it is appropriate for public safety to be produced by one provider. Government serves as a fairly well-accepted single provider that is responsive to citizens' desires for services and equity.

There are additional reasons for government involvement in public safety. Economists consider public safety to be a *public good*. The basic difference between a public good and other types of goods and services is that a public good is consumed by all persons whether or not they pay for it. It is impossible, or at least very costly, to provide a public good for a single individual's benefit. For example, if the highway patrol removes hazards from the road, it is impossible to prevent a single, non-paying motorist from benefiting from that service.

Why must government be involved in the provision of public goods such as public safety? If the provision of public safety is left to private markets, not enough public safety will be provided from society's point of view. This is because when one individual decides how much public safety to purchase, he/she considers only the benefits he/she receives from public safety and does not take into account the benefits others receive. An individual hiring his/her own police force will consider only the benefits he/she receives when deciding how many police officers to hire and will not consider the benefits received by others. As a result, from society's point of view, too few officers will be hired. To resolve this problem, government is needed to ensure that the appropriate amount of public safety is provided for its citizens.

In addition, because many people benefit from public safety services, under a private system each person would have an incentive to withhold his/her own financial support for public safety services. This would be a rational option since the individual could benefit from public safety services that other people have purchased without spending any of his/her own resources. This *free rider* phenomenon would exacerbate the under-provision of public safety and could result in an unfair distribution of the burden of supporting public safety services. Thus, it is desirable for government to allocate the benefits as well as the costs of public safety.

Federal, State and Local Roles

In the United States there are three basic levels of government each with its own powers to provide services and raise revenues: federal, state, and local. A multilevel governing system such as this raises an important question. What is the best way to allocate responsibilities for the provision of public safety among each level of government?

In general, the level of government best suited for the provision of public safety depends on which citizens benefit from the good or service being provided. The federal government should undertake the provision of goods that have benefits collectively consumed on the national level. For example, the federal government supplies national defense since all citizens, regardless of state or locality, collectively benefit from it. Similarly, state and local governments should undertake the provision of those goods and services whose benefits are collectively consumed by citizens within a certain geographical area. For example, public safety services that usually result in locally consumed collective benefits are police and fire protection, municipal courts, and local jails and prisons. Public safety services that usually result in collective benefits consumed state-wide are highway patrols, state courts, and state correctional facilities.

The primary advantage of local, state, and federal supply of public safety services is that it allows each level of government to accommodate the particular desires of its citizens. The more decentralized the government, the easier it is to accommodate the particular needs of the population. However, diversifying the responsibility of providing public safety between local, state, and federal governments can also lead to inefficiencies. A lack of coordination between jurisdictions may lead to duplication of services as well as inconsistent application of rules and regulations. Furthermore, government provision of public safety on a small scale can result in higher per-unit costs because scale economies cannot be realized.

The Crisis In Corrections

Perhaps the most pressing public safety issue facing policy makers today is the tug-of-war being waged between the proponents of fiscal conservatism and the proponents of a "get tough" criminal justice system.

Responding to the public outcry condemning the ever increasing rate of violent and drug-related crimes, state legislatures across the nation have enacted tougher sentencing practices in an attempt to deter the commission of crimes, keep criminals off the streets longer, and enhance consistency in sentencing and prison time served. However, these new practices are being threatened by a shortage of prison beds and the high costs of supporting an expanding prison population. Legislatures have become increasingly reluctant to devote resources to the construction of new prisons and the renovation of old facilities.

Today the "crisis in corrections" has reached a critical level. By the end of 1984, state prison systems were being operated at 112 percent of capacity; that is, 382,000 people were being held in state prison facilities that were designed to hold 341,989 inmates. In fact, in 1984 nearly every state prison system in the U.S. was operating at or above capacity (United States Department of Justice, 1984).

The situation has continued to deteriorate. At the end of 1987 the state prison systems were being operated at 120 percent of capacity while more than 40,000 people were being held in a federal prison system designed to hold 29,000 inmates (*The Wall Street Journal*, March 21, 1989). Recently, California increased the capacity of its prison system, the largest in the country, to 49,767 inmates; unfortunately, there are more than 86,000 people currently being held in California prisons (*New York Times*, November 26, 1989).

Corrections departments in many states are under extreme pressure to relieve prison crowding. In more than half the states at least one prison facility is being operated under a court order to reduce prison crowding.

The situation in the State of Arizona is much the same. In April of 1989, the Arizona Department of Corrections was operating at 102 percent of capacity. At this time, the department reported an adult prison capacity of 12,280 and an adult inmate population of 12,415 with an additional 153 people held in county jails awaiting admission to state facilities.

Why has prison overcrowding been allowed to reach such a critical level? Building and operating state prison facilities is very costly. In Arizona, the average new bed construction cost is about $36,000 per bed and annual operating expenses are over $17,000 per inmate. In fiscal year 1986/87 state governments' expenditures on corrections accounted for 51 percent of their total justice system expenditures and in Arizona they accounted for 61 percent of the total. Legislators are becoming more and more reluctant to ask taxpayers for the additional revenues needed to fund prison systems.

The lack of taxpayer willingness to bear the costs of a "get tough" criminal justice system is beginning to cause many states to re-evaluate mandatory sentencing policies, to tailor sentencing to available prison resources, and to examine alternatives to incarceration.

Interstate Comparisons Of Public Safety Expenditures

In order to make meaningful interstate comparisons of public safety expenditures, it is necessary to use a data source that is consistent across states. The most consistent data concerning public safety expenditures are compiled by the U.S. Bureau of the Census and the U.S. Department of Justice. Tables 15-1 and 15-2 present data on state and local public safety expenditures for selected fiscal years.

Table 15-1 reports total state and local expenditures per capita for the United States as a whole, Arizona, and comparison states in 1979 and 1987. The data indicate that Arizona's total public safety expenditures per capita were about 20 percent above average in

1979 with police protection and protective inspection and regulation the categories most above average. By 1987, Arizona's expenditures per capita had risen to nearly 26 percent above average. Police protection remained high above the U.S. average, but inspection and regulation expenditures were about average in 1987. Arizona corrections and judicial expenditures both experienced large increases relative to the U.S. average during the period. Corrections grew from 17 to 45 percent above average, while the judicial system grew from 4 to 32 percent above average. Of the comparison states, California and Nevada spent more per capita than Arizona in both years, Colorado spent more than Arizona in 1979 but less in 1987, and New Mexico, Texas, and Utah spent less than Arizona in both years.

Table 15-1
State and Local Government Public Safety Expenditures
($ Per Capita)

1978/79

	Judicial	Police	Corrections	Fire	Inspection and Regulation	Total
Total U.S.	$13.44	$54.36	$24.64	$22.92	$9.24	$124.61
Arizona	13.94	72.57	28.79	20.68	13.39	149.37
California	15.30	69.84	36.41	31.93	15.79	169.28
Colorado	14.12	55.25	23.66	22.71	7.79	123.53
Florida	13.37	64.61	25.58	23.34	9.11	136.01
Nevada	19.27	85.10	41.05	41.57	22.48	209.47
New Mexico	10.01	47.39	23.35	19.07	9.11	108.92
Texas	9.92	40.94	14.65	18.07	6.01	89.59
Utah	10.31	44.30	17.75	17.18	9.51	99.04
AZ % US	103.7	133.5	116.8	90.2	144.9	119.9

1986/87

	Judicial	Police	Corrections	Fire	Inspection and Regulation	Total
Total U.S.	$41.52	$101.42	$68.35	$44.82	$18.16	$274.27
Arizona	54.95	128.43	99.20	43.55	19.00	345.13
California	60.06	144.91	108.67	77.08	39.18	429.90
Colorado	45.27	117.01	59.32	44.00	15.02	280.61
Florida	46.52	123.59	74.41	45.66	20.11	310.31
Nevada	67.30	134.88	119.74	78.04	47.09	447.05
New Mexico	39.69	95.26	69.62	34.18	17.98	256.71
Texas	29.59	82.12	49.59	36.60	12.16	210.06
Utah	31.12	82.25	60.08	29.16	15.12	217.73
AZ % US	132.3	126.6	145.1	97.2	104.6	125.8

Sources: *Government Finances*, U.S. Bureau of the Census and *State and Metropolitan Area Data Handbook*, 1982, U.S. Bureau of the Census.

Table 15-1 illustrates that, nationally, police protection dominates the public safety category with corrections second at about 70 percent of the police expenditure level. The 1987 pattern was similar in Arizona with corrections expenditures reaching approximately 77 percent of police expenditures.

Table 15-2 reports per capita public safety expenditures made by state government only. As the table shows, Arizona state government also spends more than average on public safety. Looking at expenditures by category, Arizona is far above average for corrections and police, and about average for inspections and regulation. For judicial expenditures, however, the state spent only 65.8 percent of the national average in 1987. Arizona's per capita state expenditures were the highest of any comparison state for both police and corrections as well as for total public safety expenditures.

<table>
<tr><td colspan="6">Table 15-2
State Government Public Safety Expenditures
($ Per Capita)</td></tr>
<tr><td colspan="6">1986/87</td></tr>
<tr><td></td><td>Judicial</td><td>Police</td><td>Corrections</td><td>Inspection and Regulation</td><td>Total (Excl. Fire)</td></tr>
<tr><td>Total U.S.</td><td>$17.61</td><td>$16.63</td><td>$48.08</td><td>$12.02</td><td>$94.35</td></tr>
<tr><td>Arizona</td><td>11.58</td><td>24.35</td><td>73.74</td><td>12.12</td><td>121.79</td></tr>
<tr><td>California</td><td>6.89</td><td>22.07</td><td>67.09</td><td>22.53</td><td>118.57</td></tr>
<tr><td>Colorado</td><td>24.23</td><td>15.35</td><td>38.43</td><td>9.75</td><td>87.76</td></tr>
<tr><td>Florida</td><td>21.57</td><td>17.22</td><td>42.27</td><td>10.89</td><td>91.95</td></tr>
<tr><td>Nevada</td><td>8.92</td><td>12.23</td><td>57.63</td><td>32.60</td><td>111.38</td></tr>
<tr><td>New Mexico</td><td>32.94</td><td>18.61</td><td>52.57</td><td>13.52</td><td>117.64</td></tr>
<tr><td>Texas</td><td>5.48</td><td>8.64</td><td>31.18</td><td>7.60</td><td>52.89</td></tr>
<tr><td>Utah</td><td>15.77</td><td>15.67</td><td>52.20</td><td>12.55</td><td>96.19</td></tr>
<tr><td>AZ % US</td><td>65.8</td><td>146.4</td><td>153.4</td><td>100.8</td><td>129.1</td></tr>
</table>

Note: State Government expenditures include amounts that are passed through to local governments.

Source: *State Government Finances*, U.S. Bureau of the Census.

Table 15-3 reveals that the state contribution to total state and local public safety expenditures in Arizona was about average in 1987 at 40 percent. All of the comparison states except Utah and New Mexico exhibited a lower share of state financing. Arizona's state share of judicial expenditures was 21 percent only half of the U.S. average share. This explains Arizona's low standing on state judicial expenditures per capita despite its above-average total state and local judicial spending. State shares of judiciary expenditures exhibited the widest range of any category among the comparison states with Arizona, California, Nevada, and Texas below average; and Colorado, Florida, New Mexico, and Utah above. States contributed the largest share of financing in the corrections and inspection and regulation categories providing an average of 70 percent and 66 percent respectively.

Table 15-3
State Government Public Safety Expenditures
as a Share of Total State and Local Public Safety Expenditures
(percentages)

1986/87

	Judicial	Police	Corrections	Inspection and Regulation	Total (Excl.Fire)
Total U.S.	42.2	16.4	70.3	66.2	41.1
Arizona	21.1	19.0	74.3	63.8	40.4
California	11.5	15.2	61.7	57.5	33.6
Colorado	53.5	13.1	64.8	64.9	37.1
Florida	46.4	13.9	56.8	54.1	34.7
Nevada	13.2	9.1	48.1	69.2	30.2
New Mexico	83.0	19.5	75.5	75.2	52.9
Texas	18.5	10.5	62.9	62.5	30.5
Utah	50.7	19.0	86.9	83.0	51.0

Note: State Government expenditures include amounts that are passed through to local governments.

Source: *State Government Finances* and *Government Finances*, U.S. Bureau of the Census.

It is useful to ask whether there is some justification for Arizona spending significantly more than average on public safety. Are there characteristics of the state that require greater levels of public safety spending? In fact, as shown in Table 15-4, Arizona has a high crime rate especially in property crime. In 1987, Arizona's property crime rate was 33 percent above the national average. Arizona's violent crime rate was about average and lower than that of California, Florida, Nevada, New Mexico, and Texas. Compared to violent crimes, property crimes make up a much larger portion of total crime rates. Arizona's total crime rate was 30 percent above average.

Thus, it appears that Arizona's higher-than-average public safety expenditures are driven, at least in part, by above-average crime rates. Of the comparison states, only Florida and Texas had higher total crime rates than Arizona in 1987. It is also likely that other state characteristics not considered here such as geography and visitor traffic, policy decisions on crimes, and political tastes for security, affect public safety expenditures.

<table>
<tr><td colspan="4" align="center">Table 15-4
1987 Crimes Rates
(Crimes Per 100,000 Population)</td></tr>
<tr><td></td><td align="center">Violent
Crime</td><td align="center">Property
Crime</td><td align="center">Total</td></tr>
<tr><td>U.S.</td><td align="center">609</td><td align="center">4,940</td><td align="center">5,550</td></tr>
<tr><td>Arizona</td><td align="center">612</td><td align="center">6,576</td><td align="center">7,189</td></tr>
<tr><td>California</td><td align="center">918</td><td align="center">5,588</td><td align="center">6,506</td></tr>
<tr><td>Colorado</td><td align="center">468</td><td align="center">5,984</td><td align="center">6,451</td></tr>
<tr><td>Florida</td><td align="center">1,024</td><td align="center">7,479</td><td align="center">8,503</td></tr>
<tr><td>Nevada</td><td align="center">695</td><td align="center">5,675</td><td align="center">6,371</td></tr>
<tr><td>New Mexico</td><td align="center">628</td><td align="center">5,919</td><td align="center">6,547</td></tr>
<tr><td>Texas</td><td align="center">632</td><td align="center">7,091</td><td align="center">7,722</td></tr>
<tr><td>Utah</td><td align="center">230</td><td align="center">5,388</td><td align="center">5,619</td></tr>
<tr><td>Arizona % of U.S.</td><td align="center">100.5</td><td align="center">133.1</td><td align="center">129.5</td></tr>
<tr><td colspan="4">Note: The sum of violent and property crime rates may not add to total due to rounding.</td></tr>
<tr><td colspan="4">Source: Statistical Abstract of the U.S., U.S. Bureau of the Census.</td></tr>
</table>

Public Safety Expenditures In Arizona

Table 15-5 presents data on actual expenditures made by the Department of Public Safety (DPS), the Department of Corrections (DOC), and the Arizona Judiciary in total during the past ten years. Column two of the table displays expenditures in nominal dollars; that is, the data in column two have not been adjusted for inflation. Column three displays these expenditures as a percentage of total state general fund expenditures. Column four displays these expenditures in real 1988 dollars, and column five displays real per capita public safety expenditures.

The data in Table 15-5 show that nominal expenditures on public safety have increased from $85 million in fiscal year 1978-79 to $325 million in fiscal year 1987-88. This represents an average increase of 16 percent per year. However, focusing on nominal expenditures gives a distorted view of what has actually happened to public safety expenditures in Arizona because nominal figures do not account for inflation or population growth. As also shown in Table 15-5, real expenditures on public safety have increased from $141 million in fiscal year 1978-79 to $325 million in fiscal year 1987-88. This is an average increase of 9.7 percent per year. In addition, real per capita expenditures have grown from $53.58 in 1979 to $93.00 in 1988, an average annual increase of 6.3 percent.

The data in Table 15-5 also indicate that public safety expenditures have grown faster than the state budget as a whole. The share of state funds devoted to public safety has risen modestly from 8.3 percent in FY 1978-79 to 12.4% in FY 1987-88. Note, however, that most of this increase has occurred in the last four years.

<table>
<tr><td colspan="5">Table 15-5
State Government Public Safety Expenditures in Arizona</td></tr>
<tr><td>Fiscal
Year</td><td>Nominal
Expenditures
(millions)</td><td>Share of Total
General Fund
Expenditures</td><td>Real
Expenditures
(millions)</td><td>Per Capita
Real
Expenditures</td></tr>
<tr><td>(1)</td><td>(2)</td><td>(3)</td><td>(4)</td><td>(5)</td></tr>
<tr><td>1978-79</td><td>$ 85.303</td><td>8.3%</td><td>$141.232</td><td>$53.58</td></tr>
<tr><td>1979-80</td><td>100.040</td><td>8.9%</td><td>143.837</td><td>52.55</td></tr>
<tr><td>1980-81</td><td>124.307</td><td>8.5%</td><td>162.058</td><td>57.51</td></tr>
<tr><td>1981-82</td><td>154.854</td><td>9.8%</td><td>191.694</td><td>66.31</td></tr>
<tr><td>1982-83</td><td>159.517</td><td>9.0%</td><td>194.462</td><td>65.63</td></tr>
<tr><td>1983-84</td><td>179.271</td><td>9.3%</td><td>206.600</td><td>67.36</td></tr>
<tr><td>1984-85</td><td>213.522</td><td>10.0%</td><td>234.387</td><td>73.48</td></tr>
<tr><td>1985-86</td><td>254.434</td><td>11.1%</td><td>275.522</td><td>83.09</td></tr>
<tr><td>1986-87</td><td>297.704</td><td>12.5%</td><td>309.818</td><td>90.62</td></tr>
<tr><td>1987-88</td><td>325.230</td><td>12.4%</td><td>325.230</td><td>93.00</td></tr>
<tr><td>Average
Annual
Increase
1979-88</td><td>16.0%</td><td></td><td>9.7%</td><td>6.3%</td></tr>
</table>

Note: Real figures are in 1988 dollars. Amounts include state operating expenditures of the Department of Public Safety and the Department of Corrections and total State expenditures on the judicial system.

Source: Department of Administration *Annual Financial Reports*, Joint Legislative Budget Committee *Appropriations Reports*, The Arizona Courts *Judicial Reports*, Department of Corrections *Data Handbook for the Symposium on Corrections*.

In order to understand what factors have contributed to the rise in real expenditures on public safety, it is necessary to investigate the historical pattern of expenditures of each of these three departments individually.

The Arizona Department of Public Safety

The Arizona Department of Public Safety was established in 1969. This Department consists of five bureaus: Criminal Investigation, Highway Patrol, Administration,

Telecommunications, and Criminal Justice Support. DPS's primary responsibilities are to monitor Arizona's highways; to enforce Arizona's criminal statutes, including the areas of narcotics, organized crime, and liquor distribution; and to provide investigative assistance to local, county, state, and federal criminal justice agencies.

Table 15-6 presents data on actual expenditures made by DPS from state appropriated funds during the past ten years. Over the period, expenditures made by DPS have increased from $39 million to $75 million. This is an average increase of 7.6 percent per year. Real expenditures, on the other hand, have increased from $53 million to $63 million. This represents an average increase of only 1.8 percent per year. In fact, from FY 1986-87 to FY 1987-88 real expenditures made by DPS fell by more than $1 million.

Table 15-6
Arizona Department of Public Safety Operating Expenditures

Fiscal Year	Nominal Expenditures (millions)	Real Expenditures (millions)	Per Capita Real Expenditures
1978-79	$38.735	$53.354	$24.33
1979-80	41.557	49.708	21.83
1980-81	50.881	55.185	23.54
1981-82	57.853	59.581	24.77
1982-83	54.888	55.667	22.58
1983-84	59.866	57.398	22.49
1984-85	65.364	59.693	22.49
1985-86	70.924	63.895	23.16
1986-87	73.878	63.964	22.49
1987-88	75.191	62.555	21.50
Average Annual Increase 1979-88	7.6%	1.8%	-1.4%

Note: Real Figures are in 1988 dollars.

Source: State of Arizona, *Appropriations Report*, Joint Legislative Budget Committee.

In addition, real DPS expenditures per capita have been relatively constant over the last ten years. They were at their ten-year low point in 1988 at $21.50 which is $3.27 below the ten-year high reached in 1982.

The Arizona Department of Corrections

The primary responsibility of DOC is to serve and protect the citizens of the State by imprisoning those individuals legally committed to the Department. The department consists of six divisions: Administration, Inspections and Investigations, Adult Institutions,

Juvenile/Community Services, Human Resources/Development, and Arizona Correctional Industries. The Legislature and the Governor recently enacted a law to establish Juvenile Correctional Services as an independent agency, effective July 1, 1990.

Table 15-7 presents data on real and nominal expenditures made by DOC during the past ten years. Nominal expenditures have increased from $41 million in FY 1978-79 to $206 million in FY 1987-88. This is an average increase of 19.6 percent per year. Real expenditures have increased from $68 million to $206 million. This represents an average increase of approximately 13.1 percent per year. Real per capita expenditures more than doubled during the period growing from $25.87 to $58.94.

Table 15-7 Arizona Department of Corrections Operating Expenditures			
Fiscal Year	Nominal Expenditures (millions)	Real Expenditures (millions)	Per Capita Real Expenditures
1978-79	$ 41.185	$ 68.188	$25.87
1979-80	50.425	72.501	26.49
1980-81	66.292	86.424	30.67
1981-82	88.733	109.843	37.99
1982-83	95.484	116.401	39.28
1983-84	109.204	125.852	41.03
1984-85	133.707	146.772	46.01
1985-86	163.368	176.908	53.35
1986-87	190.013	197.745	57.84
1987-88	206.129	206.129	58.94
Average Annual Increase 1979-88	19.6%	13.1%	9.6%

Note: Real Figures are in 1988 dollars.

Source: Arizona Department of Corrections, *Data Handbook for the Symposium on Corrections*.

While Table 15-7 indicates that corrections expenditures have grown dramatically, Table 15-8 reveals that the state has actually reduced the amount spent per inmate. The data in Table 15-8 display DOC expenditures per inmate in both real and nominal terms. As Table 15-8 indicates, the average daily population of Arizona's state prisons has increased approximately 14.5 percent per year for the past ten years with the largest annual increase coming between 1981 and 1982. However, the data also show that real expenditures per inmate have actually fallen over the past ten years from a high of $16,139 in FY 1978-79 to $14,418 in FY 1987-88. This result clearly indicates that the increase in DOC expenditures is due primarily to the increase in the prison population and that, in real terms, DOC has been able to contain operating costs per inmate.

If DOC expenditures have been driven by the increase in prison population, then it is important to ask what factors have been responsible for the increase in prison population. While many factors affect the rate of growth of the State's prison population, perhaps the most important factors have been the changes made to the criminal code in the late 1970's and the corresponding enactment of mandatory sentencing. These changes include the establishment of pre-determined sentences for specific crimes requiring incarceration for certain convictions and also requiring sentences of specific lengths. These changes may have had an impact both on the likelihood of convicted persons being sent to prison and on the length of time they stay there. Because the distribution of sentence lengths affects the size of the prison population for many years, it is quite possible that the effects of mandatory sentencing will not be fully played out until the mid or late 1990s.

Table 15-8
Arizona Department of Corrections Operating Expenditures Per Inmate

Fiscal Year	Average Daily Population	Nominal Expenditures Per Inmate	Real Expenditures Per Inmate
1978-79	3,515	$11,717	$16,139
1979-80	3,716	13,570	16.232
1980-81	4,042	16,401	17,788
1981-82	5,218	17,005	17,513
1982-83	6,209	15,378	15,597
1983-84	7,369	14,819	14,208
1984-85	8,468	15,790	14,420
1985-86	9,064	18,024	16,238
1986-87	10,404	18,263	15,812
1987-88	11,894	17,330	14,418

Note: Average daily population includes both adult and juvenile prisoners.

Source: Arizona Department of Corrections, *Data Handbook for the Symposium on Corrections*

We can get some idea of the impact of mandatory sentencing legislation on prison population by regressing average daily population in Arizona's state prison facilities, ADPADC, on average daily population lagged one year, ADPADC(-1), and a dummy variable, D. The dummy variable reflects the implementation of the mandatory sentencing legislation in 1982; that is, it is one from 1982 on and zero otherwise. The data used in the regression are for fiscal years 1972-73 to 1987-88 and the results are reported in Exhibit 15-1 below.

Both regressors are positive and significant and explain over 99 percent of the variation in average daily population. The coefficient on the dummy variable, D, indicates that mandatory sentencing caused the prison population to increase an average of 760 inmates (or about 14 percent) per year. Since from 1981-82 to 1987-88 average real expenditures per inmate were $18,000 per year, this result implies that if mandatory sentencing had not been implemented, then the state would have saved $13.7 million per year in expenditures on Corrections.

<table>
<tr><td colspan="3">Exhibit 15-1
Arizona's State Prison Population</td></tr>
<tr><td colspan="3">Ordinary Least Squares Estimation

Dependent Variable: ADPADC
16 observations used for estimation from 1973 to 1988</td></tr>
<tr><td>Regressor</td><td>Coefficient</td><td>t-Statistic</td></tr>
<tr><td>C
ADPADC(-1)
D</td><td>134.33
1.03
759.95</td><td>1.01
26.50
3.68</td></tr>
<tr><td>R-Squared
DW-statistic
Mean of Dependent Variable</td><td colspan="2">0.99
1.99
5,380.30</td></tr>
</table>

Once the system has experienced the full effect of mandatory sentencing and other factors that have been driving prison population growth, prison population will reach its new steady state level and prison population growth from that point on should be approximately equal to state population growth (or growth in male population aged 17-25, the portion of the population most linked to criminal activity).

The Arizona Judicial System

The judicial branch of the Arizona government consists of the Arizona Supreme Court, the Court of Appeals, the Superior Court, and the Justices of the Peace and Municipal Courts. The Arizona Supreme Court consists of five justices and has administrative authority over all courts in the state. The Supreme Court's constitutional authority includes appellate review, the issuance of extraordinary writs, and the power to makes rules concerning procedural matters in all courts.

The Court of Appeals has two divisions. Division One consists of twelve judges and is located in Phoenix; Division Two consists of five judges and is located in Tucson. The Court of Appeals reviews matters appealed from the Superior Court except for criminal cases involving sentences of life imprisonment or death which are appealed directly to the Supreme Court.

The Superior Court is a trial court with general jurisdiction and is empowered to hear cases involving real property, civil claims of $2,500 or more, felonies and misdemeanors, probate matters, and dissolution or annulment of marriage. As of June 30, 1988 the Superior Court consisted of 101 judges.

Justices of the Peace and Municipal Courts have jurisdiction to hear class 1, 2, and 3 misdemeanor cases and to conduct preliminary investigations of felonies. Traffic violation cases and civil lawsuits account for much of the caseloads of these courts.

The Arizona judiciary is funded mainly by state and local governments. Municipal funds support the Municipal Courts, county funds support Justice of the Peace courts, and state funds support the Supreme Court and the Court of Appeals. Funding for the Superior Court comes from both the State and the counties. Table 15-9 presents data on statewide judicial expenditures. Over the past ten years the state has played an increasing role in funding the Arizona judiciary. This has resulted from the State choosing to increase its fiscal support for the probation programs of the Superior Court. Thus, the state share of total funding increased from 10 percent to 25 percent over the past ten years, while the county share decreased from 74 percent to 60 percent. Total Judicial system nominal expenditures increased at an average annual rate of 14.4 percent, while total expenditures in real terms grew at an average rate of 8.2 percent.

Table 15-9
State, County, Municipal, and Federal Funds as a Percentage of Total Expenditures of the Arizona Judicial System

Fiscal Year	State Funds	County Funds (%)	Municipal Funds (%)	Federal Funds (%)	Total Funds (millions)
1978-79	10.4	73.5	11.9	4.2	$ 52.0
1979-80	12.4	71.1	12.1	4.4	65.4
1980-81	10.2	74.0	13.2	2.6	69.5
1981-82	10.7	73.5	13.2	2.6	77.4
1982-83	10.3	73.4	13.9	2.4	88.5
1983-84	10.8	73.3	15.1	0.8	94.6
1984-85	13.5	70.2	16.0	0.3	107.8
1985-86	15.1	66.9	17.5	0.5	132.8
1986-87	22.2	62.5	14.9	0.5	152.5
1987-88	25.0	59.5	15.0	0.5	175.3

Note: Includes both capital and operating expenditures.

Source: The Arizona Courts, *Judicial Reports*.

Table 15-10 presents data on state funds expended by the Arizona Judiciary. Nominal expenditures have increased from $5 million in FY 1978-79 to $44 million in FY 1987-88. This is an average increase of over 26 percent per year. Real expenditures have increased from $9 million to $44 million which is an average increase of 19.4 percent per year. Real per capita state Judicial expenditures in 1988 were more than three and a half times the 1979 amount.

Table 15-10			
State Expenditures of the Arizona Judicial System			
Fiscal Year	**Nominal Expenditures (millions)**	**Real Expenditures (millions)**	**Per Capita Real Expenditures**
1978-79	$ 5.383	$ 8.912	$ 3.38
1979-80	8.058	11.586	4.23
1980-81	7.134	9.300	3.30
1981-82	8.268	10.235	3.54
1982-83	9.145	11.148	3.76
1983-84	10.201	11.756	3.83
1984-85	14.451	15.863	4.97
1985-86	20.142	21.811	6.58
1986-87	33.813	35.189	10.29
1987-88	43.910	43.910	12.56
Average Annual Increase 1979-88	26.3%	19.4%	15.7%
Note: Real Figures are in 1988 dollars.			
Source: The Arizona Courts, *Judicial Reports*.			

The bulk of the increase in state judicial expenditures has occurred during the last four fiscal years. This is due primarily to the implementation of several special programs affecting probation services. These programs include State Aid For Probation Services, State Aid Enhancement, Adult and Juvenile Intensive Probation Supervision, and the Juvenile Probation Services Fund. Table 15-11 displays the annual state expenditures on these programs since 1984, which have grown from virtual nonexistence to almost $26 million in 1988.

The Juvenile Probation Services Fund was created in 1987 by combining an existing court program with a program that had previously been funded in the budget of the Department of Economic Security. The majority of funding for this program supports the placement of children in residential settings as an alternative to commitment to DOC. In FY 1987-88, expenditures on this program were $12.3 million.

The Adult and Juvenile Intensive Probation Supervision programs are special probation programs created to help alleviate prison over-crowding by diverting non-violent offenders from prison. They involve stricter rules and closer supervision than ordinary probation. State expenditures on these two programs have grown from $0.2 million in FY 1984-85 to $8 million in FY 1987-88. In FY 1987-88, over 1,000 adult offenders alone were supervised at an annual cost of about $4,000 per offender.

<table>
<tr><td colspan="7" align="center">Table 15-11
Probation-Related State Judicial Expenditures
(thousands of dollars)</td></tr>
<tr><td>Fiscal
Year</td><td>Adult
Intensive
Probation</td><td>Juvenile
Intensive
Probation</td><td>Juvenile
Probation
Services</td><td>State
Aid
Enhancement</td><td>Probation
State Aid</td><td>Total</td></tr>
<tr><td>1983-84</td><td>$ ---</td><td>$ ---</td><td>$ ---</td><td>$ ---</td><td>$ 652.5</td><td>$ 652.5</td></tr>
<tr><td>1984-85</td><td>159.9</td><td>---</td><td>1,346.4</td><td>632.5</td><td>685.2</td><td>2,824.0</td></tr>
<tr><td>1985-86</td><td>1,979.2</td><td>---</td><td>2,394.2</td><td>1,354.4</td><td>729.9</td><td>6,457.7</td></tr>
<tr><td>1986-87</td><td>4,867.8</td><td>4,426.7</td><td>12,724.4</td><td>4,282.4</td><td>1,371.0</td><td>27,572.3</td></tr>
<tr><td>1987-88</td><td>4,720.0</td><td>3,249.8</td><td>12,337.3</td><td>4,197.4</td><td>1,319.2</td><td>25,823.7</td></tr>
<tr><td colspan="7">Source: The Arizona Courts, Judicial Reports.</td></tr>
</table>

The State Aid For Probation Services and the State Aid Enhancement programs were designed to assist local governments in funding probation programs of the Superior Court. The State Aid For Probation Services program provides discretionary funding to each Superior Court in the state for maintaining and improving juvenile probation services. The State Aid Enhancement program provides funding for maintaining the statutorily-required average supervision ratio of 60 adult probationers per probation officer. With this funding, the State has borne the costs of increasing probation caseloads leading to the increase in state share of total funding and the decrease in the county share, discussed above. As shown in Table 15-11, state expenditures on these two programs combined have grown from $0.6 million in FY 1983-84 to $5.5 million in FY 1987-88.

In FY 1987-88, these probation service programs alone accounted for over $25.8 million, or over 58 percent, of state judicial expenditures. Whether or not expenditures on these probationary programs can be justified on fiscal grounds will depend on whether or not they are offset by decreases in the rate of growth of corrections expenditures. Unfortunately, at this time there is not enough reliable data concerning the impact of these new probationary programs on state prison population to make this determination.

Summary of Trends In Expenditures

Inflation-adjusted public safety expenditures in Arizona have more than doubled in the last ten years. A historical investigation of expenditures made by DPS, DOC, and the Judiciary reveals that the increase in public safety expenditures is primarily due to increased spending on the judiciary and corrections. Further, it appears that the primary reason for the increase in state funds devoted to the Judicial system is the implementation of several programs dealing with adult and juvenile probation, while the primary reason for the increase in state funds devoted to corrections is the rise in the number of individuals incarcerated each year.

Other Policy Issues

The structure of public safety programs is ultimately determined by citizens' values regarding security, justice, and the proper resolution of disputes. There are a number of policy issues related to these values facing the State now and for the future.

New Law Enforcement Technologies

Technological advances in the law enforcement area can have a significant impact on public safety expenditures. DPS is currently planning for future implementation of two new technologies that will increase the efficiency of criminal investigations and increase the probability of identifying and convicting criminal suspects. These technologies are automated fingerprinting and DNA printing.

The automated fingerprint identification system (AFIS) is a new law enforcement tool that matches fingerprints found at crime scenes and taken from suspects with the computer-stored fingerprints and records of known offenders in a very short amount of time. The technology saves countless hours of labor required to match prints manually. While DPS does not currently have a statewide AFIS, it did pursue an agreement with California to access their AFIS. In FY 1987-88 approximately 17,000 Arizona arrest fingerprint records were placed in the California AFIS database.

The other new technological development in law enforcement is DNA printing. DNA analysis of blood, skin, hair, etc. provides a genetic fingerprint that can positively identify an offender. DPS has begun training its personnel in the use of DNA testing and estimates that it may take two to five years to implement the system fully.

Both of these technologies will increase Arizona's efficiency in apprehending criminals and will reduce investigative labor expenditures per case. The ultimate impact on total expenditures, however, is uncertain. Both technologies require substantial initial investments in equipment and training as well as annual operating costs. As these technologies enable law enforcement agencies to process greater numbers of cases in a given amount of time, total expenditures may actually increase. In addition, if these technologies lead to more arrests and convictions, as expected, they will result in increased costs for both DOC and the Judicial system.

State Funding of the Judicial System

Another policy option that has a major effect on public safety expenditures is what share the state should contribute to support the operation of Arizona's judicial system. In its 1989 report, The Commission on the Courts, a commission appointed by Chief Justice Francis X. Gordon to develop long range plans and recommendations for the Arizona Judiciary, has recommended that the state provide full funding of the entire state and local judicial system. One of the disadvantages of decentralized provision of judicial services is that administrative inefficiencies may arise because of duplication of programs or lack of economies of scale. In addition, decentralization can lead to inconsistencies in administration. This point is particularly relevant for Arizona's courts.

Since the Municipal, Justice of the Peace, and Superior courts are funded locally, the operation of these courts is affected to a large degree by the willingness and ability of local governments to provide funds. This type of funding scheme leads to natural disparities in resources available for courts across the state. Counties and cities with relatively strong economic bases can provide a higher quality of public safety to their citizens, while those counties and cities experiencing difficult economic conditions can not provide the same quality of judicial services.

State funding of the entire court system would result in administrative efficiencies and could equalize the level and quality of judicial services for all citizens across the state. The fiscal impact of full state funding would depend on how fast the program is implemented, and how the state financed its new responsibility. As proposed by the Commission, a shift to state funding could be initially expenditure neutral for the state if state aid to cities and counties were reduced to compensate for the added State Judicial expenditures.

Alternatives to Incarceration

Several programs arc being discussed and/or implemented by the Department of Corrections in an attempt to reduce expenditures by reducing prison population without endangering the citizens of the state. These programs include shock incarceration, home arrest, and community punishment.

The DOC has recommended a shock incarceration program for young first-time offenders. This program is based on a military boot camp model. It is intended to "shock" individuals with a "preview" of prison life and to develop self-esteem and self-control to encourage them to become law abiding citizens. In Arizona the program consists of four months of strenuous physical exercise and labor as well as academic instruction.

A home arrest program has been approved by the state Legislature as an alternative to incarceration. Offenders selected for the program will complete the last part of their sentences in the community under home arrest. This enables them to be employed and become re-integrated with society. When not at work, these individuals are restricted to their homes. They will wear an electronic monitoring device that alerts parole officers when offenders leave their home or work.

The Community Punishment program was authorized in 1987-88 and funded by the state for the first time in 1990-91. It is a set of programs and services for people placed on probation that emphasize financial restitution to victims, community service work, individualized medical and job training services for probationers, and supervision and control of the probation population. The program is intended to divert individuals from state prisons and county jails.

The success of these programs in reducing costs depends upon the eligibility rules that are established and the utilization of the programs in practice. If people who would otherwise have been incarcerated are instead assigned to these programs, then costs will be reduced. The potential exists, however, for these programs to be used as substitutes for regular probation or parole. If this occurs, then costs will increase because the per-person cost of these alternatives is higher than the cost of probation or parole.

Chapter 16

Financing State and Local Highways

Alberta H. Charney and Craig M. Horn

The Conceptual Role of Government
In Providing Highway Services

Highways serve several different purposes. They provide access to land, they provide a community service function by facilitating the movement of persons and property for social and production purposes, and they provide a means of long-distance transportation and inter-community mobility.

The purpose of a specific road determines the level of government (federal, state, or local) that should provide the road. To the extent that a road provides only local access to urban or rural areas, it is appropriately provided by local governments (city and county). State governments provide roads that perform this function to the extent that the flows of persons and property cross county borders. When highways are used as a means of long-distance inter-community travel, they are appropriately provided by the state or federal government. The federal government has primary responsibility for roads connecting major communities across state lines while the states are responsible for connecting communities within a given state.

The purpose of a road also determines the appropriate type of revenue sources to use for funding. Historically, when highways were used almost exclusively for local transportation, they were financed from general local taxes. The provision of highways was considered a benefit to the general public and therefore financed like other local government services. If a specific road is for local access, it may be appropriately financed by local general taxes. This philosophy still applies in most areas and local governments use general taxation to provide at least some local roads.

In contrast, highways that are used for intercity or interstate travel cannot and should not be funded by local general taxes for several reasons. First, it is not feasible to finance all highways with local general taxes because it would be necessary to broaden the base to the state or federal level since benefits are accruing to individuals outside the local area. Second, highways are not pure public goods benefitting all equally, thus it is inappropriate to use only general taxes. In addition, exclusive use of general taxation, whether local, state, or federal, to support the entire highway system would result in an unfair competitive advantage for highways over other modes of travel, *i.e.*, railroads and airways for intercity traffic and mass transit for intracity traffic. Therefore, state and federal highways are funded almost exclusively by "user chargers," or taxes and fees levied on owners and operators of motor vehicles because of their use of public highways.

The interactions among the three levels of government both in terms of highway usage and in funding have become extremely complex over time. Interstate roads were designed to connect major population centers. In addition, cities tend to grow up around highways. Thus, parts of the interstate system currently are used for urban commuting. A significant portion of local spending on roads in many states is derived from highway monies collected by the state and distributed to county and city governments. The federal government has provided funding not only for highways but also for some of the capital needs of mass transit.

The federal government undertook a much more significant role in transportation issues following World War II. During this period, which can be characterized as a building phase, the federal government funded major improvements to the nation's highway and transit services. To promote the beneficial use of the highways and to integrate these roadways into a uniform system for national defense, construction of the National System of Interstate and Defense Highways began. Also, during this time, the capital investment needs of mass transit were facilitated by the Urban Mass Transportation Act of 1964.

Today, the problems extend beyond building the necessary highway infrastructure; rather, the problems now include the maintenance and preservation of existing systems and how best to alleviate the congestion and pollution found primarily in urban areas.

The Benefit Principle of Taxation and User Fees

In the private sector of the economy, persons pay for private sector output. Since consumers must maintain a balanced budget and they must pay for what they purchase, consumers are forced to make trade-offs among the private goods until they arrive at the mix of goods that maximizes their utility. At the same time, producers of each private good allocate resources and factors of production to produce those goods in the least expensive way. In addition, producers of different private goods compete among themselves for resources. Consumption and production are said to be *efficient* when markets clear (that is, the mix and quantity of private goods produced exactly matches the mix and quantity of private goods demanded by consumers at a set of prevailing prices), when no consumer can be made better off by changing his/her mix of purchases and when no additional private goods and services can be produced with the available resources.

Certain goods and services provided by government convey direct benefits to individuals in the sense that services received by individuals are rival and exclusionary. Any government service yielding at least partial direct benefits can be financed by charges instead of general taxes. Or, if the use of charges per se is difficult, certain taxes may be applied indirectly on a complementary product in lieu of charges, *e.g.*, fuel taxes.

Highways are publicly owned transportation facilities that are necessary to the operation of motor vehicles. As such, highways are viewed as providing benefits to highway users. Highway-user taxation is designed to recover from highway users that portion of highway costs that are allocable to those users.

The use of a price system, when possible, to finance government services can lead to efficiency in the allocation of resources. Financing a government service by a user charge allows the price system and the market, rather than a political process, to determine the amount of the government service to produce. Consequently, the use of user charges can facilitate an efficient allocation of resources given appropriate pricing policies. In the short run, an appropriate set of user charges prevents excessive utilization of the service by rationing available facilities among users. Over the long run, when facilities can be adjusted, user charges (*i.e.*, prices) provide a basis for making decisions regarding expansion.

In the case of highway user charges, efficiency requires that the benefit principle be applied among various user groups and among users within a given group. Efficient pricing among user groups requires that those users that impose higher maintenance and operation costs on the system (*e.g.*, heavy trucks) be assessed comparatively higher user charges.

Weight fees paid at the time of registration can be designed to insure that each weight group pays a different fee according to the cost each imposes on the system. However, because users within each weight group do not travel the same number of miles, benefit principle taxation requires that users within a weight group pay according to their use of the highways.

Efficiency can be achieved if fixed highway costs (costs which do not vary with traffic volume or highway use) are paid for with fees that do not vary with usage while variable highway costs are paid for out of highway taxes that vary with highway use.

Efficient Pricing of Highways

The basic theory of highway finance requires users to pay an amount per vehicle-mile equal to the short-run marginal costs they impose on the roadbed and society. In the absence of congestion on the roads, this marginal cost (per vehicle-mile) would include operation costs of the vehicle (which are paid for by the user), road maintenance costs associated with that user, depreciation and interest costs, and all other costs associated with highway use.

Short-run marginal costs also include all other government costs associated with highway use such as the marginal costs of other government-provided services to highway users that vary with use, *e.g.*, police and highway administration, portions of budgets for planning, electricity for lighting, public health, coroner, city/county/state attorney, municipal, superior and juvenile courts, and the fire department and paramedics.[1] Short-run marginal costs also include costs associated with negative externalities of automobile operation, namely pollution and accidents, and the associated costs of illness and death such as foregone wages and hospital bills.[2]

Optimal user fees will differ among vehicle types because marginal maintenance costs differ among vehicle classes. The damage that a vehicle inflicts on pavement is proportional to the vehicle's "equivalent standard axle loading" (ESAL), where one ESAL equals the wear caused by a single axle bearing 18,000 pounds.[3]

When a highway has reached its point of maximum flow, the addition of one more vehicle will slow the flow and increase the travel time of all other vehicles. The marginal driver considers only his/her own private costs in deciding whether or not to use the highway and fails to consider the costs that his/her trip imposes on all other drivers. In this instance, there is a divergence between private marginal costs and social marginal costs. Efficiency calls for imposing a congestion toll which equals the difference between social marginal costs (which include the costs of wear and tear on other vehicles, the value of other drivers' time lost due to congestion, and costs associated with increased hazard) and private marginal costs.[4]

Congestion charges, as well as marginal user charges, would differ among vehicle types because trucks and buses, which are larger than automobiles and accelerate more slowly, create more congestion. Of course, this is true only to the extent that trucks and buses utilize the roads during periods of congestion. For example, if trucks travel only during off-peak periods, they should pay no congestion toll at all.[5]

Under certain assumptions,[6] two operating rules would lead to both optimal utilization of an existing transportation network and, ultimately, a long run optimum network. These rules are: (1) establish short run marginal cost prices for the use of each link in an existing network. Doing so would require levying congestion tolls equal to the difference between the short run marginal social costs and short run private costs of trips. And, (2) alter the size of each link to the point where the toll revenues generated by it equal the costs to the authority of providing the link, *i.e.*, maintenance and other operating costs, depreciation and imputed interest on invested capital.[7]

Without an efficient pricing scheme on congested urban roads, the tendency is to "solve" the congestion problem by continually expanding capacity until there is no congestion. However, as capacity is expanded and congestion costs are reduced, individual highway users' private marginal costs also fall resulting in an even greater demand for those urban roads. Consequently, roads are expanded until an acceptable level of congestion is reached. Under most financing schemes, very little of this congestion cost is allocated directly to peak-load users. Rather, it is spread over all highway users and/or collected from non-users through general taxes.

Highway Funding Sources

Most state government highway expenditures are funded primarily by revenues from registration fees, motor fuel taxes, federal highway funds, taxes on commercial motor carriers, and in some states, vehicle-related property taxes. Sources of funding for local governments in most states include state-shared highway revenues, county-based sales and motor fuel taxes, local developer fees, and other general sources of revenue for local governments. In Arizona, local governments are limited in their ability to impose highway-user taxes.

First-Structure Taxes

Motor vehicle registration fees are imposed for vehicle identification and the privilege of using the state's highways. Registration fees are referred to as a first-structure highway use tax because they were the first type imposed and because they are imposed on a per-vehicle basis and therefore do not vary with use. Second and third-structure taxes, which are discussed below, were developed to improve the overall efficiency of highway user taxes.

The registration fee for private vehicles can be a flat fee per vehicle; a fee based on the weight of the vehicle, the vehicle's rated horsepower, or a combination of both; or a percentage of the vehicle's original price. Registration fees for commercial vehicles are usually based on the weight of the vehicle either unladen or the maximum gross weight with cargo.

While imposing reasonable charges for vehicle identification, registration fees are not appropriate for efficient pricing of highways. Although it may be possible to devise a schedule for registration fees so that the fee would be in proportion to the costs imposed by each highway-user group, the fee for each vehicle within that group is based on average responsibility. The fact that a vehicle may travel significantly more miles than another within the same group cannot be accounted for by registration fees.

In Arizona, all motor vehicles (including automobiles, pick ups, vans, truck tractors, but excluding motorcycles) are assessed an annual eight dollar fee at registration. (Motorcycle registration fees are nine dollars, the additional one dollar funding motorcycle-related education programs.) The annual registration fee for commercial tractor-trailer combination trucks is either $16 or $57 ($8 for registration of the truck tractor and an additional $8 or $49 fee that depends on the gross weight of the trailer or semi-trailer).

Commercial vehicles also pay a four dollar Commercial Registration Fee. In addition, a Gross Weight Fee is imposed on each commercial vehicle ranging from $7.50 for vehicles below 8,000 pounds to $918 for vehicles up to 80,000 pounds, the maximum gross weight allowed on Arizona highways without a special overweight permit.

Persons registering a vehicle for personal use are also assessed a Vehicle License Tax. This in-lieu property tax is assessed at the rate of four percent of the vehicle's statutory value. When a newly purchased vehicle is registered in Arizona, the vehicle is assigned a value equal to 60 percent of the manufacturer's base retail price. For each succeeding year, this value is reduced by 15 percent. The minimum Vehicle License Tax assessed on any vehicle is $30.

Commercial vehicles can be subject to the Vehicle License Tax, the Additional Highway Use Tax,[8] or both. Arizona-based commercial vehicles that travel solely within Arizona are subject to the Vehicle License Tax, the same as private use vehicles. Foreign-based commercial vehicles that travel through Arizona for a single trip or are proportionally registered in Arizona only are subject to the Additional Highway Use Tax. Arizona-based commercial vehicles that are proportionally registered in Arizona and other states first are assessed the Vehicle License Tax and then, if the fee imposed under the Additional Highway Use Tax exceeds the Vehicle License Tax, the amount in excess of the Vehicle License Tax is assessed as the Additional Highway Use Tax.

Total registration fees for Arizona-based commercial vehicles that only travel within Arizona are the sum of the Motor Vehicle Registration Fee, the Commercial Vehicle Fee, the relevant Gross Weight Fee, and the Vehicle License Tax. Total fees for proportionally registered commercial vehicles (which include the Additional Highway Use Tax) are pro-rated based on the vehicle's use of Arizona's highways.[9] If a vehicle is used in commercial activity within Arizona 40 percent of the time (as determined by the ratio of miles traveled within Arizona to total miles traveled by the vehicle), then the owner must pay 40 percent of the total registration fees that would be required had the vehicle been fully engaged in commerce within Arizona.

In most states, including Arizona, registration fees are not efficient in assigning charges for highway use in proportion to the costs imposed by each user. Under existing Arizona law, registration fees for commercial vehicles can be vastly different. As Table 16-1 shows, the manner in which Arizona assesses registration fees on proportionally registered vehicles is the reason for this difference.

Assume an Arizona business owns a new 80,000 pound gross weight truck that will travel all of its 40,000 miles within Arizona. To register this vehicle in Arizona, the vehicle's owner will pay an $8 Motor Vehicle Registration Fee for the tractor and an additional $49 for the trailer. The owner also must pay the $4 Commercial Vehicle Fee and $918 for the Gross Weight Fee. If this new truck has a base retail price of $100,000, then the Vehicle License Tax is $2,400. The total cost to register this Arizona-based vehicle will be $3,379.

If this same vehicle was based in another state and travels one-half of its total 80,000 miles within Arizona, then the total cost to register this vehicle would be only $1,037. When computing total registration fees, the vehicle's owner would enter into his/her calculations the same $8 and $49 for the Motor Vehicle Registration Fee, the same $4 for the Commercial Vehicle Fee, and the same $918 for the Gross Weight Fee as an Arizona owner. The foreign-based vehicle would not be subject to Arizona's Vehicle License Tax, however. Instead, Arizona assesses an Additional Highway Use Tax of $1,095 on the vehicle.

Table 16-1
Arizona Registration Fees For Commercial Vehicles
(Fees for Arizona-based and Foreign-based Vehicles)

Suppose two new 80,000 pound gross weight tractor-trailer combination trucks, with base retail prices of $100,000, are registered in Arizona. One is Arizona-based and travels all of its 40,000 miles within Arizona. The other is based in another state and travels 40,000 of its 80,000 total miles within Arizona.

Total Arizona registration fees for each vehicle would be:

Arizona-based Truck	
Motor Vehicle Registration Fees	
For Tractor	$ 8
For Trailer	49
Commercial Vehicle Fee	4
Gross Weight Fee (80,000 pounds)	918
Vehicle License Tax (4% of $60,000 value)	2,400
Additional Highway Use Tax ($1,095 maximum)	0*
Total Registration Fees	3,379
Foreign-based Proportionally Registered Truck	
Motor Vehicle Registration Fees	
For Tractor	$ 8
For Trailer	49
Commercial Vehicle Fee	4
Gross Weight Fee (80,000 pounds)	918
Vehicle License Tax (Foreign-based Vehicles Exempt)	0
Additional Highway Use Tax ($1,095 maximum)	1,095
Sub-total	2,074
Times apportionment factor for proportional registration (40,000 of 80,000 total miles traveled within Arizona)	0.50
Total Registration Fees	1,037

* Since this vehicle is Arizona-based and not proportionally registered, the Additional Highway Use Tax does not apply.

The sum of these fees is $2,074. This would be equivalent to the total cost for a foreign-based owner who registers a vehicle that would travel solely within Arizona. Since the vehicle used in this example only travels one-half of its total miles within Arizona, *i.e.*,

40,000 miles in Arizona, the $2,074 must be pro-rated by the factor 0.50, or 50 percent, to determine the actual registration fees paid by the non-Arizona owner.

This example shows that Arizona's registration fees are not imposed in relation to use of the highways; therefore, they are not efficient. It is also interesting that Arizona's fees contain a "bias" against Arizona-based commercial vehicle owners.

Second-Structure Taxes.

Motor fuel taxes, imposed on a cents-per-gallon basis, historically have been the most important revenue source for highways. They are called second-structure highway use taxes because they vary with miles driven. The main benefits of the fuel tax relate to the improved efficiency (vis-a-vis registration fees) associated with its direct relationship to use of the highways (as measured by miles traveled) and the relatively low administrative costs. All other things being the same, users, private or commercial, who utilize the highways more than other users will pay higher fuel taxes.

State gasoline taxes (including Arizona's) are imposed on distributors when the fuel is refined, blended or imported into the state. Imposing the tax on distributors and not on retailers or users facilitates the administration of the tax by minimizing the number of taxpayers and the cost of compliance.

In October, 1989, Arizona's 17 cents per gallon gasoline excise tax was the same as that imposed in North Dakota and Maine (see Table 16-2). Nineteen states and the District of Columbia imposed higher gasoline taxes. Excise taxes in other states ranged from a low of 7.5 cents per gallon in Georgia to 22 cents per gallon in Nebraska with the average rate nationally being approximately 15.80 cents.[10]

Arizona, like other states, imposes a use fuel tax on users of special fuels (primarily diesel fuel) to compensate the state for the use of its highways. The primary highway users of these special fuels are heavy, multi-axle commercial trucks and buses. Unlike the gasoline tax, the use fuel tax is more often imposed on the individual user which significantly increases the costs associated with record-keeping, collection and compliance enforcement.[11] If the fuel tax were imposed on distributors, it is possible that the user would avoid the tax by refueling outside the state and driving through thereby not compensating the state for the use of its highways.

The use fuel tax is truly a "use" tax. During each reporting period, highway users are required to report the number of miles traveled within the state for each vehicle. Depending on the type of vehicle, and therefore, the fuel efficiency (miles per gallon of fuel) expected for that vehicle, the user computes the amount of fuel that was consumed within the state. The tax liability is simply the number of gallons "used" within the state multiplied by the use fuel tax rate. If the user actually pays taxes to a vendor for fuel purchased in the state, then the fuel taxes already paid are deducted to arrive at the net tax liability.

In October, 1989, Arizona's excise tax on diesel fuel (also 17 cents per gallon) ranked twenty-second amongst all states and the District of Columbia. The state with the lowest tax rate was Georgia (7.5 cents per gallon) while Iowa had the highest rate (22.5 cents per gallon). Throughout the nation, the average excise tax rate for diesel fuel was approximately 15.97 cents per gallon. However, in addition to the excise tax on diesel fuel, five states imposed "additional motor carrier fuel taxes" on heavy, multi-axle commercial trucks and buses (see Table 16-2). When these taxes are added to the excise taxes on diesel fuel, the average fuel tax paid by heavy-duty commercial vehicles was 16.62 cents per gallon.

Table 16-2 State Tax Rates on Motor Fuel (Page 1 of 2)					
	Motor Fuel Excise Taxes				
State	**Gasoline**	**Diesel Fuel**	**Additional Motor Carrier Fuel Taxes**	**State Ad Valorem Taxes (percent)**	**Local Option Taxes Allowed**
Alabama	13	14			L
Alaska	8	8			L
Arizona	17	17			
Arkansas	13.5	12.5			
California	9	9		4.75	L
Colorado	20	20.5			
Connecticut	20	20		3[1]	
Delaware	16	16			
D. C.	18	18			
Florida	9.7[2]	9.7[2]		5[2]	L
Georgia	7.5	7.5		3	L
Hawaii	11	11		4	L
Idaho	18	18			
Illinois	16	18.5	4.1*	6	L
Indiana	15	16	11	5	
Iowa	20	22.5			
Kansas	15	17			
Kentucky	15*	12*	7.2*		
Louisiana	16	16		4	L
Maine	17	20			
Maryland	18.5	18.5			
Massachusetts	11*	11*			
Michigan	15	15		4	
Minnesota	20	20			
Mississippi	18	18			L
Missouri	11	11			
Montana	20	20			L (none currently imposed)
Nebraska	22*	21.1*			
Nevada	16.25	20			L
New Hampshire	14	14			
New Jersey	10.5	13.5			
New Mexico	16.2	16.2			L (none currently imposed)
New York	8	10	4		L (mass transit; NYC lead pollution)
North Carolina	20.9*	20.9*			
North Dakota	17	17			

Table 16-2 (Page 2 of 2)					
	Motor Fuel Excise Taxes (cents/gal.)				
States	**Gasoline**	**Diesel Fuel**	**Additional Motor Carrier Fuel Taxes**	**State Ad Valorem Taxes (percent)**	**Local Option Taxes Allowed**
Ohio	18*	18*			
Oklahoma	16	13			
Oregon	16	16			L
Pennsylvania	12	12	6	6[1]	
Rhode Island	20*	20*			
South Carolina	16	16			
South Dakota	18	18			L
Tennessee	21[3]	17[3]			L (mass transit)
Texas	15	15			
Utah	19	19			
Vermont	16	17	5		
Virginia	17.5	16			L (mass transit)
Washington	18	18			L (none currently imposed)
West Virginia	20.35[4]	20.35[4]		5	
Wisconsin	20.8*	20.8*			
Wyoming	9	9			

* Excise tax rates vary quarterly or annually based on the wholesale price of fuel, highway maintenance costs, or fuel consumed. In Illinois, only "Additional Motor Carrier Fuel Taxes" vary.

[1] Connecticut and Pennsylvania: Gross receipts tax on first purchase of motor fuel by distributors. In the others states, the ad valorem taxes are general sales taxes.

[2] Florida: Combined excise and sales taxes. The motor fuel excise tax is 4 cents per gallon. A 5 percent sales tax also is imposed. The minimum sales tax is 5.7 cents per gallon.

[3] Tennessee: Includes 1 cent per gallon for Special Petroleum Products Tax.

[4] West Virginia: Combined excise and sales taxes. The motor fuel excise tax is 15.5 cents per gallon. A 5 percent sales tax also is imposed. Currently, the sales tax is set at 4.85 cents per gallon.

Source: Commerce Clearing House, Inc., *State Tax Guide*, Chicago, Il., October, 1989, and taxing authorities in various states.

Most states impose motor fuel excise taxes on a flat cents-per-gallon basis. However, in eight states the excise tax incorporates either a flat rate per gallon plus an additional variable rate, generally based on the average wholesale price of fuel within the state, or a variable rate with a minimum cents-per-gallon floor. (Refer to Table 16-2 for these variable tax states.) For example, in October, 1989, North Carolina's motor fuel excise tax of 20.9 cents per gallon included a flat rate of 17 cents plus an additional amount equal to the greater of 7 percent of the average wholesale price per gallon or 3.5 cents per gallon. In Ohio and Wisconsin, the variable portion of the excise tax is tied to highway maintenance costs and the amount of fuel consumed in the state during the previous year. Revenues associated with the variable portion of the fuel tax in these two states will respond closely to changes in the costs of highway provision.

In addition to motor fuel taxes, twelve states imposed general sales taxes on the purchase of gasoline for highway use with some of these states including both federal and state fuel taxes in the taxable base. Revenues from ad valorem motor fuel taxes are related to both the price of fuel and the number of gallons purchased and thus to the use of the highways. To the extent that it relates to usage, the tax is efficient. However, fuel price fluctuations have little relation to either highway use or the costs for construction and maintenance of highways. In this regard, a sales tax on fuel is considered inferior to a fuel tax with a rate that adjusts with the costs of building and maintaining highways.

An advantage of ad valorem fuel taxes is that the tax can offset some of the losses in fuel taxes associated with declines in fuel consumption during periods of high fuel prices. For example, during periods of high fuel prices, the consumption of fuel and the use of highways declines, the consequence of which is a potential decline in highway user revenues. An ad valorem tax, imposed as a percentage of the value of sale, would generate additional revenues during this period to counteract the associated reduction in other highway user revenues.

Eighteen states also allowed local option taxes on motor fuel sold within their jurisdictions (see Table 16-2). These taxes include motor fuel excise taxes and general sales taxes. It is interesting to note that some local governments impose taxes on motor fuels to assist the funding of mass transit in urban areas while New York City also imposes a "pollution" tax on leaded motor fuels.

Third-Structure Taxes

Economic efficiency requires users to pay the marginal costs associated with their use of the highways. These costs are related to the weight of the vehicle and the level of use (vehicle miles traveled). Gasoline and use fuel taxes assign higher costs to those who make greater use of the highways since greater use requires the purchase of more fuel and, therefore, the payment of more fuel taxes. However, studies have shown that heavy vehicles impose costs that significantly exceed the additional fuel taxes associated with their lower miles per gallon. By incorporating both vehicle weight and highway use, third-structure taxes can efficiently assign costs to each highway user.

In 1982, Arizona imposed a Motor Carrier Tax based on the declared maximum gross weight of the commercial vehicle and the distance within Arizona that the vehicle travels. Such a tax is often referred to as a "weight-distance tax." Although weight-distance taxes have been politically controversial, they are an efficient means to tax highway users.

Commercial vehicles in excess of 12,000 pounds gross weight are subject to Arizona's Motor Carrier Tax. To save administration costs, owners of vehicles with gross weights between 12,001 and 26,000 pounds pay an annual tax (from $64 to $119) depending only on weight, not weight and the actual miles traveled each year. Heavier vehicles, those in excess of 26,000 pounds, pay the tax based upon gross weight and the actual number of miles traveled within Arizona, therefore, paying taxes more closely related to the marginal costs associated with their use of the highways. Tax rates for these heavy vehicles increase progressively from 1.3 cents to 8.0 cents per mile.

Revenues from the Motor Carrier Tax have steadily increased since its imposition. These revenue increases reflect the increasing use of heavier trucks by motor carriers and not increased rates for the Motor Carrier Tax. In fact, the rate schedule for the Motor Carrier Tax has remained unchanged since 1982.

Third-structure taxes used in other states include the ton-mile tax and the diesel differential tax. Both are designed to achieve what Arizona's weight-distance tax does, but they do so less efficiently. For example, a diesel differential tax is generally imposed by states in an attempt to increase highway user payments of heavy trucks relative to lighter trucks or automobiles without having to impose a weight-distance or a ton-mile tax. The argument for imposing a diesel differential tax is that since heavy trucks utilize diesel fuel imposing a higher (or differential) tax on diesel fuel relative to gasoline will result in higher highway user fees on trucks. The diesel differential can improve efficiency when the state highway revenue structure includes only first and second structure taxes and fees. However, the diesel differential is clearly inferior to a weight-distance tax which can be adjusted to coincide closely with the costs associated with each vehicle weight class.

A ton-mile tax is similar, but inferior, to a weight-distance tax. A weight-distance tax is a tax that is based on the number of vehicle miles traveled. The tax rate varies across weight classes in such a way that heavy trucks pay proportionately more per mile than would be indicated by their weight. That is, truck A, that weighs twice as much as truck B, would pay more than twice as much per mile traveled as truck B. The weight-distance tax may be designed in such a way that the per-mile tax rate varies across weight classes proportionally to the distribution of costs imposed by those weight classes. A ton-mile tax cannot be fine tuned to be proportional to the distribution of costs across weight classes. It is generally imposed as x-cents per ton-mile (tons carried times the number of miles those tons are carried). The ton-mile tax, therefore, varies with miles traveled and with tons carried. However, with a ton-mile tax, truck A, carrying 80,000 lbs., and traveling one mile would pay the same ton-mile tax as truck B, carrying 20,000 lbs. traveling four miles, even though truck A inflicts substantially more damage on the pavement than truck B.

Earmarked Highway User Funds

The Federal Government and most states, including Arizona, earmark highway-user revenues in a special fund which is dedicated to highway purposes. For most government functions, earmarking is considered a poor budgeting procedure because it constrains certain revenue sources to particular expenditure categories, and as expenditure priorities change, it is difficult to change earmarked revenues in a corresponding fashion. In the case of highway financing, however, earmarking is appropriate and in line with the benefit approach when taxes are imposed in lieu of charges. In this instance, a linkage between highway user revenue sources and expenditures is efficient in charging for variable costs and distributing costs according to benefits received.

Highway User Revenue Fund

Generally, "highway user revenues" are all monies received from registration fees, taxes, penalties and interest. In Arizona, these revenues are deposited into an earmarked highway fund called the Highway User Revenue Fund (HURF). Table 16-3 details HURF monies by major revenue source since Fiscal Year 1976. Following 1980, Arizona began earmarking a portion of the state's Vehicle License Tax for highways. Currently 31.5 percent of the Vehicle License Tax is deposited into HURF. The "other" category in Table 16-3 includes a portion of the revenues generated by the Vehicle License Tax. In years when revenues from this source grow faster than 7 percent, some of the "excess" is deposited into HURF.

HURF monies are distributed to the State Highway Fund; to counties, with special distributions going to the two major urban areas; and to incorporated cities and towns within Arizona.

State Highway Fund

Arizona's State Highway Fund includes HURF monies remaining after distribution to cities, towns and counties; monies received from counties (including bond proceeds) that are credited to a special account in the Fund to aid in financing dedicated projects within the county; federal funds for use in Federal-aid programs; and monies deposited into the State's General Fund from the disposal of various properties used by the Arizona Department of Transportation (ADOT).

Expenditures from the State Highway Fund may be used for the wages and salaries of ADOT personnel; the purchase of equipment and supplies; the engineering, construction, improvement, and maintenance of state and Federal-aid highways; and for assistance in relocating persons or businesses along rights-of-way. When expending monies from the Fund, Arizona, like most states, prioritizes spending to receive federal matching funds.

Local Highway Revenues

The major revenue sources for local highway expenditures in most states are state-shared highway revenues, local non-highway taxes (primarily property tax revenues), and local developer fees. Some states allow local governments to impose local vehicle fees, local motor fuel taxes (ad valorem taxes or at fixed rates per gallon), or local general sales taxes with revenues earmarked for highway purposes.

In Arizona, local governments are not allowed to impose local vehicle fees or motor fuel taxes. County governments are allowed to impose a general sales tax with revenues earmarked for highways or mass transit. Local general sales taxes (or payroll taxes) that fund mass transit or highways in urban areas are not uncommon in other states. However, depending on the type of roads being funded by these monies, the use of a general sales tax may be an inefficient source of highway revenues.

Table 16-3
Revenues Deposited into Arizona Highway User Revenue Fund (HURF) By Source, Fiscal Years 1976 - 1989
($ thousands)

Fiscal Year	1976	1977	1978	1979	1980	1981	1982
Motor Vehicle Fuel Tax	106,336	111,507	120,017	127,584	122,898	120,432	122,344
Motor Vehicle Registration Fee	37,386	40,118	41,827	46,402	49,019	48,726	59,043
Motor Carrier Tax*	11,180	12,602	15,386	17,152	19,760	20,292	18,161
Operators' License & Miscellaneous Fees	10,394	11,583	12,843	13,940	14,838	15,819	16,419
Motor Vehicle License Tax						8,353	23,097
Other							
Total Highway User Revenue Fund	$165,296	$175,810	$190,073	$205,078	$206,515	$213,622	$239,064

Fiscal Year	1983	1984	1985	1986	1987	1988	1989
Motor Vehicle Fuel Tax	151,159	194,774	223,651	257,445	309,541	314,928	336,898
Motor Vehicle Registration Fee	59,844	63,127	66,658	77,622	74,727	79,090	80,338
Motor Carrier Tax	55,187	70,326	78,148	86,834	92,704	98,707	104,710
Operators' License & Miscellaneous Fees	16,373	18,776	20,416	21,862	23,821	22,996	23,402
Motor Vehicle License Tax	34,035	42,595	54,336	61,834	69,030	79,240	80,125
Other	4,590	0	3,310	5,644	10,205	12,422	20,512
Total Highway User Revenue Fund	$321,188	$389,598	$446,519	$511,241	$580,028	$607,383	$645,985

* Prior to Fiscal Year 1983, the Motor Carrier Tax was a "gross receipts tax," not the current weight-distance tax.

Source: Administrative Services Division, Arizona Department of Transportation.

Federal Highway Funds

Federal assistance in the funding of state and local highways has significantly evolved since 1921 when federal aid was first authorized for the integration of a network of principal roadways important to interstate, statewide and regional travel (now called the Federal-aid Primary System). Since that time, additional federal aid has been authorized for the Federal-aid Secondary System (rural major collector roads); the urban extensions of both Federal-aid Primary and Secondary roads; the Federal-aid Interstate System; a separate Federal-aid Urban System (roadways within municipalities having populations of 5,000 or more persons); and various safety and bridge-related programs.[12]

The Federal-aid highway program generally refers to all highway construction and improvement activities funded by the Federal Highway Administration (FHWA) and administered by state or local transportation agencies. The Federal-aid program is a reimbursement program. To obtain federal aid for highway construction and improvements, states or local governments develop plans, enter into contracts, and supervise construction with the approval of the FHWA. As projects are completed, the FHWA reimburses the agencies for a portion of the costs incurred. The proportion of funds reimbursed for each project (so-called federal matching funds) is determined by the type of project involved. By statute, Interstate System construction and improvement projects are financed on a 90-percent federal, 10-percent state matching basis while other Federal-aid highways are financed on a 75-percent federal, 25-percent state matching basis.[13] In states, such as Arizona, where public lands exceed 5 percent of the area, the federal share is proportionally increased. Federal funding provides nearly 94% of construction costs for Interstate projects and 92% of construction costs for other Federal-aid highway projects in Arizona.

Historically, federal aid was only available for the construction of Federal-aid highways. Since the 1970s, however, increasing emphasis has been placed on the preservation and reconstruction of highways and bridges. Separate special authorizations have provided monies for bridge rehabilitation and replacement and the resurfacing, restoration, rehabilitation and reconstruction of the nation's Interstate highways (Interstate 4R funds). With limited exceptions, federal monies are not provided for maintenance (snow removal, shoulder work, etc.) of Federal-aid highways. The financial responsibility for the maintenance of these highways lies with state or local governments.

The federal matching funds available to the states from the Federal-aid program are derived from the Federal Highway Trust Fund administered by the FHWA. The Highway Trust Fund is a "pay-as-you-go" fund which is financed from the proceeds of federally imposed highway user-related taxes, motor fuel taxes and other highway-related excise taxes. The amount of funds available to each state during any fiscal year is determined by the total funds appropriated for each program and the formulas used to apportion these monies amongst the various states.[14] These formulas give weight to population, area, road mileage and relative project completion costs.[15] The monies apportioned to the states during each federal fiscal year need not be expended during the fiscal year authorized. The program allows a "grace period" of at least two years for states to plan and implement their projects.

Highway Expenditures

Highway expenditures differ from other government expenditure categories in several important respects. First, highway expenditures tend to be driven by highway revenues. Unlike most state government services which are funded with appropriations from the state's general fund, highways are generally paid for from the proceeds of earmarked highway revenues. Although legislatures could, if they so desired, appropriate general fund revenues to highways, there is reluctance to do so given that there is an earmarked fund set aside for that purpose. As a result, state highway expenditures are not increased without the legislature developing and passing a specific earmarked revenue package to fund the increase.

Second, highways are capital investments. That is, they are investments that have a very long useful life. Highways usually have a 20-year design life, *i.e.*, they are designed to last and to meet the expected demand for highway services over a 20-year period. This aspect of highway financing results in expenditures occurring in lumps as particular projects are developed and constructed.

Third, highway expenditures in any given year can greatly exceed or be substantially less than highway revenues in that same year. This is not contradictory to the first issue raised above. The reason for the differential between expenditures and revenues is that a large portion of highway expenditures is funded initially through the sale of bonds which are paid back over time (usually over a 20-year period) from highway revenues. Consequently, there are periods in which current expenditures significantly differ from current revenues.

It is important to recognize these basic differences between the provision of highway services and other government services when making interstate comparisons of per capita highway expenditures. Table 16-4 presents total per capita expenditures (state and local, including those financed with federal funds) on highways in Arizona and eleven other western states for selected years from 1960 through 1980 and each year following 1980. Note that each state's per capita highway expenditures are expressed relative to U.S. per capita highway expenditures.

Only western states are used in this comparison. This is because the provision of highways, unlike other government services, depends not only on population levels and population characteristics but also on geographic characteristics such as terrain, the concentration of population in urban areas, and the expansiveness of rural areas. Arizona is similar to other western states in these characteristics. In addition, the western region has, in general, grown more rapidly than the U.S. as a whole resulting in increased pressures for government expenditures on roads.

Figures in Table 16-4 indicate that Arizona's per capita expenditures on highways from 1960 through 1983 were approximately 5 to 10 percent higher than that of the U.S. as a whole with the exception of 1983 when per capita expenditures were slightly less than that of the U.S. Beginning in 1984, Arizona's per capita highway expenditures grew relative to U.S. per capita expenditures. By 1987, the last year for which data are available, Arizona's per capita highway expenditures exceeded the comparable U.S. figure by almost 70 percent.

With the exception of California, every other western state exceeded the U.S. per capita highway expenditures for the majority of years presented in Table 16-4. Arizona per capita highway expenditures were, on average, 15 percent higher than the U.S. per capita expenditures for the entire 1960 through 1987 period. Only three of the western states, California, Texas, and Colorado, had per capita expenditures less than Arizona when averaged over the 1960 through 1987 period. California's per capita highway expenditures

Table 16-4
Per Capita Total State and Local Highway Expenditures Relative to the U.S.
(U.S. Per Capita Level Equals 100)

	1960	1965	1970	1975	1980	1981	1982	1983	1984	1985	1986	1987	Average 1960-87
Arizona	103.00	113.51	102.91	104.49	106.82	112.88	109.73	97.50	115.69	128.72	134.32	169.50	114.67
California	85.49	96.94	100.35	75.58	66.41	67.15	65.11	65.10	66.13	65.79	61.96	65.82	81.02
Colorado	106.97	111.83	93.60	104.95	111.59	108.03	115.09	116.65	125.87	115.80	120.16	115.97	108.00
Idaho	146.81	163.66	145.77	149.96	122.89	118.38	112.82	122.71	129.12	127.50	124.33	117.15	137.93
Montana	169.51	221.28	209.34	153.66	211.21	208.82	168.82	178.59	192.80	195.20	203.02	176.97	193.54
Nevada	159.76	265.54	158.61	145.56	160.25	164.58	142.03	157.75	144.26	147.23	141.27	129.99	168.20
New Mexico	111.99	143.85	131.67	124.46	132.15	137.70	178.93	181.00	181.13	148.74	141.48	148.42	136.09
Oregon	133.85	159.92	113.27	121.37	122.20	123.43	127.27	107.70	107.65	109.37	99.83	107.08	123.24
Texas	111.30	96.10	98.32	94.58	109.21	115.29	128.54	101.02	93.65	85.91	112.12	112.19	99.52
Utah	111.02	151.51	138.73	96.38	129.97	124.87	110.05	106.70	132.84	148.88	121.43	100.06	120.76
Washington	98.66	128.10	125.59	125.50	132.04	141.63	137.05	147.26	123.32	139.44	106.09	116.18	126.01
Wyoming	267.39	356.89	277.40	239.08	259.35	298.74	330.44	316.87	345.36	358.28	342.65	306.65	292.72

Source: Compiled from *Government Finances*, U.S. Department of Commerce, Bureau of the Census, various years.

averaged only 81 percent of the U.S. for the 1960 through 1987 period. Texas' per capita expenditures, on average, matched those of the U.S. for the 1960 through 1987 period while Colorado's per capita expenditures exceeded the U.S. figures by approximately eight percent. The remaining states had average relative per capita expenditures higher than Arizona.

Table 16-5 compares, by year, Arizona's per capita highway expenditures with average per capita expenditures in eleven other western states. It should be noted that the averages presented in Table 16-5 are simple averages over the eleven states. Consequently, Wyoming's very high per capita expenditures are given the same weight as each of the other states. Arizona's per capita expenditures were between 65 and 80 percent of the simple average of the other eleven western states from 1960 through 1984. Beginning in 1985, Arizona's per capita expenditures, relative to the other eleven states, began increasing, and by 1987, Arizona's per capita expenditures were 25 percent higher than the other eleven states.

Table 16-5
Per Capita Total State and Local Highway Expenditures -
Arizona Relative to Other Western States
(Western States Average per Capita Level Equals 100)

Arizona Relative to:	1960	1965	1970	1975	1980	1981
Western States	75.39	65.87	71.07	80.32	75.45	77.19
Western States excluding Wyoming	83.37	73.77	78.24	87.66	82.30	86.17

Arizona Relative to:	1982	1983	1984	1985	1986	1987
Western States	74.69	66.97	77.50	86.22	93.85	124.59
Western States excluding Wyoming	85.35	75.90	89.22	100.26	109.06	142.46

Note: The western states include: California, Colorado, Idaho, Montana, Nevada, Oregon, Texas, Utah, Washington, and Wyoming.

Source: Compiled from U.S. Department of Commerce, Bureau of the Census, *Government Finances*, various years.

If Wyoming is removed from the western state average, Arizona's per capita expenditures were 75 to 90 percent of the other western states from 1960 through 1984, approximately the same in 1985, and greater than the other western states by 9 percent in 1986 and by 42 percent in 1987. Thus, while Arizona's current per capita expenditures are higher than its comparable states, the past expenditure levels were substantially less. This comparison suggests that Arizona under-invested in highways for many years and is currently "catching-up" in development of its highway infrastructure.

It should be noted that two major changes in Arizona's highway finances occurred in the early to mid-1980s which account for the rapid growth in expenditures. First, the state of Arizona began issuing highway revenue bonds in 1980. Prior to that year, the state built highways on a pay-as-you-go basis. Second, in 1985, the legislature passed laws permitting counties to use general sales taxes to finance both highways and public transit. The maximum allowable county sales tax for each of these uses is approximately one-half of one percent (actually 10 percent of the state's sales tax rate). Three counties, including the county containing the Phoenix metropolitan area, have enacted sales taxes for highway use. Use of the sales tax for public transit has not yet received voter approval.

Tables 16-4 and 16-5 compare Arizona's highway expenditures adjusted for the size (measured by population) of the state to other comparable western states. However, current highway expenditures are not solely a function of current population. Rather, current highway expenditures are a function of current and past population (*i.e.*, population growth) relative to past highway expenditures. For example, a slow-growing state would not be expected to have the same highway expenditures as a state that has experienced a five to six percent annual population growth rate for the previous 10 to 20 years even though current population levels are identical. In addition, the durable nature of highways makes a year by year comparison of per capita expenditures suspect.

Thus, a second method of comparing highway expenditures across states is to compare the sum of highway expenditures over a period of time with the increase in population over the same time period. Table 16-6 presents, for Arizona, the U.S. and the eleven comparison western states, the 10-year sum of deflated highway expenditures (in 1977 dollars) divided by the 10-year change in population. The first three columns present the calculations for total highway expenditures for the 10 years prior to 1970, 1980, and 1987, respectively. The last three columns present the calculations for capital outlays only. These measures of highway expenditures, summed over 10 years and divided by population change, are proxies for added capacity relative to population change.

Table 16-6
10-Year Sum of Highway Expenditures Relative to
10-Year Population Change Real Dollars per Added Person
(in 1977 Dollars)

	Total Expenditures			Capital Outlays		
	1961-1970	1971-1980	1978-1987	1961-1970	1971-1980	1978-1987
Arizona	5,621	2,924	3,861	4,357	1,905	2,649
California	6,329	4,935	3,165	4,660	2,765	1,433
Colorado	6,372	4,658	6,048	4,095	2,744	2,986
Idaho	30,627	5,962	10,835	20,854	3,588	6,791
Montana	109,901	18,511	42,583	84,847	12,269	26,526
Nevada	5,894	3,488	4,085	4,545	2,036	2,575
New Mexico	27,683	5,868	8,111	20,044	3,289	4,900
Oregon	11,256	6,054	7,111	7,350	3,376	6,080
Texas	9,426	4,289	4,224	6,912	2,846	3,009
Utah	11,272	3,951	5,225	8,649	2,683	3,316
Washington	9,813	7,320	7,388	6,883	4,349	4,438
Wyoming	486,799	8,151	8,151	385,138	5,690	13,900
United States	11,755	10,547	10,132	8,004	6,089	5,494

Source: Compiled from *Government Finances*, U.S. Department of Commerce, Bureau of the Census, various years. Authors' calculations as described in text.

The 1987 figure for total expenditures in Arizona means that for each new person added to the state from 1978 to 1987, the state spent $3,861 (in $1977) on highways. Capital outlays for each additional person were $2,649 over the same period. Arizona's 10-year capital outlay, per person added, for the 1978-1987 period was lower than other western states except California and Nevada and only 45 percent of the comparable figure for the U.S. In the decade prior to 1980, Arizona's capital outlays relative to the state's population growth were the lowest of all the western states and less than one-third that of the U.S. In the decade prior to 1970, Arizona's capital spending was lower than all western states except for Colorado, spending just over half of what the U.S. spent on capacity relative to added population. Again, these figures strongly suggest that Arizona has been under-investing in highways for many years, relative to other western states and relative to the U.S., when capital outlays, used as a proxy for increases in capacity, are compared to population growth.

Policy Implications

Arizona imposes a variety of highway user fees and taxes that are suitable for establishing an efficient revenue structure. Arizona's revenue sources include: flat fees and fees that vary with weight, taxes that vary with use (fuel taxes), and taxes that vary with use and weight (weight-distance tax). A combination of these existing taxes and fees can distribute the cost responsibility among users in an efficient and fair manner.

This section presents policy issues relevant for Arizona and many other states.

Indexing

State imposed highway fees and taxes do not keep pace with increases in the costs of constructing and maintaining highways. Registration fees and weight fees are imposed per vehicle and, while they increase with the number of registered vehicles, they do not increase with inflation and, therefore, do not keep up with the costs of constructing and maintaining highways. Fuel taxes and weight-distance taxes increase with the level of activity (*e.g.*, gallons consumed or miles driven), but they do not keep up with increases in the costs of highway provision.

Because of this and because highway costs have been increasing, the purchasing power of almost all of these revenue sources decreases over time unless the legislature continually intervenes and increases fees and tax rates. There is reluctance on the part of legislators to do this since increasing taxes is politically unpalatable. Indexing highway user fees and tax rates would eliminate this problem. Note that indexing would not increase current revenues; it merely assures that future highway revenues keep pace with inflation (and maintain purchasing power).

There are several alternative measures that may be used for indexing highway fees and tax rates including a highway construction cost index, a highway maintenance and operation cost index, a weighted average of construction and maintenance indices or a general measure of inflation such as the GNP deflator. With indexing, highway revenues would automatically keep up with the costs of providing highway services. Consequently, any further legislative increase in the tax would signal a desire to increase the level of highway services provided rather than simply to maintain existing service levels.

Congestion Fees

Highway congestion occurs because individuals make a decision to enter a highway based only on their own private costs and not on the costs they impose on others. Optimal highway pricing requires that these individuals be assessed a toll.

While there are many toll roads in the United States, the purpose of these tolls generally is only to provide revenues to pay for construction costs. The philosophy of the Federal-aid highway program historically has been to allow no tolls on highways that receive federal funds.[16] However, prior to 1969 federal law did allow the imposition of tolls to reimburse the states for their share of the costs associated with the construction of new highways, bridges and tunnels. By using federal highway funds, the states agreed to eliminate the tolls when their share of construction costs had been repaid. In addition, federal law requires that existing Interstate highways not be withdrawn from the system and converted into toll roads.[17]

No cities in the United States impose congestion tolls, *per se*.[18] The costs of collecting the toll and the congestion created by toll booths has generally precluded use of tolls on most highways. Recent technological advances, *i.e.*, electronic tolls, have led to the field-testing of congestion tolls in Hong Kong. Under this system, vehicles are electronically monitored as to when they enter and leave congested zones. The toll is computed electronically and bills are periodically sent to the highway user.

An alternative to congestion tolls are time of day permits which a user would have to purchase and display if they used the congested highway during peak periods. Permits could be bought daily, weekly, monthly, or annually. However, it would not be appropriate to offer significant discounts for commuters buying monthly or annual permits since the purpose is to tax the peak-user. Time of day permits, like all flat fees, are inefficient when compared to a congestion toll because they do not vary with miles driven. However, time of day permits do impose higher costs on rush hour commuters relative to non-rush hour travelers which is appropriate since the former are responsible for the congestion and the capacity required to relieve that congestion. Time of day permits would be easier to implement and administer than congestion tolls. Time of day permits have been used in Singapore.

Local Highway-User Taxes and Fees

In the state of Arizona, enabling legislation and possibly a constitutional amendment would be required before local governments (counties or cities) could impose local option fuel taxes and vehicle fees.

Local vehicle fees are comparable to state registration fees but they are paid to local governments for the privilege of using local roadways. Local vehicle fees, since they do not vary with the use of the road, suffer from the same inefficiencies that exist for state vehicle fees. However, the use of general taxation for the provision of roads is also inefficient in that non-users are required to pay the same as heavy users. Consequently, local fees would be an improvement over the current situation in Arizona by permitting counties to levy a first-structure use fee on users of local roads.

Local option fuel taxes are efficient in the sense that they vary with usage. They suffer from all the disadvantages of state-imposed fuel taxes, in particular, the use of fuel does not increase proportionately with damage costs imposed by heavier vehicles. To the extent that the revenue is to be used to provide urban roads for the use of local residents and businesses, this method of raising revenues is reasonably efficient.

One compliance problem is that individuals may buy fuel outside the local government's jurisdiction to avoid the tax. In many states, this poses no problem because of the geographic expanse of most counties and the urban concentration of population within those counties.

Imposing Highway Fees and Taxes for Non-Highway Purposes

Currently, highway fees are imposed solely for the purpose of generating revenues for the construction and maintenance of roads. The above discussion on the economics of highway financing suggests that the framework for imposing highway user fees could be broadened to deal with externality problems, particularly pollution, and to include other governmental costs, such as police and court costs, associated with highway use.

Currently in Arizona, an air quality fee is imposed annually on each registered vehicle. The flat fee does not vary with usage and, thus, is not a perfect pollution fee. A fuel tax surcharge (indexed) could be imposed as a pollution fee. This would have several advantages. First, it would internalize to the user of motor fuels some of the social health costs associated with pollution. A fuel tax surcharge would force the user of motor fuels (and therefore the polluter) to incur at least a portion of the costs of pollution. The result would be a reduction in total fuel consumption, a shift from highways to mass transit, and a reduction in pollution levels.

Second, the dollars raised from a pollution surcharge could logically be expended to support urban mass transit which is viewed as a way of abating pollution, to provide additional funding for Arizona Department of Environmental Quality programs, or to provide a source of revenue for the Arizona Health Care Cost Containment System (AHCCCS) on the basis that some health problems are caused or aggravated by pollution.

Although a fuel surcharge could be imposed statewide, it would be more efficient to impose it only in the two urban areas since pollution is a problem only in those areas. A fuel surcharge imposed in the urban areas is identical to imposing a local fuel tax (many states permit local areas to impose fuel taxes) except these revenues would *not* be earmarked for road maintenance and construction.

References

American Association of State Highway and Transportation Officials, *Highway Cost Allocation Study Activity Report*, February, 1989.

Commerce Clearing House, Inc., *State Tax Guide*, Chicago, Il., October, 1989.

Due, John F., and Ann F. Friedlaender. (1977) *Government Finance: Economics of the Public Sector*. Sixth Edition. Richard D. Irwin, Inc. Homewood, Illinois 60430.

Keeler, T., and K. Small. (1977) "Optimal Peak-Load Pricing, Investment, and Service Levels on Urban Expressways." *Journal of Political Economy* 85, No. 1, pp. 1-25.

Kraus, Marvin (1981) "Indivisibilities, Economies of Scale, and Optimal Subsidy Policy for Freeways." *Land Economics* 57, No. 1 (February), pp. 115-121.

Locklin, D. Philip (1972) *Economics of Transportation*. Seventh Edition. Richard D. Irwin, Inc., Homewood, Illinois 60430, 1972.

McGuire, Therese and Robert D. Ebel, Eds. (1986). *Final Report of the Minnesota Tax Study Commission*, Butterworth Legal Publishers, St. Paul, Minnesota.

Mills, Edwin S., and Bruce W. Hamilton. (1984) *Urban Economics*. Scott Foresman and Company, Glenview, Illinois.

Mohring, Herbert (1976) *Transportation Economics*. Ballinger Publishing Company (A Subsidiary of J.B. Lippincott Company), Cambridge, Massachusetts.

Morrison, Steven A. (1987) "The Theory of Optimal Highway Pricing and Investment: Comment." *Southern Economic Journal* 53 (3). pp. 779-782.

Musgrave, Richard A., and Musgrave, Peggy B. (1988) *Public Finance in Theory and Practice, 5th Edition*. McGraw-Hill Book Company, New York, New York.

Pogue, Thomas F. (1986) "Minnesota Highway User Taxes: Issues and Alternatives. *Final Report of the Minnesota Tax Study Commission*, edited by Robert D. Ebel and Therese J. McGuire, Butterworth Legal Publishers, St. Paul, Minnesota.

Small, Kenneth A. (1990) "Urban Transportation Economics." *Fundamentals of Pure and Applied Economics*, Harwood Academic Press.

Strotz, Robert H. (1965) "Urban Transportation Parables." *The Public Economy of Urban Communities*, edited by Julius Margolis. Resources for the Future, Inc. Washington, D.C. 20036. pp. 127-169.

Transportation Board of the State of Arizona, Department of Transportation, *Official Statement: Transportation Excise Tax Revenue Bonds (Maricopa County Regional Area Road Fund) 1988 Series A*, 1988.

U.S. Department of Commerce, Bureau of the Census, *Government Finances*, various years.

U.S. Department of Transportation, Federal Highway Administration, *Financing Federal-Aid Highways*, November, 1987.

U.S. Department of Transportation, Federal Highway Administration, *Highway Statistics*, 1987.

U.S. Department of Transportation, Federal Highway Administration, Bureau of Public Roads (1968), *The Role of Third Structure Taxes in the Highway User Tax Family*. Prepared for the Office of Research and Development by the University of Mississippi, Bureau of Business and Economic Research, Contract No. CPR 11-8029.

Endnotes

1. See Keeler and Small (1977) for a discussion of these other items. They estimate that the per vehicle-mile costs for these other government items in the San Francisco Bay Area were $0.0045 (in $1977). More recently, Small (1990) argues that municipal government subsidization of automobile travel is approximately $0.019 per vehicle mile ($1987). This excludes direct municipal disbursements for highways ($0.032 per vehicle mile in $1987).

2. Small (1990) estimates pollution costs associated with automobile emissions to be approximately $0.003 per mile ($1987) -- roughly equivalent to an extra $0.06 per gallon on the gasoline tax. In the same article, he estimates the cost of accidents which are external to the individual decision to drive to be $0.10 to $0.13 per vehicle mile.

3. See Morrison (1987).

4. See Mohring (1976), Keeler and Small (1977), Strotz (1965).
5. If they travel during congested periods, Morrison (1987) has estimated that buses and trucks should pay congestion fees 1.6 to 2.0 times that of automobiles.
6. This discussion assumes constant returns to scale. See Morrison (1987), Keeler and Small (1977) and Mohring (1976). There are differences of opinion as to the structure of highway cost functions.
7. Mohring (1976). Keeler and Small (1977) and Kraus (1981) estimate optimal congestion tolls for various areas under different conditions. Keeler and Small find congestion tolls ranging from 2 to 3 cents ($1977) per vehicle-mile on rural-suburban roads up to 6 to 13 cents on most central city roads. They estimate optimal tolls for expressway users in the San Francisco Bay Area of up to 35 cents ($1977) per vehicle-mile on downtown roads. Kraus (1981) computes the optimal congestion toll per vehicle-mile for various traffic volumes and obtains comparable results. Since the optimal congestion tolls are substantially higher than user charges paid by most U.S. commuters, commuter auto traffic is being subsidized.
8. The Additional Highway Use Tax, a registration fee based on the weight and age of the vehicle, was enacted to simplify registration of foreign-based commercial vehicles.
9. Most states are members of the International Registration Program (IRP) which serves as a clearinghouse for the collection of proportional registration fees from motor carriers.
10. Includes the combined excise and sales tax rates for Florida and West Virginia.
11. To minimize these costs, many states (including Arizona) are members of the International Fuel Tax Agreement (IFTA) which serves as a clearinghouse for the payment of fuel taxes by motor carriers.
12. Federal-aid highway programs are authorized by Title 23 U.S. Code.
13. Certain special purpose programs, e.g., safety-related projects, can receive up to 100 percent federal funding.
14. The Surface Transportation And Uniform Relocation Assistance Act of 1987 (PL 100-17) appropriated program monies through Federal Fiscal Year 1991 and extended other provisions of the Federal-aid program through Fiscal Year 1993.
15. The FHWA publication *Highway Statistics* details apportionment formulas by program.
16. Title 23 U.S. Code Sections 129 and 301.
17. There could be future changes in the "no tolls" philosophy of the Federal-aid highway program particularly for urban areas. The Surface Transportation Act of 1987 authorized federal matching monies for seven pilot toll facilities. The law allows states participating in this pilot program to use toll financing and federal aid for new and expanded capacity construction of non-Interstate highways, bridges or tunnels. The federal share for such projects is 35 percent.
18. Many cities charge tolls on bridges and certain road segments. However, these tolls are imposed on all users whether the road is congested or not.

Part IV:
Local
Government
Finance

Chapter 17

Financing Local School Districts

Thomas A. Downes and Thomas F. Pogue

Arizona spends more on public elementary and secondary education than any other government activity, $2.4 billion for the 1987/1988 school year, about $4,200 per student. Real (inflation adjusted) expenditures increased at an average annual rate of 3.5 percent from 1980 through 1988; real expenditures per student increased at an average annual rate of 1.9 percent during that period.

This chapter is concerned with several broad questions about these expenditures. How have Arizona education expenditures changed over time and how do they compare to other states? What are the main purposes of state aid to local school districts? What is the appropriate division of school funding responsibility between state and local governments? Is total spending distributed among districts so that educational opportunities do not depend on where students attend school? Are school taxes distributed fairly among Arizona taxpayers, regardless of where they reside and own property? The aim of this chapter is to provide a factual background for examination of these questions and to identify some major school finance issues currently facing policymakers in Arizona and other states.

Trends

Tables 17-1 and 17-2 show how school district revenues and expenditures changed during the 1980s. From 1979/80 to 1987/88, nominal spending doubled from $1.17 to $2.38 billion increasing at an average annual rate of 8.9 percent. Most of this growth was due to inflation and the growth of the student population; real per-student spending grew at an average annual rate of only 1.9 percent. Table 17-2 shows that in 1981 there was a major shift of funding responsibility from local districts to the state. The state general fund share of school finance continued to rise in the early 1980s but decreased steadily in the three most recent school years. The local share has correspondingly increased in recent years and is now just slightly below the state general fund share. Despite this recent trend reversal, the state general fund share was somewhat greater in 1988 than in 1980 and the local share was somewhat lower in 1988 than in 1980.

Table 17-1
Arizona School District Expenditures, School Years 1980-88

School Year	Total Expenditures			Maintenance and Operation Expenditures		Capital Expenditures	
	Nominal (millions)	Real (millions)	Real Per Student	Real (millions)	Real Per Student	Real (millions)	Real Per Student
1979-80	$1171	$1428	$2860	$ 988	$1978	$127	$255
1980-81	$1323	$1473	$2927	$1004	$1996	$133	$264
1981-82	$1411	$1459	$2929	$1019	$2047	$129	$260
1982-83	$1537	$1501	$3015	$1046	$2102	$127	$255
1983-84	$1634	$1523	$3034	$1066	$2124	$118	$236
1984-85	$1738	$1547	$3012	$1175	$2288	$124	$242
1985-86	$1953	$1675	$3182	$1274	$2421	$138	$262
1986-87	$2216	$1837	$3342	$1368	$2488	$131	$239
1987-88	$2379	$1889	$3330	$1430	$2521	$124	$219
Ave. Annual Growth Rate: 1980-88	8.9%	3.5%	1.9%	4.6%	3.0%	-0.3%	-1.9%

* Includes expenditures from capital outlay and adjacent ways funds.

Note: Expenditures from federal projects, state projects, debt service, food services and other funds are not shown separately above but are included in the total. Expenditures from the school plant, bond building, auxiliary operation, intergovernmental agreements, indirect costs and unemployment insurance funds are not included in the total. Real magnitudes are 1982 dollars, calculated using GNP deflator for state and local government purchases of goods and services.

Source: Arizona Department of Education *Annual Report of the Superintendent of Public Instruction*, 1979-80 through 1987-88 editions.

<table>
<tr><td colspan="7">Table 17-2
Arizona School District Revenues School Years 1980-88</td></tr>
<tr><td>School
Year</td><td>Total
Revenues[1]
(millions)</td><td>Percent
From
Federal
Funds</td><td>Percent
From
State
General
Fund</td><td>Percent
From
County
Funds</td><td>Percent
From
Local
Funds</td><td>Percent
From
Other
Funds[2]</td></tr>
<tr><td>1979-80</td><td>1202.0</td><td>10.2</td><td>37.2</td><td>0.14</td><td>48.9</td><td>3.6</td></tr>
<tr><td>1980-81</td><td>1287.4</td><td>8.8</td><td>47.9</td><td>2.7</td><td>33.8</td><td>6.9</td></tr>
<tr><td>1981-82</td><td>1346.9</td><td>7.1</td><td>49.1</td><td>3.4</td><td>33.9</td><td>6.4</td></tr>
<tr><td>1982-83</td><td>1413.0</td><td>6.6</td><td>50.4</td><td>3.8</td><td>32.8</td><td>6.5</td></tr>
<tr><td>1983-84</td><td>1532.3</td><td>N/A</td><td>N/A</td><td>N/A</td><td>N/A</td><td>N/A</td></tr>
<tr><td>1984-85</td><td>1759.6</td><td>N/A</td><td>N/A</td><td>N/A</td><td>N/A</td><td>N/A</td></tr>
<tr><td>1985-86</td><td>2045.9</td><td>7.7</td><td>47.6</td><td>3.4</td><td>33.8</td><td>7.5</td></tr>
<tr><td>1986-87</td><td>2163.7</td><td>6.4</td><td>45.4</td><td>3.7</td><td>37.6</td><td>7.0</td></tr>
<tr><td>1987-88</td><td>2410.6</td><td>5.6</td><td>43.8</td><td>3.8</td><td>40.3</td><td>6.4</td></tr>
</table>

[1] Excludes revenue to the following funds: school plant, bond building, auxiliary operations, intergovernmental agreements, indirect costs, and unemployment insurance. Revenues do not include fund balances or transfers.

[2] Includes state equalization aid paid from endowment earnings, food service fees, and other fees and special revenue funds.

Source: Arizona Department of Education, *Annual Report of the Superintendent of Public Instruction*, 1980/81 through 1987/88 editions.

Table 17-3 displays Arizona trends in teacher salaries and in numbers of teachers and students. Between 1980 and 1988, real teacher salaries increased while the teacher/student ratio remained virtually constant. These trends imply improved educational opportunities if average teacher productivity has increased in line with the increase in real teacher salaries. However, to the extent that productivity has not increased, higher salaries and costs have been necessary just to hold constant the per-student level of educational services. Therefore, unless we know how productivity has changed, we do not know whether the growth of real per-student spending, shown in Table 17-3, has been rapid enough to maintain the level of educational services offered by Arizona schools.

Table 17-4 shows the relative importance of various revenue sources in financing schools for Arizona, the U.S., and a set of comparison states. In 1986, the national average share of state aid in total K-12 financing was 46.8 percent; in Arizona the corresponding percentage was 46.9. The importance of state aid in financing local schools has increased over the past three decades. In 1962, state aid accounted for only 37.2 percent of school funds nationally and 34.1 percent in Arizona. The share provided by local taxes in Arizona (almost all of which are property taxes) has diminished from 48.6 percent in 1962 to 33.2 percent in 1986 following the long-term and nationwide trend that has reduced reliance on local property taxation for school finance and increased reliance on state-level taxes. For the neighboring states, the state share in 1985/86 ranged from 39.2 percent in Colorado to 75.6 percent in New Mexico. Nationally, the range was greater, from 6.7 percent in New Hampshire to 85 percent in Hawaii (which has a state school system rather than a local district system).

Table 17-3
Trends in Salaries, Number of Teachers, and Student-Teacher Ratio,
School Years 1980-88

School Year	Teacher Salaries			Number of Teachers	Number of Students	Student/ Teacher Ratio
	Nominal (millions)	Real (millions)	Real Per Teacher			
1979-80	N/A	N/A	N/A	27,228	499,281	18.3
1980-81	N/A	N/A	N/A	26,689	503,192	18.9
1981-82	$512	$529	$19,838	26,669	498,053	18.7
1982-83	554	541	20,624	26,227	497,723	19.0
1983-84	570	531	20,169	26,348	501,900	19.0
1984-85	902	802	29,731	26,982	513,478	19.0
1985-86	656	563	20,097	28,005	526,295	18.8
1986-87	775	643	22,030	29,187	549,726	18.8
1987-88	847	672	21,838	30,795	567,384	18.4
Average Annual Growth Rate: 1980-88	8.4%	4.0%	1.6%	1.5%	1.6%	

Note:	Real magnitudes are 1982 dollars, calculated using GNP deflator for state and local government purchases of goods and services.

Source:	Arizona Department of Education. *Annual Report of the Superintendent of Public Instruction*, 1979-80 through 1987-88 editions.

Census data indicate that Arizona's total direct expenditures on elementary and secondary education were slightly above average in 1986-87, measured on either a per capita or a per student basis or compared to personal income (Table 17-5). Current expenditures per student were 1 percent below the national average and similar to current expenditure levels in neighboring states. In contrast, Arizona's per-student capital expenditures were almost three times the national average and also higher than in neighboring states. This relatively high capital spending reflects Arizona's rapid population growth and the resulting need for construction of new schools and other capital outlays.

Table 17-4
Long Term Trends in School Finance:
Arizona, U.S., and Comparison States Distribution of Revenue Sources to School Districts

State	State Aid as Percent of Total Revenue[1]		Federal Aid as Percent of Total Revenue		Own Revenue as Percent of Total Revenue[2]		Tax Revenue as Percent of Total Revenue	
	1985-86	1961-62	1985-86	1961-62	1985-86	1961-62	1985-86	1961-62
U.S. Average	46.8	37.2	6.1	1.5	45.6	59.2	30.4	51.0
Arizona	46.9	34.1	8.0	3.8	42.0	55.9	33.2	48.6
California	65.2	37.5	6.4	2.2	27.5	59.0	20.3	53.7
Colorado	39.2	22.4	4.0	4.3	56.7	61.1	46.4	54.2
Florida	52.8	44.4	7.0	2.3	40.2	52.8	30.4	38.4
Illinois	38.7	19.8	5.7	0.5	55.5	79.7	46.0	73.2
Minnesota	51.3	38.0	4.9	0.2	42.8	58.5	33.4	52.3
New Mexico	75.6	68.4	12.7	6.9	11.7	24.6	6.9	19.1
NewYork	40.8	47.0	4.0	0.7	55.2	51.7	29.6	46.6
Texas	44.1	46.1	15.0	1.6	49.4	52.1	41.0	41.7
Utah	56.0	47.2	5.7	2.5	38.3	50.3	30.8	43.3

[1] Does not include federal aid distributed by the state.
[2] Consists of taxes, charges, fees, parent government contributions, and other. Virtually all taxes are property taxes.

Source: For 1985-86, U.S. Department of Commerce, Bureau of the Census, *Finances of Public School Systems in 1985-86*. For 1961-62, U.S. Department of Commerce, Bureau of the Census, *1962 Census of Governments: Finances of School Districts*, Vol. 4, No. 1.

<table>
<tr><td colspan="6">Table 17-5
Elementary and Secondary Education
Expenditures Interstate Comparisons 1986-1987</td></tr>
<tr>
<td>State</td>
<td>Total Expenditures Per Capita</td>
<td>Total Expenditures Per $1,000 Personal Income</td>
<td>Total Expenditures Per Pupil</td>
<td>Capital Expenditures Per Pupil</td>
<td>Current Expenditures Per Pupil</td>
</tr>
<tr><td>Arizona</td><td>$697.87</td><td>$48.76</td><td>$4,420.64</td><td>$879.45</td><td>$3,541.19</td></tr>
<tr><td>California</td><td>642.66</td><td>36.06</td><td>4,060.77</td><td>221.59</td><td>3,839.18</td></tr>
<tr><td>Colorado</td><td>726.91</td><td>46.64</td><td>4,290.54</td><td>560.52</td><td>3,730.02</td></tr>
<tr><td>Nevada</td><td>578.35</td><td>35.33</td><td>3,612.03</td><td>328.08</td><td>3.283.94</td></tr>
<tr><td>New Mexico</td><td>677.53</td><td>57.06</td><td>3,604.63</td><td>451.86</td><td>3,152.76</td></tr>
<tr><td>Utah</td><td>644.70</td><td>56.72</td><td>2,603.64</td><td>209.38</td><td>2,394.27</td></tr>
<tr><td>U.S. Average</td><td>$650.30</td><td>$45.13</td><td>$3,913.70</td><td>$321.83</td><td>$3,591.87</td></tr>
<tr><td>Arizona % of U.S. Average</td><td>107%</td><td>108%</td><td>113%</td><td>273%</td><td>99%</td></tr>
</table>

Note: Expenditure figures represent total direct general expenditures by state and local governments. Total expenditures are equal to the sum of current (operation and maintenance) expenditures and capital expenditures.

Source: For population and state personal income, *Significant Features of Fiscal Federalism* 1989 Edition, Volume 1, Advisory Commission on Intergovernmental Relations. For expenditures, U.S. Bureau of the Census, *Governmental Finances*. For enrollment, U. S. Department of Education, Center for Education Statistics, "Common Core of Data" Survey.

Rationales For State Aid

In Arizona and most other states, state aid to local school districts is the primary means by which state government contributes to school financing. Arizona's state aid funded about 45 percent of spending in 1987/88. Its main assistance programs, which account for about 99 percent of aid, are *basic* state aid (equalization assistance) and *additional* state aid (aid that pays part of the property taxes levied on owner-occupied housing). Some aid is also dispensed as grants to districts for specific programs (such as vocational education and chemical abuse prevention) and as formula-driven assistance for students whose education is a state responsibility.

Two broad rationales are typically offered for state aid to school districts. The most widely accepted is that without state aid, public education and its financing would be unfair for both students and taxpayers. These potential inequities first became important school finance issues in the 1920s, when the concept of equalizing school aid was introduced. They continue to be important today. Indeed, the historical failure of states to provide equal protection (even-handed treatment of individual students and taxpayers) has led to numerous challenges of the constitutionality of state school systems since the early 1970s. And virtually every state has overhauled its school finance system with the aim of reducing taxpayer and student inequities. The second rationale is that local districts, acting without either financial incentives or regulations from state government, may choose to spend too much or too little from an efficiency perspective on education, either in total or on specific activities.

Fairness for Taxpayers

Two principles of fairness are commonly used in evaluating systems of government finance: horizontal equity and vertical equity. When ability to pay is the basis for taxation, horizontal equity requires that taxpayers who have equal abilities to pay (are similar in income, wealth, and family responsibilities) bear equal tax burdens.[1] Vertical equity is concerned with the question of how to tax persons who have different taxpaying abilities because they differ in income, wealth, and family responsibilities. These principles apply to school finance as well as to taxation in general.

Horizontal equity. With perfect horizontal equity, persons with the same income and wealth would pay the same taxes for a given level of school spending regardless of where they reside within the state. Although widely regarded as desirable, horizontal equity usually cannot be achieved if schools are fully funded by local taxes. The reason is that school districts typically differ significantly in their fiscal capacities, their abilities to finance school spending from their own revenue sources. Because property taxes are the main source of local revenues, differences in fiscal capacities are indicated by differences in the per-student value of taxable property (Pogue, 1989). In 1987/88, per-student property value in Arizona school districts ranged from $808 to $6,400,897; the wealthiest district had over 8,000 times the fiscal capacity of the poorest district.

When there are such large differences in fiscal capacity, financing schools completely from local sources is likely to be unfair for taxpayers and students alike.[2] The fundamental problem that arises because of fiscal capacity differences is that individuals are treated unfairly relative to one another. The problem is not that some *areas* of the state fare differently; differences among areas are of concern only to the extent that they generate unfair differences in the treatment of *individuals*.[3] Either the per-student level of school spending or the property tax rate required to finance that spending must vary from district to district. In this case, horizontal equity for taxpayers can be achieved *only* by funding part or all of education spending with taxes that apply uniformly throughout the state, taxes that do not depend on where within the state an individual resides or owns property. To promote horizontal equity, most states, including Arizona, collect funds with uniform state-level taxes and distribute them as equalization aid to local school districts, districts with lower property values and higher costs receive more aid. Reducing the horizontal inequities that arise because of intrastate differences in the school taxes borne by persons with the same income and wealth is therefore one of the main purposes of equalization aid.

Any state tax, sales, income, property, or other, can be used to finance state equalization aid provided that it applies uniformly throughout the state. Therefore, equalization of school tax burdens across districts *does not require* reduced reliance on property taxes, the traditional source of local school funds, nor does it require increased funding from income or sales taxes. The choice of taxes to finance schools can be made *independently* of the decision about the share to be financed with state aid and the share to be financed with locally collected revenues. Arizona presently finances its equalization aid mainly with general fund revenues that come from income and sales taxes, but it also effectively levies a statewide property tax to finance part of equalization aid. A county levy of $0.50 per $100 of primary assessed value is mandated and applies uniformly throughout the state. This county aid funded 8.7 percent of Arizona's $1.04 billion in equalization aid for 1987/88. Increased equalization aid in Arizona could be funded by an increase in the county levy or by any tax levied by the state.

Vertical equity. Another frequently suggested rationale for state aid is that the state has more equitable revenue sources at its disposal than local districts which in Arizona and most other states must rely on property taxes. In this view, property taxes are regressive in comparison to state income and sales taxes. State aid, financed with state sales and income taxes, is seen as a means of achieving a more equitable distribution of tax burdens *across income classes* than can be achieved if schools are financed fully with property taxes. However, vertical equity is enhanced by increased state aid only if property taxes are more regressive than income and sales taxes.

Fairness for Students

Even-handed treatment of students is another purpose of state aid. A basic and difficult question is what constitutes fair treatment. One answer is that the same amount should be spent on the education of each student. State aid should be allocated so as to equalize per student spending across districts. As an alternative answer, some have argued that equal spending per student does not provide equal educational opportunities because the costs of educational activities vary across districts and with the type of student being educated. According to this second view, fairness requires that a specified set of educational programs and opportunities be made available to all students in a state even if doing so results in unequal per-student spending. That is, fairness requires that each student's educational *opportunities* be independent of where within the state he or she attends public school. But it does not require that all students be brought to the same level of educational achievement as measured by standardized test scores or otherwise. Because funding is easy to quantify and control, the fairness goal is often expressed in terms of cost-adjusted expenditures per student. Thus, equity in expenditures is used as a proxy for equity in educational opportunity.

Educational costs vary from district to district for a number of reasons. Per-student costs may be related to a district's total enrollment (because of economies of scale) and the geographic dispersion of its students. Costs also depend on student characteristics such as whether students are gifted or handicapped, use English as a second language, or live in low-income households. Education of high school students is generally thought to be more costly per student than education of elementary students.

Formulas for distributing state school aid typically adjust in some fashion for interdistrict variation in the costs of providing a specified set of programs. The accuracy of these adjustments determines whether state aid serves the objective of making basic educational opportunities independent of where students attend school. For the most part, this chapter will not evaluate Arizona's present methods of adjusting for cost differences. However, it does provide a preliminary investigation into the relevance of certain cost factors.

Spillover Effects

Because of population mobility, persons educated in one area often become residents and citizens of another. Educational policies followed in a particular school district may therefore affect persons who reside in other areas within the state and nation. Some of the benefits of K-12 education, particularly those that take the form of better citizenship, may "spill over" the boundaries of school districts. The costs of poor education may likewise spill over; persons who are poorly educated because of a particular district's policies may migrate to other areas of the state and become unemployed and welfare-dependent.

Individual districts may spend too little, either in total or on particular programs, if they fail to recognize and give appropriate weight to the spillover effects of their policies. State school aid can be a potential remedy for such deficiencies in spending if it is structured as a matching grant that gives districts more aid when they spend more from their own sources. When aid is directly linked to total local spending, it provides an incentive for districts to spend more in total than they would otherwise spend. When aid is linked to spending on a particular program or activity, it provides an incentive for that spending.

Local Control

The reasons given above for state aid reflect problems that can be eliminated by having state government take full responsibility for K-12 education and its financing. But full state funding conflicts with the apparently widespread desire for locally managed schools. State government would not likely provide all of the funds for local schools without also taking a major role in managing schools and formulating educational policy.[4] Some degree of local control is desirable because local districts may be better able than the state to assess and respond to the particular needs and interests of their students. Also, flexibility, experimentation, and innovation are likely to increase as local control increases. Maintaining a significant degree of local control over school policy, while pursuing goals of taxpayer and student equity, is therefore a third rationale for state school aid.

Arizona's Present System: How Does It Work?

Since 1980, the Arizona Legislature has made a number of major changes in the state's school finance system. The intent of these changes has been to reduce interdistrict variation in property tax levies for schools, equalize educational opportunities by limiting variation in per-student spending that is not tied to variation in costs, reduce reliance on property taxation for school finance, and limit the growth of property taxes.

To achieve these objectives, the state has placed limits on revenues that individual districts can raise and spend, placed a constitutional limit on overall school spending, provided state equalization aid to school districts, and provided additional state aid to pay part of the primary property tax levies on owner-occupied residential property.

Equalization Aid

The formula for distributing equalization aid makes adjustments for interdistrict differences in both fiscal capacities and costs. The objective is to offset differences in costs and property wealth so that each district can finance a target level of spending, referred to as the equalization base, with a property tax rate that does not exceed a specific tax rate. This rate is termed the *qualifying tax rate* (QTR). For districts that have both elementary and secondary students, the current (1989) QTR is $4.72 per $100 of primary assessed value. For districts that have only elementary students or only high school students, the rate is $2.36 per $100.[5]

Equalization aid is calculated separately for the elementary and high school components of a district's enrollment using the following formulas:

1. equalization aid based on elementary enrollment
   = elementary equalization base
   - (0.0236 x primary assessed value of property).
2. equalization aid based on high school enrollment
   = high school equalization base
   - (0.0236 x primary assessed value of property).

A district can receive aid based on one or both types of enrollment. The first calculation determines the aid received on the basis of elementary enrollment, and the second calculation determines the aid received on the basis of high school enrollment. A district receives no aid only if both calculations yield an amount that is less than or equal to zero.

A district's equalization base is a limit on the revenue that it can raise and spend for maintenance and operation and capital outlay. This base is calculated using statutorily defined formulas that take into account the number and characteristics of the district's students, the costs of transporting those students, the years of experience of the districts' teachers, whether district enrollment is declining, and whether the district is small or isolated. Student characteristics are relevant in determining aid because some students are relatively costly to educate. A district can spend more than its equalization base limit under conditions described below.

Equalization aid is financed by both state and county revenues. Counties are required to collect $0.50 per $100 of primary assessed value to finance equalization aid. This county contribution to the financing of equalization aid amounted to $91 million in 1987/88. The state provides the remainder of the equalization aid through general fund appropriations and endowment earnings from the Permanent Common School Fund. In 1987/88 the general fund financed $910 million in equalization aid and endowment earnings contributed $43 million. Thus, total equalization aid in 1987/88 amounted to $1,044 million.

Block Grant Approach

Although the equalization base is calculated on the assumption that some students are more costly to educate than others, there is no requirement that districts actually spend more on those students. In fact, there is no requirement that districts spend any set minimum amount on education. In 1987/88, 25 percent of the districts spent less than their equalization base.

Because Arizona's state aid comes with no specific spending requirements, it functions as a "block grant." This approach to dispensing state aid presumes that local districts are better able than the state to assess the educational needs of their students and to determine how best to meet those needs. It allows much more local discretion in the spending of state aid than the pre-1980 system allowed. Districts do risk losing their aid allocation if they do not comply with certain state program requirements, but apart from this, aid is not a means of encouraging districts to spend for programs and activities of the state's choosing.

Spending Above Equalization Base Limits

A district may spend in excess of its equalization base for a number of reasons specifically authorized by statute. In particular, with a voter approved "budgetary override," a district's maintenance and operations spending may exceed its revenue control limit, the main component of its equalization base, by up to 10 percent. Overrides to improve academic achievement in grades K-3 are also possible with voter approval. In addition, the equalization base limits do not apply to "small" districts.[6]

In 1987/88, maintenance, operation, and capital outlay spending by all districts ($1.95 billion) exceeded their total equalization base ($1.78 billion) by 10 percent. The average tax rate required to fund these override levies was $0.46 per $100 of assessed value with a range from $3.03 per $100 of assessed value in the Superior Unified district to $0.0037 per $100 in the Ruth Fisher district. This very large range is due in part to the large variation in school district fiscal capacity.

Additional State Aid

Additional state aid, also called the homeowner's rebate, pays 56 percent of the primary school levy on owner-occupied residential property up to a maximum of $500. It also pays the amount by which the primary tax levies of all governments exceed 1 percent of the market value of such property. A homeowner never pays the portion of her property taxes that is offset by additional state aid. Instead, that portion of the levy on her home is paid directly by the state to the school district.

Additional state aid does not increase the total funds available to a school district; instead, it shifts part of the cost of schools from local property taxation to state-level taxes, mainly sales and income taxes. It also reduces the school tax burden on homeowners relative to other types of taxpayers. Because it lowers the cost of school spending to homeowners, it may make them more willing to support increases in school spending.

Arizona's Present System: Is It Fair?

Any assessment of the fairness of Arizona's school finance system must be based upon a standard of student equity. For the following discussion, we assume the standard of student equity discussed above: fairness requires that a set of basic educational programs and opportunities be available to all students and that a student's educational opportunities be independent of where she attends public school.

To be useful in allocating resources, this broadly stated ideal must be translated into dollars. The equalization base approximates such a dollar standard. Through weights and adjustments to the formula, the state attempts to adjust for interdistrict differences in the costs of providing elementary and secondary education. *If these adjustments are correct,* then even-handed treatment of students requires that each district's actual spending for maintenance, operation, and capital be the same as its equalization base. The fairness of Arizona's system, from the student perspective, is indicated by the extent to which districts' actual spending coincides with their equalization bases.

Given this concept of student equity, taxpayer equity is achieved if the *property tax rate required* to finance the equalization base level of spending *is the same* for all districts. If this is the case, persons who have the same property wealth pay the same taxes to provide a given level of school services (the equalization base level) regardless of where they reside and own property. The remainder of this section documents the extent to which Arizona's present system meets these standards for student and taxpayer equity.

Student Equity

A district's per-student equalization base measures the average amount that it can spend on maintenance and operations and capital outlays for the education of each of its students except for budget overrides and statutorily specified categories of expenditures that can be budgeted outside equalization base limits. The top panel of Table 17-6 shows that the maximum equalization base per student is more than five times the minimum. This wide variation reflects adjustments made for presumed interdistrict differences in costs that arise out of differences in student and district characteristics. Transportation cost adjustments, which are quite large for a few districts, are responsible for much of this variation (compare the top and middle panels of Table 17-6). Capital cost adjustments account for very little of the variation which can be seen by comparing the top and middle panels of Table 17-6.

Tables 17-7 and 17-8 show how districts' actual spending varied relative to their equalization bases in 1987/88. Actual spending exceeded the equalization base in 75 percent of the districts and fell short of the base in 25 percent of the districts. For the middle one-half of all districts (from the 25th to the 75th percentiles), spending exceeded the equalization base between 0.6 and 14 percent. Approximately 75 percent of Arizona's student population attended school in these districts. For all districts, expenditures ranged from more than double the equalization base to half the base.

Much of the variation in Tables 17-7 and 17-8 reflects the fact that spending by small districts is not limited. Also, some districts receive enough federal impact aid that they can spend above their equalization bases while levying no property tax. Under Public Law 81-874, which governs the distribution of federal impact aid, they must be allowed to do so.[7] When small districts and districts with a zero primary property tax rate are eliminated, expenditures vary much less relative to equalization bases as shown in Table 17-8. Considerable variation remains, with spending ranging from 18 percent below to 92 percent above the equalization base and 25 percent of the districts spent more than 11 percent above their equalization bases.

Table 17-9 shows that very few students attended school in "low" expenditure districts. Most of the variation is on the high side with approximately forty percent of the state's students attending school in districts that spent more than 10 percent above their equalization base. Thus, there appears to be a fairly widespread desire for school spending above the designated equalization base.

Table 17-6
Variation in Per-Student Equalization Base SY 1987-88
(in dollars per student)

	Mean	Minimum	Maximum	Maximum Relative To Minimum
Equalization base per student				
all districts	3,971	2,957	15,009	5.1
02 districts	3,535	3,043	5,311	1.7
03 districts	4,909	3,295	15,009	4.6
04 districts	3,821	2,957	8,562	2.9
05 districts	3,997	3,336	6,125	1.8
Equalization base minus transportation revenue control limit per student				
all districts				
02 districts	3,521	2,712	7,747	2.9
03 districts	3,332	2,972	5,225	1.8
04 districts	3,859	2,712	7,743	2.9
05 districts	3,489	2,885	7,747	2.7
	3,618	3,204	4,732	1.5
Equalization base minus transportation and capital outlay and capital levy revenue control limits per student				
all districts	3,122	2,246	7,409	3.3
02 districts	2,926	2,597	4,786	1.8
03 districts	3,482	2,246	7,409	3.3
04 districts	3,096	2,533	7,188	2.8
05 districts	3,153	2,767	4,208	1.5

Note: Districts of type 01 are omitted; total number of districts in tabulation is 218. The number of students in a district is measured by its unweighted ADM (average daily membership). Unweighted ADM, also termed state aid ADM, is the number of students for which the district receives state aid. Arizona school districts are labelled with a number according to their type. Type 02 districts are unified districts with the responsibility for educating students in grades K-12. Type 03 districts are elementary districts that have financial responsibility for the education of the high school students residing within district boundaries. These districts pay tuition to other districts to educate their high school students. Type 04 districts have responsibility for elementary students only, and type 05 have responsibility for high school students only.

Source: Arizona Department of Education and author's calculations.

<table>
<tr><td colspan="6">Table 17-7
Ratio of Actual Maintenance, Operation, and
Capital Outlay Spending to Equalization Base, 1987-88</td></tr>
<tr><td>District
Type</td><td>Mean</td><td>Minimum</td><td>Maximum</td><td colspan="2">Percentiles[*]</td></tr>
<tr><td>02</td><td>1.14</td><td>0.88</td><td>2.00</td><td>99</td><td>2.27</td></tr>
<tr><td>03</td><td>1.08</td><td>0.52</td><td>2.43</td><td>95</td><td>1.64</td></tr>
<tr><td>04</td><td>1.10</td><td>0.77</td><td>2.30</td><td>90</td><td>1.34</td></tr>
<tr><td>05</td><td>1.14</td><td>0.98</td><td>2.00</td><td>75</td><td>1.14</td></tr>
<tr><td>all districts</td><td>1.12</td><td>0.52</td><td>2.43</td><td>50</td><td>1.06</td></tr>
<tr><td></td><td></td><td></td><td></td><td>25</td><td>1.006</td></tr>
<tr><td></td><td></td><td></td><td></td><td>10</td><td>.93</td></tr>
<tr><td></td><td></td><td></td><td></td><td>5</td><td>.88</td></tr>
<tr><td></td><td></td><td></td><td></td><td>1</td><td>.70</td></tr>
</table>

[*] This part of the table reads as follows: The percentage of districts shown in the first column had spending ratios below the number shown in the second column. For example, 99 percent of all school districts had a ratio of actual spending to their equalization base of less than 2.27.

Note: Total number of districts in this tabulation is 208: 86 of type 02, 41 of type 03, 65 of type 04, and 16 of type 05. Number of omitted districts by type: zero for types 02 and 05; 9 for type 03; 1 for type 04. Districts were omitted if they had either no students, no teachers, or no information on tuition paid.

Source: Arizona Department of Education and authors' calculations.

Spending above the equalization base tends to be positively related to property wealth; the correlation between property value per student and the ratio of expenditures to the equalization base is 0.29. This result is consistent with the view that it is easier for relatively wealthy districts to take advantage of statutorily authorized opportunities for spending in excess of the equalization base limit. Evidence that this advantage is not offset by state aid is the -0.24 correlation between equalization aid per student and the ratio of expenditures to the equalization base. This negative correlation indicates that even though districts with low property value and/or high costs receive more equalization aid, they nevertheless spend less per weighted student than wealthier districts.

The variation in districts' spending relative to their equalization bases shown in Tables 17-7 and 17-8 signals significant inequality of educational opportunity. This is true regardless of whether the formulas that determine districts' equalization bases correctly adjust for interdistrict differences in per-student education costs.

On the one hand, if the cost adjustments are accurate, then each district's costs vary in proportion to its equalization base. Districts that spend more relative to their equalization base provide more educational services than districts that spend less. To a first approximation, equalizing educational opportunities in this case requires that the ratio of spending to equalization base be the same for all districts.

Table 17-8
Ratio of Actual Maintenance, Operation, and
Capital Outlay Spending to Equalization Base
Larger Districts with Positive Primary Tax Rate, 1987-88

District Type	Mean	Minimum	Maximum	Percentiles[*]	
02	1.11	0.88	1.92	99	1.87
03	1.02	0.82	1.15	95	1.28
04	1.06	0.93	1.21	90	1.18
05	1.09	0.98	1.26	75	1.11
all districts	1.08	0.82	1.92	50	1.06
				25	1.01
				10	.98
				5	.95
				1	.85

[*] This part of the table reads as follows: The percentage of districts shown in the first column had spending ratios below the number shown in the second column. For example, 99 percent of these school districts had a ratio of actual spending to their equalization base of less than 1.87.

Note: Total number of districts in this tabulation is 148: 72 of type 02, 14 of type 03, 47 of type 04, and 15 of type 05. Number of omitted districts by type: 14 for type 02; 36 for type 03; 19 for type 04; and 1 for type 05. Districts were omitted if they had either no students, no teachers, or no information on tuition paid. From the remaining 208 districts, districts were omitted if they had either a primary tax rate of zero or a student count less than 100 for 05 districts or less than 125 for 02, 03, and 04 districts.

Source: Arizona Department of Education and authors' calculations.

On the other hand, if the cost adjustments are inaccurate, then aid is *not* being distributed in a manner that equalizes districts' ability to provide educational services. To the extent that there is less than full adjustment for cost differences, the equalization base and state aid are too low for higher cost districts and too high for lower cost districts. Lower cost districts will therefore be able to provide more educational services than higher cost districts. The opposite will be true to the extent that there is over-compensation for actual cost differences. The likely consequence of inaccurate adjustment for cost differences is therefore unequal provision of educational services and inequality of educational opportunity.

Table 17-9
Number of Students in High and Low Expenditure Districts, 1987-1988[*]

	High Expenditure Districts			Low Expenditure Districts		
Type of District	Number of Students	Percent of Total Students	Number of Districts	Number of Students	Percent of Total Students	Number of Districts
02	152,343	26.9	39	2,873	0.5	3
03	1,829	0.3	12	526	0.1	9
04	43,812	7.7	18	1,458	0.3	3
05	27,739	4.9	6	0	0.0	0
All	225,723	39.8	75	4,857	0.9	15

[*] "High" expenditure districts are those with maintenance, operation and capital spending more than 10 percent above the district equalization base; "low" expenditure districts spent more than 10 percent below the equalization base.

Note: Total number of students in the state is 567,384. Total number of districts in this tabulation is 208: 86 of type 02, 41 of type 03, 65 of type 04, and 16 of type 05. Number of omitted districts by type: zero for types 02 and 05; 9 for type 03; 1 for type 04. Districts were omitted if they had either no students, no teachers, or no information on tuition paid.

Source: Arizona Department of Education and author's calculations.

Are current adjustments for interdistrict differences in costs in fact accurate? Probably not, for two reasons. First, the formulas used to calculate districts' equalization bases were, for the most part, set at the time of the 1980 reworking of the school finance system. While there have been some revisions, the formulas have essentially been unchanged since then. Yet there is little reason, for example, to expect that the relative costs of teaching handicapped and non-handicapped students have remained unchanged since 1980. The tools and techniques for educating students vary across time as do the costs of teachers, books, and other resources. As a result, the weights assigned to particular types of students and other cost adjustments may now fail to account accurately for cost differences. Second, the formulas do not include adjustments for all district and student attributes that may generate interdistrict cost differences.   For example, they do not allow for the likelihood that a student's performance is directly influenced by the attributes of her peers. If she attends school in a district that has a large fraction of economically disadvantaged students, then she may not do as well on standardized measures of performance as she would in a district with a less disadvantaged student body. In short, deficiencies of the formulas currently used in calculating equalization bases may well create inequities in the education provided by different school districts even if each district spends precisely the amount of its equalization base.

Taxpayer Equity

To determine how well the Arizona system measures up to the ideal of horizontal taxpayer equity, we must first define the level of educational services for which tax rates are to be compared. As explained above, the obvious choice is the equalization base since it is the level of spending used in the calculation of equalization aid. Taxpayer equity would require in this case that every district be able to finance its equalization base by levying the same property tax rate.

The top panel of Table 17-10 shows the wide interdistrict variation in per-student property value. Because of this variation, the tax rates required to finance the equalization base level of spending with no state aid or other revenue sources would be, in fact, far from equal.[8] Hypothetical tax rates, shown in the second panel of Table 17-10, are calculated on the assumption that each district utilizes no revenue sources other than property taxes and equalization aid to fund the equalization base. Despite the wide range of these tax rates, the rate required to fund the equalization base in *most* districts is equal to the present qualifying tax rate. Only 39 out of 223 districts (17 percent) had enough property value to be able to finance the equalization base level of spending at a rate less than their QTR.[9] Thus, property owners in 184 of the districts are treated fairly relative to one another, but as a group they are treated unfairly relative to property owners in the 39 higher property value districts.

Because a district's actual spending can exceed or fall below its equalization base and because in practice districts can draw on revenue sources other than property taxes and equalization aid, variation in actual tax rates is greater than variation in the hypothetical rates required to finance the base (see the third panel of Table 17-10). Over 100 districts levied primary tax rates that were less than the QTR in 1987/88.

Variation in the rates required to finance equalization bases more clearly indicates unfairness than variation in actual rates. The variation in hypothetical rates reflects dispersion of property wealth -- the fact that some districts have relatively high property wealth per student and therefore can fund the full equalization base with a tax rate below the qualifying tax rate. In contrast, relatively high or low actual rates may reflect decisions by district residents or governing boards to spend more or less.

Equality Of Outcome: Another Perspective On Student Equity

Student equity can be defined in terms of either educational opportunity or educational outcomes. As explained in the preceding section, cost-adjusted expenditure per student is, in principle, an appropriate indicator of educational opportunity. For it to be also an indicator of educational outcomes there must be a direct link between spending and outcomes such as high school completion rates and student performance on standardized tests. If there is no such link, equalizing cost-adjusted per student expenditures, as Arizona attempts to do with its present system of state school aid, may not achieve equity defined as equal educational outcomes. It will, of course, still promote the important goal of equal educational opportunity.

<table>
<tr><th colspan="5" align="center">Table 17-10
Variation in Property Tax Rates and
Property Tax Bases, SY 1987-88</th></tr>
<tr><th></th><th>QTR[1]</th><th>Mean</th><th>Minimum</th><th>Maximum</th></tr>
<tr><td>Dollars of Primary assessed value,
per student[2]</td><td></td><td></td><td></td><td></td></tr>
<tr><td>   02 districts</td><td></td><td>32,090</td><td>808</td><td>518,221</td></tr>
<tr><td>   03 districts</td><td></td><td>244,717</td><td>5,030</td><td>6,400,897</td></tr>
<tr><td>   04 districts</td><td></td><td>72,863</td><td>2,450</td><td>570,708</td></tr>
<tr><td>   05 districts</td><td></td><td>115,793</td><td>55,200</td><td>399,569</td></tr>
<tr><td>   All districts</td><td></td><td>93,182</td><td>808</td><td>6,400,897</td></tr>
<tr><td>Hypothetical tax rate required to fund
equalization base, dollars per $100 of
PAV[3]</td><td></td><td></td><td></td><td></td></tr>
<tr><td>   02 districts</td><td>4.72</td><td>4.58</td><td>0.84</td><td>4.72</td></tr>
<tr><td>   03 districts</td><td>4.72</td><td>3.83</td><td>0.06</td><td>4.72</td></tr>
<tr><td>   04 districts</td><td>2.36</td><td>2.28</td><td>0.79</td><td>2.36</td></tr>
<tr><td>   05 districts</td><td>2.36</td><td>2.30</td><td>1.40</td><td>2.36</td></tr>
<tr><td>Actual primary tax rate, 1987-88,
dollars per $100 of PAV</td><td></td><td></td><td></td><td></td></tr>
<tr><td>   02 districts</td><td>4.72</td><td>3.86</td><td>0.00</td><td>7.45</td></tr>
<tr><td>   03 districts</td><td>4.72</td><td>3.26</td><td>0.00</td><td>9.80</td></tr>
<tr><td>   04 districts</td><td>2.36</td><td>2.13</td><td>0.00</td><td>3.57</td></tr>
<tr><td>   05 districts</td><td>2.36</td><td>2.55</td><td>1.51</td><td>5.41</td></tr>
<tr><td>Actual secondary tax rate, 1987-
1988, dollars per $100 of SAV[4]</td><td></td><td></td><td></td><td></td></tr>
<tr><td>   02 districts</td><td></td><td>1.83</td><td>0.00</td><td>10.14</td></tr>
<tr><td>   03 districts</td><td></td><td>0.26</td><td>0.00</td><td>2.17</td></tr>
<tr><td>   04 districts</td><td></td><td>0.81</td><td>0.00</td><td>3.99</td></tr>
<tr><td>   05 districts</td><td></td><td>0.52</td><td>0.00</td><td>1.50</td></tr>
<tr><td>   All districts</td><td></td><td>1.10</td><td>0.00</td><td>10.14</td></tr>
</table>

[1] QTR = qualifying tax rate, in dollars per 100 dollars of primary assessed value.

[2] Total number of districts in this tabulation is 208: 86 of type 02, 41 of type 03, 65 of type 04, and 16 of type 05. Number of omitted districts by type: 0 for types 02 and 05; 9 for type 03; 1 for type 04. Districts were omitted if they had either no students, no teachers, or no information on tuition paid. Number of students, measured by unweighted or state aid ADM, is the number of students for which a district receives state aid.

[3] Districts of type 01 are omitted; total number of districts in tabulation is 218.

[4] SAV = secondary assessed valuation.

Source: Arizona Department of Education and authors' calculations.

On its face, it seems reasonable that increased expenditures would lead to improved student performance. And, in practice, simple correlations between expenditures and measures of student performance, such as district average (mean) scores on standardized tests, are often positive. But such simple correlations do not allow for the possibility that districts with higher expenditures may also have students with more innate ability. If innate ability determines performance, the positive correlation between expenditures and performance may only exist because of the positive correlation between expenditures and ability.

When researchers have carefully accounted for student ability, they have *not* found a consistent relationship between performance and either expenditures or inputs to the schooling process (Hanushek, 1986). The assumption that increases in expenditures can be translated into improved outcomes is therefore a controversial one which to date is not supported by strong evidence.

Performance and Expenditures: Evidence from Arizona

We have used Arizona data to estimate how expenditures affect performance when the influence of student and school district characteristics is also taken into account. This is the information needed to understand how a state's school finance system affects student equity defined in terms of outcomes.

Given the complexity of the schooling process and the likelihood that districts pursue a number of objectives, there is no single measure of student performance that would be ideal for comparison across all districts. We chose as primary indicators of student performance the district means of students' raw scores on the Iowa Test of Basic Skills (3rd and 6th grades) and the Stanford Achievement Test (11th grade). We computed for each district a basic score equal to the sum of the raw scores on the English, reading, and mathematics sections of the test.[10] We also included the dropout rate as a measure of student performance to allow for the possibility that districts differ in the value placed on student retention.

Table 17-11 presents information on the 1987/88 distributions of test scores and dropout (retention) rates. Scores do exhibit noticeable dispersion. Whether reducing this dispersion would require a reworking of the equalization base formula can only be judged by determining the extent to which the dispersion is due to interdistrict differences in the average innate ability of students, to differences in per-student expenditures, or to some combination of peer group and environmental factors that make students in some districts more costly to teach than students in other districts.

The correlations of Table 17-12 offer an initial look at the relationship between expenditures and student performance. From this table, it does not appear that expenditures have a positive effect on scores. Instead, test scores and expenditures exhibit a statistically strong *negative* correlation. Similarly, the correlation between the dropout rate and measures of expenditure is *positive*. Although these correlations do not support the view that increases in expenditures can be translated into improved performance, they also do not rule out that possibility. There could be other causal factors, which are inversely correlated with expenditures, that are overriding any positive effect expenditures have on student performance. There could be aspects of performance that are not adequately measured by test scores.

The general problem we face is one of isolating the separate effects on performance of environmental factors (student and district characteristics) and resources used in the teaching process. Linear regression is a technique for estimating the separate effects of several variables on a variable of interest. Therefore, using data from the 1986/87 and 1987/88 school years, we regressed district means of standardized test scores of 11th graders on resources used in the teaching process (teachers, aides and other classified employees, supplies and materials, etc.) and on student characteristics. (For a thorough discussion of the estimation of such education production functions, see Hanushek, 1986.) Table 17-13 presents two representative regressions.

<table>
<tr><td colspan="5">Table 17-11
Distributions of Student
Performance Measures in 1987-88</td></tr>
<tr><td>Variable</td><td>Mean</td><td>Standard
Deviation</td><td>Minimum</td><td>Maximum</td></tr>
<tr><td>Basic test score, Grade 6</td><td>207.89</td><td>26.87</td><td>110.5</td><td>295.0</td></tr>
<tr><td>Basic test score, Grade 11</td><td>152.46</td><td>13.44</td><td>113.5</td><td>175.6</td></tr>
<tr><td>Basic test score, Grade 12</td><td>158.86</td><td>14.12</td><td>112.6</td><td>183.5</td></tr>
<tr><td>Dropout rate</td><td>8.90</td><td>4.11</td><td>0.0</td><td>23.7</td></tr>
</table>

Note: Standard deviation is a statistical measure of dispersion.

Source: Arizona Department of Education and authors' calculations.

<table>
<tr><td colspan="4">Table 17-12
Correlations between Expenditure
Measures and Performance Measures, 1987-88</td></tr>
<tr><td></td><td>M & O
Expenditures Per
Weighted ADM</td><td>Total Expenditures
Relative to
Equalization Base</td><td>Equalization
Aid Per
Weighted ADM</td></tr>
<tr><td>Basic score, Grade 6</td><td>-.03</td><td>-.19*</td><td>-.33*</td></tr>
<tr><td>Basic score, Grade 11</td><td>-.14</td><td>-.23*</td><td>-.44*</td></tr>
<tr><td>Basic score, Grade 12</td><td>-.15</td><td>-.26*</td><td>-.39*</td></tr>
<tr><td>Dropout rate</td><td>.21*</td><td>.16</td><td>.27*</td></tr>
</table>

* Indicates correlation is statistically significant at the .05 level.

Note: A correlation coefficient of 1.00 is a perfect, positive correlation, while a
        correlation coefficient of -1.00 indicates a perfect, negative correlation.

Source: Arizona Department of Education and authors' calculations.

Table 17-13
Estimates of the Education Production Function Dependent Variable: Log of District Mean of Basic Scores of Eleventh Graders
(Asymptotic standard errors in parentheses)

Independent Variables	Model 1 Coefficients	Model 2 Coefficients
Intercept	0.6287* (0.1746)	0.7749* (0.1427)
Log of teachers TEI** (in per pupil terms)	0.2181* (0.0529)	0.1285* (0.0414)
Log of other certified employees per pupil	-0.0117 (0.0199)	0.0258 (0.0156)
Log of materials and supplies expenditures per pupil	-0.0078 (0.0135)	0.0112 (0.0135)
Log of classified employees per pupil	-0.1088* (0.0287)	0.0144 (0.0208)
Log of weighted average daily membership (WADM)	-0.1157* (0.0462)	-0.0569 (0.0442)
Log of average daily membership (ADM)	0.1318* (0.0475)	0.0870 (0.0463)
Fraction of district's students with limited English proficiency	-0.6557* (0.1041)	-0.1335 (0.0961)
Square of fraction of students with limited English proficiency	0.4845* (0.0978)	0.1450 (0.0773)
Fraction of district's students who were Hispanic		-0.1574* (0.0254)
Fraction of district's students who were Native Americans		-0.3151* (0.0286)
Fraction of district's students who were Black		-0.5252* (0.1378)

Notes: 1. Test scores were the basic score calculated for the Stanford Achievement test. Data are from the 1986/87 and the 1987/88 school years. The parameters are constrained to be the same across time.
2. Coefficients marked with an asterisk are significant at the 5 percent level.
3. Standard errors are consistent against heteroskedasticity and first-order autocorrelation.
4. ** Teacher Experience Index

Regression model 1 shows the estimated effects on test scores of educational inputs, average daily membership (included to allow for possible scale economies), weighted average daily attendance (a measure of statutorily recognized influences on a district's ability to translate dollars into performance), the fraction of students in the district with limited English proficiency, and the square of this variable.[11]   The results confirm the expectation that limited English proficiency tends to be associated with relatively low test scores, but they also indicate that several of the input measures are negatively correlated with test scores. For example, districts with more classified employees per pupil tend to have lower test scores, all else equal. The only input that is positively correlated with test scores is the number of teachers per student adjusted for the teacher experience index. However, these results should be interpreted with caution because potentially important district and student characteristics may not have been taken into account.

The need for caution is confirmed by the second regression equation which also includes measures of the ethnic composition of the districts. It shows that the negative correlation between input measures and test scores observed in the first equation was attributable to the correlation of input mixes with ethnic composition. In this second regression, each of the inputs is positively correlated with performance; the coefficients on the inputs are jointly significant;[12] and the coefficient on the teachers-per-student measure is individually significant. These results reinforce the conclusions reached in an Arizona Department of Education study which examined the relationship between student performance and the "at risk" status of students. In that study, differences in the fraction of minority students and the fraction with limited English proficiency explained much of the interdistrict variation in test scores.

Policy Implications

The estimated production functions in Table 17-13 provide a tentative answer to the question of how educational outcomes might be enhanced in districts with large fractions of disadvantaged students. They imply that increased aid to districts with high concentrations of such students would raise test scores and thus reduce disparities in student performance if the aid is channeled into expenditures for teachers, teacher aides, and other inputs to the schooling process.

At the same time, considering that the link between inputs and student performance estimated in this and other studies, surveyed in Hanushek (1986), is relatively weak, increases in unconditional (lump sum) aid may not be the best means of achieving greater equity of educational outcomes. That is not to say that increased aid should not be part of the effort to improve equity. But, as Hanushek (1989) and others have suggested, aid should be structured to provide teachers and school administrators with incentives to seek the most effective programs. For example, seed money might be targeted initially to districts with high fractions of educationally disadvantaged students with future aid contingent on improved student performance. Careful consideration would have to be given to the question of how to measure performance. Clearly, it is in no one's interest to provide incentives only to teach students how to perform well on standardized tests. Nevertheless, once appropriate performance measures are chosen, performance-based aid (more than unconditional aid) encourages schools to seek a mix of programs that best achieves these performance goals.

Conclusion And Potential Policy Changes

Since 1980 Arizona has enacted changes in its school finance system that on balance reduce interdistrict variation in tax rates and spending. However, as the data in Tables 17-7 through 17-10 show, there remains considerable unevenness in the treatment of both students and taxpayers.

Although the current state aid formula allows all districts to spend their equalization base amount by levying *no more* than the qualifying tax rate, several districts are able to spend the base amount while levying primary tax rates substantially *below* the qualifying tax rate. In addition, the aid formula exerts no equalizing effect on expenditures allowed above the equalization base. Due to the extreme variation in property wealth in the state, school districts have varying capabilities to finance bond issues, expenditure overrides, and items statutorily placed outside the equalization base limits. As Bishop and Richardson note (1988:11), some districts cannot take advantage of these types of spending "because of the prohibitive effect on the tax rate, and among those who do use them, the impact on the rate varies considerably from a few cents in one district to several dollars in another."

As districts have expressed a greater desire to spend above their equalization base (see Table 17-9), the Legislature has responded by allowing extra budget capacity above equalization base limits. While this increased budget capacity has permitted more extensive local choice, it also has increased the opportunity for "unequalized" spending.

This section identifies several means of moving toward more uniformity in tax rates and per-student expenditures, assuming that it is desirable to do so. The section also explores the feasibility of permitting greater choice while maintaining student and taxpayer equity.

Minimum Tax Rate

To reduce variation in tax rates and local effort, the state can require that property in *all* districts be subject to taxation at a specified minimum rate in order to finance the equalization base level of spending. One means of doing so is the following. Define the minimum rate as the qualifying tax rate for state aid. Then for each district, calculate the difference between its equalization base and the revenue that it could obtain by taxing its property at the qualifying tax rate. If this difference is positive, the district receives equalization aid in that amount just as it does under the present system. If the difference is negative, the district pays the difference as an "equalization property tax" into a fund to finance state aid. Equalization aid and the equalization property tax are thus determined by the formulas:

1. equalization aid = EB - (QTR x PAV/100)
2. equalization property tax = (QTR x PAV/100) - EB

where the first formula applies in districts that cannot finance their equalization base with the qualifying tax rate, and the second applies in districts that can. If EB - (QTR x PAV/100)=0 then the district neither receives aid nor contributes to the equalization aid fund. With this system, each district's local effort is the qualifying tax rate multiplied by the primary assessed value of its property. This is the amount that the district must obtain from sources other than state aid to finance its equalization base.

Applying this system statewide in 1987-88 would have yielded more than enough to finance the equalization base in 16 districts and generated a surplus totalling $89 million.

This surplus would have been collected and placed in the state aid fund and distributed to other school districts to cover the cost of lowering the qualifying tax rate. Of this $89 million, $69 million (or 78 percent) would have come from one district, Ruth Fisher Elementary. Tax rates would have been lower and aid would have been higher in 178 of 208 districts.[13] Unlike the present system, property located in wealthy parts of the state would have been taxed at the qualifying tax rate to help provide the equalization base level of educational services in each district. Each district would have been able to fund the equalization base amount with the same primary property tax rate, and equally situated taxpayers would have been subject to the same school district primary property tax rates regardless of where they reside or own property. The result would have been horizontally equitable treatment of taxpayers at the equalization base level of spending.

This example clearly shows that it is not necessary to increase state funding of schools in order to equalize the tax rate required to finance a target level of spending such as the equalization base. Neither is it necessary to substitute state-level income and sales taxes for local property taxes. This means that the question of whether to change the distribution of aid so as to increase horizontal equity for students and taxpayers can in principle be separated from the question of whether to increase or decrease reliance on state funds and particular taxes. The latter is mainly a question of vertical (rather than horizontal) equity that extends beyond school finance. Its resolution requires comparison of the incidence of property, income, and sales taxes.

Increasing state aid, financed with uniform state-level taxes, would, of course, reduce variation in the local property tax rates required to fund the equalization base. In principle, if state aid were increased to the point that local revenue finances an insignificant part of total school spending, then the horizontal taxpayer inequities described above would likewise be insignificant. But school finance would no longer be a joint state-local responsibilty. Therefore, Arizona must choose (explicitly or implicitly) between the present wide variation in tax rates and either a minimum property tax, increased funding from statewide taxes, or some combination of the two.[14]

Access to Overrides

Much of the variation in actual spending, especially in spending relative to the equalization base, is due to the uneven use of overrides. This uneven use reflects, in part, the large variation in per-student property wealth and in the tax rate required to finance an override. The rates required to fund a 10 percent override in 1986/87 ranged from $0.009 to over $3 per $100 of assessed value (Arizona Legislature, 1987), and the range of variation and ranking of districts has not changed significantly since then. The districts using overrides tend to be those that can do so at relatively low tax rates. Although a number of districts with low property wealth and high tax rates have overrides in effect currently, the average levy for the current overrides ($0.71 per $100 of assessed value) is less than the average required if all districts financed a 10 percent override (that average is just under $1.00).

Access to overrides can be made more uniform only by either increasing the revenue that relatively low wealth districts derive from levying a given tax rate or decreasing the revenue that relatively wealthy districts derive from levying the same rate. One relatively simple means of doing so would be to have the state share in the costs of overrides according to a "power equalizing" formula:

$$\text{override aid per student} = t \times (V^* - V)$$

for $V \leq V^*$, where V^* is valuation per student in a hypothetical reference district, V is valuation per student in the district for which override aid is being calculated, and t is the override tax rate levied by that district. A district would not receive aid if its per-student valuation exceeds the valuation of the reference district -- if V exceeds V^*. With aid distributed in this manner, levying a given tax rate, for example $1 per $100 of valuation, would yield the same amount of revenue per student in all districts with a valuation less than or equal to the reference district valuation of V^*. The state would thus supplement the revenues raised by a low wealth district whose residents choose to tax themselves to spend above their equalization base.

Determining override aid by the above power-equalizing formula does not equalize the increase in per-student *educational services* that can be obtained from a given override levy since per-student costs vary across districts. Instead, levying a given override tax rate increases the availability of educational services more in low cost districts than in high cost districts.

Furthermore, power-equalizing aid does not, in general, equalize the increase in educational services that districts will *choose* to provide with override spending. The reason is that for districts with $V \leq V^*$, the power equalization formula decreases the cost of an additional dollar of spending to V/V^*. (In the absence of power equalization, an additional dollar of spending costs a district one dollar of local resources.) With power equalization, districts with low valuations may therefore be more willing to approve an override than districts with valuations close to V^*. The cost of an override is also lower for districts with valuations above V^* than for districts with valuation of V^*. Because of this "price" effect, educational services provided through overrides are unlikely to be equalized, even if the effect of wealth (property value) differences is eliminated by defining the reference district as the district with the highest valuation per student. Nonetheless, power equalization can reduce the (inverse) correlation between district resources and the use of overrides.

If override aid is financed from state taxes, the state's cost increases as the reference district valuation increases, and it is greatest when the reference district is the wealthiest and access to overrides is fully equalized. Because of the extremely wide variation in per-student valuation, it would be very costly for Arizona to provide full equalization. Therefore, it would probably be necessary to provide equalization for only a fraction of districts, for example, the poorest half.

Providing override aid need not increase the state's total aid costs. The state can reduce its equalization aid (by increasing the qualifying tax rate) to compensate for the expected cost of override aid. And this can be done without sacrificing horizontal equity in the distribution of equalization aid.

Retaining the present upper limits on overrides (10 percent in most instances) may be called for as a means of limiting the state's outlay for override aid. A limit may also be justified as a means of limiting inequalities in the availability of educational opportunities.

Spending Outside Equalization Base Limits

The state can reduce variation in districts' spending relative to their equalization bases by eliminating statutory provisions for spending outside the limits for purposes such as excess utilities, excess insurance, and desegregation costs. There is a two-part rationale for doing so. First, to the extent that the need to spend for these purposes varies significantly across districts, that fact should be allowed for in calculating the equalization base. Adjusting equalization bases for these cost differences seems just as appropriate as adjusting for transportation cost differences. Second, to the extent that these provisions are *not* valid adjustments for high or extra costs, they should be eliminated completely. A district could still spend for these purposes, but in doing so it would have to remain within its equalization base limit. All adjustments for genuine interdistrict differences in costs would then be reflected in the equalization base, and spending above the equalization base would be limited to overrides.

The pressures that have led to expanded options for overrides and spending above the equalization base limit reflect in part a desire by some districts to spend more than the limits allow and the willingness of legislators to find some means of allowing districts to spend above the limits if they are able and willing to do so *from their own sources*. The recent trend has therefore been to allow greater spending but to do so in a manner that conflicts with student equity. Had the legislature allowed spending to increase *on an equalized basis* for property-rich and property-poor districts alike, it would have had to increase either total equalization aid or the qualifying tax rate. Both of these options were apparently politically unattractive. The lesson to be drawn from the Arizona experience of the past decade is that allowing greater local choice will necessarily reduce student equity. The citizens of Arizona and their elected representatives must decide the appropriate tradeoffs between these two conflicting goals. The policy options discussed here cannot eliminate the need to make tradeoffs, but they can help the state's citizens understand the main alternatives.

References

Amemiya, Takeshi. 1985. *Advanced Econometrics*. Harvard University Press, Boston.

Arizona Department of Education. 1989. *The "At Risk" Status of Arizona School Districts*.

Arizona Department of Education. 1988a. *Education Statistics*, June.

Arizona Department of Education. 1988b. *Annual Report of the Superintendent of Public Instruction, 1987/88*.

Arizona Legislature. 1987. *School Finance in Arizona: 1980/81 through 1986/87*. A Report to the Joint Legislative Committee to Study Funding Priorities of the Public School System. Phoenix.

Arizona Legislature, Joint Legislative Committee to Study Funding Priorities of the Public School System. 1989. *1988 Final Report*. Phoenix.

Bishop, C. Diane and Judy Richardson. 1988. *The Role of the State in Financing Elementary and Secondary Education in Arizona*. Prepared for the Joint Select Committee on State Revenues and Expenditures. Arizona Department of Education. Phoenix.

Coleman, James S. *et al.* 1966. *Equality of Educational Opportunity*. Washington: U.S. Department of Health, Education, and Welfare, Office of Education.

Downes, Thomas A. 1989. "Evaluating the Impact of the Serrano Decision and Proposition 13 on the Provision of Public Education in California." *Mimeograph*, Northwestern University.

Feldstein, Martin S. 1975. "Wealth Neutrality and Local Public Choice in Education." *American Economic Review*. 65 (March): 75-89.

Hanushek, Eric A. 1986. "The Economics of Schooling: Production and Efficiency in the Public Schools." *Journal of Economic Literature*. 24 (September): 1141-1177.

Hanushek, Eric A. 1989. "Expenditures, Efficiency, and Equity in Education: The Federal Government's Role." *American Economic Review.* 79 (May):46-51.

Lockwood, Robert C. 1988. *Public School Finance in Arizona.* Arizona House of Representatives. Phoenix.

Lockwood, Robert C. 1989. *Legislation: Public Schools.* Arizona House of Representatives. Phoenix.

Pogue, Thomas F. 1989. "School District Fiscal Capacity: Measurement and Equalization," *Proceedings of the Eighty-Second Annual Conference on Taxation, National Tax Association.*

Verstegsen, Deborah. 1988. *School Finance at a Glance.* Education Commission of the States. Denver.

Endnotes

1. When taxes are based on benefits received, horizontal equity requires equal tax burdens for persons who benefit equally from governmental services.

2. The fundamental problem that arises because of fiscal capacity differences is that individuals are treated unfairly relative to one another. The problem is not that some areas of the state fare differently; differences among areas are of concern only to the extent that they generate unfair differences in the treatment of individuals.

3. Disparities in fiscal capacity may lead to another problem: essentially identical businesses that are located in different school districts may pay different taxes. Such differential taxation may lead businesses to favor low-tax over high-tax districts even if the latter are more desirable except for taxes.

4. Among the states, only Hawaii has chosen to finance most of its K-12 education spending with state-level taxes; management responsiblility is also at the state level.

5. Since 1980, Arizona has assigned two distinct values to most property parcels: "limited" and "full cash" values. Limited value cannot exceed full cash value, and the annual rate of increase of limited value cannot exceed the larger of either 10 percent or 25 percent of the difference between cash value and the previous year limited value. "Primary" taxes, used to finance the maintenance and operation expenditures of counties, cities, and school districts, are levied on limited (or primary) assessed values. "Secondary" taxes, used to finance debt retirement, voter approved overrides, and spending by special service districts, are levied on full cash (or secondary) values.

6. Small districts are elementary districts with a student count of 125 or less; high school districts with 100 or less; unified districts with 125 or less in grades K-8, or 100 or less in grades 9-12. There were 48 such districts in 1988/89. While small districts may have special spending needs due to their size, it is not clear why they should be completely free of the expenditure limits that apply to other districts. It should be possible to define equalization base limits that allow for any additional costs faced by small districts just as factors that affect the costs of larger districts have been taken into account when defining their equalization base limits.

7. The federal government distributes "impact aid," P.L. 81-874 funds, to support the education of students living on federally owned lands where property taxes cannot be levied such as Indian reservations and military bases.

8. Equalization aid is designed to reduce variation in the local tax rate required to fund the equalization base.
9. By design of the equalization formula, no district has to impose a tax rate greater than the qualifying tax rate to fund the equalization base.
10. Similar results were obtained with scores on individual test components (reading, math, etc.). The conclusions we draw below do not depend on our decision to use aggregate scores.
11. Including the squared value of the fraction of students with limited English proficiency allows for the possibliltiy of a nonlinear relationship between student performance and that variable. A nonlinear relationship could arise if there are either economies or diseconomies of scale in providing specialized teaching for students with limited English proficiency.
12. By jointly significant we mean that the coefficients on the input variables *taken as a group* differ significantly from zero. For discussion of such joint significance tests, see Amemiya (1985).
13. Districts that have both elementary and secondary students would have been able to finance spending in the amount of their equalization bases with a tax rate of $4.06 versus $4.72 at present; the corresponding rates for districts that have only one type of student are $2.03 and $2.36. An alternative approach would be to merge the wealthy districts with other less wealthy districts so that none of the merged districts is able to fund fully its equalization base with revenues obtained by levying the QTR. Then the question of what to do with excess revenues would not arise.
14. The long-term, nationwide trend in school finance has been a shift from reliance on local revenues, usually property taxes, to greater reliance on state aid raised through state-level taxes. This shift has reduced horizontal taxpayer inequities, but it is not the only available means of doing so.

Chapter 18

Unrestricted State Aid to Cities and Counties

Michael E. Bell

Over the last decade, our federal system has undergone a significant realignment of revenue raising and spending responsibilities. As a result, state and local governments face added pressure on their revenue raising systems at a time when these governments confront taxpayer revolts and compete more aggressively for firms and families.

The purpose of this chapter is to examine trends in one source of local revenue, state aid to local governments in Arizona. The chapter describes how the relative importance and composition of state aid has changed over time. The chapter then addresses two fundamental policy issues associated with unrestricted state assistance to local governments: (1) does the distribution of state aid compensate for fiscal disparities among local jurisdictions? and (2) do local governments substitute state revenues for local own-source revenues?

The next section identifies trends in state assistance in Arizona and its neighboring states. A description of specific state assistance programs in Arizona and trends in spending levels follows. The next section evaluates the impact of unrestricted state assistance programs in Arizona on fiscal disparities across local governments in the state. The final section summarizes the major findings and conclusions of the analysis.

Interstate Comparisons Of State Assistance To Local Governments

Arizona state government allocates a larger share of its expenditures (40.4 percent) for local assistance than states nationally (30.5 percent). As Table 18-1 indicates, in the aggregate, local governments in Arizona rely on state assistance for a slightly larger share of general revenues (35.8 percent) than do local governments nationally (33.3 percent). However, counties and school districts in Arizona receive somewhat less support from state aid than similar jurisdictions nationally, while cities rely on state assistance as a source of revenue to a somewhat greater extent than cities nationally. This section presents a discussion of the importance of state aid to local governments in Arizona and compares Arizona to several other states.[1]

In 1987, local governments in Arizona received $2.1 billion in assistance from the state government equal to $648 *per capita*. While Arizona's *per capita* state assistance to local governments was 14 percent above the national average ($567), it ranked in the middle of the seven comparison states in Table 18-1. California ($971) provided the greatest amount of state aid *per capita* to local governments and Texas ($389) provided the least.

Table 18-1
State Assistance To Local Governments:
***Per Capita* Aid And As A Share Of General Revenues**

	Per Capita Aid				
	1966--67	**1971--72**	**1976--77**	**1981--82**	**1986--87**
Arizona	$ 94	$174	$305	$450	$648
California	148	256	410	698	971
Colorado	98	153	263	363	459
Florida	66	124	257	340	489
Nevada	103	187	271	569	702
New Mexico	131	206	345	619	737
Texas	63	101	172	293	389
Utah	89	135	242	338	458
U.S.	94	168	281	414	567

	Share Of Local General Revenues (Percent)				
	1966-67	**1971-72**	**1976-77**	**1981-82**	**1986-87**
Arizona	33.4	36.5	37.2	37.3	35.8
California	32.4	34.6	35.2	44.7	44.0
Colorado	29.7	29.9	29.3	26.8	24.4
Florida	24.8	30.2	33.8	30.4	28.7
Nevada	26.3	32.7	28.0	39.9	37.0
New Mexico	47.9	50.3	53.1	57.0	48.9
Texas	28.3	28.4	27.7	27.6	24.5
Utah	38.2	37.9	38.3	31.3	32.5
U.S.	31.5	33.4	33.7	34.0	33.3

Source: U.S. Census Bureau, *Government Finances*, various years

Over the 20 years reflected in Table 18-1, state assistance to local governments in Arizona increased 588 percent compared to an increase of 505 percent for local governments nationally. *Per capita* state assistance to local governments in Arizona increased from 100 percent of the national average in 1967 to 114 percent in 1987.

Data in the second panel of Table 18-1 show that local governments in all comparison states (except Utah), and the nation as a whole, increased their "dependence" on state assistance from 1967 to 1972. That is, the share of total local general revenues coming from state assistance increased between 1967 and 1972. No trend is discernible from 1972 to 1982, local governments in four states became more dependent and local governments in three states became less dependent on state aid as a source of general revenues. From 1982 to 1987, however, local governments in Arizona and all comparison states (except Utah) mirrored the national trend of reduced reliance on state assistance as a share of local general revenues. The recent trend toward more self reliant local governments may be an important harbinger of structural change in our federal system in the 1990s as a result of what John Shannon, former Executive Director of the Advisory Commission on Intergovernmental Relations, has characterized as the Reagan administration's legacy of fend-for-yourself-federalism.

At the same time that state aid has declined in relative importance, local governments in Arizona and the nation have also sustained significant cuts in federal aid. The data in Table 18-2 indicate that for local governments nationally and in Arizona, California, Colorado, and Florida, federal aid *per capita* peaked in 1982. Local governments in these states received significantly less federal aid *per capita* in 1987 and their relative reliance on federal aid declined from 1982 to 1987 (see second panel in Table 18-2).

For the other comparison states (Nevada, New Mexico, Texas and Utah) *per capita* federal aid increased throughout the period (except in New Mexico from 1977 to 1982). In spite of the continued increase in *per capita* federal aid in these states, the relative importance of federal aid (expressed as a share of local general revenues) declined from 1982 to 1987. The sole exception is Nevada where federal aid has accounted for an average of 5.3 percent of local general revenues since 1977.

For local governments nationally, federal aid decreased between 1982 and 1987 by $10 *per capita* and state aid increased by $153 *per capita*. In those states where federal aid declined between 1982 and 1987 (by an average of $15 *per capita*), state aid increased (by an average $179 *per capita*). Alternatively, in those states where federal aid continued to increase over the 1982 to 1987 period (by an average of $12 *per capita*), state aid grew more slowly (by an average of $117 *per capita*). While this sample is very small, these trends suggest some degree of replacement of state assistance for declining federal assistance at least in the aggregate.

Despite the growth in *per capita* state aid, local governments nationally, in Arizona, and in six of the seven comparison states are more self sufficient in 1987. For all comparison states except Utah, the share of total local general revenues from own-source revenues increased between 1982 and 1987 (See Table 18-3). In fact, the trend toward local self sufficiency has been emerging over the last 10 years. Local governments in Arizona and all comparison states, except California and Nevada, generated a larger share of general revenues from own-sources in 1987 then they did a decade earlier.[2] However, local governments in Arizona and three comparison states (California, Florida, and Nevada) generated a smaller share of general revenues in 1987 than they did in 1967. Local governments in the other four comparison states were more self sufficient financially in 1987 than during the previous 20 years.

State assistance in Arizona, and other states, is not allocated uniformally across all types of local governments. For example, school districts in Arizona depend on state assistance for 49.5 percent of their total general revenues. This is slightly less than school districts nationally which receive 52.8 percent of their general revenues from state assistance.

In 1987, counties in Arizona received 29 percent of their total general revenues from state assistance, somewhat less than the national average of 32 percent. The Arizona share is up slightly from 27 percent in 1977. In contrast, counties nationally reduced their reliance on state assistance over this ten year period falling from 35 percent to 32 percent of general revenue.

Table 18-2				
Federal Assistance To Local Governments				
***Per Capita* Aid And As A Share Of Local General Revenues**				

	Per Capita Aid				
	1966-67	**1971-72**	**1976-77**	**1981-82**	**1986--87**
Arizona	$11	$24	$70	$88	$ 80
California	12	25	77	88	73
Colorado	10	25	62	79	64
Florida	8	16	78	97	74
Nevada	14	20	53	73	101
New Mexico	25	49	87	78	89
Texas	6	16	53	63	65
Utah	9	14	58	62	69
U.S.	10	22	78	91	81

	Share Of Local General Revenues (Percent)				
	1966-67	**1971-72**	**1976-77**	**1981-82**	**1986-87**
Arizona	4.0	5.0	8.6	7.3	4.4
California	2.7	3.4	6.6	5.6	3.3
Colorado	3.0	4.9	7.0	5.9	3.4
Florida	3.0	3.8	10.2	8.7	4.4
Nevada	3.5	3.5	5.5	5.1	5.3
New Mexico	9.1	11.8	13.3	7.1	5.9
Texas	2.8	4.5	8.5	6.0	4.1
Utah	4.0	4.1	9.2	5.8	4.9
U.S.	3.2	4.3	9.3	7.5	4.8

Source: U.S. Census Bureau, *Government Finances*, various years.

Cities in Arizona relied on state assistance for about one-quarter of their general revenues in 1977 and 1987. This was slightly more than cities nationally which received 23 and 21 percent of their general revenues from state assistance in 1977 and 1987, respectively.

In summary, the state of Arizona devotes a larger share of its expenditures to local assistance than states nationally. However, state assistance is a smaller share of general revenues in counties and school districts in Arizona than it is nationally but somewhat more important for cities. This seemingly contradictory evidence reflects lower direct state expenditures and higher direct local expenditures in Arizona than in the nation as a whole. In other words, while the State of Arizona allocates a greater than average share of its limited expenditures to local governments, local governments have greater than average spending responsibilities in the state's relatively decentralized system. Thus, local governments in Arizona must still finance a near-average portion of their expenditures from own-source revenues.

Table 18-3
Local Own-source Revenues:
***Per Capita* And As A Share Of Local General Revenues**

	Per Capita Own-Source Revenues				
	1966-67	**1971-72**	**1976-77**	**1981-82**	**1986-87**
Arizona	$177	$279	$444	$667	$1082
California	297	458	676	775	1164
Colorado	223	333	571	912	1355
Florida	193	270	426	680	1144
Nevada	275	421	644	783	1096
New Mexico	118	156	218	389	680
Texas	154	239	395	706	1133
Utah	134	207	332	680	882
U.S.	194	313	475	711	1054
	Share Of Local General Revenues (Percent)				
	1966-67	**1971-72**	**1976-77**	**1981-82**	**1986-87**
Arizona	62.7	58.5	54.2	55.4	59.8
California	65.0	61.9	58.2	49.7	52.7
Colorado	67.3	65.2	63.7	67.3	72.2
Florida	72.2	65.9	56.1	60.9	67.0
Nevada	70.2	73.7	66.5	54.9	57.7
NewMexico	43.1	37.9	33.6	35.9	45.2
Texas	68.9	67.1	63.8	66.5	71.4
Utah	57.8	58.1	52.4	62.9	62.6
U.S.	65.3	62.3	57.0	58.5	61.9

Source: U.S. Census Bureau, *Government Finances*, various years.

State Assistance To Cities And Counties In Arizona

The economic theory of intergovernmental grants identifies two separate roles for aid from one government to another.[3] The first role is to correct for positive interjurisdictional spillovers. A spillover (or externality) occurs when the benefits of a locally provided public good or service accrue to non-residents. In this case, the jurisdiction will provide a level of public goods and services which is too low from a society-wide perspective because local decision makers do not take into account the benefits received by non-residents.

In order to encourage the local government to provide more of the public good benefiting non-residents, an appropriate solution is for other affected jurisdictions to subsidize local provision at a rate that reflects the level of benefit accruing to non-residents. Examples of goods and services with spillover benefits include local transportation systems, education systems, recreation facilities, public welfare programs and publicly provided safety. The form of grant to best accomplish this objective is an open-ended matching categorical grant.[4] An example of such a categorical program in Arizona is the Highway User Revenue Fund (HURF) which provides state assistance for highways, streets, roads and bridges although the grant program is not open-ended.

The second primary role for intergovernmental grants identified in the literature is to facilitate fiscal equalization or to mitigate the impact on local jurisdictions and their residents of unequal fiscal resources and needs (fiscal disparities). Jurisdictions vary in terms of their wealth (and needs) so different tax rates will be necessary to provide equal expenditures (or equal levels and/or quality of public services). As a result, individuals of equal income living in different jurisdictions may pay substantially different shares of their income for the same level or quality of public services. In other words, horizontal inequities may occur.

Capitalization of these tax and expenditure differences into property values may mitigate some of the horizontal inequity problem. However, imperfect mobility will likely result in a system whereby relatively wealthy jurisdictions can provide a given level of service at a lower tax rate and lower tax-inclusive price of housing than less wealthy jurisdictions.

On equity grounds, intergovernmental assistance may be desirable if the tax price faced by individuals of equal income in different jurisdictions providing a standard level and quality of service differ because one jurisdiction is less wealthy than another. Specifically, if a less wealthy jurisdiction finds it prohibitively expensive to achieve a given minimum standard, then grants to relatively poor jurisdictions can be justified. Because states define local revenue raising and expenditure responsibilities, state general assistance is most appropriate for addressing such distributional objectives. An example of such aid in Arizona is the Urban Revenue Sharing program which is state assistance to cities and towns that can be used for any local government purpose, *i.e.*, it is unrestricted revenue to the jurisdiction.

The State of Arizona has over two dozen programs providing both categorical and unrestricted state assistance to local governments. Generally, these programs are grouped into two categories: (1) what are commonly referred to as state shared revenues, and (2) state appropriated funds for local assistance.

State shared revenues include the personal and corporation income tax, general sales tax, motor fuel tax, motor vehicle license tax, lottery receipts, liquor license tax, in-lieu watercraft license tax, gas and fuel tax used for watercraft, fire insurance premium tax and fines, penalties and forfeitures collected by the courts for criminal offenses and traffic violations. Some of these shared revenue programs provide unrestricted assistance to local governments in Arizona. Other programs provide categorical assistance to local governments for specific purposes (for example, motor fuel taxes and lottery revenues are earmarked for transportation).

In Arizona, many of the state shared revenues are traditionally referred to as shared taxes. However, these funds are really state aid to local governments from earmarked revenue sources. That is, the funds come from state revenue sources, local governments have no control over the amount of revenue collected, and the funds are distributed by formula rather than returned to the jurisdiction of origin. This is in contrast to local income taxes in Maryland, for example, which are truly shared tax revenues since local governments accept the state's definition of taxable income, but each jurisdiction sets its own tax rate, and the revenues collected by the state are returned to the jurisdiction of origin. Despite this distinction, the term shared revenues will be used in this chapter in reference to state taxes earmarked for assistance to local governments.

The budgetary process distinguishes state appropriated funds for local assistance from state shared revenues: in the first category, the legislature annually determines the funding for specific purposes, while in the second category, the amount of aid is determined by formulas written in statute, and specific state revenue sources generate the aid amounts.

State appropriated funds for local assistance include school equalization assistance programs, health and hospital aid (five programs), law enforcement and justice planning grants (five programs), flood control aid, library grants, and disaster aid. Virtually all of these programs provide categorical assistance to local governments in Arizona for specific purposes; local governments have little discretion over how the funds are spent. The revenues generated under these programs in 1987 are illustrated in Table 18-4.

The data in Table 18-4 indicate that shared sales and income tax revenues were the largest sources of state assistance to cities in 1982 accounting for 65 percent of state aid received. By 1987, the share of state aid received by cities from these two programs declined to 53 percent. The largest single state aid program to cities in 1987 was the Highway User Revenue Fund providing $188 million in revenues and representing almost 40 percent of all state aid received.

For counties in Arizona, the largest single state aid program, in both 1982 and 1987, was state shared sales tax revenues. However, by 1987, the share of state aid received by counties coming from this program was only 47 percent, down significantly from 60 percent just five years earlier. Over this period, state aid to counties for highways increased from 15 to 26 percent of aid received and health and hospital reimbursements increased from 10 to 16 percent of state assistance received. In 1982, the counties provided essentially all medical care to indigents. However, by 1987, the state had assumed responsibility for this service and contracted to either private vendors or the individual counties to provide the service. State funds for this activity are classified as state aid to counties.

Over the period 1982 to 1987, for both cities and counties in Arizona, there was a clear shift in the relative importance of state assistance from unrestricted grant assistance (funded from general revenues) to categorical assistance (funded primarily by user fees). The major exception is categorical state assistance for health and hospitals which is funded out of general revenues. This trend in state assistance, from programs funded out of general revenues to programs funded by user fees (primarily transportation programs), is mirrored at the federal level over the last ten years. Thus, to the extent that state and federal unrestricted assistance equalized fiscal disparities, reductions in this assistance would exacerbate fiscal disparities across jurisdictions.

Table 18-4

State Assistance to Local Governments in Arizona

	Cities			Counties		
	Amount	Percent Distribution		Amount	Percent Distribution	
	1987	1982	1987	1987	1982	1987
State Shared Sales Tax	$129,825,249	37.8	26.9	$199,224,683	60.0	46.9
State Shared Income Tax	124,073,530	27.3	25.7	--	--	--
Highway User Revenues	188,302,686	21.8	39.0	111,264,330	14.9	26.2
Local Transportation Assistance Fund	23,337,603	5.8	4.8	--	--	--
County Transportation Assistance Fund	--	--	--	7,649,999	0.0	1.8
Health Aid and Reimbursements	*	1.5	0.0	--	--	--
Health and Hospital Reimbursement	--	--	--	69,665,423	10.5	16.4
Housing and Community Development	3,092,945	0.3	0.6	--	--	--
Law Enforcement Grants	952,888	0.2	0.2	22,661,610	0.5	5.3
Water and Sewer Grants	471,936	1.8	0.1	--	--	--
State Liquor Tax	--	--	--	734,631	0.0	0.2
Airport License Tax	*	0.7	0.0	--	--	--
Fire Insurance Premium Tax	217,937	0.0	0.0	--	--	--
Disaster Aid	390,381	0.0	0.1	--	--	--
Flood Control Aid	--	--	--	1,771,332	0.4	0.4
Manpower Training (CETA) Grants	N/A	1.4	0.0	--	--	--
Job Partnership Training Act	5,921,545	0.0	1.2	--	--	--
All Other State Grants	6,613,477	1.5	1.4	11,936,444	13.6	2.8
Total Revenue From State	$483,200,177	100.0	100.0	$424,908,452	100.0	100.0

* Revenue source no longer exists.

Source: Census survey data collected by Arizona State University and adjusted by Arizona Fiscal 2000 committee staff; also, U.S. Census Bureau.

The Urban Revenue Sharing program (shared state income tax revenues) and the shared sales tax are the two largest state general assistance programs for cities in Arizona. State shared sales taxes are the largest state general assistance program for counties.

Urban Revenue Sharing

Each year, cities and towns in Arizona are entitled to receive 15 percent of the net income taxes collected in the fiscal year two years prior to the current year. For example, in fiscal 1987 cities and towns received state assistance from 1987 income tax collections equal to 15 percent of income tax collections in fiscal 1985.[5] In fiscal 1987 total estimated distributions in this program amounted to $129.8 million. This represents an increase of 44 percent from the 1982 distribution of $90.1 million. Over this period, however, the relative importance of this source of revenue declined from 38 to 27 percent of total state aid received by cities.

These funds are distributed to cities and towns based on the relation of each jurisdiction's population to the total population of all incorporated cities and towns in the state. In other words, if a city has 5 percent of the population living in incorporated cities and towns in the state, it will receive 5 percent of the funds distributed through the Urban Revenue Sharing program.

This distribution mechanism raises four main concerns. First, since the amount distributed this year is a function of tax collections two years earlier, the program may exacerbate cyclical budgetary pressures at the state level. For example, Table 18-5 shows the annual percentage change in Urban Revenue Sharing distributions, state personal income and state population from 1976 to 1988. Growth in state population and personal income tend to move in the same general direction (correlation coefficient of .655); when population is growing rapidly so is personal income and when population is growing more slowly so is personal income.

Alternatively, growth in state assistance to local governments through the Urban Revenue Sharing program changes independently of or slightly inversely to growth in state personal income (correlation coefficient of -.349) and state population (correlation coefficient of -.243). These results are consistent with the argument that the Urban Revenue Sharing program may exacerbate state finances over the course of the business cycle, but the results suggest the impact is not great. Also, to the extent that local revenue systems are sensitive to cyclical fluctuations in the state's economy, such state aid may compensate for lost local revenues and provide countercyclical stability for local governments (if not the state government).

Second, a jurisdiction's share of the total distribution is affected by the actions of others. For example, the incorporation of new cities and towns reduces the share going to existing jurisdictions. As new cities and towns incorporate, the total population living in incorporated areas will increase. Since each jurisdiction's allocation reflects its share of the total population living in incorporated areas, a jurisdiction's share will fall if there are new incorporations even if its own population increased.

This raises the third concern, that because the allocation of funds to individual jurisdictions is based on the jurisdiction's share of the population living in incorporated cities and towns, state aid may or may not have any relation to the actual fiscal needs of the jurisdiction. This issue is examined in more depth later in this chapter.

Finally, there is a technical concern with the consistency of the population data used to make the annual allocation of Urban Revenue Sharing funds. The U.S. Census Bureau completes comprehensive population counts for each jurisdiction only every 10 years, the most recent being the 1980 census. These population estimates become the basis for distributing state assistance to cities and towns until the next formal census. However, if a jurisdiction chooses, it may pay the Census Bureau to perform a special census halfway between the formal reports. For example, 45 of Arizona's 81 cities had a detailed population census provided by the U.S. Census Bureau in 1985.[6] These mid-decade census numbers become the baseline for the population estimates for these jurisdictions and generally benefit rapidly growing jurisdictions.

<table>
<tr><td colspan="4">Table 18-5
Annual Percent Change in Urban Revenue Sharing Distributions,
State Personal Income and Population, 1977 to 1988</td></tr>
<tr><td>Fiscal Years</td><td>Percent Change Urban Revenue Sharing</td><td>Percent Change State Personal Income</td><td>Percent Change State Population</td></tr>
<tr><td>1976-77</td><td>14.1</td><td>N/A</td><td>3.3</td></tr>
<tr><td>1977-78</td><td>3.6</td><td>18.7</td><td>3.7</td></tr>
<tr><td>1978-79</td><td>15.8</td><td>18.3</td><td>4.8</td></tr>
<tr><td>1979-80</td><td>18.3</td><td>14.3</td><td>3.8</td></tr>
<tr><td>1980-81</td><td>25.5</td><td>12.9</td><td>3.0</td></tr>
<tr><td>1981-82</td><td>20.7</td><td>5.0</td><td>2.6</td></tr>
<tr><td>1982-83</td><td>13.1</td><td>10.1</td><td>2.5</td></tr>
<tr><td>1983-84</td><td>12.9</td><td>12.4</td><td>3.5</td></tr>
<tr><td>1984-85</td><td>15.8</td><td>11.3</td><td>4.0</td></tr>
<tr><td>1985-86</td><td>13.0</td><td>9.2</td><td>3.9</td></tr>
<tr><td>1986-87</td><td>14.3</td><td>6.2</td><td>3.1</td></tr>
<tr><td>1987-88</td><td>5.2</td><td>N/A</td><td>2.3</td></tr>
<tr><td colspan="4">Source: Census survey data collected by Arizona State University and adjusted by Arizona Fiscal 2000 committee staff; also, U.S. Census Bureau.</td></tr>
</table>

<u>Shared State Sales Tax Collections</u>

For nearly 50 years the state has shared some portion of its sales tax revenues with local governments. As discussed in Chapter 8 on the general sales tax, prior to 1959 the state relied exclusively on a transactions privilege tax for state sales tax revenues. About half of this revenue was divided among the state, the counties, and the cities according to a distribution formula. The remaining unearmarked portion went directly into the state's general fund. However, between 1959 and 1986 several changes were made in the state's sales tax which complicated the distribution process.

In 1986, the transaction privilege tax was consolidated with the education excise tax, the special education excise tax and the business excise tax into a single sales tax. This consolidated sales tax is divided into two parts to reflect the historical treatment of sales tax revenues: first, there is the sales tax which is shared among cities, counties and the state; second, there is the non-shared base which is allocated directly to the state's general fund. Typically, the distribution base is composed of 1 percentage point of the total tax rate applied to most taxable activities. However, for some activities like retail sales and restaurant and bar sales, the distribution base is 2 percentage points. See Table 18-6 for a detailed listing of the tax collections for the distribution base and the non-shared base for each taxable activity in 1988.

Table 18-6
State Sales Tax Collections by Class, 1988

Classification	Distribution Base	Nonshared	Total Sales Tax Collections
Transportation and Towing	$ 204,638	$ 818,496	$ 1,023,134
Nonmetal Mining, Oil and Gas	1,268,293	2,694,750	3,963,043
Mining Severance	15,439,211	3,829,262	19,268,473
Timbering Severance	446,078	111,398	557,476
Utilities	31,492,358	125,970,866	157,463,224
Communications	7,227,879	28,911,509	36,139,388
Railroads and Aircraft	232,724	930,832	1,163,556
Private Car and Pipelines	24,727	98,908	123,635
Publishing	184,130	736,427	920,557
Printing	3,111,204	12,439,367	15,550,571
Local Advertising	12,090	6,087	18,177
Restaurants and Bars	52,858,287	79,245,091	132,103,378
Amusements	5,628,878	8,442,949	14,071,827
Rentals of Real Property	31,346,780	27,423,996	58,770,776
Rentals of Personal Property	25,607,507	38,408,069	64,015,576
Contracting	42,501,214	170,182,828	212,684,042
Wholesale Feed	529,734	462,944	992,678
Retail	315,096,800	472,590,542	787,687,342
Hotel/Motel	14,235,577	14,235,511	28,471,088
Agricultural Equipment	0	517,384	517,384
Rental Occupancy Tax	58,778	29,385	88,163
Use Tax	0	61,797,123	61,797,123
License Fees	0	379,479	379,479
Total	$537,506,889	$1,050,263,203	$1,597,770,090

Source: Arizona Department of Revenue, *Annual Report*, 1988.

The revenue in the distribution base is divided, by formula, among cities, counties and the state. Cities receive 25 percent of the revenue in the distribution base, counties receive 38.08 percent, and 36.92 percent of the total goes into the state general fund.

The city and county "pots" are then divided among all eligible governments. In 1988, the city pot was $136.9 million, an increase of 5.5 percent over the 1987 amount. The city pot is allocated in the same manner as the Urban Revenue Sharing assistance. Specifically, each jurisdiction receives a share of the total pot that is equal to its share of the total population living in incorporated cities and towns.

In 1988, the county pot totaled $208.5 million, an increase of 5.5 percent over 1987. The distribution formula for the county pot is more complicated. First, each county's share of net assessed valuation located in all counties (secondary valuations) and of sales tax collections are calculated. These shares are then averaged to determine each county's share of the pot. However, if any one county has a share more than 63.35 percent of the pot, its allocation is capped at 63.35 percent and the remaining funds are allocated to the other counties. In allocating any residual, all counties are first held-harmless at their shared sales tax allocation in the previous fiscal year. If there are still funds in the residual pot, 35 percent is distributed to the remaining counties equally, and 65 percent is distributed among the counties based on population.

With regard to the distribution of the city pot, the concerns expressed about the allocation of the Urban Revenue Sharing funds are equally applicable here. With regard to the county allocation formula, since the funds are allocated on the basis of net assessed values, as well as origin of tax collections, there is additional redistribution inherent in the program. Thus, the major concern is whether the funds are being allocated in a way that redresses or exacerbates existing fiscal disparities.

As mentioned above, 38.08 percent of the revenues collected from the shared sales tax base are distributed to the counties by formula rather than returned to the jurisdiction where they were collected. If the distribution were based on county of origin, each county would receive 38.08 percent of the amount collected in that county, and the distribution of payments to each county would reflect the distribution of actual collections and the distribution of taxable sales.

Because sales tax collections are reported on a county-by-county basis, the flow of collections and allocations can be compared on such a basis. Table 18-7 lists shared sales tax collections (distribution base) and county allocations for all 15 counties in Arizona. The last column in Table 18-7 reports each county's actual allocation relative to the 38.08 percent share they would have received if funds were allocated based on origin of collection.

Seven of the counties in the state received distributions that were within plus or minus 5 percent of their 38.08 percent share (Coconino, Graham, Maricopa, Pima, Pinal, Santa Cruz and Yavapai). Three counties were net exporters of shared sales tax revenues because they received significantly less than their 38.08 percent share of revenues collected in the county, Greenlee (69 percent), Yuma (89 percent) and Gila (90 percent). Gila and Greenlee counties received a smaller share of their collections because mining properties in those counties declined thereby reducing their allocations. Those counties would have received larger allocations if allocations had been based on origin of collections.

Five counties are importers of shared sales tax revenues since their allocations are substantially greater than 38.08 percent of their collections; Apache (297 percent), Cochise (110 percent), La Paz (123 percent), Mohave (110 percent), and Navajo (134 percent). This difference, between the amount collected and the amount received, represents one measure of redistribution to/from each county as a result of the shared sales tax distribution formula.

<table>
<tr><td colspan="4" align="center">Table 18-7
State Shared Sales Tax Collection And Distribution -- 1988</td></tr>
<tr><td align="center">County</td><td align="center">Distribution Base
Collected By State</td><td align="center">Actual Allocation
To County</td><td align="center">Actual Allocation
Relative To County
Share*</td></tr>
<tr><td>Apache</td><td>$2,525,978</td><td>$2,855,747</td><td>297</td></tr>
<tr><td>Cochise</td><td>8,293,393</td><td>3,476,947</td><td>110</td></tr>
<tr><td>Coconino</td><td>15,376,368</td><td>5,837,146</td><td>100</td></tr>
<tr><td>Gila</td><td>6,769,665</td><td>2,333,551</td><td>90</td></tr>
<tr><td>Graham</td><td>1,886,119</td><td>707,622</td><td>98</td></tr>
<tr><td>Greenlee</td><td>5,531,327</td><td>1,455,429</td><td>69</td></tr>
<tr><td>La Paz</td><td>1,789,534</td><td>841,691</td><td>123</td></tr>
<tr><td>Maricopa</td><td>348,953,086</td><td>131,829,415</td><td>99</td></tr>
<tr><td>Mohave</td><td>10,193,126</td><td>4,281,442</td><td>110</td></tr>
<tr><td>Navajo</td><td>9,153,549</td><td>4,659,465</td><td>134</td></tr>
<tr><td>Pima</td><td>94,902,301</td><td>34,663,653</td><td>96</td></tr>
<tr><td>Pinal</td><td>13,228,953</td><td>4,928,417</td><td>98</td></tr>
<tr><td>Santa Cruz</td><td>3,401,036</td><td>1,252,506</td><td>97</td></tr>
<tr><td>Yavapai</td><td>13,269,112</td><td>5,223,667</td><td>103</td></tr>
<tr><td>Yuma</td><td>12,233,345</td><td>4,143,925</td><td>89</td></tr>
<tr><td>Total</td><td>$547,506,892</td><td>$208,490,623</td><td>100</td></tr>
</table>

* County share is 38.08 percent of the distribution base. For example, the Apache County share is $961,892 ($2,525,978 times 0.3808).

Source: Census data adjusted by staff of the Arizona Joint Select Committee on State Revenues and Expenditures.

Impact Of Intergovernmental Assistance

As discussed above, intergovernmental grants serve two roles in providing financial assistance from one government to another.[7] First, intergovernmental grants correct for interjurisdictional spillovers. Second, intergovernmental grants facilitate fiscal equalization or mitigate the impact on local jurisdictions and their residents of unequal fiscal resources and expenditure needs (fiscal disparities).

Based on this theory of intergovernmental grants, public finance economists generally identify two questions evaluating the impact of intergovernmental grants: first, is the intergovernmental assistance distributed in a manner that equalizes for fiscal disparities across jurisdictions? and second, does the intergovernmental assistance stimulate additional local spending or does it substitute for local own-source revenues? In the first instance, variations in *per capita* grants across jurisdictions are explained in terms of fiscal capacity, fiscal effort and expenditure needs.[8] In the second instance, variations in local expenditures, in the aggregate or for specific functions, are explained in terms of variations in expenditure need, fiscal capacity and intergovernmental grants.[9]

One of the findings of this empirical literature is that the form in which assistance is given has important implications for the degree of equalization attained and the extent of expenditure growth or revenue substitution realized. Too often, however, the intergovernmental aid variables included in such empirical analysis are an aggregate of all aid types into one variable thus obscuring the differential impact of various types of aid. Arizona's two intergovernmental aid programs distributing general assistance to cities provide a unique opportunity to focus on the equalization and stimulative/substitution effects of truly lump-sum grants to local governments.

General Local Revenue Sharing and Fiscal Equalization: The Case of Shared Revenues in Arizona Cities

The discussion and analysis that follow focus on 41 of the 83 cities in Arizona in 1987. Of those 83 cities, 45 commissioned a special census since 1980 which provided detailed data on population and housing characteristics. Of these 45 cities, four had their special census conducted when they incorporated while the other 41 had the census conducted in 1985. Therefore, only those 41 cities with consistent data are used in the analysis.

Equalization. To evaluate the equalizing impact of unrestricted state assistance, the extent to which the distribution of such aid compensates for fiscal disparities across jurisdictions is analyzed. For the cities examined here, *per capita* total local own-source revenues in 1987 ranged from $991 and $1,347 in Gilbert and Page, respectively, to $101 and $112 in Chino Valley and Guadalupe, respectively. The average for the 41 cities is $512. The coefficient of dispersion, which measures the degree of variation from the average across all cities, is 43 percent indicating a substantial variation in *per capita* local own-source revenues across these cities.

In an effort to measure total unrestricted resources available to local governments, *per capita* local own-source revenues were added to *per capita* shared revenues received from the Urban Revenue Sharing and shared sales tax programs. When these totals are examined, the range in *per capita* resources is from $1,097 and $1,452 in Gilbert and Page respectively, to $206 and $218 in Chino Valley and Guadalupe, respectively. The average for all 41 cities is $618. More importantly, the coefficient of dispersion for the distribution of *per capita* local own-source revenues plus total shared revenues is 36 percent indicating that while there is still substantial variation in *per capita* resources available to local governments in Arizona, the degree of variation is reduced by adding shared revenues. In other words, state shared revenues tend to reduce, to some extent, fiscal disparities across cities.

While these aggregate data indicate that there is some equalization in resource availability across the cities examined, they do not test directly the hypothesis that shared revenues are allocated in a manner that compensates for variations across cities in fiscal capacity, fiscal effort or expenditure needs. Unfortunately, from a statistical perspective, state shared revenues distributed to cities through the Urban Revenue Sharing and state shared sales tax programs are allocated on a *per capita* basis. As a result, there is virtually no variation across the 41 cities examined here in the *per capita* value of these state aid variables. Thus, these aid variables cannot be used to test the equalization hypothesis with traditional multivariate analysis.

Substitution of State Aid for Local Own-Source Revenues. In evaluating the impact of state aid on local governments, a second hypothesis to test is whether state aid stimulates additional local spending or merely substitutes state revenues for local own-source revenues. This hypothesis is generally tested by the determinant type studies discussed above. In such studies, the dependent variable is some measure of local own-source revenues or expenditures *per capita* while one of the independent variables is a measure of *per capita* state aid received by the local government. Once again, however, because the Urban Revenue Sharing and shared sales tax programs in Arizona allocate funds to cities on a *per capita* basis, there is no variation across cities in the *per capita* value of these aid variables. As a result, a traditional determinant type model cannot be tested directly.

While the hypothesis that aid substitutes state revenues for local own-source revenues cannot be tested directly with traditional methodology, available data can be examined to identify tendencies which may or may not be consistent with the hypothesis. For example, of the 41 cities examined here, 18 have no real property tax collections. Since all 41 receive general state assistance through the Urban Revenue Sharing and shared sales tax programs, there is a suggestion that state tax revenues substitute for local property taxes.

To examine this substitution hypothesis more directly, data were collected on local fiscal capacity, local fiscal effort and the extent to which each local jurisdiction relied on general state aid through the Urban Revenue Sharing and shared sales tax programs. Using local finance data provided by the Arizona Joint Select Committee on State Revenues and Expenditures, the fiscal capacity of a local jurisdiction in Arizona can be measured by property wealth *per capita* as well as sales tax base *per capita*.

Fiscal effort measures reflect the degree to which a local jurisdiction actually takes advantage of or uses its own revenue sources. Using data provided by the Arizona Joint Select Committee on State Revenues and Expenditures, fiscal effort measures used here include local real property tax collections, local sales tax collections and total own-source revenues expressed both in *per capita* terms and relative to the average income of the jurisdiction.

Actual revenues raised relative to population or income reflect the size of the base and the ability of the jurisdiction to tax that base. One important factor that influences the ability of a jurisdiction to access a particular base is the ability to export taxes to non-residents. Thus, the above effort measures are modified to reflect the ability of the jurisdiction to export taxes. For example, variables measuring the percent of the city's real property tax base in residential use and the share of the sales tax attributable to utilities and hotels were constructed. The higher the percentage of a local jurisdiction's real property tax base in residential property the smaller the opportunity to export property taxes to non-residents. Similarly, the greater the share of sales tax collections coming from utilities and hotels, the greater the ability to shift taxes to non-residents.[10]

Examination of data on fiscal capacity, fiscal effort and reliance on general state assistance suggests some interesting tendencies. For example, cities in Arizona tend to take advantage of their local sales tax options. Those cities that have large sales tax bases have high sales tax collections, but those with limited sales tax bases have low sales tax collections.

To test the substitution hypothesis, local reliance on state general assistance was correlated with measures of sales tax base and effort. The correlations suggest that those cities with low *per capita* sales tax bases tend to rely more heavily on general state assistance through the Urban Revenue Sharing and shared sales tax programs. Similarly, those cities with low *per capita* sales tax collections (or low sales tax collections relative to income) tend to rely more heavily on state general assistance.

These findings suggest that state general aid may equalize for sales tax base disparities across cities. The relative importance of such aid tends to be greater for those cities with limited sales tax collections. In other words, the data suggest that sales tax collections are low because the base is low, and reliance on state assistance is relatively high, at least in part, to compensate for limited fiscal capacity.

Carrying out a similar analysis for local real property taxes leads to somewhat different conclusions. Unlike the case for the local sales tax, there is essentially no relation between a jurisdiction's *per capita* wealth, *per capita* real property tax collections and the local property tax burden (real property tax collections as a share of income).

To test the substitution hypothesis, local reliance on state general assistance was correlated with measures of local real property tax base and effort. In contrast to the case for the sales tax, there is not a strong relation between a jurisdiction's reliance on general state assistance and its *per capita* wealth. However, there is a somewhat stronger inverse relationship between the reliance on general state assistance and the local property tax burden (both *per capita* and relative to income). That is, cities with relatively low property tax burdens tend to rely more heavily on state general assistance.

Summary

Arizona provides unrestricted state assistance to cities through the Urban Revenue Sharing and shared sales tax programs. These shared tax revenues are allocated to cities in Arizona on a *per capita* basis.

Based on the preliminary statistical analysis presented here, there is some evidence that the resulting allocation of state grant funds does equalize fiscal resources across jurisdictions and that there may be some compensation for variations in sales tax bases across cities. Alternatively, the analysis suggests that these state aid programs may substitute state revenues for local property taxes, but the evidence is inconclusive.

On a general policy level, one can raise questions, based on the evidence in this chapter, about the purpose of general state aid to local governments. What are the major policy objectives associated with these programs? How does the current distribution formula address those objectives? Are these resources being used most efficiently?

In this context, an important issue is whether state revenues are being substituted for local revenues. For example, local real property taxes are relatively low in Arizona. In fact, 31 of the state's 83 cities did not have real property tax collections in 1987. Thus, if the formula for allocating state shared revenues to cities is to be reviewed, one area of potential interest may be to consider including elements in the distribution formula to encourage local governments to maintain some local fiscal effort as a prerequisite for receiving state shared revenues.

Endnotes

1. For interstate fiscal comparisons, data published by the Census Bureau are used because they are the most consistent data across states available. However, Census data for any individual state may not exactly correspond with data published by that state.

2. California voters approved Proposition 13 in 1978 which reduced local reliance on the property tax and increased reliance on state assistance. Nevada voters approved a tax-shift plan in 1981 which substituted state assistance financed by the state sales tax for local property taxes.

3. The economic theory of intergovernmental grants is synthesized in Wallace E. Oates, *Fiscal Federalism*, (New York: Harcourt Brace Jovanovich, 1972).

4. For example, see chapters by Rafuse and by Huckins and Carnevale in Michael E. Bell (ed.), *State and Local Finances in an Era of New Federalism*, Research in Urban Economics, Volume 7, (Greenwich, Connecticut: JAI Press, 1988).

5. In fiscal year 1986, the state distributed $108.6 million to cities and towns under the Urban Revenue Sharing program. Of that amount, $99.6 million came from income tax collections in fiscal 1986 while the remaining $9.1 million was set aside from fiscal 1985 receipts. See Table 31 in *Arizona Department of Revenue: 1988 Annual Report*.

6. Four of these cities had their special census done in the year when they incorporated, not in 1985.

7. See Wallace E. Oates, *Fiscal Federalism*, (New York: Harcourt, Brace and Jovanovich, 1972).

8. For a general discussion of these issues see U.S. Department of Treasury, Office of State and Local Finance, *Federal-State-Local Fiscal Relations*, (Washington D.C.: Government Printing Office, September 1985) pp. 174-93; and Jerry C. Fastrup, "Fiscal Capacity, Fiscal Equalization and Federal Grant Formulas" in U.S. Department of Treasury, Office of State and Local Finance, *Federal-State-Local Fiscal Relations, Technical Papers, Volume I*, (Washington D.C.: Government Printing Office, September 1986), pp. 41-62. For a more recent approach to evaluating fiscal equalization of state grants to central cities see John Yinger and Helen F. Ladd, "The Determinants of State Assistance to Central Cities," *National Tax Journal*, Volume 42, No. 4, December 1989, pp. 413-28.

9. For a summary of this literature see Larry E. Huckins and John T. Carnevale, "Federal Grants-In-Aid: Theoretical Concerns, Design Issues, and Implementation Strategy," in Michael E. Bell (editor), *State and Local Finances in an Era of New Federalism*, Research in Urban Economics, Volume 7, (Greenwich, Connecticut: JAI Press, 1988), pp. 41-62.

10. Yinger and Ladd define a measure of local revenue raising capacity that essentially merges the concepts of fiscal capacity and fiscal effort discussed here. Thus, the concept of exporting is critical to their definition of fiscal, or revenue raising, capacity. Yinger and Ladd, "Determinants of State Assistance to Central Cities," op. cit.

Chapter 19

The Theory and Rationale of Local Property Taxation

Wallace E. Oates

The purpose of this chapter is to "think" about the property tax: to try to understand what, in principle, is the tax base; who really pays the tax; and what its effects are both on the operation of private markets and on decisions in the public sector. These are issues that economists have explored (and argued about) over many decades. In the last twenty years, a body of theoretical and empirical work has helped to clarify the answers to these questions. In consequence, this chapter seeks largely to explain the "current thinking" on the nature of the property tax.[1]

One of the tricky aspects of tax analysis is that things are not always what they seem. It is one thing to levy a tax on a particular set of individuals or economic units (*e.g.*, corporations) but quite another to determine who actually bears the burden of the tax. The entities upon whom the legal liability for the tax is placed can often, by adjusting their economic behavior in certain ways, pass the tax along to someone else. The owners of a business firm *may*, for example, be able to pass on at least some of the taxes levied on their enterprise by raising the prices that they charge their customers. As we shall see, this process of the "shifting of taxes" (as economists call it) is also present in various (and subtle) ways in the functioning of the property tax.

The chapter begins by examining the nature of the tax base. What is it that is taxed under the property tax? We then move to a consideration of a property tax in a national setting. What if the federal government were to tax property nationwide? Although this is obviously not the way the tax is employed in this country, the discussion helps to clarify some of the basic properties of the tax. However, in the United States and in many foreign countries as well, the property tax is mainly a local tax. And, as we shall see, placing the tax in a local setting introduces a whole new dimension to its analysis. To some extent, one can think of the tax as representing a kind of "price" that residents of a local community pay in order to live in the community and consume the public services that are provided there. As a local levy, the property tax has some intriguing implications for the way local fiscal decisions will be made with some important asymmetries between the behavior of owner-occupants and those who reside in rental units. And these implications suggest some ideas about how the tax might be structured to make it more effective.

One particular modification to the tax has received special attention among policy makers, the movement toward a heavier taxation of land relative to the structures on the land. The proposal for a land tax has a long and rich history in the United States dating back to Henry George in the nineteenth century. Although its use has been quite limited, in some places (notably the city of Pittsburgh) property taxation has taken a form under which land is taxed much more heavily than buildings. Proponents of this measure claim that this modification has set off a building boom in the city that has been an integral part of its economic rejuvenation. In view of the interest in this experience, we shall devote some attention later in the chapter to urban land taxation where we shall assess the validity of these claims.

What is Taxed Under the Property Tax?

In its most comprehensive form, the property tax would include within its base the value of all property: land, buildings, producer and consumer durable goods (like machines, automobiles, and kitchen appliances), business inventories, holdings of government bonds and cash, etc. In short, it would be a tax on capital, on all forms of wealth (aside from "human capital"). In fact, there have been periods in our history when the property tax encompassed many of these forms of personal property. However, in recent times, there has been a tendency to narrow the definition of the tax base to so-called "real property"; that is, to land and the value of any structures or other improvements to the land. For purposes of discussion, we shall thus take the tax base to be land and structures on the land.

The tax bill under the property tax is determined by multiplying the tax rate (typically an ad valorem, a percentage rate) times the value of the property including the value of both the land and buildings. Since most parcels of property are sold only infrequently, some mechanism is needed to determine the value of the property. This is accomplished through an assessment procedure under which a public official, the assessor, assigns a value to the property equal either to the estimated market value or some fraction thereof. The tax bill thus equals the tax rate times the assessed value of the property.

The property tax, not only in the United States but in numerous other countries, is a major source of public revenues. Its distinguishing role in most countries has been as a primary source of tax revenues for local governments. But it will be helpful in understanding the nature of the tax to begin with an examination of the effects of a nationwide tax on property.

A National Property Tax

Suppose that the federal government were to levy a national tax on the market value of land and structures with the same tax rate applicable in all areas. The legal liability for the tax would thus rest on property owners. Each property owner would receive a periodic tax bill (annually perhaps) equal to the nationwide tax rate multiplied by the estimated market value of his or her property. From the perspective of home owners, the tax would effectively be a tax on housing consumption. For business enterprises, it would be a cost of doing business.

Although it is clear upon whom the legal liability would rest, it is much less clear who would bear the true "burden" of the tax. As suggested in the introduction to this chapter, economic agents often can adjust their activities so that they avoid the tax and "shift" its burden onto others. A tax on a firm, as we noted, may be "shifted forward" to customers in the form of higher prices. But this by no means exhausts the possibilities. Under some circumstances, the taxes on a business can be "shifted backwards" onto the labor the firm employs through a reduction in wages. If, for example, a firm is earning the minimum profit needed to keep it in business, and if it sells its output in a large market so that it effectively has little control over the price it receives, then it may have little choice; it either pays lower wages to its employees or it closes its doors. If the firm's workers have no opportunities for equivalent employment elsewhere, they may well be willing to accept lower wages rather than moving on to inferior jobs elsewhere. In this case, the tax on the firm has effectively been shifted backwards onto those employed by the firm.

To understand further the process of tax shifting, we examine a particular case that has special relevance, as we shall see shortly, to property taxation. Consider a piece of urban land that the owner rents to a business enterprise. Following sound business practices, we assume that the owner has found the most profitable use for this land so that the maximum rental income is being earned. Were the owner to raise the rent any higher, there would be no takers and the land would lie vacant. Suppose now that the government decides to levy a tax on this land. How would the land-owner respond? A little thought suggests that there is really nothing that the owner can do to avoid the tax and pass it on to someone else. The owner who tries to raise the rent will lose the tenant and be worse off than by absorbing the tax and settling for a reduced net (after-tax) income. This is a case where there is no shifting of the tax. The individual upon whom the legal liability rests has no avenues open through which to avoid the tax and hence must bear the full burden.[2]

In other instances, there will exist such avenues or alternatives so that taxes can be shifted. Think, for instance, of a tax on the purchase of a certain commodity. Buyers of the good have an obvious way to avoid at least some of the tax; they can reduce the level of their purchases (perhaps even to zero). Similarly, a heavy tax on a business firm in a particular locality may be avoided by moving elsewhere. Shifting thus involves finding ways in which to alter one's economic behavior so as to avoid paying the tax. Where no such alternatives exist (as in the case above of our land-owner), shifting cannot take place.

With this as background, let us return to our examination of a national property tax on land and structures. Such a tax would tend to decrease the demand for housing and business property. As we have seen, there is little that land-owners can do to circumvent such a decline in demand; since the alternatives are very limited, they basically must accept the lower land rent and absorb the part of the tax that applies to the value of land. Moreover, the reduced demand for structures will have somewhat similar effects on owners of capital. As capital flows out of the housing industry (and the construction industry more generally) and seeks "employment" in other industries, it will tend to depress the return to capital throughout the economy. From this perspective, a national property tax takes the form of a tax on land and capital throughout the economy.[3] Interestingly, this would suggest that such a tax is likely to be progressive. It would come primarily from capital (rather than wage) income. Since income from capital (and land) constitutes a much larger fraction of the income of higher income groups, the tax would fall more heavily on the relatively wealthy.

Although we have been considering a hypothetical national tax on property, the discussion does have some relevance to a system of local property taxation. If all localities were to employ roughly similar forms and levels of property taxation, then the system as a whole would resemble markedly a national tax on property. And the conclusion, following this line of analysis, would be that the tax is not regressive (as sometimes thought) but progressive in that the tax burden on higher income households would constitute a larger percentage of their incomes than would the burden on lower income persons.

While all this is of some interest, it is seriously incomplete as a description of the property tax. The property tax is primarily a local tax over which local jurisdictions exercise some discretion. And this element of local discretion in the setting of the tax rate provides a wholly different way of thinking about the tax.

The Property Tax as a Local Tax

The character of the property tax is seen in quite a different light when it is placed in the framework of local taxation. Consider, for example, a metropolitan area consisting of a central city and numerous smaller suburban municipalities containing extensive residential areas. An individual who works in the metropolitan area will typically have a considerable range of choice among municipalities in which to reside. Each of these municipalities will offer its own particular menu of schools, parks, and other public services and amenities. From this perspective, the individual will see the prospective property tax liability for a particular community as the "price" for living in that community and consuming the array of services provided there.

In this setting, the local property tax functions much like a price in the private sector; it effectively indicates to a prospective resident the cost of public services. In fact, economists often refer to such a tax liability as the "tax-price" of local services. We can thus envision an urban setting in which individual homeowners "shop" for a community of residence and in which the available services (such as the quality of the local schools and the level of public safety) play a major role in the choice of a jurisdiction. In a famous and seminal paper, Charles Tiebout (1956) introduced this view:

> *Just as the consumer may be visualized as walking to a private market place to buy his goods, the prices of which are set, we place him in the position of walking to a community where the prices (taxes) of community services are set. Both trips take the consumer to market. There is no way in which the consumer can avoid revealing his preferences in a spatial economy. Spatial mobility provides the local public-goods counterpart to the private market's shopping trip* (p. 422).

As a local tax, the property tax effectively becomes a price for public services. It represents, to some extent at least, a price paid for benefits received or a "benefit tax".

"Capitalization" and Its Implications

This view of local finance carries with it some additional, and more subtle, elements with profound implications for the effective and equitable functioning of the system. These implications are often overlooked in deliberations (and court decisions) over the desirability of local property taxation. Essential to these implications is the well-documented phenomenon of "capitalization."

As a general concept, capitalization refers to the adjustment of the price of an asset to reflect the whole stream of future benefits and costs that are associated with ownership of the asset. The asset of interest here is a place of residence, a dwelling unit, in a particular municipality. In this context, capitalization refers to the adjustment of house prices to reflect not only the future "housing services" provided by the structure itself but also the whole array of neighborhood and community characteristics *and* the tax liability attached to the house.

The point is straightforward. People will be willing to pay more for a particular house if, by living there, they have access to excellent public services: local schools of high quality, high levels of public safety, and so on. Or, put more technically, the value of a superior set of local amenities will tend to be *capitalized* into higher market values for houses, and the increase in market value will reflect (approximately) the value in monetary terms of the entire *future* stream of these services.

Capitalization is not limited only to these amenities. It will also tend to reflect levels of taxation. If houses in a particular jurisdiction are taxed especially heavily (without offsetting higher levels of local services), their market value will be depressed relative to the price of similar houses in other areas. High levels of local taxes will thus tend to be *capitalized* into lower property values.

These are not irrelevant economic abstractions. Nearly everyone is aware of the premia that houses command in the areas with the best public schools. There are dozens of statistical studies of local finance in which economists have measured these premia and confirmed the existence of capitalization of differentials both in levels of services and local taxes.[4] In fact, such studies have been employed "in reverse" to derive estimates of what people are willing to pay for improved amenities. For example, by comparing the selling prices of houses in a part of a metropolitan area with relatively clean air with the prices of comparable houses in a more polluted part of the area, economists have provided estimates of the monetary value that individuals place on cleaner air.[5]

We can note one immediate implication of the discussion. It does not follow that higher taxes in a particular locality will depress property values and economic activity if they are accompanied by higher levels of local services. This important point was recognized long ago by the eminent English economist, Alfred Marshall, who wrote in the Eighth Edition (1949, originally published in 1920) of his monumental *Principles of Economics*, that "remunerative rates [that is, local property taxes used to provide local services of value] ... ably and honestly administered, may confer a net benefit on those who pay them; and an increase in them may attract population and industry instead of repelling it" (p. 794).

The net effect of new programs on property values will clearly depend on the value of additional services relative to the increase in taxes required to finance them. If new taxes are used to provide worthless programs, then they will tend to depress local house prices. But if they provide extensions of local services that people value over and above the increment to taxes needed to pay for them, then as Marshall suggested, they will provide a net benefit to the community and will result in an appreciation of the value of local property.

Capitalization and Fairness

The phenomenon of capitalization also has a very important (and rarely noticed) implication for the *fairness* of a system of local property taxation. We often hear that the local property tax is an unfair tax because the size of the tax base per resident varies significantly from one jurisdiction to another. A municipality, for example, with a large commercial and industrial tax base will typically be able to finance local services with lower tax rates and hence lower tax bills on residential property.

This argument is not so compelling as it may, on first glance, appear. First, from our discussion of capitalization, it is clear that we should expect house prices in high-tax jurisdictions to be, other things equal, commensurately lower. This implies that a family who chooses to purchase a house in such a high-tax community is not being treated unfairly. It is being compensated for the future stream of higher tax payments by paying a lower price for a house. And market forces will tend to make such housing-price differentials reflect (approximately) the extent of the higher tax payments. We thus find that in a system of local finance, fairness is (to some extent at least) self-policing. Adjustments in house prices through the process of capitalization will take place so that fiscal differentials across local jurisdictions tend to manifest themselves in offsetting differences in house prices. What appears to be unfair may not be so.

There is also a second reason to be cautious about the unfairness argument. The augmentation of the local tax base with substantial quantities of commercial and industrial property is typically not an unmixed blessing. Business firms often bring with them congestion, noise, pollution, and other side effects that adversely affect the local environment. There is thus a real cost to enlarging the local tax base with nonresidential property in terms of reduced environmental quality. In fact, many relatively wealthy, residential communities have chosen to adopt restrictive zoning ordinances that prohibit altogether the location of business enterprise within their borders. This suggests that to some extent at least, the tax payments of commercial and industrial firms should be thought of as compensation to the jurisdictions for these side effects not as a pure "windfall." Moreover, some of these added tax revenues must be used to finance the extension of local public outputs (roads, police protection, etc.) needed to service these firms.[6]

The point then is that we should not take tax base per resident as an unambiguous measure of fiscal well-being. State aid programs, for example, that distribute funds by a formula incorporating tax base per capita can have some perverse redistributional results. In some instances, such programs can direct more funds into relatively wealthy residential jurisdictions that have zoned out commercial-industrial property than into poorer areas with a large business tax base. In one study of local finance in Northeastern New Jersey (a state heavily dependent on local property taxation), an examination of the relationship between the level of income in suburban municipalities and levels of property tax rates did *not* find a significant correlation between the two. In fact, certain high income jurisdictions that had zoned out commercial-industrial property had among the highest effective tax rates in the area.[7] It is not necessarily the case that municipalities with relatively wealthy residents have relatively low tax rates.

At the same time, this does not mean that there is no place for a well designed program of equalizing intergovernmental grants. Differentials in current house prices may compensate to a substantial degree for certain fiscal inequities (and it is important to be aware of this). But the citizenry may still wish to make available to school districts, for example, a certain level of funding per student so that districts with a high proportion of children or with a relatively small tax base do not have inordinately higher levels of tax payments per household. Such programs should be designed carefully, however, to ensure that the funds go in relatively large amounts to the jurisdictions in most need, and need should not be determined solely by tax base per resident.

Property Taxation and Local Fiscal Choice

In addition to providing an equitable distribution of the tax burden and minimizing distortions to the private market system, a good tax system should foster effective fiscal decision-making. From this "public-choice" perspective, we should ask whether or not the property tax is likely to encourage the right sorts of local fiscal decisions. The basic idea is that a tax provides a set of "signals" to citizen-taxpayers as to the cost of providing local services. Just as the prices of products in the private sector guide consumer decisions by indicating what has to be sacrificed to obtain a particular commodity, so taxes in the public sector should provide a clearly visible and accurate signal of the costs of public services.

If taxes are largely hidden or don't reflect the costs of public services, then the residents of a jurisdiction will be more likely to make poor decisions on levels of local public programs. For example, if a local government financed its services by a tax on local corporations, there might be little sense among residents as to what these services actually cost. Residents would not pay taxes directly and would have a hard time knowing what a new park, for instance, would really cost each of them. Such uncertainty is not likely to encourage responsible fiscal choices.

Local property taxes get reasonably good marks on this measure of tax effectiveness, at least as they apply to homeowners. Property taxes tend to be fairly visible. Local homeowners receive tax bills either quarterly or annually, and these bills provide an indication of the cost to residents of local services.[8] In some instances, local tax rates may be tied explicitly to budgets that are subject to a local referendum so that the cost "signals" to residents are quite clear indeed.

Local property taxes, in contrast, do not provide such clear cost signals to occupants of rental units. Property taxes in this country are paid by owners of property so that it is the landlord, not the tenant, who is formally the taxpayer on rental property. This does not mean, of course, that renters do not bear the burden of the tax. Following our earlier discussion of shifting of taxes, there is good reason to believe that property taxes on rental units will be shifted forward in the form of higher rents. If, for example, higher taxes are used to provide better schools, parks, and roads in a particular municipality, then prospective renters will be willing to pay higher rents to live in this jurisdiction in order to enjoy the higher levels of amenities. Thus, we should expect property taxes on rental dwellings to be shifted forward on to tenants.

The difficulty is that the shifting process may not be *visible*. Renters may not be aware of the fact that they are paying for improved local services. This all may sound rather abstract and hypothetical. But there is some very striking evidence on this matter. Economists have undertaken numerous econometric (statistical) studies of patterns of local spending across jurisdictions. In study after study, the same remarkable finding emerges. Other things held equal, communities with a larger percentage of renters spend more on public services per capita. This finding is buttressed by some further studies of voting behavior on bond referenda and fiscal-limitation measures. These latter studies find that renters are much more likely to vote in favor of bond issues to expand local services and to vote against fiscal-limitation proposals than are homeowners.[9]

Why is it that renters apparently favor larger public budgets than owner-occupants? One explanation could be that renters have higher demands for public services, but there is little reason or evidence to suggest that renters have preferences that are more strongly inclined to public education, police protection, etc., than do home owners. An alternative explanation, the one suggested above, is that renters are subject to a form of "fiscal illusion."[10] They do not perceive that they are paying for higher levels of public services and, as a result, quite naturally push for expansion in the local public budget to finance higher levels of public outputs. Alternatively, it is possible that property taxes are not fully shifted forward into higher rents or that this takes place only with a long lag so that renters really don't pay their full share of the costs of local services. Whichever of these two explanations is correct, there will be a tendency for renters to support spending measures beyond the levels justified by the benefits and costs of the proposed programs.

The problem, in short, is that the property tax does not seem to give clear signals to renters of the costs of local services and leads them to support larger local public budgets. Is this problem resolvable short of replacing property taxation with some other source of local revenue? The answer, in principle at least, is yes. One way to remove this source of illusion is to levy property taxes directly on renters themselves rather than on landlords. If property taxes are, in fact, shifted forward in the form of higher rents, this would not alter the actual burden of the tax. Renters would simply pay the tax directly to the government and pay a commensurately lower rent to the landlord.

The levying of property taxes on tenants is not a practice that is employed in this country. But it is standard practice in Britain, where "local rates" (as the property tax is called there) are levied directly on the occupant, not the owner, of a residence. Taxing tenants rather than landlords may be somewhat more cumbersome administratively, but it would seem to have the advantage of making local taxes more visible and, in this way, of encouraging more responsible local fiscal choices.[11]

A Note on Property Taxation in Central Cities

The view of the local property tax that emerges from the preceding discussion is one of a "tax-price" that serves to guide individual location decisions and community fiscal choices. This view is an appealing and compelling one when we think of a large system of suburban municipalities within which mobile households select a community of residence. Such households effectively "shop" among communities and choose a place to live that provides them with desirable housing and local services.

This perspective, however, may provide a less compelling description of the way the tax functions in larger central cities where choices are much more circumscribed. For various sorts of reasons, some segments of the population may find themselves effectively bound to the center city with a much more limited range of housing and fiscal options. In this setting, particularly for occupants of low-income rental units, the preceding view of the role of local property taxation may be misleading. Large city landlords, for example, may exercise considerable market power in the determination of rents. The analysis of the shifting of the property tax in this rather different setting is a complex problem, one that is often further complicated by the existence of programs of rent controls. Under some such programs, for example, increases in property taxes are allowed to be passed forward directly in the form of higher rents.

The local property tax may well be a much more regressive tax in this setting than it is in the suburban sector, and it may function less well as an effective guide for making sound local fiscal decisions. There is a stronger case here for reduced reliance on property taxation with more revenues from other sources. A further alternative is a possible restructuring of the tax along the lines to be discussed in the next section.

Land Taxation

An intriguing alternative to a tax base consisting of land and structures is a base limited solely to the unimproved value of land. The proposal for a land tax has a long, rich history. In the nineteenth century, the U.S. reformer Henry George made an impassioned plea in his *Progress and Poverty* (1929, originally published in 1879) for a tax system consisting of a single levy, a tax on land. George saw economic progress as a perverse process in which the fruits of this progress tended over time to take the form of "unearned increments" to the value of land. Land, unlike industry and population, George reasoned, is fixed in quantity. And the growth of population and industry must inevitably put upward pressure on the price of the fixed stock of land. A squeeze on wages and profits would follow with the gains from economic growth taking the form of increased land rents to idle landowners. Economic justice, in George's view, required that these "unearned increments" be taxed away by a levy on the value of land. George contended that the revenues from this single source would be sufficient to finance the entire public budget. His proposal was "To abolish all taxation save that upon land values" (p. 406). Such a tax would change the character of society:

> *By sweeping away this injustice ... we shall remove the great cause of unnatural inequality in the distribution of wealth and power; we shall abolish poverty; tame the ruthless passions of greed; dry up the springs of vice and misery...and make tyranny and anarchy impossible* (p.545).

Strong claims for tax reform!

Although their objectives are somewhat more modest, economists too have found the proposal for land (or site) value taxation to be of interest. Taxes on improvements have an undesirable economic effect; they discourage building activity. A project that is otherwise socially attractive in that its economic benefits exceed their costs can be rendered unprofitable by the pecuniary disincentive created by the tax. As a result, certain socially desirable improvements to land may be deterred by the property tax.

A tax limited solely to land value may avoid these distortionary side effects. As we saw earlier, since a landowner's most profitable employment of a land parcel will be unaffected by a tax on rental income, a land tax will not directly affect decisions on land use. In the economist's lingo, a tax on land rents is a "neutral" tax that does not (in a direct way) alter the terms on which economic decisions are made.[12] A pure tax on land rents, under the traditional view, will be capitalized fully into land prices such that the price net of the tax will fall by the full amount of the tax. The gross price to users of the land will remain unchanged.

Land taxation thus has a real appeal as an alternative to the taxation of land and buildings in that it avoids certain costly distortions in the use of the economy's scarce resources. At the same time, it has some attractions (as Henry George pointed out) in terms of fairness. Income from land rents tends to accrue disproportionately to higher income groups so that a tax on this form of income will be a progressive tax. Both on grounds of equity and of the efficient use of economic resources, land taxation seems to have much to commend it.

Actual experience with land taxation is limited, but there is some. In the United States, the city of Pittsburgh and some smaller jurisdictions in Pennsylvania have made use of a "graded" property tax under which the land component of the property tax base is taxed at a higher rate than structures. For over fifty years, Pittsburgh taxed land at a rate equal to twice that on structures. In 1979, the city raised the tax on land to four times that on structures and then to five. Reports from Pittsburgh claim that these shifts in the rate structure of the graded system have been followed by a dramatic rise in the total value of building permits issued. Some observers have attributed this surge in construction activity to the movement away from the taxation of buildings although there remains the difficult issue of separating out the influence of the tax from other factors affecting the development of the city.

At any rate, there is at least a *prima facie* case on both theoretical and empirical grounds for a systematic consideration of replacing the property tax with a system of land taxation or at least of going some distance in that direction by introducing a graded system that would tax land at a higher rate than buildings.

What are the likely effects of such a reform in local taxation? Some have argued that land taxation will discourage speculative activity and bring vacant land into use more rapidly. The basic contention is that the higher taxes on land will increase the cost of holding land idle and will thereby force speculators to bring vacant land into use more quickly. This is seen as desirable, particularly in city areas where certain parcels of land may sit vacant for long periods of time in the hands of speculators, while development proceeds at the outer reaches of the city. In this way, land taxation, so the argument goes, will help to contain the process of "urban sprawl."

Careful analysis suggests that there is some validity to this claim. As Brian Bentick (1979) and David Mills (1981) have shown, a tax on land *value* (rather than on *rental* income from land) will alter incentives in favor of the earlier development of land parcels. The point can be made in terms of a simple illustration. Suppose that a landowner can sell a parcel of land for immediate development for $100,000. Assume further that the going rate of return on alternative investments is 10 percent so that the owner could take the receipts from the sale and invest them at 10 percent. But suppose that the owner has an alternative. The land could lay idle and a year later sell for $115,000. Clearly, it is in the owner's interest to keep the land off the market and realize what is effectively a rate of return of 15 percent through its future sale. Suppose, however, that the local government introduces a tax on land at a rate of 6 percent of its value. The *net* rate of return for the delayed sale would now be only 9 percent (15 percent less the 6 percent per annum due in land taxes). The profitable option in the presence of the land tax would thus be to sell the land for immediate development. The general principle emerging from this hypothetical case is that land value taxation raises the rate of return on speculative land holding that is required to make such speculation profitable. To be more precise, we see that in order for holding land idle to be profitable, the prospective rate of increase in its price must exceed the sum of the yield on alternative investments and the tax rate on land value. An increased rate of land value taxation will indeed tend to discourage the holding of vacant land.

We should not conclude too quickly that this is always a good thing. There may well be cases where it is socially desirable to hold land vacant until time for a superior development alternative. It is possible that a land tax could lead, in certain instances, to excessively early development in inferior uses. Whatever the answer is to this question, it seems clear that land value taxation will discourage the holding of vacant land and this may be desirable in urban centers.

Under a graded system, the counterpart to an increased rate of land taxation is a reduced rate of taxation on buildings. It is straightforward to show that this will tend to encourage building activity and to lead to a more capital-intensive use of land (*i.e.*, more structures per unit of land).[13] Certain other effects are less clear. One might suppose that the higher tax on land under the graded system will necessarily lead to a fall in land prices. But this need not be so. The impetus to building will give rise to an increase in the demand for land on which to place the structures. This increase in the demand for land will put upward pressure on its price thus having an opposite effect on land prices from the tax. As Brueckner (1986) shows, the outcome on balance is not fully predictable. There is some presumption that the effect of the land tax will predominate so that land prices will fall somewhat, but it is not inconceivable that the building demand effect could prove the stronger so that land prices could, in fact, rise under a graded system.

This is obviously a complicated matter. One should be wary of studies that purport to describe the effects of the shift from a standard property tax system to a graded system. Often these studies simply take *existing* assessed values and calculate the changes in tax liabilities by multiplying the projected new tax rates times these assessed values. Such estimates are likely to be highly misleading. For the reform of the tax system will itself have major effects on the relative values of different properties. As these changed market values become reflected in revised assessments, the pattern of changes in tax liabilities is likely to look quite different from that predicted on the basis of existing property value assessments.

There remain a number of questions concerning land value taxation that have not been fully answered. These include such matters as the adequacy of land as a tax base. Since in most metropolitan areas, the buildings on land constitute much the larger component of the value of the property, there is some concern that a radical shift towards land taxation would be unable to provide needed local revenues. On another issue, the separate assessment of land from buildings raises some tricky conceptual and practical problems concerning the way in which land values should be calculated for tax purposes.[14]

In view of the limited experience with land taxation and the uncertainty concerning some of its effects, there are reasons for having real reservations about a major reform of local property taxation that would involve the complete replacement of the property tax by a levy on land. However, in view of the fiscal (and general economic) plight of many center cities, there is a case for a serious consideration of the introduction of a graded tax system in urban centers. Such a reform in city taxation, involving a substantial shift from the taxation of buildings to land, could make a real contribution to the rejuvenation of the urban economy.[15]

Local Property Taxation: A Summing Up

The picture of local property taxation that emerges from this discussion is a mixed one. The tax is certainly not perfect, but there is no perfect tax. The real issue is how it stacks up against the feasible alternatives for raising local revenues.

From the perspective of fairness, the property tax comes off reasonably well. As we have discussed, to the extent that local governments across the nation rely on the tax, it resembles to some extent a nationwide tax on property. This suggests that some significant part of the burden of the tax will rest on individuals receiving income from capital implying that it is a progressive tax. Under the older view of the tax which saw it simply as a levy on housing consumption, it was taken to be regressive since it was seen as an excise tax on a "necessity." However, more careful studies of the property tax even in these terms suggest that this may not be the case. When measured properly against "permanent income" (which irons out temporary fluctuations in income), most studies suggest that housing expenditure is a relatively constant fraction of income at all income levels. Higher income households, on average, spend about the same fraction of their income on housing as do lower income families. Thus, if the tax were simply taken to be a levy on housing consumption, it would be (on average) neither progressive or regressive. It would be (roughly) a proportional tax.[16]

The fairness issue arises in a different way when the tax is seen as a local tax. Here the property tax has been criticized because of the disparities in the size of the tax base across different localities. Jurisdictions with a concentration of commercial and industrial property will tend to have much larger tax bases per capita than purely residential jurisdictions. But, as we have discussed, this criticism is to some extent misleading, since the capitalization of fiscal differentials implies that higher taxes will tend to be offset by commensurately lower housing prices.

It should be recognized, moreover, that this particular criticism of disparities in local tax bases will apply to virtually any local tax instrument. A system of local income or sales taxes, for example, would produce tax bases that vary significantly from one jurisdiction to another. The issue of disparities in local tax bases is thus not so much a matter of the particular tax that is employed. More generically, it is a matter of relying on local taxation. The way to eliminate such disparities is to move away from taxation at the local level to state taxes.

The most radical solution would be to do away with local taxation altogether and simply finance local services from funds provided under intergovernmental grant programs from the state. This approach, however, seriously undermines local autonomy and responsibility in fiscal decision making. If local services are funded by the state, residents in a particular jurisdiction will have powerful incentives to seek expansion in various local programs since most of the funds will come from taxpayers elsewhere in the state. Local revenue decisions will become wholly the result of political negotiations between state and local governments. There will be little genuine local discretion.

For local fiscal choice to have real economic meaning, it is imperative that local residents bear the costs of their decisions to adjust levels of local services. The populace must be in a position to weigh the benefits from public programs against their costs. For this to occur, local governments must have their own tax system with which to confront residents in making decisions on levels of local expenditure. Local taxes with local discretion over tax rates are, in short, essential for an economically meaningful local public sector.

This does not mean that there is no scope whatsoever for reducing some of the disparities in local tax bases. If handled properly, certain kinds of equalizing grants from the state government can be used to even out local tax bases somewhat without severely compromising the incentives for effective local fiscal decisions. As discussed in Chapter 18, the state government may provide more generous funding assistance to relatively poor jurisdictions to help them provide adequate levels of public services. A state may wish, for example, to provide a grant per student to local school districts, where the magnitude of the grant varies inversely with (among other things) the school district income and/or tax base per pupil. What is important is that after these grants are incorporated into the local budget, any decisions concerning adjustments to local spending and service levels should come primarily from locally raised revenues. Put slightly differently, local services should be financed primarily by local taxes *at the margin*. In this setting, whenever the local electorate (or its elected representatives) is considering an adjustment to levels of local public services, it will have to weigh this adjustment against the fiscal costs.

Assuming then that local government needs its own major revenue source, how does the local property tax compare with the major alternative sources of local revenue? The three major candidates to replace the property tax are local sales taxes, income taxation, and/or user fees. Sales taxes have some serious shortcomings as a local revenue source, sufficiently serious that they cannot be recommended as the *primary* source of own revenues in a setting with many small local governments. First, the sales tax base is likely to vary widely among jurisdictions. Communities that are primarily residential would have to levy very high tax rates to generate the requisite revenues from their small volume of retail sales. In fact, differentials in tax bases and tax rates would probably be a good deal more dramatic under a local sales than under a local property tax were it to be the major local tax. Second, significant sales tax differentials would give rise to costly trips among jurisdictions as consumers sought to save money by making their purchases in low tax rate communities. Even large cities (and states to some extent) have experienced losses in sales from having tax rates that are higher than those in neighboring jurisdictions. And, third, sales taxes do not receive good marks on a fairness criterion based on ability-to-pay. The tax (depending on how the base is defined) tends to be somewhat regressive.

The sales tax, in short, has little promise as a full replacement for local property taxation. There is some scope (notably in larger cities) for a modest reliance on a local sales tax as a supplementary revenue source, but it is not to be recommended as the major local tax instrument.

This discussion, incidentally, raises an important point. The potential mobility of economic activity imposes a major constraint on local taxation. The taxation of certain goods or forms of productive activity in a particular jurisdiction creates incentives for movement elsewhere to escape payment of the tax. This is quite clear, for example, in the case of local sales taxation. One advantage of the local property tax is that at least one component of the tax base, land, is immobile. Local officials can tax land without the fear that it will depart! The part of the property tax that falls on structures is less innocuous in this respect. A heavy local tax may discourage new building activity and may lead the owners of existing structures, in the long run, not to replace their factories or apartments but to move elsewhere. There is thus some potential for movement in response to local property taxation, but it is generally less than under most other taxes (like those on sales).

A second alternative tax base is local income. Some local governments in the United States (mainly cities and counties) levy their own taxes on personal income. This often consists of "piggybacking" on the state income tax; that is, adding a couple of percentage points to the state tax rate which is then collected by the state and returned to the locality. Local income taxation has some appeal. It is quite a visible tax, and it is generally regarded as a progressive tax so that it gets good marks on equity grounds. However, it is not demonstrably superior in these respects to local property taxation. The local supplement to most state income taxes is not, in practice, very progressive.

Moreover, local income taxation encounters the mobility problem to some extent. A jurisdiction that opts for relatively high tax rates runs the risk of deterring the entry of new households, especially those with above-average incomes that would have relatively large tax payments. Individuals may chose to reside in neighboring localities with lower tax rates.[17]

In addition, there is something to be said for avoiding excessive reliance in the economy as a whole on any single tax instrument. The federal government and most state governments rely on the income tax as a primary revenue source and there has been considerable concern that income tax rates have become sufficiently high to discourage various forms of productive activity. Measures to lower tax rates have been justified in terms of reducing these disincentives. For this reason, local government may contribute to an improved overall tax system by avoiding further use of the income tax and sticking with the revenue source that has historically been almost exclusively its own.

Finally, property taxation promises a more stable source of local revenues than does a local income tax. Personal income exhibits considerable sensitivity to cyclical movements in the economy so that the tax base under a local income tax will tend to rise and fall with movements in the economy. The property tax base, in contrast, depends upon the assessed valuation of the properties on the tax rolls; this tends to change little over the course of the business cycle. As a result, local property taxation provides a relatively stable, predictable flow of revenues into the local treasury.

The other major local revenue source is user fees. There is a strong economic case, as discussed in Chapter 10, for the use of such fees. They represent a form of "benefit taxation" in that the users of the service are the ones who pay for it. They also perform the valuable role of a "price" in limiting the use of the service to cases where the benefits provided (as measured by individuals' willingness-to-pay) exceed the cost of the service. In this sense, a system of fees provides a kind of "market test" for the provision of local public services. The difficulty is that many local services are "public" in character. They are consumed collectively by the community so that the imposition of fees is not feasible. It is hard to see, for example, how a locality could charge its residents for their individual levels of usage of such things as local roads, police protection, etc. Fees can be used for the financing of a limited number of local services, but they cannot supplant the need for a major source of local tax revenues.

In summary, local property taxation emerges as a quite defensible source of local revenues. Although it has historically been the subject of heavy criticism, the tax, especially when compared to the alternative sources of local revenues, appears to have been excessively maligned. As we have seen, the local property tax gets reasonably good marks on various fairness criteria. Moreover, in those instances where it has been thought to be inequitable, a variety of measures (including circuit breakers and homestead exemptions and credits) have been introduced to provide tax relief.[18] Disparities in the tax base across jurisdictions have been smoothed somewhat through the use of equalizing intergovernmental grants. In short, states and localities have introduced provisions to remedy what are seen as the major sources of inequities under the tax.

The property tax provides a reasonably visible measure of the costs of local services to residents (at least to homeowners), and in this way encourages the weighing of benefits against costs in the design of local programs. As we have discussed in this chapter, there are some reforms that merit serious consideration to enhance the effectiveness of the tax. There is a strong case for amending administrative procedures to charge tenants in rental units directly for their share of the tax rather than taxing them indirectly through landlords. In addition, where economic decline of the center cities is an issue, there are real grounds for considering the modification of the property tax to a graded system that would tax land at a substantially higher rate than structures. Overall, the property tax provides local government with a reasonably fair and effective source of revenues -- one that is sufficiently flexible to accommodate modifications to enhance its equity and effectiveness.

A Note on State Property Taxation and Fiscal Limitations

This chapter has explored the property tax as a local tax. There are some states (including Arizona) where, in addition to local government, the state also taxes property. Is this desirable or to be discouraged?

In the older tax administration literature, some fiscal specialists put forth as a "principle" of taxation in a federal system the so-called doctrine of "separation of sources." According to this principle, each level of government should have its own sources of tax revenues with no overlap; one level of government should not encroach on a tax base employed by another level. This principle has not been given much notice in the evolution of our federal fiscal system. There are obviously lots of instances of "shared tax sources" (including, for example, federal, state, and, in some instances, local taxation of personal income).

As a rigid principle, "separation of sources" has little to commend it. But there is a grain of truth as regards property taxation in state and local finance. The argument in this chapter is that, all things considered, the property tax is the best major tax instrument available to local government. It is thus important that local government have primary access to this tax base without having the scope of its fiscal decisions circumscribed by state reliance on the property tax.

How might state use of property taxation undermine local fiscal autonomy? Were states to place heavy demands on property taxation, it might push rates of property tax (state plus local) to undesirable levels and put pressures on local government to reduce their own property tax levies. Very high rates on any single tax source can have serious distorting effects on the economy. In fact, it can be shown that the distorting side effects from taxes tend to rise disproportionately with the level of the tax rate.[19] Any inequities associated with a certain tax will likewise become magnified with a heavier reliance upon it.

The implication is that state government should exercise some care in its use of property taxation; it probably should not make extensive use of this tax base for fear that it could impinge on local fiscal choices. There is little danger of this if states make only modest use of the property tax as a supplementary source of tax revenues. Especially if the revenues from this source are employed as intergovernmental grants to local government, they will reduce the extent to which local governments need to tax property. Property taxation, in short, should not constitute a major source of state revenues, but there are no powerful objections to its use as an incremental, supplementary source of state tax monies.

Finally, there is the issue of fiscal limitations. Many states, again including Arizona, have introduced a variety of measures that restrict the fiscal activities of state and local government. As discussed in Chapter 21, these measures include limits on property taxes (such as the famous Proposition 13 in California) and various restrictions on levels of spending and growth in spending and tax revenues. While such limitations may have their own role to play, it is important to recognize their potential impact on local fiscal decision-making. As we have stressed in this chapter, local property taxes serve an essential function as a kind of "price" for public services. The local citizenry, in making fiscal decisions on the whole range of local programs, must weigh the benefits of these programs against the prospective increase in local property tax bills. Suppose, however, that (as in California) local property taxes are consistently bumping against an upper limit. Then there is no scope for the tax to play its role as a "price" for local services. Any increments to local programs must then be funded in some other manner either by revenues from another tax source or from additional grant funds from the state.

This suggests that states should think carefully about the design of fiscal limitations to ensure that they do not effectively undermine the proper conduct of local fiscal decision-making. In particular, it is critical that *at the margin*, the local electorate be aware of the costs of its decisions. For the property tax to provide a cost signal to local residents, there must be some scope for local property tax bills to vary with local choices on public programs. A limitation measure that essentially fixes local property tax payments thus compromises the capacity of the tax to fulfill its allocative function in local finance.

References

Aaron, Henry J., *Who Pays the Property Tax: A New View* (Washington, D.C.: The Brookings Institution, 1975).

Advisory Commission on Intergovernmental Relations, *Changing Public Attitudes on Governments and Taxes* (Washington, D.C.: ACIR, 1988).

Bentick, Brian L., "The Impact of Taxation and Valuation Practices on the Timing and Efficiency of Land Use," *Journal of Political Economy*, vol. 87 (August, 1979), pp. 859-868.

Bradford, David F., and Wallace E. Oates, "Suburban Exploitation of Central Cities and Governmental Structure," in H. Hochman and G. Peterson, eds., *Redistribution Through Public Choice* (New York: Columbia University Press, 1974), pp. 43-92.

Brueckner, Jan K., "A Modern Analysis of the Effects of Site Value Taxation," *National Tax Journal*, Vol. 39 (March, 1986), pp. 49-58.

Ebel, Robert D., and James Ortbal, "Direct Residential Property Tax Relief," *Intergovernmental Perspective*, vol. 15 (Spring, 1989), pp. 9-14.

Fischel, William A., "Fiscal and Environmental Considerations in the Location of Firms in Suburban Communities," in E. Mills and W. Oates, eds., *Fiscal Zoning and Land Use Controls* (Lexington, Mass.: D.C. Heath, 1975), pp. 119-174.

Freeman III, A. Myrick, *The Benefits of Environmental Improvement* (Baltimore: Johns Hopkins Press, 1979).

George, Henry, *Progress and Poverty* (New York: Random House, The Modern Library, 1929).

Holland, Daniel M., ed., *The Assessment of Land Value* (Madison, Wisconsin: University of Wisconsin Press, 1970).

Marshall, Alfred, *Principles of Economics*, Eighth Edition (New York: Macmillan, 1949).

Mills, David E., "The Non-Neutrality of Land Taxation," *National Tax Journal*, Vol. 34 (March, 1981), pp. 125-129.

Netzer, Dick, *Economics of the Property Tax* (Washington, D.C.: The Brookings Institution, 1966).

Oates, Wallace E. "The Effects of Property Taxes and Local Public Spending on Property Values: An Empirical Study of Tax Capitalization and the Tiebout Hypothesis," *Journal of Political Economy*, Vol. 77 (Nov./Dec., 1969), pp. 957-971.

__________. "The Effects of Property Taxes and Local Public Spending on Property Values: A Reply and Yet Further Results," *Journal of Political Economy*, Vol. 81 (July/Aug., 1973), pp. 1004-1008.

______________. "Property Taxation," in J. Eatwell et al., eds., *The New Palgrave Dictionary of Economics, Vol. 3* (London: Macmillan, 1987), pp. 1034-1035.

______________. "On the Nature and Measurement of Fiscal Illusion: A Survey," in Geoffrey Brennan *et al.*, eds., *Taxation and Fiscal Federalism* (Sydney: Australian National University Press, 1988), pp. 65-83.

______________. "The Reform of Local Property Taxation: A Public Choice Perspective," unpublished paper (1989).

Rosen, Harvey S., *Public Finance* (Homewood, III.: Richard D. Irwin, Inc., 1985).

______________. and Fullerton, David J., "A Note on Local Tax Rates, Public Benefit Levels, and Property Values," *Journal of Political Economy*, Vol. 85 (April, 1977), pp. 433-440.

Tiebout, Charles, "A Pure Theory of Local Expenditures," *Journal of Political Economy*, vol. 64 (Oct. 1956), pp. 416-424.

Endnotes

1. For lucid explications of the theory of the property tax, see Henry Aaron (1975) and Harvey Rosen (1985, Chapter 18). An older, standard source on the property tax is Dick Netzer (1966). A recent and more succinct treatment is available in Wallace Oates' entry on "Property Taxation" in *The New Palgrave Dictionary of Economics 1987*.

2. This is an instance of the more general case of a tax on a commodity that is fixed in supply. Such a tax falls wholly on the owner of the good.

3. This is the so-called "new view" of the "incidence" (*i.e.*, the pattern of the tax burden) of the property tax. For more extended discussions of this issue, see Henry Aaron (1975) and Harvey Rosen (1985, Chapter 18).

4. See, for example, Wallace Oates (1969 and 1973) and Harvey Rosen and Donald Fullerton (1977).

5. For a discussion of this approach to measuring the benefits of environmental services, see A. Myrick Freeman (1979, Chapter 6).

6. For a more extended discussion of this view of commercial and industrial property (including some empirical findings), see William Fischel (1975).

7. See David Bradford and Wallace Oates (1974).

8. The tax is admittedly somewhat less visible where it is included as part of a monthly mortgage payment.

9. For a summary of this evidence, see Wallace Oates (1989).

10. For a discussion of fiscal illusion and its application to renters, see Wallace Oates (1988).

11. An alternative to taxing tenants would be to exclude them from voting on local fiscal measures. The limitation of the right to vote in local elections to property owners was once a common practice in this country, but it is now unconstitutional following a U.S. Supreme Court decision. More generally, it would seem undesirable both on grounds of fairness and of full representation of preferences to exclude the interests of a significant constituency of the community in determining the menu of public outputs.

12. As we shall see momentarily, this proposition requires a qualification for a tax on land *value*. A land value tax can influence the choice between alternative improvements to land in the case where one project promises its benefits at a time earlier than another.

13. For a rigorous treatment of the effects of introducing a graded system of property taxation, see Jan Brueckner (1986).

14. See Daniel Holland (1970) for a useful collection of papers addressing the assessment issue.

15. The case for extending land taxation outside the city to suburban jurisdictions seems less compelling. There would be some legitimate objections in terms of fairness to such a reform in largely residential areas. Rather than weighing land and house values equally, a graded system would tax more heavily those families that had relatively modest houses on comparatively large-size lots. It would thus tend to encourage relatively land-intensive dwellings in residential areas.

16. For a further discussion of this point, see Henry Aaron (1975, Chapter 3).

17. Interestingly, the mobility problem may be eased to some extent by the capitalization of local income taxes. Efforts to avoid jurisdictions with relatively high taxes (that are not compensated for by superior amenities) will result in a decreased demand for housing. Thus, new entrants into such communities will tend to be compensated for their higher tax payments by lower housing prices.

18. See Robert Ebel and James Ortbal (1989) for a recent and comprehensive survey, state by state, of the various provisions in effect to provide direct residential property tax relief.

19. For the simple case of an excise tax on a single commodity, it can be shown that the welfare losses from the tax (over and above the revenues that it generates) are directly proportional to the *square* of the tax rate.

Chapter 20

Real Property Classification

John H. Bowman

Property classification subjects different types of property to different levels of taxation as a matter of explicit policy. Over the last two decades, many states have adopted *de jure* real property classification systems. The move to classification, the antithesis of tax uniformity, is part of a long-continuing series of swings in property tax policy.

Historically, property taxation has moved in cycles, starting with selective coverage of some forms of property, moving to general coverage of most, if not all, types of property, and then moving back toward more selective coverage. Scholars have traced this repeating cycle through many centuries in Europe and, more recently, in the United States (Lynn, 1967).

In the U.S., general taxation of property was achieved in the mid-nineteenth century. Typically, all property, real and personal, was to be assessed at market value and all property within a given taxing unit was subjected to the same statutory tax rate. Such uniformity has been in retreat, however, for most of the twentieth century. The retreat is seen in the declining importance of personal property in the tax base,[1] and in the many and varied "relief" programs for various components of the real property base. These include homestead exemptions, use-value assessment of agricultural land, and circuit breakers, as well as classification.

How Is Classification Accomplished?

General Approaches to Classification

The essence of classification is that different effective tax rates, the amount of tax as a percentage of market value, are established for different property types (*i.e.*, classes).[2] Because the tax amount is the product of the tax base (assessed value) times the statutory tax rate, effective rate differentials can be accomplished in several ways:
- Uniform nominal tax rates can be applied to assessed values that represent different percentages of market value;[3]
- Different nominal tax rates can be applied to assessed values that represent the same percentage of market value for all properties;
- Uniform nominal tax rates can be applied to uniform assessed values with the tax amount is reduced via credits that are not uniform; and/or
- Two or more of the preceding approaches can be combined.

In fact, these approaches encompass all forms of direct property tax relief[4]: homestead exemptions, circuit breakers, tax credits, and use-value assessment laws all result in nonuniform effective tax rates. While the line between classification and other direct relief approaches is rather indistinct, common use of the terms suggests perceived differences. This chapter follows the convention. The term *classification* is used to describe a comprehensive, or general, tax differentiation across property uses. The basic difference is in the generality of classification versus the selective nature of other relief approaches. A classification scheme allocates every taxable property to some particular class of property and establishes interclass differentials.

Practice Among Classification States

A 1986 study found real property classification in 21 states and the District of Columbia (Table 20-1). Several classification programs, including Arizona's, prescribe differentials for both real and personal property. While the first state adoption of real property classification came in 1913 (Minnesota), the recent trend toward *de jure* classification commenced in 1968, when Arizona became the fourth state to implement a comprehensive classification program.[5]

The most common approach to classification (18 states) sets assessed values at different percentages of market value. Four states require uniform assessments but provide that different nominal tax rates be used for different classes of property. Two states in the first group (Minnesota and Ohio) also use tax credits to effect further differentiation.

As of 1986, the number of classes ranged from two to 34. The most common number was four, found in seven states and the District of Columbia, another six states had only two classes, and 17 had four or fewer. Minnesota had the largest number of classes, while Arizona's nine classes gave it a rather distant second place. Actually, some of these numbers are not very precise. As notes to Table 20-1 show, the actual number of different percentages used to establish effective-rate differentials differs from the professed number of classes in a half-dozen states. Also, some states' credits are intertwined with their classification systems (*e.g.*, Minnesota and Ohio). Often, therefore, it is difficult to determine just what makes up a "class."[6]

The degree of intended nonuniformity among the classes also varies across the states. In 1986, most states intended differentials of 3:1 or less (Table 20-1, last column). The smallest differential was 1.11:1 (North Dakota). The largest differentials existed in Minnesota (27.5:1), Arizona (20:1), and Montana (10:1). While the ratios shown here are not entirely comparable from state to state, they do support the conclusion that Arizona established one of the highest degrees of effective property tax rate differentiation in 1986. (Table 20-1 does not report ratios for states in which differentials are set locally or in which differentials are not fixed but may change over time, based on a formula).

Residential property typically is the most favored class, but this often is broken into subclasses among which differences are sometimes striking. Most common is the distinction between owner-occupied and renter-occupied residences; this distinction is drawn in Alabama, Arizona, District of Columbia, Minnesota, Oregon, and West Virginia.

Utility properties often are placed in a separate class to be taxed at higher effective rates. This policy is found in Arizona, but the differentials have been reduced in recent years, partly in response to new federal law below.

Table 20-1 — Selected Features of State Real Property Classification				
			Effective Tax Rate Differentials	
State	**Date Established**	**Number of Classes**	**Introduced by**	**High/Low**
Alabama	1972	3	Value (i)	3:1
Arizona	1968	9 (a)	Value (i)	20:1
California*	1978	2	Value	(m)
Colorado	1985	2	Value	1.38:1
District of Columbia	1978	4	Rate (i)	1.67:1
Illinois	1973	7 (b)	Value (j,k)	2.5:1
Iowa	1978	4	Value	(m)
Kansas	1986	4 (c)	Value	2.5:1
Louisiana	1978	4 (d)	Value	2.5:1
Massachusetts	1979	4	Rate (l)	(m)
Minnesota	1913	34 (e)	Value, credit	27.5:1
Mississippi	1982	2	(i)	2:1
Missouri	1985	3	Value	2.67:1
Montana	1917	6 (f)	Value	10:1
New York	1981	4; 2 (g)	Value	(m)
North Dakota	1981	4 (c)	Value (j,l)	1.11:1
Ohio	1979	2	Value	(m)
Oregon	1979	2	Rate, credit	(m)
South Carolina	1976	5 (h)	Value (i)	2.63:1
Tennessee	1973	3	Value	2.2:1
Utah	1983	3	Value	1.67:1
West Virginia	1934	4	Value, Rates (i)	4:1

* California nonuniformities arise from Proposition 13 provisions that restrict assessed value increases to no more than 2% annually for properties that are unchanged and that have not changed ownership since a base year. (a) Arizona uses 2 different value measurements for each classification, with different percentages for the 2 measures in 1 class, for a total of 10 percentages; (b) 5 percentages used for 7 classes; (c) 2 percentages used for 4 classes; (d) 3 percentages used for 4 classes; (e) number of classes is unclear -- 15 different percentages used in 34 separate listings under 14 numbered classes; (f) 8 percentages used for 6 classes; (g) 4 classes mandated for New York City and Nassau County, 2 classes optional elsewhere; (h) 4 percentages for 5 classes; (i) owner-occupied housing is favored within the residential class; (j) structures with relatively few units are favored over larger structures within the residential class; (k) applies only in Cook County; (l) local option (for New York, also see note [g]); (m) differentials created by local choice or by state formula that precludes summary ratio calculation.

Source: Adapted from John H. Bowman, "Real Property Classification: The States March to Different Drummers." *Proceedings of the Seventy-ninth Annual Conference on Taxation.* Columbus, Ohio: National Tax Association-Tax Institute of America, 1987.

In several states, property location affects rates. In West Virginia, real property (except owner-occupied residences and farms) is taxed more heavily if it is inside a municipality. Classification in Illinois applies only in Cook County. New York mandates classification for New York City and Nassau County only but allows local choice (within bounds set by the state) as to adoption of classification and the degree of differentiation across classes for other New York localities. Massachusetts also provides guidelines within which localities can determine for themselves how the tax load is to be distributed across four state-defined classes.[7] Thus, some states use their classification programs to promote local choice or to avoid state-level decisions which almost certainly would produce losers as well as gainers among voters.

These and other differences in the details of classification make generalizations difficult and averages often meaningless.

Why Classify Property?

What explains the movement toward real property classification? Is there some compelling logic that reveals a critical flaw in the notion that property tax burdens (effective rates) should be uniform?

While some philosophical arguments in favor of classification have been offered, and often defended vociferously, it seems that the major explanation for recent developments is of a more practical, political nature. Over the years, assessors often departed from legally prescribed uniformity thus creating *de facto* classification. As John Shannon has noted:

> *It is not unusual to discover that various classes of property are being assessed at different rates.... This extra-legal system for distributing the property-tax burden among various classes of property owners takes on special political significance because any decision to raise all assessments to full value would cause a radical redistribution of the tax load. Homeowners in particular might be forced to pay higher taxes.* (Shannon, 1967, p.51)

Fear of "political repercussions," Shannon goes on to argue, makes state policy makers reluctant to enforce full-value (uniform) assessment laws.

Steven Gold suggests that state officials often are unwilling to enforce uniformity: "The great majority of states which have classified their property tax have done so in order to legalize a pattern of extra-legal favoritism which had previously existed and which was threatened by court mandates to adhere to the law." (Gold, 1984, p.96) Assessment law and practice can be reconciled by changing either, and many states have found it easier politically to change the legal standard. Accordingly, the explosion of *de jure* real property classification adoptions over the last two decades has changed property tax *outcomes* less than property tax *law*.

While most property classification adoptions have sought to codify existing extra-legal differences in an attempt to avoid politically painful redistributions of the property tax burden, total avoidance of redistribution is not possible. First, uniformity within a class still is required. Moreover, assessment nonuniformity tends to increase with the passage of time between reassessments. This is because different properties experience different changes in value over time, both among and within classes. Thus, if it has been several years since the last reassessment (not an uncommon situation across the U.S.), a reassessment will involve redistribution of the property tax even *within* a class. In fact, New York State found that, "The shifts *within* each major class of property (*i.e.*, residential, farm, vacant and commercial) continue to create a greater redistribution of property tax burden than that occurring *between* classes." (*1980 Revaluations*, 1980)

California has sought to avoid the shifts in tax burden *among current property owners* caused by reassessment through the rather simple expedient of abolishing general reassessments. Property is revalued at its sales price when property is transferred, but otherwise the annual change in value is limited to no more than two percent. This feature of Proposition 13 classifies properties according to date of sale, or transfer, a practice cast in doubt by a recent U.S. Supreme Court decision.[8] Perhaps the California system and the more conventional classifications reflect a belief that taxing on the basis of current market value is unfair at least as it relates to some properties. Despite its rather obvious popular appeal, this view generally is opposed by public finance economists. The arguments on both sides are considered below.

How Does Arizona Classification Compare?

Property taxation in Arizona has reflected the general developments of U.S. property taxation which Arthur Lynn has summarized as follows:

> *Since 1900, and more particularly since 1930, property-tax development has included (a) the repeal or modification of uniform-rule provisions and the classification of property for tax purposes; (b) the exemption of particular types and categories of property from ad valorem taxation and, in some instances, the substitution of in-lieu taxes so that the property tax has steadily lost its general character; ... significant changes have come primarily in periods of crisis or under the impact of quite glaring inequities.* (Lynn, 1967, p.15-16)

Arizona property taxation initially required that all taxable property be taxed uniformly. "Laws of 1912, Chapter 23 created the Arizona State Tax Commission ... to assure that all property of every class, kind, and character were assessed uniformly and at full cash value." (Perry & Stein, 1986, p.43) Over the years, the generality eroded. Examples of the changes include subjecting flight property to a special tax instead of the general tax (1951), establishing a different means of determining the value of oil and gas producing properties (1959), exempting business inventories (1964), and exempting household personal property in non-commercial uses (1968). While there were some exceptions to the trend away from uniformity (*e.g.*, bringing financial institutions under personal property tax coverage in 1970), the general pattern was that of moving toward a less general tax (Perry & Stein, 1986, p.43-52).

Of primary interest was the abandonment in 1967 (effective in 1968) of the principle of uniformity for those properties remaining in the tax base, replacing taxation of full cash value with taxation of varying fractions of full cash value for each of five property classes (Perry & Stein, 1986, p.45).

The Arizona classification system is typical, in that it introduces tax differentials via nonuniform assessments, but atypical in that it employs more classes and produces greater differentials than most states. Arizona also is typical of classification states in that *de jure* classification was adopted when a court decision threatened to redistribute the property tax load by ending existing *de facto* nonuniformity.

Antecedents of Classification

Despite the legal requirement of assessing property, regardless of its nature, at 100 percent of full cash (market) value, actual assessment ratios prior to the 1967 adoption of classification reveal nonuniformity. Data for 1966 show an overall real property assessment ratio of 15.4 percent, while residential, commercial and industrial, acreage and farms, and vacant lots were assessed, respectively, at 18.2, 12.4, 8.7, and 7.3 percent.[9] Data for prior years also reveal *de facto* classification in Arizona.

The status quo was disrupted by a legal challenge to the *de facto* classification.[10] In *Southern Pacific Company v. Cochise County*, the Arizona Supreme Court in 1963 held that existing practice clearly was contrary to the statutory standard [A.R.S. section 42-227] requiring that property of all types be assessed at full cash value.

This was the start of the "crisis" that Lynn has argued often acts as the catalyst for "significant changes" in property taxation. In 1967 the Arizona legislature adopted classification and created a new state-level Department of Property Valuation to value centrally assessed properties and to oversee local assessors' administration of the property tax laws (Perry & Stein, 1986, p.44-45). Also, other tax structure and state aid changes were made to reduce reliance on property taxes.

In opting for classification, Arizona had a comparatively easy task because, in contrast to many states, the Arizona constitution did not require uniformity across all types, or classes, of property: "All taxes shall be uniform upon the same class of property within the territorial limits of the authority levying the tax." [Arizona Constitution, Article IX, section 1] The Arizona Supreme Court in its 1963 decision had, in fact, made explicit note of the legislative prerogative to classify property and to require assessments at different levels of full cash value [92 Ariz. at 403] which may have nudged the legislature in that direction.

Development of Arizona Classification

The initial classification system divided taxable property into five classes. Statutory assessment ratios (the percentages of full cash value used as assessed value, the tax base) were 18 percent for agricultural, residential, and certain other properties (Class 4); 25 percent for commercial and industrial properties (Class 3); 40 percent for most public utilities (Class 2); 60 percent for other public utilities (railroads, private car companies, and flight property) as well as standing timber and mines (Class 1); and 100 percent for oil and gas producing properties (Class C).

Assuming these assessment targets were met, effective tax rates within any taxing unit would be 5.56 times as high for oil and gas properties as for agricultural and residential properties. Over the ensuing two decades, there were two related trends: a proliferation of classes and a downward drift in the assessment ratios. As a result, uniformity declined. The number of classes almost doubled from five to nine and the relative assessment in the highest-assessed class increased from 5.56 to 20 times that of the lowest-assessed class.[11]

Considering the classes as they were defined in 1988, Table 20-2 reveals 47 assessment-ratio changes (including five new classes) with 39 decreases and eight increases (Table 20-3).

Table 20-2
Summary of Property Classes in Arizona, 1988

Class	Rate (%)	Description
1	30	Producing mines and mining claim property and standing timber.
2	30	Property used to provide local telecommunications service, gas, water and electric utility company property, and pipeline company property.
3	25	Commercial and industrial property not included in other classes.
4	16	Mainly agricultural properties and vacant land.
5	10	Residential property not used for profit (owner occupied).
6	15	Leased or rented residential property.
7	24	Railroad operating property, private car company property, and airline flight property.
8	5	Historic property as defined in Arizona Revised Statutes, Section 42-139.
C	100	Producing oil and gas company property.

Source: *State and County Abstract of the Assessment Roll 1988.* Phoenix, Arizona: Arizona Department of Revenue, Central Information Services, 1988, pp. vi-vii.

The new classes generally are assessed at especially low ratios thus contributing to the increased spread in effective rates. The first additional class, Class 5, was created to provide more favorable treatment of owner-occupied residences. Worthy of special note is Class 7, railroad and airline operating property. It was discrimination against such property that led to the challenge to the previous *de facto* classification in the 1963 *Southern Pacific* case which precipitated the Arizona legislature's 1967 adoption of *de jure* classification. Such property historically was assessed at high levels relative to other property by many states, including Arizona, which initially included it in Class 1 assessed at 60 percent. In prevailing in court, the railroad won the battle but lost the war as states legalized higher rates on this class of property. Ultimately, however, the national government gave the railroads at least part of the victory they had sought in courts in Arizona and elsewhere with a requirement that railroad property could not be taxed more heavily than other commercial and industrial property.[12] Class 7 was created to satisfy this requirement.

Classes 3 and C are the only ones with the same assessment ratios in both 1988 and 1968 (25 percent and 100 percent, respectively), and only Class C experienced no change over the years. Assessment ratio changes were few in the early years; the first three occurred in 1974. At least two assessment ratio changes occurred in each year between 1981 and

1988, for a total of 30. Either directly or indirectly, 1980 legislation accounted for 26 of the 30 changes since 1980 shown in Table 20-3.

Table 20-3 History of Assessment Ratios for Arizona Property Classes, As Defined by 1988 Law, 1968-1988 (Percentages of Value)[a]										
	1988 Property Class[b]									
Year	**1**	**2**	**3**	**4**	**5**	**6**	**7**	**8**	**9**[c]	**C**
1968	60	40	25	18	18	25	60	18	60	100
1969	60	40	25	18	18	25	60	18	60	100
1970	60	40	25	18	18	25	60	18	60	100
1971	60	40	25	18	18	25	60	18	60	100
1972	60	40	25	18	18	25	60	18	60	100
1973	60	40	25	18	18	25	60	18	60	100
1974	60	50	27	18	**15**	25	60	18	60	100
1975	60	50	27	18	15	25	60	18	60	100
1976	60	50	27	18	15	27	60	18	60	100
1977	60	50	27	18	15	27	60	**8**	60	100
1978	60	50	27	18	15	23	60	8	60	100
1979	60	50	27	18	15	21	36	8	36	100
1980	**52**	**44**	25	**16**	**10**	18	34	8	34	100
1981	52	44	25	16	10	18	36	8	36	100
1982	52	44	25	16	10	18	34	5	34	100
1983	**38**	**38**	25	16	10	18	30	5	30	100
1984	**36**	**36**	25	16	10	18	23	5	23	100
1985	**34**	**34**	25	16	10	17	26	5	13	100
1986	**32**	**32**	25	16	10	16	27	5	13.5	100
1987	**30**	**30**	25	16	10	15	22	5	11	100
1988	30	30	25	16	10	15	24	5	12	100
Exhibit: Changes										
Up	6	7	1	1	2	6	6	2	7	0
Down	0	0	1	0	0	1	4	0	3	0

[a] Prior to 1980, the percentages were applied to full cash value; since 1980, they have been applied to both full cash value and limited property value.

[b] Changed assessment ratios are boldfaced. Classes 1-4 and C are the original classes; the others were added as follows: 5 (1973); 6 (1976); 8 (1977, at first as Class 7); 7 (1980); and 9 (1984). Assessment ratios for years prior to the creation of a current class are those for the class from which the new class was created.

[c] Class 9, Scenic or Historic Railroad property, was eliminated as a separate class in 1988.

Source: Paul Perry and Randie Stein, eds., *State of Arizona Tax Handbook 1985*, (Phoenix, Arizona: Joint Legislative Budget Committee, 1986), pp. 43-86, and updates through 1988; and A.R.S section 42-227.

Interestingly, the 1980 legislation ultimately will reduce effective-rate differentials, but assessment ratios will decline still more. Specifically, that legislation (1) scheduled annual reductions for Classes 1 and 2 until both reached 25 percent by 1992 (accelerated by 1982 law to reach 25 percent by 1990), and (2) linked the assessment ratio for Class 7 (railroad property) to the average for other commercial and industrial property in the prior year. Due to budgetary pressures, however, the assessment ratios for Classes 1 and 2 were frozen temporarily at 30 percent by 1988 legislation.

Finally, 1980 legislation added a second measure of value, limited property value (LPV), in addition to full cash value (FCV), for all real property (except Classes 1, 2, and C) and mobile homes. Since then, each assessment ratio has been applied to both of these measures so that each real property parcel has two taxable values. These two bases underlie two different sets of levies. Specifically, LPV is the base for "primary" taxes and FCV is the base for "secondary" taxes. Secondary taxes are those levied (1) for debt service, (2) voter-approved overrides of tax limits, and (3) levies of special districts. All other property taxes are primary taxes, the bulk of all property taxes, about 75 percent in 1988.

While the LPV concept was developed as a way to restrict the growth of the base for most property taxes, the formula applicable since 1983 has required an increase in LPV even when market value did not increase so long as LPV was below FCV [A.R.S. section 42-201.02]. Given this formula and lower growth in market values in the state in recent years, the gap between LPV and FCV has narrowed and, in many instances, closed.

Tax Shares and Effective Rates Under Classification

Convention is to express the level of property taxes in relation to property values. The most logical measure of property value for this purpose is market value, a reasonably objective measure of the worth of a parcel of property.[13]

Arizona law provides that properties be appraised at market value: "For property tax purposes the full cash value of all taxable property shall be determined at its market value." [A.R.S section 42-227 A] Thus, the full cash value (FCV) figures readily available in Arizona tax data represent the assessors' estimates of market value. Full cash value is the starting point for determination of the taxable values used in calculating secondary taxes.

Implementing Classification

Arizona classification causes taxes to be levied on percentages of value (*i.e.*, assessment ratios or classification ratios) that differ across classes. Moreover, those classification ratios are applied to two measures of value: full cash value (FCV) for secondary taxes and limited property value (LPV) for primary taxes. For Classes 1, 2, and C, LPV = FCV, but for the other classes, the two can differ. Statewide data for 1988 show that LPV overall was equal to 92.3 percent of FCV and to the following percentages of FCV by property class (*State and County Abstract of the Assessment Roll 1988*, 1988):

LPV As a Percentage of FCV by Property Class								
Class	**1**	**2**	**3**	**4**	**5**	**6**	**7**	**8**	**C**
LPV %	100.0	100.0	89.0	78.0	97.7	94.9	83.4	98.0	100.0

Thus, while LPV was as much as 22 percent below FCV (Class 4, agricultural property), it was below FCV by only five percent or less for residential properties (Classes 5 and 6).

Calculating taxes due on various properties involves several steps. For secondary taxes, for example:

- The full cash (market) value estimate is made for each parcel by the assessor;
- Any exempt amount is subtracted from each parcel's gross FCV;
- This net FCV is then reduced to the secondary assessed value by application of the classification ratio for the appropriate class;[14]
- The secondary tax rate of each taxing authority in which a parcel lies is multiplied times the secondary assessed value to determine the tax due each authority, and these amounts are summed to determine the total secondary tax for that parcel.

The same process is completed for primary taxes except that FCV is replaced by LPV. LPV gross, exempt, and net amounts may differ from their FCV counterparts. Also, because primary and secondary taxes are for different purposes, and in some cases even for different authorities, the tax rates are different. As shown below, primary taxes accounted for about three-fourths of Arizona property taxes in 1988.

Once both the secondary and primary taxes have been calculated for each parcel, the total property tax to be raised by Arizona state and local governments from each parcel has been determined. If the one percent constitutional limit on a Class 5 property would be exceeded, the property tax is reduced and the state reimburses the local government for the lost tax funds. The sum of all these taxes across the nearly two million parcels determines the aggregate property tax levy in Arizona. In 1988, this was $1,918.7 million.[15]

Actual 1988 tax data aggregated from individual taxing authorities are used below to consider the end results of property taxation under Arizona classification. A hypothetical case is then presented to abstract from the effects of locational differences across classes.

<u>Actual Overall Results</u>

Relating total property taxes levied, primary plus secondary, to the amount of full cash value less exemptions (net FCV) shows that property taxes averaged 1.52 percent of net FCV statewide (Table 20-4). Average effective tax rates for the several classes individually ranged from 0.55 percent (Class 8) to 15.17 percent (Class C), a ratio of about 28:1. However, neither of these extremes accounted for much of the total tax levy; together they represented less than 0.02 percent of the levy. Among classes of property accounting for at least 10 percent of the statewide aggregate levy, the range of rates was from 1.10 percent (Class 5) to 2.18 percent (Class 3), about a 2:1 ratio.

Some of the results are rather striking. For example, Class 5 accounts for 46.2 percent of net FCV but only 33.4 percent of total taxes, a 28 percent reduction in tax share below base share (Table 20-4). For Class 3, tax share (27.9 percent) is 43 percent above base share (19.6 percent).

A caveat is in order here. These differences are not attributable solely to classification. This can be seen by the fact that Classes 1 and 2 both were assessed at 30 percent of FCV and LPV for 1988 yet their effective tax rates were 3.52 percent and 2.00 percent, respectively. This disparity between classes treated equally under classification largely reflects the effects of location. Different taxing authorities impose different rates of tax, and the various classes of property are distributed unevenly across taxing jurisdictions. Classes concentrated in low-tax authorities fare relatively well.

Table 20-4
Percentage Distributions (by Class) of Arizona Property Tax Base,
Tax Amounts, and Effective Tax Rates (ETR) Statewide, 1988

Class		Net FCV	Secondary Tax	Net LPV	Primary Tax	Total Tax	ETR[*]
No.	Rate						
1	30.0	0.613	1.460	0.679	1.397	1.413	3.52
2	30.0	10.233	11.096	11.347	14.202	13.398	2.00
3	25.0	19.552	29.278	16.870	27.451	27.924	2.18
4	16.0	12.866	14.280	10.827	11.672	12.347	1.46
5	10.0	46.172	32.050	49.589	33.919	33.435	1.10
6	15.0	10.359	11.429	10.494	11.043	11.143	1.64
7	24.0	0.201	0.351	0.188	0.314	0.324	2.45
8	5.0	0.002	0.001	0.002	0.001	0.001	0.55
C	100.0	0.002	0.055	0.002	0.002	0.015	15.17
Total		100.0	100.0	100.0	100.0	100.0	1.52
Exhibit: Amounts in millions of dollars		125,834.2	496.7	113,476.8	1,422.0	1,918.7	

[*] Total tax as a percent of Net FCV.

Source: Calculated from unpublished data provided by the Arizona Department of Revenue.

Results with Uniform Statewide Tax Rates

A clearer impression of the effects of classification can be formed if we abstract from the influence of interarea differences in tax rates. This is done by applying the same statewide, uniform rate to the net taxable assessed values in each class. Such rates were calculated separately for secondary taxes and primary taxes using actual statewide aggregate data for 1988 and dividing the aggregate net secondary (primary) tax base by the aggregate secondary (primary) tax actually levied for 1988 (Table 20-5). The rates produced hypothetical uniform taxes by class that summed exactly to the amounts levied as secondary and primary taxes in 1988; *i.e.*, the exercise is revenue-neutral so that differences between calculated and actual effective rates are not attributable to an overall revenue effect.

Table 20-5
Comparisons of Actual Property Tax to a Hypothetical Statewide
Uniform Property Tax Based on Average Rates for 1988[a]
(Rates and ETRs in Percents; Dollars in Thousands, Except Totals in Millions)

Class		Secondary Taxes (on FCV)				Actual Total Taxes	
No.	Rate	Net FCV[b]	Assessed Value[c]	Actual Tax	Hypothetical Tax[d]	Amount	ETR[e]
1	30.0	$ 771,038	$ 231,311	$ 7,251	$ 5,560	$ 27,112	3.52
2	30.0	12,876,536	3,862,961	55,109	92,849	257,057	2.00
3	25.0	24,603,185	6,150,796	145,415	147,839	535,766	2.18
4	16.0	16,190,108	2,590,417	70,925	62,263	236,905	1.46
5	10.0	58,099,843	5,809,984	159,184	139,648	641,517	1.10
6	15.0	13,035,655	1,955,348	56,766	46,998	213,806	1.64
7	24.0	253,523	60,845	1,742	1,462	6,209	2.45
8	5.0	2,399	119	3	3	13	0.55
C	100.0	1,959	1,959	275	47	297	15.17
Total		125,834.2	20,663.7	496.7	496.7	1,918.7	1.52

Class		Primary Taxes (on LPV)				Hypothetical Total Taxes		
No.	Rate	Net LPV[b]	Assessed Value[c]	Actual Tax	Hypothetical Tax[d]	Amount	ETR[e]	H/A[f]
1	30.0	$ 771,038	$ 231,311	$ 19,861	$ 17,962	$ 23,521	3.05	0.87
2	30.0	12,876,536	3,862,961	201,948	299,962	392,811	3.05	1.53
3	25.0	19,144,098	4,785,434	390,351	371,638	519,478	2.11	0.97
4	16.0	12,286,481	1,965,837	165,981	152,649	214,911	1.33	0.91
5	10.0	56,272,580	5,627,258	482,333	436,961	576,608	0.99	0.90
6	15.0	11,908,592	1,786,289	157,040	138,707	185,705	1.42	0.87
7	24.0	213,238	51,177	4,467	3,974	5,436	2.14	0.88
8	5.0	2,288	114	10	9	12	0.49	0.89
C	100.0	1,959	1,959	23	152	199	10.17	0.67
Total		113,476.8	18,312.9	1,422.0	1,422.0	1,918.7	1.52	1.00

[a] Statewide average effective tax rate and revenue were held constant for both primary and secondary taxes taken separately.
[b] FCV (secondary) or LPV (primary) after exemptions but before application of assessment rates.
[c] Net assessed value: gross base times assessment rate.
[d] Tax rates, calculated as explained in the text, applied to the tax bases are 0.0240358051 for FCV (secondary) and 0.0776507437 for primary (LPV).
[e] Effective tax rate, as percentage of net FCV.
[f] Total hypothetical tax divided by total actual tax.

Source: Calculated from unpublished data provided by the Arizona Department of Revenue.

Comparison of the actual and the hypothetical uniform tax amounts and effective tax rates in the last two columns of Table 20-5 shows that factoring out the effect of location changes the story somewhat. The Class 5 ETR drops under the uniform tax indicating that owner-occupied residential property values are concentrated in areas where tax rates are relatively high. (Other direct property tax relief, which is concentrated on Class 5 properties, is ignored here.[16]) In fact, this is true for all classes except Class 2. Although still substantial, the range of effective tax rates across classes is narrower under the uniform tax than under the actual tax. Also, Classes 1 and 2 have equal ETRs under the hypothetical tax.

Expressing the hypothetical tax amounts as percentages of their actual tax equivalents summarizes the differences more conveniently. This reveals that every class other than Class 2 would have lower taxes for the class as a whole if a uniform rate were applied statewide; Class 8, which has the highest ETR under both the actual and hypothetical taxes, would enjoy the largest reduction. Clearly, differences in local tax rates and in the distribution of properties across localities contribute significantly to some of the differences in actual interclass ETRs.

Evaluation Of Classification: Arizona As A Case Study

After adopting formal classification over two decades ago, Arizona left the system relatively unchanged for several years. In the late 1970s and early 1980s, however, a number of changes were made that have added to the complexity and to the degree of assessment-ratio differentiation. The prescribed assessment level is 20 times as great for Class C (100 percent) as for Class 8 (five percent). While neither of these classes accounts for a significant portion of full cash value, classification alters their relative shares quite dramatically. It alters the relative shares of other classes of property somewhat less dramatically.

Class 5, owner-occupied residences, is a logical basis for comparison for it contains more parcels and more full cash value than any other class. The Class 5 assessment ratio is 10 percent. Among the nine classes, only Class 8 is assessed at a lower fraction of value. Relative to Class 5, Class C is assessed 10 times as high; Classes 1, 2, 3, and 7 are assessed anywhere from 2.4 to three times as high; and Classes 6 and 4 are assessed 50 and 60 percent higher, respectively. (Remember that classification does not tell the whole story; other property tax relief programs further reduce the Class 5 effective net tax rate.)

Fairness (equity) often is given as the rationale for classification, but critics suggest that classification is unfair. What is the logical basis for the differences in effective property tax rates intended by the Arizona classification system? To some extent, property taxes may rest on the benefits-received rationale. If this logic is accepted,[17] is it likely, for example, that renter-occupied residences of a given value receive 50 percent more benefits than owner-occupied residences of the same value? Do the relative benefits of most types of business property warrant taxing it 2.5 to three times as heavily as owner-occupied residential property? For both questions, a "no" answer seems appropriate.

Property taxation also may rest upon the ability-to-pay rationale. The basic notion is that, all else equal, people with property are better off (are in a higher economic position) than those without and that, among those with property, economic position (ability to pay) rises with the value of property. Market value is the standard measure of property value as discussed immediately below. However, classification advocates argue that market value is not a good proxy for ability to pay. Of course, if ability to pay does not differ across alternative property uses in proportion to the the tax differences produced by classification, then, rather than promote equity, classification contributes to inequity. Moreover, differences in tax liability per $100 of market value might discourage investment in higher-taxed property uses and thus also have implications for efficiency.

Market Value As a Tax Base: Equity Considerations

The property tax is levied on accumulated assets, or wealth, which is one measure of ability to pay tax. Value is not absolute or inherent in a given object. Market value, the price a property would command in an arm's-length transaction between a willing buyer and a willing seller, is the traditional measure used:

> *An estimate of market value, or value in exchange, is the purpose of most valuation assignments. Such an estimate reflects the appraiser's interpretation of the buyers and sellers in the marketplace and the conditions that prevail when property is offered for sale. (The Appraisal of Real Estate, 1983, p.39)*

Market transactions are voluntary actions by people dividing their available dollars among many alternative uses in ways that they believe are in their own best interests. Thus, market value is an objective measure of value that reveals what people think property is worth. Current market values can logically also be used in valuing properties not sold recently because people who purchased their properties many years ago have the option of selling. If they choose not to, implicitly they are saying that they value the property at least as highly as the market price it would be expected to command.

These considerations suggest that a dollar's worth of value in any type, or class, of property represents the same wealth (ability to pay taxes) as a dollar's worth of any other type of property. The implication is that taxes should be a uniform percentage of market value across property types.

Income-Production Argument

Not all agree with this view. An opposing view is given succinctly by the following statement:

> *The reason we have the classification system is that ... it is just inherently unfair to tax non-income-producing properties at the same level of market value that income-producing properties are taxed. Income-producing property, by virtue of the fact that it is what it is, generates more wealth for its owners, whereas non-income-producing property is a drain, if it is anything, on its owner. In other words, it is sterile and unproductive -- all you do is live in it and you do not make any money out of it. (Lyons, 1967, p.217)*

In this view, two property owners who have properties with equal market value and who, for simplicity, are equally situated in all other important respects, do not have equal ability to pay property taxes if one owns income-producing property and the other does not.

If the basic point is granted, what guidance does the observation provide for setting relative property tax amounts? Very little; it says only that the income-producing property should pay more. It does not indicate whether the appropriate difference is 10 percent, 25 percent, 100 percent, 300 percent, or some other amount. There is no objective way to determine this which helps to explain why relative taxes are different across the states with classification and why they often change in response to political influence within a given state.

How seriously can one take the argument that owner-occupied homes are "sterile and unproductive" and "a drain" on their owners? It implies that all who own homes or aspire to own homes are irrational. Under this view, those with mansions, or any homes that provide more than very basic shelter, deserve the pity of others not saddled with such liabilities. Is pursuit of "the American dream" of homeownership truly the pursuit of folly? That so many people willingly put so much money into their homes suggests that homeownership is neither folly nor unproductive. Homes provide their owners with valued services. If they did not, people would behave differently; large, expensive, feature-laden homes would not command resources in the markets, and average home size and luxury features would not be increasing.

But homes do command resources in voluntary transactions so the prices paid must indicate the value placed on them by owners even, as already noted, by people who have not purchased their properties recently because they have the option of selling.

Finally, it must be noted that homeowners, the class that receives the bulk of the relief provided by classification, also receive tax breaks under income tax provisions. Whereas income-producing property's income stream is taxed as part of the income tax base, the non-monetary benefits from homeownership are not. Yet the tax and interest costs of homeownership are permitted as deductions from the income tax base effectively offsetting other income of homeowners. If income production is to be a consideration in varying property tax effective rates, a case could be made that the *higher* ETRs should be imposed on *non-income-producing* property, the opposite of conventional classification.

Cash-Flow Argument

Another, but related, argument by those who oppose reliance upon market value as the base for property taxation starts with the observation that all taxes are paid out of income. It is then noted that the property tax is a tax on accumulated asset value, not on current income, which means that at times the amount of tax may be uncommonly large in relation to income. The resultant cash-flow squeeze sometimes is said to provide the justification for general relief from property taxes for non-income-producing properties.

While cash-flow problems are both real and serious for certain property owners in any given year, they do not justify across-the-board relief for homeowners which suspends the logic of a tax on asset value. Such broad relief is not sufficiently targeted. It decreases the revenue yield of the property tax at any given nominal rate or it requires a higher rate on other properties to provide a given level of revenue. In short, costs are imposed in granting such relief. Property ownership is relatively concentrated, and most would feel that those who own property are better off (*i.e.*, have more economic and taxpaying capacity) than those who do not; thus, property tax relief tends to provide a subsidy from the have-nots to the haves (Aaron, 1975). If the cash-flow problem is deemed to require a legislative solution, then rather narrowly targeted relief mechanisms, such as deferrals or circuit breakers, are more equitable than broad relief to all homeowners.

Departures from the objective base of market value create inequities and open the door to making tax liabilities reflect lack of political influence more than value of property. Effective-rate differences of 20:1 or 10:1 are incredibly large. Even differences of 3:1, 2:1, or 1.5:1 are large enough to pose equity problems.

The following summarizes the major considerations which, on balance, favor basing property taxes on a uniform percentage of market value:

- Market value is an objective measure of value determined through voluntary transactions that reveal what people think property is worth;
- Even non-income-producing property (owner-occupied housing) provides benefits of value to its owners who otherwise would choose not to be owners or at least to own less;
- Homeowners already are subsidized by income tax provisions which omit from the tax base their benefits from homeownership while permitting property taxes and mortgage interest to be offset against other income;
- Once the tie to a uniform percentage of market value is broken, relative property taxes tend to be determined on the basis of differences in political power rather than on differences in economic capacity; and
- The cash-flow problems experienced by some property owners do not justify broad, across-the-board relief to whole classes of owners. More targeted relief mechanisms are available that address the problem.

Efficiency Considerations

In Arizona, all other things (including location) equal, property tax liability is 50 percent to 200 percent higher for a given investment in rental property or other business property than for the same investment in the investor's own home. Such penalties for the higher-assessed classes may affect investment decisions at the margin.

Tax provisions that directly influence economic behavior are said to be non-neutral, and tax-induced differences in relative prices can be shown to lead to inefficient allocation of resources producing an "excess burden" of taxation that exceeds the sum of the revenue and the costs of administration and compliance efforts incurred in raising that revenue (Browning & Browning, 1987, p.309-315). Excess burden, simply stated, means that society fails to get as much utility (satisfaction or benefit) as possible from available resources. Tax administration and compliance costs above those that are necessary to raise a given amount of revenue also are a source of excess burden.

Effective-rate differences across states or localities, or property uses, if not offset by differences in valued services, tend to make the higher-tax areas less attractive to investors in property. Within any given area, effective-rate differences tend to alter the relative attractiveness of holding different forms of property.

In the U.S., tax preferences for owner-occupied housing are bestowed both by income taxes and by classification or other property tax concessions to homeowners. These tend to stack the deck in favor of investment in homes to the detriment of investment in business assets. Even if, at the margin, another dollar of investment in a home (first or second) appears to an investor to offer lower returns (monetary or otherwise) before taxes than investment in a factory or retail facility; for example, *after-tax* returns still may favor housing. A property tax on business property that is 2.5 to three times as heavy as that on owner-occupied housing, as in Arizona, can tip the scales in favor of housing investment, and state and federal income tax concessions to housing will reinforce the property tax bias. Such non-neutralities may help explain both the increase in average house size and price and the relatively poor United States productivity record in recent decades.

An earlier study concluded that classification violates the criterion of tax neutrality arguing that if deadweight utility loss is to be minimized, then real estate, as an input to the productive process (including homes, which produce housing services for their owners), "... ought to be taxed uniformly according to the optimal tax literature. Obviously, a classified property tax would violate this rule because it would tax real estate in different land uses at different rates." (Sonstelie, 1978, p.240)

The tendency for tax differentials to influence economic decisions is quite clear. The question, of course, is how strong that tendency is -- whether differentials of the magnitude in Arizona property classification are large enough to have a significant influence on the location of activity.

The empirical literature on the effects of taxes on economic choices provides some relevant insights (Fisher, 1988). While other factors rank ahead of taxes, the influence of taxes sometimes is significant. A recent study of interstate differences in employment growth, for example, found that "... the overall increase in tax effort has a negative and statistically significant effect on overall employment growth and on employment growth in manufacturing, retail trade and services." (Wasylenko, 1986, p.506) This study did not include a separate property tax variable. Another considered the effects of taxation on capital mobility using both the usual state-level average tax variables and a new tax variable which was specific to industry and state and also was focused on the marginal rather than the average tax on an additional investment outlay (Parke, 1987). While the traditional tax variables were statistically insignificant, the new, more refined variable indicated that higher taxes on capital are associated with lower capital investment.

"The evidence... suggests that tax differentials probably have significant effects on the location of firms and differences in intra-regional employment growth." (Wasylenko, 1986, p.227) Several of the substate studies included effective property tax differentials, rather than overall tax levels; and in many instances, though not all, the property tax variables were statistically significant in explaining differences in business activity. The findings from one study that considered different industries are instructive. Wasylenko found, using data for localities in the Milwaukee area, that effective property tax rate differences had significant and negative effects on manufacturing and wholesale trade (industries whose markets are largely outside a given locality, so that alternative locations are acceptable) but were not significant for four other industries operating in more localized markets (Wasylenko, 1986, p.225-26).

In summary, the literature suggests that economic decisions are affected by differences in tax levels consistent with theory. Sensitivity to tax differences, however, depends upon other circumstances. These might be summarized as differences in price-sensitivity (elasticity). The larger the number of options available (*e.g.*, the greater the number of acceptable locations for a given venture), the more sensitive will the final decision be to tax differentials. In other words, if there is only one possible location for a given project, and if that project will be executed regardless of cost (at least within some broad range) because the overall return from the venture is expected to be high, then the level of taxes in that location will have no effect on the decision. But if multiple locations are equally suitable, or nearly so, while taxes at the different locations are quite different (and expected to remain so), then a rational investor would be expected to choose the most profitable (lowest tax) alternative.

The evidence is largely from differences in interstate and interlocal tax levels and effective rates rather than differences in effective rates across different uses of property. Extension of the findings to this latter situation seems warranted, however, because investment dollars are mobile across types of investment as well as across localities. Differences in sensitivity to tax differences are to be expected here, too, for demand for certain types or uses of property will be more inelastic than for others.

Efficiency considerations tend to suggest uniformity to meet the objectives of tax neutrality and maximum benefit from available resources. Recognizing that demands are not completely insensitive to price, however, suggests that perfect neutrality is unlikely, so minimal interference in decisions from the tax system is the best that can be hoped for. Because different uses of property are likely to be characterized by demands with different degrees of sensitivity to price, a non-uniform (classified) tax system may be warranted in an attempt to maximize tax neutrality and benefit from available resources. Demand for owner-occupied residences may be less elastic than for most other uses (Sonstelie, 1978, p.240-41), however, so the heaviest taxes would tend to be on owner-occupied residences, the opposite of current classification in Arizona and other states.

Tax Capitalization: A Caveat

A caveat is in order here. Tax differences have no effect on economic decisions if those differences have been fully *capitalized* (*i.e.*, if property prices have adjusted to reflect the present value of expected taxes). Thus, removal of capitalized tax differentials caused by classification might be opposed on the ground that they no longer affect decisions and their removal would create windfall losses and gains. But removal of uncapitalized differentials probably is desirable. As Aaron has observed:

> *The key to capitalization is the existence of persistent tax differentials, whatever the motive for their creation. Permitting the continuance of unintentional inequalities in tax burdens that are not capitalized can be justified only if the cost of removing them is considered excessive.* (p.64)

Aaron's context was assessment error; the argument applies equally to *intentional* inequalities, though, as his first sentence indicates.

At most, only partial capitalization of Arizona tax differences stemming from classification can have occurred. There can be no capitalization for properties not sold since the advent of classification. Moreover, full capitalization is not likely even for properties that have sold in part because details of the Arizona classification system have been changed several times. Unstable and unpredictable differences do not facilitate full and rapid capitalization.

Administration and Compliance Costs

If classification were removed, what costs would be affected? An obvious category is political costs for it has been argued that minimization of feared political costs led to the adoption of *de jure* classification initially. This cost, however real to current officeholders, is what economists call a transfer cost. That is, it generates winners to offset losers. Transfers occur, but overall societal well-being is not affected.

Other costs are more important to the overall well-being of society. The current system entails large costs for administrators and for taxpayers. The extra time and effort spent on property taxes because of classification could be used in other ways; hence, a real opportunity cost is incurred. For example, administrators have to make certain determinations in order to classify property, and often they must defend their decisions in legal proceedings or less formal encounters. A 1984 law requires a new, annual verification process for eligibility for Class 5 status, and imposes new penalties on violators in an effort to avoid improper (illegal) receipt of the special and substantial subsidies that classification bestows on owner-occupied residences (Perry & Stein, 1986, p.52). The need for this results from the fact that classification taxes rental residences 50 percent more heavily than owner-occupied residences. Some units change from one status to another, and thus tax liabilities change. Changes from rented to owned can be expected to be reported, but the opposite changes apparently are not always reported voluntarily. Perhaps some false representations are made even with the recent changes. But the new procedure to try to assure proper compliance adds costs for all administrators and owner-occupants, even in cases where there was no impropriety.

Illegal actions aside, when gains (tax savings, or subsidies) can be gotten, it is rational to incur costs up to the amount of the expected benefit. In some cases, this may mean simply working within the existing system to gain more favorable treatment legally. An example would be seeking change in the shares of a mixed-use property that are assigned to each of the classes involved. But when the existing classes do not seem quite right, for whatever reason, then actions to change the system may be undertaken. Remember that there is no single logical structure of relative tax treatments that is "right." The whole system is up for grabs. Within rather broad limits, the differentials can be whatever legislators can be prevailed upon to provide. As a former Minnesota tax commissioner stated of that state's experience with classification, the longest of any state:

> ... there is no logical stopping point once you start a classification of property. We started with four classes and we now have some twenty different classes. I think the fact that we have only twenty classes of property is a tribute to the legislature, because had they yielded to all the pressures involved we could easily have had over two hundred. (Hatfield, 1967, p.242)

That assessment was made over twenty years ago, about the time Arizona was embarking upon classification. A more recent count shows that Minnesota has succumbed to the pressures to add more classes (Table 20-1), but that higher count does not do justice to the complexity of the system that has evolved there (Bowman, 1986).

Meanwhile, as discussed in an earlier section, the Arizona system has changed many times, with the addition of new classes, changes in the assessment ratios of established classes, and the reassignment of certain properties from one class to another. Introduction of limited property value as an additional base for property taxes, and the partitioning of taxes into "primary" and "secondary" portions levied on the two different bases, also added a new dimension to Arizona classification. A four-inch stack of paper is needed to provide only brief summaries of legislative consideration of bills introduced in the last five years seeking changes related to the Arizona classification system.

Such changes present costs that result from uncertainty thus violating the tax criterion of predictability. They also tend to create greater complexity which makes it more difficult for taxpayers to know how they are being treated and how that compares with the treatments accorded others. Those who do not understand the manner in which their taxes are determined may come to mistrust the political system that created the maze of provisions. Such mistrust could impose a sizable, although intangible, cost.

The more immediate point, however, is that significant costs are incurred in the drafting of legislative bills, analyses of those bills, hearings and lobbying efforts on those bills, etc. Such costs are real, and they are incurred because the determination of relative tax treatments has been opened up to resolution by political influence and strength. While it is rational for individuals and groups hoping to make gains (reduced taxes) to incur such costs up to the level of expected tax savings, their efforts constitute a deadweight loss to society, for they are made at the expense of other, more productive uses of the same time and resources. The broader question, then, is whether it is rational for the state to encourage the expenditure of resources.

Summary And Conclusion

While classification often is defended as necessary for equity, the case that classification produces inequity can be made at least as easily. Efficiency is a more precise concept than equity, but its empirical measurement is not easy. Available evidence, however, shows that differentials in effective property tax rates alter economic decisions in some circumstances thus violating the efficiency criterion and producing excess burdens. Further efficiency losses result from administrative and compliance costs imposed by classification as well as from taxpayers' efforts to gain more favorable tax treatments in what is, in essence, a system of negotiated property tax liabilities.

If a classified system is deemed a political necessity, consideration should be given to placing the details in the state constitution. This can reduce greatly the periodic changes thus lending more stability and lowering the costs associated with classification. West Virginia's constitutional, four-class system has endured without change since 1934. Keeping the number of classes rather small reduces the number of border areas which also should hold down the costs of classification, and avoiding truly large differentials can further curb the harmful aspects of classification. Moderation also may be necessary to avoid federal intervention to change state policies that violate constitutional requirements. The states' latitude in property tax policy, while considerable, is not absolute. Numerous U.S. Supreme Court decisions over the years illustrate both these points. Recent federal legislation limiting the taxation of railroad and airline property relative to other business property provides a specific example of restrictions on state discretion.

In general, the case for property taxation based on a uniform percentage of market value is stronger than that for a classified system with effective-rate differentials. Moreover, to the extent that an efficiency justification can be made for classification, it seems to suggest placing the heaviest burdens on owner-occupied residences, the opposite of current classification.

References

Aaron, Henry J. *Who Pays the Property Tax? A New View.* Washington, D.C.: Brookings Institution, 1975.

Allegheny Pittsburgh Coal Company v. County Commission of Webster County, West Virginia, 109 S.Ct. 633 (1989).

The Appraisal of Real Estate, 8th ed. Chicago, Illinois: American Institute of Real Estate Appraisers, 1983.

Beebe, Robert L. and Richard J. Sinnott. *In the Wake of Hellerstein: Whither New York?* Albany, New York: New York Executive Department, Division of Equalization and Assessment, 1977.

Bowman, John H. "Direct Property Tax Relief in Minnesota: An Analysis." Chapter 13 in R. D. Ebel and T. J. McGuire, eds., *Final Report of the Minnesota Tax Study Commission: Volume 2, Staff Papers.* St. Paul, Minnesota: Butterworths, 1986, pp. 281-332.

Bowman, John H. "Real Property Classification: The States March to Different Drummers." *Proceedings of the Seventy-ninth Annual Conference on Taxation.* Columbus, Ohio: National Tax Association-Tax Institute of America, 1987, pp. 288-96.

Bowman, John H., John L. Mikesell, Frederick D. Stocker, and David Carr. *City of Buffalo Revaluation and Revenue Study.* Washington, D.C.: Academy for State and Local Government, August 1982.

Browning, Edgar K. and Jacquelene M. Browning. *Public Finance and the Price System,* 3rd ed. New York, New York: Macmillan Publishing Company, 1987.

Commerce Clearing House. *State Tax Reporter,* Looseleaf State and Local Tax Service. Chicago, Illinois: Commerce Clearing House, continually updated.

Fisher, Ronald C. *State and Local Public Finance.* Glenview, Illinois: Scott, Foresman and Company, 1988.

Gold, Steven D. "The Changing Shape of Property Tax Relief Since the Late 1960s," in *Legal Problems in Property Assessment and Taxation.* Chicago, Illinois: International Association of Assessing Officers, 1984, pp. 87-117.

Gold, Steven D. *Property Tax Relief.* Lexington, Massachusetts: Heath/Lexington Books, 1979.

Hatfield, Rolland F. "Minnesota's Experience with Classification." *The Property Tax: Problems and Potentials.* Princeton, New Jersey: Tax Institute of America, 1967, pp. 239-44.

Hellerstein, Jerome R. and Walter Hellerstein. *State and Local Taxation: Cases and Materials,* 5th ed. St. Paul, Minnesota: West Publishing Co., 1988.

Lynn, Arthur D., Jr. "Property-Tax Development: Selected Historical Perspectives." R. W. Lindholm, ed., *Property Taxation USA.* Madison, Wisconsin: University of Wisconsin Press, 1967, pp. 7-19.

Lyons, Thomas G. "The Classification Issue in Illinois." *The Property Tax: Problems and Potentials.* Princeton, New Jersey: Tax Institute of America, 1967, pp. 216-20.

1980 Revaluations: Property Tax Shift Analysis. Albany, New York: New York Executive Department, Division of Equalization and Assessment, 1980.

Papke, Leslie. "Subnational Taxation and Capital Mobility: Estimates of Tax-Price Elasticities." *National Tax Journal,* 40(June 1987): 191-203.

Perry, Paul and Randie Stein (eds.). *State of Arizona Tax Handbook 1985*. Phoenix, Arizona: Joint Legislative Budget Committee, 1986.

Shannon, John. "Conflict between State Assessment Law and Local Assessment Practice." R. W. Lindholm, ed., *Property Taxation USA*. Madison, Wisconsin: University of Wisconsin Press, 1967, pp. 39-63.

Sonstelie, Jon. "The Classified Property Tax." *Technical Aspects of the District's Tax System: Studies and Papers Prepared for the District of Columbia's Tax Revision Commission*, Submitted to the Committee on the District of Columbia, U.S. House of Representatives. Washington, D.C.: Government Printing Office, 1978, pp. 233-60.

State and County Abstract of the Assessment Roll 1988. Phoenix, Arizona: Arizona Department of Revenue, Central Information Services, 1988.

U.S. Bureau of the Census, *1967 Census of Governments, Volume 2, Taxable Property Values*. Washington, D.C.: Government Printing Office, 1968.

U.S. Bureau of the Census, *1987 Census of Governments, Volume 2, Taxable Property Values*. Washington, D.C.: Government Printing Office, 1989.

Wasylenko, Michael. "Local Tax Policy and Industry Location: A Review of the Evidence." *Proceedings of the Seventy-eighth Annual Conference on Taxation*. Columbus, Ohio: National Tax Association-Tax Institute of America, 1986, pp. 222-28.

Wasylenko, Michael and Therese McGuire. "Jobs and Taxes: The Effect of Business Climate on States' Employment Growth Rates." *National Tax Journal*, 38 (December 1985): 497-511.

Endnotes

1. Between 1956 and 1986, the real property component of the nationwide property tax base rose from 75 percent to 85 percent (1987 Census of Governments, viii). Both figures assign state-assessed property to the personal property category and, thus, would be somewhat higher if the real estate component could be isolated.

2. This section draws upon Bowman (1986).

3. Although similar results can, and often do, emerge *de facto* from poor administration of uniformity provisions, only legally intended (*de jure*) effective rate differentials are considered here.

4. Indirect property tax relief is effected outside the property tax, e.g., by introduction of nonproperty taxes or intergovernmental aids to reduce reliance on property taxation. Direct property tax relief results from changes within the property tax including homestead exemptions and classification.

5. Classification systems differentiating between real and personal property were more common than those extending differentials into real property.

6. For a discussion of Minnesota, where the situation no doubt is the most complex and confusing, see Bowman (1986). In addition, agricultural use-value assessment programs make counting classes more difficult. While nearly all states have such programs, they generally are not included as part of a real property classification system (1987 Census of Governments: Appendices A & C). But an exception is Kansas where the differentiation between agricultural land and "other" real property arises from the

different underlying value concepts (market value and use value) rather than from different assessment rates.

7. Information on what actual practice has emerged from the local-option arrangements in Massachusetts and New York is not readily available, but in 1986 classification was not widespread in either state (Bowman, 1987, fn 13).

8. The defined classes must be defensible against charges of denial of equal protection. In January 1989, the U.S. Supreme Court held that different assessment levels for recently sold properties via-a-vis those not recently sold could not be permitted to exist more than temporarily (*Allegheny Pittsburgh Coal Company v. County Commission of Webster County, West Virginia* [1989]). This case and its possible application in California and beyond were the subject of a session at the 1989 annual meeting of the National Tax Association.

9. The Census Bureau prepares and reports size-weighted ratios (1967 Census of Governments: Table 9). Census Bureau ratios may differ from those of any given state, due to such matters as sampling, screening for arm's-length sales, and the Census Bureau's inclusion of only "ordinary real estate" which in 1967 excluded parcels with values in excess of $250,000. This latter aspect would have affected commercial and industrial properties, in particular.

10. Unless specifically noted otherwise, the following brief review of legal aspects of Arizona's move to classification (including the bracketed text references) is based upon Beebe and Sinnott (1977) pages 7-86.

11. This summary is based upon Perry and Stein (1986), pages 43-86 and periodic updates.

12. By 1976 legislation, Congress forbade state and local governments to tax railroad property more heavily than other commercial and industrial property, and in 1982 this was extended to airline property (Hallerstein & Hallerstein, 1988, pp. 48-49).

13. This chapter uses assessors' estimates of market value without adjustment for assessor error, in part because satisfactory adjustment was not possible and in part because it seems likely that assessor performance would not be affected materially even by fundamental change in classification provisions.

14. Mixed-use properties are apportioned between the classes and the appropriate portions are carried in each class in which the parcel belongs, for both FCV and LPV [A.R.S section 42-227 E].

15. Property tax relief measures that reduce individual tax bills to property owners but that do not reduce the property tax revenue to the taxing authorities, such as the homeowners' rebate, are *not* reflected in this paper, as noted earlier.

16. Those programs, not reflected in the numbers in this paper, include the homeowners' rebate under which the state pays 56% of a homeowner's primary school tax up to relief limit of $500. A cap on homestead property taxes at one percent likewise benefits Class 5. In addressing overall tax burdens, these and other property tax relief programs, including classification and exemption policies, need to be considered together to determine the net effect of the various state policies.

17. Property tax liabilities often may not correspond very well to either benefits received from, or costs imposed for, public services for such major services as education and public safety. Low-valued properties, for example, may impose greater costs for fire protection than high-valued ones; more police patrols may be needed in areas with low property values; and the tax dollars per child in school may be greater in areas with high valued property.

Chapter 21

Local Property Tax
And Expenditure Limits

Ronald C. Fisher and Mary N. Gade

Expenditure and property tax limitations attracted national attention with the tax revolt of the late 1970s and early 1980s. State legislation was designed to increase the constraints on local government taxing and spending power. The limits targeted property tax rates, property tax assessment increases, and the growth in property levies, total revenues, or expenditures. The nominal effectiveness of these limits in reducing the growth of their targeted sources seems to have varied widely. The fundamental fiscal issue is whether these limits have caused localities to alter their fiscal behavior, and, how or whether, the nature of the programs is such that the limits have not been constraining.

Local governments in Arizona face expenditure and property tax restrictions as a result of Constitutional amendments adopted in 1980. These Arizona fiscal limitations provide an incentive for localities to substitute other revenue sources for the limited property taxes if the limits are binding. In addition, any potential effects of the limits may be mitigated by opportunities to override or supercede the limits either by direct voter approval or substitution among fiscal categories.

We pursue two parallel approaches in examining the effects of Arizona's fiscal limits. First, we compare the (county and city) levels and mix of both revenues and expenditures before and after limits came into effect. Observed changes in fiscal behavior can be related to specific provisions of the limits. Second, we use an analytical model of local government fiscal decisions to examine statistically whether there is evidence of an overall change in the pattern of fiscal behavior at the county level as a result of the limits. Our results suggest that the limits themselves do not appear to have reduced the growth of expenditures and property taxes in Arizona throughout the 1980s, although the limits seem to have induced localities to rely more on borrowing.

Description Of Limits

Counties, cities, and community college districts in Arizona face limits to the growth of primary property tax levies and to expenditures[1]. Primary property tax levies are limited to increases of 2 percent per year over the base year (1980) in addition to increases as a result of new construction. The property tax levy limit does not apply to taxes or special assessments for the payment of long-term bond principal or interest or to taxes for special purpose districts (including improvement districts), and the levy limit can be exceeded by a vote of the people. The limit is increased to allow for new construction ("property not taxed in the prior year") but is also decreased if property is demolished or no longer exists.[2]

Expenditures of counties, cities, and community college districts are limited to percentage increases sufficient to maintain constant real per capita spending. The expenditure limit is the product of the percentage increases in the general price level and population (student population for the community college districts) since the base year of 1980. Counties and cities can change the base year by popular vote; cities can suspend the expenditure limit over a given time period (by adopting an alternative limit by popular vote); and the limits can be exceeded to respond to natural or manmade disasters. For counties and cities, the limit does not apply to expenditures paid from funds from the sale of bonds, to federal intergovernmental aid, to state intergovernmental aid if covered under the state expenditure limit (as specific-purpose state aid is), to the amounts counties distribute to schools, to expenditures for city hospitals (if supported before January 1, 1980), to amounts accumulated to purchase land or structures, or to gifts, interest, or dividends received. Expenditures by all school districts together are similarly limited to the percentage increases in the general price level and student population. The cumulative allowed total school expenditure under the limit is the 1980 base amount plus changes in inflation and population plus 10 percent. There are also expenditure limits that apply to each individual school district.

The Constitutional amendment also imposed an overall limit on total primary property taxes levied on any individual owner-occupied home equal to 1 percent of the property value. This limit applies to the primary property taxes levied by all local governments on a home but does not include primary property taxes levied by school districts that are rebated to the taxpayer through the homeowner's rebate, to taxes or special assessments levied to pay principal or interest on long-term bonds, to taxes or assessments levied by special purpose districts, or to taxes approved by an election to exceed a fiscal limit. Property value is limited to a 10 percent annual rate of increase when computing this limit. If the 1 percent limit is reached for any owner-occupied residential property, the tax above that amount is paid by the state government to the school district. In essence, then, the state pays from other revenue sources for school property taxes that would exceed the one percent limit.

It is worth noting that Arizona operated with a different statutory local government property tax limit for many years prior to the Constitutional amendments adopted in 1980. The prior limit restricted the annual growth in property tax levies of counties and municipalities to no more than 10 percent although a number of specific categories were exempt from the limit and there was an option for voted overrides. The new 2 percent levy limit for primary property taxes net of new construction may be more restrictive than the prior 10 percent overall levy limit except in areas where there is very substantial new construction. On the other hand, the new expenditure limit essentially has been of the same order of magnitude as the prior levy limit given the rate of population increase in Arizona and inflation rates in the 1980s.

Expenditures

It appears that the expenditure limits generally have not been constraining in the 1980s for three reasons: (1) the substantial growth in population and the price level, (2) the institutional features of the limit which exempt a number of spending categories, and (3) the ability of cities, particularly, to adopt voter-approved alternatives to the limit.

County Expenditures

The expenditure limit was designed to allow spending to grow in direct proportion with the growth in population and prices. The combination of about 38 percent growth in population and a 68 percent increase in the price level allowed for a 131 percent increase in the expenditure limit for all counties together from the base year of 1979-80 to 1989-90. In the first ten year period of the expenditure limit, allowed county expenditures grew at an average rate of 13 percent per year.

In fiscal year 1981-82, just after implementation of the current limit, only Maricopa county was spending at the limited amount. In aggregate, the counties were spending $70 million less than allowed in the limited expenditure categories. Because of the substantial growth in the limits throughout the 1980s, only two counties were at their spending limit by 1986-87 which is the first piece of evidence suggesting the limits did not constrain spending. All counties together were still more than $63 million below the limited amount. Other than the two at the limit, only two other counties had utilized even 90 percent of their limit.

The second reason the expenditure limit did not constrain spending at the county level is that the limit does not apply to a number of categories of county expenditures. In 1981-82, the limit did not apply to about one-third of county expenditures. By 1986-87, the limit applied to less than half (46 percent) of total county expenditures. Over the five year period from 1982 to 1987, the total county expenditure limit increased by about 39 percent, a substantial increase, but still much less than the growth of total expenditures (111 percent) or expenditures in the limited categories (47 percent). Expenditures not subject to the limit did increase much faster than spending in the limited categories, an important change in county fiscal behavior, although it did not produce the reduction in the growth of spending apparently intended by the limit.

As a result, total county expenditures increased much faster than population and prices while county expenditures in the limited categories remained less than the limited amounts. From fiscal year 1981-82 to fiscal year 1986-87, actual per capita county expenditures increased by 77 percent, from $187 to $278, which corresponds to an average annual increase of more than 12 percent. The 12 percent increase in per capita spending is twice as great as the average annual increase in prices (6 percent) over this same time period. Such substantial increases in per capita expenditures were broadly representative of the situation in most counties. Although the limit became marginally tighter in the limited categories over these years, in general it was not constraining.

The growth of county expenditures and the shift from limited expenditures to expenditures not subject to the limits also seem consistent with the results of a comparison of the distribution of county expenditures by function for 1981-82 and 1986-87. Expenditures increased faster than average (leading to an increase in that function's share of total expenditures) for public safety, highways, welfare, debt service, and other capital expenditures.

The changes in the distribution of county expenditures reflect changes in state or federal grants, new state mandated programs, changes in relative costs, and the fact that the limits affect some but not all programs. The main components of county budgets not covered by the expenditure limit are federal grants, specific-purpose state grants that are covered by the state spending limit, county distributions to schools, and expenditures financed by the sale of bonds. So if grants were increased for a particular function, as they were for highways, expenditures could rise outside the limit. Indeed, highway expenditures is one category that substantially increased in importance. Similarly, counties desiring an increase in infrastructure can borrow and spend funds outside the limit. The increase in the debt service expenditure share does reflect an increase in outstanding debt not just a rise in interest rates. On the other hand, expenditures grew less than average in the general government category, health, education, recreation, and sanitation.

City Expenditures

For fiscal year 1989-90, the expenditure limit for all cities in aggregate is nearly 142 percent greater than the base limit in the base year of 1979-80. Thus, in the first ten year period of the expenditure limit, allowed city expenditures grew at an average rate of 14 percent per year. This substantial increase in the expenditure limit resulted from the combination of 45 percent growth in the population in cities and a 68 percent increase in the price level.

Since 1982, actual city expenditures in aggregate also increased rather substantially. Per capita city expenditures in aggregate increased by 56 percent, from $480 to $634. This corresponds to an average annual increase in per capita spending of more than 9 percent, substantially more than can be accounted for by the inflation rate in this five year period (about 6 percent per year).

An additonal reason why the expenditure limits generally have not been constraining for cities is that cities may adopt, through voter approval, alternative expenditure limits for a four-year period. The alternative limits allow for greater expenditures than the state limits. Commonly, the alternative limit simply states that the city council will adopt annually an expenditure limitation and that expenditures will be no greater than revenues. Essentially, then, the alternative city expenditure limit option is a voter-approved exemption or suspension of the state-imposed limit for a four-year period substituting annual decisions of the city council. Through 1987, 42 of the 81 cities (in 1982) had adopted an alternative voter-approved expenditure limitation. Thirty-three of these cities have reauthorized continued use of an alternative expenditure limitation for a second four-year period which implies that an alternative limit was adopted in fiscal years 1981-82 or 1982-83. The success of cities in adopting alternative expenditure limits suggests that the limit law has not been constraining. Moreover, this suggests that in many cities residents do not perceive that the growth of expenditures has been out of control; citizens have been willing to support higher spending. Municipalities also may choose to approve permanent adjustments in the 1979-80 base limit used to compute the expenditure limitation and they may approve a one-year override of their expenditure limitation.

All of these institutional features of the limit allow local governments to exempt themselves through voter approval. In fact, as shown in Table 21-1, the actual limited expenditures of the cities with alternative limits in 1987 account for about 69 percent of the total actual limited expenditures in the state. The state-imposed limit has been suspended for more than two-thirds of city expenditures intended to be covered by the limit.

Some city expenditures are excluded from the expenditure limitation. The major exclusions are expenditures financed by the sale of bonds, by federal aid, and by some types of state aid (for instance, highway aid). Total actual limited expenditures are just 58 percent of the total expenditures for municipalities, as shown above.

Table 21-1 City Expenditures And Expenditure Limits: 1987		
		Percent of Total
Total Expenditures	$2,295,057,315	100.0
Cities with Alternative Limits	1,408,123,615	61.4
Cities with State-Imposed Limits	886,933,700	38.6
Actual Limited Expenditures	1,333,190,390	100.0
Cities with Alternative Limits	916,638,492	68.8
Cities with State-Imposed Limits	416,551,898	31.2
Expenditure Limitation	1,807,372,569	100.0
Cities with Alternative Limits	1,308,223,987	72.4
Cities with State-Imposed Limits	499,148,582	27.6
Actual Limited Expenditures As A Percentage Of Total Expenditures	58.09	
Cities with Alternative Limits	65.10	
Cities with State-Imposed Limits	46.97	
Source: City annual expenditure limitation reports.		

Given that the expenditure limits generally have not been constraining for cities, one would not expect the limits to have altered the pattern of city spending. Indeed, there has been very little change in the functional distribution of city expenditures since 1982. Expenditures for highways and streets and for culture and recreation services have become somewhat more important in city budgets in aggregate, and the expenditure shares for public safety and sanitation services have declined. None of these changes are very dramatic, however, and likely have resulted from a number of different forces not related to the limit.

Revenues

The combination of the property tax levy limit and restriction on primary assessed values in Arizona was expected to reduce the growth of property taxes below that which would occur if the limits were not in place. However, it appears that the limits did not curtail the growth of aggregate property taxes and revenues throughout the 1980s for several reasons: (1) the substitution of other revenue sources, (2) the exclusions permitted for secondary taxes and specific purpose taxes, (3) the substantial growth in new construction, and (4) the override provision.

County Revenues

The growth of total county property taxes has been substantial despite the levy limit. Aggregate county property taxes increased by more than 82 percent and per capita county property taxes by nearly 54 percent from 1982 to 1987. Real per capita county property taxes increased from $62 to nearly $80. In aggregate, the share of county revenues provided by property taxes in 1987 was identical to that in 1982, nearly 30 percent. Reliance on property taxes for revenue increased in 9 counties over these years (including Pima) and decreased in 5 (including Maricopa).

Among other county revenue sources, the share provided by federal government grants declined by about half, from 9.6 percent in 1982 to 4.9 percent in 1987. Indeed, the nominal amount of federal intergovernmental aid in 1987 was the same as in 1982, so that all growth in county revenue arose from state and local sources. The share of county revenue provided by state grants rose modestly from 33 to 34 percent. On the other hand, the share of revenue from charges and other sources increased substantially in aggregate, from 20.8 percent in 1982 to 25.5 percent in 1987. Focusing on user charges and special assessments only, however, half of the growth is accounted for by hospital charges and almost all of the dollar magnitude of growth occurred in Maricopa and Pima counties. This growth in charges seems to reflect general economic growth and the rapid increase in health care costs rather than any general and broad substitution of charges for property taxes.

Because the base year for computing the property tax limit is 1979-80, it is possible that counties responded to the new limit in fiscal year 1980-81 which would not have shown up in the data discussed above. In fact, changes in the distribution of county revenues from 1978-79 to 1981-82 show that there was a very substantial decline from 36.9 to 31.2 percent in county reliance on property taxes over this time period. However, there was a major structural change in county property taxes that occurred in the same years. Prior to 1981, county governments were required to levy property taxes to finance teacher retirement funds. Beginning with 1981, counties no longer levied property tax for that purpose. Budgeted teacher retirement payments by counties for fiscal year 1979-80 were nearly $60 million. When those payments were eliminated, county property tax collections were actually lower in 1980-81 than in 1979-80, and the property tax share of revenue declined correspondingly. If the $60 million of teacher retirement payments by counties had continued in fiscal year 1981, the share of revenue provided by the property tax would have been essentially the same as in 1980. Therefore, the change in county property tax reliance between 1979-80 and 1980-81 was not due to any effects of the new property tax limit.

Part of the reason for the overall growth in county property taxes from 1982 to 1987 is that there has been a substantial shift by counties toward use of secondary property taxes, perhaps in response to the levy limit. The levy limit does not apply to secondary taxes although they are voter-approved. Per capita primary taxes grew by 41.5 percent from 1982 to 1987 while per capita secondary taxes grew by 168 percent. In 1982, primary property taxes accounted for nearly 91 percent of total county property taxes but only about 84 percent in 1987. Although seven counties collected no secondary tax in 1982, only two still collected no secondary property tax in 1987.

County secondary taxes are used to pay the principal and interest on bonds and to finance certain special districts such as fire and library districts. Most of the increase in county secondary property taxes since 1982 can be traced to increased borrowing and the resulting debt service payments. The substantial increase in the share of county expenditures for debt service has already been noted. A statistical analysis relating the change in county secondary taxes from 1982 to 1987 to changes in county debt service payments supports the hypothesis that the growth in secondary taxes reflects increased borrowing. In the regression equations shown below for both the change in total and per capita secondary taxes, the change in debt service exerts a positive and statistically significant effect on the change in secondary taxes. Each dollar increase in county debt service is associated with a $0.72 to $0.73 increase in county secondary taxes.

$$\text{Change In Secondary Tax} = 369893.4 + .73 \text{ Change In Debt Service}$$
$$(\text{Adjusted } R^2 = .87) \qquad (.54) \qquad (9.13)$$

$$\text{Change In Per Capita} = 3247.1 + .72 \text{ Change In Per Capita Debt Service}$$
$$\text{Secondary Tax} \qquad (1.42) \qquad (4.0)$$
$$(\text{Adjusted } R^2 = .51)$$
$$\text{(t-statistics in parantheses)}$$

Another major reason for the rapid growth of allowed primary and total county property taxes is the increase in property value from new construction. Recall that new construction increases the levy limit and thus allows growth in total and perhaps even per capita primary property taxes. Without new construction, primary taxes could increase only 2 percent per year. In fact, as shown in Table 21-2, if there had been no new construction since 1986 and the county property tax limits grew at the allowed 2 percent rate from 1986 to 1987, the 1987 limit would be only 67.6 percent of its actual value. Clearly, without the substantial construction in Arizona in recent years, the county property tax limits would be much lower than they are now.

County primary taxes include a tax of $0.50 per $100 of primary net assessed value, which is levied by state law and transferred to school districts. This component of the county primary tax is not counted toward the counties' primary tax limits. After this component of the county primary tax is removed, it appears as if county primary property taxes were essentially at the limited amount in both 1982 and 1987. Roughly half the counties remained below their primary tax limits only by very modest amounts. Therefore, without the growth in new construction to boost the limited amounts, the primary levy limits would likely have been very restrictive.

Because of the substantial increase in property values throughout the 1980s, the ratio of county taxes to the full cash value of property, *i.e.*, the effective rate of tax, declined from 1982 to 1987 for both primary and total county taxes. The effective rate for total county taxes was 0.34 percent in 1982 and 0.32 percent in 1987. The effective rate for primary taxes declined from 0.31 percent in 1982 to 0.27 percent in 1987. There has been very little change in the effective rate of total property taxes since 1982 because counties apparently substituted secondary taxes for the limited primary taxes.

There is an opportunity for counties to override the property tax levy limit through a popular vote. Although overrides for a seven-year period have been proposed in half of the counties in Arizona, they have been defeated in all but one of those cases. The evidence presented above suggests a possible reason why most of the county levy limit override proposals were defeated. Even with the levy and expenditure limits, both property taxes and county expenditures increased substantially in many counties.

<table>
<tr><td colspan="4" align="center">Table 21-2
Actual County Levy Limits Compared To
Hypothetical Limits In The Absence Of New Construction</td></tr>
<tr><td align="center">County</td><td align="center">1987
Actual Limits</td><td align="center">1987 Hypothetical
Limits[*]</td><td align="center">Hypothetical
As % Of Actual</td></tr>
<tr><td>Apache</td><td>$ 619,771</td><td>$ 178,866</td><td>28.86</td></tr>
<tr><td>Cochise</td><td>8,188,058</td><td>6,546,151</td><td>79.95</td></tr>
<tr><td>Coconino</td><td>1,937,344</td><td>1,458,561</td><td>75.29</td></tr>
<tr><td>Gila</td><td>6,832,901</td><td>4,854,266</td><td>71.04</td></tr>
<tr><td>Graham</td><td>1,288,705</td><td>1,198,492</td><td>93.00</td></tr>
<tr><td>Greenlee</td><td>175,979</td><td>159,825</td><td>90.82</td></tr>
<tr><td>La Paz</td><td>1,493,165</td><td>N/A</td><td>N/A</td></tr>
<tr><td>Maricopa</td><td>91,896,522</td><td>55,237,171</td><td>60.11</td></tr>
<tr><td>Mohave</td><td>7,241,386</td><td>5,170,427</td><td>71.40</td></tr>
<tr><td>Navajo</td><td>1,664,685</td><td>1,346,488</td><td>80.89</td></tr>
<tr><td>Pima</td><td>84,703,903</td><td>61,945,252</td><td>73.13</td></tr>
<tr><td>Pinal</td><td>16,547,141</td><td>11,399,866</td><td>68.89</td></tr>
<tr><td>Santa Cruz</td><td>2,892,472</td><td>1,926,726</td><td>66.61</td></tr>
<tr><td>Yavapai</td><td>9,450,465</td><td>6,356,099</td><td>67.26</td></tr>
<tr><td>Yuma</td><td>5,680,264</td><td>N/A</td><td>N/A</td></tr>
<tr><td>Total^{**}</td><td>$233,439,332</td><td>$157,778,190</td><td>67.6</td></tr>
</table>

[*] Represents 2% growth in the 1982 levy limit every year through 1987.
^{**} Totals exclude La Paz county.

Source: Property Tax Oversight Commission.

City Revenues

Cities and towns are subject to the same type of property tax levy limit as the counties. The annual growth of primary property taxes is restricted to 2 percent plus revenue from new construction (or minus revenue from property that no longer exists). Property taxes comprise a relatively small share of city revenues in Arizona, about 6 percent, and that share was the same in 1987 as in 1982. This stable aggregate pattern is rather deceiving however. Although the share of revenue from property taxes declined in almost half of the 75 major cities from 1982 to 1987, it increased in 13 cities, including Phoenix and Tucson, two cities that together account for two-thirds of all city property taxes. It is noteworthy that nearly all of the cities with no change in property tax reliance actually levy no property tax.

Among other city revenue sources, the main changes in the aggregate since 1982 are a substantial decline in the share of revenue from federal intergovernmental grants and modest increase in the shares for state intergovernmental revenue and local sales taxes. Again, the aggregate picture is deceiving. There is quite a substantial variation among the cities and towns in both the share of revenue from these various sources and the change in those shares over this period.

Although the aggregate share of city revenues from property taxes has remained stable, there has been substantial growth in the amount of city property taxes since 1982 and a shift toward greater use of secondary property taxes. Total city property taxes increased by more than 93 percent from 1982 to 1987, an annual average rate of increase of about 14 percent. Primary city property taxes alone increased more than 47 percent. But the geographic pattern was very uneven. The bulk of the increase in city property taxes occurred in cities in Maricopa, Pima, and Yavapai counties.

As a result of the much faster growth in city secondary property taxes over this period, primary taxes declined from 53 percent of total city property taxes in 1982 to about 41 percent in 1987. As with counties, the increase in city secondary taxes reflects increased voter-approved borrowing with the principal and interest paid by a secondary tax. It is important to remember that absent new construction limited primary property taxes could increase only two percent annually without voted overrides. As with counties, then, new construction must have added substantially to the allowed city primary tax levies. In fact, in 1987, city primary taxes in aggregate were about $5 million below the aggregate city tax limit substantially more below the limit than in 1982 ($1 million).

It is clear, then, that city property taxes have grown substantially despite the levy limits and that city primary property taxes generally remain below the limits. This growth has occurred partly because of substantial new construction and partly because of a shift toward greater use of secondary property taxes that are not covered by the limit.

Modeling Local Fiscal Behavior In Arizona

An alternative to examining the fiscal changes in individual localities is to use an analytical model of local fiscal behavior to examine the influence of various factors on past fiscal decisions. Our approach is to use a standard model of local government expenditure and revenue choice and to estimate the model statistically for county governments for two periods, and examining changes in per capita expenditures and changes in the share of revenues from property taxes from 1977 to 1982 and from 1982 to 1987. The first period was a period of transition including those years just before the current Arizona fiscal limits were adopted and the first two years that they applied (1980-81 and 1981-82). The second period allows us to consider any longer-run adjustments to the limits after their initial effects.

The fiscal model to be estimated relates expenditures and revenues selected by county governments to the resources available in the community (income and intergovernmental grants), the cost of providing services (population), tastes of community residents, and any important statutory details (see Fisher, 1989 for additional discussion of these kinds of models). The fiscal model is represented for counties by the following equations:

$$EXP_t = a_0 + a_1 POP_t + a_2 PCY_t + a_3 PIR_t + a_4 MUN_t + a_5 Z_t + e_1$$
$$PT_t = b_0 + b_1 EXP_t + b_2 PCY_t + b_3 PIR_t + b_4 Z_t + e_2$$

where EXP_t = per capita expenditures, POP_t = population, PCY_t = per capita income, PIR_t = per capita intergovernmental revenue, MUN_t = number of municipalities in the county, Z_t = county-specific factors, and PT_t = property tax share of total revenue. In the case of expenditures, differences in population may require differences in per capita spending if costs are not proportional to population. If costs increase faster than population, then a_1 would be positive. Increases in per capita income and intergovernmental revenue are expected to increase the demand for local services leading to greater expenditures. If so, a_2 and a_3 would be positive. It may be that expenditures by municipalities can substitute for spending by county governments. If so, then as new municipalities are formed in counties, county expenditures may decline, and a_4 would be negative. The other variable, Z_t, relates to specific characteristics or fiscal details in selected counties which may apply for only some years, such as any limit overrides that have been adopted.

Given a selected level of expenditures, a county must use a set of revenues sufficient to pay for those expenditures. The equation for the share of revenue collected from property taxes is an attempt to examine whether differences in property tax reliance among the counties are related to any of the economic factors included. Issues examined include whether counties with higher per capita spending or income rely more on property taxes, whether intergovernmental grants substitute for property taxes, and whether overrides to limits matter.

We examine the changes in per capita expenditures and property tax shares for the 15 counties over two periods, 1977 to 1982 and 1982 to 1987. We assume that residents' preferences in a county do not change over the period, therefore, those variables are eliminated. Because property tax reliance depends on the selected level of expenditures, which itself depends on many of the same variables as does property tax reliance, we use a two-stage least squares regression technique to estimate the model.

The estimations are shown below. For the changes from 1982 to 1987 we have the following results:

$$\text{Exp} = .189 \text{ Pop} + .041 \text{ Pcy} + .937 \text{ Pir} - 67.049 \text{ Mun} + 173.585 \text{ Apache}$$
$$\phantom{\text{Exp} =} (.93) \qquad (4.18) \qquad (3.03) \qquad (3.76) \qquad (3.32)$$
$$\text{Adjusted } R^2 = .68 \qquad \text{F-statistic} = 7.69$$

$$\text{Pt} = -.0001 \text{ Exp} + .00004 \text{ Pcy} - .0014 \text{ Pir} - .0001 \text{ Gila} + .2557 \text{ Apache}$$
$$\phantom{\text{Pt} =} (.71) \qquad (3.86) \qquad (4.78) \qquad (5.26) \qquad (4.78)$$
$$\text{Adjusted } R^2 = .84 \qquad \text{F-statistic} = 18.44$$

The results for the 1977 to 1982 changes are as follows:

$$\text{Exp} = -.161 \text{ Pop} + .039 \text{ Pcy} - .241 \text{ Pir} - 6.217 \text{ Mun} + .125 \text{ Gila}$$
$$\phantom{\text{Exp} =} (.60) \qquad (2.04) \qquad (.30) \qquad (.19) \qquad (3.53)$$
$$\text{Adjusted } R^2 = .36 \qquad \text{F-statistic} = 2.84$$

$$\text{Pt} = -.0002 \text{ Exp} - .00004 \text{ Pcy} - .0012 \text{ Pir} - .0004 \text{ Gila} - .3111 \text{ Apache}$$
$$\phantom{\text{Pt} =} (.10) \qquad (.69) \qquad (1.70) \qquad (.19) \qquad (4.32)$$
$$\text{Adjusted } R^2 = .47 \qquad \text{F-statistic} = 3.84$$
$$\phantom{\text{Adjusted }} \text{t-statistics in parantheses})$$

The effects on per capita expenditures in the 1982 to 1987 period are very consistent with the economic evidence reported for many different state-local governments over a number of years. Increases in per capita income are associated, in a statistically significant way, with small increases in per capita spending. Each one dollar difference in per capita income among counties is associated with about a $.04 difference in per capita spending (all else constant). Similarly, increases in intergovernmental revenues lead to increases in per capita spending. Per capita spending by county governments is lower in counties with a greater number of municipal governments. This is consistent with the idea that as more cities are created, they take on service responsibilities from the counties leading to lower per capita county spending. There is also clear and strong statistical evidence that the change in per capita spending over these years in Apache county was significantly greater than can be explained by changes in the other variables. Apache county adopted, through voter approval, a substantial override of their expenditure limit. Apparently this override reflects a desire to increase expenditures substantially in the county, a desire that was fulfilled. Finally, it does not appear that per capita spending varies in any systematic way with county population.

The results for the change in county per capita expenditures from 1977 to 1982 are very similar to those for the subsequent five-year period with the notable exception of the effect of intergovernmental revenue and the number of municipalities. Unlike the latter period, it appears that changes in per capita intergovernmental revenue had no systematic effect on county per capita spending form 1977 to 1982. This period was one of transition in intergovernmental aid with a dramatic increase in the importance of federal intergovernmental grants and several changes in state aid programs. Except for the two differences described above, the expenditure equations show very similar growth patterns in the two periods. These results seem consistent with the examination of county expenditure growth discussed previously in this paper. Essentially, county expenditures have continued to grow in recent years in a way that does not seem to have changed dramatically since adoption of the limits.

The results concerning the property tax share of county revenue for the 1982 to 1987 period also are consistent with the view that total property tax reliance and fiscal behavior did not change greatly between these periods. Higher-income counties tend to rely on property taxes to a somewhat greater degree, but the effect is small. A $1,000 difference in per capita income is associated with a 4 percentage point difference in the percent of revenue from property taxes. On the other hand, increases in per capita intergovernmental revenue are associated with decreases in property tax reliance. Intergovernmental aid substitutes to some degree for local property tax revenue. This is consistent with the effect of changes in intergovernmental revenue on expenditures reported above. A $1.00 increase in per capita intergovernmental revenue is associated with an increase in per capita spending of less than one dollar which allows the remaining intergovernmental aid to be used to lower property taxes.

There is no strong statistical evidence that property tax reliance among counties varies in any systematic way with county spending. But there is strong statistical evidence that property tax reliance is greater in Apache county (which adopted an expenditure limit override) and smaller in Gila county than can be explained by the other economic variables. Interestingly, however, there is no evidence that property tax reliance is greater than can be explained by these economic factors in Greenlee county, the one county that has approved an override of the property tax limit.

The estimated equation for changes in property tax reliance in the earlier 1977 to 1982 period is similar. Intergovernmental aid and property taxes are substitutes for each other in both periods. The only differences between the two periods are that differences in income in the earlier period are not associated at all with differences in property tax use, and Apache county relied to a statistically significant degree less on property taxes than suggested by its other characteristics, just the opposite of its situation in the latter five years.

Recall that there was a dramatic, one-time decrease in property tax reliance among counties between fiscal years 1979-80 and 1980-81 which resulted from the ending of county government property tax levies for teacher retirement payments. Because of this change, we re-estimated the property tax share equations after adjusting the data for the retirement payments. The coefficients did not change much.

School District Property Taxes And The Homeowner's Rebate

From 1982 to 1987 total property taxes levied by school districts increased 112 percent and per capita taxes by more than 78 percent. Such a growth rate is particularly noteworthy because school districts account for more than half of total property taxes in the state, a share that has been increasing due to this rapid growth. Primary school taxes alone increased by more than 96 percent. Because school property taxes are collected from the same base as county and city taxes, the differences in property tax growth rates among counties (82 percent), cities (93 percent), and school districts (112 percent) may be due to (1) the absence of a levy limit for schools, (2) the homeowner's rebate for school property taxes, (3) changes in equalizing state school aid, or (4) differences in taxpayer/voter attitudes toward schools compared to general purpose local governments. The apparent ineffectiveness of the levy limit in restricting the growth of overall property taxes for cities and counties in Arizona suggests that the growth in school district property taxes may be due to a large extent to the homeowner's rebate.

Under the homeowner's rebate program in Arizona, the state government reimburses school districts for 56 percent of school district primary property taxes on individual owner-occupied homes, up to a maximum of $500 per home. This amount is not collected by the district from the taxpayer but collected directly from the state government. In 1987-88, the state government paid school districts more than $150 million in homeowner rebates, an amount equal to more than 19 percent of total school district property taxes. The average rebate paid per student is $286 although there is substantial variation among the districts. The $500 maximum for the rebate has not been a substantial constraint to date as less than 2 percent of the homeowner properties hit that maximum in 1987-88. Only 15 percent of the residential properties in the state receive more than a $250 rebate. The average rebate per home is $123.

The relatively large magnitude of the rebate at the margin and the small number of taxpayers who reach the maximum suggests that a powerful incentive is provided for increasing school primary taxes and spending. The most important feature of the rebate program from the point of view of individual homeowner/taxpayers is that the rebate reduces the marginal cost of property tax increases as long as the rebate is less than the maximum. If the $500 maximum is reached, the taxpayer must pay the school property tax above the limit (up to 1 percent of value). However, as long as primary property taxes on the home are below $500, an increase in the school property tax of $1.00 per home only costs the average homeowner an additional $0.44. Essentially, the school district can get the state government to pay an additional $0.56 for each additional $0.44 collected from local homeowners. In addition, if the tax rate is increased, the district receives additional primary tax from nonresidential properties.

By reducing the marginal cost of school property taxes, homeowners may be induced to demand and vote for greater school property taxes and spending. Because the maximum is generally not constraining, the average marginal cost of school primary property taxes on homeowners for all districts in the state is $0.45. Whether this incentive actually works to cause an increase in school primary taxes and spending depends on a number of factors. Some analysts believe that taxpayers are not aware of the rebate or that taxpayers may not understand how the rebate reduces their cost of additional school spending. Even if taxpayers understand the rebate and desire more spending as a result, other analysts argue that more spending may not occur particularly if there is no vote on school taxes or budgets or if voter participation is low.

A number of other states provide rebates or credits for a fraction of homeowner (or renter) property taxes in a manner similar to the Arizona rebate. A common feature of many of these programs is the reduction in the marginal cost of property tax increases to taxpayers receiving the rebate or credit. Research by Fisher and Rasche (1984), Rubinfeld and Wolkoff (1983), and Fisher (1988) for Michigan and Bell and Bowman (1987) for Minnesota provide evidence that state programs that reduce the marginal cost of property taxes to taxpayers result in an increase in the level of property taxes selected. Detailed taxpayer awareness about the rebate program may not be necessary. The community simply receives additional state government payments from increasing its primary tax rate. Local officials can publicize this additional state money as a reason for the rate increase.

Although we provide no direct test of this hypothesis, the per capita property taxes of school districts increased much more (78 percent) than those of counties (53 percent), cities (58 percent), and community college districts (39 percent) since 1982. The differences in the growth rates of per capita primary property taxes, to which the rebate applies, are even more striking, as shown in Table 21-3.

The rebate reduces the marginal cost of homeowner tax increases by 56 percent. Even if taxpayers respond by only a small magnitude to cost reductions, such a large cost reduction could explain the difference in growth rates of primary taxes shown above. A price elasticity of demand for education service of just 0.33 (in absolute value) is sufficient, given the large price reduction, for explaining all of the difference in primary tax growth between community colleges and school districts. And a price elasticity of 0.33 is very consistent with the economic evidence.

Table 21-3
Percentage Growth Of Per Capita
Primary Property Taxes 1982 To 1987

Counties	41.5
Cities	47.0
Community Colleges	60.0
School Districts	96.3

The incentive to increase school primary property taxes caused by the homeowner's rebate is expected to differ among school districts however. First, the rebate provides an advantage and a greater incentive to increase school primary taxes in districts with relatively more homeowner residents than renter residents (the state credit for property taxes for renters is much smaller). Second, the rebate is likely to create a greater incentive for tax increases in districts with relatively more residential than nonresidential property.

The rebate equals as much as 34 percent of school property taxes in some districts and practically none in others where individual homes are not an important part of the tax base. The importance of the rebate relative to primary property taxes in a school district depends on the ratio of the primary taxable value of homes to the total taxable property value. The homeowner's rebate favors districts where homes are relatively more important in the tax base. Because a rebate or credit is not available for school primary taxes on manufacturing and commercial property, an increase in the school primary tax rate will increase homeowner taxes by a smaller percentage than nonresidential primary property taxes.

Summary

Overall, the level and reliance on property taxes and the level and growth of total expenditures by local governments in Arizona do not appear to have been reduced in the 1980s by the constitutional expenditure and property tax limits. The institutional features of the limits appear to have rendered them ineffective. Where the expenditure limits might have been constraining, the voters have overridden them or, in the case of cities, adopted alternatives that are not constraining. When asked to override levy limits, voters in many cases said no. But their preferences for containing property taxes would presumably have been communicated to elected officials through the political process, even in the absence of state-imposed limits, and substantial increases in property taxes were allowed under the limits in any case. It is hard to find evidence in the data for any major positive changes in local government fiscal behavior attributable directly to the limits.

The main changes in local fiscal behavior that seem attributable to the limits are an increase in the use of voter-approved secondary taxes and an increase in borrowing by counties and cities to finance capital expenditures. The secondary taxes are then used to pay the debt service and principal on the bonds. This seems largely an intended result of the fiscal limits and one that, as yet, does not seem to have been abused (by using debt for operating expenses, for instance).

One criticism of the property tax levy limit is that differences among counties in property tax level and reliance when the limit was adopted have been maintained perpetuating substantial intercounty differences in property tax use and rates. It is clearly true that there are substantial differences in county effective property tax rates and that the distribution in 1987 is nearly identical to that in 1982. For instance, the effective property tax rate was 0.22 percent in 1987 for Maricopa county and 0.49 percent for Santa Cruz despite the fact that the counties had approximately equal per capita expenditures. The comparative effective tax rates were 0.23 and 0.48 percent in 1982. The difference in effective tax rates in Maricopa and Santa Cruz counties reflects greater reliance on the property tax in Santa Cruz (37 percent of revenue) compared to Maricopa (26 percent). Maricopa offsets its lower reliance on property taxes (and federal aid as well) with greater reliance on user charges, 26 percent of revenue in Maricopa compared to 10 percent in Santa Cruz. If the ratio of charges exported to nonresidents is no different than the share of property taxes exported, then residents bear the same burden in both counties despite large differences in property tax levels.

Santa Cruz county could conceptually attempt to mirror the revenue distribution of Maricopa by raising or adopting new user charges and lowering property taxes. (Of course, major differences in the economic base of the two counties may make this infeasible, but that is not due to the levy limit.) On the other hand, conceptually it would be more difficult for

Maricopa to attempt to mirror Santa Cruz which would require a major increase in reliance on and effective rates of the property tax. Such a change would be restricted by the levy limit and could likely be accomplished only with voter approval. The point, of course, is that differences in revenue structure, and thus levels of various revenues, may arise from differences in spending and differences in economic conditions as well as from the constraints of the fiscal limits.

The levy limit has also been criticized because no adjustment is made for exogenous changes in intergovernmental revenue. The amount of federal aid to counties in Arizona was the same in 1987 as 1982, thus it accounts for a much smaller share of revenue in the latter year. If the infusion of new federal aid induces localities to lower property taxes rather than increase spending, a subsequent decrease in that aid requires an increase in local taxes just to maintain constant services. If a tax limit is imposed after federal aid has been increased and local taxes lowered, the locality is blocked from returning to their prior position once the aid is reduced. Given that federal aid to localities peaked in the late 1970's and declined substantially in the 1980s, the timing of the new property tax limit could have been particularly troublesome. The opportunity to substitute secondary for primary taxes mitigated this potential difficulty.

Indeed, one might inquire why it is that many localities remain below their tax and expenditure limits? In those cases, some other forces (political competition, intergovernmental competition, financial market constraints, the political beliefs of public officials) have caused local governments to levy lower property taxes and spend less than allowed by the state limits. It is possible that the limits are largely irrelevant, overridden by voters when the limits are lower than desired and ignored by voters when they are higher than desired. Accountability and efficiency are achieved when local voters have the opportunity to make their own independent fiscal decisions. By creating the opportunity to vote on secondary taxes and by voting for alternative limits, the 1980 fiscal changes in Arizona seem to have achieved accountability but not reductions in taxes and spending.

References

Advisory Commission on Intergovernmental Relations, *State Limitations on Local Taxes and Expenditures*, Report A-64, Washington D.C., February 1977.

Advisory Commission on Intergovernmental Relations, *Significant Features of Fiscal Federalism*, 1985-86 Edition, Washington D.C., December 1986.

Advisory Commission on Intergovernmental Relations, *Significant Features of Fiscal Federalism*, 1988 Edition, Volume I, Report M-155, Washington D.C., December 1987.

Advisory Commission on Intergovernmental Relations, *Significant Features of Fiscal Federalism*, 1988 Edition, Volume II, Report M-155II, Washington, D.C., July 1988.

Advisory Commission on Intergovernmental Relations, *Significant Features of Fiscal Federalism*, 1989 Edition, Volume I, Washington, D.C., July 1988.

Arizona Department of Economic Security, Population Statistics Unit, "Total Estimated Population for Arizona Counties and Cities," March 1989.

Arizona Department of Revenue, *State and County Abstract of the Assessment Roll*, 1981.

Arizona Department of Revenue, *State and County Abstract of the Assessment Roll*, 1986.

Arizona Department of Revenue, "Summary of Property Tax Levies," September 1987.

Arizona Joint Select Committee on State Revenues and Expenditures, *Final Report*, Volumes 1 and 2, November 1989.

Arizona Joint Select Committee on State Revenues and Expenditures, Property Tax Data File, June 1989.

Bell, Michael E. and John H. Bowman, "The Effect of Various Intergovernmental Aid Types on Local Own-Source Revenues: The Case of Property Taxes in Minnesota," *Public Finance Quarterly*, 15 (July 1987): 282-97.

Ebel, Robert D. and James Ortbal, "Direct Residential Property Tax Relief," Intergovernmental Perspective, U.S. Advisory Commission on Intergovernmental Relations, Spring 1989, 9-14.

Fisher, Ronald C. and Robert H. Rasche, "The Incidence and Incentive Effects of Property Tax Credits: Evidence from Michigan," *Public Finance Quarterly*, 12 (July 1984): 291-319.

Fisher, Ronald C., "Intergovernmental Tax Incentives and Local Fiscal Behavior," Michigan State University, 1988.

Fisher, Ronald C., *State and Local Public Finance*, Scott, Foresman and Company, Glenview, Illinois, 1989.

Rubinfeld, D.L. and M.L. Wolkoff, "The Distributional Impact of Statewide Property Tax Relief," *Public Finance Quarterly*, 11 (1983):131-153.

State of Arizona, *Annual Expenditure Limitation Report for Cities and Counties*, June 1987.

U.S. Department of Commerce, Bureau of the Census, *1977 Census of Governments*, "Finances of County Governments," Washington, D.C., May 1979.

U.S. Department of Commerce, Bureau of the Census, *1982 Census of Governments*, "Finances of County Governments," Washington, D.C.

U.S. Department of Commerce, Bureau of the Census, *1987 Census of Governments*, "Governmental Organization," Washington, D.C., 1989.

U.S. Department of Commerce, Bureau of the Census, *Current Population Reports*, Series P-24, Series P-25, Series P-26, various numbers and years, Washington, D.C.

U.S. Department of Commerce, Bureau of the Census, "Governmental Finances in 1981-82," Washington, D.C., 1983.

U.S. Department of Commerce, Bureau of the Census, "Governmental Finances in 1982-83," Washington, D.C., 1984.

U.S. Department of Commerce, Bureau of the Census, "Governmental Finances in 1986-87," Washington, D.C., 1988.

Endnotes

1. Primary property taxes are general purpose local taxes. Direct voter approval is not required to levy primary taxes within the limits, but the tax base is restricted. Secondary property taxes are voter-approved for specific purposes and not restricted by the limits.

2. This primary property tax limit is cumulative in that the allowed tax in year t is $(1.02)^t$ multiplied by the tax in 1980, ignoring new construction. Thus, if taxes do not increase by 2 percent in one year, they may increase by more than 2 percent in another.

Part V:
Conclusion

Chapter 22

General Fund Projections: Quantifying the Structural Deficit

Mark W. Watson

The primary goal of this chapter is to quantify the "structural deficit" that faced Arizona in the Fall of 1989. By "structural deficit" I mean a systematic bias in the fiscal system leading to a shortfall of revenues over expenditures. To quantify the structural deficit, forecasts of expenditures and revenues are constructed for the year 2000. These forecasts are constructed under the assumption that Arizona's fiscal system remains essentially unchanged from 1989 through 2000. Revenues and expenditures are projected to grow over the forecast period because of natural growth in the revenue and expenditure bases. The structural deficit can be quantified as the difference between the trend rate of growth in expenditures and the trend rate of growth in revenues.

The most important conclusion of this chapter is that Arizona faces a large structural deficit. A significant change in the current fiscal system will be required to eliminate this deficit. Assuming no change in the fiscal system, real revenues are forecast to increase at an average annual rate of 4.0 percent during the 1990s while real expenditures are forecast to increase at an average annual rate of 5.6 percent. The forecasts imply a budget deficit amounting to nearly one quarter of total general fund revenues in fiscal year 2000.

The next section of this chapter provides a summary of the expenditure and revenue forecasts. The third section summarizes the key assumptions underlying the forecasts and systematically traces the fiscal implications of alternative assumptions. The purpose of this exercise is twofold. First, it provides a measure of the uncertainty that surrounds the forecasts. For example, forecasts associated with average annual real personal income growth of 3.5 percent and 4 percent are compared. The difference in the two forecasts provides an indication of the forecast uncertainty associated with future economic growth. Second, many assumptions used in the forecast relate directly to policy variables under the control of the state government. Tracing out the fiscal implications of these assumptions provides an indication of the fiscal consequences of alternative fiscal policies. The final section of this chapter contains a ten year history of general fund revenues and expenditures. This section is included in this chapter for two purposes. First, it provides a summary of much of the data on the expenditure and revenue categories discussed in the other chapters. Second, it compares the historical trends in revenues and expenditures to the trends in the projections. An appendix to this chapter contains a detailed summary of the forecast methodology used to construct the individual forecasts.

As mentioned above, the forecasts presented in this chapter were constructed with the following question in mind, how does the trend in expenditure growth compare to the trend in revenue growth, given the current fiscal system? This question highlights two important characteristics of the projections. First they have been constructed to shed light on the trends in expenditures and revenues. Second, the assumptions underlying the forecasts were chosen to reflect the characteristics of the *current* fiscal system. Since the forecasts focus on the trends or long run properties of revenues and expenditures, they abstract from variability associated with short run phenomena such as the business cycle. To highlight the long run nature of the forecasts we report only forecast values for FY 1995 and FY 2000. Moreover, the forecasts are not meant to predict what will happen over the decade of the 1990s but rather to predict what will happen absent any policy interventions by the state.

As noted throughout this chapter, all dollar figures are in 1988 dollars so that price inflation has been netted out from the calculations. Consequently, all growth rates discussed in this chapter represent growth in the value of real goods and services.

Revenue and Expenditure Forecasts -- Results

A summary of the revenue and expenditure forecasts for FY 1995 and 2000 is given in Table 22-1. Detailed forecasts by revenue and expenditure category are displayed in Table 22-2. Table 22-1 shows that real revenues are forecast to increase by 60 percent from $2,563 million in 1988 to $4,099 million in 2000, an average annual increase of 4.0 percent. On the other hand, real expenditures are forecast to increase 93 percent over the same twelve year period, an average annual increase of 5.6 percent. The forecasts imply a budget deficit of $932 million in 2000 which represents 23 percent of total revenues in that year.

Table 22-1 General Fund Revenue and Expenditure Forecast 1988-2000: Summary (Millions of $1988)			
	1988	1995	2000
New Revenues	2563	3360	4099
Expenditures	2612	4034	5031
Surplus or [Deficit]	[49]	[674]	[932]
Surplus or [Deficit] (% of New Revenue)	[2]	[20]	[23]

Note: The $49 million 1988 deficit was financed by a fund balance of $55 million available on July 1, 1987.

Source: Arizona Department of Administration (1988) and author's projections (1995 & 2000)

Table 22-2 provides a more detailed picture. Over the 1988-2000 period, sales and use tax revenue is projected to increase by 50 percent (an average annual increase of 3.5 percent), income tax revenue is projected to increase by 74 percent (4.7 percent per year on

Table 22-2 General Fund Revenue and Expenditure Forecast 1988-2000 (Millions of $1988)			
	1988	**1995**	**2000**
Revenue			
Sales and Use Tax Revenue	1250	1581	1878
Income Tax Revenue	873	1203	1518
Other Tax Revenue	440	576	703
Revenue Total	**2563**	**3360**	**4099**
Expenditure			
Public Safety			
Department of Public Safety	77.90	88.46	97.18
Corrections	206.10	355.20	425.84
Courts	43.90	101.19	127.00
Total	**327.90**	**544.85**	**650.02**
Health Care			
AHCCCS Acute Care	165.70	360.05	547.46
ALTCS	4.60	93.49	127.93
DHS - Beh. Hlth.1	61.70	98.05	121.03
DHS - Other	35.20	39.52	44.93
Total	**267.20**	**591.11**	**841.35**
K-12 Education			
Total	1057.20	1609.81	1940.34
Higher Education			
Universities	429.50	557.56	708.17
Community Colleges	67.60	78.91	92.97
Total	**497.10**	**636.46**	**801.14**
Natural Resources			
Environmental Quality	23.10	31.00	39.10
Water Resources	12.07	12.10	12.10
Parks	6.60	8.30	9.90
Game and Fish	24.40	30.00	35.60
Land	7.70	9.90	12.00
Other	1.10	1.10	1.10
Total	**74.97**	**92.40**	**109.80**
Welfare			
Total	231.50	355.47	482.89
Selected Capital Expenditures			
Higher Education	18.53	23.55	29.64
Corrections	0.00	24.98	8.56
Total	**18.53**	**48.53**	**38.20**
Other General Fund			
Total	138.30	155.62	166.82
Expenditure Total	**2612.70**	**4034.25**	**5030.55**
Source: Arizona Department of Administration (1988) and author's projections (1995 & 2000)			

average), and other revenues are projected to increase by 60 percent (4.0 percent per year). Over the 1988-2000 period, total health care expenditures are projected to increase by 215 percent (10 percent per year), welfare expenditures to increase by 108 percent (6.3 percent per year), total public safety expenditures (including courts) to increase by 98 percent (5.9 percent per year), education (K-12 and higher education) to increase by 76 percent (4.8 percent per year), natural resources to increase by 46 percent (3.2 percent per year), and other general fund expenditures to increase by 21 percent (1.6 percent per year).

These results present a clear picture of a structural deficit in Arizona's fiscal system in 1989. Most of the expenditure areas are projected to increase faster than the major revenue sources. Figure 22-1 plots the expenditure and revenue projections. The structural deficit shows up in the figure as the increasing gap between the revenue and expenditure projections. Expenditures are forecast to increase faster than revenues leading to an increasing "deficit gap" between the two projections.

Since Arizona's structural deficit is large, the changes required to eliminate the deficit are large. For example, Table 22-2 reveals that slowing the growth of expenditures on total health care, welfare, and corrections would go only part way toward eliminating the deficit. To eliminate the deficit using these expenditure categories only, would require a capping their real expenditure levels at essentially their 1988 levels throughout the 1990s. That is, there could be no increase in real expenditures for health care, welfare, or corrections during the 1988-2000 period.

Revenue and Expenditure Forecasts -- Methodology and Assumptions

The forecasts summarized in Tables 22-1 and 22-2 were constructed using a variety of different forecasting techniques, each requiring its own set of specific assumptions. In many respects, the forecasting exercise that is carried in this chapter is different from "optimal" forecasting discussed in standard econometrics or statistics textbooks. First, and most important, the forecasts that we present are conditioned on the characteristics of the current fiscal system. After all, the purpose of the forecasting exercise is to quantify certain characteristics of the current fiscal system. Thus, historical trends in revenues and expenditures are useful only to the extent that they are consistent with the characteristics of the current fiscal system. Second, and this is more of a technical statistical concern, for many expenditure categories there is very little historical data. Standard statistical techniques that rely on regression or similar methods are likely to be very unreliable. There just is not enough historical data to accurately estimate the parameters of a statistical model.

Rather than rely on statistical models, most of the expenditure forecasts were constructed using information and expert judgements from a variety of sources. The primary source for each expenditure category's forecast was the author of the chapter for that category. Thus, Downes and Pogue who studied K-12 education (see Chapter 17) also provided forecasts for K-12 education. These forecasts were then modified based on discussions with experts in Arizona government and with the editors of this volume.

Since each expenditure and revenue category was forecast using a different method, a detailed discussion of each method would take us too far afield. Instead, a detailed discussion is provided in the appendix to this chapter, and Table 22-3 provides an overview of the key assumptions underlying the forecasts. (A careful reader of the appendix will note

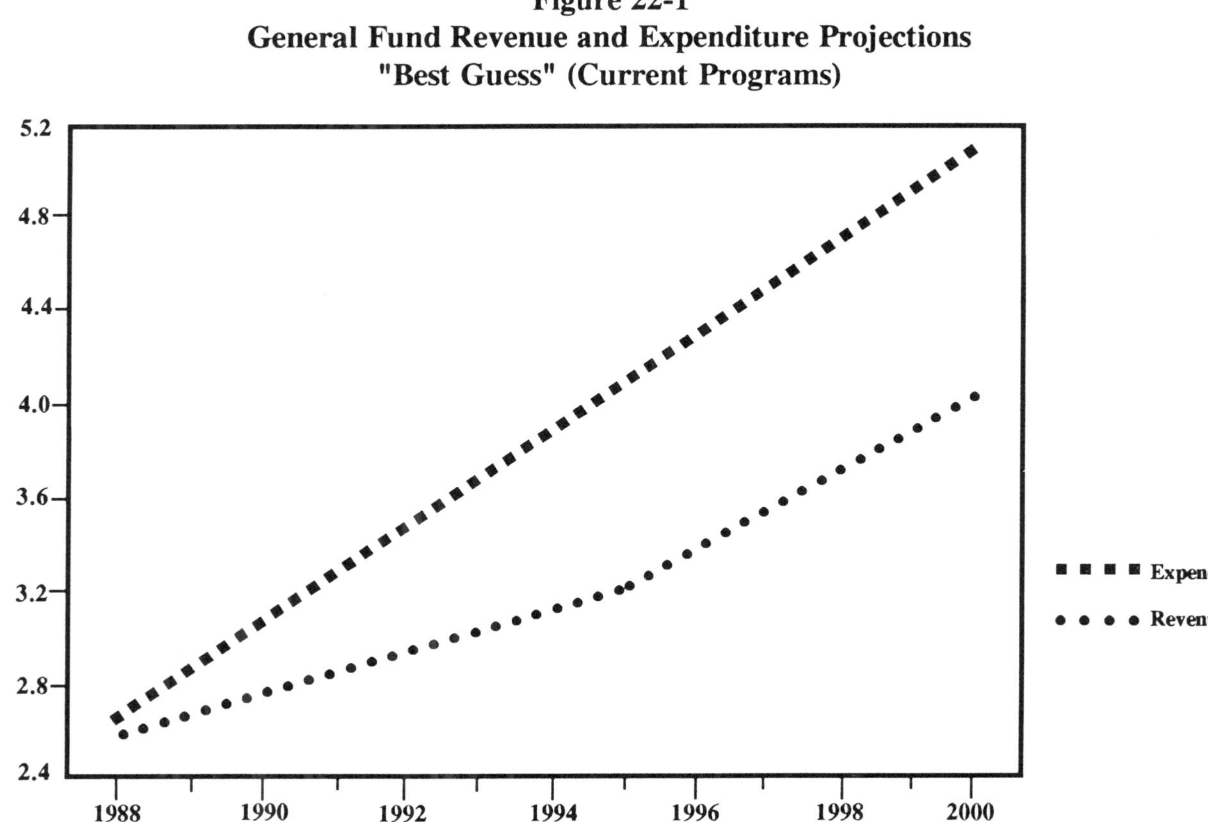

Source: Published agency data.

that the assumptions listed in Table 22-3 are sometimes simplifications of the actual assumptions used.) Table 22-3 lists, for each expenditure and revenue category, the critical assumptions that form the basis of the projection. Thus, the revenue projections were calculated assuming that the historical relationship between the growth in tax collections and the growth in Arizona's employment and personal income would continue throughout the 1990s, that employment would grow at an average annual rate of 2.8 percent, and that personal income would grow at an average annual rate of 3.5 percent during the forecast period. Similarly, the projection for the Department of Corrections is based on the assumption that the inmate population would grow by an average annual rate of 5.4 percent and that expenditures per inmate would grow by an average annual rate of 0.3 percent during the forecast period.

<table>
<tr><td colspan="3" align="center">Table 22-3
Summary of Annual Forecast Assumptions</td></tr>
<tr><td>Revenue</td><td>Wage and Salary Employment Growth 1991-2000
Real Personal Income Growth 1991-2000
1990 Sales and Use Revenues
1990 Income Tax Revenues</td><td>2.8%
3.5%
$13-
31.4
$952.7</td></tr>
<tr><td>Expenditures</td><td>Public Safety
  Department of Corrections
    Growth in real expenditures per inmate
    Growth in inmate population
  Courts
    Growth in State + County expenditures
  Department of Public Safety
    Growth in expenditures
Health Care
  AHCCCS Acute Care
    Growth in client base
    Growth in real medical care cost
    Growth in utilization
    State's share of total cost
  ALTCS
    Growth in client base
    Growth in real medical care cost
    Growth in utilization
    Federal share of total cost
    County share of total cost
  DHS Non-behavioral Health
    Growth rate
  DHS Behavioral Health
    Expendiures in 1993
    Growth in expenditure 1993-2000
    Federal share of total expenditure</td><td>

0.3%
5.4%

5.4%

1.9%

3.0%
3.0%
2.5%
48.0%

4.0%
0.5%
1.5%
60.4%
$87.9

2.6%

$170.0
4.3%
47.0%</td></tr>
</table>

Table 22-3 Continued		
Expenditures *Continued*	**Higher Education**	
	Enrollment growth 1988-1995 (Univ.)	2.2%
	Enrollment growth 1995-2000 (Univ.)	3.3%
	Enrollment growth 1988-1995 (Com. Col.)	2.2%
	Enrollment growth 1995-2000 (Com. Col.)	3.3%
	Growth in expend. per pupil (Univ.)	1.6%
	Growth in expend. per pupil (Com. Col.)	0.0%
	K-12 Education	
	Enrollment growth 1988-1995	3.4%
	Enrollment growth 1995-2000	1.9%
	Growth in expend. per pupil growth	1.9%
	State's Share of total expenses	47.0
	Welfare	
	Growth in AFDC enrollment	6.3%
	Growth in expenditures per enrollee	0.0%
	Natural Resources	
	Growth rate	3.2%
	Selected Capital Expenditures	
	Higher Education ratio of capital to operating expenses	3.7%
	Corrections renewal of luxury tax 1995-2000	
	Other General Fund Expenditures	
	Growth rate 1991-1995	1.7%
	Growth rate 1995-2000	1.4%
Notes:	Growth rates represent average annual growth rates over the forecast period. All dollar figures are in $1988.	

The assumptions listed in the table were chosen to reflect the "best guesses" of outside factors (*e.g.*, population) or of policy factors (*e.g.*, expenditures per AFDC recipient) as reflected in the current fiscal system. As an example, assumptions concerning the growth in wage and salary employment and in K-12 enrollments are based on the population projections provided in Chapter 3, and expenditure growth per pupil is assumed to be at a level that maintains the relative position of Arizona schools (see Chapter 17).

While Tables 22-1 and 22-2 show the "best guess" forecasts using these assumptions, there are two important reasons to construct forecasts using alternative assumptions. First, there is inherent uncertainty surrounding many assumptions concerning outside factors and varying the assumptions makes it possible to quantify the uncertainty in the forecast. For example, the economy may be more or less robust than is implied by our "best guess" assumption of personal income growth. Varying the assumption concerning personal income growth within a reasonable interval produces a range of reasonable forecasts for revenues and expenditures. This is a nonrigorous, but useful way to construct a confidence interval for the forecasts. The second reason for providing alternative assumptions is that many assumptions concern variables directly under the control of policymakers. Varying these assumptions provides insight into the effect of specific policies on general fund revenues and expenditures of the state. As an example, a reduction in the assumed rate of growth of the inmate population in Arizona's prisons helps quantify the fiscal implications of the elimination of Arizona's mandatory sentencing law.

Alternative assumptions and their net revenue/expenditure implications are shown in Table 22-4. The table lists the "best guess" assumption (also displayed in Table 22-3), an "alternative" assumption, and the FY 2000 net impact on revenues minus expenditures. For example, the first row of the table shows that if personal income growth averages 4.0 percent per year over the forecast period rather than the "best guess" assumption of 3.5 percent, the net revenue/expenditure position of the state will increase by $194 million in FY 2000. Thus, the "best guess" $932 million FY 2000 deficit shown in Table 22-1 will fall by $194 million to $738 million. The effects of changing the "best guess" assumptions are symmetric: if personal income growth averaged 3.0 percent over the forecast period (0.5 percent less than the "best guess" assumption of 3.5 percent) the deficit would increase by $194 million rather than decline.

Many of the alternative assumptions listed in Table 22-4 were chosen not for realism but rather to indicate the quantitative importance of the assumptions for the forecasts. Most alternative assumptions concerning growth rates for expenditures are one half their "best guess" counterparts. Cutting the rate of growth of the AHCCCS client base in half reduces FY 2000 expenditures by $81 million while cutting the rate of growth of the Department of Public Safety in half reduces FY 2000 expenditures by $11 million.

The alternative assumptions for 1990 tax revenue show how the forecasts can be used for policy evaluation. The alternative assumptions consider a 20 percent increase in FY 1990 tax revenues which then increase at the "best guess" rates between 1990 and 2000. The projections indicate that a FY 1990 20 percent increase in sales and use tax revenues ($266 million) reduces the FY 2000 deficit by $376 million; a FY 1990 20 percent increase in income tax revenues ($190 million) reduces the FY 2000 deficit by $304 million. Slowing the introduction of the state's behavioral health care programs appears to have little impact on the FY 2000 deficit. Reducing projected DHS behavioral health expenditures from $170 million in FY 1993 to $136 million (a 20 percent reduction), reduces the FY 2000 deficit by only $24 million.

Eliminating the structural deficit requires either expenditure reductions, revenue increases or both. In terms of Figure 22-1, the deficit gap can only be eliminated by making the revenue line more steep or by making the expenditure line less steep. Two extreme policies which accomplish this are shown in Table 22-5. The first policy increases revenues and leaves expenditures at their "best guess" current program level; the second policy reduces expenditures and leaves revenues at their "best guess" current program levels. These policy experiments are not recommendations but rather are meant to illustrate the magnitude of the required cuts in expenditures and increases in revenues necessary to eliminate the FY 2000 deficit.

Table 22-5 considers a policy that increases FY 1990 income tax revenues by $587 million (an increase of 62 percent) and then allows revenues to increase throughout the 1990s at their "best guess" rates. This policy increases FY 2000 revenues by $936 million which eliminates the deficit. Similar results follow from a FY 1990 increase in the sales and use tax. However, because sales and use tax revenues are projected to increase more slowly than income tax revenues, the 1990 sales and use tax increase necessary to eliminate the deficit would have to be larger than the income tax increase required to eliminate the deficit. Thus, an increased reliance on the income tax increases the responsiveness of the fiscal system to trend growth in employment and income.

<table>
<tr><th colspan="4" align="center">Table 22-4
Year 2000 Fiscal Impact of Alternative Assumptions</th></tr>
<tr><th align="center">Assumption</th><th align="center">Best Guess</th><th align="center">Alternative</th><th align="center">Net FY2000
Impact</th></tr>
<tr><td>Revenue</td><td></td><td></td><td></td></tr>
<tr><td> Real Pers. Income Growth 1991-2000</td><td align="center">3.5%</td><td align="center">4.0%</td><td align="right">$194</td></tr>
<tr><td> 1990 Sales and Use Revenues</td><td align="center">$1331.4</td><td align="center">$1597.7</td><td align="right">376</td></tr>
<tr><td> 1990 Income Tax Revenue</td><td align="center">$952.7</td><td align="center">$1143.2</td><td align="right">304</td></tr>
<tr><td></td><td></td><td></td><td></td></tr>
<tr><td>Expenditures</td><td></td><td></td><td></td></tr>
<tr><td> Department of Corrections</td><td></td><td></td><td></td></tr>
<tr><td>   Growth in expenditures per inmate</td><td align="center">0.3%</td><td align="center">0.0%</td><td align="right">13</td></tr>
<tr><td>   Growth in inmate population 1989-2000</td><td align="center">5.4%</td><td align="center">2.7%</td><td align="right">122</td></tr>
<tr><td> Courts</td><td></td><td></td><td></td></tr>
<tr><td>   Growth in State+County expenditures</td><td align="center">5.4%</td><td align="center">2.7%</td><td align="right">55</td></tr>
<tr><td> Department of Public Safety</td><td></td><td></td><td></td></tr>
<tr><td>   Growth in expenditures</td><td align="center">1.9%</td><td align="center">0.85%</td><td align="right">11</td></tr>
<tr><td> Health Care</td><td></td><td></td><td></td></tr>
<tr><td>   AHCCCS Acute Care</td><td></td><td></td><td></td></tr>
<tr><td>   Growth in client base</td><td align="center">3.0%</td><td align="center">1.5%</td><td align="right">81</td></tr>
<tr><td>   Growth in real medical care cost</td><td align="center">3.0%</td><td align="center">1.5%</td><td align="right">81</td></tr>
<tr><td>   Growth in utilization</td><td align="center">2.5%</td><td align="center">1.25%</td><td align="right">69</td></tr>
<tr><td>   ALTCS</td><td></td><td></td><td></td></tr>
<tr><td>   Growth in client base</td><td align="center">4.0%</td><td align="center">2.0%</td><td align="right">38</td></tr>
<tr><td>   Growth in utilization</td><td align="center">1.5%</td><td align="center">0.75%</td><td align="right">15</td></tr>
<tr><td>   DHS Non-behavioral Health</td><td></td><td></td><td></td></tr>
<tr><td>   Growth rate</td><td align="center">2.6%</td><td align="center">1.3%</td><td align="right">5</td></tr>
<tr><td>   DHS Behavioral Health</td><td></td><td></td><td></td></tr>
<tr><td>   Expenditures in 1993</td><td align="center">$170</td><td align="center">$136</td><td align="right">24</td></tr>
<tr><td>   Growth in expenditure 1993-2000</td><td align="center">4.3%</td><td align="center">2.15%</td><td align="right">16</td></tr>
<tr><td> Higher Education</td><td></td><td></td><td></td></tr>
<tr><td>   Growth in expend. per pupil (Univ.)</td><td align="center">1.6%</td><td align="center">0.8%</td><td align="right">63</td></tr>
<tr><td>   Growth in expend. per pupil (Com. Col.)</td><td align="center">0.0%</td><td align="center">1.6%</td><td align="right">[20]</td></tr>
<tr><td> K-12 Education</td><td></td><td></td><td></td></tr>
<tr><td>   Growth in expend. per pupil growth</td><td align="center">1.90%</td><td align="center">0.85%</td><td align="right">$226</td></tr>
<tr><td> Welfare</td><td></td><td></td><td></td></tr>
<tr><td>   Growth in AFDC enrollment</td><td align="center">6.3%</td><td align="center">3.15%</td><td align="right">147</td></tr>
<tr><td>   Growth in expenditures per enrollee</td><td align="center">0.0%</td><td align="center">1.0%</td><td align="right">[60]</td></tr>
<tr><td> Natural Resources</td><td></td><td></td><td></td></tr>
<tr><td>   Growth Rate</td><td align="center">3.2%</td><td align="center">1.6%</td><td align="right">18</td></tr>
<tr><td> Capital Expenditures</td><td></td><td></td><td></td></tr>
<tr><td>   Corrections: Luxury tax not extend 1995-2000</td><td></td><td></td><td align="right">19</td></tr>
<tr><td> Other General Fund Expenditures</td><td></td><td></td><td></td></tr>
<tr><td>   Growth rate</td><td align="center">1.6%</td><td align="center">0.8%</td><td align="right">15</td></tr>
</table>

Notes: The column labeled "Best Guess" shows the assumptions underlying the projections in Table 22-1 and 22-2. The column labeled "Net FY 2000 Impact" shows the FY 2000 change in net Revenues minus Expenditures that obtains when the "Best Guess" assumption is replaced with the "Alternative" assumption. All dollar amounts shown in the table are in millions of $1988.

Table 22-5
Balanced Budget Alternatives

Increase Revenues

Assumption	Best Guess	Alternative	Net FY2000 Impact
1990 Income Tax Revenue	$952.7	$1540.0	$936
Growth In Total Revenues	4.0%	5.8%	936

Decrease Expenditures

Assumption	Best Guess	Alternative	Net FY2000 Impact
Department of Corrections			
Growth in inmate population 1989-2000	5.4%	2.7%	$122
Courts			
Growth in State + County expenditures	5.4%	2.7%	55
Department of Public Safety			
Growth in expenditures	1.9%	0.85%	11
Health Care			
AHCCCS Acute Care			
Growth in client base	3.0%	1.5%	81
Growth in utilization	2.5%	1.25%	69
ALTCS			
Growth in client base	4.0%	2.0%	38
Growth in utilization	1.5%	0.75%	15
DHS Non-behavioral Health			
Growth rate	2.6%	1.3%	5
DHS Behavioral Health			
Expenditures in 1993	$170	$120	36
Growth in expenditure 1993-2000	4.3%	2.15%	16
Higher Education			
Growth in expend. per pupil (Univ.)	1.6%	0.7%	71
K-12 Education			
Growth in expend. per pupil	1.90%	0.7%	257
Welfare			
Growth in AFDC enrollment	6.3%	3.15%	147
Natural Resources			
Growth rate	3.2%	1.6%	18
Growth In Total Expenditures	5.7%	3.8%	$941

Notes: The column labeled "Best Guess" shows the assumptions underlying the projections in Table 22-s 1 and 2. The column labeled "Net FY 2000 Impact" shows the FY 2000 change in net Revenues minus Expenditures that obtains when the "Best Guess" assumption is replaced with the "Alternative" assumption. All dollar amounts shown in the table are in millions of $1988.

Table 22-5 considers eliminating the deficit by across the board expenditure cuts. Again, these cuts are not meant to be policy recommendations or to represent spending priorities but to be illustrative examples of the magnitude of expenditure savings associated with various policy changes. Enrollment levels in health and welfare programs and the rate of growth of the inmate population are restricted to one half of their "best guess" rates. (To put these cuts in perspective, note that they reduce the FY 2000 prison population from a "best guess" level of 23,208 to 18,344 and the number of AFDC enrollees in FY 2000 from a "best guess" level of 198,000 to 138,000.) Expenditures per pupil in K-12 and higher education are assumed to increase at the average rate of growth of labor productivity in Arizona (0.7 percent). These cuts reduce FY 2000 expenditures by $941 million which eliminates the FY 2000 deficit.

Revenues and Expenditures -- 10 Year History

Ten year histories of general fund revenues and expenditures are shown in Tables 22-6 and 22-7; all figures are in 1988 dollars ($1988). In real terms, revenues increased at an average annual rate of 2.6 percent over the last decade. During the same period, Arizona's population increased at an average rate of 3.2 percent thus real general fund revenue collections per capita fell by an average rate of 0.6 percent during the past decade. The revenue history shows that over the 1980s Arizona increased its reliance on the income tax while reducing its reliance on the property tax. The share of general fund revenues from the income tax increased from 28 percent in 1979 to 34 percent in 1988, while the corresponding property tax share fell from 7 percent to 2 percent.

The expenditure history shows that real expenditures increased at an average annual rate of 3.8 percent over the last decade. Public safety expenditures had the largest percentage increases with an average annual growth rate of 8.9 percent. Health and welfare expenditures posted an average annual increase of 6.4 percent while education expenditures grew at an average annual rate of 2.5 percent.

There are important similarities and differences between the trends in historical revenue and expenditure patterns over the last decade and the projections of revenues and expenditures in the next decade. Income tax revenue growth is forecast to continue at essentially the same rate. The growth in sales and use tax revenue is forecast to decline relative to its value in the 1980s reflecting a slowdown in wage and salary employment growth. On the expenditure side, health and welfare expenditures are forecast to continue their rapid growth. Indeed, the forecasts suggest more rapid growth in the 90s than in the 80s. Expenditures for public safety and corrections are also forecast to increase faster than the rate of population growth in the 90s, but the growth will not be as great as during the 80s. During the 1979-1988 period, general fund expenditures on education lagged behind population growth. Expenditures increased at an average annual rate of 2.5 percent while total population grew at an average annual rate of 3.2 percent. This trend is forecast to be reversed in the next decade. The forecasts for general fund education expenses call for annual average growth of 4.5 percent, nearly 2 percent higher than the projected increase in population. Since education expenditures are by far the largest component of the budget, this projected change in its trend has a dramatic effect on the projected FY 2000 deficit. If education were to continue its 1979-1988 trend growth of 2.5 percent over the next decade, rather than the "best guess" forecast of 4.5 percent, the projected FY 2000 budget deficit would decline by $651 million.

Table 22-6
General Fund New Revenues

Function	1979		1980		1981		1982		1983	
	$1988	% of Total	$1988	% of Total	$1988	% of Total	$1988	% of Total	$1988	% of Total
Sales and Use	916.0	46.37	917.5	47.95	790.7	39.78	714.4	39.22	744.6	38.97
Total Income Taxes	561.1	28.40	583.9	30.52	637.4	32.07	599.9	32.94	695.1	36.37
Property	142.4	7.21	60.5	3.16	122.3	6.15	108.7	5.97	93.8	4.91
Other Taxes	234.8	11.89	225.4	11.78	229.1	11.53	194.0	10.65	200.1	10.47
Total Tax	1854.3	93.87	1787.3	93.41	1779.6	89.53	1617.0	88.77	1733.6	90.72
Other Revenue	121.2	6.13	126.0	6.59	208.1	10.47	204.6	11.23	177.4	9.28
Total Revenue	1975.4	100.00	1913.4	100.00	1987.7	100.00	1821.6	100.00	1910.9	100.00

Function	1984		1985		1986		1987		1988		Ave % Growth 1979-1988
	$1988	% of Total	$1988	% of Total	$1988	% of Total	$1988	% of Total	$1988	% of Total	
Sales and Use	1019.0	47.98	1171.4	50.38	1225.7	50.62	1248.8	49.61	1250.1	48.77	3.16
Total Income Taxes	733.7	34.55	800.0	34.41	821.4	33.92	868.2	34.49	873.5	34.08	4.53
Property	92.9	4.38	60.2	2.59	59.4	2.45	61.6	2.45	62.3	2.43	-7.93
Other Taxes	175.1	8.24	208.6	8.97	220.2	9.09	229.5	9.12	244.6	9.54	0.41
Total Tax	2020.8	95.15	2240.2	96.35	2326.7	96.08	2408.2	95.67	2430.5	94.83	2.74
Other Revenue	102.9	4.85	84.8	3.65	94.9	3.92	108.9	4.33	132.6	5.17	0.91
Total Revenue	2123.7	100.00	2325.0	100.00	2421.6	100.00	2517.1	100.00	2563.1	100.00	2.64

Source: Arizona Department of Administration *Annual Financial Reports* and author's calculations.

Table 22-7
General Fund Expenditures

	1979		1980		1981		1982		1983	
	$1988	% of Total	$1988	% of Total	$1988	% of Total	$1988	% of Total	$1988	% of Total
General Government										
Courts	8.91	0.50	11.58	0.68	9.30	0.43	10.23	0.52	11.14	0.57
Other GG	103.17	5.75	94.55	5.52	113.81	5.21	96.97	4.92	83.74	4.28
GG Total	112.08	6.25	106.13	6.20	123.11	5.64	107.20	5.44	94.88	4.84
Health and Welfare										
DHS	81.97	4.57	77.35	4.52	93.48	4.28	85.20	4.32	77.55	3.96
DEQ	0.00	0.00	0.00	0.00	0.00	0.00	0.00	0.00	0.00	0.00
AHCCCS	0.00	0.00	0.00	0.00	0.00	0.00	0.72	0.04	26.64	1.36
DES	197.61	11.02	186.12	10.87	224.45	10.28	203.14	10.31	182.94	9.34
Other HW	2.74	0.15	2.59	0.15	2.92	0.13	2.66	0.13	3.13	0.16
HW Total	282.31	15.74	266.06	15.53	320.86	14.70	291.71	14.81	290.27	14.82
Insp. and Reg.	28.64	1.60	26.69	1.56	33.68	1.54	30.20	1.53	25.40	1.30
Education										
Univ	325.45	18.14	307.00	17.92	361.24	16.55	337.33	17.12	309.13	15.78
DEd	819.10	45.66	784.49	45.80	1028.52	47.11	923.82	46.89	979.44	50.01
CC	62.46	3.48	55.66	3.25	61.59	2.82	49.22	2.50	48.72	2.49
OtherEd	12.90	0.72	11.61	0.68	11.32	0.52	10.68	0.54	11.52	0.59
Ed Total	1219.91	68.01	1158.75	67.65	1462.68	66.99	1321.04	67.06	1348.81	68.87
Public Safety										
Corrections	85.05	4.74	99.12	5.79	136.70	6.26	137.89	7.00	129.90	6.63
DPS	29.59	1.65	25.22	1.47	43.13	1.98	41.38	2.10	31.04	1.58
OtherPS	10.65	0.59	10.32	0.60	15.01	0.69	10.62	0.54	9.61	0.49
PS Total	125.30	6.99	134.66	7.86	194.84	8.92	189.89	9.64	170.55	8.71
Transportation	0.14	0.01	1.40	0.08	9.89	0.45	6.13	0.31	2.94	0.15
Natural Resources										
Dept. Water Res.	12.32	0.69	9.78	0.57	27.35	1.25	12.01	0.61	15.14	0.77
Other NR	13.06	0.73	9.32	0.54	10.97	0.50	11.81	0.60	10.45	0.53
NR Total	25.38	1.41	19.10	1.12	38.32	1.76	23.82	1.21	25.59	1.31
Expenditure Total	1793.76	100.00	1712.79	100.00	2183.38	100.00	1969.99	100.00	1958.44	100.00

Table 22-7 Continued

	1984		1985		1986		1987		1988		Average % Growth 1979-1988
	$1988	% of Total	$1988	% of Total	$1988	% of Total	$1988	% of Total	$1988	% of Total	
General Government											
Courts	11.75	0.56	15.86	0.70	21.81	0.88	35.89	1.44	43.91	1.68	17.29
Other GG	90.62	4.34	114.63	5.08	150.73	6.08	131.71	5.27	130.13	4.98	2.35
GG Total	102.37	4.90	130.49	5.78	172.54	6.96	167.60	6.70	174.04	6.66	4.50
Health and Welfare											1.40
DHS	73.91	3.54	78.20	3.47	89.06	3.59	99.60	3.98	94.22	3.61	
DEQ	0.00	0.00	0.00	0.00	0.00	0.00	0.00	0.00	9.30	0.36	
AHCCCS	94.17	4.51	138.51	6.14	150.47	6.07	132.82	5.31	187.19	7.16	
DES	183.15	8.77	190.91	8.46	214.51	8.65	230.41	9.22	230.75	8.83	1.56
Other HW	3.61	0.17	3.74	0.17	3.59	0.14	3.72	0.15	3.52	0.13	2.54
HW Total	354.85	16.98	411.36	18.23	457.64	18.46	466.55	18.66	524.99	20.09	6.40
Insp. and Reg.	25.71	1.23	26.85	1.19	30.44	1.23	32.20	1.29	34.42	1.32	1.86
Education											
Univ	345.06	16.52	360.96	15.99	403.44	16.27	424.27	16.97	452.43	17.32	3.35
DEd	982.87	47.04	1024.50	45.40	1050.74	42.38	1032.62	41.30	1021.61	39.10	2.23
CC	48.66	2.33	46.49	2.06	57.98	2.34	67.08	2.68	68.09	2.61	0.87
OtherEd	10.05	0.48	10.74	0.48	12.85	0.52	13.54	0.54	14.85	0.57	1.42
Ed Total	1386.62	66.37	1442.69	63.93	1525.02	61.50	1537.51	61.50	1556.98	59.59	2.47
Public Safety											
Corrections	135.55	6.49	155.22	6.88	177.51	7.16	194.45	7.78	207.42	7.94	9.32
DPS	52.79	2.53	62.74	2.78	72.17	2.91	61.20	2.45	77.93	2.98	10.17
OtherPS	11.14	0.53	8.23	0.36	8.79	0.35	9.16	0.37	7.50	0.29	-3.45
PS Total	199.48	9.55	226.19	10.02	258.47	10.42	264.81	10.59	292.86	11.21	8.86
Transportation	0.10	0.00	0.87	0.04	0.14	0.01	3.81	0.15	2.53	0.10	33.87
Natural Resources											
Dept. Water Res.	10.51	0.50	8.07	0.36	19.31	0.78	11.31	0.45	12.93	0.50	0.49
Other NR	9.59	0.46	10.30	0.46	16.04	0.65	16.27	0.65	13.95	0.53	0.66
NR Total	20.10	0.96	18.37	0.81	35.35	1.43	27.58	1.10	26.88	1.03	0.58
Expenditure Total	2089.23	100.00	2256.81	2100.00	2479.59	100.00	2500.06	100.00	2612.70	100.00	3.83

Source: Arizona Department of Administration Annual Financial Reports and author's calculations.

Summary

As stated in the introduction, the primary purpose for preparing revenue and expenditure projections for the next decade was to quantify the "structural deficit" facing Arizona. The structural deficit is generated by differences in the growth rates of expenditures and revenues. The projections suggest that a large structural deficit is built into the 1989 Arizona fiscal system. This deficit amounts to roughly one-fourth of general fund revenues or $932 million in FY 2000. To address this structural deficit, policymakers must change the fiscal system to increase the trend rate of growth in revenues or decrease the trend rate of growth in expenditures. Neither option will be popular, but the analysis in this chapter suggests that a mix of expenditure growth reductions and revenue growth increases is unavoidable.

Appendix

This appendix contains a summary of the forecasting techniques and assumptions used to construct the projections that appear in Table 22-2.

Revenue Projections

The revenue forecasts were based on equations estimated by Dennis Hoffman and Don Schlagenhauf of Arizona State University:

$$R_t = -0.68 + 0.98\,t + 0.49\,E_t$$
$$O_t = -2.65 + 1.37\,Y_t$$
$$I_t = 0.80 + 0.88\,Y_t + 0.32\,E_t$$

where:

R_t = percentage real growth in retail sales tax revenue,

O_t = percentage growth in the remaining components of Sales and Use (S&U) tax revenue,

I_t = percentage real growth in personal income tax revenue,

Y_t = percentage real growth in Arizona personal income, and

E_t = percentage growth in Arizona wage and salary employment.

These equations were estimated by ordinary least squares using data from 1972 through 1987. (The equation for I_t used data through 1988).

The equation for personal income tax growth was used to forecast total income tax receipts. The equations for sales and use tax show negative intercepts, reflecting a downward drift in these variables, holding personal income and employment constant. Presumably this downward drift reflects changes in the S&U tax structure over the sample period. Thus, the S&U equations may not reflect the 1989 fiscal system but rather the evolution of the tax code during the 1980s and thus are inappropriate for forecasting current policy. For the projections, the equations were modified by assuming that S&U tax revenues would increase one for one (in percentage terms) with Arizona personal income.

The assumptions concerning the annual rate of growth in wage and salary employment and real personal income used in the "best guess" forecasts were:

	1989	1990-2000
Wage and Salary Employment	2.35%	2.8%
Personal Income (Real)	2.90%	3.5%

The 1989 wage and salary employment projections are from Hoffman and Clark ("Revenue Projections for Major Components of the Arizona General Fund: FY 1988/1989 and FY 1989/1990," November 1988 revision, Table 8.) The 1989 Personal Income projection is from the JLBC Appropriations Report (FY 1989, page 363). Wage and salary employment projections for 1990-2000 are based on the age 18+ population growth projections developed in Chapter 3. The 1990-2000 personal income growth rates equal the wage and salary employment growth rates plus a projected 0.7 percent increase in personal income per employee. This is approximately equal to the average rate of increase in U.S. personal income per (non-agricultural) employee during the 1970-1988 and 1980-1988 time periods.

Projections for total general fund revenues were calculated from the projections of S&U tax and income tax revenues by assuming that these components would provide a constant fraction of total general fund revenue over the 1989-2000 time period.

Expenditures Projections

Public Safety

Department of Corrections (DOC). Forecasts for DOC were based on forecasts of expenditures per inmate and the growth in prison population. Expenditures per inmate were forecast using an AR(1) time series model. The estimated model was:

$$e_t = 8.26 + .55e_{t-1}$$

where e_t denotes expenditures per inmate in thousands of $1988. Forecasts were constructed using a base FY 1988 cost per inmate of $17,330 per year.

The prison population was forecast by assuming that the rapid growth of the late 1980s was somewhat transient and would decline to the rate of population growth by FY 2000. In particular, it was assumed that the growth rate would decline linearly from 9.0 percent in 1989 to 2.5 percent in 2000. This yielded an average annual growth rate from 1989-2000 of 5.4 percent.

Courts. It was assumed that the sum of state plus county court expenditures were proportional to "case load." Case load was assumed to grow at the same rate as prison population (discussed above.) Thus, the projections used a unit elasticity of total court expenditures with respect to prison population. The relative contribution of the state to the total court expenditures increased over the 1980s as the state supported a growing share of probation costs. County expenses were assumed to increase by 5 percent in 1989 and decline (linearly) to a growth rate of 2.5 percent in 2000. The state was assumed to pay the difference between the total increase and that increase paid by the counties.

Department of Public Safety (DPS). Forecasts were constructed using a regression model that included the DPS expenditures and Arizona population lagged one year.

Health Care

Arizona Health Care Cost Containment System (AHCCCS) Acute Care and Arizona Long Term Care System (ALTCS). Projections are based on constant growth assumptions over the 1989-2000 period. Total annual growth is decomposed into (i) growth in client base, (ii) growth in real cost of medical care, and (iii) growth in utilization. The growth rate assumptions used in the projections were:

	AHCCCS	ALTCS
Growth in Client Base	3.0	4.0
Real Medical Costs	3.0	0.5
Utilization	2.5	1.5

These growth rates were then applied to the following base expenditures:

AHCCCS, FY 1989 Expenditures (Millions of $1988)   315.2
ALTCS, FY 1990 Expenditures (Millions of $1988)   301.9

This yielded total projected expenditures for the two categories. The state was assumed to pay 48 percent of AHCCCS acute care expenditures. The Federal share of ALTCS was assumed to be 60.4 percent and the Counties were assumed to contribute a fixed $87.9 million per year. The residual is assumed to be paid by the state.

<u>Department of Health Services (DHS)</u>

Non-Behavioral Health. Real expenditures in this category were projected to increase at the rate of population growth (2.6 percent per year).
Behavioral Health. This projection is based on a report prepared for the state by Peat, Marwick Main & Co (PMM). That report presents forecasts of behavioral health expenditures for FY 1993. These were converted to $1988 using an annual inflation rate of 4.09 percent (the value assumed by PMM). The 4.3 percent real growth rate (used by PMM for 1990-1993) was used for the 1993-2000 projection. It was assumed that the Federal government would pay 47 percent of total expenditures and the state would pay the remainder.

<u>K-12 Education</u>

These forecasts were based on the assumption that enrollments would increase at the rate of school age population growth during the 1988-2000 period and that real expenditures per pupil would increase at a rate equal to their average values during the 1980s. The specific assumptions were:

	1988-1995	1995-2000
Student Growth Rate	3.38%	1.87%
Expenditure per Pupil Growth Rate	1.90%	1.90%

<u>Higher Education</u>

Total expenditures were assumed to increase by the rate of "headcount" growth plus the growth in expenditures per student. The specific growth rate assumptions employed were:

	Head Count		Expenditures Per Student	
	1988-1995	1995-2000	1988-1995	1995-2000
University	2.23	3.33	1.56%	1.56%
Community College	2.23	3.33	0.00%	0.00%

1988 expenditure bases for the forecasts were:

Universities: $429.4 (Millions $1988)
Community Colleges: $67.6 (Millions $1988)

The student head count assumptions were based on the 1986 "Future Needs of the State Task Force on Education and Public Expenditures" report. The assumed growth in expenditures per student was equal to one half of the average annual growth over 1980-1988 for Universities.

Water Resources

Expenditures were assumed to remain constant in real terms. The average value of expenditures during 1981-1990 period (in $1988) was used to determine the forecast for the 1991-2000 period. The data in 1981 and 1986 were dropped from the average as outliers.

Arizona State Parks Board - Operating Expenditures

Forecasts are generated from a regression model in which park expenditures were regressed on a constant and state population. The model was estimated using data from 1980 to 1989.

Environmental Quality

Forecasts are generated from a regression model in which EQ expenditures were regressed on a constant and total state income. The model was estimated using data from 1980 to 1989. State income was forecast to increase an average 3.9 percent (annual rate) over the forecast period.

State Land

Same forecasting method as Arizona State Parks Board - Operating Expenditures

Game and Fish

Same forecasting method as Arizona State Parks Board - Operating Expenditures

Other Natural Resources

Forecasts were generated from a linear time trend regression. The model was estimated using data from 1978 to 1990.

<u>Welfare</u>

A very good indicator of welfare expenditures is AFDC expenditures. For the total Department of Economic Security (DES) expenditure projections it was assumed that the state's welfare expenditure was proportional to AFDC expenditures. One rationalization for this assumption is that historically AFDC expenditures have been approximately constant. Thus, the growth rate in state DES expenditures was assumed to equal the growth in AFDC enrollment plus the growth in AFDC expenditures per enrollee. The specific assumptions employed were:

Growth in AFDC enrollment: 6.3%
Growth in expenditures per enrollee: 0.0%

During 1980-1988 AFDC enrollment grew at an annual average rate of 8.94 percent while population grew at 3.11 percent. The 1987-1988 growth in AFDC was particularly large. From 1980-1986 AFDC enrollment grew at an average annual rate of 7.99 percent while population grew at 3.25 percent. During the 1990s AFDC growth was assumed to slow but remain much higher than the rate of growth in population. In particular it was assumed the ratio of AFDC to population growth during the 1990s would equal its 1980-1986 historical value.

<u>Selected General Fund Capital Expenditures</u>

During the 1980s higher education capital expenditures financed by the general fund averaged 3.7 percent of higher education operating expenses. This relationship was assumed to continue during the 1990s.

Total capital expenditures for corrections were projected based on 1990 prison capacity of 13,124, the projections of prison population discussed above and estimated capital cost per bed of $36,000. In 1989, corrections' capital expenditures were financed entirely by the corrections fund. The projections suggest that this fund would be inadequate to finance the necessary capital expenditures in the 1990s. The necessary additional funds were assumed to be supplied out of the general fund. The luxury tax, which is earmarked to the corrections fund, expires in FY 1995 under current law. The projections assume that the tax would be extended until at least FY 2000.

<u>Other Expenditures</u>

In 1988, the specific categories discussed above accounted for approximately 94 percent of general fund expenditures. The largest remaining categories were General Government (excluding Courts) and Inspection and Regulation. Over the 1979-1988 period the expenditures not specifically covered above increased by 2.0 percent in real terms, while population over the same period increased by 3.0 percent. For the projections we assumed that this category of expenditures will continue to increase at a rate 1 percent slower than the population. Thus, during the 1988-1995 period we assume that "other" expenditures will increase by 1.7 percent and during the 1995-2000 period "other" expenditures will increase by 1.4 percent.